The Promise of **Artificial Intelligence**

This book, along with any associated content or subsequent updates, can be accessed at https://hdl.handle.net/10986/45296.

AI Disclosure Statement

Claude Sonnet 4.6 and 5, DeepSeek Chat, GPT-5 mini, Gemini 1.5 Flash, and Opus 4.6 and 4.8 were used for coding and labeling unstructured data. The World Bank's internal mAI interface using ChatGPT 5 and Copilot was used to improve clarity and shorten text in earlier drafts. All uses and outputs of AI were closely monitored by the team. All analytical judgments, policy interpretations, and conclusions were developed, reviewed, and verified by the author team.

Reproducible Research Repository
https://reproducibility.worldbank.org

A reproducibility package is available for this book in the Reproducible Research Repository at https://reproducibility.worldbank.org/catalog/624.

Scan to see this and prior editions of the *World Development Report*.

The Promise of
Artificial Intelligence

WORLD BANK GROUP

1818 H Street NW, Washington, DC 20433
Telephone: 202-473-1000; Internet: www.worldbank.org

1 2 3 4   29 28 27 26

ISSN: 0163-5085
ISBN: 978-1-4648-2331-2
e-ISBN: 978-1-4648-2357-2
DOI: 10.1596/978-1-4648-2331-2

Artificial Intelligence: Page ii has information on the use of AI tools in the development of this work.

Cover image: The cover image was generated using OpenAI / ChatGPT image generation on June 24, 2026.

Cover design: Ivanna Locmanidis, Sergio Andres Moreno Tellez, and Greg Wlosinski, World Bank Creative Services.

The Library of Congress Control Number has been requested.

The manufacturer's authorized representative in the European Union for product safety is Mare Nostrum Group B.V., Doelen 72, 4831 GR Breda, The Netherlands. Email: gpsr@mare-nostrum.co.uk.

Contents

Boxes

Figures

Maps

Tables

Foreword

The debates over artificial intelligence (AI) have devolved into exercises in self-absorption in most developed economies. Silicon Valley is racing for the holy grail—an all-purpose intelligence that outthinks the human mind. Major economies are locked in a contest for global technological supremacy. White-collar workers are losing sleep over chatbots coming to take their jobs.

Developing economies should tune out much of this noise. This Report—the first comprehensive assessment of AI's implications for the rest of the world—shows why. AI has thrown them a lifeline they should grasp before it slips away. Doing so does not oblige them to burn a trillion dollars on the ultimate large language model. It does not require them to show the door to armies of office workers. AI's potential for them is at once more basic and more radical. For the first time, it could put scarce knowledge about what matters most for economic progress within the reach of millions—through a text message, a voice call, and a variety of other low-cost but sharp instruments for clinics, courts, schools, farms, and small businesses.

If handled well, AI could help lift global growth to its strongest pace since the golden years of the 2000s, delivering tangible benefits to people in developing economies as well. This 2026 edition of the *World Development Report* shows that even if AI fails to live up to all its hype, developing economies would still be better off than they are today: The worst-case estimates suggest that potential growth rates in developing economies would rise above the dismal average of the first half of the 2020s. At a time when development progress has dipped to a 75-year low, nothing else on the horizon offers as much upside. Such an opportunity might not come again any time soon.

Of course, nothing worthwhile ever comes without risk. AI could close off a promising route to middle-class employment in many developing economies, threatening call-center work and entry-level jobs in software, finance, and business services. It could worsen electricity and water shortages. It could deepen dependence on foreign technology—and force poorer countries to choose between rival AI systems controlled by the most powerful nations. It could bring an array of other unwanted outcomes: greater income inequality, stealthier misinformation, and political repression.

This litany of dangers, however, only strengthens the case for immediate action. Developing economies cannot afford to watch new AI technologies from the sidelines: The experience from earlier waves of innovation shows that the costs of defensiveness or passivity are simply too high. The first Industrial Revolution—the age of steam power and machines of mass production—left those outside the mainstream in the dust. At its outset, Britain was roughly four times richer per person than India. By the end of the 20th century, it was 10 times richer. The gap had widened into an impossible-to-bridge chasm.

This time around, developing economies must determine their own destiny. *World Development Report 2026* offers them a road map. Until now, concrete evidence about AI's impact on the developing world has been scant. This Report starts to fill that void. It provides the first detailed assessment of how people, businesses, and governments in poorer countries are using AI, what is holding them back, and where the largest gains are likely. It offers a simple framework to decode AI and strike a sensible blend of measures to adopt, adapt, and advance AI-based technologies. Finally, based on the facts and framework, it provides low- and middle-income countries—and even small high-income economies—the essentials of a potent national strategy.

As a rule, developing economies today have more to gain—and less to fear—from AI than richer ones, our analysis finds. Less than a tenth of their jobs are susceptible to AI automation, compared with more than a third in high-income economies. Yet the upside is substantial: One out of every six developing-economy jobs would be enhanced rather than replaced, only slightly less than the share in high-income economies. AI, for example, might enable the judiciary to radically reduce caseloads, help teachers to prepare better lessons, assist nurses in interpreting a medical scan, or guide a farmer on when to plant and which pesticides to avoid.

It costs little, moreover, to reap such benefits—no need for massive investments in data centers or large language models. AI can help solve important problems involving narrow tasks even when local computing power is limited, electricity is unreliable, and internet service is dodgy. *Small AI* models can be constructed to run offline on just about any hardware. For most developing economies, the first step of AI adoption will involve exactly such models: The immediate benefits are most likely to come from off-the-shelf AI tools.

These are not pie-in-the-sky predictions. It is already happening on a significant scale. One in five small firms surveyed across six developing economies already uses AI chatbots—only modestly below the share in the United States. So far, AI use is often shallow, concentrated on information searches, writing, and translation rather than deeper changes in how businesses and governments operate. Even so, the effects on public services have been impressive. In Bangladesh, for example, AI-generated medical imaging has increased by 40 percent per day the number of patients screened for diabetes-related eyesight problems. In India, AI weather forecasts produced savings of as much as $560 per small farmer in the state of Telangana.

AI, however, is unusually sensitive to context: A tool that works in one country may fail in another unless it is adapted to local languages, institutions, and ways of working. In Nigeria, a medical AI trained on data from wealthy countries recommended more laboratory tests than local conditions warranted. In Ghana, by contrast, the Rori AI tutoring system was designed for basic phones and weak internet connections. Delivered by text message, it produced nearly a full year of mathematics learning for as little as $5 per student. For most developing economies, the greatest opportunity lies in adapting AI to local needs.

Over time, they may also seek greater control over the technologies they rely on. That need not mean pursuing "AI sovereignty" by building every layer of an AI supply chain themselves. A more practical way to reduce dependence on a single country is to buy models, cloud services, and other AI tools from many countries—and make sure they can work together and be swapped out without requiring the entire system to be rebuilt. India's UPI and Brazil's Pix—national instant-payment networks that connect banks, fintech firms, and payment apps—show how this might work. By giving many providers access to the same underlying system, they promote competition and make it easier to add or replace one provider without rebuilding the entire network.

World Development Report 2026 urges developing economies to adopt an *optimistic* mindset. Still agrarian and reliant on small enterprises, poorer economies are less likely to suffer large-scale job losses: AI is more likely to lend their workers a hand than put them out of work. And wielded adroitly, AI could help extend otherwise costly medical, legal, educational, and agricultural services to underserved billions—doing in a decade what might otherwise take a century.

Time is of the essence. AI is spreading much faster and is more context-specific than earlier general-purpose technologies like steam power, electricity, and the internet. That calls for policies that poor countries can afford and implement now—not later. Most developing economies do not yet have the wherewithal to develop AI technologies of their own, so advancement cannot be a big part of an AI strategy for them. And the context-specificity of AI-based technologies defies simple import-and-adopt approaches. For developing economies, the Report recommends strategies in which *adaptation* is the mainstay.

Implementing such a strategy requires deliberate choices. To extend medical, judicial, educational, and agricultural extension services, the Report points to *predictive* AI in back-end functions instead of generative AI at the frontline of service delivery. To mitigate against the danger of becoming overly reliant on technologies being developed in a single country, the report advises making interoperability a feature instead of aiming for sovereignty. To balance the imperatives of innovation and protection, the Report advocates encouraging industry to debate and develop voluntary standards. And perhaps most important, it recommends an emphasis on *small AI* applications diffused widely across the economy instead of big investments in large language models concentrated in a few firms.

Developing countries should leave it to the rich world to agonize over whether AI will one day doom humanity. Their own question is more immediate: Will they again arrive late to a technological revolution? Or will they use it this time to improve the lives of millions? Today's developing economies missed the first Industrial Revolution and spent the next two centuries paying the price. They cannot afford to miss this one.

Indermit Gill
Senior Vice President and Chief Economist
The World Bank Group

Acknowledgments

World Development Report 2026 was prepared by a World Bank team led by Gaurav Nayyar, who was the Director. Susan Athey (Stanford Graduate School of Business) and Ufuk Akcigit (University of Chicago) (through June 30, 2026) served as the academic leads. Joyce Antone Ibrahim served as the Report's manager. Overall guidance was provided by Indermit Gill (Senior Vice President and Chief Economist of the World Bank Group) and Somik V. Lall (Director of Strategy, Development Economics Vice Presidency). The Report was cosponsored by the Development Economics Vice Presidency and the Digital and AI Vice Presidency.

The core team comprised S Anukriti, Sharmista Appaya, Elwyn Davies, Lelys Dinarte-Diaz, Samuel Paul Fraiberger, Yi Jie Gwee, Yan Liu, Jeremy Ng, Tiago Carneiro Peixoto, Manuel Ramos Maqueda, Anja Sautmann, Katherine Stapleton, and Shu Yu.

Deepak Mishra served as an adviser to the Report's team. Aya Aboul Hosn, Sonam Tshering Gurung, Bolor Erdene Munkhbayar, Shyam Jayanti Patel, and Uzma Sahar Rauf served as research assistants. Ankit Bhatia, Alegria Burneo, Meney De La Peza Gandara, Johanna Einsiedler, Judith Gideon Mwaya, Jingyun Huang, Luke Jordan, Jennifer Rincon Amaya, Hector Segura Jimenez, Nitisha Tripati, and Matthew White also provided research assistance at various stages of the Report. Sandi Soe Lwin provided administrative support from July through December 2025. Gabriela Calderon Motta provided administrative support from January 2026 to publication. Indu Kilaru provided support at various stages of the Report.

Philip Grinsted, Boris Inderbitzin, Sharif Kazemi, Chinasa T. Okolo, Cindy Parokkil, Jonah Matthew Rexer, and Siddharth Sharma provided specific inputs.

Bruce Ross-Larson and Joseph Rebello provided developmental guidance in drafting the Report.

The team thanks the World Bank Enterprise Analysis team for coordinating the World Bank Enterprise Survey on AI Adoption. The data collection was led by David Francis and Filip Jolevski and also included Gemechu Ayana Aga, Davide Mare, Solomiya Shpak, William Soh, and Mehmet Nazim Tamkoc, under the overall supervision of Jorge Rodriguez Meza. Elwyn Davies supervised the surveys on behalf of the Report's team. Xavier Cirera, Marcio Cruz, and Kyung Min Lee provided inputs on the survey design, and Sonam Tshering Gurung and Jennifer Rincon Amaya provided research assistance. The team also thanks the World Bank AI and Data for Better Governance team for overseeing and coordinating the World Bank AI and Data for Better Governance Survey. The latter team was led by Manuel Ramos-Maqueda and Daniel Rogger and included Flavia Sacco Capurro, Robert Lipinski, Timothy Steven Lundy, Shyam Jayanti Patel, Josefina Silva Fuentealba, and Michelle Wronski.

Stephane Straub and Estefania Vergara Cobos authored box 1.2 on AI as a tool for improving infrastructure. Ghislain De Salins and William Zhang provided inputs to box 1.3 on cybersecurity. Johan Bjurman Bergman, Lana Graf, and Anastasia Nedayvoda provided substantial inputs to spotlight 1 on small AI. Gian Boeddu, Juan Carlos Izaguirre, Fredesvinda Fatima Montes, Camila Quevedo-Vega, and Maria Fernandez Vidal authored box 4.1 on financial inclusion. Parvathy Krishnakumari, Sunil Madan, and Parmesh Shah authored spotlight 2 on AI and agricultural advisory services. Megan Lang and Esther Naikal authored spotlight 4 on AI and the environment, with inputs from Stephane Straub and Estefania Vergara Cobos. Lulit Mitik Beyene and Mei Mei Aileen Lam provided inputs to box 4.4 on the effects of AI in Poland. Holly Krambeck, Towera Moyo, and Ifeoluwanimi Ogbeba provided substantial inputs to box 7.3 on unlocking AI for low-resource languages. Junaid Ahmad, Mariana Dahan, and David Savage provided inputs to box 7.5 on investment guarantees. Luke Jordan coauthored box 8.2 on readiness of governments.

The communications and engagement strategy was led by a team comprising Aliza Marcus, Karolina Mazurkiewicz, Kristen Milhollin, and Shane Romig. Multimedia support was provided by a team comprising Amin Elsiwi, Andrew Gilhooly, and James Sullivan, under the supervision of Pete Von Elling, with multilingual support by Edy Semaan and Andrea Tapia. Roula Yazigi provided web and online services.

Special thanks are extended to Mark McClure, who coordinated and oversaw formal production of the Report, and to the World Bank's Formal Publishing Program, including Cindy Fisher, Patricia Katayama, and Jewel McFadden. Mary C. Fisk facilitated the multiple translations of the overview and main messages by the Translations and Interpretation team, coordinated by Wendy Wei Chang Spadavecchia. Deborah Appel-Barker managed the printing and electronic conversions of the Report and the many ancillary products.

The Report was edited by Michael Harrup and Nancy Morrison and proofread by Catherine Farley, Gwenda Larsen, and Honora Mara. Robert Zimmermann verified the Report's extensive citations and assisted with the copyediting. The design team of the World Bank's Global Corporate Solutions unit designed the cover and the interior layout. Luisa Lopez helped design some of the Report's figures and infographics. Datapage supplied typesetting services.

Dayana Leguizamon provided the team with resource management support.

The team extends a special thanks to the following organizations for hosting consultation sessions throughout the preparation of the Report: African Institute for Data Science and Artificial Intelligence (AfriDSAI) (University of Pretoria), Asian Development Bank Institute (ADBI), Delhi School of Economics, Fondazione Bruno Kessler, Global Center for Economic Growth (University of Chicago), Infosys Limited, Institute for Economic Development (World Bank Group), Saudi Competitiveness and Business Center, World Bank Group–Saudi Arabia Knowledge Hub, and Zhejiang Provincial Department of Finance (China). Relatedly, the team also thanks colleagues at various World Bank country offices who assisted with logistics and stakeholder engagements. Special thanks to Kenan Karakulah, Sandi Soe Lwin, and Grace Soko for their help with coordination and high-level engagement strategies.

The team expresses its sincere gratitude to the World Trade Organization (WTO), Peking University, Zhejiang University, and the Asian Infrastructure Investment Bank (AIIB) for their collaboration and engagement in the preparation of *World Development Report 2026*. We are especially grateful to Director-General Ngozi Okonjo-Iweala, Deputy Director-General Johanna Hill, and Chief Economist Robert W. Staiger of the WTO; President Jiayi Zou and Chief Economist Erik Berglöf of AIIB; Professor Justin Yifu Lin and Dean Huang Yiping of the National School of Development, Peking University; and Vice President Jianghong Zhou and Vice Dean Sen Gong of Zhejiang University for valuable insights and feedback.

The team is grateful for the guidance, comments, and inputs provided by other World Bank Group colleagues, particularly Ayhan Kose (Deputy Chief Economist of the World Bank Group and Director of the Prospects Group, Development Economics Vice Presidency), Norman Loayza (Director, Policy Indicators Group, Development Economics Vice Presidency), Aaditya Mattoo (Director, Research Group, Development Economics Vice Presidency), all managers in the Development Economics Research Group, and all chief economists in the World Bank vice presidencies and regions. The team is also grateful for the guidance, comments, and inputs provided by World Bank Group colleagues from the Budget and Procurement Vice Presidency; Communications and External Relations Vice Presidency; Department of the Managing Director and World Bank Group Chief Administrative Officer; Development Finance Vice Presidency; Digital and AI Vice Presidency; East Asia and Pacific Region; Eastern and Southern Africa Region; Europe and Central Asia Region; Independent Evaluation Group; Information and Technology Solutions; Infrastructure Vice Presidency; Integrity Vice Presidency; International Finance Corporation; Latin America and the Caribbean Region; Legal Vice Presidency; Middle East, North Africa, Afghanistan, and Pakistan Region; Outcomes Department; People Vice Presidency; Planet Vice Presidency; Prosperity Vice Presidency; South Asia Region; and Western and Central Africa Region. The team thanks the many World Bank colleagues who offered written comments during the formal World Bank Group–wide review process. These comments provided invaluable guidance at a crucial stage in the production of the Report.

The team gratefully received suggestions and guidance from a high-level advisory panel: Abdullah Alswaha (Minister of Communications and Information Technology, Saudi Arabia), Karan Bhatia (Global Head, Global Affairs and Public Policy, Google), Rumman Chowdhury (Founder, Humane Intelligence), Amal El Fallah Seghrouchni (Minister of Digital Transition and Administrative Reform, Morocco), Ryu Je-Myung (Vice Minister of Science and ICT, Republic of Korea), Kate Kallot (CEO and Cofounder, Amini), S. Krishnan (Secretary, Ministry of Electronics and Information Technology, India), Albert Park (Chief Economist, Asian Development Bank), Amandeep Singh Gill (Under-Secretary-General and Secretary-General's Special Envoy for Digital and Emerging Technologies, United Nations), and Bosun Tijani (Minister of Communications, Innovation and Digital Economy, Nigeria).

The team received suggestions and inputs from an academic advisory committee: David H. Autor (Massachusetts Institute of Technology), Daniel Björkegren (Columbia University), Nicholas Bloom (Stanford University), Erik Brynjolfsson (Stanford University), Bhaskar Chakravorti (Tufts University), James Evans (University of Chicago), Avi Goldfarb (University of Toronto), Aziz Z. Huq (University of Chicago), Michael Kremer (University of Chicago), David Leslie (Queen Mary University of London), Vukosi Marivate (University of Pretoria), Arvind Narayanan (Princeton University), Ziad Obermeyer (University of California, Berkeley), Benjamin Rosman (University of the Witwatersrand), Sunita Sarawagi (Indian Institute of Technology [IIT] Bombay), Catherine

Tucker (Massachusetts Institute of Technology), and Yi Zeng (Institute of Automation, Chinese Academy of Sciences, University of Chinese Academy of Sciences).

In addition, the team consulted with many other academics and is grateful for their inputs: Hamed Abdelhaq (An-Najah National University, West Bank and Gaza), Ashraf Abdelwahab (American University of Cairo), Fatima K. Abu Salem (American University of Beirut), Rachel Adams (African Observatory on Responsible AI), Ibrahim Adeyanju (Federal University Oye-Ekiti, Nigeria), Rebecca Adler-Nissen (University of Copenhagen, Denmark), Philippe Aghion (College de France and INSEAD), Luca Aiello (IT University of Copenhagen, Denmark), Khondaker Abdullah Al Mamun (United International University, Bangladesh), Justice Kwame Appati (University of Ghana), Elliot Ash (ETH Zürich, Switzerland), Beakal Gizachew Assefa (Addis Ababa Institute of Technology [AAiT] and Addis Ababa University, Ethiopia), Jasmin Baier (University of Oxford, United Kingdom), Elefelious Getachew Belay (Addis Ababa University, Ethiopia), Luigi Benfratello (Politecnico di Torino [Polytechnic University of Turin], Italy), Asrat Mulatu Beyene (Addis Ababa Science and Technology University, Ethiopia), Johanne Bruffaerts (Epitech Bénin), Joanna Bryson (Hertie School, Germany), Altan Cakir (Istanbul Technical University, Türkiye), Maggie Chen (George Washington University, United States), Zhao Chen (China Center for Economic Studies, Fudan University), Munther A. Dahleh (Massachusetts Institute of Technology, United States), Sanmay Das (Virginia Polytechnic Institute and State University, United States), Sonali Das (University of Pretoria, South Africa), Leon Derczynski (IT University of Copenhagen, Denmark), David Eaves (University College London, United Kingdom), José Ramón Enríquez (Stanford University, United States), James Evans (University of Chicago, United States), Nick Feamster (University of Chicago, United States), Kiran Garimella (Rutgers University, United States), Marko Grobelnik (Jozef Stefan Institute, Slovenia), Robert Grossman (University of Chicago, United States), Sivaramakrishnan R. Guruvayur (Amrita Vishwa Vidyapeetham, India), César Hidalgo (Toulouse School of Economics, France), Yuki Higuchi (Sophia University, Japan), Abdulnasir Hossen (Sultan Qaboos University, Oman), Jingbo Huang (United Nations University Institute in Macau Special Administrative Region, China), Bogdan Ionescu (National University of Science and Technology Politehnica Bucharest, Romania), Seiro Ito (Institute of Developing Economies, Japan External Trade Organization [JETRO]), Aleksandar Jeremović (Singidunum University, Serbia), Zhiyuan Jiang (Shanghai University, China), Benjamin F. Jones (Northwestern University, United States), Roman Jurowetzki (Aalborg University Business School, Denmark), Ezra Karger (Federal Reserve Bank of Chicago), Taro Katsurai (JICA Ogata Sadako Research Institute for Peace and Development, Japan), Kefayatullah Khairkhah (Badakhshan University, Afghanistan), Zubair Khalid (Lahore University of Management Sciences, Pakistan), Gul Muhammad Khan (University of Engineering and Technology Mardan, Pakistan), Hannah Rose Kirk (University of Oxford, United Kingdom), Rembrand M. Koning (Harvard Business School, United States), Anton Korinek (University of Virginia, United States), Ponnurangam Kumaraguru (International Institute of Information Technology [IIIT] Hyderabad, India), Anish Kurien (Artificial Intelligence Institute of South Africa and AI Hubs, Tshwane University of Technology), Cassey Lee (Institute of Southeast Asian Studies [ISEAS]–Yusof Ishak Institute, Singapore), Lixing Li (National School of Development, Peking University, China), Zhikuo Liu (School of Economics, Fudan University, China), Ciira wa Maina (Dedan Kimathi University of Technology, Kenya), Bilal Mateen (University of Birmingham, United Kingdom), Antonio Minniti (University of Bologna, Italy), Joel Mokyr

(Northwestern University, United States), Jabu Mtsweni (Council for Scientific and Industrial Research [CSIR], South Africa), Deeparghya Mukherjee (Indian Institute of Management Nagpur), Atsuko Munemura (Chiba University of Commerce, Japan), Emmanuel Mutisya (Kenya Advanced Institute of Science and Technology), Joyce Nakatumba-Nabende (Makerere University, Uganda), Yadati Narahari (Indian Institute of Science [IISc] Bangalore), Christopher Neilson (Yale University, United States), Nicky Nicholls (University of Pretoria, South Africa), Debora Nozza (Bocconi University, Italy), Victor Odumuyiwa (University of Lagos, Nigeria), Izumi Ohno (GRIPS [National Graduate Institute for Policy Studies], Japan), John Olukuru (Strathmore University Business School, Kenya), Luca Pappalardo (Scuola Normale Superiore, Italy), Nohyoung Park (Korea University Law School), Dino Pedreschi (University of Pisa, Italy), Beata Polok (Dar Al-Hekma University, Saudi Arabia), Islem Rekik (Imperial College London, United Kingdom), Gianluigi Riva (Bocconi University, Italy), Alan Ross (Global AI Solutions, United States), Jun Saito (Japan Center for Economic Research), Aduwati Sali (Institute for Mathematical Research and Intelligent Systems [INSPEM], Universiti Putra Malaysia), Anna Salomons (Utrecht University, Netherlands), Nicu Sebe (University of Trento, Italy), Ismaila Seck (African Institute for Mathematical Sciences [AIMS], South Africa), Jonathan Shock (University of Cape Town, South Africa), Ram Singh (Delhi School of Economics, India), Josef Sivic (Czech Institute of Informatics, Robotics and Cybernetics, Czech Technical University), Tetushi Sonobe (National Graduate Institute for Policy Studies [GRIPS], Japan), Jacopo Staiano (University of Trento, Italy), Thomas Streinz (European University Institute, Italy), Milind Tambe (Harvard University, United States), Neil Thompson (Massachusetts Institute of Technology, United States), Manuel Tonneau (University of Oxford, United Kingdom), Yasushi Ueki (Institute of Developing Economies, Japan External Trade Organization [JETRO]), Lan Xue (Tsinghua University, China), Hiroyuki Yamada (Keio University, Japan), Naoyuki Yoshino (Keio University, Japan), Dandan Zhang (National School of Development, Peking University, China), and Yuan Zhang (China Center for Economic Studies, Fudan University).

The team benefited from the inputs of government agencies, international and regional organizations, think tanks, research institutes, academic institutions, civil society organizations, private sector organizations, and other organizations, including 42 Amman (Jordan); Accel (India); Adalat AI (India); Africa Practice (Botswana); Africaines In Tech (Côte d'Ivoire); African Center for Economic Transformation (South Africa); African Development Bank (AfDB); African Union Development Agency–New Partnership for Africa's Development (AUDA-NEPAD) (South Africa); AfriLabs (Nigeria); Agencia de Gobierno Electrónico y Sociedad de las Información y del Conocomiento [Agency for Electronic Government and the Information Society and Knowledge] (AGESIC) (Uruguay); The Agency Fund (United States); AI Safety Connect; AI4Bharat (India); AI Security Institute (United Kingdom); Alibaba Cloud Intelligence Group (China); Alibaba Group (China); Alpha Intelligence Capital (Luxembourg); Amazon (United States); Amini AI (Kenya); Amplifai Health (Saudi Arabia); Ant Technology Group (China); Anthropic (United States); Applied Innovation Center, Ministry of Communications and Information Technology (Arab Republic of Egypt); Arkam Ventures (India); Artificial Intelligence Council, Ministry of Industry and New Technologies (Tajikistan); Artificial Intelligence for Social Impact and Development (AI4SID) (Nigeria); Asian Development Bank (ADB); Aspen Institute (United States); Association of Southeast Asian Nations (ASEAN) Foundation; Atlas Computing (United States); Bank of Mongolia; BharathGen (India); BioForge, University of Pittsburgh

(United States); Brain and Signal Research and Analysis (BASIRA) Lab (Tunisia); Cambodia Academy of Digital Technology; Carnegie Endowment for International Peace (United States); Center for AI and Digital Policy (United States); Center for Analysis of Economic Reforms and Communication (Azerbaijan); Centre for Intellectual Property and Information Technology Law (CIPIT) (Kenya); Centre for Open Societal Systems (India); Cognitive Insights for Artificial Intelligence (United States); Communications, Space and Technology Commission (Saudi Arabia); Consumer Reports (United States); Council of Europe; Cyber Sierra (Singapore); Data-Pop Alliance (Spain); Deloitte (United Kingdom); Department of Communications and Digital Technologies (South Africa); Department of Science, Technology and Innovation (South Africa); DevData Analytics (Tanzania); Digital Egypt Pioneers Initiative; Digital Government Committee (Cambodia); Digital Rights Foundation (Pakistan); Digital Umuganda (Rwanda); E-Commerce and Digital Economy Agency, Ministry of Industry and Trade (Viet Nam); E-Mongolia; eCitizen (Kenya); EkStep Foundation (India); Etudesk (Côte d'Ivoire); Eurisko (Lebanon); European AI Office; European Bank for Reconstruction and Development (EBRD); European Commission; European Investment Bank (EIB); European Laboratory for Learning and Intelligent Systems (ELLIS) (Germany); Expo 2030 (Saudi Arabia); Federal Ministry of Information Technology and Telecommunication (Pakistan); FuturAfric Intelligence Artificielle (Côte d'Ivoire); Gates Foundation (United States); Genesys Analytics (South Africa); GitHub (United States); Global Center on AI Governance (South Africa); Google (United States); Google Research (United States); Grab (Singapore); GrowUp AI (Benin); Hangzhou Shenrui Bolian Technology Company (China); Hangzhou Yushu Technology Company (China); Homai (United States); Humain (Saudi Arabia); Humane Intelligence (United States); IDB Invest, Inter-American Development Bank Group; Independent Communications Authority of South Africa (ICASA); The Information and Communications Technology Association of Jordan-intaj; Information and Communications Technology (ICT) Authority (Kenya); Infosys (India); Innovation and Digital Development Agency (Azerbaijan); Insights for Research Polling and Training (West Bank and Gaza); Institute of Advanced Studies Kőszeg (iASK) (Hungary); Intelmatix (Saudi Arabia); Inter-American Development Bank (IDB); International Centre for Theoretical Sciences (India); International Economics Consulting (Viet Nam); International Electrotechnical Commission (IEC); International Federation for Information Processing (IFIP), United Nations Educational, Scientific and Cultural Organization (UNESCO); International Monetary Fund (IMF); International Organization for Standardization (ISO); International Research Centre on Artificial Intelligence (IRCAI); International Telecommunication Union (ITU); Ipazia (Italy); Jus Mundi; Kalaari Capital (India); Karnataka Digital Economy Mission (India); KPMG (United Kingdom); Kuwait Chamber of Commerce and Industry; Leo Capital (India); LinkedIn (United States); Logatta (Jordan); Lucidya (Saudi Arabia); Masakhane African Languages Hub; Max Planck Institute for Human Development (Germany); Meta (United States); Microsoft (United States); Microsoft AI for Good Lab (United States); Ministry of Communication Technologies and Digital Transformation (Tunisia); Ministry of Communications and Information Technology (Egypt); Ministry of Communications and Information Technology (Saudi Arabia); Ministry of Digital Economy and Entrepreneurship (Jordan); Ministry of Digital Transition and Administrative Reform (Morocco); Ministry of Electronics and Information Technology (India); Ministry of Information, Communications and The Digital Economy (Kenya); Ministry of Management and Innovation in Public Services (Brazil); Ministry of National Development Planning (Indonesia); Ministry of Science and

Higher Education (Poland); Ministry of Science, Technological Development and Innovation (Serbia); Ministry of Science, Technology and Innovation (Malaysia); Modular Open Source Identity Platform (MOSIP) (India); MOZN (Saudi Arabia); National Artificial Intelligence Center (Azerbaijan); National Artificial Intelligence Expert Council (Mongolia); National Association of Software and Service Companies (NASSCOM) (India); National Center for AI (Saudi Arabia); National Centre for Artificial Intelligence and Robotics (NCAIR) (Nigeria); National Centre for Artificial Intelligence in Society (CAISA) (Denmark); National Information Center (Saudi Arabia); National Innovation Council (Philippines); National Institution for Transforming India (NITI Aayog); National Research Council of Italy (CNR); National Technology Development Program (Saudi Arabia); NetEase Network Company (China); NETLINKS (Afghanistan); New H3C Technologies Company (China); Niramai Health Analytix (India); NVIDIA (United States); Office of the Council of State (Thailand); Omidyar Network (United States); OneOffTech (Italy); OpenAI (United States); Open Forum for AI (OFAI) (United States); Organisation for Economic Co-operation and Development (OECD) (France); Otoritas Jasa Keuangan [Financial Services Authority] (Indonesia); Palestine for Development, Palestine Investment Fund (West Bank and Gaza); Partnership on AI (United States); PATH (United Kingdom); PayGlocal (India); People+ai (India); Quintelligence (Slovenia); Qure.ai (India); RAND Europe (United Kingdom); Reserve Bank Innovation Hub (RBIH) (India); RevolutionAIze (India); Rocket Learning (India); Rookie Systems LLC (Mongolia); Sarvam AI (India); Saudi Authority for Data and Artificial Intelligence (Saudi Arabia); Sèmè City (Benin); Senira Solutions (Slovenia); Sevilla Fútbol Club (Spain); Shutterstock (United States); Smart Government II Project Implementation Unit (Mongolia); Snow Mountain AI (India); South Africa Revenue Service; STelligence (Thailand); Swiss AI Initiative (Switzerland); Takshashila Institution (India); Tencent (China); Tony Blair Institute for Global Change (United Kingdom); TROTRO Tractor (Ghana); United Nations Children's Fund (UNICEF); United Nations Development Programme (UNDP); upGrad Enterprise (India); Wa'ed Ventures (Saudi Arabia); Women's Digital League (Pakistan); World Trade Organization (WTO); Zaka AI (Lebanon); Zoom Communications (Germany); Zucchetti Group (Italy); and Zypl.ai (Tajikistan).

The team apologizes to any individuals or organizations inadvertently omitted from this list. It is grateful for the help received from all who contributed to this Report, including those whose names may not appear here. Team members also thank their families for their support throughout the preparation of this Report.

Glossary

- **Agentic AI (AI agent).** An AI system that pursues a goal by planning and carrying out a sequence of steps on its own, using external tools such as software or web search along the way, rather than answering only a single request.
- **AI stack.** The layered set of building blocks that make up AI, ranging from the hardware and computing infrastructure to the models and applications.
- **Application programming interface.** A connection that lets one software system use another's capabilities over a network. It enables an organization to send data to a model hosted elsewhere and receive results without running the model itself.
- **Augmentation.** The use of AI to complement people in tasks they continue to perform and oversee, complementing their skills rather than replacing them. It is usually contrasted with *automation*. AI can also complement physical capital and infrastructure.
- **Automation.** The use of AI to perform tasks previously carried out by people, reducing direct human involvement in doing them. It is usually contrasted with *augmentation*.
- **Benchmark.** A standardized test used to measure and compare how well AI models perform on tasks such as answering questions or reasoning through a problem.
- **Bias.** A systematic tendency in an AI model's outputs, usually traced to imbalances in its training data, that can make results unfair or inaccurate.
- **Chatbot.** An application that lets people interact with an AI model through plain language prompts, either typed or spoken.
- **Compute.** The processing power resulting from chips and related hardware needed to train and run AI models.
- **Deepfake.** AI-generated audio or video made to realistically depict people saying or doing things they did not say or do.
- **Fine tuning.** Further training that adapts an already trained, general-purpose model to a particular task or local context.
- **Foundation model.** An AI model trained on broad data that can be adapted to many different tasks and applications. Large language models are one type.
- **Frontier model.** The most advanced AI model available at a given time.
- **General-purpose technology.** A technology that affects the entire economy, improves continuously, and leads to complementary innovation. Examples include steam power, electricity, and the internet.

- **Generative AI.** AI that creates content, such as text, images, audio, or code, usually in response to a typed request, as in a chatbot.
- **Inference.** The stage at which a trained AI model produces an output from a new input, such as answering a question or scoring an application.
- **Large language model.** An AI model trained on very large amounts of data that can understand and generate content. Large language models underlie chatbots and many writing and coding tools.
- **Machine learning.** Algorithms that learn patterns from data rather than by following rules written by hand, becoming more accurate as they take into account more data.
- **AI model.** Algorithms that have been trained to recognize patterns in data, making predictions, generating new content, and taking decisions based on those patterns.
- **Model drift.** The decline in a model's performance over time as the data or conditions it meets in use move away from those it was trained on. It is one reason models are rechecked after deployment.
- **Open-source model.** A model released for anyone to use and modify, usually including its underlying code. Making a model open source grants broader rights than an open-weight release.
- **Open-weight model.** A model whose internal values (*weights*) are released publicly, so that others can download and adapt it on their own systems.
- **Parameters (weights).** The numerical values inside an AI model that encode what the model has learned during training (that is, the model's knowledge). A model's size is often described in terms of the number of its parameters, which are often loosely referred to as weights.
- **Predictive AI.** AI that forecasts outcomes or assigns scores from data, such as predicting crop yields or credit risk, rather than generating content.
- **Training.** The process of teaching an AI model to recognize patterns to make predictions, generate content, and take decisions.
- **Validation.** Checking how well a trained model performs by comparing its outputs against independently verified data, usually data the model was not trained on. Because performance can drift, models are often revalidated after deployment.

Abbreviations

AI	artificial intelligence
DPI	digital public infrastructure
EMDEs	emerging market and developing economies
EU	European Union
FAO	Food and Agriculture Organization of the United Nations
GDP	gross domestic product
GenAI	generative artificial intelligence
GPT	general-purpose technology
ICT	information and communication technology
IEC	International Electrotechnical Commission
ISO	International Organization for Standardization
LLM	large language model
MIS	management information system
NOODL	Nwulite Obodo Open Data License
OECD	Organisation for Economic Co-operation and Development
SMEs	small and medium enterprises
TFP	total factor productivity
TVET	technical and vocational education and training
UN	United Nations
UNESCO	United Nations Educational, Scientific and Cultural Organization
WTO	World Trade Organization

All dollar amounts are in US dollars unless otherwise indicated.

Overview

In brief

This Report is the first comprehensive assessment of what artificial intelligence (AI) means for 6.8 billion people living in low- and middle-income countries. It argues that AI represents a historic opportunity for these countries, potentially enabling them to overcome development challenges that have defied solution for decades. Given the scarcity of information on AI's use in developing countries, the Report sets the ball rolling on closing the gap. It uncovers new facts about how businesses and governments in developing countries are using AI—and identifies the main obstacles to greater and more productive use.

AI is a general-purpose technology, or GPT. That puts it in rare company. Steam power. Electricity. Computers and the internet. Each transformed not just one sector, but entire economies, and did so continuously, over decades. Each also followed a pattern: slow and uncertain at first, but eventually reshaping how economies produce and how societies function. AI is following a similar pattern, but on a much faster timeline. It took about 80 years for the steam engine to reach lower-income countries, 40 years for electricity, and 20 years for the internet.[1] *By contrast, middle-income countries accounted for half of ChatGPT's global traffic within six months of its launch.*[2] *Rapid diffusion on such a scale has not been seen before.*

But history also teaches us that the countries that benefited most from previous GPTs were not always the ones that came up with the underlying technology. Those that benefited had built the necessary foundations and moved fast to develop applications on top of them. The countries that did not invest in the infrastructure, skills, and institutions that such technologies required to function benefited less and felt the most pain from disruption. This lesson is directly relevant to AI: The winning approach will take advantage of the new technologies, not seek refuge from them.

In only a few years, AI has evolved from making predictions to generating content from text, audio, and video to now autonomously executing complex tasks. As it becomes more powerful and pervasive, its value as a tool for development depends on three factors. The first is capabilities. *Unlike computers or the internet, AI can perform complex thinking tasks that guide decision-making and usually require human expertise, such as diagnosing diseases, forecasting weather, or advising farmers. These skills are often in short supply in developing countries, so AI has the potential to fill important gaps.*

The second is concentration. *The most advanced AI models, the chips they rely on, and the data centers that run them are controlled by a small number of companies in just a few economies. This concentration creates dependency risks and affects whether the AI tools available will meet developing countries' needs. However, this concentration also allows countries to customize AI models without having to spend billions of dollars creating the most advanced AI systems from scratch.*

The third is complements: *the foundations that allow AI to be used safely and effectively. AI works best where reliable infrastructure, good education systems, and strong institutions are present. Developing countries often have shortages in all three. AI, moreover, needs to be customized to the local context because it learns from the data upon which it is trained. How quickly countries build these complements—and*

A reproducibility package is available for this book in the Reproducible Research Repository at https://reproducibility.worldbank.org/catalog/624.

how well governments and businesses reorganize to use AI productively—will determine how much and how fast AI improves development. In that respect, AI is no different from GPTs that have come before. Ten years ago, World Development Report 2016: Digital Dividends *called these prerequisites the analog complements to digital technologies. Today, AI requires both strong analog and digital complements to deliver its full benefits.*

What developing countries should do: Adopt and adapt, then advance

Developing countries can benefit from AI in three ways: by adopting *existing AI tools, by* adapting *AI to local needs, and by* advancing *the technology: building their own frontier AI models and the infrastructure that powers them. Each step requires more investment, skills, and infrastructure than the last.*

Advancing frontier AI models is by far the hardest and most expensive path. It requires chips, large data centers, huge amounts of training data, and world-class AI researchers. Today, only a handful of companies in a few countries can afford to do this, spending billions of dollars to train leading AI models. In 2026, the amount these companies are expected to spend on AI infrastructure is larger than the entire economies of many countries.[3]

For most developing countries, building frontier AI models is not a realistic goal in the near future. Only a small number of countries and companies have the resources to compete at that level, and progress might take years. A few countries are making inroads. Examples include India's Sarvam AI, the United Arab Emirates' Falcon, and Sub-Saharan Africa's InkubaLM, which were built from scratch to work better in local languages.

Instead, the best place to start is by adopting AI tools that already exist, such as AI tools that can make it easier for doctors to diagnose patients, farmers to improve crop decisions, and businesses to become more productive. But these benefits depend on strong analog foundations, including reliable electricity, fast internet, and basic education.

Merely adopting AI, however, will not be enough. AI systems trained in high-income countries often do not work well in other settings. In Nigeria, for example, an AI tool trained on data from high-income countries systematically recommended far too many laboratory tests because it learned medical norms that were more appropriate for Los Angeles than for Lagos.[4] *AI tools should also be designed to work for people with different levels of access to technology. For example, AI solutions will need to be delivered through voice calls on basic mobile phones for those who cannot read or afford smartphones. Simply importing an AI model does not mean it will work well locally.*

That is why adapting AI to local conditions is likely to deliver the biggest benefits for developing countries. Entrepreneurs can build on existing open AI models—such as Apertus, Bidirectional Encoder Representations from Transformers (BERT), Gemma, Llama, Mistral, and Qwen—to create AI that better understands local languages, laws, and needs. Examples include Latin America's Latam-GPT and Southeast Asia's Southeast Asian Languages in One Network (SEA-LION).

Developers can also use these models and AI coding tools to build practical applications, such as medical-imaging systems for clinics with few specialists, chatbots that advise small businesses, and AI algorithms that help governments monitor public spending. To make this possible, countries need the right digital and analog complements, including access to computing infrastructure, local-language data, and workers with AI skills.

Doing in a decade what once took a century

Many developing countries have a shortage of highly skilled people to solve complex problems. There are too few doctors to diagnose disease and too few business specialists who can grow small businesses, too few agricultural experts to support farmers, and too few skilled public officials to deliver better services. Building this expertise through education and training can take generations. AI, when it is adapted to local languages and context, can radically speed up the pace of transformation. It can put expert knowledge within reach of millions instead of just a small elite.

The benefits can radiate across the economy, society, and politics. Among economic impacts, AI can help millions of small businesses and farmers become more productive. In India, for example, AI is supporting weather forecasting systems, which have previously enabled smallholder farmers to alter their behavior in response to specific risks, causing some to increase farm expenditures by as much as one-third and others to reap net savings of as much as $560 per farmer.[5] Among social impacts, predictive AI analytics and decision support for back-office administrative work in government can have large payoffs. In Kenya, for example, the judiciary used AI to assign more than 10,000 court cases each year to more than 1,500 mediators, helping reduce a large backlog of cases.[6] Among political impacts, AI can improve transparency and accountability. In Ukraine, for example, a machine-learning tool developed by Transparency International Ukraine detects suspicious patterns in government procurement and directs citizens' complaints to law enforcement.[7]

Managing the risks

This Report urges developing countries to be deliberate about AI technologies. This means pursuing policies to actively exploit the potential of AI solutions for enterprises, households, and governments. Without this, developing countries risk losing economic dynamism and global relevance. But this active policy stance also means being aware of the accompanying risks.

On the economic side, AI is not yet replacing large numbers of jobs in most developing countries. But it is already having an impact in some industries. Countries that rely on business process outsourcing (such as call centers and back-office services) face growing pressure as AI automates more of this work. On the social side, AI can be biased if it is trained on data that do not reflect local people, languages, and cultures. It can also make it easier to spread false information, commit fraud, and carry out cybercrime. On the political side, the world's most advanced AI systems are controlled by a small number of companies, mainly in the United States and China. This means developing countries could become dependent on technology they do not control. Like all countries, they also face risks from unexpected consequences of AI.

Making AI work for development

To benefit from AI, developing countries must first and foremost keep investing in the analog foundations. They still need reliable electricity, internet access, and strong education systems, which remain inadequate in too many developing countries. In Sub-Saharan Africa, for example, nearly one-third of rural schools still do not have reliable electricity; more than two-thirds lack dependable internet access; and nearly nine out of ten 10-year-olds cannot read a simple text.[8]

Countries also need the digital building blocks for AI. They should expand access to affordable computing infrastructure (the hardware and processing power needed to train and run AI models) and build shared data resources so local developers have the local-language data needed to adapt AI to their own countries.

But these foundations are only the starting point. To encourage AI innovation, governments should create a business environment that helps start-ups raise investment and experiment with new ideas. Today's AI coding tools make it easy to build new applications, so there are already thousands of pilot AI projects. The bigger challenge is knowing which ones actually work. Governments and businesses need better evidence, along with stronger capacity to test, evaluate, buy, and expand successful AI solutions.

Finally, building public trust in AI is just as important. With limited regulatory capacity and the technology evolving fast, governments in developing countries should first leverage voluntary standards concerning impact assessments, independent audits, and testing protocols to encourage responsible AI use. Where such standards do not adequately protect people, governments should use existing laws to address harms such as unsafe AI systems, while developing flexible AI regulations that avoid creating unnecessary barriers.

Developing countries must start now

Without the right preparation, developing countries could miss AI's benefits while becoming increasingly exposed to its risks. That preparation has begun in a substantial number of developing countries, but not in the countries that need it most. As of mid-2026, more than 80 countries had published national AI strategies. But only one of the world's 25 low-income countries, Rwanda, has done so.[9] *The countries with the most to gain appear today to be the least prepared.*

It will be especially important for all developing countries not to mimic the priorities of advanced economies, where the focus is either on the peril of massive job losses or the need to win the global race to build the most advanced AI. Developing countries face different challenges. Their priority should be to use AI to improve productivity, strengthen public services, and solve local development problems. In short, they should be blinded neither by the hype nor the hysteria surrounding AI in the global headlines. Adopting, adapting, and then advancing new technologies—with care but without delay—is the proven path to prosperity. In the area of AI, that approach could enable developing countries to solve problems that have resisted solutions for generations.

" . . . AI will be either the best, or worst thing, ever to happen to humanity."

—Stephen Hawking, speech delivered at the launch of the Leverhulme Centre for the Future of Intelligence, University of Cambridge, October 19, 2016

Few technologies divide opinion as starkly as AI—both across regions of the world and between technology companies, citizens, and governments. In the United States and Asia, tech executives mostly see the bright side. In the United States, Europe, and Latin America, many citizens worry that AI could automate too many white-collar jobs, raise demand for energy, introduce algorithmic biases into decision-making, and pose risks for data privacy. In Africa, policy makers line up in the middle—enthusiastic about the possibilities that AI can bring for improving public services but anxious that AI could widen the current digital divide. Since the launch of ChatGPT in November 2022, people around the world have tuned in to conversations about AI on social media and, as Stephen Hawking did, tend to perceive only the extremes.[10]

This polarization cuts across AI's potential economic, social, and political impacts. Its *economic impacts* can shape what businesses do, how they organize their operations, and how much workers earn. AI's advice on marketing delivered through a mobile messaging app can unlock growth possibilities for small businesses. But its automation of call centers may displace workers and narrow the paths to economic growth. AI's *social impacts* can improve delivery of government services. If it improves learning in public schools, it will expand access to knowledge, but if it embeds bias in government decision-making, it can harm people. AI's *political impacts* can give people more voice and agency to fulfill their aspirations but can leave people worse off if malicious actors armed with AI spread pernicious disinformation, invade their privacy, or engage in cybercrime.

Evidence of AI's impacts—good or bad—is still evolving. Entrepreneurs, researchers, and civil society groups have created thousands of new AI applications, and the rapidly proliferating pilots in agriculture, health, and education are yielding a range of benefits. But definitive evidence that AI is accelerating economic growth, generating more and better jobs, and improving service delivery at scale—the outcomes that shape people's daily lives—is hard to find. Reconciling the myriad vantage points described earlier is easier once AI is understood as a GPT, much like steam power, electricity, computers, and the internet. The effects of AI will unfold through its initial disruption, gradual diffusion, and eventual transformation of economies, societies, and polities. These *transitional dynamics* will depend not only on changes in the production and use of AI but also on resulting spillover effects that range from changes in the demand for workers to patterns of trade and the movement of people across places.

AI as a general-purpose technology: Tuning out the noise

A *general-purpose technology* is characterized by its widespread use, its potential for continuous innovation, and its spurring of complementary innovations in industries.[11] AI fits the bill.[12] In a few short years, AI has evolved from machine-learning algorithms that make predictions to large language models that generate content from text, audio, and video, to AI agents that autonomously execute a series of tasks. AI's capabilities are also improving continuously and rapidly. In competition-level mathematics, AI leaped from well below the best human performers to parity in only a few years (2021–24), and AI performance on PhD-level science questions exceeded human parity within a year (2023–24).[13] In its evolution from *predictive* to *generative* to *agentic*,[14] AI has spawned innovative applications in medical imaging, weather forecasting, personal tutoring, and much more.

Viewing AI as a GPT becomes even more useful when examining the mechanisms that determine its role in the development process (refer to figure O.1). First, unlike previous technologies, AI enhances *capabilities* to perform nonroutine cognitive functions that guide decision-making and are often in short supply in developing countries. Second, the production of AI models and the related hardware and data centers is *concentrated* in a few countries—even more so than previous technologies—and linked through global value chains. These value chains shape developing countries' access to the capabilities of AI, which can be customized to build and use AI solutions that fit their context. Third, the effectiveness of AI solutions to raise the capabilities of individuals, businesses, and governments depends on the presence and quality of *complements* (particularly data that AI learns from, but also infrastructure, skills, institutions, and the like), which tend to be less available in developing countries, and the removal of organizational frictions, which tend to abound.

Figure O.1 AI's capabilities, concentration, and complements determine its economic, social, and political impacts through the pathways of adoption, adaptation, and advancement

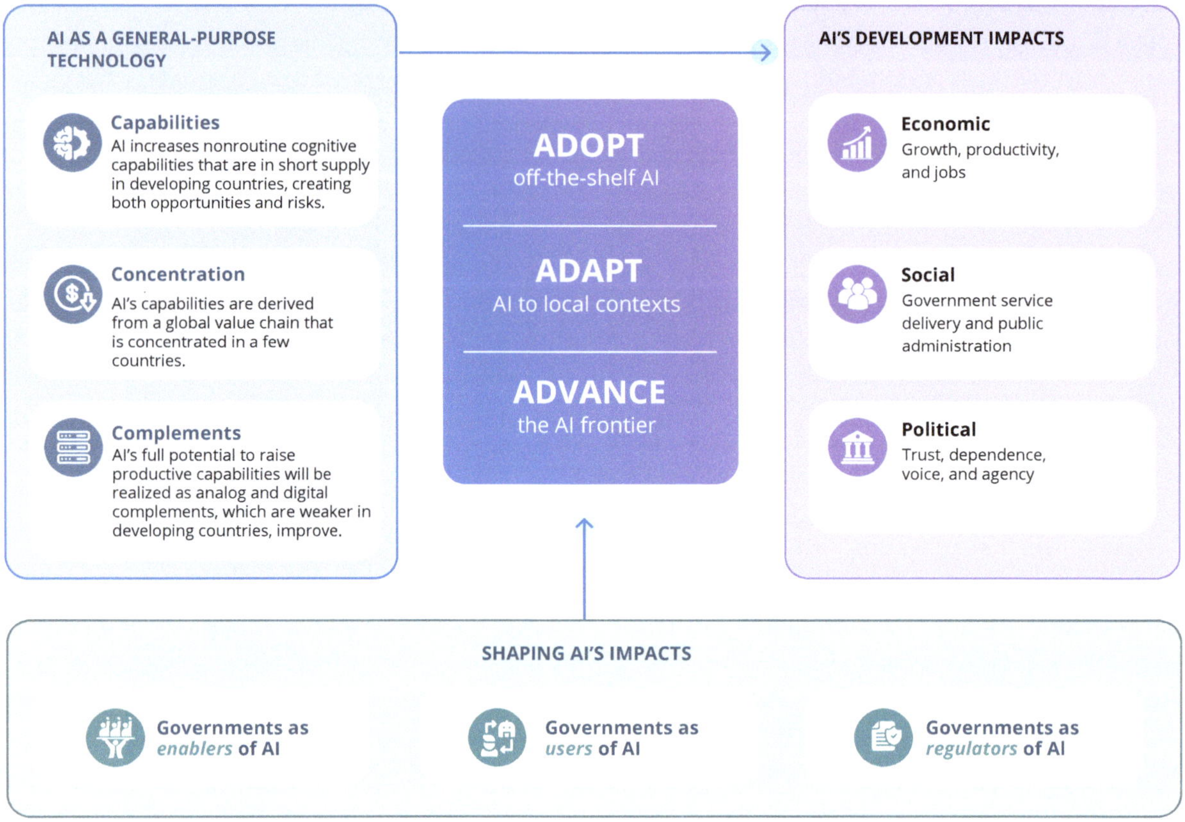

Source: WDR 2026 team.
Note: AI = artificial intelligence.

Capabilities: AI can do in a decade what might otherwise take a century

AI is "an umbrella term for a set of loosely related technologies."[15] AI's capabilities support nonroutine cognitive or analytical tasks that require judgment, contextual understanding, and problem solving.[16] This can be extremely helpful in developing countries, where capabilities to perform many cognitive tasks are scarce, costly, or undersupplied—too few teachers and too few health care professionals are a case in point.[17] Businesses now use AI across tasks that range from summarizing information, writing, and analyzing data to translation, customer interaction, and software development (refer to figure O.2). Governments use AI to guide the allocation of resources, disseminate citizen alerts, improve forecasting, enhance frontline services, and provide virtual assistants for citizen engagement.

Many developing countries face shortages of highly skilled workers. AI can help by enabling less experienced workers to perform more advanced cognitive tasks, allowing some work to be shifted away from scarce specialists and making existing workers more productive. First, if AI automates more expert tasks within an occupation, it lowers the entry requirements for people to carry out the work in that occupation.[18] There is evidence of such *leveling up*

Figure O.2 Businesses use AI for a wide range of tasks, including summarizing information, writing, analyzing data, translating, interacting with customers, and developing software

Average share of firms across sample countries that report using AI, by function, 2026 (%)

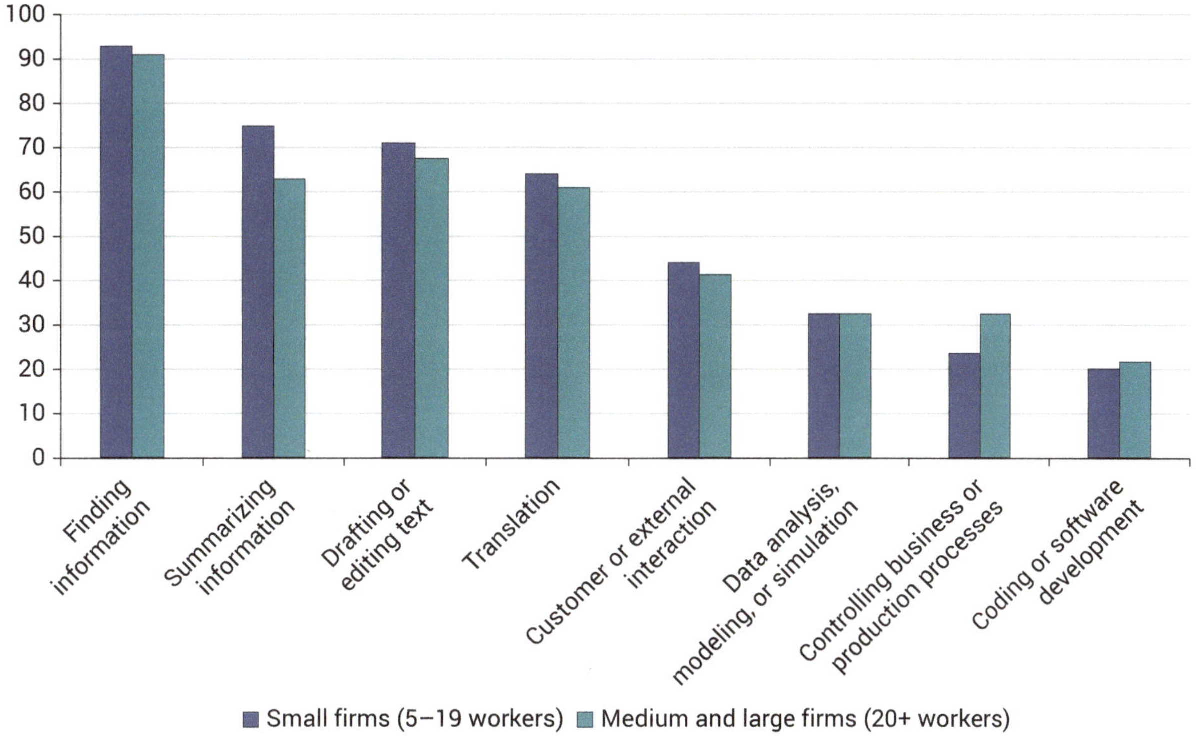

Source: WDR 2026 team, based on World Bank Enterprise Survey on AI Adoption.

Note: The sample includes formal firms with five or more employees, in manufacturing, construction, and services. The samples are as follows: India (1,355 firms), Jordan (358), Kenya (360), Mexico (603), Nigeria (777), Thailand (360), United States (392). Microdata are available at Enterprise Surveys (data portal), World Bank, https://www.enterprisesurveys.org/en/data. AI = artificial intelligence.

across cognitive occupations, including customer support,[19] professional writing,[20] and software development.[21] Second, AI can shift a given cognitive task to adjacent occupations that employ people with less expertise, such as shifting the task of medical-image screening from scarce medical specialists to lower-level health care providers.[22] Third, AI makes people more productive at what they currently do. For example, generative AI tools improve the quality of instruction in schools by supporting teachers with lesson planning, generating learning materials matched to students' skill levels, and providing quicker feedback on student work.

AI, however, can also have undesirable effects: It can eliminate some jobs, increase inequality, enable new forms of fraud and cybercrime, and weaken people's skills if they become overly dependent on it. It could, for example, displace call center jobs or exacerbate electricity shortages in developing countries. Fraudsters are already using AI to create deepfakes. Other malicious actors could use AI to launch cyberattacks, enlarging vulnerabilities for developing countries where institutional checks and balances are typically weaker.[23] In the classroom, moreover, there are early signs of *cognitive offloading*—students are letting AI do some of the thinking and learning they would otherwise do for themselves.[24] In the workplace, AI's negative impact on the demand for entry-level workers[25]—for example, in software services—can reduce opportunities to learn on the job.[26] Finally, because today's AI systems are largely designed in high-income countries, they might not fit the cultures, laws, languages, or social norms of developing countries.

The impact of AI-powered capabilities will depend not only on what AI can do in principle, but also on how quickly and widely AI diffuses, in practice. Today, AI is spreading across the globe faster than previous general-purpose technologies. High-income countries began using the steam engine, for example, about 80 years before lower-income countries adopted it widely. For electricity, the adoption lag halved to 40 years, and then it halved again to 20 years in the case of computers and the internet.[27] The diffusion of AI has been swifter still: When ChatGPT was launched in November 2022, more than 70 percent of user traffic originated from the United States, where the model was developed, but within six months, middle-income countries collectively accounted for half of ChatGPT traffic.[28] That creates a major opportunity for developing countries to catch up with the living standards in wealthier countries. Yet gaps in the intensity of use remain large. For example, nearly 25 percent of internet users in high-income countries had adopted ChatGPT on average by April 2025, compared with only 5.8 percent in upper-middle-income countries, 4.7 percent in lower-middle-income countries, and 0.7 percent in low-income countries.[29] That suggests that AI's benefits could remain concentrated in higher-income countries, at least initially.

Concentration: AI's capabilities depend on a value chain that is concentrated in a few countries

AI companies that are leading the development of AI models—and the related massive up-front investments in data centers, semiconductors, large data sets, and specialized talent—are concentrated today in a handful of countries. Most of the leading publicly listed AI companies are based in either the United States or China (refer to table O.1). So too are the world's prominent private AI companies.[30] Such concentration leads to so-called agglomeration effects, in which a deep pool of specialized talent attracts more firms and venture capital, fueling more research and start-ups, drawing in even more talent and investment. This cycle reinforces the efficient matching of top talent to leading firms, and of leading firms to capital, making it increasingly difficult for followers to catch up to AI's frontier. Little surprise, then, that the San Francisco Bay area maintains its position as the leading global AI hub.

The concentration of the most important building blocks of AI—such as advanced models, computing infrastructure, and specialized hardware—within a few companies and countries leaves developing countries potentially dependent on technologies they do not control. However, such concentration also allows developing countries to customize AI models to their local context without having to spend billions of dollars creating the most advanced systems from scratch.[31] For example, developing countries can build useful AI applications on top of existing models rather than creating the models themselves. The cost of using advanced large language models such as ChatGPT, Claude, and Gemini has declined considerably.[32] At the same time, many companies now offer large language models that are freely available or open for modification—including Apertus, DeepSeek, Falcon, Gemma, Kimi, Mistral, Llama, and Qwen.[33] These models can be downloaded, adapted to local languages and needs, and used to create new applications without requiring large investments in computing power, data, or highly specialized talent.

Table O.1 As of the end of 2025, most leading publicly listed AI-related companies are predominantly based in the United States and China

Company	Compute	Infrastructure	Data tools	Models	Applications
	Products and services				
Headquartered in the United States					
Advanced Micro Devices (AMD)	●		●		
Alphabet	●	●	●	●	●
Amazon	●	●	●	●	●
Apple	●	○	●	●	●
Cisco	●				
Meta	○	○	●	●	●
Microsoft	○	●	●	●	●
NVIDIA	●	●	●	●	●
Oracle		●	●	●	●
Palantir			●		●
Tesla	○	○	○	○	●
Headquartered in China					
Alibaba	●	●	●	●	●
Tencent		●	●	●	●
Headquartered in Taiwan, China					
Taiwan Semiconductor Manufacturing Company (TSMC)	●				
Headquartered in the Republic of Korea					
Samsung	●			○	●
SK Hynix	●				
Headquartered in the Netherlands					
ASML Holding NV	●				

● Marketed product or service ○ Used internally only

Source: WDR 2026 team, based on data of Frost et al. 2026.

Note: Firms are defined as *leading* based on supply chain presence and valuation. If a firm both sells a product or service and uses it internally, the product or service is coded as marketed. *Compute* refers to the hardware and processing power needed to train and run artificial intelligence (AI) models.

Complements: AI's capabilities have immediate effects, but its full potential will be realized as analog and digital complements improve

AI tools are becoming easier to use and customize. Today, people without formal technical skills or expensive hardware are accessing AI advice through local-language prompts in chatbots on smartphones. Similarly, AI coding assistants allow people with little or no programming experience to build applications using everyday language instead of computer code.[34]

Yet AI's full potential to raise capabilities for productive use will be realized only when the required analog and digital complements—infrastructure, skills, data systems, a good business environment, and institutions, among others—become widespread.[35] Without the right complements, AI's harmful capabilities can spread fast. For example, with legacy information technology systems and insufficient capacity to detect harmful incidents, AI can be used by malicious actors for cyberattacks.[36] This is precisely where developing countries risk losing out, because complements are typically weaker and slower to evolve—infrastructure is not built overnight, institutions are slow to adjust, and human capital accumulates gradually.[37]

Because of differences in the availability of complements across countries, AI's benefits will not be felt everywhere at the same speed. In places where people already have basic tools such as mobile phones and where AI can easily fit into existing ways of working, the impact could be rapid. Farmers, small business owners, and teachers, for example, can receive advice in their local language through voice or text messages on basic mobile phones, which are more common than smartphones in many low-income countries (refer to figure O.3). The benefits could be greater once people have access to smartphones and reliable internet connections, allowing them to use AI-powered chatbots through popular messaging apps. The benefits could be even greater when AI developers are able to tailor AI solutions to better align with local norms, culture, and regulations because local-language data are digitized.

Even when critical complements are in place, the adoption of AI may move slowly because of organizational frictions within businesses and governments. The decision-making process necessary for adoption can be arduous, going from gathering information to selection to piloting, evaluation, and implementation. Each stage requires scarce time and resources. The slow pace of change is compounded because AI adoption is a continuous process; as one bottleneck is relieved, another might emerge. For example, a pharmaceutical company using AI to discover new medicines may face capacity constraints in implementing human trials.[38]

History shows that new technologies often take time to deliver their full benefits because organizations must first change the way they work. For example, when electricity first became available, factories had to redesign their layouts before they could take full advantage of electric power, which slowed adoption.[39] Similarly, computers did not immediately boost productivity because businesses needed years to change their workflows, management practices, and operating procedures to make effective use of them.[40]

Figure O.3 Many more people in developing countries own a mobile phone than a smartphone

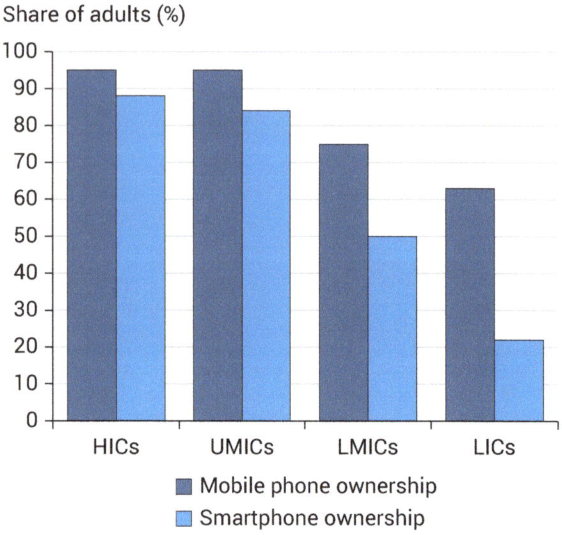

Source: WDR 2026 team, based on Klapper et al. 2025.

Note: The figure shows, by country income group, the share of the population ages 15 and above that owns a mobile phone and a smartphone. Data are as of 2024. HICs = high-income countries; LICs = low-income countries; LMICs = lower-middle-income countries; UMICs = upper-middle-income countries.

AI in developing countries: Adopt and adapt, then advance

Countries can adopt AI, adapt AI to the local context, or advance frontier AI systems themselves (refer to figure O.4). The last option is by far the most expensive, requiring enormous complementary investments in semiconductors, data centers, data, and talent. In fact, the biggest AI companies in the United States are expected to spend more than $750 billion on AI infrastructure in 2026 alone—more than the entire annual GDP of many developing countries (refer to figure O.5).[41] Because the costs are so high, only a handful of countries are likely to compete at the cutting edge of AI development.

That, however, still leaves a wide berth for developing countries to benefit from the technology. The adoption of off-the-shelf AI applications by households, businesses, and governments is a starting point. In 2025, more than half the users of ChatGPT, Claude, DeepSeek, and Gemini were in developing countries.[42]

Some AI solutions can meet users where they are—for example, through voice calls on regular mobile phones—and spur productive adoption. Even so, broader adoption will depend on local constraints: AI solutions will be less effective when providing advice to a small business owner, a court case mediator, or a teacher if electricity access is intermittent, if internet connectivity is patchy, if access to digital devices is limited, or if people cannot read. As of 2024, 32 percent of rural schools in Sub-Saharan Africa did not have regular access to electricity, 68 percent of rural schools did not have consistent internet access,[43] and 89 percent of 10-year-olds could not read and understand simple text.[44]

Adoption, in any case, will need to be supplemented with adaptation—because AI solutions are not always easily transplanted. The performance of an AI model developed in the United Kingdom

Figure O.4 Most developing countries do not need to advance the AI frontier to benefit substantially, but all need to adopt and adapt AI

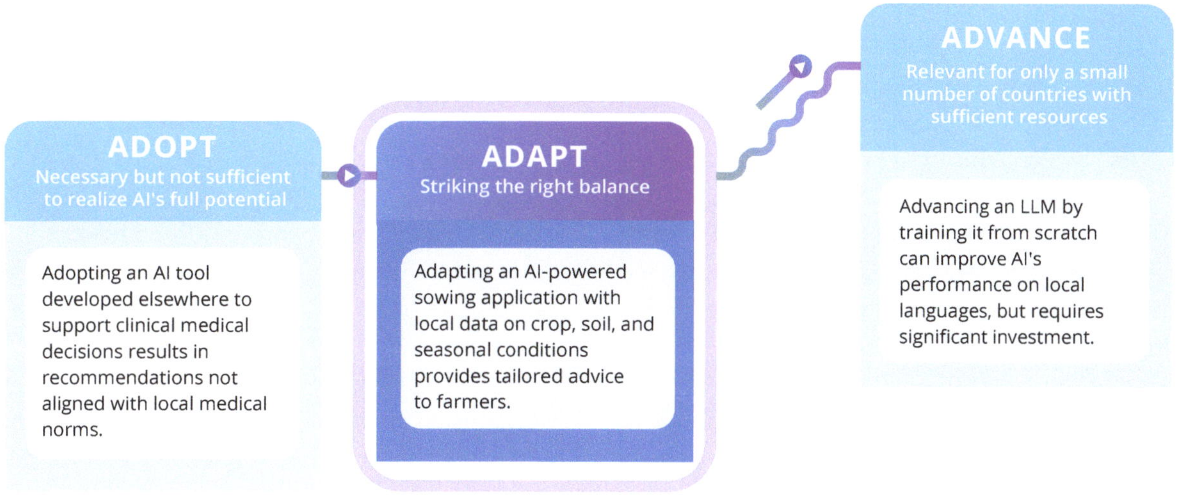

Source: WDR 2026 team.

Note: AI = artificial intelligence; LLM = large language model.

Figure O.5 The projected capital expenditures by AI hyperscalers exceeds the nominal GDP of many countries

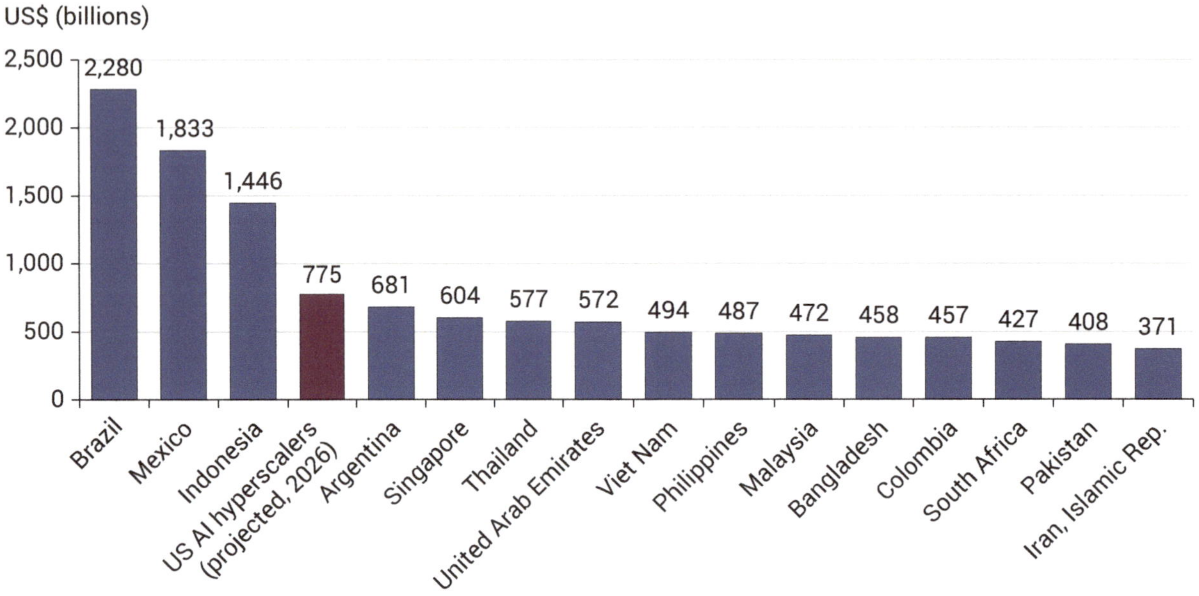

Source: WDR 2026 team, based on projected 2026 capital expenditure by Alphabet (Google), Amazon, Meta, Microsoft, and Oracle; data on GDP, Current Prices (dashboard), International Monetary Fund, https://www.imf.org/external/datamapper/NGDPD@WEO/OEMDC/ADVEC/WEOWORLD.

Note: The figure shows projected 2026 capital expenditures for AI hyperscalers (red bar; Alphabet [Google], Amazon, Meta, Microsoft, and Oracle; *AI hyperscalers* operate massive cloud infrastructures required to train and deploy AI models and applications) and 2025 nominal GDP for countries (blue bars). AI = artificial intelligence; US = United States.

to triage patients suspected of having COVID-19 declined sharply when it was tested using data from Viet Nam because patient demographics were so different.[45] Similarly, an AI tool used to screen for a complication of diabetes that affects the eyes rejected more than 20 percent of the images nurses took of patients because the lighting in the clinics did not match the lighting conditions that the model had been trained on.[46] The biggest benefits for developing countries will come when local entrepreneurs tailor AI tools to their own needs and circumstances. Doing this does not require the massive investments needed to build cutting-edge AI models, but it does require some access to computing power, data in local languages, and people with knowledge of local industries and problems. *Small AI* solutions are one important avenue of adaptation. Such solutions are grounded in specific development challenges and built for the complements that already exist in low-resource settings (refer to box O.1).

Countries can customize prediction systems like Google's Flood Hub to improve flood forecasting, for example. They can also make large language models like ChatGPT, Claude, and Gemini more useful by connecting them to local documents and knowledge or by building AI chatbots that work inside popular local messaging apps and provide business advice. Some countries are also creating AI models designed specifically for their own languages and cultures. Examples include Latin America's Latam-GPT and Southeast Asia's Southeast Asian Languages in One Network

Box O.1 Small AI, big impact

What makes artificial intelligence (AI) *small* can vary. In the tech industry, small AI refers to model size.[a] For example, small language models are trained to approach the performance of a large language model on far fewer *parameters*—the internal values that store what the model has learned.[b] Or it can be small in scope, built for one narrow task, such as identifying a crop disease or screening a medical image. Either way, small AI is built to run where the complements it depends on, such as power, internet connectivity, and digital devices, are scarce.[c] Small AI models can run offline on a phone or laptop. The model can also remain large in the cloud but can be accessed by users in low-resource settings through an application from a basic phone over a voice call or a text.

Small AI models are typically adapted from larger foundational AI models but can perform better on a narrow task—such as in the case of detecting hate speech on Nigerian Twitter.[d] Small AI applications can be built from large or small AI models and are already at work on real development challenges in a variety of areas. For example, Nuru, powered on a phone and even available offline, outperformed agricultural extension officers at diagnosing a diseased leaf.[e] Cough Against TB, built by Wadhwani AI with India's Central Tuberculosis Division, correctly flagged 9 in 10 people while screening for tuberculosis from the sound of a cough to identify who needed a test to confirm results.[f] In a randomized controlled trial across 40 Kenyan facilities, mothers who accessed the PROMPTS chatbot gained knowledge and sought care for their children and themselves more often.[g] In Ghana, Rori provides AI-powered tutoring in mathematics by text message on basic phones and weak networks; it generated nearly one full year of learning from two 30-minute weekly sessions over eight months at a cost of about five dollars per student.[h]

Source: WDR 2026 team.

a. Caballar and Stryker (2026); Kumar, Davenport, et al. (2025); Wang et al. (2024).
b. Abdin et al. (2024).
c. Chakravorti (2025); Goldin (2026).
d. Tonneau et al. (2024).
e. Mrisho et al. (2020).
f. Cough Against TB (web page), Wadhwani AI, AI Unit, Lords Education and Health Society, https://www.wadhwaniai.org/impact/healthcare-solutions/cough-against-tb/.
g. Jacaranda Health (2024).
h. Henkel et al. (2024).

(SEA-LION), which can sometimes perform better in local languages than the largest global AI models.

Over time, countries that gain experience adapting AI may begin advancing their own AI technologies from the ground up. For example, India's Sarvam AI has started developing new AI models rather than simply modifying existing ones. In Africa, Lelapa AI created InkubaLM, a model trained directly in five African languages. In the Middle East, the United Arab Emirates developed the Falcon family of AI models for Arabic. A similar pattern can be seen in the semiconductor industry. After spending decades building expertise in assembling and manufacturing computer chips, Malaysia is now moving into chip design. In 2025, a Malaysian company, SkyeChip, launched the country's first locally designed 7-nanometer chip, called MARS1000.[47]

The promise and peril of AI: Assessing its economic, social, and political impacts

Through the three pathways identified in this Report—adoption, adaptation, and advancement—AI is transforming national well-being economically (by affecting what people do and how much they earn); socially (by changing how people access public goods and services); and politically (by reshaping power relationships between countries, between governments and corporations, between corporations and individuals, and between citizens and states).

AI's economic impact: Restructuring growth, increasing productivity, and transforming jobs

In developing countries, the immediate risk of disruption from AI is limited to a small share of jobs, involving people employed in knowledge-intensive professional services. On the flip side, AI has the potential to improve the capabilities of many small businesses, in which most people are currently employed and in which they undertake manual rather than cognitive work. AI can also help productive businesses grow by reducing transaction costs. However, if complements do not evolve to match the need, gaps in productivity between small and large businesses and between developing and high-income countries are likely to widen. AI adoption will also have cascading economic effects, including by reshaping trade patterns, increasing human capital, raising energy costs, and creating economic volatility.

Immediate impacts: AI adoption will disrupt a small portion of the overall labor force in developing countries but can raise the capabilities of many small businesses

In low- and middle-income countries, about 4.5 percent of existing jobs are amenable to automation by generative AI—compared with 14.2 percent in high-income countries—while 16.2 percent of jobs are amenable to being complemented by AI (refer to figure O.6).[48] Some sectors with more cognitive jobs, such as information and communication technology (ICT), finance, and business services, are more amenable to automation by AI but employ relatively few people in developing countries.[49]

Early evidence reveals that the launch of ChatGPT reduced the demand for jobs that are more amenable to automation by AI, although the impact is much smaller in low- and middle-income countries than in high-income countries.[50] In China, the introduction of generative AI reduced job postings, with disproportionate impacts on entry-level, highly educated workers.[51] In India, the introduction of generative AI reduced monthly job postings for white-collar occupations most amenable to AI use and least complementary to AI, with disproportionate impacts on entry-level workers.[52] Even though these job displacement effects have been narrow in scope, they have outsized importance because

Figure O.6 The share of jobs amenable to AI use is lower in developing countries than in advanced economies

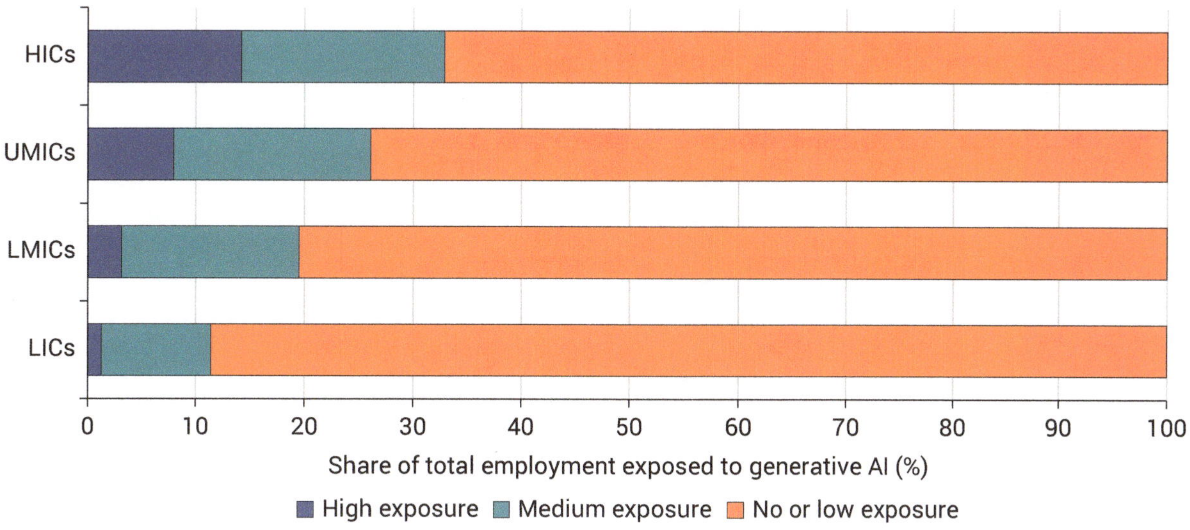

Sources: WDR 2026 team, based on Gmyrek et al. 2026.

Note: The figure displays the average score for exposure to generative AI across 137 countries (47 HICs, 38 UMICs, 35 LMICs, 17 LICs). Income classifications are for fiscal year 2027. High exposure will more likely lead to AI automating jobs, while medium exposure will more likely lead to AI complementing jobs. For details on the definitions of high exposure, medium exposure, and no or low exposure, refer to Gmyrek et al. (2026). AI = artificial intelligence; HICs = high-income countries; LICs = low-income countries; LMICs = lower-middle-income countries; UMICs = upper-middle-income countries.

knowledge-intensive services account for a growing share of middle-class jobs in developing countries and share links with other sectors.[53]

AI adoption is also expanding some jobs. The share of online job postings mentioning AI skills—those for software developers, systems analysts, and web developers—has surged since 2023, although this share was more than five times higher in high-income countries than in middle-income countries in the first half of 2025.[54]

In low-income and lower-middle-income countries, most people work in very small businesses. Nearly 90 percent work in firms with fewer than 10 people, and more than half work for themselves.[55] Most of these businesses are in agriculture, retail, and hospitality. Such small businesses can start benefiting from AI right away because AI can power up the tools they already use—messaging apps, business software, and social media (refer to figure O.7). For example, about one-fifth of small firms—those with 5 to 19 employees—across India, Jordan, Kenya, Mexico, Nigeria, and Thailand, on average, have adopted AI chatbots in their business operations compared with one-fourth of firms in the United States.[56] AI can boost productivity even in places with only basic internet or phone service, although people might need some training on how to use AI effectively. Kenya's experience illustrates both the opportunity and the challenge. A Kenyan WhatsApp-based AI assistant gave small business owners advice on managing inventory, handling customer inquiries, and creating marketing materials. But the app benefited only small-scale businesses that were already performing well and better at choosing and applying the advice they received.[57]

Figure O.7 Many businesses in developing countries already use digital technologies that facilitate the adoption of AI solutions

Share of firms using digital technology in surveyed developing countries, 2026 (%)

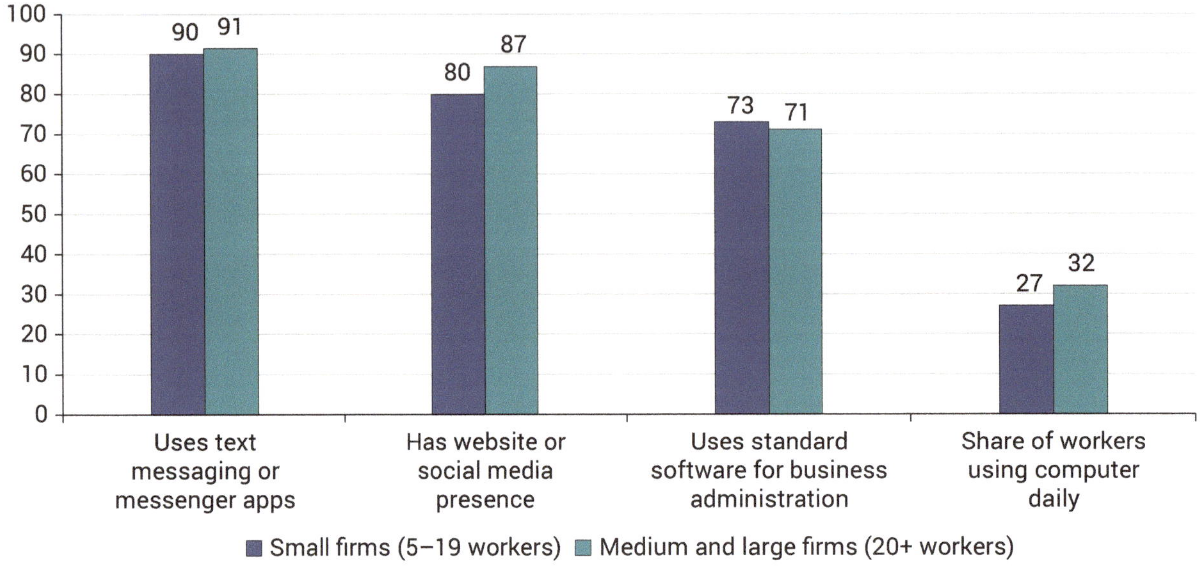

Source: WDR 2026 team, based on World Bank Enterprise Survey on AI Adoption.

Note: The figure reports data on formal firms in manufacturing, construction, and services with five or more employees. *Standard software* refers to software such as Excel. The data for surveyed developing economies average country-level indicators, with equal weight for each country. The samples are as follows: India (1,355 firms), Jordan (358), Kenya (360), Mexico (603), Nigeria (777), Thailand (360), United States (392). Microdata are available at Enterprise Surveys (data portal), World Bank, https://www.enterprisesurveys.org/en/data. AI = artificial intelligence.

Longer-term impacts: With the right complements, AI adoption can enable transformative entrepreneurship; without them, it could widen productivity gaps

Over time, AI can help small businesses and start-ups grow by making it easier to organize finances, manage customer service, create marketing materials, and reach customers in other countries.[58] Even very small businesses can use AI tools to perform tasks that once required the management resources of much larger companies. Businesses that find successful ways to use AI may be able to expand quickly and create new jobs.

Some of these opportunities will come from building AI products and services themselves. In many developing countries, start-ups backed by venture-capital investors are creating AI tools that other businesses can use.[59] Developing countries also play an important role in supplying the hardware needed for AI. About half of global exports of products used to build AI systems come from developing countries, including China, Mexico, Malaysia, Viet Nam, and Thailand, in that order, which have benefited from growing investment in semiconductors, electronics, and data center equipment.[60]

For now, AI adoption remains highly uneven. The World Bank Enterprise Survey on AI Adoption—in surveys of firms in India, Jordan, Kenya, Mexico, Nigeria, Thailand, and the United States—found that businesses with better management capabilities, past instances of product or process innovation, and better market access and labor productivity are much more likely to adopt AI. In China, the biggest benefits from AI have gone to firms that were already highly productive and located in regions with strong digital infrastructure, financial systems, and competitive markets.[61] These findings suggest that without the right complementary factors—infrastructure, skills, institutions, and venture capital that enable business dynamism—AI might do little to increase the number of successful entrepreneurs and fast-growing businesses in developing countries.

At current trends of AI adoption and with the current composition of jobs, the productivity benefits of AI are expected to be more than double in advanced economies than in developing countries.[62] About two-thirds of this gap is simply because advanced economies are adopting AI much more widely.[63] This could translate into a more sizable boost to economic growth in advanced economies; in the most optimistic scenario, AI is estimated to raise average annual potential growth from 1.2 percent to 3.6 percent in advanced economies, and from 4.1 percent to 4.9 percent in developing countries, during the 2020s.[64] Higher rates of AI adoption can result in higher potential growth in developing countries.

Cascading effects: AI could disrupt global trade patterns, increase human capital, raise energy costs, and create economic volatility

AI could change how countries grow by reshaping global trade and creating ripple effects across the economy. One example is the business process outsourcing industry—such as call centers, customer support, data processing, and back-office services—which has helped countries like India and the Philippines create jobs and grow their economies. As AI becomes better at handling many office and knowledge-based tasks, companies in wealthy countries may need fewer workers overseas to do this work. In fact, one major online freelance platform reported that jobs outsourced to developing countries fell by 39 percent in 2025, especially in occupations that AI can easily replace.[65] But the evidence is mixed: Some studies suggest AI could actually increase outsourcing by making workers more productive,[66] while others find no measurable effects.[67] AI could also affect the manufacturing sector. As robots become "smart" and able to perform complex tasks, low labor costs could become less important as a competitive advantage. This could make it harder for some developing countries to create manufacturing jobs through exports based mainly on cheap labor.

AI adoption is also likely to have other spillover effects—both positive and negative. On the positive side, AI could improve education and health care through tools such as personalized tutoring and medical decision support. Better education and health can lead to a more skilled and productive workforce, benefiting the entire economy. On the negative side, it could put pressure on prices and resources. AI data centers consume enormous amounts of electricity.[68] This could contribute to higher energy prices. Governments might also offer tax breaks and other incentives to attract AI investment. This can encourage growth, but it can also lead to too much money flowing into AI-related industries, inflating asset prices and increasing the risk of boom-and-bust cycles of growth and investment.

AI's social impact: Improving the delivery of public services

AI can help government officials do their jobs better by improving forecasts, helping them decide how to allocate scarce resources, and making it easier to track and manage government programs. AI can also help address shortages of skilled workers who interact directly with citizens—such as teachers and health care workers in government schools and hospitals—although evidence of these benefits is still limited and emerging. However, many governments face obstacles to using AI widely. They often lack clear information on which AI tools to choose, how to buy them, and how to implement them effectively. In addition, important supporting factors—such as reliable internet access, digital systems, and worker skills—are often missing, especially in government services that deal directly with the public.

AI turns government data into information that improves decision-making

AI can make a variety of back-office government functions far more efficient than they historically have been. In India, AI-supported weather forecasts are helping farmers—who relied little on information from the government and extension agents—make better production and investment choices.[69] In Kenya, the judiciary used a predictive AI algorithm to allocate more than 10,000 court cases per year to more than 1,500 mediators. This made case assignments fairer and increased the chances of successful mediation.[70] AI can also analyze large data sets to spot patterns that humans might miss in the monitoring and oversight of government programs. In Brazil, AI models use municipal audit data to predict which local governments might be at higher risk of corruption, allowing federal oversight bodies to focus their audits where problems are most likely to occur.[71] Across developing countries, government back-office use of AI applications substantially involves predictive AI, which helps officials forecast events, target scarce resources, analyze geographic information, and detect risks early (refer to figure O.8).

AI shows promise in improving the delivery of frontline public services

AI can strengthen frontline public services by helping tax officials, teachers, and health workers do their jobs more effectively. Early evidence shows that AI can save citizens time, improve teaching support, and expand access to medical screening, especially where skilled workers are in short supply. For example, Singapore's tax authority has an AI assistant that lets taxpayers check what they owe, change payment plans, and make payments. In 2024 alone, it saved taxpayers nearly 12,000 hours.[72] Similarly, generative AI tools are improving the quality of instruction in schools. In Sierra Leone, teachers increasingly used an AI assistant on WhatsApp instead of a standard web search because it provided cheaper and more useful advice on matching lessons to students' skill levels.[73] AI is also filling skills gaps in medical diagnosis. In Bangladesh, for example, AI-generated medical imaging increased the number of patients screened for a complication of diabetes by nearly 40 percent per day.[74]

Limited information on what works is slowing AI adoption in government, especially in frontline services

Governments face challenges at every step of adopting AI solutions—from choosing potential vendors and procurement systems to testing, deploying, evaluating, and improving them.[75] Yet there is little evidence or practical guidance on the best way to surmount these challenges in areas critical to the welfare of citizens: education, health care, social protection, and justice. That is a high-stakes concern: Mistakes in these areas could cause serious harm. AI algorithms can be inaccurate, biased, or poorly suited to local conditions. In Bangladesh, for example, an AI system based on mobile phone data identified poor households less accurately than traditional methods for targeting cash transfers.[76] In Nigeria, an AI tool used to support medical decisions tended to recommend more laboratory tests than were appropriate, reflecting practices common in high-income countries rather than local needs.[77]

Figure O.8 Governments in lower-income countries use AI mostly for decision support, geospatial intelligence, and early warning systems, and overwhelmingly rely on predictive AI

Types of AI used for the most common back-end tasks in low- and lower-middle-income countries

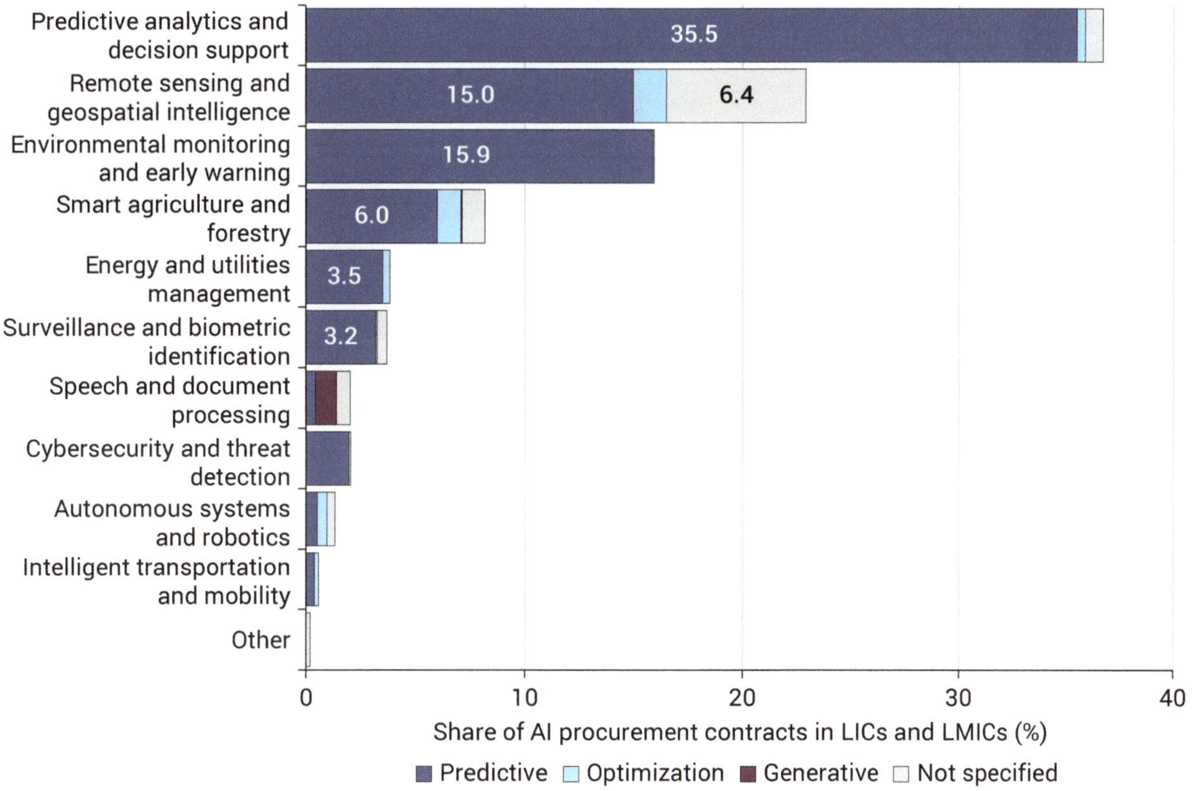

Source: WDR 2026 team, based on analysis of data on procurement contracts from Open Contracting Partnership 2025; Tenders Electronic Daily, EU Tenders, Publications Office of the European Union, https://ted.europa.eu/en/; World Bank.

Note: GPT-5 was used to classify 6,127,564 procurement contracts. The figure focuses on the 10 most frequent categories of tasks in procurement contracts classified as back end in low- and lower-middle-income countries. The sample of procurements of AI for back-end government services includes contracts from 19 low-income countries (338 contracts), 48 lower-middle-income countries (1,302 contracts), 43 upper-middle-income countries (1,190 contracts), and 40 high-income countries (11,156 contracts). Procurement contracts may not capture all possible uses of AI in government. AI = artificial intelligence; LICs = low-income countries; LMICs = lower-middle-income countries.

These issues can lead to poor decisions. Governments may delay the procurement of AI products until more evidence is available. Alternatively, they might move ahead despite insufficient evidence about what works and end up purchasing systems that are ineffective or poorly matched to their needs.

AI adoption faces bigger obstacles at the front lines of public service delivery than in government back offices

For services delivered directly to the public, the main barriers for service providers are often basic ones: limited internet access, a lack of AI tools in local languages, and shortages of digital skills (refer to figure O.9, panel a).[78] Frontline workers also need training and support to use AI effectively. In Sierra Leone, for example, early evidence shows that teachers are more likely to use AI tools when they have received guidance on how to integrate them into their work, even popular messaging apps such as WhatsApp.[79]

In government back offices, by contrast, the core constraint is usually data (refer to figure O.9, panel b). In many developing countries, government records are scattered across PDF manuals, legal documents, old computer systems, and staff knowledge rather than in organized digital databases. AI can help organize, process, and consolidate this information, but many countries have not yet undertaken the necessary investments for that to occur.

Figure O.9 **Governments in developing countries cite skills and connectivity on the front lines and data at the back end as the main obstacles to using AI to deliver public services**

Survey question: "To what extent do the following constraints prevent or limit your government's use of AI in the delivery of front-facing public services?"

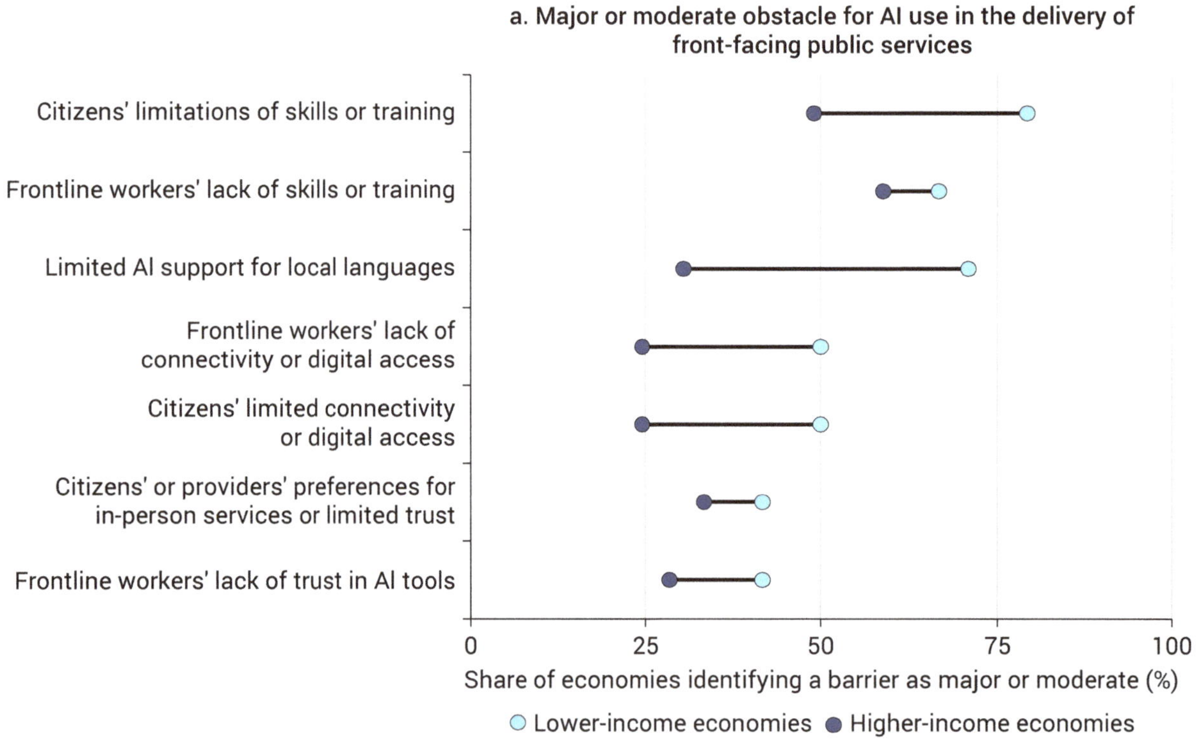

(Figure continues next page)

Figure O.9 Governments in developing countries cite skills and connectivity on the front lines and data at the back end as the main obstacles to using AI to deliver public services (*continued*)

Survey question: "To what extent do the following constraints prevent or limit your government's internal use of AI tools?"

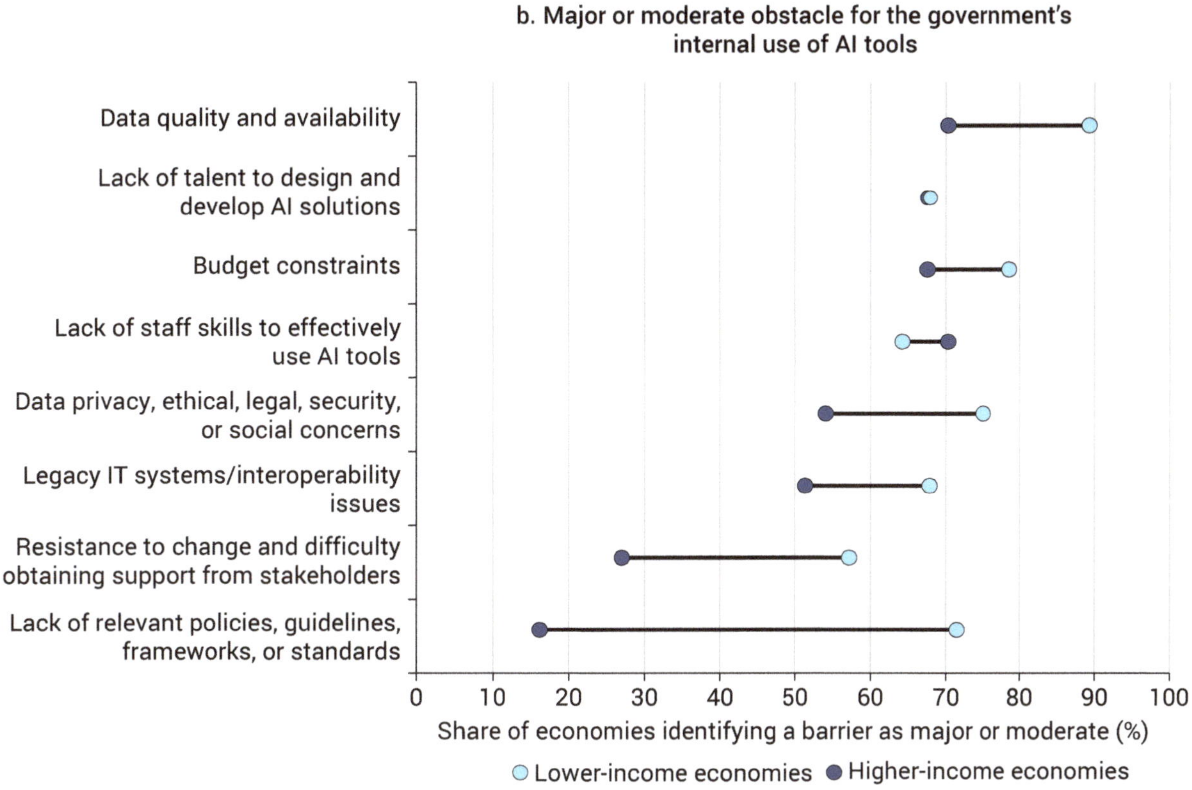

Source: WDR 2026 team, based on the AI and Data for Better Governance Survey, World Bank.

Note: The sample includes 12 low-income and 12 lower-middle-income economies (lower-income group) and 16 upper-middle-income economies and 17 high-income economies (higher-income group). AI = artificial intelligence; IT = information technology.

AI's political impact: Reshaping power within and across countries

AI is reshaping power relationships in four ways: between countries, between governments and corporations, between corporations and individuals, and between citizens and governments. Between countries, control over key parts of the AI value chain can give some nations leverage over others and limit their access to AI. Within countries, AI's benefits might not be widely shared if governments, businesses, and citizens are not aligned on the appropriate use of AI and strong institutions are lacking. AI can also be misused, giving governments new tools for surveillance and disinformation that weaken the rights and influence of citizens.

Geopolitics will shape countries' access to AI's full capabilities

Governments increasingly see AI as a foundational force shaping economic activity, national security, and global influence. Control over key parts of the AI value chain—raw materials, advanced chips, and data centers—by the world's leading powers, especially the United States and China, creates dependency risks for other countries. The availability of open AI models and the falling price of proprietary AI models (albeit for older versions) make advanced AI more accessible, but using them at scale still depends on data centers built on chips and commercial cloud services that are largely controlled by the major powers. Developing countries can reduce dependencies by sourcing these AI products and services from different countries, choosing the most suitable available technology. However, because AI systems depend on the different layers working together, this strategy can create interoperability problems and expose countries to conflicting regulations tied to technologies from different jurisdictions.

Pursuing *AI sovereignty* by building fully independent AI capabilities is an alternative in principle, but it is unlikely to deliver the desired results in practice. Investing across all layers of the AI value chain is extremely costly. Simply having a local data center cannot avoid dependencies on chips from major foreign providers. Large investments in data centers may also impose other societal costs, such as higher electricity prices.[80] Meanwhile, if several countries have built sovereign AI systems, they will be unable to benefit from global demand that lowers costs across AI systems, from model training and chip manufacturing to application development.[81] Thus, a more practical middle path is to combine open AI models with shared regional computing infrastructure, reducing dependence without requiring full AI sovereignty.

AI could deepen inequality unless policies are carefully designed

Millions of people, including in developing countries, already use AI to get practical advice, find information, and complete everyday tasks.[82] However, early evidence suggests that a growing share of the economic gains from AI is going to owners of technology and capital rather than to workers. In the European Union, regions with more intense AI patenting tend to experience a decline in the share of income earned by workers as wages, salaries, and benefits.[83] Workers who help build AI systems also earn little, in some cases. In Kenya, for example, gig workers who performed data-labeling tasks that are crucial for training frontier AI models were paid as little as $1.32 to $2.00 per hour in 2023—barely above Kenya's statutory minimum wage of about $1.20 per hour.[84]

Governments across the world are also providing subsidies and other incentives to support AI investments.[85] But if these policies are poorly designed, taxpayers could bear most of the financial risk while a small number of politically connected firms capture most of the rewards. Unless the benefits of AI are broadly shared, tensions between governments, businesses, and citizens could be exacerbated. That would limit AI's contribution to economic development.

The use of AI to misinform or monitor citizens leaves developing countries especially vulnerable

Generative AI creates possibilities for improving the integrity of information. In South Africa, biweekly AI-enabled fact-checks delivered via WhatsApp over six months improved citizens' ability to identify new misinformation.[86] In Ukraine, Transparency International Ukraine's DOZORRO applies machine learning to the government's e-procurement system, ProZorro, to flag irregularities and route citizens' complaints to law enforcement bodies.[87] However, generative AI has also been used to "sow doubt, smear opponents, or influence public debate" across countries through fake images, videos, and text.[88] Many developing countries are more vulnerable to generative AI's sophisticated manipulation of information because they lack institutional checks and balances or have weak ones. In 2025, Africa had only 66 active fact-checking organizations serving 1.5 billion people, compared with 139 in Europe serving 750 million people.[89]

The weak rule of law, few constraints on executive power, and limited space for civil society dialogue in countries can tip the balance toward AI-powered surveillance tracking citizen activity.[90] Autocracies and weak democracies are more likely to import AI surveillance technologies, such as facial recognition, following domestic political unrest.[91]

Shaping AI: Governments as enablers, users, and regulators

AI's economic, social, and political impacts in developing countries hold both promise and peril. Governments—in tandem with markets—can leverage AI's potential and guard against AI's risks as *enablers* of AI, *users* of AI, and *regulators* of AI along the pathways of AI adoption, adaptation, and advancement (refer to table O.2).

As enablers of AI, governments should focus on establishing the analog and digital complements

Table O.2 Governments shape the opportunities to adopt, adapt, and advance AI as enablers, users, and regulators

<table>
<tr><th rowspan="2">AI pathway</th><th colspan="3">Government role</th></tr>
<tr><th>Enabler of AI</th><th>User of AI</th><th>Regulator of AI</th></tr>
<tr><td>Adopt
(use off-the-shelf AI)</td><td>• Build foundational infrastructure and skills.
• Share information about what AI can do.
• Build AI as public infrastructure.
• Avoid tax and other regulatory policies that encourage replacing workers with AI.</td><td>• Make government data AI-ready.
• Invest in staff capacity.</td><td rowspan="3">• Start with voluntary standards.
• Use existing laws to address AI risks now.
• Build AI rules that can adapt over time.
• Work with other countries to keep AI rules compatible internationally.</td></tr>
<tr><td>Adapt
(build AI solutions that incorporate the local context)</td><td rowspan="2">• Expand access to computing infrastructure.
• Invest in better data.
• Invest in AI-related technical skills.
• Create a business environment where entrepreneurs can thrive.</td><td rowspan="2">• Create better systems to buy, test, evaluate, and improve AI solutions.
• Use government procurement to crowd in local AI solutions if they work better in the local context.</td></tr>
<tr><td>Advance
(participate in frontier AI development)</td></tr>
</table>

Source: WDR 2026 team.

Note: The policy recommendations for adapting and advancing AI solutions are qualitatively similar but quantitatively different. For example, investments in computing infrastructure, data, and AI-related technical skills are significantly larger in AI advancement relative to AI adaptation. AI = artificial intelligence.

that enable the productive adoption and adaptation of AI by the private sector. As users of AI, governments should leverage their position as anchor customers to scale up AI adaptation. As regulators of AI, governments should rely on voluntary standards as a starting point, while using existing legal instruments to counter social harms where voluntary standards fall short. Standards, whether voluntary or mandatory, should draw on international cooperation to guard against regulatory fragmentation across countries.

Countries are already making these choices. As of June 2026, more than 80 countries had published national AI strategies (refer to map O.1). However, countries with the most to gain from AI might be the least prepared. For example, among 25 low-income countries, only one—Rwanda—had published a dedicated AI strategy, compared with more than half of high-income countries.

Governments as enablers: Invest in analog and digital complements for the productive adoption and adaptation of AI

As enablers of AI, governments should focus on strengthening the analog complements—reliable electricity, broadband connectivity, and foundational literacy—necessary for the productive adoption of AI by small firms and farms. These are areas where the private sector may not invest sufficiently. In themselves, these analog complements do not guarantee productive AI use—businesses may be unaware of AI solutions, unable to access AI solutions if those solutions require subscriptions, or use AI solutions to substitute for workers because regulations increase hiring and firing costs. Governments should therefore fill information gaps about AI solutions, build AI as public infrastructure, and reform regulations

Map O.1 Very few low-income countries have published national AI strategies

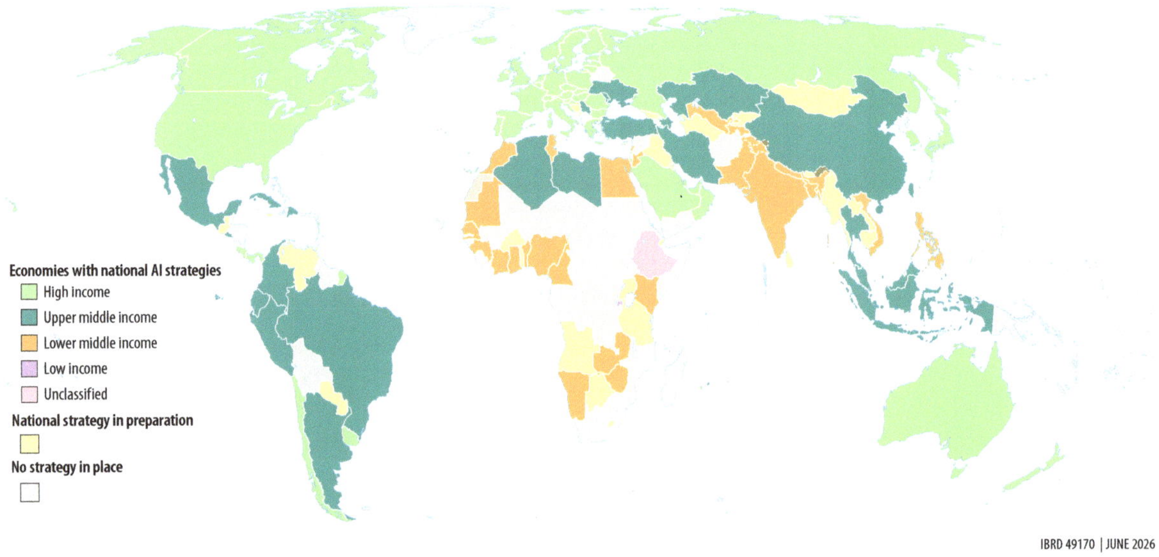

Source: WDR 2026 team, based on Radu 2026.

Note: The map includes published strategies for which the full text could be found online as of June 2026. World Bank income classifications for 2025 were therefore used. For the purposes of this analysis, a national AI strategy is defined as a stand-alone, government-led framework defining a country's vision and action plan for artificial intelligence (AI). Ethiopia has a national AI strategy, but its income level was unclassified in 2025. For Lebanon and Switzerland, published sector-based strategies are included. South Africa is not included as an economy with a strategy because of the withdrawal of the Draft National AI Policy in April 2026. *National strategy in preparation* refers to AI strategies under development, from early stages of consultation to near-final drafts.

that create incentives for businesses to replace workers with AI.

To foster the development of AI applications that are adapted to the local context, governments can help by expanding access to data, computing infrastructure, and digital skills and increasing support for local entrepreneurship. Without these analog and digital complements, local business will have fewer opportunities to compete in the market, innovate, and adapt AI to meet domestic needs.

Strengthen the analog complements to support the productive adoption of AI

Build foundational infrastructure and skills to widen access to AI

Governments have an important role in providing the basic infrastructure upon which AI depends, especially in remote areas where the private sector is unlikely to invest.[92] This includes electricity and internet access in schools, hospitals, and public service centers. In Mali, for example, improving the reliability of a community health care worker mobile app more than doubled the chances that workers completed the minimum expected number of home visits.[93] Governments can also make it easier for people and businesses to use digital technologies by reducing taxes on low-cost smartphones, computers, and other digital devices.[94]

Governments should also invest in the basic skills that help people benefit from AI, including literacy, numeracy, reasoning, basic digital skills, and teamwork. These skills make it easier to learn how to use new technologies and adapt as jobs change.[95] Building them starts with high-quality formal education from an early age. In Rwanda, for example, the government is introducing AI-awareness modules in secondary schools as part of its broader digital transformation strategy.[96]

Share information about what AI can do

Even when businesses have internet access, electricity, and the skills to use AI, many still do not adopt it because they do not know which AI tools work, what they cost, or how they can be deployed to improve their business. In developing countries, businesses say that lack of information and lack of finance are the two biggest reasons they either do not use AI products or do not expand AI's use (refer figure O.10). Evidence from a recent study of more than 500 start-ups around the world shows that entrepreneurs who learned how other businesses had successfully used AI identified more ways to apply AI across their own operations.[97] Governments can help by making it easier for businesses to find AI solutions—for example, through online directories, industry-specific registries, or technology advisers who match AI providers with potential users.[98]

Build AI as public infrastructure

Governments can also expand access to AI by making low-cost open and interoperable AI tools in local languages more widely available through digital public infrastructure, an approach that would be especially beneficial to people employed in agriculture, small retail, and other microenterprises. Brazil's Pix payment system, Estonia's X-Road data exchange, and India's Unified Payment Interface (UPI) exemplify the approach. All were designed as reusable foundations for digital public infrastructure.[99] When AI runs on public rails, its benefits can diffuse more widely and quickly.

Avoid tax and other regulatory policies that encourage replacing workers with AI

Tax systems in many high-income countries make it cheaper for businesses to invest in automation than to hire workers. In the United States, for example, businesses today pay a tax of less than 5 percent when buying automation equipment or software. By contrast, over the last four decades, businesses have paid an average rate of 25 percent in payroll and income taxes for hiring workers to perform the same tasks.[100] Tax differences of this kind can encourage businesses to use AI to replace workers rather than to

Figure O.10 Lack of information and finance are the biggest reasons businesses do not adopt and scale up AI solutions

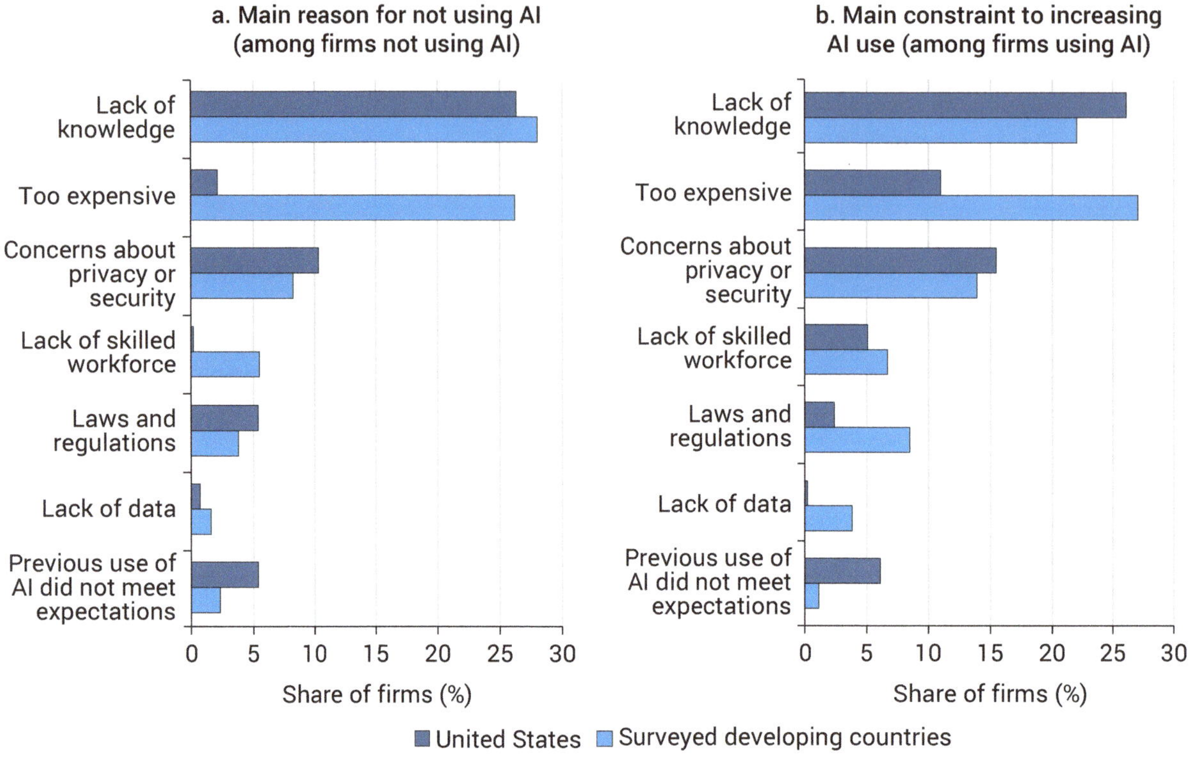

Sources: WDR 2026 team, based on World Bank Enterprise Survey on AI Adoption; Davies et al. 2026.

Note: Firms could select only one option. The figure covers formal firms with five or more employees, pooling data across all countries (averaging country-level indicators). The data for surveyed developing countries average country-level indicators, with equal weight for each country. The samples are as follows: India (1,355 firms), Jordan (358), Kenya (360), Mexico (603), Nigeria (777), Thailand (360), United States (392). Microdata are available at Enterprise Surveys (data portal), World Bank, https://www.enterprisesurveys.org/en/data. AI = artificial intelligence.

help them become more productive. Governments in developing countries—where millions of people are joining the workforce each year—should avoid taxes and other regulatory policies that make the purchase of AI software more attractive than hiring or retaining workers.

Build the analog and digital complements that enable local businesses to adapt AI

Expand access to affordable computing infrastructure

Because data centers needed for AI development are concentrated among a handful of large companies in high-income countries, developing countries will need to rely on cloud services to meet their immediate needs. In larger middle-income countries, private investment in local data centers can help businesses adapt AI to local needs—because faster data transmission enables AI tools to respond more quickly to users while supporting the growth of local AI companies. Governments can also improve access to AI compute by making it easier for foreign companies to invest in local data centers. That is already happening: developing countries now collectively account for about 40 percent of new foreign direct investment projects in data centers worldwide.[101] Smaller economies can reduce costs by working together—for example, by adopting common rules that attract private investment or by jointly financing regional data centers, as the African Union has done.[102] Governments can further help small businesses, start-ups, and researchers by offering compute at lower cost, as India has done through its INDIAai mission.[103] In lower-income countries, where many people still lack reliable electricity and internet access, governments should balance support for data centers with investments in the physical and digital complements necessary for AI to thrive.

Invest in better data

Governments can help make the data needed to build AI solutions more widely available. One option is to make more public data—especially administrative data in local languages—open for AI developers to use.[104] The government of India's BHASHINI initiative, for example, has significantly increased the accessibility of public records.[105] Governments can also work with universities and civil society to create more open data sets. In Africa, the Masakhane project is building language data sets from African speakers for use in AI training data.[106] Strong data-sharing agreements that give local communities a say in how their data are used can build trust and encourage more people to participate.[107] In Ghana, researchers from the Kwame Nkrumah University of Science and Technology are developing realistic synthetic data[108] for applications in health care and agriculture.[109] Finally, governments can help small businesses gain access to high-quality data owned by private companies through grants, vouchers, or other financial support, as the European Union's Horizon 2020 initiative has shown.[110]

Invest in AI-related technical skills

Countries need more people with the technical skills to adapt and advance AI—especially in fields such as computer science, data science, cybersecurity, AI ethics, and systems engineering.[111] Governments can help by ensuring that these subjects are taught in universities and vocational schools, in ways that allow workers to keep learning throughout their careers. Partnerships between businesses, universities, and governments can support this objective. Singapore, for example, has introduced AI into its national school curriculum, with an emphasis on using AI safely and responsibly.[112] In Morocco, industry federations work with the government to provide training on AI applications in sectors such as agriculture and manufacturing.[113] Governments can also draw on the expertise of skilled professionals living abroad by engaging the diaspora and creating incentives for AI research and innovation hubs.

Create a business environment in which entrepreneurs can experiment and thrive

AI makes it easier to start and grow a business by giving entrepreneurs better access to information, customers, and decision-making tools. It also encourages more productive businesses to grow while less competitive ones either improve or leave the market. But these benefits will materialize only if governments create a business environment that supports innovation and entrepreneurship.[114] The gap in financing start-ups is particularly acute, and venture capital markets in most low- and middle-income countries are weak. In many African countries, for example, local entrepreneurs struggle to raise funding because most investment comes from foreign investors, and investment often goes disproportionately to domestic business owners with foreign connections.[115] Governments can support blended finance combining public and private monies as well as partial credit guarantees to help AI solution developers raise capital and experiment. Governments can also help by making it easier to start and close businesses, attracting foreign investment, and keeping markets open to trade.

Governments as users: Wield buying power to support AI solutions that are adapted to local needs

Governments can play an important role in helping countries adapt AI to local needs by becoming early users and buyers of AI. They hold vast amounts of data and deliver many services that require AI solutions tailored to local languages, laws, and conditions. By testing, evaluating, and buying AI products, governments can reduce the risks of developing new AI solutions and create demand for AI products designed for local needs—especially when the private sector is slow to do so. This will require governments to invest in staff capacity.

Make government data AI-ready

Governments already collect huge amounts of information—from censuses, tax records, and birth and death registries to court records, land records, and social programs. Much of this information, however, is either still on paper, incomplete, or scattered across multiple agencies, making it difficult to use. The first step is to digitize old records and convert them into structured, machine-readable data that AI systems can analyze. In Brazil, for example, the VICTOR system converts scanned court documents into machine-readable text. It has reduced the amount of time it takes to determine eligibility for an appeal to the Brazilian Supreme Federal Court from 40 minutes to just 5 seconds.[116]

Governments should also connect data across agencies instead of keeping them in separate systems. Some countries already are doing this. In India's Telangana state, the TGDeX data exchange platform brings together data from sectors such as health care and agriculture so they can be used more effectively.[117] More broadly, *digital public infrastructure*—such as digital IDs, digital payment wallets, and secure data-sharing platforms—can help create standardized, linked records that different government agencies can share and use.

Create better systems to buy, test, evaluate, and improve AI solutions

Even as AI applications proliferate around the world, the evidence remains limited regarding what works and what does not (refer to figure O.11). As a result, many AI projects never move beyond small pilot programs. To fix this, governments need better ways to buy, monitor, and evaluate AI systems. Procurement should be based on clear performance standards, so AI tools are measured against agreed-upon benchmarks. For example, the World Health Organization's benchmark for AI systems that screen for tuberculosis prioritizes the detection of positive cases and lowers the risk of false negatives in its recommendations for follow-up.[118] Buying AI solutions is different from purchasing traditional software because AI systems improve over time as they are tested, refined, and adapted to local needs.[119] Governments therefore need procurement processes that support ongoing learning and improvement rather than one-time purchases. Governments should also work with universities and research institutions to evaluate whether AI solutions actually improve outcomes and provide good value for money.[120] Shared evidence and public benchmarks can help countries identify which AI applications are worth scaling up and avoid the problem of running too many pilot projects that are never expanded.[121]

Use government procurement to crowd in local AI solutions for uses in which the local context matters greatly

Governments often have the data needed to use AI to improve public services, but they usually lack the expertise to build AI applications themselves. That makes procurement the main mechanism for bringing AI into government services. Used well, government procurement can encourage privately developed local AI solutions that are aligned with public goals. This approach is similar to the one taken for the development of vaccines, in which governments commit in advance to buying successful products. This approach is especially useful in areas such as health care, education, and the justice system, in which AI that is poorly adapted to local conditions can cause serious harm. It also makes sense for AI tools that provide broad public

Figure O.11 Few AI health interventions have been evaluated well enough to justify large-scale deployment

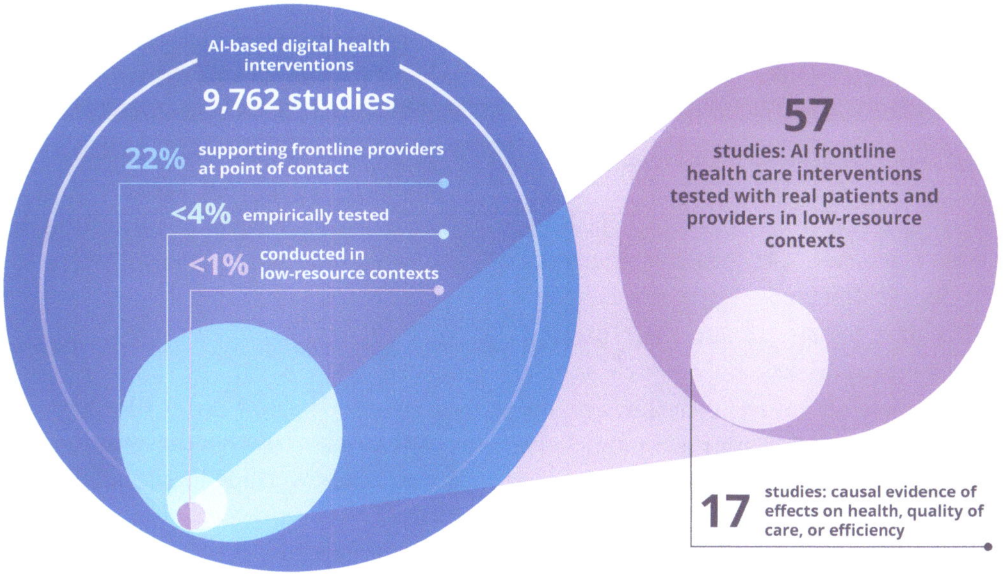

Source: Sautmann and Weinert 2026.

Note: Low-resource contexts refers to contexts in low- and middle-income countries, as well as low-resource settings in high-income countries. AI = artificial intelligence.

benefits, such as digital teaching assistants or digital public infrastructure.

When buying AI, governments should avoid becoming dependent on a single vendor. Contracts should make it easy to switch providers by requiring that data be able to be accessed and transferred to another system.[122] Vendors should also be rewarded for collecting data that helps measure whether the AI solution is working as intended, and for continually improving it.[123] One way to do this is through performance-based contracts, in which vendors are paid based on the results they deliver rather than for simply providing the technology.[124]

Invest in staff capacity to make AI work

Governments need people with the skills to buy, deploy, maintain, and improve AI systems over time. The skills most needed to do this are not training AI models, but understanding user workflows, evaluating vendor claims, and safely connecting government data to AI tools.

The starting point is recruiting experienced practitioners from academia, nonprofits, and the private sector in government departments and specialized digital agencies, as well as using partnerships with research institutes and universities. Such talent can hit the ground running. In Brazil, for example, the use of AI tools by digital teams improved productivity and helped accelerate service delivery across 53 projects.[125] Empowering digital teams in the decision-making process around AI solutions can help consolidate these benefits. Building *AI literacy*—understanding what AI can and cannot do, when its use is appropriate, and how to interpret its outputs—across the broader civil service also matters. Many governments around the world report that training and capacity building would make the biggest difference for responsible AI use.[126] In India, the iGOT Karmayogi has enabled more than 1.3 million government officials to complete AI-related courses.[127]

Governments as regulators: Build trustworthy AI, using voluntary standards and flexible rules

AI can create real benefits, but it also comes with real risks. Poorly designed AI systems can discriminate against people, violate their privacy, create cybersecurity risks, and reduce public trust. When people do not trust AI, they are less likely to use it in ways that improve public services and productivity. Building trustworthy AI systems does not require governments to start from scratch. They can begin by encouraging the use of voluntary standards for trustworthy AI and by enforcing existing laws in circumstances in which AI creates risks. Clear rules give businesses confidence to develop and use AI responsibly. Over time, governments should build a flexible AI governance system that regularly reviews new developments, fills regulatory gaps, strengthens enforcement, and adapts as the technology changes. Policy makers should build on what already works, test new approaches when needed, and systematically involve businesses, researchers, civil society, and citizens in shaping AI policy. International cooperation is also important so that countries do not create conflicting rules.

Start with voluntary standards

Voluntary standards—such as guidelines for AI safety testing, auditing, transparency, and risk management—are a good starting point for AI governance.[128] Already, more than 800 AI-related standards have been published or are under development.[129] These standards have several advantages. They are created by technical experts in industry, they focus on preventing problems before they occur, and they can be updated much faster than legislation. Voluntary standards, however, are not enough on their own. Companies may not fully account for the broader social risks of AI, especially when commercial incentives conflict with the public interest.[130] Developing countries also often have limited influence over how these standards are created because they have fewer resources and less representation in international standards-setting processes.[131]

Use existing laws to address AI risks now

AI can create harm faster than governments can create new laws. Rather than waiting for AI-specific legislation, governments should use the laws they already have to protect people. Existing laws on data protection, consumer protection, human rights, intellectual property, and cybersecurity, for example, already provide important tools for managing many AI risks. Governments in several developing countries have begun to do exactly that. Senegal's Commission for Personal Data Protection blocked the use of facial recognition to monitor employees because of privacy concerns.[132] The Constitutional Court of Colombia ruled that AI cannot replace human judgment in court decisions.[133] In the Philippines, the government temporarily blocked Grok over concerns about AI-generated sexually explicit content until stronger safeguards were in place.[134]

Build AI rules that can adapt over time

Governments should review their existing legal frameworks to identify where AI creates new challenges and decide whether those gaps can be addressed by updating current laws or warrant the introduction of new ones.[135] Some countries are already updating existing regulations. Singapore, for example, has clarified how machine learning can be used for software in medical devices. Other countries have updated election laws to address AI-generated deepfakes. In some cases, new regulations will be needed—for example, to improve transparency around AI training data, prohibit especially harmful uses of AI, limit AI-enabled surveillance without consent, and regulate government purchases of high-risk AI systems. Strong enforcement and compliance is just as important as good laws. Many developing countries already have modern consumer protection and privacy laws, but lack the resources to enforce them effectively.[136] Regulatory *sandboxes* can help by providing a controlled environment in which companies can test AI tools before wider deployment.[137]

Work with other countries to keep AI rules globally compatible

Countries should avoid creating AI regulations that conflict with one another. Shared principles make it easier to avoid a regulatory race to the bottom while allowing AI companies—especially smaller firms—to operate across multiple markets without facing different rules everywhere.

Developing countries should participate actively in international discussions on AI governance. Forums such as the United Nations Global Dialogue on AI Governance give governments, businesses, and civil society an opportunity to shape global AI policy together.[138] Regional cooperation is also important. For example, the Association of Southeast Asian Nations has developed guidance to make AI governance more consistent across all member countries,[139] while the Council of Europe's Framework Convention on Artificial Intelligence and Human Rights, Democracy, and the Rule of Law promotes AI systems that respect human rights, democracy, and the rule of law.[140] The Framework Convention's signatories include the European Union, the United States, Canada, Japan, Israel, and Uruguay. Developing countries should also participate in international standards-setting processes[141] so they can help shape the technical standards that define trustworthy AI rather than simply adopting standards created elsewhere.

The future of AI's impacts depends on the choices made today

No one knows exactly how far or how fast AI will advance. If you listen to leading AI companies in Silicon Valley or follow technology podcasts on social media, you might be inclined to think that artificial general intelligence—AI that can match human thinking in almost any task—is just around the corner. Others are already talking about even more powerful AI systems. Rather than trying to predict whether or when these breakthroughs will happen, this Report focuses on a more practical question: How can countries use AI to improve people's lives? For developing countries, the answer will depend less on how capable AI becomes and much more on how widely, effectively, and responsibly AI is used to address real economic, social, and political challenges.

There is much to learn from previous waves of transformative technology. Digital technologies spread quickly, but many developing countries did not see the full economic and social benefits because the right supporting conditions were missing, as the *World Development Report 2016: Digital Dividends* showed.[142] The same has been true for the explosion of data, much of whose value in developing countries remains untapped, as the *World Development Report 2021: Data for Better Lives* noted.[143] AI has even greater potential, but whether it delivers on that promise will depend on the policy decisions governments make today.

For developing countries, the priority should be to use AI to expand people's capabilities and improve opportunities for them. Governments can help by making AI easier to access, ensuring that it works in local languages and is suited to local conditions, and investing in the digital infrastructure, skills, and institutions needed to support it. At the same time, they must reduce the risks of AI so that its benefits exceed its harms. With the right policies, countries can move beyond today's multitude of small pilot projects and shift toward deploying AI at scale to improve public services, strengthen businesses, and raise living standards. That is the only way AI can fulfill its promise as a transformative tool for development.

Notes

1. Comin and Mestieri (2018); Gill (2020).
2. Liu and Wang (2026).
3. Sajadieh et al. (2026).
4. McPeak et al. (2024).
5. Burlig et al. (2025); Government of India (2026); Vallangi (2026).
6. Analysis of mediation data by the WDR 2026 team, based on Farabi et al. (2026).
7. Yukins and Kelman (2022).
8. World Bank (2023).
9. Radu (2026).
10. Refer to "LCFI [Leverhulme Centre for the Future of Intelligence] Launch: Stephen Hawking—Event Recordings," https://www.lcfi.ac.uk/resources/cfi-launch-stephen-hawking.
11. Bresnahan and Trajtenberg (1995).
12. AI-related technologies, including big data, data mining, data science, machine learning, and natural language processing, conform to these criteria (Goldfarb et al. 2023). More recently, with substantially fewer resources than ever before, the coding tools of generative AI have helped create software because the code is verifiable. The speed of progress might be slower in other application domains in which human feedback is typically needed to verify outputs.
13. Maslej et al. (2025).
14. *Predictive AI* uses statistical and machine learning models for prediction or classification tasks. *Generative AI* creates new content, such as text, images, or audio. *Agentic AI* executes a series of tasks independently based on goals, context, and learning gained during the process.
15. Narayanan and Kapoor (2024).
16. Bick et al. (2025); Felten et al. (2023).
17. There were 2.9 physicians per 10,000 people in Sub-Saharan Africa in 2019, far below the global average of 16.7. Physician-patient densities were also low (less than 10 per 10,000) in the Middle East and North Africa and in South Asia (Haakenstad et al. 2022). Similarly, the average student-teacher ratio in primary schools across low-income countries is approximately 40:1, compared with about 15:1 in high-income countries. Refer to UIS Data Browser (dashboard), Institute for Statistics, United Nations Educational, Scientific, and Cultural Organization, https://databrowser.uis.unesco.org/.
18. This will lower wages if demand for the work does not increase (Autor and Thompson 2025).
19. Brynjolfsson, Li, et al. (2025).
20. Noy and Zhang (2023).
21. Cui et al. (2026).
22. Autor (2024).
23. The restricted release of Anthropic's Claude Mythos exemplifies the tension that AI's capabilities can be used by criminals to threaten cybersecurity much more quickly than large organizations can prepare cyber systems to guard against such attacks.
24. Students researching a question with the help of large language models produced less relevant cognitive responses (Stadler et al. 2024). Students who were given unrestricted access to such models bypassed opportunities for "desirable difficulty" and performed worse on subsequent knowledge tests (Barcaui 2025; Bastani et al. 2025).
25. Brynjolfsson, Chandar, et al. (2025); Brynjolfsson et al. (2026); Hosseini and Lichtinger (2025).
26. Gans (2025).
27. Comin and Mestieri (2018); Gill (2020).
28. Liu and Wang (2026).
29. Liu and Wang (2026).
30. Anthropic and OpenAI are headquartered in the United States, as is SpaceX (which went public in June 2026). ByteDance, DeepSeek, and Moonshot AI are based in China.
31. The diffusion of frontier knowledge that enables countries to catch up rapidly has been described as an advantage of technological backwardness (Gerschenkron 1962).
32. For example, the cost of processing 1 million tokens with models that have performance similar to GPT-3.5, the model that powered the first released version of ChatGPT, fell from about $20 in late 2022 to only $0.07 by late 2024. Comparable reductions in price are taking place across a range of AI models (Maslej et al. 2025). These price reductions refer to a given model capability, not the latest frontier model.
33. Open weights allow AI developers to run the AI model on their own computer systems, customize the model, examine it for safety or bias, and develop applications without relying solely on one provider. Open-source models provide transparency and customization, allowing those that are building AI applications to access the model weights, but also the model architecture, training data, and even source code, with minimal licensing restrictions.
34. Generative AI products can also be used to accelerate the process of turning *unstructured data* that cannot be organized, indexed, or queried effectively in a traditional database management system into *labeled data* that are formatted for machine learning algorithms.
35. For example, the use of predictive machine learning algorithms to make forecasts requires large amounts of data and specialized talent to build the

AI model and to integrate it with databases and software systems.

36. In 2022, a ransomware attack compromised multiple ministries across the government of Costa Rica, forcing the government to declare a national emergency (Assenza et al. 2026; Murray and Srivastava 2022).
37. As of 2025, the intensity of generative AI chatbot use by consumers was significantly higher in countries with better physical infrastructure (fast internet and access to electricity), higher human capital (higher literacy rates and higher average years of schooling), and stronger institutions (in government effectiveness and regulatory quality) (Liu and Wang 2026). These estimates account for differences in levels of per capita GDP.
38. Jones (2025).
39. David (1990).
40. Bresnahan et al. (2002); Brynjolfsson et al. (2021).
41. Global private investment in AI in 2025 was more than 20 times larger in the United States—at $285 billion—than in China, which occupied second position. The remaining countries that constituted the top 15 were the United Kingdom, France, Canada, India, Germany, Israel, Australia, Saudi Arabia, Singapore, Republic of Korea, Belgium, Japan, and Sweden (Sajadieh et al. 2026).
42. WDR 2026 team, based on Semrush (Software as a service platform), Semrush Holdings, https://www.semrush.com/. The data on the number of ChatGPT users are based on unique IP (Internet Protocol) addresses/devices. Therefore, a person using multiple devices or in different locations may be counted more than once.
43. UNESCO (2023).
44. World Bank (2023).
45. Yang et al. (2024).
46. Beede et al. (2020).
47. Poon (2025).
48. These estimates might understate AI's potential to complement workers because they are based on existing tasks and do not consider any new tasks that AI could perform. Following Gmyrek et al. (2026), occupations are considered exposed to generative AI if they fall within exposure gradients 1–4 as defined in the ILO-NASK AI exposure index (Gmyrek et al. 2025). This threshold captures approximately 25 percent of all occupations under ISCO-08 codes. Other studies, such as Cazzaniga et al. (2024), report higher shares of employment exposed to AI because they use the median occupation as their cutoff. If the median ILO-NASK score is used as the cutoff instead of the threshold that sits closer to the top quartile, the share of employment exposed to GenAI is comparable with the shares found in Cazzaniga et al. (2024).
49. WDR 2026 team, based on Gmyrek et al. (2026) and data of ILOSTAT (dashboard), International Labour Organization, https://ilostat.ilo.org/; WDI (World Development Indicators) (dashboard), World Bank, Washington, DC, https://datatopics.worldbank.org/world-development-indicators/.
50. Huang et al. (2026).
51. Li et al. (2026).
52. World Bank (2025c). These findings conform to evidence from the United States, where employment among early-career workers (ages 22–25) in occupations highly amenable to automation by AI use fell by 13 percent between late 2022 and 2025 (Brynjolfsson, Li, et al. 2025).
53. Nayyar et al. (2021).
54. WDR 2026 team analysis, based on Lightcast data covering more than 100 countries globally. Refer to Lightcast Data (dashboard), Lightcast, https://lightcast.io/products/data/overview.
55. Based on ILOSTAT (dashboard), International Labour Organization, https://ilostat.ilo.org/.
56. WDR 2026 team, based on World Bank Enterprise Survey on AI Adoption; Davies et al. 2026.
57. Otis et al. (2024).
58. AI's capabilities are reducing trade costs, which can help businesses in developing countries become internationally competitive. AI-powered solutions facilitate compliance with complex regulations, such as with the European Union (EU) Carbon Border Adjustment Mechanism (CBAM), whereby the integration of machine learning into data platforms is helping firms collect, manage, and report emissions data more efficiently (Nexer 2025). AI can improve the efficiency of border procedures, such as through the automatic verification of sanitary and phytosanitary (SPS) standards certificates (Turchetto Júnior 2025). AI can also lower communication costs. The introduction of a machine translation system thus increased international trade on eBay by 17.5 percent (Brynjolfsson et al. 2019).
59. WDR 2026 team, based on the data of Digital Business Indicators (database), World Bank, https://www.worldbank.org/en/research/brief/digital-business-indicators.
60. The share of AI-enabling goods in world trade increased from about 13 percent to nearly 17 percent between 2023 and the end of 2025.
61. Luo et al. (2024). This reinforces evidence from the United States that shows that AI adoption depends on the characteristics of businesses (Akcigit et al. 2026).
62. WDR 2026 team, based on Acemoglu (2025); Aghion and Bunel (2024); Baily et al. (2023); Bergeaud (2024); Filippucci et al. (2025).
63. WDR 2026 team, based on Acemoglu (2025).
64. WDR 2026 team, based on Acemoglu (2025); Aghion and Bunel (2024); Baily et al. (2023); Bergeaud (2024); Filippucci et al. (2025); World Bank (2026).
65. Betai and Chen (2026).
66. Stapleton and O'Kane (2021).
67. Bastos and Nayyar (2026).
68. IEA (2026).
69. In the state of Telangana, statistical forecasts of the rainy season enabled farmers to alter their behavior in response to weather-related risks (Burlig et al. 2025). The Government of India subsequently delivered AI-based weather forecasts to more than 30 million farmers across the country,

providing most with advanced prediction of the rainy season earlier than ever before (Government of India 2026).
70. Analysis of mediation data by the WDR 2026 team, based on Farabi et al. (2026).
71. Ash et al. (2025).
72. OECD (2025b).
73. Björkegren et al. (2025).
74. Abramoff et al. (2023). The condition, diabetic retinopathy, is a leading cause of preventable blindness in the working population. It is projected to affect 160 million adults by 2045 (Teo et al. 2021).
75. For example, among thousands of published articles on AI in health care, less than 0.2 percent provide causal evidence of the effects on health care quality or efficiency in low-resource contexts (Sautmann and Weinert 2026).
76. Aiken et al. (2025).
77. McPeak et al. (2024).
78. Based on findings from the AI and Data for Better Governance Survey of governments conducted by the World Bank for this Report. The survey's findings focus on the use of, barriers to use of, and governance of AI, highlighting key differences across countries according to income level. The survey included a core module for digital agencies (or ministries of digital transformation or the equivalent), as well as two modules each for the following sectors: health, education, tax, public finance, civil service, and procurement. The survey was sent to relevant authorities in 129 economies. Respondents in 60 economies completed at least one of the modules, with 57 economies responding to the core module, including 12 low-income economies (Burkina Faso, Burundi, Central African Republic, Democratic Republic of Congo, Ethiopia, Malawi, Mali, Niger, Federal Republic of Somalia, South Sudan, Uganda, Republic of Yemen); 12 lower-middle-income economies (Benin, Bhutan, Cambodia, Arab Republic of Egypt, Kenya, Lao PDR, Lesotho, Myanmar, Nepal, Nigeria, Tajikistan, West Bank and Gaza); 16 upper-middle-income economies (Argentina, Azerbaijan, Bosnia and Herzegovina, Brazil, Ecuador, Guatemala, Jordan, Kazakhstan, Kosovo, Malaysia, Mexico, Peru, Philippines, Thailand, Türkiye, Ukraine); and 17 high-income economies (Australia, Austria, Belgium, Canada, Chile, Costa Rica, Czechia, Greece, Hungary, New Zealand, Panama, Poland, Portugal, Saudi Arabia, Singapore, United Arab Emirates, Uruguay). Kim et al. (2026).
79. Choi et al. (2024).
80. Anand and Mookerjee (2026); Mozur et al. (2025); Pooler (2026).
81. Refer to Clayton et al. (2025) for a general discussion on how excessive fragmentation can lead to a self-reinforcing fragmentation doom loop.
82. Chatterji et al. (2025).
83. Minniti et al. (2025).
84. Perrigo (2023). The demand for AI content moderation work also exposes workers to deeply disturbing imagery. A 2023 lawsuit by Kenyan content moderators against Meta and Sama alleged exposure to traumatic content without adequate psychological support, leading to diagnoses of depression and anxiety (Espada 2023).
85. In Uzbekistan, for example, the government has introduced policies to attract AI-related investments through tax exemptions and discounted electricity rates for data centers (Reuters 2025).
86. Bowles et al. (2025).
87. Kelman and Yukins (2022).
88. Funk et al. (2023, 1).
89. Ryan (2025).
90. Acemoglu and Johnson (2023).
91. Beraja et al. (2023).
92. Private investment in infrastructure can also help close the digital divide. For example, foreign satellite technology providers, such as OneWeb, SpaceSail, and Starlink, have bypassed the prohibitive costs of laying terrestrial fiber in remote regions in Bangladesh, Brazil, Nigeria, and Rwanda. In India, the progressive liberalization of the telecom sector—culminating in 100 percent foreign direct investment—has spurred competition and large-scale network rollouts, helping drive affordable data and rapid internet take-up.
93. Yang et al. (2021).
94. The removal of the 16 percent value added tax on mobile handsets in Kenya in 2009 increased handset purchases by 200 percent and internet penetration by more than 50 percent (Deloitte and GSMA 2011). It is estimated that the welfare costs of handset taxes are more than three times the revenue these taxes raise (Björkegren 2019).
95. World Bank (2018); World Bank et al. (2022).
96. Ministry of Education, Rwanda (2026).
97. Kim et al. (2026). In Czechia, capacity building and peer learning programs that exposed firms to how a variety of AI tools work increased the adoption of AI within firms by 26 percent (Pereira-López et al. 2025).
98. Cirera et al. (2020). In Nigeria, a marketplace platform providing quality ratings for professional business service providers shifted the preferences of purchasing firms toward more highly rated providers (Anderson and McKenzie 2021).
99. Velmet (2026); World Bank (2025a).
100. Acemoglu and Johnson (2023).
101. Large middle-income countries, including Brazil, India, and Malaysia, stand out as the main recipients of such data-center foreign direct investment. In December 2025, Microsoft announced a $17.5 billion data-center investment in India, which is expected to be implemented by 2029 (Aykut et al. 2026).
102. African Union (2024).
103. MeitY (2026).
104. Administrative data are information collected routinely by government departments and agencies to administer programs and deliver services.
105. Kumar, Sarin, et al. (2025).
106. Nekoto et al. (2020).
107. Data licensing frameworks in Africa, such as the Nwulite Obodo Open Data License (NOODL), ensure that the communities generating these assets maintain structural ownership of the data (Verhulst et al. 2025).

108. Synthetic data are artificially generated data that mimic the characteristics and patterns of real-world data.
109. Muinde (2025); Mwigereri et al. (2025). A combination of lung ultrasound image data from real patients with simulated data yielded better results in the detection of lungs infected with COVID-19 (Zhao et al. 2024).
110. Mitra and Niakaros (2023).
111. Martins-Neto et al. (2026).
112. MOE (2026).
113. CGEM (2025).
114. Successful entrepreneurship ultimately depends on talent, ideas, capital, market access, and a supporting ecosystem of financial institutions, researchers, incubators, and policy makers (Cruz and Zhu 2023; Grover et al. 2019).
115. Colonnelli et al. (2026).
116. Becker and Ferrari (2020). Large language models can now learn directly from unlabeled scanned documents, which makes digitalization 100 times less expensive than manual processes (Bäcker-Peral et al. 2025).
117. Data for Public Good (2026).
118. WHO (2026).
119. Athey (2025).
120. For example, evidence shows that people face difficulties in taking in and using information provided by an automated decision support system, either overrelying on it or overruling it at the wrong time (Agarwal et al. 2023; Mosier and Manzey 2019; Nielsen et al. 2025; Stevenson and Doleac 2024).
121. Governments can also integrate AI safety guardrails into public procurement to shape responsible AI practices. In Chile, ChileCompra has pioneered bidding documents that require AI vendors to demonstrate transparency, conduct risk assessments, and ensure data quality from the outset.
122. Hagiu and Wright (2025); OECD (2025a).
123. Athey (2025).
124. For example, refer to Kremer et al. (2022). Government procurement of AI applications also needs to ensure the safety of sensitive government and citizen data. For high-sensitivity tasks, the AI model might need to be hosted on a trusted centralized data platform.
125. For details, refer to Serpro (Serviço Federal de Processamento de Dados, Federal Data Processing Service) (homepage), https://www.serpro.gov.br/.
126. Lundy et al. (2026).
127. For details, refer to CBC (Capacity Building Commission) (web page), https://cbc.gov.in/about-cbc.
128. World Bank (2025d).
129. Hennessy et al. (2026). They provide organizations with guidance on how to adopt an AI risk management system (NIST AI Risk Management Framework–National Institute of Standards and Technology (United States); ISO/IEC 42001 International Organization for Standardization/International Electrotechnical Commission); how to conduct an AI impact assessment (ISO/IEC 42005); and how to measure and test levels of transparency (IEEE 7001-2021–Institute of Electrical and Electronics Engineers).
130. Hennessy et al. (2026); Smuha and Yeung (2025).
131. Galvagna (2023); World Bank (2025d).
132. Tsebee and Oloyede (2024).
133. Valenzuela (2025).
134. Trajano (2026).
135. Bennett Moses (2017); Maas (2025).
136. World Bank (2025b).
137. World Bank (2024).
138. If countries are too small to engage meaningfully in global AI governance, such as in Africa, the governments can use regional groupings, such as the African Union, regional economic communities, the Continental AI Strategy, and the AfCFTA Digital Trade Protocol.
139. ASEAN (2024).
140. For details, refer to COE (2024).
141. World Bank (2025d).
142. World Bank (2016).
143. World Bank (2021).

References

Abdin, Marah, Jyoti Aneja, Hany Awadalla, et al. 2024. "Phi-3 Technical Report: A Highly Capable Language Model Locally on Your Phone." *arXiv:2404.14219v4 [cs.CL]*, August 30, Cornell University. https://doi.org/10.48550/arXiv.2404.14219.

Abramoff, Michael D., Noelle Whitestone, Jennifer L. Patnaik, et al. 2023. "Autonomous Artificial Intelligence Increases Real-World Specialist Clinic Productivity in a Cluster-Randomized Trial." *npj Digital Medicine* 6 (October): 184. https://doi.org/10.1038/s41746-023-00931-7.

Acemoglu, Daron. 2025. "The Simple Macroeconomics of AI." *Economic Policy* 40 (121): 13–58. https://doi.org/10.1093/epolic/eiae042.

Acemoglu, Daron, and Simon Johnson. 2023. *Power and Progress: Our Thousand-Year Struggle over Technology and Prosperity*. PublicAffairs. https://www.hachettebookgroup.com/titles/daron-acemoglu/power-and-progress/9781541702547/?lens=publicaffairs.

African Union. 2024. "Continental Artificial Intelligence Strategy: Harnessing AI for Africa's Development and Prosperity." African Union. https://au.int/sites/default/files/documents/44004-doc-EN-_Continental_AI_Strategy_July_2024.pdf.

Agarwal, Nikhil, Alex Moehring, Pranav Rajpurkar, and Tobias Salz. 2023. "Combining Human Expertise with Artificial Intelligence: Experimental Evidence from Radiology." NBER Working Paper 31422 (July), National Bureau of Economic Research. https://doi.org/10.3386/w31422.

Aghion, Philippe, and Simon Bunel. 2024. "AI and Growth: Where Do We Stand?" Working Paper (June), Federal Reserve Bank of San Francisco. https://www.frbsf.org/wp-content/uploads/AI-and-Growth-Aghion-Bunel.pdf.

Aiken, Emily L., Anik Ashraf, Joshua Evan Blumenstock, Raymond Guiteras, and Ahmed Mushfiq Mobarak. 2025. "Scalable Targeting of Social Protection: When Do Algorithms Out-Perform Surveys and Community Knowledge?" NBER Working Paper 33919 (June), National Bureau of Economic Research. https://www.nber.org/papers/w33919.

Akcigit, Ufuk, Craig A. Chikis, Emin Dinlersoz, and Nathan Goldschlag. 2026. "Attention (and Money) Is All You Need: Why Universities Are Struggling to Keep AI Talent." NBER Working Paper 34964 (March), National Bureau of Economic Research. https://www.nber.org/papers/w34964.

Anand, Ram, and Ishika Mookerjee. 2026. "Malaysia Draws First Data Center Protest over Pollution and Water." *Technology* (blog), February 7. https://www.bloomberg.com/news/articles/2026-02-07/malaysia-draws-first-data-center-protest-over-pollution-water.

Anderson, Stephen J., and David J. McKenzie. 2021. "What Prevents More Small Firms from Using Professional Business Services? An Information and Quality-Rating Experiment in Nigeria." Policy Research Working Paper 9614, World Bank. https://doi.org/10.1596/1813-9450-9614.

ASEAN (Association of Southeast Asian Nations). 2024. "ASEAN Guide on AI Governance and Ethics." ASEAN. https://asean.org/wp-content/uploads/2024/02/ASEAN-Guide-on-AI-Governance-and-Ethics_beautified_201223_v2.pdf.

Ash, Elliott, Sergio Galletta, and Tommaso Giommoni. 2025. "A Machine Learning Approach to Analyze and Support Anticorruption Policy." *American Economic Journal: Economic Policy* 17 (2): 162–93. https://doi.org/10.1257/pol.20210618.

Assenza, Giacomo, William Zhang, and Francesca Spidalieri. 2026. "Building Cyber Resilience at National Scale: Why Strategy Matters More Than Ever." *Digital Transformation* (blog), January 26. https://blogs.worldbank.org/en/digital-development/building-cyber-resilience-at-national-scale--why-strategy-matter.

Athey, Susan Carleton. 2025. "Presidential Address: The Economist as Designer in the Innovation Process for Socially Impactful Digital Products." *American Economic Review* 115 (4): 1059–99. https://www.aeaweb.org/articles?id=10.1257/aer.115.4.1059.

Autor, David H. 2024. "Applying AI to Rebuild Middle Class Jobs." NBER Working Paper 32140 (February), National Bureau of Economic Research. https://www.nber.org/papers/w32140.

Autor, David H., and Neil Thompson. 2025. "Expertise." *Journal of European Economic Association* 23 (4): 1203–71. https://doi.org/10.1093/jeea/jvaf023.

Aykut, Dilek, Selcuk Ozyurt, K. Jung, and Estefania Vergara Cobos. 2026. *Data Center and AI Investment in EMDEs: Risks and Opportunities*. DEC Private Markets–IFC/Infrastructure Chief Economist Office, World Bank Group.

Bäcker-Peral, Verónica, Vitaly Meursault, and Christopher Severen. 2025. "Can LLMs Credibly Transform the Creation of Panel Data from Diverse Historical Tables?" Working Paper WP 25–28 (September), Research Department, Federal Reserve Bank of Philadelphia. https://doi.org/10.21799/frbp.wp.2025.28.

Baily, Martin Neil, Erik Brynjolfsson, and Anton Korinek. 2023. "Machines of Mind: The Case for an AI-Powered Productivity Boom." *Research* (blog), May 10. https://www.brookings.edu/articles/machines-of-mind-the-case-for-an-ai-powered-productivity-boom/.

Barcaui, André. 2025. "ChatGPT as a Cognitive Crutch: Evidence from a Randomized Controlled Trial on Knowledge Retention." *Social Sciences and Humanities Open* 12 (November): 102287. https://doi.org/10.1016/j.ssaho.2025.102287.

Bastani, Hamsa, Osbert Bastani, Alp Sungu, Haosen Ge, Özge Kabakcı, and Rei Mariman. 2025. "Generative AI Without Guardrails Can Harm Learning: Evidence from High School Mathematics." *PNAS, Proceedings of the National Academy of Sciences* 122 (26): e2422633122. https://doi.org/10.1073/pnas.2422633122.

Bastos, Paulo, and Gaurav Nayyar. 2026. "Artificial Intelligence and International Trade in Services: Evidence from the United States." Background paper prepared for *World Development Report 2026: The Promise of Artificial Intelligence,* World Bank. https://www.worldbank.org/en/publication/wdr2026/brief/world-development-report-2026-background-papers.

Becker, Daniel P., and Isabela Ferrari. 2020. "VICTOR, the Brazilian Supreme Court's Artificial Intelligence: A Beauty or a Beast?" In *Regulação 4.0: Desafios da Regulação Diante de Um Novo Paradigma Científico*, vol. 2, edited by Daniel P. Becker and Isabela Ferrari. Editora Revista dos Tribunais. https://www.jusbrasil.com.br/doutrina/secao/victor-the-brazilian-supreme-court-s-artificial-intelligence-a-beauty-or-a-beast-regulacao-40-desafios-da-regulacao-diante-de-um-novo-paradigma-cientifico/1198075998.

Beede, Emma, Elizabeth Baylor, Fred Hersch, et al. 2020. "A Human-Centered Evaluation of a Deep Learning System Deployed in Clinics for the Detection of Diabetic Retinopathy." In *CHI '20: Proceedings of the 2020 CHI Conference on Human Factors in Computing Systems*, edited by Regina Bernhaupt, Florian Floyd Mueller, David Verweij, and Josh Andres. Association for Computing Machinery. https://doi.org/10.1145/3313831.3376718.

Bennett Moses, Lyria. 2017. "Regulating in the Face of Sociotechnical Change." In *The Oxford Handbook of Law, Regulation and Technology*, edited by Roger Brownsword, Eloise Scotford, and Karen Yeung. Oxford University Press. https://doi.org/10.1093/oxfordhb/9780199680832.013.49.

Beraja, Martin, Andrew Kao, David Y. Yang, and Noam Yuchtman. 2023. "AI-tocracy." *Quarterly Journal of Economics* 138 (3): 1349–1402. https://doi.org/10.1093/qje/qjad012.

Bergeaud, Antonin. 2024. "The Past, Present and Future of European Productivity." Paper presented at the European Central Bank's ECB Forum on Central Banking, "Monetary Policy in an Era of Transformation," Sintra, Portugal, July 1–3. https://www.ecb.europa.eu/pub/pdf/sintra/ecb.forumcentbankpub2024_Bergeaud_paper.en.pdf.

Betai, Nehai, and Maggie Chen. 2026. "Automation Without Borders: Generative AI and Cross-Border Service Outsourcing." Paper presented at the Georgetown University–World Bank Fourth Annual AI in Action (AIA) Conference, "Making AI Work: What Firms and Workers Need," Washington, DC, January 26. https://thedocs.worldbank.org/en/doc/2770aa5def57e42a6d2449c90d6cf974-0070062026/original/10-Chen.pdf.

Bick, Alexander, Adam Blandin, and David J. Deming. 2025. "The Rapid Adoption of Generative AI." NBER Working Paper 32966, rev. (February), National Bureau of Economic Research. https://www.nber.org/papers/w32966.

Björkegren, Daniel. 2019. "The Adoption of Network Goods: Evidence from the Spread of Mobile Phones in Rwanda." *Review of Economic Studies* 86 (3): 1033–60. https://doi.org/10.1093/restud/rdy024.

Björkegren, Daniel, Jun Ho Choi, Divya Budihal, Dominic Sobhani, Oliver Garrod, and Paul Atherton. 2025. "Could AI Leapfrog the Web? Evidence from Teachers in Sierra Leone." *arXiv:2502.12397v3 [cs.CY]*, December 2, Cornell University. https://doi.org/10.48550/arXiv.2502.12397.

Bowles, Jeremy, Kevin Croke, Horacio Larreguy, Shelley Liu, and John Marshall. 2025. "Sustaining Exposure to Fact-Checks: Misinformation Discernment, Media Consumption, and Its Political Implications." *American Political Science Review* 119 (4): 1864–87. https://doi.org/10.1017/S0003055424001394.

Bresnahan, Timothy F., Erik Brynjolfsson, and Lorin M. Hitt. 2002. "Information Technology, Workplace Organization, and the Demand for Skilled Labor: Firm-Level Evidence." *Quarterly Journal of Economics* 117 (1): 339–76. https://academic.oup.com/qje/article-abstract/117/1/339/1851770.

Bresnahan, Timothy F., and Manuel Trajtenberg. 1995. "General Purpose Technologies 'Engines of Growth'?" *Journal of Econometrics* 65 (1): 83–108. https://doi.org/10.1016/0304-4076(94)01598-T.

Brynjolfsson, Erik, Bharat Chandar, and Ruyu Chen. 2025. "Canaries in the Coal Mine? Six Facts About the Recent Employment Effects of Artificial Intelligence." Working Paper (November 13), Stanford Digital Economy Lab, Stanford University. https://digitaleconomy.stanford.edu/publication/canaries-in-the-coal-mine-six-facts-about-the-recent-employment-effects-of-artificial-intelligence/.

Brynjolfsson, Erik, Bharat Chandar, and Ruyu Chen. 2026. "Canaries, Interest Rates, and Timing: More on the Recent Drivers of Employment Changes for Young Workers." *News* (blog), February 9. https://digitaleconomy.stanford.edu/news/canaries-interest-rates-and-timinga-more-on-recent-drivers-of-employment-changes-for-young-workers/.

Brynjolfsson, Erik, Xiang Hui, and Meng Liu. 2019. "Does Machine Translation Affect International Trade? Evidence from a Large Digital Platform." *Management Science* 65 (12): 5449–60. https://pubsonline.informs.org/doi/abs/10.1287/mnsc.2019.3388.

Brynjolfsson, Erik, Danielle Li, and Lindsey R. Raymond. 2025. "Generative AI at Work." *Quarterly Journal of Economics* 140 (2): 889–942. https://doi.org/10.1093/qje/qjae044.

Brynjolfsson, Erik, Daniel Rock, and Chad Syverson. 2021. "The Productivity J-Curve: How Intangibles Complement General Purpose Technologies." *American Economic Journal: Macroeconomics* 13 (1): 333–72. doi:10.1257/mac.20180386.

Burlig, Fiona, Amir Jina, Erin M. Kelley, Gregory V. Lane, and Harshil Sahai. 2025. "Beliefs, Forecasts, and Investments: Experimental Evidence from India." Working Paper (October), Agricultural Technology Adoption Initiative, Abdul Latif Jameel Poverty Action Lab, Massachusetts Institute of Technology; Center for Effective Global Action, University of California, Berkeley. https://www.atai-research.org/the-value-of-forecasts-experimental-evidence-from-india/.

Caballar, Rina Diane, and Cole Stryker. 2026. "What Are Small Language Models?" *IBM Think* (blog). https://www.ibm.com/think/topics/small-language-models.

Cazzaniga, Mauro, Florence Jaumotte, Longji Li, Giovanni Melina, Augustus J. Panton, Carlo Pizzinelli, Emma Rockall, and Marina M. Tavares. 2024. "Gen-AI: Artificial Intelligence and the Future of Work." IMF Staff Discussion Note SDN 2024/001 (January), International Monetary Fund. https://www.imf.org/-/media/files/publications/sdn/2024/english/sdnea2024001.pdf.

CGEM (General Confederation of Moroccan Enterprises). 2025. "Launch of the AI Xcelerate Morocco Program." *Activities* (blog), December 9. https://cgem.ma/en/activites/launch-of-the-ai-xcelerate-morocco-program/.

Chakravorti, Bhaskar. 2025. "How to Make AI More Useful." *Foreign Policy: Argument* (blog), October 27. https://foreignpolicy.com/2025/10/27/ai-use-cases-developing-world/.

Chatterji, Aaron K., Thomas Cunningham, David J. Deming, et al. 2025. "How People Use ChatGPT." NBER Working Paper 34255 (September), National Bureau of Economic Research. https://www.nber.org/papers/w34255.

Choi, Jun Ho, Oliver Garrod, Paul Atherton, Andrew Joyce-Gibbons, Miriam Mason-Sesay, and Daniel Björkegren. 2024. "Are LLMs Useful in the Poorest Schools? TheTeacher.AI in Sierra Leone." *arXiv:2310.02982v2 [cs.CY]*, February 1, Cornell University. https://doi.org/10.48550/arXiv.2310.02982.

Cirera, Xavier, Marcio Jose Vargas da Cruz, Elwyn Adriaan Robin Davies, et al. 2020. "Policies to Support Businesses Through the COVID-19 Shock: A Firm-Level Perspective." Policy Research Working Paper 9506, World Bank. https://documents1.worldbank.org/curated/en/188461610547807479/pdf/Policies-to-Support-Businesses-through-the-COVID-19-Shock-A-Firm-Level-Perspective.pdf.

Clayton, Christopher, Matteo Maggiori, and Jesse Schreger. 2025. "A Theory of Economic Coercion and Fragmentation." NBER Working Paper 33309, rev., National Bureau of Economic Research. https://www.nber.org/papers/w33309.

COE (Council of Europe). 2024. "Council of Europe Framework Convention on Artificial Intelligence and Human Rights, Democracy and the Rule of Law." Council of Europe Treaty Series 225, Vilnius, Lithuania, September 5. https://rm.coe.int/cets-225-en-docx/48802bf168.

Colonnelli, Emanuele, Marcio Jose Vargas da Cruz, Mariana De La Paz Pereira-López, Tommaso Porzio, and Chun Zhao. 2026. "Startups in Africa." NBER Working Paper 35261 (May), National Bureau of Economic Research. https://www.nber.org/papers/w35261.

Comin, Diego A., and Martí Mestieri. 2018. "If Technology Has Arrived Everywhere, Why Has Income Diverged?" *American Economic Journal: Macroeconomics* 10 (3): 137–78. https://doi.org/10.1257/mac.20150175.

Cruz, Marcio Jose Vargas da, and Tingting Juni Zhu. 2023. *Developing Entrepreneurial Ecosystems for Digital Businesses and Beyond: A Diagnostic Toolkit*. International Development in Practice Series. World Bank. https://openknowledge.worldbank.org/server/api/core/bitstreams/343b62c3-f6b5-4000-a1e4-5c973f97a235/content.

Cui, Kevin Zheyuan, Mert Demirer, Sonia Jaffe, Leon Musolff, Sida Peng, and Tobias Salz. 2026. "The Effects of Generative AI on High-Skilled Work: Evidence from Three Field Experiments with Software Developers." *Management Science*. Published ahead of print, February 27. https://doi.org/10.1287/mnsc.2025.00535.

Data for Public Good. 2026. "CDPG-Associated Initiatives 'TGDeX' and 'GDI' Honoured at The Economic Times GovTech Awards 2026." Media Release, March 19. https://dataforpublicgood.org.in/media-releases/cdpg-associated-initiatives-tgdex-and-gdi-honoured-at-the-economic-times-govtech-awards-2026/.

David, Paul A. 1990. "The Dynamo and the Computer: An Historical Perspective on the Modern Productivity Paradox." *American Economic Review* 80 (2): 355–61. https://www.academia.edu/11211365/The_Dynamo_and_the_Computer_An_Historical_Perspective_on_the_Modern_Productivity_Paradox.

Davies, Elwyn, David Francis, Filip Jolevski, Gaurav Nayyar, Katherine Stapleton, and Shu Yu. 2026. "Adopting Fast and Slow: Cross-Country Evidence on Business Adoption of AI." Background paper prepared for *World Development Report 2026: The Promise of Artificial Intelligence*, World Bank. https://www.worldbank.org/en/publication/wdr2026/brief/world-development-report-2026-background-papers.

Deloitte and GSMA. 2011. "Mobile Telephony and Taxation in Kenya." Deloitte LLP and GSMA. https://www.gsma.com/solutions-and-impact/connectivity-for-good/public-policy/wp-content/uploads/2012/03/mobiletelephoneandtaxationinkenya.pdf.

Espada, Mariah. 2023. "Facebook Content Moderators Sue Meta over Layoffs in Kenya." *Time* (blog), March 20. https://time.com/6264621/facebook-content-moderators-lawsuit-kenya/.

Farabi, Shafkat, Didac Marti Pinto, Wei Lu, et al. 2026. "SMaRT: Online Reusable Resource Assignment and an Application to Mediation in the Kenyan Judiciary." *arXiv:2602.18431v2 [cs.CY]*, June 26, Cornell University. https://doi.org/10.48550/arXiv.2602.18431.

Felten, Edward W., Manav Raj, and Robert Seamans. 2023. "How Will Language Modelers Like ChatGPT Affect Occupations and Industries?" *arXiv:2303.01157v2 [econ.GN]*, March 18, Cornell University. https://doi.org/10.48550/arXiv.2303.01157.

Filippucci, Francesco, Peter N. Gal, Katharina Laengle, and Matthias Schief. 2025. "Macroeconomic Productivity Gains from Artificial Intelligence in G7 Economies." OECD Artificial Intelligence Paper 41 (June), Organisation for Economic Co-operation and Development. https://www.oecd.org/en/publications/macroeconomic-productivity-gains-from-artificial-intelligence-in-g7-economies_a5319ab5-en.html.

Frost, Jon, Kumar Rishabh, and Vatsala Shreeti. 2026. "Global Giants in the AI Supply Chain." *BIS Bulletin* 122 (February), Bank for International Settlements. https://www.bis.org/publ/bisbull122.pdf.

Funk, Allie, Adrian Shahbaz, and Kian Vesteinsson. 2023. "Freedom on the Net 2023: The Repressive Power of Artificial Intelligence." Freedom House. https://freedomhouse.org/sites/default/files/2024-10/FOTN2023Final24.pdf.

Galvagna, Christine. 2023. "Inclusive AI Governance: Civil Society Participation in Standards Development." Discussion Paper (March), Future of Regulation Series, Ada Lovelace Institute. https://www.adalovelaceinstitute.org/report/inclusive-ai-governance/.

Gans, Joshua S. 2025. "If AI and Workers Were Strong Complements, What Would We See?" *Mess and Magic* (blog), August 30. https://joshuagans.substack.com/p/if-ai-and-workers-were-strong-complements.

Gerschenkron, Alexander. 1962. *Economic Backwardness in Historical Perspective*. Belknap Press. https://www.hup.harvard.edu/books/9780674226005.

Gill, Indermit Singh. 2020. "Whoever Leads in Artificial Intelligence in 2030 Will Rule the World Until 2100." *Commentary* (blog), January 17. https://www.brookings.edu/articles/whoever-leads-in-artificial-intelligence-in-2030-will-rule-the-world-until-2100/.

Gmyrek, Pawel, Janine Marie Berg, Karol Kamiński, et al. 2025. "Generative AI and Jobs: A Refined Global Index of Occupational Exposure." ILO Working Paper 140 (May), International Labour Organization. https://www.ilo.org/sites/default/files/2025-05/WP140_web.pdf.

Gmyrek, Pawel, Mariana Viollaz, and Hernán Jorge Winkler. 2026. "Disruption Without Dividend? How the Digital Divide and Task Differences Split GenAI's Global Impact." Policy Research Working Paper 11328 and background paper prepared for *World Development Report 2026: The Promise of Artificial Intelligence*, World Bank. https://www.worldbank.org/en/publication/wdr2026/brief/world-development-report-2026-background-papers.

Goldfarb, Avi, Bledi Taska, and Florenta Teodoridis. 2023. "Could Machine Learning Be a General Purpose Technology? A Comparison of Emerging Technologies Using Data from Online Job Postings." *Research Policy* 52 (1): 104653. https://doi.org/10.1016/j.respol.2022.104653.

Goldin, Nicole. 2026. "Small AI, Big Results." *Blog Post* (blog), January 17. https://unu.edu/cpr/blog-post/small-ai-big-results.

Government of India. 2026. "Government Conducts AI-Based Pilot for Local Monsoon Forecasting to Support Kharif Sowing Decisions." Ministry of Agriculture and Farmers Welfare, PIB, March 17, 2026 (Release ID: 2241412). https://www.pib.gov.in/PressReleasePage.aspx?PRID=2241412&reg=1&lang=1.

Grover, Arti Goswami, Denis Medvedev, and Ellen Olafsen. 2019. *High-Growth Firms: Facts, Fiction, and Policy Options for Emerging Economies*. World Bank. https://hdl.handle.net/10986/30800.

Haakenstad, Annie, Caleb Mackay Salpeter Irvine, Megan Knight, et al. 2022. "Measuring the Availability of Human Resources for Health and Its Relationship to Universal Health Coverage for 204 Countries and Territories from 1990 to 2019: A Systematic Analysis for the Global Burden of Disease Study 2019." *Lancet* 399 (10341): 2129–54. https://www.thelancet.com/journals/lancet/article/PIIS0140-6736(22)00532-3/fulltext.

Hagiu, Andrei, and Julian Wright. 2025. "Artificial Intelligence and Competition Policy." *International Journal of Industrial Organization* 103 (Part A, December): 103134. https://doi.org/10.1016/j.ijindorg.2025.103134.

Henkel, Owen, Hannah Horne-Robinson, Nessie Kozhakhmetova, and Amanda Lee. 2024. "Effective and Scalable Math Support: Experimental Evidence on the Impact of an AI-Math Tutor in Ghana." In *Artificial Intelligence in Education: Proceedings of the 25th International Conference on Artificial Intelligence in Education (AIED 2024)*, edited by Andrew M. Olney, Irene-Angelica Chounta, Zitao Liu, Olga C. Santos, and Ig Ibert Bittencourt. Communications in Computer and Information Science Series, vol. 2150. Springer Nature. https://link.springer.com/chapter/10.1007/978-3-031-64315-6_34.

Hennessy, Orla, Roxana Radu, and Nora von Ingersleben-Seip. 2026. "Who Leads AI Standardization? Geopolitics in a Fragmented Standards Landscape." RegulAite Working Paper 05/2026, University of Amsterdam. https://www.regulaite.eu/images/pdf/HennessyRaduvonIngerslebenSeip2026.pdf.

Hosseini, Seyed Mahdi, and Guy Lichtinger. 2025. "Generative AI as Seniority-Biased Technological Change: Evidence from U.S. Résumé and Job Posting Data." Del Seminar Series, Stanford Digital Economy Lab, Stanford University, Stanford, CA, September 22. https://digitaleconomy.stanford.edu/event/seyed-m-hosseini-and-guy-lichtinger-generative-ai-as-seniority-biased-technological-change-evidence-from-u-s-resume-and-job-posting-data/.

Huang, Jingyun, Yan Liu, He Wang, and Shu Yu. 2026. "Who Takes the Hit? The Uneven Impacts of Generative AI on Labor Demand Across Countries." Background paper prepared for *World Development Report 2026: The Promise of Artificial Intelligence*, World Bank. https://www.worldbank.org/en/publication/wdr2026/brief/world-development-report-2026-background-papers.

IEA (International Energy Agency). 2026. *Key Questions on Energy and AI*. World Energy Outlook Special Report. IEA. https://www.iea.org/reports/key-questions-on-energy-and-ai.

Jacaranda Health. 2024. "Jacaranda Launches Open Source LLM in Five African Languages." *Blog*, August 16. https://jacarandahealth.org/jacaranda-launches-open-source-llm-in-five-african-languages/.

Jones, Benjamin F. 2025. "Artificial Intelligence in Research and Development." NBER Working Paper 34312 (October), National Bureau of Economic Research. https://www.nber.org/papers/w34312.

Kelman, Steven, and Christopher R. Yukins. 2022. "Overcoming Corruption and War: Lessons from Ukraine's ProZorro Procurement System." GW Paper Series 2022-60, *NCMA Contract Management Magazine* July: 22–27. https://scholarship.law.gwu.edu/cgi/viewcontent.cgi?article=2887&context=faculty_publications.

Kim, Hyunjin, Dahyeon Kim, and Rembrand Koning. 2026. "Mapping AI into Production: A Field Experiment on Firm Performance." INSEAD Working Paper 2026/20/STR (March 30), INSEAD. https://doi.org/10.2139/ssrn.6513481.

Klapper, Leora F., Dorothe Singer, Laura Starita, and Alexandra Norris. 2025. *The Global Findex Database 2025: Connectivity and Financial Inclusion in the Digital Economy*. World Bank. http://hdl.handle.net/10986/43438.

Kremer, Michael Robert, Jonathan Levin, and Christopher M. Snyder. 2022. "Designing Advance Market Commitments for New Vaccines." *Management Science* 68 (7): 4786–4814. https://doi.org/10.1287/mnsc.2021.4163.

Kumar, Ajay, Thomas H. Davenport, and Randy Bean. 2025. "The Case for Using Small Language Models." *AI and Machine Learning* (blog), September 8. https://hbr.org/2025/09/the-case-for-using-small-language-models.

Kumar, Santosh, Gouri Sarin, and Rishita Aggarwal. 2025. "BHASHINI: Transforming Maha Kumbh Through Multilingual Innovation." January 16, Research Unit, Press Information Bureau. https://static.pib.gov.in/WriteReadData/specificdocs/documents/2025/jan/doc2025116486101.pdf.

Li, Lixing, Zhencen Liu, Anqi Wang, He Wang, and Shu Yu. 2026. "Now Hiring: Firm-Level Adoption of Generative AI in China." Background paper prepared for *World Development Report 2026: The Promise of Artificial Intelligence*, World Bank. https://www.worldbank.org/en/publication/wdr2026/brief/world-development-report-2026-background-papers.

Liu, Yan, and He Wang. 2026. "Who on Earth Is Using Generative AI?" *World Development* 199 (March): 107260. https://doi.org/10.1016/j.worlddev.2025.107260.

Lundy, Timothy, Shyam Jayanti Patel, Manuel Ramos-Maqueda, Daniel Rogger, Flavia Sacco Capurro, and Josefina Silva Fuentealba. 2026. "How Is Government Using AI?" Background paper prepared for *World Development Report 2026: The Promise of Artificial Intelligence,* World Bank. https://www.worldbank.org/en/publication/wdr2026/brief/world-development-report-2026-background-papers.

Luo, Shuang, Wenting Lei, and Peng Hou. 2024. "Impact of Artificial Intelligence Technology Innovation on Total Factor Productivity: An Empirical Study Based on Provincial Panel Data in China." *National Accounting Review* 6 (2): 172–94. https://www.aimspress.com/article/doi/10.3934/NAR.2024008.

Maas, Matthijs M. 2025. "Sociotechnical Change: AI as Regulatory Rationale and Target." In *Architectures of Global AI Governance: From Technological Change to Human Choice*, edited by Matthijs M. Maas. Oxford University Press. https://doi.org/10.1093/9780198 8455.003.0006.

Martins-Neto, Antonio Soares, Yan Liu, Saloni Khurana, and Juan Manuel Porras Lopez. 2026. "Click, Code, Earn: The Returns to Digital Skills." Policy Research Working Paper 11313 and background paper prepared for *World Development Report 2026: The Promise of Artificial Intelligence*, World Bank. https://www.worldbank.org/en/publication/wdr2026/brief/world-development-report-2026-background-papers.

Maslej, Nestor, Loredana Fattorini, Raymond Perrault, et al. 2025. *Artificial Intelligence Index Report 2025*. April. AI Index Steering Committee, Institute for Human-Centered Artificial Intelligence, Stanford University. https://hai.stanford.edu/assets/files/hai_ai_index_report_2025.pdf.

McPeak, Grady, Anja Sautmann, Ohia George, et al. 2024. "An LLM's Medical Testing Recommendations in a Nigerian Clinic: Potential and Limits of Prompt Engineering for Clinical Decision Support." In *Proceedings: 2024 IEEE 12th International Conference on Healthcare Informatics, ICHI 2024*, edited by Zhe He, Yi Guo, and Jiang Bian. Institute of Electrical and Electronics Engineers. https://doi.org/10.1109/ICHI61247.2024.00094.

MeitY (Ministry of Electronics and Information Technology). 2026. "IndiaAI Mission Expands AI Ecosystem with Affordable Compute and Startup Support." Press Release, March 25. https://www.digitalindia.gov.in/press_release/indiaai-mission-expands-ai-ecosystem-with-affordable-compute-and-startup-support/.

Ministry of Education, Rwanda. 2026. "Rwanda Achieves Major AI Education Milestone: First Round of National Day of AI Training Reaches 5,000 Teachers." February 11. https://www.mineduc.gov.rw/news-detail/in-rwanda-first-round-of-national-day-of-ai-training-reaches-5000-teachers.

Minniti, Antonio, Klaus Prettner, and Francesco Venturini. 2025. "AI Innovation and the Labor Share in European Regions." *European Economic Review* 177 (August): 105043. https://www.sciencedirect.com/science/article/pii/S0014292125000935.

Mitra, Alessio, and Konstantinos Niakaros. 2023. "The Horizon Effect: A Counterfactual Analysis of EU Research and Innovation Grants." Working Paper 2023/08, R&I Paper Series, Directorate-General for Research and Innovation, European Commission. https://data.europa.eu/doi/10.2777/584781.

MOE (Ministry of Education, Singapore). 2026. "Artificial Intelligence in Education." *Education in SG* (blog), June 2. https://www.moe.gov.sg/education-in-sg/educational-technology-journey/edtech-masterplan/artificial-intelligence-in-education.

Mosier, Kathleen L., and Dietrich Manzey. 2019. "Humans and Automated Decision Aids: A Match Made in Heaven?" In *Human Performance in Automated and Autonomous Systems: Current Theory and Methods*, edited by Mustapha Mouloua and Peter A. Hancock. CRC Press. https://d-nb.info/1223023044/34.

Mozur, Paul, Adam Satariano, and Emiliano Rodríguez Mega. 2025. "From Mexico to Ireland, Fury Mounts over a Global A.I. Frenzy." *Technology* (blog), October 20. https://www.nytimes.com/2025/10/20/technology/ai-data-center-backlash-mexico-ireland.html.

Mrisho, Latifa Mbwana, Neema Aldo Mbilinyi, Mathias Ndalahwa, et al. 2020. "Accuracy of a Smartphone-Based Object Detection Model, PlantVillage Nuru, in Identifying the Foliar Symptoms of the Viral Diseases of Cassava: CMD and CBSD." *Frontiers in Plant Science* 11 (December 17): 590889. https://doi.org/10.3389/fpls.2020.590889.

Muinde, Ezra. 2025. "Synthetic Data: What It Means for Africa." *Medium* (blog), January 8. https://medium.com/@ezra.muinde/synthetic-data-what-it-means-for-africa-1802d7cedcd3.

Murray, Christine, and Mehul Srivastava. 2022. "How Conti Ransomware Group Crippled Costa Rica—Then Fell Apart." *Financial Times* (blog), July 9. https://www.ft.com/content/9895f997-5941-445c-9572-9cef66d130f5?syn-25a6b1a6=1.

Mwigereri, Dorcas G., Nigel T. Kamotho, Akbar K. Waljee, et al. 2025. "Synthetic Data Generation of Health and Demographic Surveillance Systems Data: A Case Study in a Low- and Middle-Income Country." *JAMIA Open* 8 (6): ooaf137. https://doi.org/10.1093/jamiaopen/ooaf137.

Narayanan, Arvind, and Sayash Kapoor. 2024. *AI Snake Oil: What Artificial Intelligence Can Do, What It Can't, and How to Tell the Difference*. Princeton University Press. https://press.princeton.edu/books/hardcover/9780691249131/ai-snake-oil.

Nayyar, Gaurav, Mary Hallward-Driemeier, and Elwyn Davies. 2021. *At Your Service? The Promise of Services-Led Development*. World Bank. https://hdl.handle.net/10986/35599.

Nekoto, Wilhelmina, Vukosi Marivate, Tshinondiwa Matsila, et al. 2020. "Participatory Research for Low-Resourced Machine Translation: A Case Study in African Languages." *arXiv:2010.02353v2 [cs.CL]*, November 6, Cornell University. https://doi.org/10.48550/arXiv.2010.02353.

Nexer. 2025. "Nexer and Stibo Systems Launch AI Solution for CBAM Management." Press Release, February 12. https://nexergroup.com/news/mynewsdesk/nexer-and-stibo-systems-launch-ai-solution-for-cbam-management-3368270/.

Nielsen, Magnus Lindgaard, Jonas Skjold Raaschou-Pedersen, Emil Chrisander, et al. 2025. "Trading Off Performance and Human Oversight in Algorithmic Policy: Evidence from Danish College Admissions." *arXiv:2411.15348v2 [cs.CY]*, April 22, Cornell University. https://doi.org/10.48550/arXiv.2411.15348.

Noy, Shakked, and Whitney Zhang. 2023. "Experimental Evidence on the Productivity Effects of Generative Artificial Intelligence." *Science* 381 (6654): 187–92. https://www.science.org/doi/10.1126/science.adh2586.

OECD (Organisation for Economic Co-operation and Development). 2025a. *Governing with Artificial Intelligence: The State of Play and Way Forward in Core Government Functions*. OECD. https://www.oecd.org/content/dam/oecd/en/publications/reports/2025/06/governing-with-artificial-intelligence_398fa287/795de142-en.pdf.

OECD (Organisation for Economic Co-operation and Development). 2025b. *Tax Administration 2025: Comparative Information on OECD and Other Advanced and Emerging Economies*. OECD. https://www.oecd.org/content/dam/oecd/en/publications/reports/2025/11/tax-administration-2025_6360fad8/cc015ce8-en.pdf.

Otis, Nicholas G., Rowan Clarke, Solène Delecourt, David Holtz, and Rembrand Koning. 2024. "The Uneven Impact of Generative AI on Entrepreneurial Performance: Evidence from a Field Experiment in Kenya." Working Paper 24-042, Harvard Business School, Harvard University. https://www.hbs.edu/ris/Publication%20Files/24-042_567db548-5b24-4182-b703-9d5ef1328043.pdf.

Pereira-López, Mariana De La Paz, Stephen J. Anderson, Leonardo Iacovone, Andreas Menzel, Florian Anselm Münch, and Rahul Suhag. 2025. *Creating Ecosystems for Innovation in a Post-Coal Region: Evidence from an RCT in the Czech Republic*. Strengthening Monitoring and Evaluation of Innovation Programs in the EU Series, June 18. World Bank. https://documents1.worldbank.org/curated/en/099062725130041014/pdf/P171223-48a49632-7dc2-41ab-8161-8c1e8e4f67c1.pdf.

Perrigo, Billy. 2023. "Exclusive: OpenAI Used Kenyan Workers on Less Than $2 per Hour to Make ChatGPT Less Toxic." *Time* (blog), January 18. https://time.com/6247678/openai-chatgpt-kenya-workers/.

Pooler, Michael. 2026. "Why Isn't the Energy Used by People? China's Global AI Push Hits Resistance." *Brazilian Economy* (blog), April 21. https://www.ft.com/content/001dec5b-9e13-4a23-9dc5-dda537a47ae3.

Poon, Elim. 2025. "Malaysia Launches First Local Edge AI Processor, MARS1000." *Technology* (blog), August 25. https://www.thestar.com.my/business/business-news/2025/08/25/malaysia-launches-first-local-edge-ai-processor-mars1000.

Radu, Roxana. 2026. "The Global Landscape of National AI Strategies." Background paper prepared for *World Development Report 2026: The Promise of Artificial Intelligence*, World Bank. https://www.worldbank.org/en/publication/wdr2026/brief/world-development-report-2026-background-papers.

Reuters. 2025. "Uzbekistan Sets Up Tax-Free Zone for AI to Attract Foreign Investors." *World* (blog), November 7. https://www.reuters.com/world/asia-pacific/uzbekistan-sets-up-tax-free-zone-ai-attract-foreign-investors-2025-11-07/.

Ryan, Erica. 2025. "2025 Census: Fact-Checkers Persevere as Politicians, Platforms Turn Up Heat." *Fact-Checking News* (blog), June 19. https://reporterslab.org/latest-news/.

Sajadieh, Sha, Loredana Fattorini, Raymond Perrault, et al. 2026. *Artificial Intelligence Index Report 2026*. April. Stanford, CA: AI Index Steering Committee, Institute for Human-Centered Artificial Intelligence, Stanford University. https://hai.stanford.edu/assets/files/ai_index_report_2026.pdf.

Sautmann, Anja, and Jonas Weinert. 2026. "Artificial Intelligence Interventions to Support Frontline Healthcare Workers in Low-Resource Settings: A Review." Background paper prepared for *World Development Report 2026: The Promise of Artificial Intelligence*, World Bank. https://www.worldbank.org/en/publication/wdr2026/brief/world-development-report-2026-background-papers.

Smuha, Nathalie A., and Karen Yeung. 2025. "The European Union's AI Act: Beyond Motherhood and Apple Pie?" In *The Cambridge Handbook of the Law, Ethics and Policy of Artificial Intelligence*, edited by Nathalie A. Smuha. Cambridge Law Handbooks Series. Cambridge University Press. https://www.cambridge.org/core/books/cambridge-handbook-of-the-law-ethics-and-policy-of-artificial-intelligence/european-unions-ai-act/D41DE1DB8D6A8C7319DB82598410F5DA.

Stadler, Matthias, Maria Bannert, and Michael Sailer. 2024. "Cognitive Ease at a Cost: LLMs Reduce Mental Effort but Compromise Depth in Student Scientific Inquiry." *Computers in Human Behavior* 160 (November): 108386. https://doi.org/10.1016/j.chb.2024.108386.

Stapleton, Katherine, and Layla O'Kane. 2021. "Artificial Intelligence and Services Offshoring." https://drive.google.com/file/d/1evN3SdPqfuPzFsJTRopmvqBWuN9UNVvw/view.

Stevenson, Megan T., and Jennifer L. Doleac. 2024. "Algorithmic Risk Assessment in the Hands of Humans." *American Economic Journal: Economic Policy* 16 (4): 382–414. https://doi.org/10.1257/pol.20220620.

Teo, Zhen Ling, Yih-Chung Tham, Marco Yu, et al. 2021. "Global Prevalence of Diabetic Retinopathy and Projection of Burden Through 2045: Systematic Review and Meta-Analysis." *Ophthalmology* 128 (11): 1580–91. https://doi.org/10.1016/j.ophtha.2021.04.027.

Tonneau, Manuel, Pedro Vitor Quinta de Castro, Karim Lasri, et al. 2024. "NaijaHate: Evaluating Hate Speech Detection on Nigerian Twitter Using Representative Data." In *Proceedings of the 62nd Annual Meeting of the Association for Computational Linguistics, Volume 1: Long Papers*, edited by Lun-Wei Ku, Andre Martins, and Vivek Srikumar. Association for Computational Linguistics. https://aclanthology.org/2024.acl-long.488.pdf.

Trajano, Karryl Kim Sagun. 2026. "What the Grok Bans in Southeast Asia Tell Us About AI Governance." *The Interpreter* (blog), January 19. https://www.lowyinstitute.org/the-interpreter/what-grok-bans-southeast-asia-tell-us-about-ai-governance.

Tsebee, Dorcas, and Ridwan Oloyede. 2024. "DPAs and AI Regulation in Africa." *News* (blog), November 6. https://iapp.org/news/a/dpas-and-ai-regulation-in-africa.

Turchetto Júnior, Carlos Roberto. 2025. "Facilitating Safe Trade of Animal-Origin Foods: The Role of Digital Health Certificates and Standardized Requirements." March, Thematic Session on Innovative Regulatory Approaches to Facilitate Safe Trade, WTO SPS Committee, World Trade Organization. https://www.wto.org/library/events/event_resources/sps_1703202510/718_2174.pdf.

UNESCO (United Nations Educational, Scientific and Cultural Organization). 2023. *Global Education Monitoring Report, 2023: Technology in Education, A Tool on Whose Terms?* UNESCO. https://unesdoc.unesco.org/ark:/48223/pf0000385723.

Valenzuela, Daniel Peña. 2025. "From Code to Constitution: The Constitutionalization of Artificial Intelligence in Colombia's Case I." *Chambers: Article* (blog), August 25. https://chambers.com/articles/from-code-to-constitution-the-constitutionalization-of-artificial-intelligence-in-colombia-s-case-l.

Vallangi, Neelima. 2026. "AI-Driven Weather Forecasts for Climate Adaptation in India." *Nature Climate Change* 16: 102. https://doi.org/10.1038/s41558-025-02521-9.

Velmet, Aro. 2026. "Database Politics: Informational Infrastructure and Network Utopias in Soviet and Post-Soviet Estonia." *Internet Histories* 10 (1–2): 45–64. https://doi.org/10.1080/24701475.2026.2639221.

Verhulst, Stefaan G., Adam Zable, Andrew Zahuranec, and Peter Addo. 2025. "Reimagining Data Governance for AI: Operationalizing a Social License for Data Reuse." Technical Report 78 (April), Agence française de développement. https://www.afd.fr/sites/default/files/2025-05-01-53-37/RT_78_VA_BAT.pdf.

Wang, Fali, Zhiwei Zhang, Xianren Zhang, et al. 2024. "A Comprehensive Survey of Small Language Models in the Era of Large Language Models: Techniques, Enhancements, Applications, Collaboration with LLMs, and Trustworthiness." *arXiv:2411.03350v2 [cs.CL]*, December 28, Cornell University. https://doi.org/10.48550/arXiv.2411.03350.

WHO (World Health Organization). 2026. "Tuberculosis." Fact Sheet, March 24. https://www.who.int/news-room/fact-sheets/detail/tuberculosis.

World Bank. 2016. *World Development Report 2016: Digital Dividends*. World Bank. https://www.worldbank.org/en/publication/wdr2016.

World Bank. 2018. *World Development Report 2018: Learning to Realize Education's Promise*. World Bank. https://www.worldbank.org/en/publication/wdr2018.

World Bank. 2021. *World Development Report 2021: Data for Better Lives*. World Bank. https://doi.org/10.1596/978-1-4648-1600-0.

World Bank. 2023. *Kenya Country Economic Memorandum: Seizing Kenya's Services Momentum*. World Bank. https://documents1.worldbank.org/curated/en/099072623125529056/pdf/P177156008ee600bc0bf75078832b97b48f.pdf.

World Bank. 2024. *Global Trends in AI Governance: Evolving Country Approaches*. World Bank. https://doi.org/10.1596/42500.

World Bank. 2025a. "Digital Public Infrastructure and Development: A World Bank Group Approach." Digital Transformation White Paper, vol. 1 (March), World Bank. https://doi.org/10.1596/42935.

World Bank. 2025b. "Global Regulations, Institutional Development, and Market Authorities Perspective Toolkit (GRIDMAP): Data Markets Module." July, World Bank. https://documents1.worldbank.org/curated/en/099082225093534862/pdf/P179766-0d673a3c-c406-4e92-9fb4-16f8a771eb87.pdf.

World Bank. 2025c. *Jobs, AI, and Trade*. South Asia Development Update, October. World Bank. https://doi.org/10.1596/978-1-4648-2291-9.

World Bank. 2025d. *World Development Report 2025: Standards for Development*. World Bank. https://doi.org/10.1596/978-1-4648-2275-9.

World Bank. 2026. *Global Economic Prospects, June 2026*. World Bank. https://www.worldbank.org/en/publication/global-economic-prospects.

World Bank, UNESCO (United Nations Educational, Scientific and Cultural Organization), UNICEF (United Nations Children's Fund), FCDO (Foreign, Commonwealth, and Development Office, UK), USAID (United States Agency for International Development), and BMGF (Bill and Melinda Gates Foundation). 2022. "The State of Global Learning Poverty: 2022 Update." Conference Edition, June 23, World Bank. https://thedocs.worldbank.org/en/doc/34035a49acb5700ce8b118aeda81a5cb-0510022023/original/TheStateOfLearningPoverty-Feb2023Update-03-08-23.pdf.

Yang, Jane E., Diego Lassala, Jenny X. Liu, et al. 2021. "Effect of Mobile Application User Interface Improvements on Minimum Expected Home Visit Coverage by Community Health Workers in Mali: A Randomised Controlled Trial." *BMJ Global Health* 6 (11): e007205. https://doi.org/10.1136/bmjgh-2021-007205.

Yang, Jenny, Nguyen Thanh Dung, Pham Ngoc Thach, et al. 2024. "Generalizability Assessment of AI Models Across Hospitals in a Low-Middle and High Income Country." *Nature Communications* 15 (September): 8270. https://doi.org/10.1038/s41467-024-52618-6.

Zhao, Lingyi, Tiffany Clair Fong, and Muyinatu A. Lediju Bell. 2024. "Detection of COVID-19 Features in Lung Ultrasound Images Using Deep Neural Networks." *Communications Medicine* 4 (March): 41. https://www.nature.com/articles/s43856-024-00463-5.

Part 1

Decoding AI: Capabilities, Concentration, and Complements

Artificial intelligence (AI) means different things to different people. Some people focus on algorithmic techniques, whereas others highlight aspects of humanlike behavior and even autonomy. In practice, *AI* is often used to refer to a broad category of applications ranging from prediction tools, virtual assistants, translating and transcribing tools, and chatbots to autonomous robots and vehicles. Given this diversity and in the absence of a universally agreed-upon definition, how can we better understand what AI means for development? Part 1 identifies three salient characteristics of AI: its *capabilities*, its *concentration*, and the *complements* needed to customize and deploy it (refer to figure P1.1). Each chapter begins by explaining what one characteristic means and then examines the implications of that characteristic for developing countries.

The main message of chapter 1 is that AI's ability to perform or help accomplish more expert tasks matters greatly for developing countries. These countries need skilled workers (and the skills they offer) acutely in areas such as health care, agriculture, and government administration, but the supply of such workers is limited. AI's expanded set of *capabilities* effectively expands the supply of skills available. But although AI could have substantial potential benefits for developing countries, the benefits are neither equally distributed among geographic areas and population segments nor guaranteed to materialize. There is the possibility of adverse distributional outcomes, and AI can also enhance the harmful capabilities of malicious actors. Moreover, access to AI depends on conditions that developing countries may not always be able to control.

Chapter 2 points out that the layers of the AI stack (applications, AI models, data, infrastructure, and hardware) are *concentrated* in a few economies, and many layers are served by only a handful of companies. These characteristics affect how developing countries can access the capabilities of AI. Doing so by building components of the most advanced layers of the AI stack is difficult, but accessing the capabilities of AI by adopting and adapting what has been built by others is more feasible and relatively less expensive. For instance, open models offer a lower-cost opportunity to build locally relevant applications that can help address shortages of skilled professionals. Nevertheless, access to AI technologies alone does not guarantee that countries will benefit from them, because the effectiveness of these technologies depends on how well they fit specific contexts in developing countries.

Figure P1.1 The salient characteristics of AI have significant implications for development

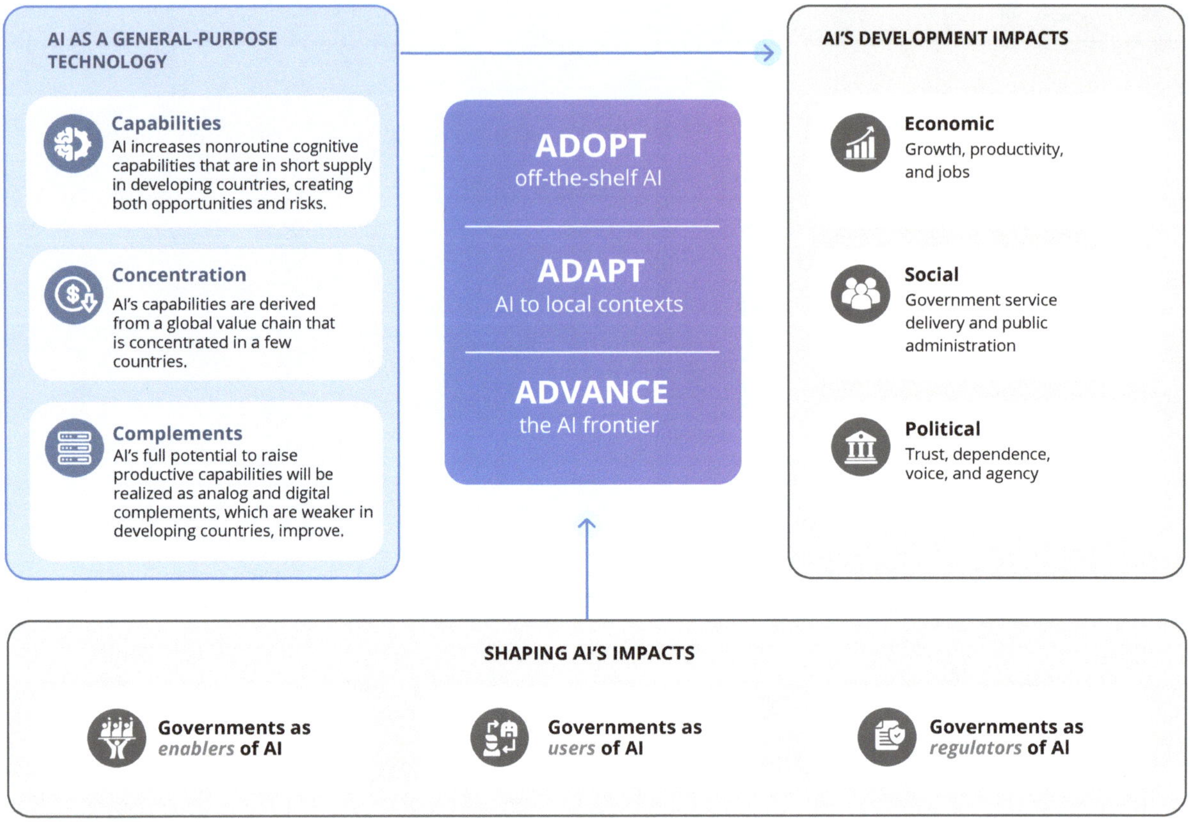

Source: WDR 2026 team.
Note: AI = artificial intelligence.

Chapter 3 emphasizes the importance of complements in adopting and adapting AI. AI's potential depends not only on the context in which it will be used, but also on the context in which it has been developed. If those contexts are disconnected—a so-called contextual mismatch—AI will not work well. Realizing the full potential of AI for development therefore requires the right *complements* to be in place to adopt AI applications and to tailor them to the context in which they are deployed. AI's capabilities, including harmful ones, can spread quickly. Whether AI ultimately does more good than harm will depend on how quickly the complements are put in place.

Spotlight 1, following chapter 3, highlights the importance of complements. In many developing countries, access to electricity, the internet, and smartphones remains far from universal. The spotlight highlights the power of *small AI,* which involves designing applications taking into account the complements that already exist in settings constrained by limited resources.

Collectively, these three chapters and the spotlight indicate that the impact of AI on development warrants neither unbridled optimism nor pervasive pessimism. Opportunities exist to enhance development through AI, but developing countries should remain vigilant to potential harms and risks and ensure that they establish the complementary factors needed to achieve the potential gains as well as the safeguards essential to prevent harms and risks from coming to fruition. Only then will AI's potential for development be realized.

1

Capabilities: The Power of AI to Alleviate Skill Shortages

Main messages

- **AI is improving and spreading at extraordinary speed**
  Developing economies should move beyond shallow usage and experiment to put AI to productive uses that expand the capabilities of workers, firms, and governments.
- **AI can now assist with tasks once requiring expert judgment**
  Use AI to recognize patterns and support decision-making in fields such as health, agriculture, data analysis, writing, translation, and software development.
- **AI can expand scarce skills without waiting a generation**
  Employ AI to perform expert tasks or enable more workers to carry them out, expanding access to expertise in health, education, agriculture, and other fields.
- **AI's benefits are neither equal nor guaranteed**
  Manage AI's unequal impacts, strengthen institutional safeguards, and protect against job displacement, fraud, cyberattacks, surveillance, and other misuse.

Introduction

In 2023, researchers deployed a chatbot powered by artificial intelligence (AI) in Kenya to provide real-time advice to maize farmers via WhatsApp.[1] The chatbot could answer questions about planting and pest and soil management. Government extension officers had traditionally performed this task during occasional farm visits. At about the same time, in India, customer service representatives at a firm that outsources business processes were learning that the same technology was taking over tasks like looking up customer accounts, providing standard troubleshooting for customer issues, and offering scripted responses to customer questions.

These two stories capture opposite aspects of the same underlying technology. For the farmers in Kenya, AI supplied a capability that was previously scarce. For the customer service representatives in India, it replaced a capability that workers were

A reproducibility package is available for this book in the Reproducible Research Repository at https://reproducibility.worldbank.org/catalog/624.

already supplying. Why can the same technology result in such different outcomes?

Examining tasks provides a good starting point for understanding this difference. As AI's capabilities increase, it can increasingly perform the types of nonroutine cognitive tasks that once required specialized trained professionals. This point has particular significance for developing countries, which have long faced shortages in the skills needed for work involving these kinds of tasks. Health care offers an instructive example. Developing economies have growing populations, and demand for health care there is increasing, yet many of these countries face acute shortages of health care workers.

AI could have substantial potential upsides for these economies, because technology tends to have the greatest impacts where the resource that it augments is in shortest supply; however, the potential gains are neither equal among groups affected nor guaranteed. AI can also enhance the harmful capabilities of malicious actors such as hackers. Finally, access to AI depends on conditions that developing countries may not always be able to control.

The technology: AI is not new, but it is expanding in scope, improving continuously, and diffusing rapidly

The conceptual foundations of AI can be traced back to the Turing test, posited in the early 1950s, which evaluates whether a machine's responses are distinguishable from those of a human.[2] Early AI in the 1960s relied on symbolic systems created with custom-coded instructions. ELIZA, a widely referenced chatbot from that era, used basic pattern-matching techniques, primarily derived from specific individual *scripts*, to conduct a conversation with a user.[3] Machine learning techniques, which predict the value of a target variable based on many input variables,[4] gained salience in the 1990s, enabling applications such as filtering of spam emails and credit scoring. However, these techniques' reliance on human experts to label target variables specific to certain tasks, especially for data in the form of images or text, limited their scalability.

The 2010s marked a turning point, with advances in computing hardware, large-scale labeled data sets like ImageNet,[5] and better methods for improving the performance of machine learning models.[6] These developments enabled *deep learning*: brain-inspired neural network models that can automatically discern abstract features of data directly. This in turn led to major breakthroughs in image and speech recognition, as well as the ability of AI models to analyze and understand text (*natural language processing*), which gave rise to a range of task-specific applications such as Apple's Siri, Amazon's Alexa, Google Assistant, and Microsoft's Cortana. Three features of the recent technological trajectory of AI that are consistent with features of trajectories of earlier general-purpose technologies, such as electricity, deserve particular attention.[7]

Scope

AI's capabilities are expanding in scope. AI has been described as a prediction machine that depends on data, statistical models, and judgment.[8] Over time, the power of this machine has increased, marked by a shift from narrow, task-specific models to flexible, large language models that learn patterns from massive, unlabeled, and often multimodal data sets involving elements such as text, images, and code.[9] Large language models can generalize across tasks they were not explicitly trained for.[10] These models underpin the success of chatbots such as ChatGPT, Claude, DeepSeek, and Gemini, among many others, which can generate text, images, code, and other outputs in response to simple prompts. The versatility of these chatbots has resulted in their use across a variety of applications, including software development tools.

As a result of such versatility and in part because there is no universally agreed upon definition, *AI* is often used today as "an umbrella term for a set of loosely related technologies. ChatGPT has little in common with, say, software that banks use to evaluate loan applicants."[11] AI's expanding scope mirrors the technology's evolution from predictive AI to generative AI to agentic AI (refer to box 1.1), as illustrated by its growing footprint across every facet of society.

Box 1.1 AI's expanding scope: The three main types of AI explained

Predictive AI uses statistical and machine learning methods for prediction or classification tasks. Machine learning methods can analyze historical as well as real-time data to detect patterns, generate forecasts, make recommendations, or guide decisions regarding optimization. Examples include extracting insights from unstructured data, such as images, audio, and text, to analyze radiology scans and using aerial imagery from drones to detect crop disease. Similarly, machine learning predictions based on past data have optimized responses to food crises, detected fraud in financial markets, and guided resource allocation in government programs.

Generative AI creates content, such as text, images, or audio. Most generative AI in use today involves large language models, such as Anthropic's Claude models, DeepSeek's models, Google's Gemini models, and OpenAI's GPT models. These models can perform a wide variety of tasks, such as answering questions, generating content, and assisting with coding. Large language models can be used to build AI chatbots (for purposes such as medical diagnosis or personalized tutoring) that can provide specific advice or assistance. Generative AI tools, including chatbots, can summarize documents, draft legal contracts, generate educational materials, and engage in customer service interaction.

Agentic AI combines predictive and generative AI with capabilities of reasoning and interacting with the broader environment in which AI operates to execute a series of tasks independently based on goals and context, as well as learning gained during the execution process. Early-stage examples of AI agents (that is, tools that employ agentic AI) include self-driving cars and software programming assistants such as Claude Code and OpenAI's Codex.

These three types of AI often build on one another, with each subsequent type expanding upon the capabilities of the previous types. Generative AI, for example, predicts, just as predictive AI does, in addition to creating outputs that are accessible to users who lack specialized skills. It can also interface with predictive AI systems by making their results easier to access and understand. Likewise, agentic AI relies on both predictive and generative capabilities to accomplish tasks.

Source: WDR 2026 team.

In the economic space, fintech lenders in India and Latin American countries are using AI-driven credit scoring to extend loans to small businesses and workers who lack formal banking histories. In delivery of social services, countries are deploying AI in *front-end* functions like health care and teaching, as well as in *back-end* administrative functions, expanding the effectiveness and reach of such services. In the political realm, AI-generated deepfakes are already affecting elections across the world, including those in developing countries.[12] Collectively, these examples demonstrate that AI serves as a general-purpose technology, actively transforming economic activities, delivery of public services, and politics, all of which are examined in dedicated chapters in part 2 of this Report.

In addition, at a time when the production of ideas has been slowing down because each new discovery requires more researchers and resources,[13] the expanding set of capabilities of AI, in its most powerful form, can relax this constraint and accelerate the creation of knowledge itself. For example, Google DeepMind's AlphaFold has successfully predicted protein folding structures, a 50-year-old challenge in the field of molecular biology, which paves the way for finding cures for diseases.[14] AI's ability to create knowledge, as a particularly potent form of innovation, is key for long-term economic growth, as illustrated by the work of three recent Nobel laureates in economics, Philippe Aghion, Peter Howitt, and Joel Mokyr.[15]

Continuous improvement

AI is improving continuously. Performance benchmarks that were state of the art just months ago are being surpassed routinely. In performance on competition-level mathematics, AI leaped from well below the best human performers to parity in only a few years (2021–24), and AI performance on doctorate-level science questions exceeded human parity within less than one year (2023–24).[16] At the time of writing, the technological frontier is shifting toward advanced AI agents that not only generate content but also plan actions, interact with tools, and execute tasks.[17] The performance of AI agents is improving rapidly, with the length of tasks they can complete doubling every seven months.[18] Crucially, these improvements are not confined to laboratory settings. Many are rapidly being incorporated into products and services that are accessible at relatively low cost, although risks of inconsistent performance may exist. The next frontier is physical, where AI is integrated into robots designed to detect, process, and respond to conditions in the real world.[19]

The continuous improvements in AI performance are attributable to AI model architecture, training techniques, data sets, and computing power. Computing speed is estimated to be doubling roughly every 2.5 years per dollar spent on chips.[20] Furthermore, research has shown that AI algorithms can analyze and optimize the layouts of computer chips, potentially strengthening computing power even further.[21] Such developments are perpetuating a feedback loop of escalating progress in which AI discoveries drive further improvements in algorithms and hardware optimizations.[22]

Rapid diffusion

AI is diffusing rapidly, making it easier to produce new products and services. Its capabilities are embedded in everyday products and services, which are used by either final consumers or by businesses in their production processes. The evolution of AI's capabilities from predictive to generative has reduced access barriers for adopting AI solutions. For example, generative AI advisory chatbots can be accessed using plain (local) language prompts on smartphones, enabling people without formal technical skills or expensive hardware to use them.[23] This is illustrated by Digital

Green's FarmerChat app, which reaches thousands of farmers in South Asia and Africa, using generative AI to answer queries in several local languages and diagnosing crop issues from uploaded images.[24]

With each past wave of general-purpose technologies, the lag in adoption between high- and lower-income countries has been shrinking. Evidence suggests that the lag in adoption was cut from about 80 years for the steam engine to 40 years for electricity and then to about 20 years for computers and the internet.[25] AI's faster diffusion, compared with those of previous general-purpose technologies, conforms to and accelerates this pattern. Lags in adoption between developing and developed countries are showing signs of disappearing. Whereas it took the internet six years to reach 3 percent of the population in developing countries after crossing that threshold in developed ones, the lag shrank to only five months for ChatGPT (measured based on unique Internet Protocol addresses or devices) (refer to figure 1.1).

When ChatGPT was launched in November 2022, more than 70 percent of user traffic originated from the United States, where the underlying model was developed, but within six months, following the release of ChatGPT 3.5, middle-income countries collectively accounted for half of ChatGPT traffic. India, Brazil, the Philippines, and Indonesia, all middle-income countries, were the remaining four of the top five countries in terms of ChatGPT traffic by the end of March 2024.[26]

Figure 1.1 ChatGPT is reaching users in substantially less time than it took the internet to do so

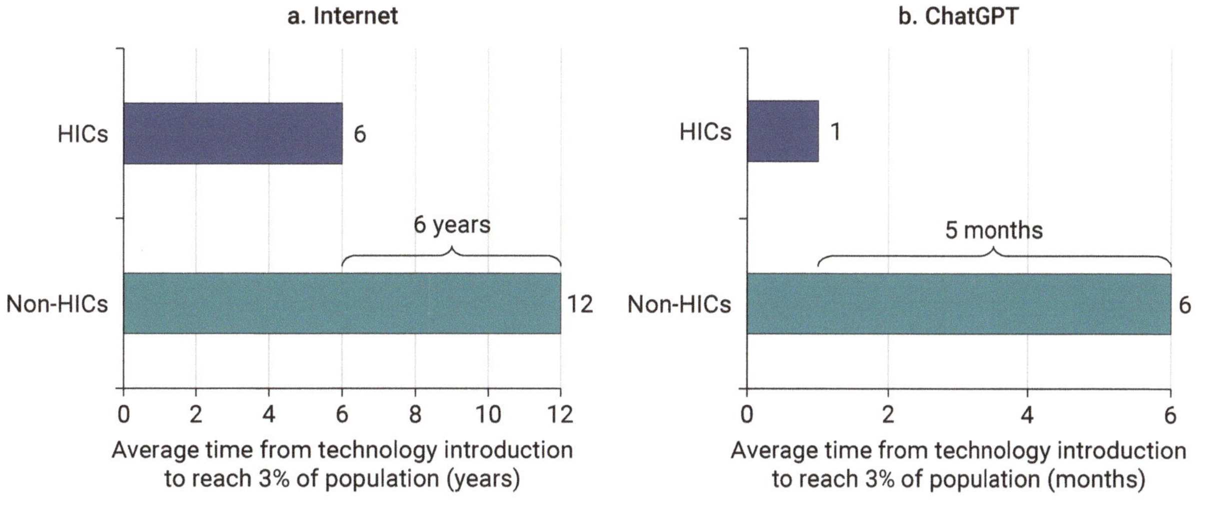

Source: WDR 2026 team, based on data of Metreau et al. 2026; Semrush (Software as a service platform), Semrush Holdings, https://www.semrush.com/; WDI (World Development Indicators) (dashboard), World Bank, https://datatopics.worldbank.org/world-development-indicators/; and World Population Prospects (dashboard), Population Division, Department of Economic and Social Affairs, United Nations, https://population.un.org/wpp/.

Note: The share of the population using ChatGPT is measured by dividing the number of monthly ChatGPT users (taken from Semrush data) by the population in the corresponding year. The data on the number of ChatGPT users are based on unique IP (Internet Protocol) addresses or devices. Thus, a single individual using multiple devices or using one device in separate locations may be counted more than once. Months are used for ChatGPT because the data are available by month. Income classifications refer to World Bank classifications for fiscal year 2027. HICs = high-income countries.

Figure 1.2 AI adoption rates among firms in developing countries have surged

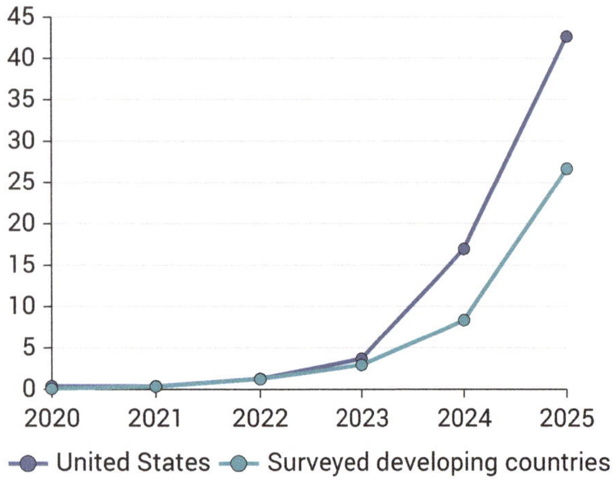

Source: WDR 2026 team, based on World Bank Enterprise Survey on AI Adoption; Davies et al. (2026).

Note: Data are from the responses to the World Bank Enterprise Survey on AI Adoption question "When did this business first start using any AI technologies?" and cover only formal firms with at least five employees. The data for surveyed developing countries average country-level indicators, with equal weight for each country. The sample sizes are as follows: India (1,355 firms); Jordan (358); Kenya (360); Mexico (603); Nigeria (777); Thailand (360); United States (392). Microdata are available at Enterprise Surveys (data portal), World Bank, https://www.enterprisesurveys.org/en/data. AI = artificial intelligence.

Data from the World Bank Enterprise Survey on AI Adoption show that between 2023 and 2025, several developing economies experienced a rapid surge in AI adoption among formal firms with at least five employees. On average, among the group of surveyed developing countries, less than 5 percent of such firms used AI in 2022, but by 2025, this figure had risen to over 25 percent (refer to figure 1.2).

Although AI adoption in developing countries is increasing, the available data offer no information on the intensity of use and whether AI is being used for casual interactions such as leisure or in ways that meaningfully enhance capabilities of workers, firms, and other economic actors.[27] Chapter 4 discusses how the gaps in AI adoption rates between developed and developing countries are wider when simple and more complex types of adoption are distinguished (*rapid diffusion, shallow adoption, slower transformation*). The transformative potential of AI ultimately depends on the extent to which it is deployed for productive purposes as opposed to leisure.

Notwithstanding the limitations on data about the use of AI, the three features discussed in this section—scope, continuous improvement, and rapid diffusion—suggest that AI has the potential to increase capabilities widely. This potential may be substantial in regard to developing economies, because the gaps that AI can fill appear to be the largest there.

From technology to tasks: AI is now able to perform nonroutine cognitive tasks, facilitating decision-making

At the most granular level, AI affects tasks.[28] Tasks, in turn, are intrinsically linked to decision-making, because they inform, support, or carry out decisions. For example, teaching includes a variety of tasks, such as planning and delivering lessons, assessing student work, supporting students' development, and communicating with parents and colleagues. Teachers also make choices matching educational plans to student needs.

Previous general-purpose technologies, such as computers, have largely executed or supported routine cognitive tasks,[29] whereas physical robots have mostly engaged in routine manual tasks.[30] These previous technologies have largely left nonroutine cognitive tasks in the domain of skilled human labor, because such tasks were hard to break down fully into explicit and repeatable rules. They require judgment, contextual understanding, and problem solving. AI is markedly different from earlier general-purpose technologies in terms of the tasks to which it can be applied. Its predictive, generative, and agentic functions perform and support the types of nonroutine cognitive tasks that previous technologies could not tackle.

Thus, jobs that rely more heavily on nonroutine cognitive tasks are more likely to be classified as more amenable to generative AI than are those involving manual tasks (refer to figure 1.3). In the world of work, these types of tasks have typically been concentrated in knowledge-intensive jobs such as those held by information and communication technology professionals and technicians, managers, business professionals, and administrative professionals.[31] Small business owners and smallholder farmers, who make decisions such as where to source supplies, how to get the best prices for their products, and when and what to sell or plant, also perform nonroutine cognitive tasks.

For jobs in some of these occupations, such as information and communication technology, the task mix varies by country income levels. Such jobs in high-income economies tend to involve higher levels of nonroutine cognitive tasks and lower levels of routine manual tasks (refer to panel a in figure 1.3) than in developing countries (refer to panel b in the figure). Although this divergence reflects a combination of factors, it suggests that workers in lower-income countries may lack the skills needed to perform the more analytically demanding components of these jobs, pointing to underlying skill gaps.

Why is AI capable of performing nonroutine cognitive tasks that were beyond the reach of previous technologies? Consider an agricultural extension officer in rural Kenya trying to diagnose a diseased crop from a farmer's description and a blurry photo of a leaf, or a health worker deciding whether a child's symptoms point to a condition requiring urgent referral. Before the rising capabilities of AI were available, it was difficult to automate such tasks because the low-quality images (in the agriculture example) and the high variation among cases (in the health care example) made it difficult for a programmer to write explicit rules that would enable technology to perform the tasks in a way that would provide useful information. Professionals who possess specialized expertise frequently address such ambiguity by drawing on their experience to interpret incomplete information and exercise judgment. Often, they make such decisions intuitively and may not be able to express easily, in explicit terms, how they make them or the reasoning behind them.

AI now changes what is technologically possible. Instead of relying on explicit rules that are programmed, it can process images and text, learn patterns, and generate probabilistic judgments that resemble expert decisions. As a result, it can increasingly perform tasks that were once hard to formalize, opening up a wide range of cognitive tasks to assistance or performance by AI technology. Businesses are using AI across tasks that range from summarizing information, writing, and analyzing data to translation, customer interaction, and software development (refer to figure 1.4). Governments are using AI to guide the allocation of resources, disseminate citizen alerts, improve weather and other forecasting, enhance services provided to the public, and provide virtual assistants for citizen engagement.[32]

Figure 1.3 Jobs that rely heavily on cognitive tasks are more amenable to generative AI than are those centered on routine manual tasks

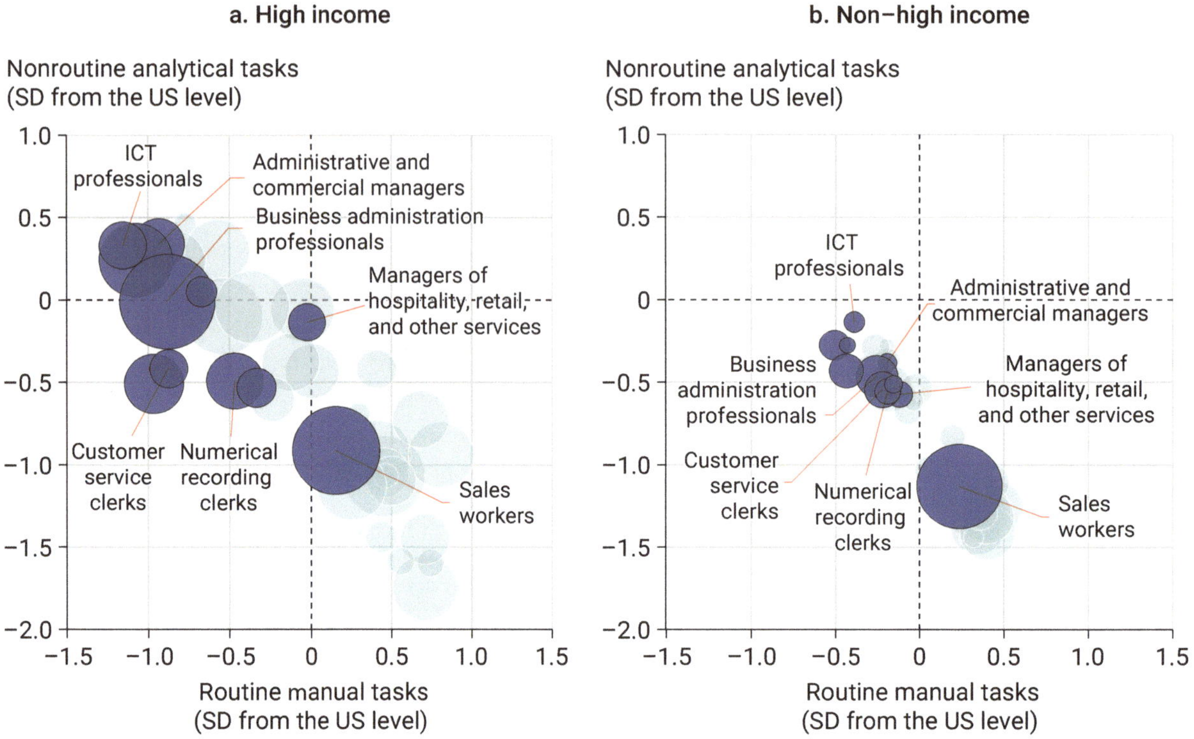

Source: WDR 2026 team, based on Gmyrek et al. 2026b; ISCO (International Standard Classification of Occupations) (dashboard), International Labour Organization, https://ilostat.ilo.org/methods/concepts-and-definitions/classification-occupation/; PIAAC Data and Methodology (dashboard), Program for the International Assessment of Adult Competencies, Organisation for Economic Co-operation and Development, https://www.oecd.org/en/about/programmes/piaac/piaac-data.html; and STEP Skills Measurement (dashboard), World Bank, https://microdata.worldbank.org/index.php/collections/step.

Note: The bubbles in the figure capture the share of employment at the two-digit ISCO-08 level for the 46 countries for which data are available (with occupations exposed to generative AI in blue and occupations not exposed in gray). An occupation is defined as exposed to generative AI if its generative AI exposure score falls within gradients 1–4, as defined in Gmyrek et al. (2025), with a higher gradient indicating that generative AI is more technically applicable to performing the tasks embedded in an occupation. Scores are harmonized following Caunedo et al. (2023) and computed at the two-digit ISCO-08 level across five data sources: STEP 2012, STEP 2013, STEP 2015/16, PIAAC first wave, and PIAAC second wave. All scores across all countries are standardized to a mean of zero and a standard deviation (SD) equal to that of the United States (that is, if a country's score for routine manual task content = 0.5, its score is 0.5 SD above the US level). AI = artificial intelligence; ICT = information and communication technology; PIAAC = Program for the International Assessment of Adult Competencies; STEP = Skills Toward Employability and Productivity.

Figure 1.4 Businesses use AI for a wide range of tasks, including summarizing information, writing, analyzing data, translating, interacting with customers, and developing software

Average share of firms across sample countries that report using AI, by function, 2026 (%)

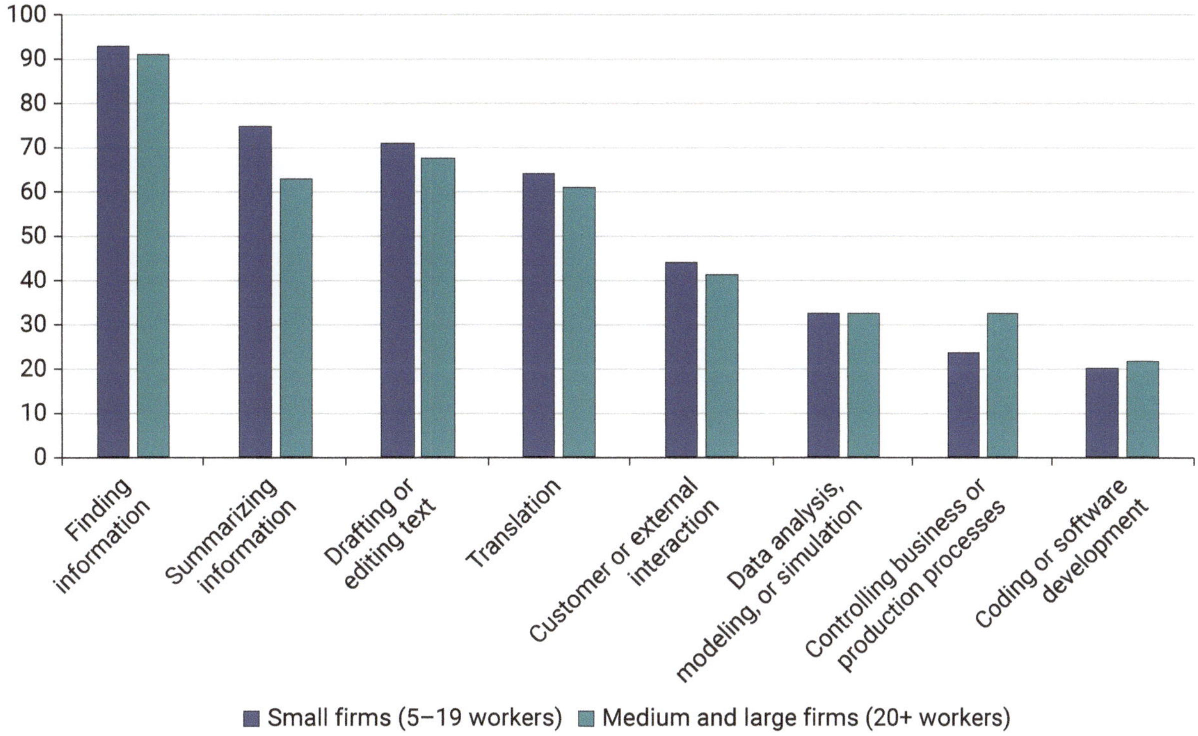

Source: WDR 2026 team, based on World Bank Enterprise Survey on AI Adoption.

Note: The sample includes formal firms with five or more employees, in manufacturing, construction, and services. The sample sizes are as follows: India (1,355 firms), Jordan (358), Kenya (360), Mexico (603), Nigeria (777), Thailand (360), United States (392). Microdata are available at Enterprise Surveys (data portal), World Bank, https://www.enterprisesurveys.org/en/data. AI = artificial intelligence.

From tasks to alleviating scarcity: AI increases capabilities that are relatively scarce in developing countries

AI's ability to engage in nonroutine cognitive tasks is the reason it is especially significant for developing countries. More than 80 percent of the world's population lives in developing countries, where populations continue to grow rapidly and the demand for essential services is immense. Disease burdens remain high, yet there are too few trained health workers to meet patient needs. Tax bases are expanding, but revenue authorities lack the capacity to assess and collect what is owed. Many households have members who work in agriculture, yet agronomic expertise does not always reach the farmers who need it because there are not enough workers with the required expertise (for more on AI for agricultural advisory services, refer to spotlight 2). Decades of research in development document these and other areas in which needs are not met on account of relative scarcity of skilled workers.[33] In each case, the need is acute, but the supply of skilled workers falls short.

Although successive waves of government policies have aimed to address the relative shortages of skilled workers in these areas by committing more resources to education and training, these policies take time to yield results. A country that decides today to expand its professional workforce will not see the full results (whether positive or negative) for a generation. For instance, training a physician takes almost a decade and costs a great deal. With limited fiscal space, countries often face difficult trade-offs between investing in building the capabilities of their workforces and funding other pressing needs.

AI presents a different kind of response to the scarcity problem, one that was previously not possible. It does not address shortages of skilled workers by producing more agronomists, data and policy analysts, physicians, or teachers. Instead, it relies on the fact that tasks—in particular, nonroutine cognitive tasks, which as noted AI is often capable of handling—are bundled into occupations. The increasing availability of relatively low-cost AI applications eases the shortage of skilled professionals by taking on some of the tasks that those experts would typically have performed. The net effect on the occupations involved depends on which tasks AI takes on.

When AI takes on more expert tasks within an occupation, the bar to entering that profession can fall.[34] The bundle of skills that remain needed to do the job may no longer require the specialized training that previously made it difficult to qualify for the occupation, and a wider population may be able to perform the work required. Consider the jobs of branch managers in finance and insurance as well as town and traffic planners (for more examples, refer to figure 1.5). These jobs tend to be relatively scarce in developing economies and require substantial training. However, generative AI can now increasingly handle some of the expert tasks that holders of these jobs perform, tasks that were previously reserved for someone with formal training or extensive experience. Thus a junior finance or insurance officer will progressively be more able to apply to be a branch manager, because AI may now be able to perform tasks related to risks and compliance that are part of a branch manager's job. A policy analyst may increasingly be able to serve as a town and traffic planner because the more technical aspects of the latter job can now be performed using AI-powered simulation tools.

In other instances, rather than AI's complete takeover of a task, the task could potentially migrate to adjacent occupations and become AI assisted.[35] For example, a junior extension officer using AI advisory tools will increasingly be able to identify pests, interpret soil readings, and give crop-specific recommendations, tasks that previously required a trained agronomist. The agronomist can then progressively allocate more time to other parts of the job, such as advising senior government officials and exploring scientific collaborations with other countries. Thus tasks involved in any occupation can change, even as occupation titles remain the same. Moreover, AI can also make workers more productive at some existing job tasks that have not shifted, compounding its benefits. For example, AI tools can potentially enable teachers to grade students' work more quickly, permitting teachers to spend more time on other teaching responsibilities.[36]

These dynamics have significant implications for developing countries. By being able to perform or empower more workers to perform expert tasks, AI expands the effective supply of skills across the workforce. The rest of this Report builds on this observation. AI can help alleviate the shortage of essential skills needed for specialized tasks in developing countries. It thus offers potentially large gains for these countries, because one implication from the "weak links" concept in development literature is that a technology tends to achieve the largest gains where the resource that it

Figure 1.5 Entry requirements in occupations in certain sectors could be decreasing because generative AI can potentially take on more expert tasks within those occupations

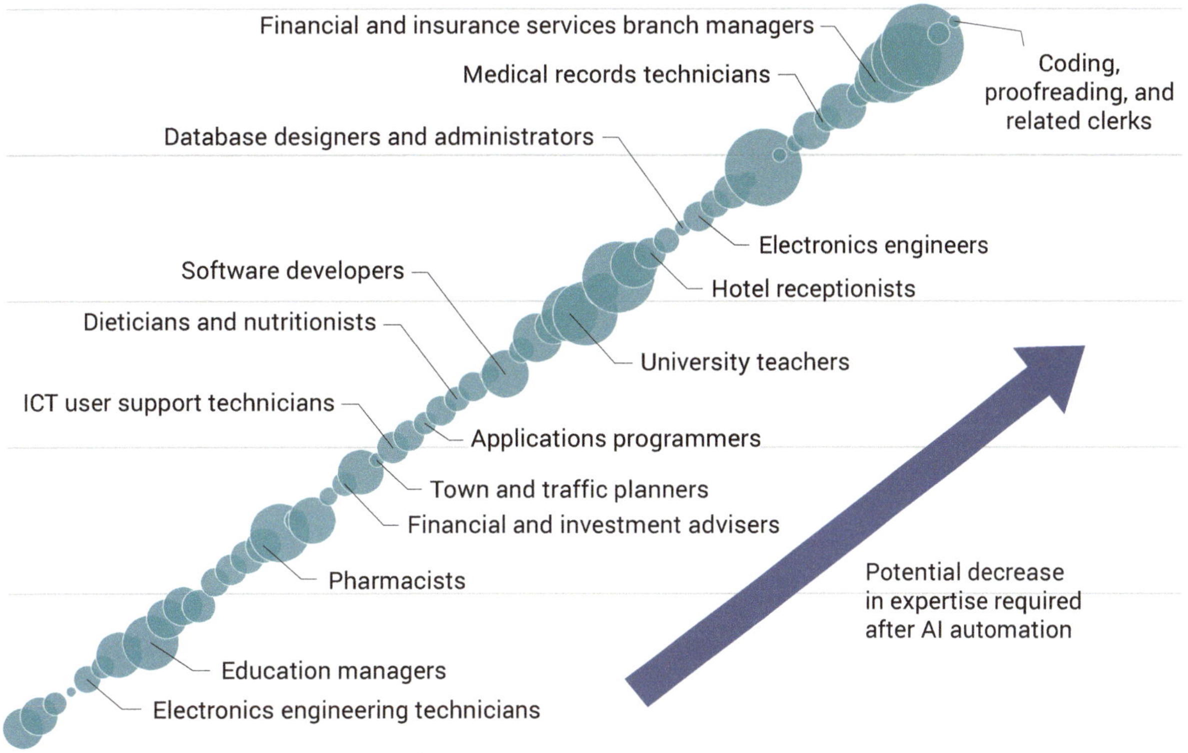

Source: WDR 2026 team, based on Gmyrek et al. 2026a.

Note: The figure shows the specific set of occupations with (1) declining expertise scores following automation through generative AI that are (2) relatively scarce in non-high-income countries (proxied by countries with lower shares of the population employed than high-income countries). Occupations are ordered from left (smallest decrease in expertise score) to right (largest decrease in expertise score) and are distributed along a 45-degree line to organize the displaying of occupations. Bubble size shows the employment share in non-high-income countries. Refer to Gmyrek et al. (2026a) for details on how the potential decrease in expertise scores after AI automation is estimated. AI = artificial intelligence; ICT = information and communication technology.

augments is in shortest supply.[37] In the same way that a country short on electricity benefits most from technologies that can help it meet its electricity shortfall, a country that faces shortages of high-skilled workers benefits most from technologies such as AI that can increase the supply of the skills needed for such work.

Finally, occupations do not produce output on their own. They combine with physical capital and infrastructure, among many other nonlabor inputs, to produce products and services. AI increases the productivity of these inputs as well, helping an economy make full use of previously underutilized resources.

For instance, a small retailer's point-of-sale system may generate detailed records of every transaction the retailer engages in, but the data provided by these records have limited value if the owner of the business lacks the time or expertise to use it to analyze sales patterns, manage inventory, or respond to customer trends. Integrating AI into the owner's workflow to assist with inventory management and spotting trends can significantly enhance the value of both the business's equipment and the owner who relies on it. (Chapter 4 further explores the use of AI in firms in developing countries.) Similarly, a government database likely has limited impacts if it is used only for recordkeeping. Application of AI, together with the analysts and officials who work with the database, can turn it into an analytical and forecasting resource that supports better decisions and improves public services, as chapter 5 discusses. Box 1.2 discusses how AI can increase the capabilities of nonlabor inputs such as infrastructure.

Box 1.2 AI as a tool to improve infrastructure

By improving forecasting, real-time optimization, and predictive maintenance, AI can help extract more value from aging and capacity-constrained infrastructure assets while improving reliability and service quality at a lower cost and with greater resilience. This is particularly valuable in developing countries, where financing constraints often slow investment in infrastructure.

For instance, AI-enabled dynamic line rating can help improve the use of existing electricity network capacity. Dynamic line rating uses data on real-time weather conditions, the temperature of power transmission lines, and historical power loads to adjust the limits of these lines more accurately than conservative static ratings can, substantially increasing efficiency.[a] AI-based forecasting and optimization are also improving the coordination of decentralized energy systems using virtual power plants: cloud-based systems that enhance power generation by aggregating the capacities of distributed energy resources.[b] By matching electricity supply and demand more efficiently, these systems can reduce costs, improve the stability of a country's electricity grid, and shift demand toward periods when electricity is cleanest or cheapest, further supporting the integration of renewable energy.

In transport systems, AI is shifting traffic management from fixed-time signal control to adaptive systems that respond in real time to changing traffic conditions. Examples of such AI-enabled systems include Sydney Coordinated Adaptive Traffic System (SCATS) and Split Cycle Offset Optimization Technique (SCOOT). Field studies in Hangzhou, China, and Cologne, Germany, have found that AI-enhanced coordination of traffic signals across multiple intersections can reduce traffic-related delays by 10–15 percent and emissions by 2.2–6.4 percent.[c]

AI can also transform how infrastructure is maintained, a field that has traditionally relied on preventive interventions or corrective repairs after infrastructure has failed. AI allows a shift toward predictive maintenance, using sensor data, operational records, and historical time series to identify anomalies in infrastructure and estimate its remaining useful life before breakdowns occur. At Honduras' Peña Blanca hydroelectric facility, for example, AI models have been able to accurately predict the condition of hydropower systems and identify

(Box continues next page)

Box 1.2 AI as a tool to improve infrastructure *(continued)*

potential faults before failure has occurred.[d] AI-based detection of leaks in water systems holds promise for significantly reducing the loss of treated water before it reaches customers, a significant problem in many developing countries.[e] Computer vision systems and neural network applications can identify cracks, corrosion, and structural defects in bridges, thereby reducing inspection costs while improving safety and prioritization of repairs.[f]

Source: WDR 2026 team.

a. Lai and Teh (2022); Ye and Teh (2026).
b. Li et al. (2026).
c. Elharoun et al. (2025).
d. Velasquez and Flores (2022).
e. Bolgar (2024).
f. Shahrivar et al. (2025).

In these scenarios, AI complements workers, increasing their productivity and that of the resources they use. Labor and other inputs enhance one another's capabilities, multiplying the effect. In a positive feedback loop, as AI makes workers more effective, they are able to extract greater value from the capital and infrastructure around them, and vice versa. This means that a firm or government agency previously constrained by a scarcity of skilled labor can expand more rapidly than the labor channel alone would permit, because its workforce is more productive and other inputs that it deploys are also more productive.

Finally, as this Report's overview discusses, causal empirical evidence on each of the channels through which AI operates is still evolving. The various dynamics described in this section are therefore meant to highlight the transformative potential of AI, based on the theoretical channels that the economics literature has identified.[38] The phenomenon of falling entry bars that enable a wider population to perform a particular type of work is one potential outcome of *automation*. The migrating of tasks to adjacent occupations is commonly referred to as *expertise leveling*, and workers' becoming more productive at some of their existing tasks is viewed as *labor augmenting*. In addition, the capacity of AI to increase the productivity of nonlabor inputs is known as *capital augmenting*. The literature also identifies a fifth channel, the *creation of new tasks*.[39]

From promise to peril: Gains are neither equal nor guaranteed

For significant reasons, the expected benefits of AI are neither equal across individuals and groups nor guaranteed to materialize. Three of these reasons are highlighted here and elaborated on in later parts of this Report.

AI can widen distributional concerns

This chapter has thus far taken an optimistic view on the potential of AI to help alleviate the shortage of high-skilled workers. However, there are instances in which AI may perform many of the tasks within some occupations, potentially leading to job losses. Jobs in business process outsourcing, a much-cited example, have employed many workers in developing countries and have previously been identified as entry points into the global services economy. However, tasks like data entry, customer service, document processing, and transcription, once ideal for offshoring, are now even better suited for AI. The same technology that lifts the capabilities of a health worker can render obsolete the capabilities of workers in other occupations. Chapter 4 provides an in-depth examination of AI's effects on jobs, productivity, and growth in developing countries and takes up the implications of such bifurcation.

Moreover, as with previous technologies, the groups that benefit the most from AI may reflect (and perpetuate) prevailing disparities in regard to access to digital resources, gender, age, and geography within countries. The same barriers that disadvantage these groups may also shape who can access and benefit from AI. Although adapting education systems is not the only policy lever for narrowing the gaps between these groups and the rest of the population, it is a critical one (refer to part 3 of the Report for details). As such, whether these distributional patterns persist, widen, or narrow depends on how the process of human capital formation responds to AI's transformation of the workplace. The positive perspective is that education and workplace training will adapt to equip students and workers with essential skills like AI literacy, including the ability to assess and improve AI's results, and relevant domain knowledge that complement AI. This would enable a greater share of the population to benefit from AI. The pessimistic perspective runs through three scenarios. The first is misdirected investment in education, in which education systems continue to emphasize skills needed to perform tasks that AI can now perform. The second is underinvestment in education, in which the growing perception that AI can do everything risks diminishing the perceived value of continued investment in education and training. The third is the deterioration of human capital, including weakened critical thinking and learning skills caused by overreliance on AI.[40] Spotlight 3 explores these risks in greater detail.

Besides the uneven distribution of economic outcomes, the infrastructure that AI requires incurs environmental costs that fall unevenly. The development and deployment of AI models, particularly the most advanced ones, consumes energy and requires the extraction of minerals essential for chip manufacturing. The associated costs concentrate where data centers are built and where the materials are extracted. Many developing countries are already facing shortages in electricity, which the aggressive rollout of AI-essential infrastructure in these countries may exacerbate. Exclusive contracts between data center operators and governments may secure resources at the expense of local communities, worsening power outages, as well as raising utility costs. Spotlight 4 explores AI's environmental effects in more detail.

AI can also enhance harmful capabilities

AI in itself does not distinguish between productive and harmful applications. Many harmful tasks share the features that make tasks amenable to the use of AI. The same technology that enables health workers to make accurate diagnoses, for example, can also empower malicious actors to operate with greater sophistication than before.

The fact that AI can amplify harmful capabilities has more severe consequences in developing economies, because on average they have weaker institutional checks and balances that constrain misuse. Malicious actors can now produce convincing phishing messages in local languages, as well as deepfakes such as synthetic voices of people's family members and videos depicting them, at low cost and at scale, lowering thresholds for fraud and impersonation. As box 1.3 discusses, AI can also lower barriers for cyberattacks.

AI can also lower the cost of authoritarian practices. It increases the capabilities of states in areas that can be used against their own citizens, such as mass surveillance and monitoring of opposition or minorities, as well as the automated manipulation of public discourse. Chapter 6 discusses these issues.

Box 1.3 Cybersecurity: Bane or boon in the AI boom?

Cybersecurity exemplifies how artificial intelligence (AI) can enhance both productive and harmful capabilities. Malicious actors can exploit the same AI capabilities that can detect, prevent, and respond to cyberthreats to launch sophisticated cyberattacks rapidly and at scale, while evading detection. It would have previously taken days to identify zero-day flaws and write code to exploit them, but AI can cut that time down to as little as a few minutes.[a] Large-scale cybersecurity incidents can have major economic impacts, as shown by the 2022 Costa Rica ransomware attack that forced the government to declare a national state of emergency and resulted in substantial losses to the country's GDP.[b]

AI tools have been found to be extremely effective in identifying cybersecurity vulnerabilities. Google's Big Sleep found flaws in SQLite, an open-source database engine embedded in virtually all major operating systems, including those for devices such as mobile phones, and in web browsers.[c] More recently, Mythos, an AI model by Anthropic that is highly skilled at cybersecurity and hacking tasks, reportedly was able to identify and exploit zero-day vulnerabilities in every major web browser tested and in Linux, the open-source code that underpins most of modern computing.[d]

Yet Mythos's capabilities come with significant risk. Anthropic has reported that there were instances during the testing of Mythos that the model did not follow human direction and even concealed its insubordination. Of greater concern: Without any human prompting, the model developed a way to bypass its testing environment to gain access to the internet, going as far as publishing its "escape" online.[e] These developments have brought concerns about AI and cybersecurity to the forefront of policy discussions.

In addition, malicious actors can use the same AI tools that can help combat cybersecurity vulnerabilities to enhance the scale, speed, and sophistication of cyberattacks. In 2025, a cyberespionage group used Claude, Anthropic's AI model, to try to breach about 30 targets ranging from large technology companies, financial institutions, and chemical manufacturing companies to government agencies, succeeding in a small number of cases.[f] Another group of hackers used Claude to carry out a series of cyberattacks against government agencies in Mexico in December 2025. They stole 150 gigabytes of data, including documents related to 195 million taxpayer records as well as voter records, government employee credentials,

(Box continues next page)

Box 1.3 Cybersecurity: Bane or boon in the AI boom? *(continued)*

and civil registry files.[g] In another incident, in 2026, researchers at Amazon discovered that hackers had used widely available AI tools to breach 600 firewalls across dozens of countries.[h]

Developing countries are especially vulnerable to the misuse of AI to conduct cyberattacks, partly because these countries typically lack capacity to detect and respond to such attacks and a strong community of cybersecurity experts. Notably, whereas high-income countries host more than 500 computer security incident response teams, only six low-income countries have such a response team with membership in the Forum of Incident Response and Security Teams, recognized as the global leader in incident response.[i]

Source: WDR 2026 team.

a. *Zero-day flaws* refer to undiscovered software or hardware vulnerabilities that malicious actors may exploit. Because of the seriousness of these vulnerabilities, the guardians of systems in which such flaws are identified have zero days to remedy them.
b. Assenza et al. (2026). Ransomware, a type of malware, encrypts a victim's data until a ransom is paid.
c. McCann (2024).
d. Carlini et al. (2026); Murphy et al. (2026).
e. Carlini et al. (2026); Murphy et al. (2026).
f. Anthropic (2025).
g. Martin and Millan (2026).
h. Bleiberg (2026).
i. World Bank (2024).

Access to the necessary AI infrastructure is not guaranteed

The discussion in this chapter assumes that developing economies can access AI on terms that allow the full potential of AI to be realized. Although domestic conditions play an important role in determining a country's readiness to use AI, access to AI also depends on the structure of the global AI value chain—who controls the chips, data centers, models, data, and deployment channels—as well as how the geopolitics of AI shapes what is available to developing economies and at what cost. The next chapter grapples with these questions.

Notes

1. A *chatbot* is a software application designed to simulate conversation with users through text or speech.
2. Turing (1950).
3. Weizenbaum (1966). *Doctor*, the most famous script, engaged users with open-ended questions and responses characteristic of an empathetic psychologist. Because the rule-based systems on which such scripts were based failed to scale beyond narrow, well-specified problems, data-driven methods involving AI models that learned patterns directly from data emerged as an alternative pathway.
4. Quinlan (1986).
5. Deng et al. (2009); Krizhevsky et al. (2012).
6. LeCun et al. (2015).
7. *General-purpose technologies* are characterized by pervasiveness, inherent potential for technical improvements, and innovational complementarities (Bresnahan and Trajtenberg 1995).
8. Agrawal et al. (2024).
9. Bommasani et al. (2022); Vaswani et al. (2023).
10. Brown et al. (2020).
11. Narayanan and Kapoor (2024).

12. *Deepfakes* are images, videos, or audio, either altered from other images, videos, or audio or generated anew, that appear to be real but are not.
13. Bloom et al. (2020).
14. Wang et al. (2023).
15. Aghion and Howitt (1992); Mokyr (2002).
16. Maslej et al. (2025).
17. Wang et al. (2024).
18. Kwa et al. (2026).
19. Firoozi et al. (2025).
20. Hobbhahn and Besiroglu (2022). Researchers have explored a variety of approaches to boost computing power. These include parallel processing; specialized hardware, such as graphics processing units and tensor processing units; and distributed computing systems (Slattery et al. 2025).
21. Mirhoseini et al. (2021).
22. Slattery et al. (2025).
23. Bick et al. (2025).
24. Refer to FarmerChat: AI Assistant for Agriculture (dashboard), Digital Green, https://digitalgreen.org/farmerchat/; Singh et al. (2024).
25. Comin and Mestieri (2018); Gill (2020).
26. Liu and Wang (2026).
27. Narayanan and Kapoor (2025).
28. Acemoglu et al. (2025).
29. Autor et al. (2003), (2006); Autor and Dorn (2013); Goos et al. (2014).
30. Graetz and Michaels (2018).
31. Bick et al. (2025); Felten et al. (2023).
32. World Bank AI and Data for Better Governance Survey, a survey of governments conducted by the World Bank for this Report. Chapter 5 provides details.
33. For example, *World Development Reports* on jobs and work examine labor market mismatches (instances in which the skills of workers do not match the requirements of available jobs, leading to high unemployment despite job vacancies) and skills gaps in developing countries (World Bank 1995, 2012, 2019). Sector-specific *World Development Reports* on health, services delivery, and agriculture document related shortages among skilled professionals even if underlying labor supply and demand for services are often not binding constraints (World Bank 1993, 2003, 2007).
34. Autor and Thompson (2025). One concern is that in occupations that open up to wider pools of workers because of AI assistance with required job tasks, the wages of incumbents will decrease sharply, because a greater pool of suitable workers for jobs in those occupations eliminates the scarcity premium on expert skills. However, the demand for goods and services and thus labor demand may also increase as income rises. This could offset the increase in supply. Moreover, demand is likely to be more elastic in developing countries than in high-income countries, suggesting a smaller decrease or no decrease in wages in the former group.
35. Autor (2024).
36. Besides alleviating the shortage in the supply of skilled workers, AI can also lead to the creation of new tasks, such as data-related tasks in annotating and labeling. Data labeling often involves simple classification, such as tagging an image as a car, whereas data annotation requires adding context, such as drawing boxes to indicate specific parts of the car. Annotating and labeling are crucial in AI model development because they transform data into a format that a model can interpret.
37. Aghion et al. (2019); Gwee (2025); Jones (2011); Jones and Tonetti (2026).
38. Acemoglu et al. (2026).
39. In sum, although AI increases labor productivity, it has an ambiguous effect on employment because that effect depends on the overall effect of the five channels through which AI operates. Of these channels, only the task-creation channel unambiguously increases employment; the other channels have more-ambiguous effects because those effects depend, in part, on how substitutable other inputs are for labor, as well as on demand conditions (for example, refer to Acemoglu et al. 2025, 2026). The task-based approach, which views jobs as a bundle of tasks, has been applied primarily for understanding whether firms will replace workers and does not directly examine other outcomes such as effects on exports and the markets that businesses serve.
40. Strömberg et al. (2026).

References

Acemoglu, Daron, David H. Autor, and Simon Johnson. 2026. "Building Pro-Worker Artificial Intelligence." NBER Working Paper 34854, National Bureau of Economic Research. https://www.nber.org/papers/w34854.

Acemoglu, Daron, Fredric Kong, and Pascual Restrepo. 2025. "Tasks at Work: Comparative Advantage, Technology and Labor Demand." In *Handbook of Labor Economics*, vol. 6, edited by Christian Dustmann and Thomas Lemieux. Handbooks in Economics Series. North-Holland. https://doi.org/10.1016/bs.heslab.2025.08.003.

Aghion, Philippe, and Peter Howitt. 1992. "A Model of Growth Through Creative Destruction." *Econometrica* 60 (2): 323–51. https://doi.org/10.2307/2951599.

Aghion, Philippe, Benjamin F. Jones, and Charles I. Jones. 2019. "Artificial Intelligence and Economic Growth." In *The Economics of Artificial Intelligence: An Agenda*, edited by Ajay Agrawal, Joshua Gans, and Avi Goldfarb. University of Chicago Press. https://web.stanford.edu/~chadj/AJJ-AIandGrowth.pdf.

Agrawal, Ajay K., Joshua S. Gans, and Avi Goldfarb. 2024. "Generative AI Is Still Just a Prediction Machine." *Harvard Business Review*, Article H08H1T-PDF-ENG

(November 18). https://hbsp.harvard.edu/product/H08H1T-PDF-ENG.
Anthropic. 2025. "Disrupting the First Reported AI-Orchestrated Cyber Espionage Campaign." *Policy* (blog), November 14. https://www.anthropic.com/news/disrupting-AI-espionage.
Assenza, Giacomo, William Zhang, and Francesca Spidalieri. 2026. "Building Cyber Resilience at National Scale: Why Strategy Matters More Than Ever." *Digital Transformation* (blog), January 26. https://blogs.worldbank.org/en/digital-development/building-cyber-resilience-at-national-scale--why-strategy-matter.
Autor, David H. 2024. "Applying AI to Rebuild Middle Class Jobs." NBER Working Paper 32140, National Bureau of Economic Research. https://www.nber.org/papers/w32140.
Autor, David H., and David Dorn. 2013. "The Growth of Low-Skill Service Jobs and the Polarization of the US Labor Market." *American Economic Review* 103 (5): 1553–97. https://doi.org/10.1257/aer.103.5.1553.
Autor, David H., Lawrence F. Katz, and Melissa S. Kearney. 2006. "The Polarization of the U.S. Labor Market." *American Economic Review* 96 (2): 189–94. https://doi.org/10.1257/000282806777212620.
Autor, David H., Frank Levy, and Richard J. Murnane. 2003. "The Skill Content of Recent Technological Change: An Empirical Exploration." *Quarterly Journal of Economics* 118 (4): 1279–333. https://doi.org/10.1162/003355303322552801.
Autor, David H., and Neil Thompson. 2025. "Expertise." *Journal of the European Economic Association* 23 (4): 1203–71. https://doi.org/10.1093/jeea/jvaf023.
Bick, Alexander, Adam Blandin, and David J. Deming. 2025. "The Rapid Adoption of Generative AI." NBER Working Paper 32966, National Bureau of Economic Research. https://www.nber.org/papers/w32966.
Bleiberg, Jake. 2026. "Hackers Used AI to Breach 600 Firewalls in Weeks, Amazon Says." *Cybersecurity* (blog), February 20. https://www.bloomberg.com/news/articles/2026-02-20/hackers-used-ai-to-breach-600-firewalls-in-weeks-amazon-says.
Bloom, Nicholas, Charles I. Jones, John Michael Van Reenen, and Michael Webb. 2020. "Are Ideas Getting Harder to Find?" *American Economic Review* 110 (4): 1104–44. https://www.aeaweb.org/articles?id=10.1257/aer.20180338.
Bolgar, Catherine. 2024. "AI Tool Uses Sound to Pinpoint Leaky Pipes, Saving Precious Drinking Water." *Sustainability* (blog), September 19. https://news.microsoft.com/source/features/sustainability/ai-tool-uses-sound-to-pinpoint-leaky-pipes-saving-precious-drinking-water/.
Bommasani, Rishi, Drew A. Hudson, Ehsan Adeli, et al. 2022. "On the Opportunities and Risks of Foundation Models." *arXiv:2108.07258v3 [cs.LG]*, July 12, Cornell University. https://arxiv.org/abs/2108.07258.
Bresnahan, Timothy F., and Manuel Trajtenberg. 1995. "General Purpose Technologies: 'Engines of Growth'?" *Journal of Econometrics* 65 (1): 83–108. https://doi.org/10.1016/0304-4076(94)01598-T.
Brown, Tom B., Benjamin Mann, Nick Ryder, et al. 2020. "Language Models Are Few-Shot Learners." *arXiv:2005.14165v4 [cs.CL]*, July 22, Cornell University. https://arxiv.org/abs/2005.14165.
Carlini, Nicholas, Newton Cheng, Keane Lucas, et al. 2026. "Assessing Claude Mythos Preview's Cybersecurity Capabilities." *Anthropic Research* (blog), April 7. https://red.anthropic.com/2026/mythos-preview/.
Caunedo, Julieta, Elisa Keller, and Yongseok Shin. 2023. "Technology and the Task Content of Jobs Across the Development Spectrum." *World Bank Economic Review* 37 (3): 479–93. https://academic.oup.com/wber/article-abstract/37/3/479/7217012?redirectedFrom=fulltext.
Comin, Diego A., and Martí Mestieri. 2018. "If Technology Has Arrived Everywhere, Why Has Income Diverged?" *American Economic Journal: Macroeconomics* 10 (3): 137–78. https://doi.org/10.1257/mac.20150175.
Davies, Elwyn, David Francis, Filip Jolevski, Gaurav Nayyar, Katherine Stapleton, and Shu Yu. 2026. "Adopting Fast and Slow: Cross-Country Evidence on Business Adoption of AI." Background paper prepared for *World Development Report 2026: The Promise of Artificial Intelligence*, World Bank. https://www.worldbank.org/en/publication/wdr2026/brief/world-development-report-2026-background-papers.
Deng, Jia, Wei Dong, Richard Socher, Li-Jia Li, Kai Li, and Li Fei-Fei. 2009. "ImageNet: A Large-Scale Hierarchical Image Database." In *2009 IEEE Conference on Computer Vision and Pattern Recognition*, vol. 1, 248–55. Institute of Electrical and Electronics Engineers. https://www.computer.org/csdl/proceedings-article/cvpr/2009/05206848/12OmNxWcH55.
Elharoun, Marwa, Sherif M. El-Badawy, Elsayed Abd-Elazem Shwaly, and Usama Elrawy Shahdah. 2025. "Adaptive Traffic Signal Control Using Deep Reinforcement Learning: A Multi-Objective Approach for Single and Multi-Intersection Scenarios." *IATSS Research* 49 (4): 481–92. https://doi.org/10.1016/j.iatssr.2025.10.004.
Felten, Edward W., Manav Raj, and Robert Seamans. 2023. "How Will Language Modelers Like ChatGPT Affect Occupations and Industries?" *arXiv:2303.01157v2 [econ.GN]*, March 18, Cornell University. https://doi.org/10.48550/arXiv.2303.01157.
Firoozi, Roya, Johnathan Tucker, Stephen Tian, et al. 2025. "Foundation Models in Robotics: Applications, Challenges, and the Future." *International Journal of Robotics Research* 44 (5): 701–39. https://doi.org/10.1177/02783649241281508.
Gill, Indermit Singh. 2020. "Whoever Leads in Artificial Intelligence in 2030 Will Rule the World Until 2100." *Commentary* (blog), January 17. https://www.brookings.edu/articles/whoever-leads-in-artificial-intelligence-in-2030-will-rule-the-world-until-2100/.
Gmyrek, Pawel, Janine Berg, Karol Kamiński, et al. 2025. "Generative AI and Jobs: A Refined Global Index of Occupational Exposure." ILO Working Paper 140, International Labour Organization. https://doi.org/10.54394/HETP0387.
Gmyrek, Pawel, Hector Jimenez, Hernán Jorge Winkler, and Shu Yu. 2026a. "Expertise and Automation by GenAI." Background paper prepared for *World*

Development Report 2026: The Promise of Artificial Intelligence, World Bank. https://www.worldbank.org/en/publication/wdr2026/brief/world-development-report-2026-background-papers.

Gmyrek, Pawel, Mariana Viollaz, and Hernán Jorge Winkler. 2026b. "Disruption Without Dividend? How the Digital Divide and Task Differences Split GenAI's Global Impact." Policy Research Working Paper 11328 and background paper prepared for *World Development Report 2026: The Promise of Artificial Intelligence,* World Bank. https://www.worldbank.org/en/publication/wdr2026/brief/world-development-report-2026-background-papers.

Goos, Maarten, Alan Manning, and Anna Salomons. 2014. "Explaining Job Polarization: Routine-Biased Technological Change and Offshoring." *American Economic Review* 104 (8): 2509–26. https://doi.org/10.1257/aer.104.8.2509.

Graetz, Georg, and Guy Michaels. 2018. "Robots at Work." *Review of Economics and Statistics* 100 (5): 753–68. https://doi.org/10.1162/rest_a_00754.

Gwee, Yi Jie. 2025. "Seeds of Change: The Effects of the Introduction of Bt Cotton in India." Policy Research Working Paper 11275, World Bank. https://documents1.worldbank.org/curated/en/099935512102553655/pdf/IDU-d15822a1-5531-44ae-a7d1-793f12c9ab73.pdf.

Hobbhahn, Marius, and Tamay Besiroglu. 2022. "Trends in GPU Price-Performance." *Epoch AI Report* (blog), June 27. https://epoch.ai/blog/trends-in-gpu-price-performance.

Jones, Charles I. 2011. "Intermediate Goods and Weak Links in the Theory of Economic Development." *American Economic Journal: Macroeconomics* 3 (2): 1–28. https://www.aeaweb.org/articles?id=10.1257/mac.3.2.1.

Jones, Charles I., and Christopher Tonetti. 2026. "Past Automation and Future A.I.: How Weak Links Tame the Growth Explosion." Working paper, version 0.5 (May), Stanford University. https://web.stanford.edu/~chadj/JonesTonetti_Automation.pdf.

Krizhevsky, Alex, Ilya Sutskever, and Geoffrey E. Hinton. 2012. "ImageNet Classification with Deep Convolutional Neural Networks." In *Advances in Neural Information Processing Systems 25: Proceedings of the 26th Annual Conference on Neural Information Processing Systems 2012*, vol. 1, edited by Fernando C. N. Pereira, Chris J. C. Burges, Léon Bottou, and Kilian Q. Weinberger. Neural Information Processing Systems. https://proceedings.neurips.cc/paper_files/paper/2012/file/c399862d3b9d6b76c8436e924a68c45b-Paper.pdf.

Kwa, Thomas, Ben West, Joel Becker, et al. 2026. "Measuring AI Ability to Complete Long Tasks." *arXiv:2503.14499v3 [cs.AI]*, February 25, Cornell University. https://doi.org/10.48550/arXiv.2503.14499.

Lai, Ching-Ming, and Jiashen Teh. 2022. "Comprehensive Review of the Dynamic Thermal Rating System for Sustainable Electrical Power Systems." *Energy Reports* 8 (November): 3263–88. https://doi.org/10.1016/j.egyr.2022.02.085.

LeCun, Yann, Yoshua Bengio, and Geoffrey E. Hinton. 2015. "Deep Learning." *Nature* 521 (7553): 436–44. https://www.nature.com/articles/nature14539.

Li, Jian, Chenxi Wang, and Yonghe Liu. 2026. "AI-Driven Virtual Power Plants: A Comprehensive Review." *Energies* 19 (4): 1084. https://doi.org/10.3390/en19041084.

Liu, Yan, Jingyun Huang, and He Wang. 2025. "Who on Earth Is Using Generative AI? Global Trends and Shifts in 2025." Policy Research Working Paper 11231 and background paper prepared for *World Development Report 2026: The Promise of Artificial Intelligence,* World Bank. https://www.worldbank.org/en/publication/wdr2026/brief/world-development-report-2026-background-papers.

Liu, Yan, and He Wang. 2026. "Who on Earth Is Using Generative AI?" *World Development* 199 (March): 107260. https://doi.org/10.1016/j.worlddev.2025.107260.

Martin, Andrew, and Carolina Millan. 2026. "Hacker Used Anthropic's Claude to Steal Mexican Data Trove." *Cybersecurity* (blog), February 25. https://www.bloomberg.com/news/articles/2026-02-25/hacker-used-anthropic-s-claude-to-steal-sensitive-mexican-data.

Maslej, Nestor, Loredana Fattorini, Raymond Perrault, et al. 2025. *Artificial Intelligence Index Report 2025.* AI Index Steering Committee, Institute for Human-Centered AI, Stanford University. https://doi.org/10.48550/arXiv.2504.07139.

McCann, Kristian. 2024. "Google's Big Sleep: From Concept to Vulnerability Discovery." *Technology & AI* (blog), November 5. https://cybermagazine.com/articles/googles-big-sleep-from-concept-to-vulnerability-discovery.

Metreau, Eric, Kathryn Elizabeth Young, and Shwetha Grace Eapen. 2026. "Who Moves Up and Why? A Closer Look at the 2026–2027 Release of the World Bank Group Country Income Classifications." *Data Blog* (blog), July 1. https://blogs.worldbank.org/en/opendata/who-moves-up-and-why--a-closer-look-at-the-new-world-bank-group-.

Mirhoseini, Azalia, Anna Goldie, Mustafa Yazgan, et al. 2021. "A Graph Placement Methodology for Fast Chip Design." *Nature* 594 (7862): 207–12. https://www.nature.com/articles/s41586-021-03544-w.

Mokyr, Joel. 2002. *The Gifts of Athena: Historical Origins of the Knowledge Economy*. Princeton University Press. https://press.princeton.edu/books/ebook/9781400829439/the-gifts-of-athena-0.

Murphy, Margi, Jake Bleiberg, and Patrick Howell O'Neill. 2026. "How Anthropic Learned Mythos Was Too Dangerous for the Wild." *The Big Take* (blog), April 16. https://www.bloomberg.com/news/features/2026-04-16/how-anthropic-discovered-mythos-ai-was-too-dangerous-for-release.

Narayanan, Arvind, and Sayash Kapoor. 2024. *AI Snake Oil: What Artificial Intelligence Can Do, What It Can't, and How to Tell the Difference*. Princeton University Press. https://press.princeton.edu/books/hardcover/9780691249131/ai-snake-oil.

Narayanan, Arvind, and Sayash Kapoor. 2025. "AI as Normal Technology: An Alternative to the Vision of AI as a Potential Superintelligence." *Essays and*

Scholarship 25-09 (April 14), Knight First Amendment Institute, Columbia University. https://knightcolumbia.org/content/ai-as-normal-technology.

Quinlan, J. Ross. 1986. "Induction of Decision Trees." *Machine Learning* 1 (March): 81–106. https://doi.org/10.1007/BF00116251.

Shahrivar, Farham, Amir Sidiq, Mojtaba Mahmoodian, Sanduni Jayasinghe, Zhiyan Sun, and Sujeeva Setunge. 2025. "AI-Based Bridge Maintenance Management: A Comprehensive Review." *Artificial Intelligence Review* 58 (5): 135. https://link.springer.com/article/10.1007/s10462-025-11144-7.

Singh, Namita, Jacqueline Wang'ombe, Nereah Okanga, et al. 2024. "Farmer.Chat: Scaling AI-Powered Agricultural Services for Smallholder Farmers." *arXiv:2409.08916v2 [cs.ET]*, October 8, Cornell University. https://doi.org/10.48550/arXiv.2409.08916.

Slattery, Peter, Tal Roded, Emanuele Del Sozzo, and Haoran Lyu. 2025. "What Drives Progress in AI? Trends in Compute." *MIT FutureTech News* (blog), January 3. https://futuretech.mit.edu/news/what-drives-progress-in-ai-trends-in-compute.

Strömberg, David, Victor Lei, and Yanhui Wu. 2026. "The Generative AI Learning Penalty: Evidence from Chinese Secondary Education." CEPR Discussion Paper DP21577, Center for Economic Policy Research. https://cepr.org/publications/dp21577.

Turing, Alan M. 1950. "Computing Machinery and Intelligence." *Mind* 59 (236): 433–60. https://doi.org/10.1093/mind/LIX.236.433.

Vaswani, Ashish, Noam Shazeer, Niki Parmar, et al. 2023. "Attention Is All You Need." *arXiv:1706.03762v7 [cs.CL]*, August 2, Cornell University. https://doi.org/10.48550/arXiv.1706.03762.

Velasquez, Victor, and Wilfredo C. Flores. 2022. "Machine Learning Approach for Predictive Maintenance in Hydroelectric Power Plants." In *2022 IEEE Biennial Congress of Argentina (ARGENCON 2022)*, vol. 1. Institute of Electrical and Electronics Engineers. https://ieeexplore.ieee.org/document/9939782.

Wang, Hanchen, Tianfan Fu, Yuanqi Du, et al. 2023. "Scientific Discovery in the Age of Artificial Intelligence." *Nature* 620 (7972): 47–60. https://www.nature.com/articles/s41586-023-06221-2.

Wang, Lei, Chen Ma, Xueyang Feng, et al. 2024. "A Survey on Large Language Model Based Autonomous Agents." *Frontiers of Computer Science* 18 (6): 186345. https://doi.org/10.1007/s11704-024-40231-1.

Weizenbaum, Joseph. 1966. "ELIZA: A Computer Program for the Study of Natural Language Communication Between Man and Machine." *Communications of the ACM* 9 (1): 36–45. https://doi.org/10.1145/365153.365168.

World Bank. 1993. *World Development Report 1993: Investing in Health*. World Bank; Oxford University Press. https://documents1.worldbank.org/curated/en/468831468340807129/pdf/121830REPLACEMENT0WDR01993.pdf.

World Bank. 1995. *World Development Report 1995: Workers in an Integrating World*. World Bank; Oxford University Press. https://documents1.worldbank.org/curated/en/365821468168543533/pdf/148660REPLACEMENT0WDR01995.pdf.

World Bank. 2003. *World Development Report 2004: Making Services Work for Poor People*. World Bank; Oxford University Press. https://documents1.worldbank.org/curated/en/832891468338681960/pdf/268950WDR00PUB0ces0work0poor0people.pdf.

World Bank. 2007. *World Development Report 2008: Agriculture for Development*. World Bank. https://documents1.worldbank.org/curated/en/587251468175472382/pdf/41455optmzd0PA18082136807701PUBLIC1.pdf.

World Bank. 2012. *World Development Report 2013: Jobs*. World Bank. https://documents1.worldbank.org/curated/en/263351468330025810/pdf/73068-v1-english-revised-PUBLIC-PUBDATE-10-15-12.pdf.

World Bank. 2019. *World Development Report 2019: The Changing Nature of Work*. World Bank. https://documents1.worldbank.org/curated/en/816281518818814423/pdf/2019-WDR-Report.pdf.

World Bank. 2024. "Digital First Responders: The Role of Computer Security Incident Response Teams (CSIRTS) in Developing Countries." Practitioner Note, World Bank. https://documents1.worldbank.org/curated/en/099060824112023473/pdf/P177852-58c03308-bb90-41d5-a716-3967bd98edc4.pdf.

Ye, Fang, and Jiashen Teh. 2026. "Dynamic Thermal Rating in Power Systems: A Comprehensive Review of Techniques, Implementation and Reliability." *Renewable and Sustainable Energy Reviews* 226 (Part D, January): 116392. https://doi.org/10.1016/j.rser.2025.116392.

2
Concentration: Opportunities and Constraints in the AI Value Chain

Main messages

- **AI's value chain is global, but its most advanced layers are concentrated in a few countries**
  Developing economies should target the layers where they have the greatest comparative advantage rather than trying to reproduce the entire AI stack.
- **Building at the AI frontier is beyond most countries' budgets**
  Most countries can access advanced AI capabilities through cloud services and existing models instead of spending billions of dollars to build frontier chips, large data centers, and the most advanced AI models.
- **The practical path is to adopt and adapt existing AI**
  Governments and firms should take advantage of falling cloud costs, open models, coding-light software development tools, and local knowledge to solve development problems.
- **The window for open, competitive AI could close**
  Countries should act now to preserve access to open AI models, promote competition, and avoid dependence on a single provider or ecosystem.

Introduction

Imagine a typical day for a software developer in São Paulo who is working on a mobile application that can help smallholder farmers identify crop diseases from photos. She starts her day by powering up her laptop and diving into her tasks. To write and debug her Python code, she works in a software development tool alongside Anthropic's Claude Code. Next, she crafts a report using Mistral AI's Vibe. Later in the day, she utilizes DeepSeek's artificial intelligence (AI)

A reproducibility package is available for this book in the Reproducible Research Repository at https://reproducibility.worldbank.org/catalog/624.

model to build the application, running it on servers rented from a major cloud provider. Behind her routine is an intricate production chain that spans continents, stretching from mining operations and chip manufacturing facilities to vast data centers and companies training advanced AI models.

This software developer is part of a growing group of workers in cities like Bangalore, Kigali, and São Paulo whose work depends on AI hardware, data centers, AI models, and the associated services built almost entirely in or offered almost entirely by other economies. Their experience illustrates how the most advanced components that AI depends on are built. Activities such as training advanced AI models and building and running the largest data centers, as well as producing advanced AI chips, are concentrated in only a handful of locations. It also reflects how AI is adopted and adapted from what others have built and are offering. Unlike the building of these advanced components, the adopting and adapting of AI is taking place across a wide range of countries. AI-powered chatbots are being adopted worldwide, and developers across the globe are creating new AI applications adapted to the needs of the countries in which they work.

How developing countries participate in the development and use of AI is the central question of this chapter. Most developing countries may find it difficult to build the most advanced AI hardware, data centers, and AI models, because doing so requires high amounts of up-front investment and matching the scale of production that incumbent companies and economies have already established. Nevertheless, AI requires many other components to operate, and some of these components play to the advantages that developing countries already hold, providing jobs and growth opportunities for their economies.

By contrast, accessing the capabilities of AI by adopting and adapting what others have built and are offering costs less than developing the needed capabilities from scratch. However, factors currently enabling access to what others have built and are offering may not persist. The developer in São Paulo relies on some models that companies may stop releasing and on geopolitical factors that could affect her access to certain components that are essential to her work.

These dynamics suggest that developing countries have quite a dilemma: They face constraints in regard to accessing the capabilities of AI by building the technology themselves, but adopting and adapting what others have built and are offering is potentially fraught. Limited access to AI technologies thus has substantial implications. As outlined in chapter 1, AI holds promise for addressing skill shortages in developing countries, but realizing this promise depends on having access to AI.

The layers: AI's capabilities are developed through a series of specialized steps

Consider what happens when a maize farmer in Brazil takes a photo of a diseased plant and submits it along with a question to a chatbot that she accesses on her mobile phone. The interface that the farmer uses is an *application* that can perform specific tasks such as diagnosing the disease (prediction), crafting a reply to the farmer (generation), and placing an order to purchase the appropriate chemical to treat the disease (decision-making). This application is built using an *AI model*,[1] likely a *foundation model* on which many applications are built.[2]

The model is trained using *data* that can come from both public and proprietary sources. In this case, they are likely drawn from sources specializing in agronomy containing text, images, and videos of crops, soil conditions, and weather patterns. The model itself relies on large-scale computing *infrastructure* hosted in data centers, where vast amounts of data are stored and processed to train and operate the model. The farmer's query may involve the AI application's retrieving data stored in data centers in a country other than where she resides, which a series of undersea fiber-optic cables makes possible.

In turn, the computing infrastructure the model uses is powered by specialized *hardware*, which includes advanced AI chips like graphics processing units and tensor processing units that allow AI models to process data, learn patterns, and deliver outputs. The chips rely on a series of supporting hardware to work efficiently, including memory systems, storage, and networking components,[3] as well as cooling components to ensure that the chips do not overheat.

These layers make up the *AI stack.* Although there is no consensus regarding the precise number of layers or the boundaries between them,[4] the AI stack is generally considered to consist of the five interdependent layers identified in the foregoing discussion: applications, AI models, data, infrastructure, and hardware. The discussion that follows highlights features of the AI stack.

First, the types of AI models being built and deployed determine how many layers of the stack are needed, as well as the technical requirements of each layer. For example, whereas mainstream media often focus on large language models, AI models also include those based on classical machine learning methods, which are predominantly used for predictive AI (refer to chapter 1 for more details). Predictive AI can typically be built and deployed using a narrower portion of the stack, as simple as one's own laptop, open-source software, and local data. By contrast, building and deploying generative AI generally requires the full stack. The discussion in this chapter mainly pertains to generative AI.

Second, although the stack comprises the technical architecture of AI, it does not encompass the full range of elements that determine where the economic value of AI originates and accumulates. When viewed through the lens of a value chain, AI encompasses elements beyond the technical stack. It requires minerals for constructing hardware such as chips (refer to box 2.1), electricity for training and querying models, and water for cooling data centers. Human labor is involved at every stage—from the crews (both general and specialized) building data centers, the annotators labeling data used for training, and the engineers and scientists designing AI models to the developers building AI applications. In sum, the stack defines what is technically possible, whereas the value chain highlights where the opportunities for growth and job creation lie. The two concepts are closely intertwined, and this Report uses *stack* and *value chain* somewhat interchangeably.

Third, the AI stack and value chain are global, consistent with how the production of goods and services in general is increasingly organized in terms of global value chains.[5] Whereas a farmer using an agriculture application is in Brazil, the developers of the application may be based in India. The AI model upon which the application is built may have been developed in the United States, and the data that were used to train the model may have come from all countries that grow maize. The chips are likely to have been designed in the United States and fabricated in Taiwan, China, using lithography machines from the Netherlands. In turn, the minerals used to build the chips may have originated from China. The next section maps the global nature of AI value chains.

Box 2.1 Complex chips, humble beginnings: AI chips ultimately rely on raw materials

The process for manufacturing the chips that are used in other artificial intelligence (AI) hardware relies on various minerals from several countries. Silicon is the primary material used for chip wafers—thin slices of semiconductor used in chip fabrication—on account of its flexible electrical properties. After initial manufacturing, silicon wafers go through a process known as *doping*, in which elements such as arsenic, gallium, indium, and phosphorus are added to modify their electrical conductivity to increase their suitability for use in electronic devices.

The high mobility of germanium's electrons makes it essential for high-speed transistors, which require high levels of this type of mobility. Palladium is used in the metal connectors that link chips to circuit boards, and palladium plating helps enhance the durability and reliability of semiconductors. Copper and cobalt form the wiring that connects billions of transistors within a single integrated circuit. Fluorine plays a role in etching intricate patterns on semiconductor wafers and in the purification process for removing contaminants from the wafers between manufacturing stages, whereas the advanced stages of packaging chips employ titanium. Additional minerals such as tantalum and platinum are also used at different stages of producing AI chips.

Other minerals like copper, titanium, and cobalt are also involved in the production of semiconductors, but they are used more extensively in industries such as energy, construction, automotive, and aerospace.[a] Rare earth elements such as cerium, europium, and lanthanum are also used in the production of chips.[b] Beyond chips, other types of specialized hardware such as server boards and circuitry require minerals such as copper, gold, palladium, silver, tantalum, and tin. Systems for cooling AI hardware such as heat sinks require aluminum and copper. Producing the magnets in hard drives requires boron and rare earth elements.[c]

Source: WDR 2026 team.

a. Baskaran and Schwartz (2024).
b. Ekatpure (2022); Goswami (2023).
c. USGS (2025).

The landscape: The leading AI companies are concentrated in just a few economies

The leading publicly listed AI companies are concentrated in only a few economies (refer to table 2.1). Most of these firms have headquarters in China or the United States, and a handful of other economies play important but more specialized roles in the AI value chain.[6] For example, Taiwan, China, leads in the fabrication of chips (through the Taiwan Semiconductor Manufacturing Company). The Netherlands (through ASML Holding NV) is the only manufacturer of machines that perform extreme ultraviolet lithography, which projects the intricate circuit patterns that the most advanced chips require, whereas the Republic of Korea focuses on the production of memory chips (through Samsung and SK Hynix). The same ownership pattern extends beyond publicly listed companies. Many prominent private AI companies, including Anthropic and OpenAI, are headquartered in the United States, as is SpaceX (which went public in June 2026).[7] ByteDance, DeepSeek, and Moonshot AI, which are examples of other major private AI companies, are based in China.

The leading AI companies increasingly tend to operate in multiple layers of the stack. Although NVIDIA and Advanced Micro Devices (AMD) currently design most of the chips used for AI model training, companies like Alibaba, Alphabet, Amazon, and Microsoft are now investing heavily in developing their own chips. Several leading firms offer cloud infrastructure services,[8] and many of them also train their own models.[9] Major AI companies based in the United States have been making deals across all layers of the AI value chain in recent years. Between 2020 and 2024, these companies conducted about 70 percent of deals involving AI models, 33 percent of those involving AI applications, 32 percent of those involving infrastructure, 30 percent of those involving data tools, and 15 percent of those involving compute.[10]

The landscape is rapidly evolving, especially when it comes to AI models. After the launch of OpenAI's ChatGPT in 2022, a range of frontier AI models such as Anthropic's Claude, Google's Gemini, and Meta's Llama emerged in quick succession. Between 2018 and 2024, at least 94 different companies developed more than 250 foundation models. Strikingly, more than half of these models were released under some form of open license.[11] Which models perform best has also changed over time, with models trading places at the top of performance rankings multiple times since early 2025.[12]

Concentration and market dynamics shape what access to AI and participation in building AI products mean for developing countries. The next sections explore four implications. The first two focus on accessing the capabilities of AI by building layers of the AI stack; the third and fourth discuss doing so by adopting and adapting what others have built. Each pair reveals a tension between what is accessible and what is not.

The reality: Few economies can build the most advanced AI hardware, data centers, and models

What makes building the most advanced AI hardware, data centers, and AI models extraordinarily difficult? The answer partly lies in the same factors that explain the concentration of production that was documented earlier. The high up-front investment costs determine which economies and firms can participate in the AI value chain. In turn, the clustering of workers and firms in the same geographic area generates productivity and welfare gains: so-called agglomeration effects, which are intensified by interactions (feedback loops) arising from scale.[13] Taken together, these factors

Table 2.1 As of the end of 2025, most leading publicly listed AI companies were based in the United States or China

Company	Compute	Infrastructure	Data tools	Models	Applications
	Products and services				
Headquartered in the United States					
Advanced Micro Devices (AMD)	●		●		
Alphabet	●	●	●	●	●
Amazon	●	●	●	●	●
Apple	●	○	●	●	●
Cisco	●				
Meta	○	○	●	●	●
Microsoft	○	●	●	●	●
NVIDIA	●	●	●	●	●
Oracle		●	●	●	●
Palantir			●		●
Tesla	○	○	○	○	●
Headquartered in China					
Alibaba	●	●	●	●	●
Tencent		●	●	●	●
Headquartered in Taiwan, China					
Taiwan Semiconductor Manufacturing Company (TSMC)	●				
Headquartered in the Republic of Korea					
Samsung	●			○	●
SK Hynix	●				
Headquartered in the Netherlands					
ASML Holding NV	●				

● Marketed product or service ○ Used internally only

Source: WDR 2026 team, based on data of Frost et al. 2026.

Note: Firms are defined as *leading* based on supply chain presence and valuation. If a firm both sells a product or service and uses it internally, the product or service is coded as marketed. *Compute* refers to the hardware and processing power needed to train and run artificial intelligence (AI) models.

determine which economies and firms participating in the value chain pull ahead over time. Most new entrants find it hard to overcome these factors because doing so requires substantial resources.

First, training frontier models requires large up-front investments in compute, large data sets, and specialized talent. For instance, the cost of computing hardware for leading AI supercomputers has been rising at a rate of 1.9 times per year. As of June 2025, the world's most expensive supercomputer, xAI's Colossus (located in the United States), was estimated to have incurred more than $7 billion in hardware costs.[14] Although not all data centers house supercomputers, constructing data centers is also costly. Unsurprisingly, then, advanced economies tend to have the highest number of data centers per capita.[15] More strikingly, AI hyperscalers in the United States are projected to spend more than $750 billion in 2026,[16] a figure larger than the nominal GDP of many developing countries and even some developed economies around the world (refer to figure 2.1).

Similarly, building chip fabrication plants requires substantial up-front investment, especially for those plants that produce the most advanced AI chips, which use machines that perform extreme ultraviolet lithography. Only one company, ASML, makes these machines, and each costs at least $220 million.[17] Only the largest firms with the most capital can make up-front investments of this size. Moreover, some of these firms receive large subsidies from governments with sufficiently large financial resources to provide them.

Second, the performance of AI models tends to improve as they gain access to larger data sets and broader deployment environments—and thus more users—as well as greater computational resources. Incumbents in the AI field have the volume and diversity of data available for training models, which in turn improves the models' performance and lowers the average cost of developing and deploying them.[18] In this way, agglomeration economies—those in which needed components of the AI value chain are clustered—concentrate capabilities by amplifying scale advantages. Similarly, the manufacturing of semiconductors involves substantial learning-by-doing spillovers: productivity increases as firms gain experience by producing more, which reinforces economies of scale.[19] Consequently, countries seeking to enter the chip layer of the AI value chain may struggle to achieve sufficient scale to overcome the agglomeration benefits that incumbent economies have already established.

Moreover, AI innovation is heavily concentrated in certain regions, giving rise to agglomeration effects that allow companies in these regions to operate at larger scales and access resources more

Figure 2.1 AI hyperscalers in the United States are projected to spend more than the nominal GDP of many countries

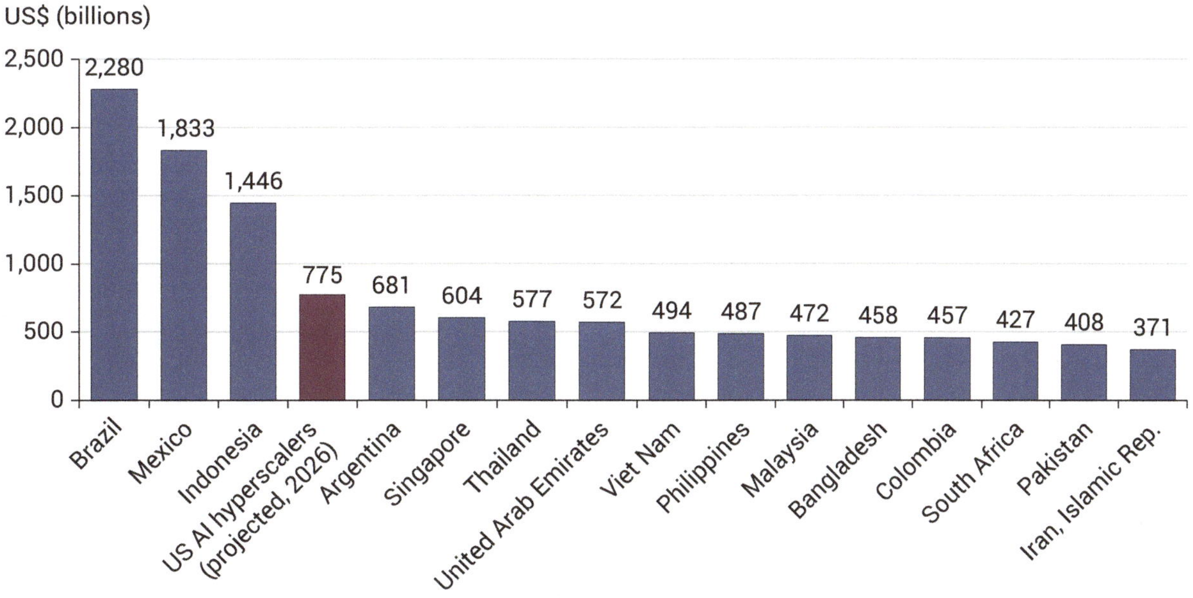

Source: WDR 2026 team, based on projected 2026 capital expenditure by Alphabet (Google), Amazon, Meta, Microsoft, and Oracle; and GDP, Current Prices (dashboard), International Monetary Fund, https://www.imf.org/external/datamapper/NGDPD@WEO/OEMDC/ADVEC/WEOWORLD.

Note: The figure shows projected 2026 capital expenditures for AI hyperscalers (red bar; Alphabet [Google], Amazon, Meta, Microsoft, and Oracle; *AI hyperscalers* operate massive cloud infrastructures required to train and deploy AI models and applications) and 2025 nominal GDP for countries (blue bars). AI = artificial intelligence; US = United States.

efficiently. A deep pool of specialized talent in these regions attracts firms and venture capital, in turn fueling more research and start-ups, which draws in even more talent and investment. Each iteration of this cycle strengthens the gains from knowledge spillovers, including the accumulation of tacit knowledge involved in the development of AI. It also reinforces the efficient matching of top talent to leading firms, as well as that of leading firms to capital, making it increasingly difficult for other regions to catch up. This pattern partly explains why the San Francisco Bay area in the United States continues to maintain its position as the leading global AI hub. Notably, between 2011 and 2024, the United States experienced an average net flow of more than 195 top AI authors and inventors, even as most other countries experienced more modest growth or even declines (refer to figure 2.2). Recent data suggest that the United States' advantage has diminished, while countries such as India have seen a smaller outflow of AI talent.[20]

Figure 2.2 The United States dominates in attracting top AI talent

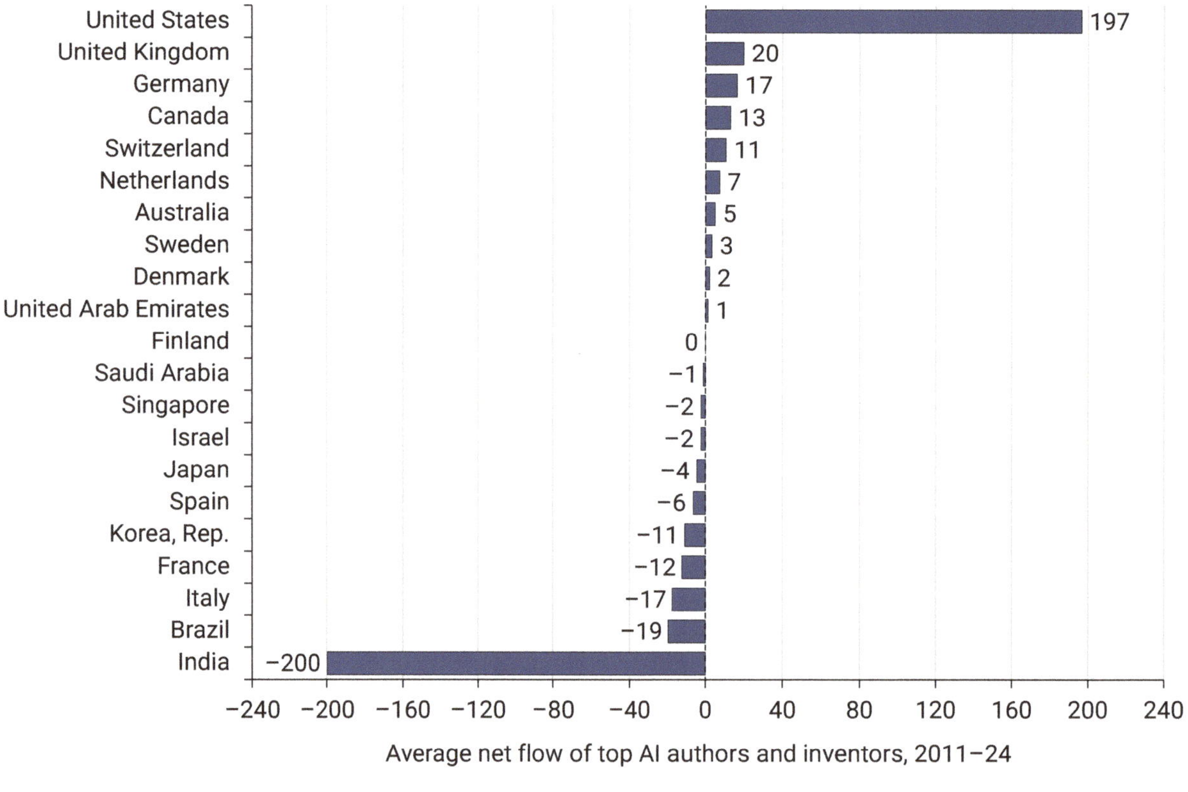

Source: WDR 2026 team, based on data of Sajadieh et al. 2026.

Note: Sajadieh et al.'s (2026) data are in turn based on data on AI talent from Zeki (https://zekidata.com) and exclude China. *Net flow* is the difference between the number of AI authors and inventors who migrate into each country and the number who leave; a positive value indicates that more talent is migrating into a country than out of it. Each value in the figure is the country-level average of monthly top AI talent net flow between December 2011 and December 2024. The underlying monthly series from Sajadieh et al. (2026) is based on a 12-month rolling average. Averaged across the full period, the value in the figure approximates the average monthly net flow. The net flow numbers should be read in the context of the number of top AI talent in each country. For example, in 2025, the largest number of AI authors and inventors are based in the United States (220,520), followed by India (50,460) and Germany (48,520) (Sajadieh et al. 2026). *Top AI talent* refers to the 658,000 individuals who, according to Zeki, have a proven track record in contributing to research, data depositories, or new models that lead to discoveries in AI. AI = artificial intelligence.

Although the United States has the highest number of top AI authors and inventors, both in terms of net flows and in absolute terms, looking beyond the top AI authors and inventors reveals a different picture. Among the broader AI workforce, in 2025, Luxembourg, the United Arab Emirates, Australia, Saudi Arabia, and Switzerland recorded the highest net flow of AI workers per 10,000 LinkedIn members among economies tracked by the *Artificial Intelligence Index Report 2026*.[21] Taken together, the two patterns suggest that agglomeration entrenches incumbency at the frontier, but short of the frontier, economies are actively building competitive AI hubs.

To summarize, then, producing the most advanced layers of the AI stack entails overcoming high up-front investment costs and generating enough scale to overcome the agglomeration benefits that incumbents have established. Most developing countries will likely find it difficult to mobilize resources needed to do this. State-led approaches require high levels of fiscal resources that most developing countries lack. The high up-front investment costs lie beyond the reach of all but the largest firms in the largest economies, constraining the entry of domestic private sector actors, and attracting foreign firms usually entails offering fiscal incentives that strain public finances, as chapter 6 highlights.

The overlooked: Participating in certain segments of the AI value chain plays to the strengths of developing countries

Most developing countries have, or could develop, the capacity to produce goods and services in parts of the AI value chain that have lower barriers to market entry. A case in point is the fabrication of mature-node chips, a vital component in the hardware that supports the functioning of advanced AI chips, as well as a wide range of everyday products, including appliances, automobiles, consumer electronics, and industrial equipment. The technological race to build advanced AI chips of ever-shrinking sizes has often overshadowed the production of these chips.[22] Although they are less cutting-edge than advanced AI chips, the demand for mature-node chips is relatively strong and consistent across a variety of uses. The importance of these chips explains why even high-income economies maintain strong positions in the segments of the AI value chain involved in their production.[23]

Facilities for making mature-node chips require significantly less resources than those for making advanced AI chips, providing a more viable pathway to building such facilities for developing economies that can marshal the resources. ASML's deep ultraviolet lithography machines, typically used to produce mature-node chips, cost between $5 million and $90 million: far less than the $220 million for its extreme ultraviolet lithography machines, used to fabricate the most advanced AI chips.[24]

In addition, and crucially, starting with back-end manufacturing, such as chip assembly, testing, and packaging, then moving to fabricating mature-node chips can help economies build the ecosystem that manufacturing in advanced AI technologies requires. Such a progression provides a pathway developing countries could follow to develop the capacities needed to build the advanced hardware in the AI value chain. For example, after accumulating decades of experience in assembly, testing, packaging, and fabricating mature-node chips, Malaysia is now diversifying into the design of relatively advanced chips. In August 2025, the Malaysian firm SkyeChip launched the country's first homegrown advanced AI chip, the 7-nanometer MARS1000.[25]

Moreover, developing economies produce a number of minerals essential to the AI stack (for some examples, refer to figure 2.3). Several rare earth minerals, key in the production of semiconductors, are

Figure 2.3 Developing countries produce a number of minerals essential to the AI stack

Shares of total world production, 2025 (%)

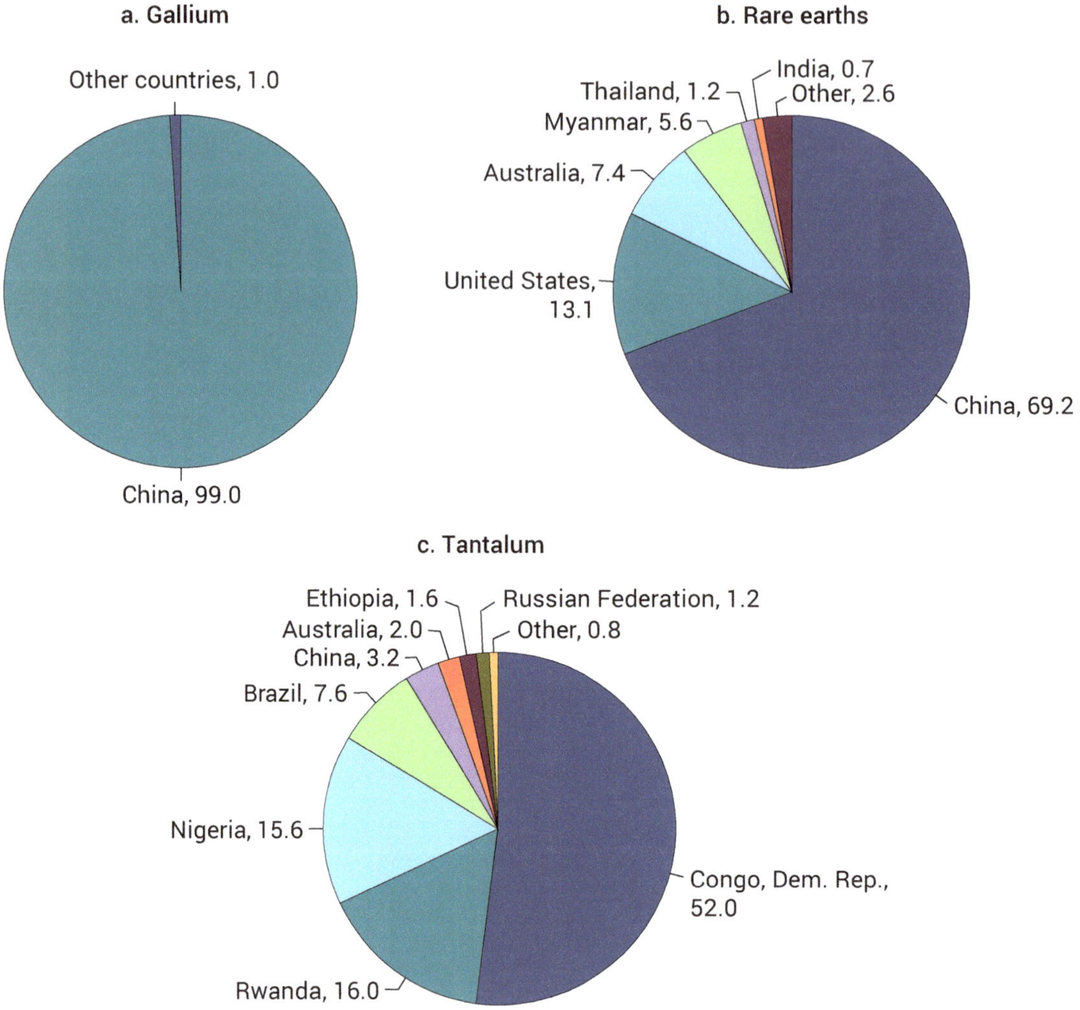

Source: WDR 2026 team, based on data of USGS 2026.

Note: Panel a shows shares of processed materials (that is, production shares). Panels b and c show production shares for raw or unprocessed materials (that is, mine production shares). AI = artificial intelligence.

predominantly produced in China, and tantalum, used in capacitors inside advanced chips, comes predominantly from the Democratic Republic of Congo. Almost all gallium, another mineral essential for high-performance semiconductors because it can increase processing speeds and energy efficiency, is a by-product of bauxite processing. Guinea has the world's largest bauxite reserves, but bauxite is also abundant in other developing economies such as Brazil, China, and Indonesia.[26] The production of gallium, on the other hand, is concentrated in China, partly because these other countries lack capabilities to process bauxite. For example, in 2022, Guinea exported 81.5 percent of its bauxite to China, and Indonesia exported a significant share to China as well until it banned bauxite exports in 2023.[27]

Tapping into the global demand for these minerals presents developing countries with opportunities for growth, but accruing the full value available through the production of these minerals may require countries to build infrastructure such as transport corridors linking mines to production facilities and ports.[28] Chapter 4 discusses in greater detail the opportunities for developing countries across the various layers of the AI stack.

The prospect: Adopting and adapting AI costs far less than building it from scratch

Several factors make adopting and adapting what others have built and are offering far less expensive than building the needed AI capabilities from scratch. First, vertical integration—an arrangement in which a company owns and integrates its supply chain—has the potential to make AI more accessible. Vertically integrated AI firms can package various layers of the AI stack into interfaces that are accessible to users that lack the technical know-how to access each layer independently from separate providers. For instance, a rural health clinic using an AI-powered diagnostic tool can benefit from an integrated system that would otherwise be expensive and difficult to access independently. Moreover, vertical integration of the AI stack may also reduce the prices for goods and services in each of the layers by removing the markup each layer would otherwise have charged if owned by an independent entity. Prices may also fall if such integration allows AI providers to optimize production and provision processes across layers, enabling them to deliver products and services more efficiently.

Second, the factors that make it challenging for most developing economies to build the most advanced AI hardware, data centers, and AI models have paradoxically rendered it comparatively affordable for these economies to "consume" these goods, because the leading AI firms have already made the initial investments in them. As a result, serving additional users adds only minimal cost. Resources for cloud computing can be purchased on an hourly basis, and the cost of using proprietary frontier AI models such as Anthropic's Claude, Google's Gemini, and OpenAI's GPT models has been declining rapidly for a given level of AI capability. For example, the cost of processing 1 million tokens—the segments of text or data that AI models process and generate—using models that have performance similar to that of GPT-3.5, the model that powered the first released version of ChatGPT, had fallen from about $20 in late 2022 to only $0.07 by late 2024. The reduction in prices has also been taking place across a range of AI models,[29] suggesting that developing economies can now access capabilities worth millions of dollars for much less than they formerly could.

Third, and perhaps most crucially, open-weight and open-source models are proliferating. Users can now download releases of open models from AI Singapore, Alibaba, Chile's National Center for Artificial Intelligence, DeepSeek, Google, Lelapa AI, Meta, Mistral AI, Sarvam AI, SwissAI, and the United Arab Emirates Technology Innovation Institute, among others, and modify them on local hardware. Direct access to these models pushes providers of proprietary models to maintain lower prices or to justify higher prices through better performance or more features.

Alongside software development platforms that enable them to create applications through graphical user interfaces with little or no need to write computer code, developers can adapt and deploy open models locally at a lower cost than proprietary models. This holds great promise for developing economies. Countries that lack sufficient numbers of agronomists, data and policy analysts, physicians, or teachers cannot simply increase the supply of these skilled professionals quickly. Open models offer such countries the opportunity to build locally relevant applications that can accomplish some of the tasks that these professionals would typically perform. For example, a research group with deep expertise in agronomy but no coding skills can now build an advisory application for farmers that is customized to local agronomic conditions. Tutoring applications aligned with a country's national curriculum can be developed. Health care applications that assist with diagnosis can increasingly be customized to account for locally prevalent diseases such as malaria and tuberculosis, which may be less common in high-income countries. Such applications expand the effective supply of skills in an economy. They arguably have the largest impact in domains in which demand for skills most strongly outpaces supply, as chapter 1 discusses.

The large increase in the number of AI projects on the developer platform GitHub over the last 15 years reflects these developments. Between 2011 and 2025, the number of such projects grew from about 150 to more than 206,000, doubling in the three years up to 2025 alone.[30] In some developing countries, AI-related activity on GitHub is not far behind that in advanced economies (refer to figure 2.4). Notably, India has more AI-related activity than any developed economy in the sample used for figure 2.4 except the United States.

Figure 2.4 AI-related activity on GitHub in middle-income countries trails that in high-income economies only slightly

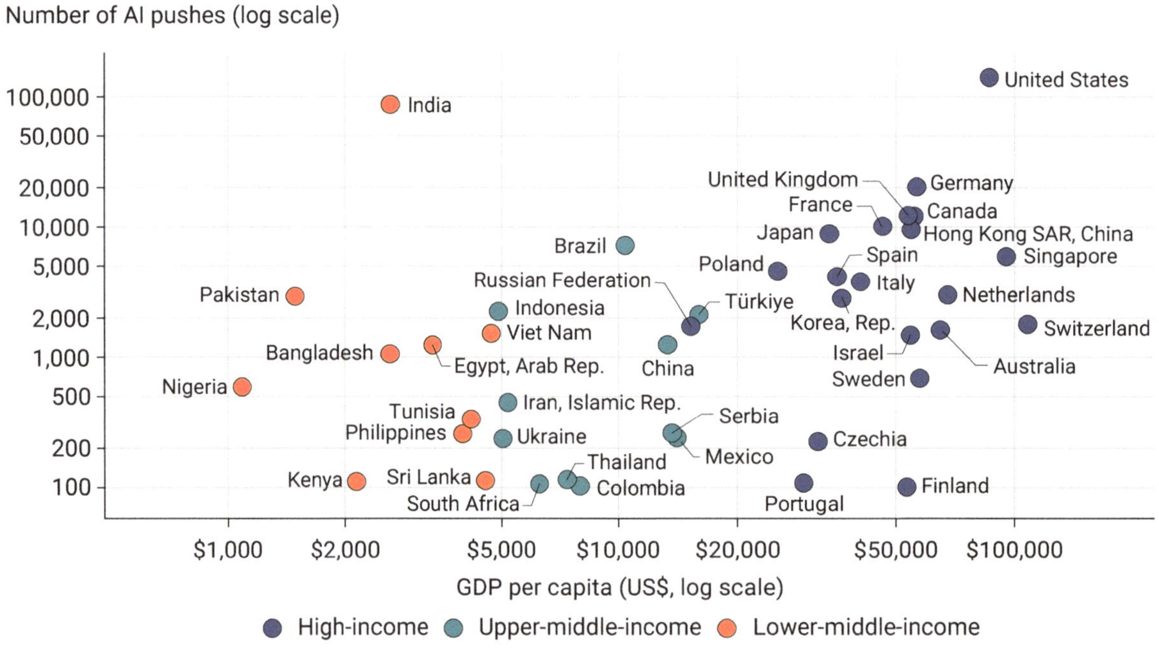

Source: WDR 2026 team, based on Git Pushes (dashboard), Innovation Graph, GitHub, https://innovationgraph.github.com/global-metrics/git-pushes; WDI (World Development Indicators) (dashboard), World Bank, https://datatopics.worldbank.org/world-development-indicators/.

Note: An *AI push* is an instance in which developers send code changes from their local computers to a shared remote repository to update the history of an AI project. Because each push typically reflects a batch of completed work, the frequency of pushes can serve as a proxy for the number of AI projects. Researchers in China often use alternatives to GitHub, such as Gitee and GitCode (Sajadieh et al. 2026), so the figure underestimates the data for China. Patterns in the figure may partly reflect population size. Data on the number of AI pushes are from 2025, while data on GDP per capita are from 2024. Viet Nam is classified as lower-middle-income in the figure per 2025 income classifications. AI = artificial intelligence.

The future: The favorable conditions today may not last

Although using AI currently costs far less than building out each layer of the AI stack from scratch, the circumstances that have enabled this may not persist. Vertical integration of the AI value chain can widen access to AI and lower prices for it, but firms can also use vertical integration to restrict competition. An integrated provider can bundle its products and services in ways that foreclose competitors by simply refusing to sell to them or by selling to them at a higher price.[31] New entrants are then forced to enter at multiple levels of the stack rather than a single level; the higher entry barriers that result limit competition. In addition, although integration can facilitate access, it can also lock users into specific AI providers, especially if a few dominant integrated AI solutions emerge from the push for vertical integration, leaving customers with no alternatives or only a few.

The future trajectory of open-weight and open-source AI models also raises concern. These models have dramatically lowered the barriers that developing countries face when seeking to build their own AI capabilities, but the window of opportunity they provide may not persist. Firms tend to open their proprietary technology when doing so increases their earnings in markets adjacent to the technology more than their losses in the market they are opening up.[32] However, firms' motivations for releasing open models may not persist over time. For example, Meta provided several high-performing open models initially but has recently been moving toward a proprietary approach. The company's newly formed Meta Superintelligence Labs have paused work on its most powerful open model, Behemoth.[33] Its recently released Muse Spark broke with Meta's previous trend toward offering open-weight models and was launched as a proprietary model instead.[34] Meta's choices reflect emerging industry trends. The *Artificial Intelligence Index Report 2026* notes that release patterns for "notable" AI models have continued to shift toward controlled access.[35] The proportion of newly released "notable" models that are open declined from a peak of 56 percent in 2020 to about 40 percent by 2025 (refer to figure 2.5).

There is disagreement regarding whether the window of opportunity for developing countries is closing. Models released under open licenses today will remain open in the future, even if their developers choose to make future models proprietary. Even so, AI is advancing so quickly that what models can do now will likely differ significantly from what they will be able to do in a few years. Moreover, the assumption that new open models will emerge may not hold, because the costs associated with training models continue to rise, and leading AI experts are increasingly joining major incumbents,[36] many of which focus on developing proprietary models. Countries that currently rely on open models risk those models' becoming outdated over time, which could result in the challenging need to repeatedly shift from obsolete versions to newer ones. The concern is most pronounced in regard to fraud detection or cyberdefense, in which using the most up-to-date models is crucial to keep pace with the rising capabilities of malicious actors.

Equally concerning is the geopolitics surrounding AI. Key layers of the AI stack function as strategic "chokepoints," because control at each layer constrains who can access the other layers. Although open-weight and open-source models solve the problem of access to models, running models at scale requires either domestic data centers, which would have to be built on chips controlled by major powers, or commercial cloud providers based in some of these countries. Those that try to source goods and services in different layers of the AI stack from multiple countries may face challenges with interoperability (for a further discussion on geopolitics, refer to chapter 6).

Figure 2.5 A closing window: The share of newly released "notable" AI models that are open has been steadily declining since 2020

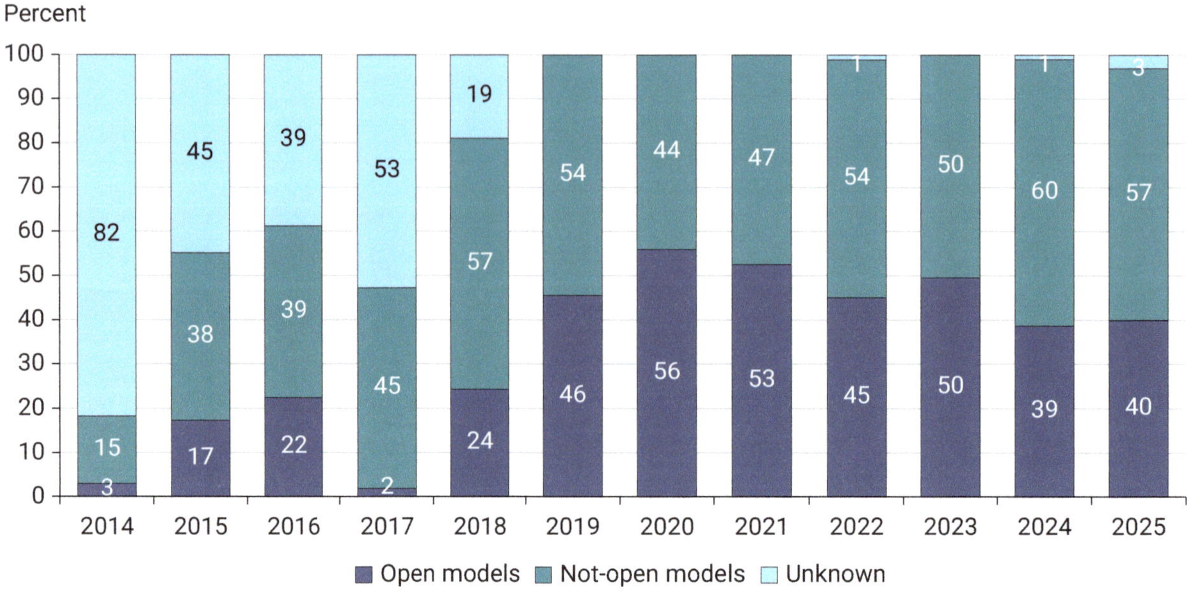

Source: WDR 2026 team, based on Sajadieh et al. 2026.

Note: Open models include those with open weights, whether their use is restricted, unrestricted, or noncommercial. *Not-open models* include those with access via applications programming interfaces, those with hosted access (no applications programming interfaces), and those that are not released. AI = artificial intelligence.

Nevertheless, the geopolitics surrounding AI should not be overstated as the primary impediment to developing countries' adoption of AI. Many developing countries that are pursuing the use of AI to improve development outcomes may face binding constraints more related to domestic factors than global ones. Although favorable access to AI technologies is necessary to gain access to the capabilities of AI, it is not sufficient to ensure it. A ministry of agriculture's chatbot that can answer queries about planting and pest and soil management yields benefits only if the underlying model is trained on data that reflect the agronomic conditions of the country where the ministry is located. A health care worker's diagnostic application is useful only if she has a smartphone, reliable electricity to charge the phone, connectivity, and the training needed to use the application. The context within which AI is used necessitates the presence of domestic complementary factors and ultimately determines whether the capabilities (highlighted in chapter 1) and the favorable conditions needed for access (described in this chapter) translate into realized gains. What this means is the subject of the next chapter.

Notes

1. *AI models* are programs that have been trained to recognize patterns in data, make predictions, generate new content, and make decisions based on those patterns, often without human intervention. They can be open source, open weight, or proprietary. *Open-source models* provide transparency and customization, allowing developers who are building AI applications to access, with minimal licensing restrictions, the model weights, architecture, training data, and even source code. Model weights are the numerical values inside an AI model that encode what the model has learned during training (that is, the model's knowledge). Open weights are important because they allow developers to run the model on their own computer systems, customize the model, examine it for safety or bias, and develop applications based on the model without relying solely on one provider. Examples of open-source models include AI Singapore's Southeast Asian Languages in One Network (SEA-LION), Allen Institute for AI's Olmo, the BigScience Large Open-science Open-access Multilingual (BLOOM) Language Model, EleutherAI's GPT-NeoX, the Swiss AI Initiative's Apertus, and Google's Bidirectional Encoder Representations from Transformers (BERT) models. *Open-weight models* allow developers to access model weights but restrict their access to other areas of the model. Examples of open-weight models include Chile's National Center for Artificial Intelligence's Latam-GPT, DeepSeek's models, Google's Gemma models, Lelapa AI's InkubaLM, and Meta's Llama models (although they are sometimes marketed as open source). A couple of OpenAI's GPT models also fall into this category. *Proprietary models* are privately owned and feature closed source code, architecture, weights, and training data. They are accessed via application programming interfaces or subscriptions. Examples include Anthropic's Claude and most of OpenAI's GPT models, even though both companies do offer some free access to these models' chatbots.
2. Jones (2023). *Foundation models* are built using methods that learn patterns from massive amounts of data. Once built, they can be applied to a wide variety of tasks and are often used to build AI applications. Some examples include Alibaba's Qwen, Anthropic's Claude, DeepSeek's models, Google's Gemini, Meta's Llama, Mistral AI's models, and OpenAI's GPT models. The most advanced foundation models that meet the highest performance benchmarks are commonly referred to as *frontier models*.
3. *Memory systems* refer to temporary storage that chips use while performing computations. Examples include random access memory (RAM) and video RAM (VRAM). *Storage* is longer term and holds data sets used for training, as well as models and outputs. It includes hard drives and solid-state drives. In a useful analogy to a typical office, a system's memory is its work desk, its storage is its filing cabinet (Kingston Technology 2020), and *networking* acts as a messenger, moving information quickly between the desk and the filing cabinet.
4. For example, in the AI stack's hardware layer, building a chip involves several specialized stages. Software tools are used to design the chip's architecture, including the placement of circuits and the number of cores (the chip components that handle tasks; more cores generally mean more computing capacity). Specialized equipment, such as machines for ultraviolet lithography (used to project circuit patterns), must be built before chip fabrication can begin. In the fabrication stage, integrated circuits consisting of numerous transistors are etched onto silicon wafers at nanometer scales. The chips then go through packaging, assembly, and testing to ensure they meet performance standards. Each stage could be considered to be a separate layer rather than grouped under one hardware layer.
5. Antràs and Chor (2022).
6. Frost et al. (2026).
7. As of June 2026, Anthropic and OpenAI had filed the initial paperwork to go public.
8. Examples include Alibaba Cloud, Amazon Web Services, Microsoft's Azure, Google Cloud, Oracle Cloud, Tencent Cloud, and ByteDance's Volcano Engine.
9. A few of these models are Apple Foundation Models (AFM), ByteDance's Doubao, Alphabet's Gemini, Tencent's Hunyuan, Meta's Llama and Muse Spark, and Amazon Nova.
10. Frost et al. (2026).
11. Wagener (2025).
12. Sajadieh et al. (2026).
13. Agglomeration effects tend to arise from the sharing of resources, the matching of talent to firms, and knowledge spillovers (Duranton and Puga 2004). If defined broadly, the network economies that characterize AI may be considered a form of agglomeration effect because they depend on the density of the users of a given product or service. Thus, a product or service becomes more valuable to each user and to the firm as more people use it.
14. Pilz et al. (2025).
15. Straub et al. (2026). China has the world's second-largest number of data centers overall, but China's per capita figure is lower than the average in advanced economies.
16. *AI hyperscalers* operate massive cloud infrastructures required to train and deploy AI models and applications.
17. Tarasov (2025).
18. Agrawal et al. (2019).
19. Goldberg et al. (2024).
20. Sajadieh et al. (2026).

21. Sajadieh et al. (2026).
22. Mature-node chips are usually larger than 22 nanometers (Sutter 2025). Advanced chips are generally smaller than 7 nanometers (Schleich and Reinsch 2023) and may be even smaller than 5 nanometers. Smaller measurements indicate higher transistor density, which enables chips to run faster and use power more efficiently.
23. See and Yuan (2024).
24. Tarasov (2025).
25. Poon (2025).
26. Baskaran and Schwartz (2024).
27. Baskaran and Schwartz (2024); Farhan (2025).
28. Countries must also be wary of the *resource curse*, whereby reliance on resource extraction can lead to economic instability, vulnerability to price volatility, and a lack of structural transformation, that is, the failure of a country's economic structure to shift over the long term to a structure that involves higher productivity, better employment opportunities, and improved living standards (Frankel 2012; Gylfason 2001; Sachs and Warner 2001; Sánchez de la Sierra 2020).
29. Maslej et al. (2025).
30. Sajadieh et al. (2026).
31. Crawford et al. (2018).
32. Lerner and Tirole (2005).
33. Tan (2025).
34. Vanian (2026).
35. Sajadieh et al. (2026). The report deems models "notable" based on the Epoch AI (2026) definition: "models that were state-of-the-art when released, have over 1,000 citations, one million monthly active users, or an equivalent level of historical significance."
36. Akcigit et al. (2026).

References

Agrawal, Ajay K., Joshua S. Gans, and Avi Goldfarb. 2019. "Economic Policy for Artificial Intelligence." *Innovation Policy and the Economy* 19: 139–59. https://doi.org/10.1086/699935.

Akcigit, Ufuk, Craig A. Chikis, Emin Dinlersoz, and Nathan Goldschlag. 2026. "Attention (and Money) Is All You Need: Why Universities Are Struggling to Keep AI Talent." NBER Working Paper 34964, National Bureau of Economic Research. https://www.nber.org/papers/w34964.

Antràs, Pol, and Davin Chor. 2022. "Global Value Chains." In *Handbook of International Economics: International Trade*, vol. 5, edited by Gina Gopinath, Elhanan Helpman, and Kenneth Rogoff. Handbooks in Economics Series. North-Holland. https://antras.scholars.harvard.edu/publications/global-value-chains.

Baskaran, Gracelin, and Meredith Schwartz. 2024. "From Mine to Microchip: Addressing Critical Mineral Supply Chain Risks in Semiconductor Production." CSIS Brief (October 7), Center for Strategic and International Studies. https://www.csis.org/analysis/mine-microchip.

Crawford, Gregory S., Robin S. Lee, Michael D. Whinston, and Ali Yurukoglu. 2018. "The Welfare Effects of Vertical Integration in Multichannel Television Markets." *Econometrica* 86 (3): 891–954. https://onlinelibrary.wiley.com/doi/abs/10.3982/ECTA14031.

Duranton, Gilles, and Diego Puga. 2004. "Micro-Foundations of Urban Agglomeration Economies." In *Handbook of Regional and Urban Economics*, vol. 4, *Cities and Geography*, edited by J. Vernon Henderson and Jacques-François Thisse. Handbooks in Economics Series 7. North-Holland. https://www.sciencedirect.com/science/chapter/handbook/abs/pii/S1574008004800051.

Ekatpure, Shubham Rajendra. 2022. "Rare Earth Elements for Semiconductor Manufacturing: Global Supply Chain and Dominance." *Journal of Marketing and Supply Chain Management* 1 (1): 1–4. https://doi.org/10.47363/JMSCM/2022(1)E109.

Epoch AI. 2026. "AI Models." Updated June 25. Epoch AI. https://epoch.ai/data/ai-models.

Farhan, Muhammad. 2025. "Indonesia Justifies Bauxite Export Ban to Boost Domestic Smelter Industry." *Jakarta Globe Business* (blog), October 15. https://jakartaglobe.id/business/indonesia-justifies-bauxite-export-ban-to-boost-domestic-smelter-industry.

Frankel, Jeffrey Alexander. 2012. "The Natural Resource Curse: A Survey of Diagnoses and Some Prescriptions." In *Commodity Price Volatility and Inclusive Growth in Low-Income Countries*, edited by Rabah Arezki, Catherine A. Pattillo, Marc G. Quintyn, and Min Zhu. International Monetary Fund. https://www.elibrary.imf.org/display/book/9781616353797/ch002.xml.

Frost, Jon, Kumar Rishabh, and Vatsala Shreeti. 2026. "Global Giants in the AI Supply Chain." *BIS Bulletin* 122 (February), Bank for International Settlements. https://www.bis.org/publ/bisbull122.pdf.

Goldberg, Pinelopi Koujianou, Réka Juhász, Nathan J. Lane, Giulia Lo Forte, and Jeff Thurk. 2024. "Industrial Policy in the Global Semiconductor Sector." NBER Working Paper 32651, National Bureau of Economic Research. https://doi.org/10.3386/w32651.

Goswami, Omanjana. 2023. "Chipping In: Critical Minerals for Semiconductor Manufacturing in the U.S." *MIT Science Policy Review* 4 (August 31): 118–26. https://sciencepolicyreview.org/wp-content/uploads/securepdfs/2023/08/MITSPR-v4-191618004005.pdf.

Gylfason, Thorvaldur. 2001. "Natural Resources, Education, and Economic Development." *European Economic Review* 45 (4–6): 847–59. https://doi.org/10.1016/S0014-2921(01)00127-1.

Jones, Elliot. 2023. "What Is a Foundation Model?" *Resource* (blog), July 17. https://www.adalovelaceinstitute.org/resource/foundation-models-explainer/.

Kingston Technology. 2020. "What Is the Difference Between Memory and Storage?" *PC Performance* (blog), October. https://www.kingston.com/en/blog/pc-performance/difference-between-memory-storage.

Lerner, Josh, and Jean Tirole. 2005. "The Economics of Technology Sharing: Open Source and Beyond." *Journal of Economic Perspectives* 19 (2): 99–120. https://www.aeaweb.org/articles?id=10.1257/0895330054048678.

Maslej, Nestor, Loredana Fattorini, Raymond Perrault, et al. 2025. *Artificial Intelligence Index Report 2025*. AI Index Steering Committee, Institute for Human-Centered Artificial Intelligence, Stanford University. https://doi.org/10.48550/arXiv.2504.07139.

Pilz, Konstantin F., Robi Rahman, James Sanders, Luke Emberson, and Lennart Heim. 2025. "Acquisition Costs of Leading AI Supercomputers Have Doubled Every 13 Months." *Data Insights* (blog), June 5. https://epoch.ai/data-insights/ai-supercomputers-cost-trend.

Poon, Elim. 2025. "Malaysia Launches First Local Edge AI Processor, MARS1000." *Technology* (blog), August 25. https://www.thestar.com.my/business/business-news/2025/08/25/malaysia-launches-first-local-edge-ai-processor-mars1000.

Sachs, Jeffrey D., and Andrew M. Warner. 2001. "The Curse of Natural Resources." *European Economic Review* 45 (4–6): 827–38. https://doi.org/10.1016/S0014-2921(01)00125-8.

Sajadieh, Sha, Loredana Fattorini, Raymond Perrault, et al. 2026. *Artificial Intelligence Index Report 2026*. April. AI Index Steering Committee, Institute for Human-Centered Artificial Intelligence, Stanford University. https://hai.stanford.edu/assets/files/ai_index_report_2026.pdf.

Sánchez de la Sierra, Raúl. 2020. "On the Origins of the State: Stationary Bandits and Taxation in Eastern Congo." *Journal of Political Economy* 128 (1): 32–74. https://doi.org/10.1086/703989.

Schleich, Matthew, and William Alan Reinsch. 2023. "Contextualizing the National Security Concerns over China's Domestically Produced High-End Chip." *Critical Questions* (blog), September 26. https://www.csis.org/analysis/contextualizing-national-security-concerns-over-chinas-domestically-produced-high-end-chip.

See, Sharon, and Yong Jun Yuan. 2024. "Is Singapore Losing Out on the AI Chip Boom?" *Business Times*, July 16. https://www.businesstimes.com.sg/singapore/bt-chip-series/singapore-losing-out-ai-chip-boom.

Straub, Stéphane, He He, Yue Li, et al. 2026. *Infrastructure Foundations: From Current Assets to Future Growth*. Sustainable Infrastructure Series. World Bank. https://openknowledge.worldbank.org/server/api/core/bitstreams/064573b1-0bff-4594-b756-ef76eba1ad06/content.

Sutter, Karen M. 2025. "U.S. Export Controls and China: Advanced Semiconductors." CRS Report R48642, Congressional Research Service. https://www.congress.gov/crs-product/R48642.

Tan, Eli. 2025. "Meta's New Superintelligence Lab Is Discussing Major A.I. Strategy Changes." *New York Times*, July 14. https://www.nytimes.com/2025/07/14/technology/meta-superintelligence-lab-ai.html.

Tarasov, Katie. 2025. "Exclusive Look at the Creation of High NA, ASML's New $400 Million Chipmaking Colossus." *CNBC Tech* (blog), May 22. https://www.cnbc.com/2025/05/22/exclusive-look-at-high-na-asmls-new-400-million-chipmaking-colossus.html.

USGS (US Geological Survey). 2025. "Key Minerals in Data Centers Infographic." July, Mineral Resources Program, USGS, US Department of the Interior. https://www.usgs.gov/media/images/key-minerals-data-centers-infographic.

USGS (US Geological Survey). 2026. *Mineral Commodity Summaries 2026*. Version 1.3 (May). National Minerals Information Center, USGS, US Department of the Interior. https://pubs.usgs.gov/periodicals/mcs2026/mcs2026.pdf.

Vanian, Jonathan. 2026. "Meta's Long-Awaited AI Model Is Finally Here: But Can It Make Money?" *CNBC Tech* (blog), April 9. https://www.cnbc.com/2026/04/09/metas-long-awaited-ai-model-is-finally-here-but-can-it-make-money.html.

Wagener, Trevor. 2025. "Intense Competition Across the AI Stack." *Competition* (blog), March 13. https://ccianet.org/articles/intense-competition-across-the-ai-stack/.

3

Complements: Customizing AI to Local Realities and Needs

Main messages

- **AI will not raise productivity on its own**
  Without complements such as electricity, internet connectivity, and workflow changes, it could be years before productivity gains emerge.
- **AI trained elsewhere may fail locally**
  AI learns from data that often underrepresent developing economies, so tools must be tested and adapted to local languages, populations, institutions, and conditions.
- **Most countries can benefit without building frontier AI**
  Use existing tools, adapt them to local needs, and develop advanced models from scratch only where resources and capabilities justify it.
- **Small AI can work where resources are limited**
  Use AI tools built for weak connectivity and narrow tasks while strengthening data, infrastructure, skills, and institutions.
- **AI should fill skill gaps, not just replace labor**
  Prioritize tools that ease skill shortages; labor-saving AI for routine work may make less sense where wages are low.

Introduction

When a research group affiliated with the University of Oxford built an artificial intelligence (AI) model for triaging patients suspected of having COVID-19, it used a handy and comprehensive data set to train the model: health records from hospital emergency departments in the United Kingdom. Yet when group members tested the model using data from two hospitals in Viet Nam, its performance declined sharply from its performance on training data, because the patient demographics and epidemiological characteristics of the population underlying the Viet Nam data were so different from those of the UK population.

A reproducibility package is available for this book in the Reproducible Research Repository at https://reproducibility.worldbank.org/catalog/624.

Similarly, in health clinics in Thailand, an AI-assisted tool developed by Google Health to screen for a complication of diabetes that affects the eyes rejected more than 20 percent of the images nurses took of patients because the lighting in the clinics did not match the lighting conditions that the model had been trained on.[1] Thus a tool designed to speed up the triage process instead generated bottlenecks. In response, nurses simply reviewed the written medical histories of patients whose images were rejected, then discharged those patients who seemed unlikely to have the condition, instead of referring them to distant specialists who were hard to reach.

These two cases—the first involving where an AI model has been built, the second concerning the conditions where it has been deployed—illustrate a problem with important implications, especially for developing countries: The potential of AI depends both on the context in which it has been developed and the context in which it will be used. If there is a disconnect between those contexts—a *contextual mismatch*—AI will not work well.

The two cases also illustrate another important point. In the first case, the model was not trained using data that reflected the characteristics of the population in the developing country (Viet Nam) where it was tested. This illustrates the absence of *customization complements,* which fit AI models and applications to the context they are deployed in and include relevant, adequate, and up-to-date data as well as technical capacity at the local level. In the second case, a crucial factor in the environment in which the model was deployed was missing: proper lighting. This highlights the absence of *deployment complements:* things that AI models and applications need to operate irrespective of the context in which they are deployed. Deployment complements include the availability of electricity and connectivity, as well as the ability of workers and organizations to effectively utilize AI, and the regulatory quality of the settings where AI models and applications are used. Realizing the full potential of AI requires tailoring AI models and applications to the setting where they are deployed, which is possible only if the right complementary factors—both the customization and deployment complements just referred to—are in place.

The technology that learns: The risk of contextual mismatches is amplified because AI's capabilities are derived from the data used to train it

Consider a tractor that is engineered for large, thousand-acre plots of monocropped corn or soybeans and relies on established supply chains for diesel fuel as well as capital financing. If the tractor is shipped to a smallholder in Sub-Saharan Africa who farms a mix of cassava, sorghum, and pearl millet on a small plot of less than one acre, it will likely be considered out of place and not work well. This example illustrates the insights of the economics literature on *inappropriate technology*. Innovations embed a mix of factors (so-called factor endowments such as land, labor, and capital), as well as the characteristics of the population, standards and regulations, and priorities of the places that produce them. This mix of factors may make some innovations inappropriate when deployed in other settings.[2]

AI follows this pattern. The institutions that build AI models are concentrated in a small number of economies, with China, the United Kingdom, and the United States dominant among them (refer to figure 3.1). As a result, the issues that AI developers focus on, the applications that AI product teams create, and the risks that AI safety researchers consider will inevitably mirror the priorities and perspectives of these economies. Unlike the tractor, however, whose contextual mismatch is physically visible, AI models, when mismatched to their intended or deployment context, hide that mismatch behind seemingly confident and expert outputs.

Figure 3.1 AI models are developed predominantly in only a few economies

Percent

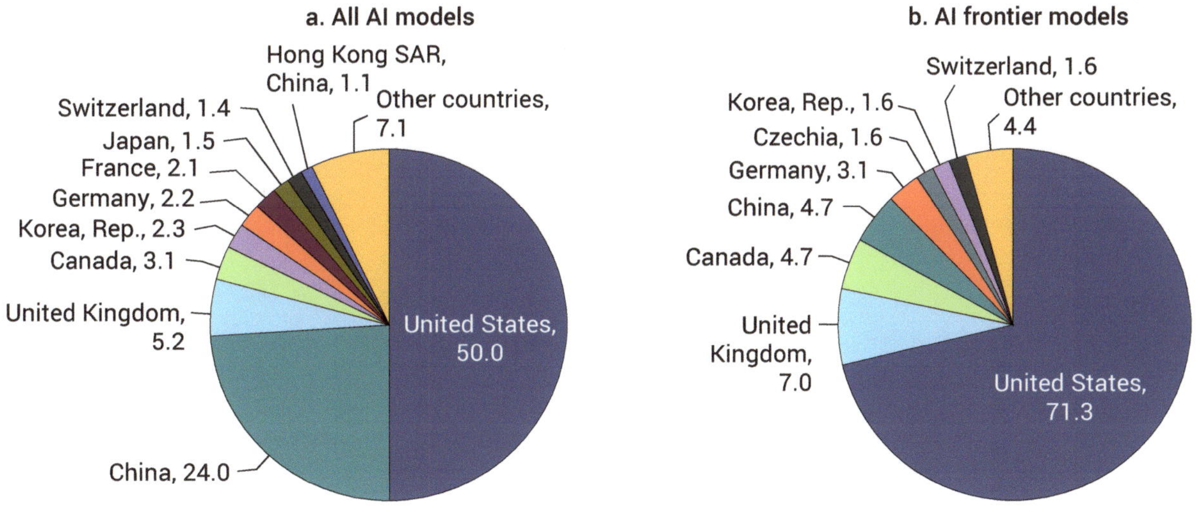

Source: WDR 2026 team, based on May 2026 data of AI Models (dashboard), Epoch AI, https://epoch.ai/data/ai-models?view=graph&tab=all.

Note: Frontier models are those ranked, at the time of their release, among the top 10 ever built, in terms of how much *compute* (the hardware and processing power needed to train and run AI models) they used, a threshold that increases over time as larger models are developed. More details on how the data were collected and the criteria for being included in the database can be found at https://epoch.ai/data/ai-models-documentation/inclusion. AI = artificial intelligence.

Furthermore, the development of AI models involves an amplified risk of contextual mismatches because, unlike the technologies that have driven previous technological waves, AI is a technology that learns, deriving its capabilities from the data used to train it. These data are overwhelmingly drawn from the internet, with content in English accounting for a disproportionate share (refer to figure 3.2, panel a). More than 60 percent of data sets on Hugging Face, a leading AI model repository,[3] are in English (refer to figure 3.2, panel b). By contrast, people who live in Africa speak more than 2,000 languages, many classified as *low-resourced* because of the lack of large-scale digitized and documented data sets (and consequently, instances of the language on which a model can be trained).[4] The effects are stark: ChatGPT recognizes only 10–20 percent of sentences written in Hausa, a language spoken by 94 million people in Nigeria.[5] Crucially, whether a language counts as high- or low-resourced tends to track the volume of available digitized data rather than the size of the population that speaks it. Some languages spoken by relatively small populations—such as Catalan, Finnish, and Swedish—are considered high-resourced because of the substantial amounts of data in those languages that have been digitized, whereas languages with far greater numbers of speakers, including Hausa, Swahili, and Zulu, remain underresourced.[6] Compounding this issue is the fact that there are many different dialects within languages. These dialects are even less well represented on the internet, which makes them especially unlikely to be included in the data that AI models are trained on.

The lack of representativeness in the data used to train AI models goes beyond language. Even within specific languages like English, the training data overrepresent the demographic and epidemiological characteristics, as well as the cultural norms and assumptions, of the people and institutions that have produced the data. Therefore, even if a team of researchers in Nigeria sought to develop

Figure 3.2 A few languages dominate the data used to train AI models
Percent

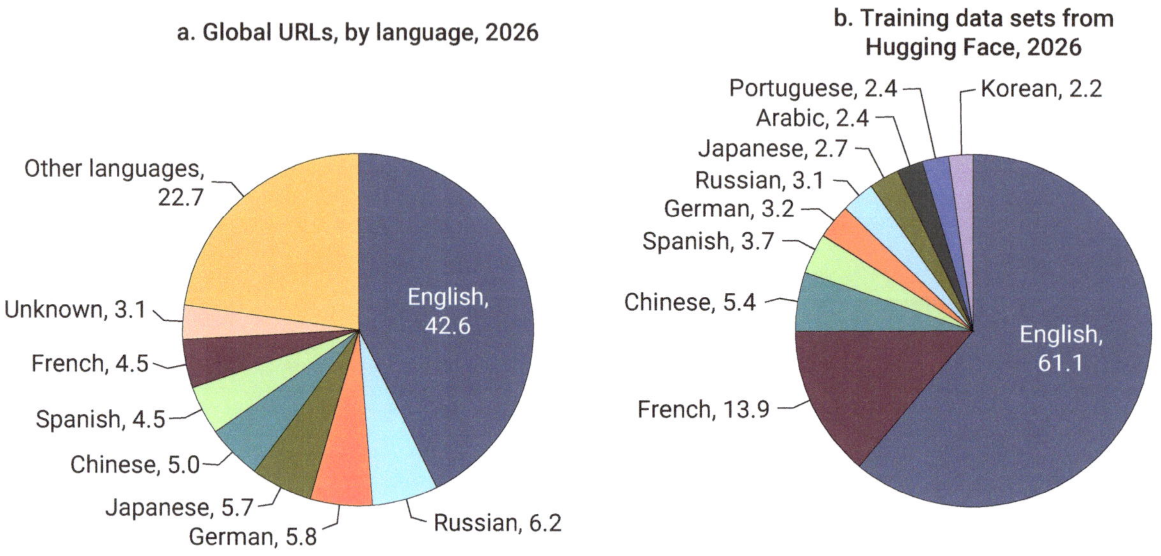

Source: WDR 2026 team, based on Distribution of Languages (table), Common Crawl Foundation, https://commoncrawl.github.io/cc-crawl-statistics/plots/languages.html; OECD 2026.

Note: Common Crawl data are as of February 2026; Hugging Face data from OECD.AI are as of June 2026. *Training data sets* include both monolingual and multilingual data sets. For panel b, the underlying data from OECD (2026) sum to more than 100 percent (refer to OECD 2026 for details). Therefore, the data in the chart have been renormalized to sum to 100 percent.

AI applications relevant for their local populations, most training data would still be dominated by English, leaving the numerous other languages used in Nigeria woefully underrepresented, and would mirror the traits of their creators.

Disparities of this kind in training data give rise to contextual mismatches when a model trained on such data is embedded in applications deployed across multiple settings, such as a chatbot on a government website responding to the queries from citizens on issues such as taxation, a diagnostic tool used in clinics, or a fraud detector deployed by banks. These applications bring together data, model, and context: Mismatches between any or all of these components are possible. Four types of mismatches are particularly common.[7]

First, AI models trained on English text perform substantially worse when prompted in other languages. Across tasks such as understanding of languages, mathematical reasoning, and answering of multichoice knowledge-based questions, accuracy gaps between model performance in high-resourced languages (English and French) and 16 low-resourced African languages average about 45 percentage points across large language models evaluated.[8] Such gaps in accuracy raise concerns, because the effectiveness of one of the most common applications of AI, chatbots, relies on users' articulating queries in their own words and receiving relevant responses. Chatbots are rendered useless when they are unable to effectively process and interpret the languages of their users.

Second, AI models that do not account for dialectal variation within a language often perform poorly. Arabic illustrates this challenge. Although more than 400 million people speak Arabic, Modern Standard Arabic differs markedly from everyday dialects such as Egyptian Arabic, Gulf Arabic, Levantine Arabic, and Maghrebi Arabic. As AI models tend to be trained and tested on formal written standard languages, those models often face a contextual mismatch in real-world use. Research shows that replacing just a single key term in a formal Arabic sentence with a corresponding term from an everyday Arabic dialect can sharply reduce model performance. In one study, a leading model's accuracy fell from 94 percent to about 65 percent when Egyptian Arabic was introduced, and another's dropped from 90 percent to about 55 percent.[9] These results suggest that applications built on models trained only on formal languages are unlikely to work well for users who primarily communicate in dialects.

Third, AI models trained on one country's data may not perform well in other countries. This type of mismatch is particularly acute in medical settings. In the example earlier in the chapter on the poor performance of an AI triage tool for COVID-19, the AI tool was making predictions based on the demographic and epidemiological characteristics of the UK population, which vary significantly from those of Viet Nam's population.[10] The tool was following the rules correctly, but for a different population than it was trained on, so its performance deteriorated.

Fourth, AI models embed the cultural norms, assumptions, and defaults of the people and institutions that have produced them, which can bias outcomes when the models are deployed in other contexts. Facial-recognition systems, designed in a limited set of countries but deployed worldwide, show large disparities in accuracy across populations, with as much as a 50 percent difference between the accuracy of predictions of the gender of women from developing countries and those for women from developed countries.[11] Similarly, researchers found that several large language models built in developed countries repeatedly associated positive qualities with certain groups in India, while ascribing negative qualities to other groups, reflecting assumptions common in the countries in which the models originated.[12] A related issue is *model collapse,* in which models trained on data generated by earlier models become increasingly less representative of real-world, human-generated data, resulting in the models' output converging toward the most common patterns in the data.[13] This phenomenon can make newer models less useful in regard to groups already underrepresented in the existing data, thereby reinforcing and even deepening contextual mismatches.

The technology that fits: Tailoring AI to the local context requires the right complementary factors

The considerations discussed in the preceding section have an important implication for development: For AI, contextual fit cannot be assumed. Realizing the full potential of AI requires tailoring AI models and the applications built using these models to the setting that they are deployed in. For this to happen, the right complementary factors for customization and deployment must be in place.

Complements for customization

The first set of complements required to unleash AI's potential are those that fit AI models and the applications built using these models to the context they are deployed in. Because the data used to train AI models shape those models' capabilities, the most basic requirement in this regard is data relevant to a particular local context, digitized, and organized in a structured manner. The data should also be available at the scale needed and of the quality necessary to meet the requirements for training models. Most developing countries lack data of this scope and caliber on account of deficiencies in the funding of national statistical systems, limited technical capacity to collect and analyze data, and weak data governance.[14] Data in many of these countries are also highly fragmented: The populations of the countries speak dozens or even hundreds of languages, and data are often scattered across informal systems or government agencies.[15]

Even when local data for training AI models are available, they are often insufficient to ensure contextual fit. To ensure the latter, they must be paired with the capacity to build applications tailored to local contexts. Techniques like retrieval-augmented generation offer a simple approach in which developers can link an existing AI model to an external database containing local data[16] and build applications that cater to local contexts. For example, the government of Buenos Aires, Argentina, enhanced Boti, its widely used WhatsApp-based chatbot, by integrating into it advanced retrieval-augmented generation technology developed in collaboration with Amazon Web Services' Generative AI Innovation Center. This upgrade was designed to improve how citizens navigate more than 1,300 complex government procedures, with the chatbot moving beyond simple keyword matching to understanding context and intent.[17]

Nevertheless, every application is ultimately built on a base model. Simple forms of customization may not be sufficient to address context mismatches, and there may be a need to modify the base model, because trying to build an application tailored to the local context will not be effective if the base model that it uses contains cultural biases or is unable to process languages that it was not trained on. For example, a model trained on languages that use Latin scripts tends to split up non-Latin scripts into many more fragments than equivalent Latin script text. The resulting fragments can fail to capture the true structure of underrepresented languages, removing important meaning and subtlety.[18] Against this backdrop, between 2020 and 2024, developers in Southeast Asia released 35 large language models specific to the region.[19] Notable examples include AI Singapore's Southeast Asian Languages in One Network (SEA-LION) and Alibaba Discovery, Adventure, Momentum, and Outlook (DAMO) Academy's SeaLLM, as well as Sea AI Lab and Singapore University of Technology and Design's Sailor. Each of these models can handle more than 10 different languages from the Southeast Asia region.

Developments of this kind extend beyond Southeast Asia. In Africa, Lelapa AI has released InkubaLM, a model that can process several African languages.[20] In the Middle East, the United Arab Emirates' Technology Innovation Institute has developed the Falcon family of models, then extended them by training them on data in the Arabic language and regional dialects.[21] In South Asia, India's Sarvam AI has released models optimized for Indian languages, and in Latin America, a consortium coordinated by Chile's National Center for Artificial Intelligence has launched Latam-GPT, trained primarily on Spanish- and Portuguese-language data from the region.[22]

As the need for modifying a model grows, so do the resources required. For instance, the most intensive forms of customizing a model require the efforts of AI engineers rather than software developers or data scientists, as well as extensive computing resources powered by advanced AI chips. As a result, choices among the different forms of model customization entail different trade-offs among cost, data requirements, and performance (refer to box 3.1).

Box 3.1 To build or not to build? An expanding set of options to customize AI to address contextual mismatches

When artificial intelligence (AI) tools do not fit a specific context, several approaches to customizing them can help narrow the gap between what exists and what is needed without incurring the cost of training models from scratch.

Fine tuning. Fine tuning involves training an existing model using smaller specialized data sets to improve its performance on specific tasks, by updating either all or some of the model's weights.[a] The latter includes techniques such as *head tuning*, which modifies the model's final layer,[b] and *low-rank adaptation*, which inserts small, trainable modules into the inner layers of the model.

Distillation. In this process, a smaller *student* model is trained to imitate a larger *teacher* model by learning from the outputs of the teacher, instead of relying on the teacher model's original training data. By training on region-specific data, for example, a student model can become more relevant to the regional context in which it will be deployed while maintaining the general abilities of the teacher model. However, concerns have been raised about whether this approach appropriates the functionality or outputs of existing models.

Continued pretraining. This is a hybrid approach between fine tuning and building models from scratch that trains an existing model on large new databases. The main difference between fine tuning and continued pretraining is that the former uses smaller data sets with the goal of improving performance on specific tasks (*behavior*), whereas the latter uses larger data sets with the goal of creating new knowledge. For example, the Latam-GPT model was built upon an existing Meta model, Llama 3.[c] Its creation was an unprecedented collaborative effort, coordinated by Chile's National Center for Artificial Intelligence, that brought together nearly 200 professionals and more than 60 institutions from 15 countries.

Building from scratch. When other methods do not adequately address contextual mismatches, the only alternative may be to develop and train a model from the ground up, a process that requires extensive data and computing power, as well as specialized talent. For example, the IndiaAI Mission, a flagship initiative by India's government that aims to make AI in India and make it work for India, selected Sarvam AI to develop local AI models. As part of its selection, the company received substantial support, including access to more than 4,000 NVIDIA H100 graphics processing unit chips for six months.[d] In February 2026, it launched two large models, having 30 billion and 105 billion parameters, trained entirely in India.[e]

Source: WDR 2026 team.

a. *Model weights* are the numerical values inside an AI model that encode what the model has learned during training (that is, the model's knowledge).
b. Models process information in successive stages called *layers.* Early layers usually detect simple patterns, while subsequent layers combine these simple patterns into increasingly abstract patterns. The final layer (often referred to as the *head*), produces the models' outputs.
c. Levy Yeyati (2025). For more details, refer to FAQ (dashboard), LatamGPT, National Center for Artificial Intelligence, https://www.latamgpt.org/en/faq.
d. Phadnis and John (2025).
e. Thaker (2026). *Parameters* may be loosely referred to as what enables the model to store information (that is, what enables it to learn).

Complements for deployment

The second set of complements needed for AI's potential to be realized concern the deployment of AI, regardless of the context in which it is deployed. The most basic of these is the physical infrastructure on which AI systems depend. Reliable electricity and adequate connectivity, for example, are preconditions for running AI applications. Even when AI applications are customized to operate in environments with limited resources, they require a minimum level of power and connectivity. Without infrastructure in these two areas to operate AI applications, other complements will not matter.

The deployment of AI also depends on the abilities of workers and organizations to use it effectively. To that end, major AI companies have expanded the *forward deployed engineering* model—in which engineers work directly with customers, who are often embedded within their teams—by making large investments in hiring workers to assist in deploying AI within enterprises.[23] Moreover, the recent increase in AI-related job postings globally indicates the significance of human capital as an essential complementary factor for AI deployment. Postings for jobs that require generative AI skills increased ninefold globally from 2021 to 2024 (refer to figure 3.3). The skills required to use AI tools effectively go beyond simply understanding the tools. They involve the ability to integrate the tools into existing, reconfigured, or new workflows and the ability to continually improve.[24] A nurse working alongside an AI-assisted diagnostic tool, for example, must know when the tool is providing

Figure 3.3 Demand for skills related to generative AI has been increasing sharply

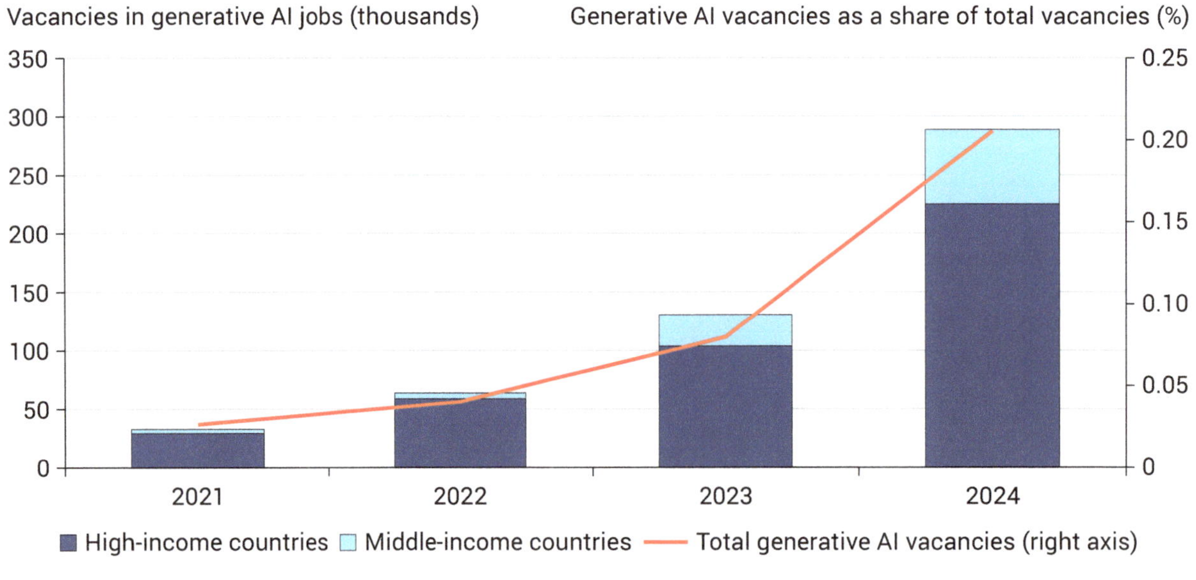

Source: WDR 2026 team, based on Lightcast Data (dashboard), Lightcast, https://lightcast.io/products/data/overview.

Note: Generative AI skills are defined as the ability to use, adapt, or develop generative AI models and applications. Generative AI-related job postings were identified using Lightcast's curated taxonomy of generative AI skills (that is, keywords) extracted from job postings. Examples include the ability to use specific types of AI models and services. A job posting is classified as requiring generative AI skills if it contains at least one generative AI-related skill. Data for upper-middle-income countries are incomplete because of extremely limited coverage for China. AI = artificial intelligence.

erroneous recommendations. Similarly, an analyst working with a chatbot needs to understand how to phrase prompts to obtain useful information. Such skills take time to develop, requiring training and a willingness to change work habits that may be engrained.

The assumption that having workers use AI tools in their jobs (*human-in-the-loop* or *human-on-the-loop*) improves the workers' performance holds true only in certain situations.[25] Factors like communication gaps, lack of trust, ethical issues, and coordination challenges can limit effective collaboration between humans and AI.[26] For this reason, it is very important that organizations have sufficient capacity to deploy AI. Managers must acquire the knowledge required to select AI applications that are relevant to the needs of their organization, and they must understand how best to determine the allocation of tasks among AI tools, employees, or a combination of the two. In addition, the higher returns from using AI tools stem from *co-invention*. That is, redesigning and coming up with new workflows that use these AI tools, as well as aligning the incentives of employees and suppliers with a new mode of production that incorporates AI.[27]

Clear regulations governing data use, liability, and the deployment of AI in specific sectors play an outsized role in the development and adoption of AI. Unclear regulations can create uncertainty for companies,[28] causing them to delay the adoption of AI technologies because they are unsure about what is permitted. Potential users of an application will not use it if its legal status is uncertain (as discussed further in chapter 9), regardless of how effective it is or how relevant it is to their local contexts. This is especially the case in areas like health care and finance, where clear and specific regulations determine how quickly new solutions are deployed. As a result, clear rules around the technical and design features of AI applications and systems, such as providing information on how the applications and systems are built and explaining the output they generate, can help organizations understand what is permitted and expected, as well as build societal trust in AI (refer to chapter 9 for further details).[29]

The customization and deployment complements rely on one another and in some instances overlap. Without deployment complements, customized models will not be able to reach the populations for which they are intended. Similarly, the absence of customization complements means that deployed AI systems will not be able to serve their intended populations effectively. Both sets of complements must be in place for the full potential of AI to be realized. The absence of either or both creates bottlenecks and constrains the pace of change.[30] This is a key insight that the Report addresses.

Nevertheless, although identifying the complements needed is a first step toward unlocking AI's potential, putting them in place is a much more challenging process. Experience shows that each new wave of general-purpose technologies has widened the gap in the intensity of technology use between higher- and lower-income countries.[31] This pattern is largely due to the challenges in putting in place the complementary factors necessary for use of these technologies.

The sections that follow highlight three reasons why AI could suffer the same fate. First, putting complements in place is a slow and continuous process; it takes decades even when conditions for doing so are favorable. Second, the complements that AI requires are often underprovided. Third, even where the required complements are in place, AI applications may still not be adopted, because it is not economically viable to do so, or simply because far too much uncertainty surrounding the expected costs and benefits remains.

The long journey: Putting complements in place is a slow and continuous process

Historically, the productivity gains from general-purpose technologies did not materialize when the technologies were invented. Instead, such gains came decades later, once organizations had reorganized themselves to take advantage of the technologies. After electricity was invented, the cost of changing factory layouts and instituting the organizational processes necessary to engineer the required technology switch slowed the pace at which factories electrified and the gains that ensued from electrification.[32] Similarly, in France during the nineteenth century, the productivity gains from mechanized cotton spinning took time to materialize, given a lengthy period of trial and error in reorganizing production to accommodate the new technology.[33] More recently, the slow rise in productivity that has accompanied the spread of computerization has been attributed to the need for complementary investments in organizational processes and other intangible capital.[34] The implication is that building complements is a slow process because some of them must be "invented," not simply put in place. AI is unlikely to be different.

Apart from the slow process of co-invention, the effectiveness of new general-purpose technologies largely depends on whether older general-purpose technologies, such as, in the case of AI, access to electricity, the internet, and computers, have been adopted. While leapfrogging over special-purpose technology is possible—for example, skipping landline telephones in favor of mobile phones—it is difficult for countries to leapfrog general-purpose technologies. Technological advancement is a cumulative process, and countries must first catch up before they can advance. The steam engine preceded electric power, and electricity was a precondition for information technology.

Similarly, AI tools are typically operated on electronic devices, such as computers and smartphones, which require access to electricity and internet connectivity. Lack of needed infrastructure may therefore constrain the wider adoption of AI in low- and middle-income countries. In low-income countries, in particular, less than half of the population has access to electricity, only about one-quarter has access to the internet, and the use of smartphones is far from universal.[35]

Building complements is a continuous process, compounding the slow pace of change. As soon as one gap is addressed, another becomes apparent. The scenario involving Google Health in the introduction of the chapter demonstrates this *moving bottleneck* phenomenon. In that scenario, once the clinics had acquired the AI-assisted diagnostic capability Google Health provided, the limiting factor shifted to the quality of lighting, which affected the clarity of the images that the clinics' nurses took. Slow internet connections worsened the problem: Uploads that had taken seconds when the tool was tested in laboratory settings took more than a minute when it was deployed in the clinics, slowing down the screening queue and limiting the number of patients who could be screened. In one clinic, the internet was down for two hours on one of the days in the study.[36] In short, accruing the full potential of AI requires managing a series of moving bottlenecks that may take a long time to clear, a point that the rest of the Report develops further.

The roadblock: Access to complements may be limited

Not only is the process of putting in place the complements required for the effective deployment of AI often slow and continuous, but these complements are often underprovided. For example, connectivity is a key requirement for the deployment of AI. Thus, a person living in a rural area without a reliable internet connection cannot use AI tools, in most instances. Even after decades of network expansion, 3.4 billion people globally still lack access to mobile internet. Of these, about 3.1 billion live in areas with mobile broadband signals but remain offline due to various reasons including high cost, and the remaining 300 million lack coverage entirely.[37] Internet access is limited partly because it is expensive to extend coverage to communities in sparsely populated, low-income regions, whereas the potential revenue from these areas is low. The irony is that the populations that AI has greatest potential to benefit—rural communities and low-income households—are those for which connectivity is least commercially attractive to provide.

The same pattern is apparent in regard to electricity, another foundational complement required by AI. Across many developing countries, state-owned distribution utilities are required to sell power at below-market prices to rural households, with the government reimbursing them for the difference. Nevertheless, reimbursements are subject to delays or disputes, and collection rates for power bills in subsidized segments remain low, but the capital expenditure per customer in rural areas is considerable. Therefore, every additional unit of electricity that distribution utilities sell to populations they are required to serve at below-market prices worsens their financial situation. To limit losses, these utilities ration the power supply to these communities by restricting access and hours of supply, which partly explains why billions of people in developing countries lack reliable access to electricity.[38] As with connectivity, the communities that could potentially benefit most from AI are the same communities for which providing this foundational complement needed for AI offers the least incentives.

The road not taken: Even where complements are in place, AI applications may still not be adopted

Even where the complements required for their implementation are in place, it may not be commercially viable for some developing countries to adopt AI-powered applications and equipment because they are relatively more expensive than *human* labor.[39] Consider retail automation driven by computer vision, a technology that allows customers to shop, pay, and exit without stopping at a checkout counter. Although several high-income countries have deployed this technology, developing countries rarely do so, because cashiers earn significantly lower wages than the outlay required for the sensors, software, and maintenance that such technologies require; the reverse is true, however, in high-income countries.

Similarly, automated cutting and sewing equipment in the garment industry has existed for decades, but countries such as Bangladesh, Cambodia, and Viet Nam seldom use it. Complements are rarely the limiting factor. Rather, the decision to not adopt the technologies behind the equipment reflects a rational response to their relatively high cost compared with that of local labor. For similar economic reasons, developing countries will likely not adopt some AI applications.[40]

These examples illustrate an important point related to the concept of inappropriate technologies discussed earlier in the chapter. In high-income countries, commercial applications tend to be designed around reducing the need for expensive labor, rather than addressing shortages of skills. The skills shortage is the more pressing issue, on the other hand, in developing countries and requires very different products. Part 3 of this Report builds on this point by discussing the role of government policies in shaping the direction of innovation in a way that serves the pressing needs of countries.

Finally, uncertainty can impede the adoption of AI applications. Decisions to adopt AI tools depend on potential users' perception of the expected costs and benefits of doing so. Uncertainty plays a big role in shaping such expectations.[41] First, there is a great degree of uncertainty about the trajectory of AI, including how quickly AI's capabilities will improve and render adoption of it in its current form obsolete, and what applications will be created and gain traction, as well as how rapidly the cost of adopting certain applications will fall. Such uncertainties make it difficult to choose the appropriate AI tools to adopt and the right time to do so. Second, firms are uncertain about how AI will reshape their own products and services. As AI improves and becomes increasingly ubiquitous, it may enhance a firm's existing offerings, but it may also render the firm's business outdated. These uncertainties may slow down the adoption of AI, even when the use of AI appears promising.

The pathways: Adopt, adapt, and then advance

Different policy objectives require different types of complements. As a result, the three observations made earlier—complements are slow to put in place, often underprovided, and even when present, do not guarantee a technology will be used—shape the set of policy options available to governments (refer to figure 3.4).

Adopting off-the-shelf AI applications such as chatbots and coding assistants can be done quickly, because the complements that they require (such as cloud storage) are generally provided by the vendors or already exist in varying degrees in most economies (such as internet connectivity). Although gains associated with adoption can be realized relatively quickly, countries may become overly dependent on external providers and end up using applications that may be poorly suited to local conditions.

Figure 3.4 Most developing countries can benefit from AI through adopting and adapting what has already been established, without needing to advance the AI frontier

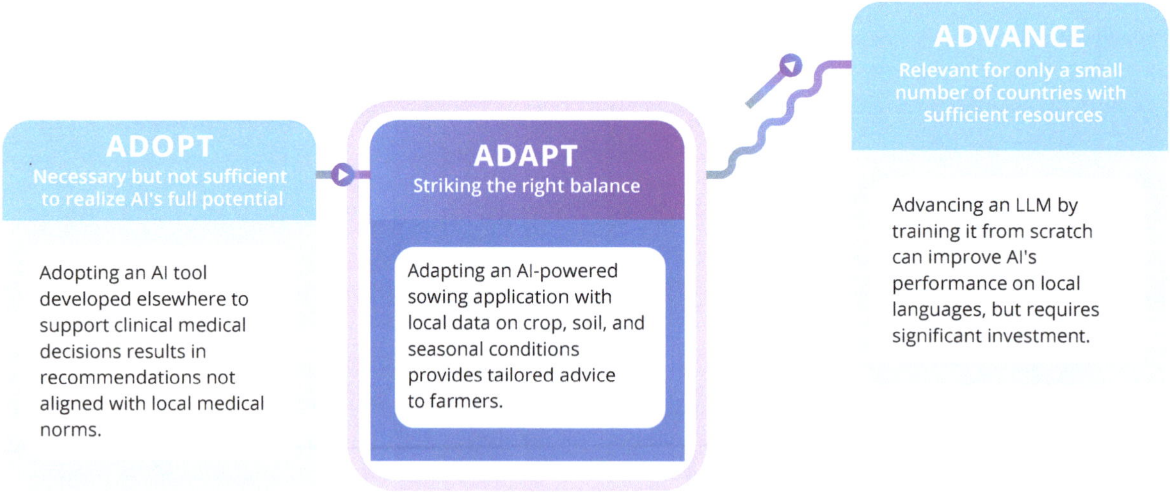

Source: WDR 2026 team.

Note: AI = artificial intelligence; LLM = large language model.

Adapting AI applications to local conditions is important, because these applications are unlikely to be effective in a particular country if they have been designed in other countries for other contexts. Such contextual mismatches have particularly serious consequences in domains like health care, in which poor performance can have serious and even fatal consequences. Local context also matters for providing tailored advice to farmers, because agroclimatic conditions vary substantially across regions and even within regions. However, whether it involves building new applications catered to the local context or modifying existing ones, adaptation typically requires access to layers of the AI stack other than the application layer such as data centers, cloud infrastructure, and models. Thus, it often requires substantially greater complements than adopting off-the-shelf solutions.

One useful approach to dealing with this problem is to design applications around the complements that already exist. Ask Viamo Anything, a voice-based generative AI service for people who lack internet access, digital devices, or digital literacy, is an example of an AI solution adapted to the context of environments with low resources. Users can dial a local number on a basic phone, ask questions orally, and then receive spoken answers on a range of topics, including health, education, agriculture, and livelihoods. Conversation data collected from Botswana, Pakistan, and Zambia show that the length of conversations on the service increases and topics broaden as users gain more experience with using it.[42] Adaptation of AI solutions to the context of low-resource environments illustrates the power of *small AI* (refer to spotlight 1). Nevertheless, designing AI around existing complements limits the scope and scale of AI's impact. The strategic question in the long term is which complements to invest in and in what order, given that bottlenecks will continually shift as each is addressed.

For some countries, AI *advancement* might come into play over time with sufficient experience in AI adaptation. Nevertheless, as discussed in the previous chapter and this one, advancing the frontier of AI involves the most expensive complements and those that require the longest time to put in place. Adopt, adapt, and then advance is thus the most viable pathway for most developing countries to acquire the capabilities of AI. Parts 2 and 3 of the Report develop this theme further.

Notes

1. Beede et al. (2020).
2. Acemoglu and Zilibotti (2001); Atkinson and Stiglitz (1969); Basu and Weil (1998); Moscona and Sastry (2025). The concept of *inappropriate technologies* is closely related to the distinction between trait-making and trait-taking technologies (Hirschman 1967; Moscona et al. 2026). *Trait-making technologies* must alter some aspect of the location to which they are being applied if they are to succeed. *Trait-taking technologies*, meanwhile, fit easily into the given social and cultural structure (Hirschman 1967).
3. In addition to AI models, Hugging Face also houses training data sets.
4. Adebara and Abdul-Mageed (2022); Joshi et al. (2020).
5. Wild (2025). With modest resources, the latest generative AI models are demonstrating increasingly robust performance in languages such as the 13 official languages in Mali (Dembele et al. 2025).
6. Adebara et al. (2025).
7. Although the discussion in this chapter mainly pertains to generative AI, the issues also affect other forms of AI to varying degrees. For example, although predictive AI often relies on nontext data, an AI application using predictive AI may produce inaccurate results if the data on which the underlying model have been trained are derived from a setting other than the setting in which the application is deployed.
8. Adelani et al. (2025).
9. Alshemali (2026).
10. Yang et al. (2024).
11. Jaiswal et al. (2024).
12. Khandelwal et al. (2024).
13. Shumailov et al. (2024).
14. World Bank (2021).
15. Kaushik et al. (2025); Marivate (2026).
16. Gao et al. (2024); Lewis et al. (2021).
17. Rappan et al. (2025).
18. Levy Yeyati (2025).

19. Noor and Kanitroj (2025).
20. Tonja et al. (2024).
21. TII (2025).
22. Levy Yeyati (2025); Thaker (2026).
23. Anthropic (2026); OpenAI (2026).
24. Steyvers and Kumar (2024).
25. *Human-in-the-loop* and *human-on-the-loop* refer to processes in which human feedback, intervention, and/or supervision are included as part of the use of AI. In *human-in-the-loop*, AI models and applications cannot complete an action without human input or approval. As for *human-on-the-loop*, AI runs on its own, but a person monitors it and can intervene, pause, or override the process.
26. Vaccaro et al. (2024).
27. Agrawal et al. (2025).
28. Baker et al. (2016).
29. Bach et al. (2024). Although trustworthy AI standards are developing, standards for AI remain fragmented and overlap across regions and institutions. Nonetheless, the various standards that are in place tend to exhibit commonalities across a number of dimensions, such as diversity, non-discrimination, and fairness; transparency; privacy and data governance; technical robustness and safety; accountability; human agency and oversight; and societal and environmental well-being, as outlined by the European Commission's High-Level Expert Group on Artificial Intelligence (Miedema et al. 2026). Regulations that address these dimensions can help ensure certainty regarding policy and can facilitate the adoption of AI.
30. Jones (2011); Kremer (1993).
31. Comin and Mestieri (2018).
32. David (1990).
33. Juhász et al. (2024).
34. Brynjolfsson et al. (2021).
35. Refer to Access to Electricity (% of Population): Low Income (data page), Electrification Dataset, World Bank, https://data.worldbank.org/indicator/EG.ELC.ACCS.ZS?locations=XM; ITU (2025); World Bank (2025). A similar pattern is evident in regard to the use of the internet for business purposes. For example, fewer than 50 percent of firms in developing economies use a website, an increase from 26 percent in the late 2000s. By contrast, more than 82 percent of firms in advanced economies use a website, an increase from 55 percent in the late 2000s (Nayyar et al. 2024). Similarly, governments in more than 80 percent of advanced economies have an online e-services portal, compared with only 38 percent in developing economies (Nayyar et al. 2024).
36. Beede et al. (2020).
37. Koetsier (2026).
38. Burgess et al. (2020).
39. Caselli and Coleman (2006).
40. Even if the adoption of a new technology is commercially viable, societies may become locked into legacy technologies for two main reasons: sunk costs (that is, the reluctance to abandon a technology—even if doing so would clearly be beneficial—because people have invested heavily in the technology) and path dependency (that is, the tendency to favor certain technologies because of prevailing structures or beliefs and values) (Allen and Donaldson 2022). Historical examples of technological lock-in, such as the QWERTY keyboard layout (David 1986), the use of ordinary water as a coolant in civilian nuclear power reactors (Cowan 1990), the use of water power instead of steam power (Hornbeck et al. 2024), and the use of electric heating as opposed to non-electric heating (Gwee and Tan 2026) demonstrate how the use of specific technologies may persist for decades even if the technologies are suboptimal in some instances.
41. Conley and Udry (2010); Dixit and Pindyck (1994); Oliva et al. (2020); Pindyck (1993).
42. Whereas users typically have only one round of conversation on one or two topics in their initial interactions with Ask Viamo Anything, the number increases to about five rounds on three to five topics after they use the service 5–10 times. For returning users, the frequency of conversations increases over time, indicating greater trust in and expanded use of the tool.

References

Acemoglu, Daron, and Fabrizio Zilibotti. 2001. "Productivity Differences." *Quarterly Journal of Economics* 116 (2): 563–606. https://doi.org/10.1162/003355301511144104.

Adebara, Ife, and Muhammad Abdul-Mageed. 2022. "Towards Afrocentric NLP for African Languages: Where We Are and Where We Can Go." In *The 60th Annual Meeting of the Association for Computational Linguistics: Proceedings of the Conference, Vol. 1 (Long Papers),* 3814–41. Association for Computational Linguistics. https://aclanthology.org/2022.acl-long.265.pdf.

Adebara, Ife, Hawau Olamide Toyin, Nahom Tesfu Ghebremichael, AbdelRahim Elmadany, and Muhammad Abdul-Mageed. 2025. "Where Are We? Evaluating LLM Performance on African Languages." In *Proceedings of the 63rd Annual Meeting of the Association for Computational Linguistics (Volume 1: Long Papers),* 32704–31. Association for Computational Linguistics. https://aclanthology.org/2025.acl-long.1572.pdf.

Adelani, David Ifeoluwa, Jessica Ojo, Israel Abebe Azime, et al. 2025. "IrokoBench: A New Benchmark for African Languages in the Age of Large Language

Models." *arXiv:2406.03368v2 [cs.CL]*, January 23, Cornell University. https://doi.org/10.48550/arXiv.2406.03368.

Agrawal, Ajay K., Joshua S. Gans, and Avi Goldfarb. 2025. "Similarities and Differences in the Adoption of General Purpose Technologies." In *Technology, Productivity, and Economic Growth*, edited by Susanto Basu, Lucy Eldridge, John C. Haltiwanger, and Erich Strassner. Studies in Income and Wealth Series, vol. 83. National Bureau of Economic Research; University of Chicago Press. https://www.nber.org/chapters/c14751.

Allen, Treb, and Dave Donaldson. 2022. "Persistence and Path Dependence: A Primer." *Regional Science and Urban Economics* 94 (May): 103724. https://doi.org/10.1016/j.regsciurbeco.2021.103724.

Alshemali, Basemah. 2026. "Dialectal Substitution as an Adversarial Approach for Evaluating Arabic NLP Robustness." *Scientific Reports* 16 (5996). https://www.nature.com/articles/s41598-026-36252-4.

Anthropic. 2026. "Building a New Enterprise AI Services Company with Blackstone, Hellman & Friedman, and Goldman Sachs." Anthropic, May 4. https://www.anthropic.com/news/enterprise-ai-services-company.

Atkinson, Anthony B., and Joseph E. Stiglitz. 1969. "A New View of Technological Change." *Economic Journal* 79 (315): 573–78. https://doi.org/10.2307/2230384.

Bach, Tita Alissa, Amna Khan, Harry Hallock, Gabriela Beltrão, and Sonia Sousa. 2024. "A Systematic Literature Review of User Trust in AI-Enabled Systems: An HCI Perspective." *International Journal of Human–Computer Interaction* 40 (5): 1251–66. https://doi.org/10.1080/10447318.2022.2138826.

Baker, Scott R., Nicholas Bloom, and Steven J. Davis. 2016. "Measuring Economic Policy Uncertainty." *Quarterly Journal of Economics* 131 (4): 1593–636. https://doi.org/10.1093/qje/qjw024.

Basu, Susanto, and David N. Weil. 1998. "Appropriate Technology and Growth." *Quarterly Journal of Economics* 113 (4): 1025–54. https://doi.org/10.1162/003355398555829.

Beede, Emma, Elizabeth Baylor, Fred Hersch, et al. 2020. "A Human-Centered Evaluation of a Deep Learning System Deployed in Clinics for the Detection of Diabetic Retinopathy." In *CHI '20: Proceedings of the 2020 CHI Conference on Human Factors in Computing Systems*, edited by Regina Bernhaupt, Florian Floyd Mueller, David Verweij, and Josh Andres. Association for Computing Machinery. https://doi.org/10.1145/3313831.3376718.

Brynjolfsson, Erik, Daniel Rock, and Chad Syverson. 2021. "The Productivity J-Curve: How Intangibles Complement General Purpose Technologies." *American Economic Journal: Macroeconomics* 13 (1): 333–72. doi:10.1257/mac.20180386.

Burgess, Robin, Michael Greenstone, Nicholas Ryan, and Anant Sudarshan. 2020. "The Consequences of Treating Electricity as a Right." *Journal of Economic Perspectives* 34 (1): 145–69. https://www.aeaweb.org/articles?id=10.1257/jep.34.1.145.

Caselli, Francesco, and Wilbur John Coleman II. 2006. "The World Technology Frontier." *American Economic Review* 96 (3): 499–522. https://www.aeaweb.org/articles?id=10.1257/aer.96.3.499.

Comin, Diego A., and Martí Mestieri. 2018. "If Technology Has Arrived Everywhere, Why Has Income Diverged?" *American Economic Journal: Macroeconomics* 10 (3): 137–78. https://doi.org/10.1257/mac.20150175.

Conley, Timothy G., and Christopher R. Udry. 2010. "Learning About a New Technology: Pineapple in Ghana." *American Economic Review* 100 (1): 35–69. https://www.aeaweb.org/articles?id=10.1257/aer.100.1.35.

Cowan, Robin. 1990. "Nuclear Power Reactors: A Study in Technological Lock-In." *Journal of Economic History* 50 (3): 541–67. https://doi.org/10.1017/S0022050700037153.

David, Paul A. 1986. "Understanding the Economics of QWERTY: The Necessity of History." In *Economic History and the Modern Economist*, edited by William N. Parker. Basil Blackwell. https://archive.org/details/economichistorym0000park/page/n7/mode/2up.

David, Paul A. 1990. "The Dynamo and the Computer: An Historical Perspective on the Modern Productivity Paradox." *American Economic Review* 80 (2): 355–61. https://www.academia.edu/11211365/The_Dynamo_and_the_Computer_An_Historical_Perspective_on_the_Modern_Productivity_Paradox.

Dembele, Alou, Nouhoum Souleymane Coulibaly, and Michael Leventhal. 2025. "The Serendipity of Claude AI: Case of the 13 Low-Resource National Languages of Mali." *arXiv:2503.03380v1 [cs.CL]*, March 5, Cornell University. https://doi.org/10.48550/arXiv.2503.03380.

Dixit, Avinash K., and Robert S. Pindyck. 1994. *Investment Under Uncertainty*. Princeton University Press. https://press.princeton.edu/books/hardcover/9780691034102/investment-under-uncertainty.

Gao, Yunfan, Yun Xiong, Xinyu Gao, et al. 2024. "Retrieval-Augmented Generation for Large Language Models: A Survey." *arXiv:2312.10997v5 [cs.CL]*, March 27, Cornell University. https://doi.org/10.48550/arXiv.2312.10997.

Gwee, Yi Jie, and Hui Ren Tan. 2026. "Locked in the Past: Old Housing and the Adoption of Electric Heating." *Explorations in Economic History* 101 (July): 101771. https://www.sciencedirect.com/science/article/abs/pii/S001449832600032X.

Hirschman, Albert O. 1967. *Development Projects Observed*. Brookings Institution Press. https://www.brookings.edu/books/development-projects-observed/.

Hornbeck, Richard, Shanon Hsuan-Ming Hsu, Anders Humlum, and Martin Rotemberg. 2024. "Gaining Steam: Incumbent Lock-In and Entrant Leapfrogging." NBER Working Paper 32384, National Bureau of Economic Research. https://www.nber.org/papers/w32384.

ITU (International Telecommunication Union). 2025. "Measuring Digital Development: Facts and Figures 2025." ITU. https://www.itu.int/itu-d/reports/statistics/facts-figures-2025/.

Jaiswal, Siddharth D., Animesh Ganai, Abhisek Dash, Saptarshi Ghosh, and Animesh Mukherjee. 2024. "Breaking the Global North Stereotype: A Global South-Centric Benchmark Dataset for Auditing and Mitigating Biases in Facial Recognition Systems." *arXiv:2407.15810v2 [cs.CV]*, July 26, Cornell University. https://doi.org/10.48550/arXiv.2407.15810.

Jones, Charles I. 2011. "Intermediate Goods and Weak Links in the Theory of Economic Development." *American Economic Journal: Macroeconomics* 3 (2): 1–28. https://www.aeaweb.org/articles?id=10.1257/mac.3.2.1.

Joshi, Pratik, Sebastin Santy, Amar Budhiraja, Kaliki Bali, and Monojit Choudhury. 2020. "The State and Fate of Linguistic Diversity and Inclusion in the NLP World." In *Proceedings of the 58th Annual Meeting of the Association for Computational Linguistics,* 6282–93. Association for Computational Linguistics. https://aclanthology.org/2020.acl-main.560.pdf.

Juhász, Réka, Mara P. Squicciarini, and Nico Voigtländer. 2024. "Technology Adoption and Productivity Growth: Evidence from Industrialization in France." *Journal of Political Economy* 132 (10): 3215–59. https://doi.org/10.1086/730205.

Kaushik, Aprajita, Capucine Barcellona, Nikita Kanumoory Mandyam, Si Ying Tan, and Jasper Tromp. 2025. "Challenges and Opportunities for Data Sharing Related to Artificial Intelligence Tools in Health Care in Low- and Middle-Income Countries: Systematic Review and Case Study from Thailand." *Journal of Medical Internet Research* 27 (February 4): e58338. https://www.jmir.org/2025/1/e58338/.

Khandelwal, Khyati, Manuel Tonneau, Andrew M. Bean, Hannah Rose Kirk, and Scott A. Hale. 2024. "Indian-BhED: A Dataset for Measuring India-Centric Biases in Large Language Models." *arXiv:2309.08573v2 [cs.CL]*, August 9, Cornell University. https://doi.org/10.48550/arXiv.2309.08573.

Koetsier, John. 2026. "3.4 Billion People Don't Have Access to Mobile Internet, Costing the Global Economy $3 Trillion." *Forbes Tech* (blog), February 18. https://www.forbes.com/sites/johnkoetsier/2026/02/18/34-billion-people-dont-have-access-to-mobile-internet-costing-the-global-economy-3-trillion/.

Kremer, Michael Robert. 1993. "The O-Ring Theory of Economic Development." *Quarterly Journal of Economics* 108 (3): 551–75. https://doi.org/10.2307/2118400.

Levy Yeyati, Eduardo. 2025. "Latam-GPT and the Search for AI Sovereignty." *Commentary* (blog), November 25. https://www.brookings.edu/articles/latam-gpt-and-the-search-for-ai-sovereignty/.

Lewis, Patrick, Ethan Perez, Aleksandra Piktus, et al. 2021. "Retrieval-Augmented Generation for Knowledge-Intensive NLP Tasks." *arXiv:2005.11401v4 [cs.CL]*, April 12, Cornell University. https://doi.org/10.48550/arXiv.2005.11401.

Marivate, Vukosi. 2026. "The Annotation Scarcity Paradox in Low-Resource NLP Evaluation: A Decade of Acceleration and Emerging Constraints." *arXiv:2605.19066v1 [cs.CL]*, May 18, Cornell University. https://doi.org/10.48550/arXiv.2605.19066.

Miedema, Emiel, Sabine Waschull, and Christos Emmanouilidis. 2026. "Towards Trustworthy Artificial Intelligence for Decision-Making: A Lifecycle Perspective on Knowledge- and Data-Driven Artificial Intelligence Systems." *Computers in Industry* 174 (January): 104409. https://doi.org/10.1016/j.compind.2025.104409.

Moscona, Jacob, Nathan Nunn, and James A. Robinson. 2026. "Searching for Fish in Trees (緣木求魚)? Economic Development When Context Matters." NBER Working Paper 34810, National Bureau of Economic Research. https://www.nber.org/papers/w34810.

Moscona, Jacob, and Karthik A. Sastry. 2025. "Inappropriate Technology: Evidence from Global Agriculture." NBER Working Paper 33500, National Bureau of Economic Research. https://www.nber.org/papers/w33500.

Nayyar, Gaurav, Regina Pleninger, Dana Vorisek, and Shu Yu. 2024. "Digitalization and Inclusive Growth: A Review of the Evidence." Policy Research Working Paper 10941, World Bank. https://doi.org/10.1596/1813-9450-10941.

Noor, Elina, and Binya Kanitroj. 2025. "Speaking in Code: Contextualizing Large Language Models in Southeast Asia." Carnegie Endowment for International Peace. https://carnegieendowment.org/research/2025/01/speaking-in-code-contextualizing-large-language-models-in-southeast-asia.

OECD (Organisation for Economic Co-operation and Development). 2026. "Training Datasets by Language and Type." Graphic (updated May 26), OECD.AI Policy Observatory, OECD. https://oecd.ai/en/data?selectedArea=ai-models-and-datasets&selectedVisualization=open-training-datasets-by-language-and-type.

Oliva, Paulina, B. Kelsey Jack, Samuel Bell, Elizabeth Mettetal, and Christopher Severen. 2020. "Technology Adoption Under Uncertainty: Take-Up and Subsequent Investment in Zambia." *Review of Economics and Statistics* 102 (3): 617–32. https://doi.org/10.1162/rest_a_00823.

OpenAI. 2026. "OpenAI Launches the OpenAI Deployment Company to Help Businesses Build Around Intelligence." OpenAI, May 11. https://openai.com/index/openai-launches-the-deployment-company/.

Phadnis, Shilpa, and Sujit John. 2025. "Sarvam May Get First IndiaAI Mission Grant, of Rs 220 Crore." *India Business* (blog), April 24. https://timesofindia.indiatimes.com/business/india-business/sarvam-may-get-first-indiaai-mission-grant-of-rs-220-crore/articleshow/120587365.cms.

Pindyck, Robert S. 1993. "Investments of Uncertain Cost." *Journal of Financial Economics* 34 (1): 53–76. https://doi.org/10.1016/0304-405X(93)90040-I.

Rappan, Julieta, Macarena Blasi, María Candela Blanco, et al. 2025. "Meet Boti: The AI Assistant Transforming How the Citizens of Buenos Aires Access Government Information with Amazon Bedrock." *Artificial Intelligence* (blog), August 28. https://aws.amazon.com/blogs/machine-learning/meet-boti-the-ai

-assistant-transforming-how-the-citizens-of-buenos-aires-access-government-information-with-amazon-bedrock.

Shumailov, Ilia, Zakhar Shumaylov, Yiren Zhao, Nicolas Papernot, Ross Anderson, and Yarin Gal. 2024. "AI Models Collapse When Trained on Recursively Generated Data." *Nature* 631 (8022): 755–59. https://doi.org/10.1038/s41586-024-07566-y.

Steyvers, Mark, and Aakriti Kumar. 2024. "Three Challenges for AI-Assisted Decision-Making." *Perspectives on Psychological Science* 19 (5): 722–34. https://doi.org/10.1177/17456916231181102.

Thaker, Naini. 2026. "Five New Sovereign AI Models Signal India's Bold Leap at AI Summit." *AI Tracker* (blog), February 23. https://www.forbesindia.com/article/ai-tracker/five-new-sovereign-ai-models-signal-indias-bold-leap-at-ai-summit/2991615/1.

TII (Technology Innovation Institute). 2025. "Middle East's Leading AI Powerhouse TII Launches Two New AI Models: Falcon Arabic, the First Arabic Model in the Falcon Series, and Falcon-H1, a Best-in-Class High-Performance Model." *News* (blog), May 21. https://www.tii.ae/news/middle-easts-leading-ai-powerhouse-tii-launches-two-new-ai-models-falcon-arabic-first-arabic.

Tonja, Atnafu Lambebo, Bonaventure F. P. Dossou, Jessica Ojo, et al. 2024. "InkubaLM: A Small Language Model for Low-Resource African Languages." *arXiv:2408.17024v2 [cs.CL]*, September 3, Cornell University. https://doi.org/10.48550/arXiv.2408.17024.

Vaccaro, Michelle, Abdullah Almaatouq, and Thomas Malone. 2024. "When Combinations of Humans and AI Are Useful: A Systematic Review and Meta-Analysis." *Nature Human Behaviour* 8 (December): 2293–303. https://doi.org/10.1038/s41562-024-02024-1.

Wild, Sarah Emily. 2025. "AI Models Are Neglecting African Languages: Scientists Want to Change That." *Nature: News* (blog), July 29. https://www.nature.com/articles/d41586-025-02292-5.

World Bank. 2021. *World Development Report 2021: Data for Better Lives.* World Bank. https://www.worldbank.org/en/publication/wdr2021.

World Bank. 2025. "Mobile-Phone Technology Powers Saving Surge in Developing Economies." Press Release 2026/002/DEC, July 16. https://www.worldbank.org/en/news/press-release/2025/07/16/mobile-phone-technology-powers-saving-surge-in-developing-economies.

Yang, Jenny, Nguyen Thanh Dung, Pham Ngoc Thach, et al. 2024. "Generalizability Assessment of AI Models Across Hospitals in a Low-Middle and High Income Country." *Nature Communications* 15 (September): 8270. https://doi.org/10.1038/s41467-024-52618-6.

1 Spotlight 1

Small AI, Big Impact

Over the past few years, frontier artificial intelligence (AI) models (the most advanced AI models available) have grown enormously in scale, making them far more capable.[1] A single model can now take on almost any cognitive task but may need hundreds of billions of parameters to run. These parameters, also referred to as *weights*, are the internal numerical values that store what models have learned. The large number of parameters needed makes such a model quite large, so it would typically be housed in a data center because of the enormous amounts of computing power and electricity it requires. A frontier model of that size costs hundreds of millions of dollars to train[2] and is out of reach for most developing countries, where some 2.2 billion people are still offline.[3] But AI solutions for most development tasks do not need anywhere near the kind of computing power that a frontier model requires. Sorting a benefits claim or flagging a fraudulent payment uses a fraction of the power needed for what a frontier model can accomplish.

Small AI fills the gap.[4] It is built to operate where the complements it depends on, such as power and connectivity, are scarce. What makes AI small can vary (refer to table S1.1). A small AI model can be a small language model, the kind that gave the term its name, trained to approach a larger model's performance on far fewer parameters.[5] Or it can be a narrow model built for a single predictive task, such as spotting a crop disease or screening a cough. Either kind can operate offline on a phone or laptop.[6] Or the model can stay large, in the cloud, but be accessed through an application from a basic phone over a voice call or a text. Either way, the model need only be good enough for the task, not the most powerful one available.

Building versus adapting small AI models

How a small AI model is made depends on what it is used for. A small foundation model meant to handle many kinds of tasks is usually adapted from an existing foundation model,[7] whether open or closed. Weights for an open model are published, so it can be operated on local hardware and even customized to a language or domain it was not specifically trained for. A closed model stays with its provider, accessed only as a service over a network. Either way, accessing a model gets easier over time. The number of parameters needed by the smallest model about as capable as the first ChatGPT shrank from 540 billion in 2022 to 3.8 billion by 2024; over the same period, the price of output at that level fell from about $20 to a few cents.[8] As the frontier of AI advances, what a small model can do keeps increasing. Some developing countries are now building foundation models of their own. Latin America's Latam-GPT adapted an open model released by Meta in the United States, whereas India's Sarvam was trained from scratch (refer to box 3.1 in chapter 3).

Table S1.1 Size decides where a small AI model can operate

Model size (number of parameters)	Memory needed	Where model can operate	Connectivity needed
Up to 10 billion	2–20 GB	Phone or laptop computer	None
10–100 billion	20–200 GB	Single server	Local network, no internet
More than 100 billion	More than 200 GB	Data center	Constant internet

Source: WDR 2026 team.

Note: The parameter and memory figures are rounded orders of magnitude for typical cases. As models are made leaner and devices grow more powerful, those with the same capability can operate on smaller and cheaper hardware. AI = artificial intelligence; GB = gigabytes (one billion bytes).

Even a small foundation model—one that can perform many tasks, from answering questions to generating images—is still hard to build. It requires heavy computing power and expertise, albeit less than frontier models, whether trained from scratch or compressed from a larger model.[9] It also must be tested broadly for safety. Building small AI for a single task is far easier. A capable team can put a model together with modest computing power and the right data. Because it does only one thing, the model can be small enough that applications based on it can run on a phone. It is also easier to trust, because a single-task model is simpler to evaluate than a general-purpose one. Applications developed from such a model are usually predictive, picking a label rather than generating text. Specialized for its task, a small model can even outdo a much larger one: A small, fine-tuned model beat a far bigger one at flagging hate speech on Nigerian Twitter.[10]

Small AI applications in practice

A model is an engine, not a car. On its own it does nothing for a user. What a nurse or a farmer actually uses is an application: a model wrapped in an interface and delivered over a call or text that users can access on a phone they already own (refer to table S1.2). The same model can power very different applications, and how its results are delivered and what it is asked to do determine its usefulness as much as the model itself. Small AI applications can be built from large or small AI models.

Nuru and Cough Against TB are predictive AI applications built for a single task. Nuru, powered on a phone and operable even offline, has proven to be more accurate than agricultural extension officers at reading a diseased leaf.[11] Cough Against TB, built by Wadhwani AI with India's Central Tuberculosis Division, correctly flagged 9 in 10 people who actually had tuberculosis—accurately enough to identify who needed a confirmatory test.[12] The other three applications in the table are generative AI applications and are not limited to very narrowly defined tasks. PROMPTS answers mothers' questions through UlizaLlama, an open model in Swahili adapted from Meta's Llama.[13] In a trial across 40 Kenyan facilities, women who accessed PROMPTS gained knowledge and sought care more often than those who did not, and more than 3 million users have now enrolled to receive PROMPTS messages.[14] Rori pairs scripted lessons in mathematics with inexpensive access through

Table S1.2 Small AI applications used in development settings

Application	Sector	What it does	How it runs
Nuru	Agriculture	Diagnoses crop disease from a leaf photo	Small model on phone, offline
Cough Against TB	Health	Screens for tuberculosis from a cough	Small model on phone, offline
PROMPTS	Health	Answers new and expectant mothers' questions in Swahili	Small model on its own server, over text
Rori	Education	Tutors mathematics by text	Large model in cloud, over text
Ask Viamo Anything	Advisory	Answers spoken questions on a call	Large model in cloud, over voice call

Source: WDR 2026 team.
Note: AI = artificial intelligence; TB = tuberculosis.

Table S1.3 How small AI and large AI compare

Characteristics	Small AI	Large AI
Capability	Lower	Higher
Response time	Lower	Higher
Cost per use	Lower	Higher
Energy per task	Lower	Higher
Connectivity needed	Lower	Higher

Source: WDR 2026 team.
Note: A model an organization creates and runs internally costs more to set up, but less per use. AI = artificial intelligence.

the cloud, holding the running cost to about $5 per student. A randomized trial in Ghana found it raised mathematics scores by approximately the equivalent of one year of learning.[15] Ask Viamo Anything answers questions over an ordinary voice call, for people with no smartphone or internet, and using it requires no reading (refer to chapter 3).

What unites these applications is fit: Each one meets people on the device and through the connection they already use. Such a close fit yields real gains (refer to table S1.3). The first is reach: These applications run on a phone people already have, over an intermittent signal or none, and serve people that frontier AI passes by. Where the model underlying an application is small, the gains compound: It uses far less power than a large one.[16] Where the model is also open, an organization can run it on its own hardware, so it pays no fees per use and its data can stay in the country where the application is used.

Small AI has its downsides too. The main one is capability. Built on a smaller model, an application can do less than one built on a larger model, and the gap is greatest for complex or open-ended tasks. It also fails more often in contexts that differ from what it has seen before. A screening tool for diabetic eye disease rejected more than one-fifth of the images nurses took, because the lighting in the clinic differed from that in its training images.[17] The rule is to match the model to the risk. A particular model's performance can be good enough for an everyday task, but the bar must be much higher for high-stakes ones, such as screening for disease. A tool should be tested where it will be used and watched as conditions change (refer to spotlight 6). Building or setting up a model takes money and skill, and whoever deploys it handles the upkeep (refer to chapter 8). Whether that pays off depends on use, because building a model is the better choice as volume grows, whereas using a model from a commercial service is cheaper when use is light.

The role of public action

Even when small AI is the right tool for a particular task, the market may not supply it. A tool serving a low-income population may never repay its cost, however cheap it is to run, because the people it helps cannot pay for the value it creates. Take languages that have little text available in digital form for training models. Even the largest AI models perform far worse in African languages than in English or French.[18] Closing the gap requires adapting a model to a particular language, which in the case of African languages, for example, may not yield large enough commercial returns. The same goes for narrow tasks inside government that are useful to government but not to any market, such as routing a citizen's request to the right office.

This is where public action comes in, to change what gets built and what lasts. Opening government data and enabling access to computing power lower the cost of building small AI. India's national AI mission did so by giving a domestic developer the chips needed to train a local language model (refer to box 3.1). *How* a government buys matters as well: Procurement that rewards an AI tool for running offline and keeping data in the country purchasing it, rather than for topping a ranking of models, makes it more likely the tool will fit the conditions in which it will operate.[19]

Small is not always better. The right tool follows from the problem and the setting, not from the size of the model behind it. For many development challenges, a small tool adapted to local conditions is the better answer, as long as being good enough is a floor to build on, not a ceiling. Building and running small tools grounds AI in a country's own context. For some developing countries, it is a first step toward advancing AI models of their own.

Notes

1. Fraiberger and Kazemi (2026); Hoffmann et al. (2022); Kaplan et al. (2020); Maslej et al. (2025).
2. Cottier et al. (2025).
3. GSMA (2025); ITU (2025).
4. Chakravorti (2025); Goldin (2026).
5. Caballar and Stryker (2024); Kumar et al. (2025); Wang et al. (2024).
6. Abdin et al. (2024).
7. *Foundation models* are large AI models trained on broad data that can be adapted to many different tasks and applications. Large language models are one type.
8. Maslej et al. (2025).
9. Zhu et al. (2024).
10. Tonneau et al. (2024).
11. Mrisho et al. (2020).
12. Refer to Cough Against TB (web page), Wadhwani AI, AI Unit, Lords Education and Health Society, https://www.wadhwaniai.org/impact/healthcare-solutions/cough-against-tb/.
13. Gichigi (2024).
14. Vatsa et al. (2025).
15. Henkel et al. (2024).
16. Luccioni et al. (2024).
17. Beede et al. (2020).
18. Adelani et al. (2025).
19. Tonja et al. (2024).

References

Abdin, Marah, Jyoti Aneja, Hany Awadalla, et al. 2024. "Phi-3 Technical Report: A Highly Capable Language Model Locally on Your Phone." *arXiv:2404.14219v4 [cs.CL]*, August 30, Cornell University. https://doi.org/10.48550/arXiv.2404.14219.

Adelani, David Ifeoluwa, Jessica Ojo, Israel Abebe Azime, et al. 2025. "IrokoBench: A New Benchmark for African Languages in the Age of Large Language Models." In *Annual Conference of the Nations of the Americas Chapter of the Association for Computational Linguistics: Proceedings of the Conference, Volume 1: Long Papers*, edited by Luis Chiruzzo, Alan Ritter, and Lu Wang. Association for Computational Linguistics. https://aclanthology.org/2025.naacl-long.139.pdf.

Beede, Emma, Elizabeth Baylor, Fred Hersch, et al. 2020. "A Human-Centered Evaluation of a Deep Learning System Deployed in Clinics for the Detection of Diabetic Retinopathy." In *CHI '20: Proceedings of the 2020 CHI Conference on Human Factors in Computing Systems*, edited by Regina Bernhaupt, Florian Floyd Mueller, David Verweij, and Josh Andres. Association for Computing Machinery. https://doi.org/10.1145/3313831.3376718.

Caballar, Rina Diane, and Cole Stryker. 2024. "What Are Small Language Models?" *IBM Think* (blog), October 31. https://www.ibm.com/think/topics/small-language-models.

Chakravorti, Bhaskar. 2025. "How to Make AI More Useful." *Foreign Policy: Argument* (blog), October 27. https://foreignpolicy.com/2025/10/27/ai-use-cases-developing-world/.

Cottier, Ben, Robi Rahman, Loredana Fattorini, Nestor Maslej, Tamay Besiroglu, and David Owen. 2025. "The Rising Costs of Training Frontier AI Models." *arXiv:2405.21015v2 [cs.CY]*, February 7, Cornell University. https://doi.org/10.48550/arXiv.2405.21015.

Fraiberger, Samuel P., and Sharif Kazemi. 2026. "Concentrated Production, Distributed Adaptation: Pathways for AI Use in Low- and Middle-Income Countries." Background paper prepared for *World Development Report 2026: The Promise of Artificial Intelligence*, World Bank. https://www.worldbank.org/en/publication/wdr2026/brief/world-development-report-2026-background-papers.

Gichigi, Allan. 2024. "Jacaranda Launches Open Source LLM in Five African Languages." *News and Resources* (blog), August 16. https://jacarandahealth.org/jacaranda-launches-open-source-llm-in-five-african-languages/.

Goldin, Nicole. 2026. "Small AI, Big Results." *Blog Post* (blog), January 17. https://unu.edu/cpr/blog-post/small-ai-big-results.

GSMA. 2025. "The State of Mobile Internet Connectivity 2025: Overview Report." September, GSMA. https://www.gsma.com/somic/overview-report/.

Henkel, Owen, Hannah Horne-Robinson, Nessie Kozhakhmetova, and Amanda Lee. 2024. "Effective and Scalable Math Support: Experimental Evidence on the Impact of an AI-Math Tutor in Ghana." In *Artificial Intelligence in Education: Proceedings of the 25th International Conference on Artificial Intelligence in Education (AIED 2024)*, edited by Andrew M. Olney, Irene-Angelica Chounta, Zitao Liu, Olga C. Santos, and Ig Ibert Bittencourt. Communications in Computer and Information Science Series, vol. 2150. Springer Nature. https://link.springer.com/chapter/10.1007/978-3-031-64315-6_34.

Hoffmann, Jordan, Sebastian Borgeaud, Arthur Mensch, et al. 2022. "Training Compute-Optimal Large Language Models." *arXiv:2203.15556v1 [cs.CL]*, March 29, Cornell University. https://doi.org/10.48550/arXiv.2203.15556.

ITU (International Telecommunication Union). 2025. "Measuring Digital Development: Facts and Figures 2025." ITU. https://www.itu.int/itu-d/reports/statistics/facts-figures-2025/.

Kaplan, Jared, Sam McCandlish, Tom Henighan, et al. 2020. "Scaling Laws for Neural Language Models." *arXiv:2001.08361v1 [cs.LG]*, January 23, Cornell University. https://doi.org/10.48550/arXiv.2001.08361.

Kumar, Ajay, Thomas H. Davenport, and Randy Bean. 2025. "The Case for Using Small Language Models." *AI and Machine Learning* (blog), September 8. https://hbr.org/2025/09/the-case-for-using-small-language-models.

Luccioni, Sasha, Yacine Jernite, and Emma Strubell. 2024. "Power Hungry Processing: Watts Driving the Cost of AI Deployment?" In *ACM FAccT '24: Proceedings of the 2024 ACM Conference on Fairness, Accountability, and Transparency*, edited by Reuben Binns, Flavio Calmon, Alexandra Olteanu, and Michael Veale. Association for Computing Machinery. https://dl.acm.org/doi/10.1145/3630106.3658542.

Maslej, Nestor, Loredana Fattorini, Raymond Perrault, et al. 2025. *Artificial Intelligence Index Report 2025*. AI Index Steering Committee, Institute for Human-Centered Artificial Intelligence, Stanford University. https://doi.org/10.48550/arXiv.2504.07139.

Mrisho, Latifa Mbwana, Neema Aldo Mbilinyi, Mathias Ndalahwa, et al. 2020. "Accuracy of a Smartphone-Based Object Detection Model, PlantVillage Nuru, in Identifying the Foliar Symptoms of the Viral Diseases of Cassava: CMD and CBSD." *Frontiers in Plant Science* 11 (December 17): 590889. https://doi.org/10.3389/fpls.2020.590889.

Tonja, Atnafu Lambebo, Bonaventure F. P. Dossou, Jessica Ojo, et al. 2024. "InkubaLM: A Small Language Model for Low-Resource African Languages." *arXiv:2408.17024v2 [cs.CL]*, September 3, Cornell University. https://doi.org/10.48550/arXiv.2408.17024.

Tonneau, Manuel, Pedro Vitor Quinta de Castro, Karim Lasri, et al. 2024. "NaijaHate: Evaluating Hate Speech Detection on Nigerian Twitter Using Representative Data." In *Proceedings of the 62nd Annual Meeting of the Association for Computational Linguistics, Volume 1: Long Papers*, edited by Lun-Wei Ku, Andre Martins, and Vivek Srikumar. Association for Computational Linguistics. https://aclanthology.org/2024.acl-long.488.pdf.

Vatsa, Rajet, Wei Chang, Sharon Akinyi, et al. 2025. "Impact Evaluation of a Digital Health Platform Empowering Kenyan Women Across the Pregnancy-Postpartum Care Continuum: A Cluster Randomized Controlled Trial." *PLOS Medicine* 22 (2): e1004527. https://doi.org/10.1371/journal.pmed.1004527.

Wang, Fali, Zhiwei Zhang, Xianren Zhang, et al. 2024. "A Comprehensive Survey of Small Language Models in the Era of Large Language Models: Techniques, Enhancements, Applications, Collaboration with LLMs, and Trustworthiness." *arXiv:2411.03350v2 [cs.CL]*, December 28, Cornell University. https://doi.org/10.48550/arXiv.2411.03350.

Zhu, Xunyu, Jian Li, Yong Liu, Can Ma, and Weiping Wang. 2024. "A Survey on Model Compression for Large Language Models." *Transactions of the Association for Computational Linguistics* 12 (November): 1556–77. https://doi.org/10.1162/tacl_a_00704.

Part 2

Assessing the Promise and Peril of AI: Its Economic, Social, and Political Impacts

Part 1 emphasized that countries can leverage AI's potential for transformational change by adopting off-the-shelf AI solutions, adapting AI solutions to local contexts, and advancing the AI frontier. Part 2 assesses how the pathways of adopting, adapting, and advancing AI are changing well-being economically (by affecting what people do and how much they earn), socially (by changing how people access public goods and services), and politically (through the ways it is reshaping power relationships between and within countries) (refer to figure P2.1).

Chapter 4 focuses on economic impacts, analyzing how AI is reshaping pathways of growth, productivity, and jobs. With most people employed in manual rather than cognitive work in developing countries, the immediate impact of AI adoption is to complement rather than displace workers. Spotlight 2 focuses on how AI adoption is alleviating the shortage of agricultural extension agents. Over time, as complementary factors—infrastructure, skills, institutions, and venture capital—develop, AI can enable productive businesses to grow. In the absence of the right complementary factors, however, AI may widen gaps in productivity between developing countries and high-income countries, where rates of AI adoption are higher. AI can also have cascading effects through disrupting trade patterns, increasing human capital, raising energy costs, and creating economic volatility.

Chapter 5 investigates social impacts, examining how AI is transforming the delivery of public services. AI's immediate impact is to raise capabilities at the back end of public administration, largely through adapting machine learning algorithms to local contexts. Adapting and adopting AI can also help overcome critical shortages of skilled personnel, such as teachers and health care workers, at the citizen-facing front end of public service delivery. The lack of evidence for selecting, procuring, and evaluating AI applications, especially at the front end, limits AI's full potential to improve the delivery of public services. The lack of complements, such as digital connectivity and skills, also constrains AI adoption at the front end of public service delivery. Spotlight 3 discusses concerns that using AI extensively to deliver education services might erode human capital in the long term.

Figure P2.1 The pathways of adopting, adapting, and advancing AI shape its economic, social, and political impacts

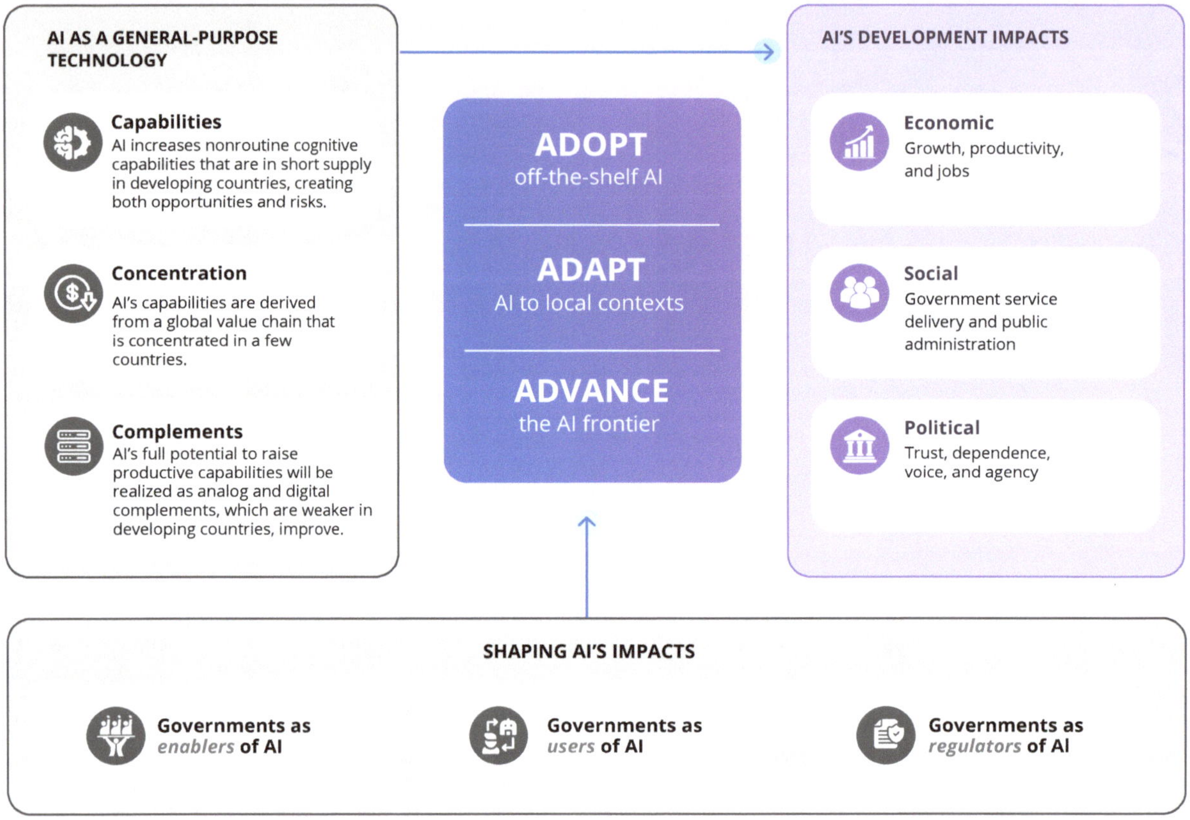

Source: WDR 2026 team.
Note: AI = artificial intelligence.

Chapter 6 explores political impacts, describing how AI is driving power asymmetries between countries, governments, corporations, and individuals. Between countries, control over key parts of the AI value chain—advanced chips and data centers—by a few companies creates dependency risks, but pursuing "AI sovereignty" comes at a high cost and with uncertain benefits. Between governments and corporations, financial incentives to attract AI investment squeeze public budgets yet provide uncertain returns. Between corporations and individuals, AI can benefit owners of AI capital more than people because of the concentration of market power. Between governments and individuals, AI can spread propaganda and enable the surveillance of citizens. Spotlight 4 discusses the environmental impacts of AI investments that traverse these axes of power.

AI's economic, social, and political impacts in developing countries are not the same as those in high-income countries. The risk of job disruption with AI is less imminent. The potential to improve the delivery of public services with AI is larger. The vulnerability of citizens to being misinformed and monitored by AI is higher in the absence of strong institutions.

4

AI's Economic Impact: Transforming Jobs, Productivity, and Growth

Main messages

- **AI could give small firms and less-skilled workers a productivity boost**
  Expand access to affordable tools and practical training so businesses can use AI to improve core functions, enter markets, and grow.
- **AI-related job losses in developing economies may be smaller overall—but painful where good jobs are scarce**
  Prepare workers in call centers, business process outsourcing, and other knowledge-intensive services to move into new tasks and jobs that complement AI.
- **AI adoption in developing economies is spreading, but productive use remains shallow and uneven**
  Help smaller firms better embed AI in their operations by building local AI applications and improving management, digital readiness, finance, worker skills, and access to markets.
- **How fast countries adopt AI matters as much as how fast AI improves**
  Accelerate broad AI adoption by strengthening the foundations for adoption—better connectivity, education, and access to finance.
- **AI could have cascading effects across sectors and countries**
  Prepare for wider effects of AI on energy demand, trade patterns, human capital, and asset prices.

A reproducibility package is available for this book in the Reproducible Research Repository at https://reproducibility.worldbank.org/catalog/624.

Introduction

Perlah works in a call center in the Philippines. Every day she answers phone calls from customers of an American bank, helping them open accounts and solve issues with their bank cards. Days are long and the work is sometimes monotonous and tiring, but the pay is decent. Perlah is glad to have this job, which exists because of the global flow of services. Overall, the sector she works in, business process outsourcing, has been an important source of job creation in the Philippines, employing about 1.3 million workers.

Artificial intelligence (AI) is penetrating the sector. Perlah is now using an AI tool that listens to her conversations and suggests ways for her to respond to queries. Sometimes it comes up with good suggestions, which saves her time looking up information. But other times, it provides a solution that is not appropriate, and she discards the advice. As voice-based AI agents become more advanced, she worries whether she can keep her job. For the moment, many of her clients prefer to speak to an actual human over the phone, but she wonders whether this will change.

Meanwhile, in Nigeria, Chioma has just started a new business developing software solutions for agricultural firms to help them predict harvest times. Finding workers with good coding skills has been a challenge; universities do not always train students to use the latest technologies. AI has made coding much faster and easier, however, allowing her and her small team to build a minimum viable product more quickly than ever to offer potential investors and customers. Her main challenge is how to break into the market and get farmers to adopt her solution.

These examples highlight the many ways through which AI is affecting firms, jobs, productivity, and economic growth in low- and middle-income countries. Some impacts are positive and others are negative, while some are predictable and others are very uncertain. This mix reflects the nature of AI as a general-purpose technology with far-reaching and complex impacts.

To trace the impacts of AI on jobs, productivity, and growth, this chapter breaks them down into three main channels: (1) the impacts of AI adoption on the production of goods, services, and ideas (*AI as an input*); (2) the impacts of the expansion of the AI value chain (*AI as an output*); and (3) *wider economic impacts* from both these channels, including those on prices and income, transaction costs, and reallocation of resources. These key channels are summarized in figure 4.1. This depiction is by no means exhaustive given AI's many complex associated (knock-on) effects.

A useful way to understand some of the mechanisms through which AI affects jobs is by using task-based labor market models.[1] As workers adopt AI, the time they spend completing a task can decrease or the quality of output they produce can increase. Both raise labor productivity. However, the reduction in time for workers to perform a task can result in labor *displacement effects* as some jobs are replaced by AI. AI adoption also creates labor *reinstatement effects* through demand for new tasks. As production costs fall, AI adoption can also result in *productivity effects*, as products become less expensive to produce and thus demand increases—which in turn requires more labor.[2] The overall (net) impacts on employment depend on the balance of these forces. Labor market effects also depend on how AI alters the composition of tasks and requirements for expertise, which can affect employment. For example, if AI decreases the requirement for expertise in an occupation, workers with less expertise can enter the labor market, potentially increasing employment.[3]

Another way to understand how AI affects jobs and productivity is to consider AI as a tool that

Figure 4.1 How AI affects jobs and productivity in low- and middle-income countries

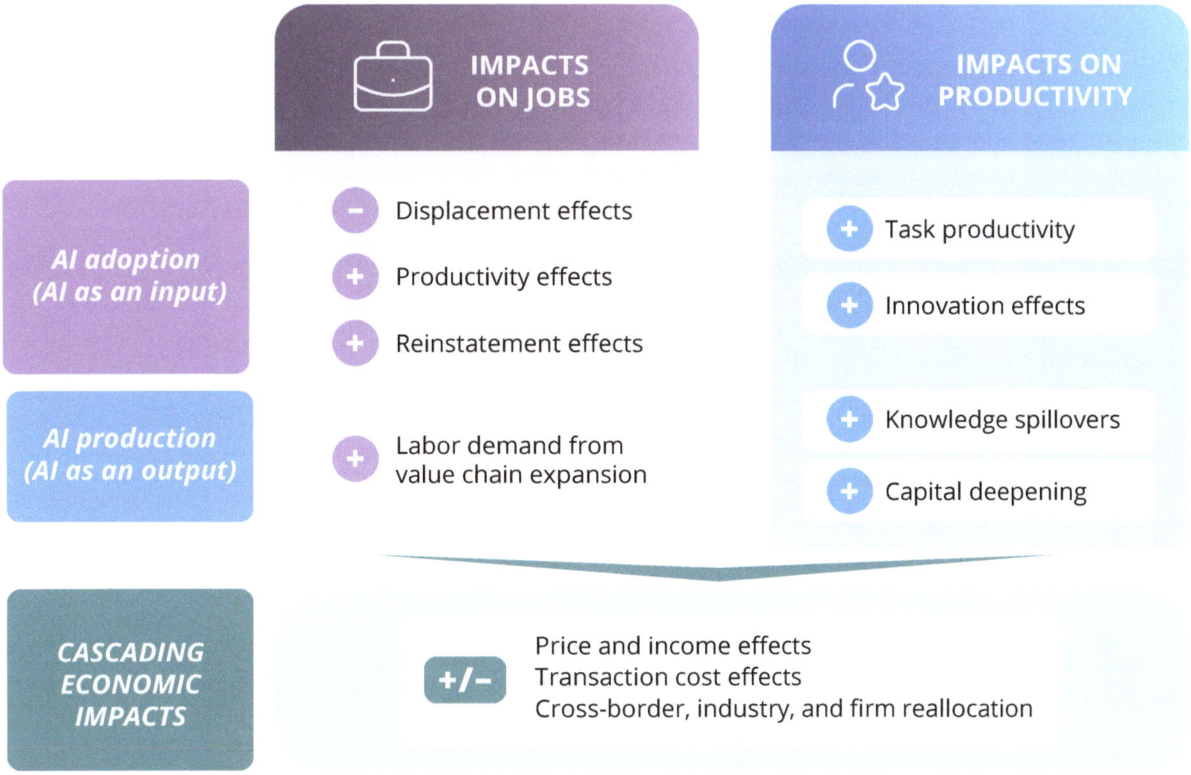

Source: WDR 2026 team.

Note: Cross-border, industry, and firm reallocation refers to the shift in economic activity across countries, industries, and firms from those that are contracting to those that are expanding. AI = artificial intelligence.

can accelerate the production of new ideas. AI can aid scientists in generating and testing questions, ideas, and designs.[4] AI has been characterized as a general-purpose metatechnology: a general-purpose technology that can be used to develop new technologies.[5] AI is already significantly affecting some parts of the process of scientific discovery, including the generation of evidence and the testing of hypotheses. AI can also speed up product innovation.[6] Low- and middle-income countries will be affected both directly by innovation at home and indirectly by innovations in other countries that spread to them.

The production of *AI as an output,* by increasing the output of goods and services that produce or enable AI technologies and solutions, can be considered a short-term supply shock that unambiguously boosts labor demand and economic growth. Chapter 2 described the value chain related to AI production, which includes several stages spanning from raw materials to chips and AI-enabling electronics, data centers, cloud computing, software, and development of AI models and applications. The production of AI as an output increases labor demand embedded in each segment of the value chain. It can also generate knowledge spillovers and deepen capital investment, raising productivity.[7]

The *cascading economic impacts* from each of these channels reach even those developing countries where AI adoption and production are limited. As AI is adopted, the main impacts include those through mechanisms affecting prices and real incomes (incomes after taking prices into account) and through lower transaction costs and reallocation of activities. By lowering the costs of inputs or raising the quality of outputs, AI adoption can decrease the prices or improve the quality and quantity of goods and services, boosting real incomes and stimulating demand for the same and other goods and services. The overall effects will depend on how sensitive income and prices are to such changes (income and price elasticities).[8] AI also lowers transaction costs such as trade and communication costs, which can expand access to markets and job opportunities. Growth in the AI value chain has indirect effects on the supply side, such as those through greater capital expenditures and energy consumption, as well as those through asset markets. By raising the productivity or output of certain industries, AI can trigger reallocation of economic activity across industries and countries. This process can raise productivity if labor moves into sectors with higher productivity or lower it if labor moves into sectors that are less suited to automation and characterized by lower productivity.[9]

This chapter explores the impacts of AI in low- and middle-income countries through these three channels. The first section explores the impacts of AI as an input on jobs and productivity. The second section explores the impacts of AI as an output on jobs and productivity. The third section explores the wider economic impacts of AI. The final section then looks to the future and evaluates different scenarios for both AI technical progress and AI adoption and how they could shape the trajectory of impacts for low- and middle-income countries over the next decade.

AI as an input: AI holds significant promise to raise productivity, but uneven patterns of adoption are concentrating both disruptions and gains

Although AI offers significant promise for raising the productivity of firms and improve firm dynamics in developing countries, AI adoption to date has been highly concentrated both within and between countries. As a result, gains in productivity, creation of high-skill jobs, and disruptions of labor markets have been uneven across firms, workers, sectors, and countries. The discussion that follows begins by examining patterns of AI diffusion across countries and firms and the factors driving those patterns. It then explores the implications of AI adoption for productivity and jobs.

AI adoption holds significant promise for increasing productivity in developing countries by raising the capabilities of small businesses and boosting entrepreneurship

In low-income and lower-middle-income countries, almost 90 percent of workers are employed in businesses with fewer than 10 people, and more than half of workers are self-employed.[10] Most people employed in these small businesses are concentrated in agriculture, retail, and hospitality services.[11] Over the near term, AI can raise the capabilities of these small businesses by providing advice on key business functions, such as inventory management or client relations.

Evidence from Enterprise Surveys on AI Adoption conducted for this Report suggests that use of AI technologies among small firms across seven countries is already pervasive.[12] Among formal firms with more than five employees in India, Jordan, Kenya, Mexico, Nigeria, and Thailand, on average, about 20 percent have recently used an AI chatbot in their business operations, compared with 34 percent in the United States (refer to figure 4.2, panel a).[13] These businesses use AI for a wide variety of tasks, including summarizing information, drafting and translating text, and interacting with customers. The rapid diffusion and adoption of AI has been facilitated in particular by firms that have already incorporated digital tools into their business operations. More than three-fourths of firms across these countries already use business messenger apps, social media apps, and standard software packages (refer to figure 4.2, panel b). This pattern suggests that if a suitable generative AI (GenAI) solution to boost firm productivity is developed, businesses could adopt it quickly—even firms typically considered to be unlikely adopters. In Nigeria, for example, 21 percent of firms that primarily use handwritten records to administer their businesses are adopting AI in some form, mostly by using AI chatbots that are easily accessible through mobile phones.

AI can help entrepreneurs and young firms experiment with low-cost AI tools to perform tasks that were once out of reach: designing websites, running targeted marketing campaigns, and creating professional content without specialized teams or large up-front investments. AI can also improve access to financial services (refer to box 4.1). As a result, AI can reduce barriers to entry for firms and help productive firms expand. Firms' discovery of viable business models can unlock rapid growth and job creation. *AI-native businesses*—firms set up with AI technologies at their core rather than retrofitted—do not have to undergo costly organizational adjustment to have the technology fit their operations.[14]

Thus, the rapid adoption of generative AI tools provides an opportunity to increase the productivity of smaller firms and facilitate the entry of new firms. However, to realize productivity gains, firms might need complementary investments, such as basic training on how to use AI

Figure 4.2 Firms' rapid adoption of AI has been facilitated by their earlier adoption of complementary digital technologies

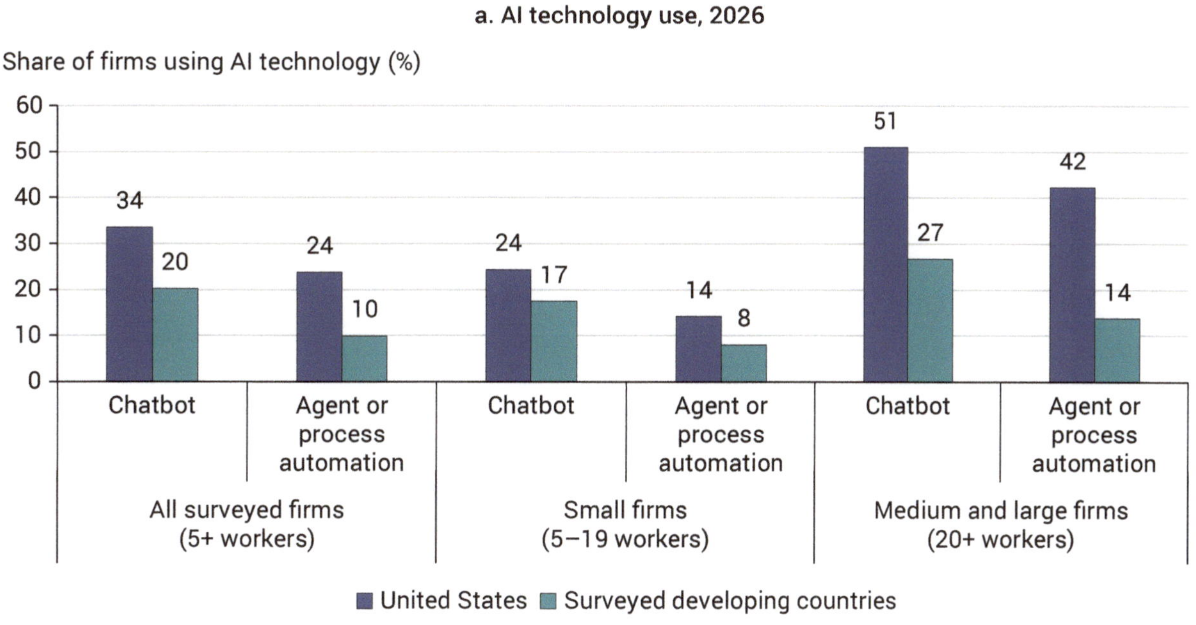

(Figure continues next page)

Figure 4.2 Firms' rapid adoption of AI has been facilitated by their earlier adoption of complementary digital technologies *(continued)*

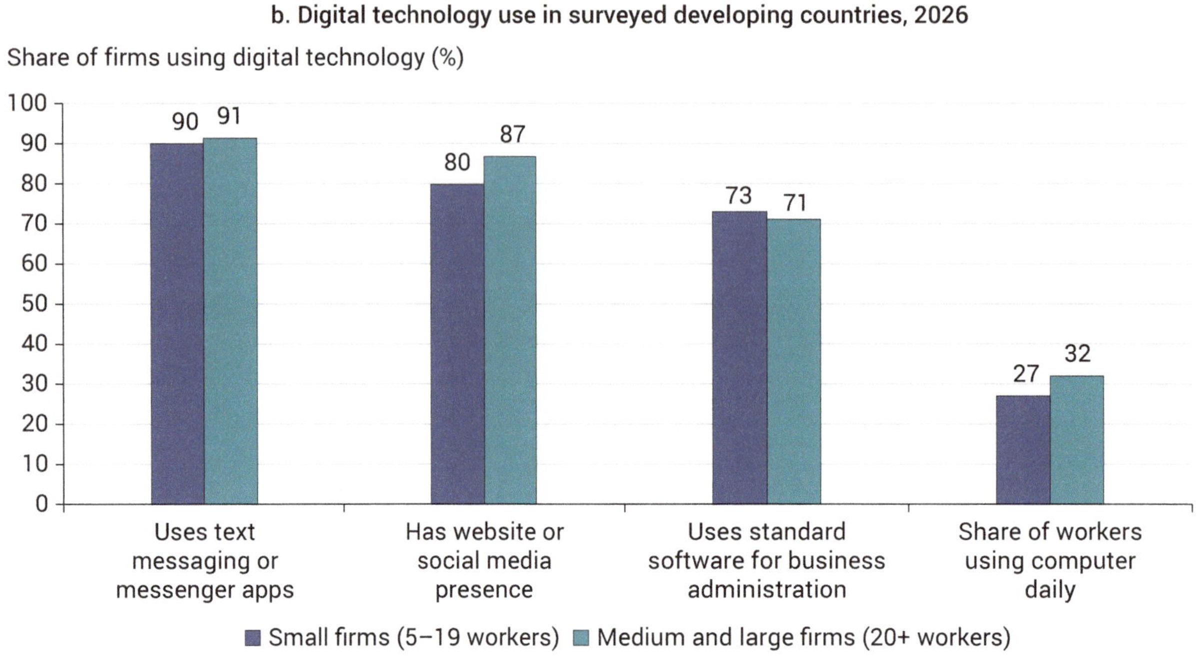

Source: WDR 2026 team, based on World Bank Enterprise Survey on AI Adoption.

Note: The figure reports data on formal firms in manufacturing, construction, and services with five or more employees. In panel a, *chatbot* refers to the share of firms using interactive AI chatbots (such as ChatGPT). *Agent or process automation* refers to the share of firms using AI agents to perform tasks independently or using AI for workflow or process automation. In panel b, *standard software* refers to software such as Excel. The data for surveyed developing countries average country-level indicators, with equal weight for each country. The samples are as follows: India (1,355 firms); Jordan (358); Kenya (360); Mexico (603); Nigeria (777); Thailand (360); United States (392). Microdata are available at Enterprise Surveys (data portal), World Bank, https://www.enterprisesurveys.org/en/data. AI = artificial intelligence.

tools. In Kenya, for example, an AI-powered business mentor for small business owners was successful in improving business performance, although it failed to do so for less profitable businesses that struggled to use AI tools effectively.[15] In Czechia, a combination of capacity building, peer learning, and exposure to a variety of AI tools not only increased the adoption of AI within firms (by 26 percent), but also established new business connections and increased firm growth.[16] A global study with start-ups from both middle- and high-income countries showed that sharing information about successful AI adoption by other firms within an accelerator program increased adoption by 44 percent and almost doubled revenues.[17]

Box 4.1 Leveraging AI to expand financial inclusion

Advances in artificial intelligence (AI) are expanding financial inclusion for individuals and micro-, small, and medium enterprises (MSMEs) that have been underserved by traditional banking institutions. AI-driven scoring models leverage alternative data (for example, mobile money transactions, digital payments data, e-commerce activity, and records of utility and telecommunications use) to assess the creditworthiness of borrowers without formal credit histories. These models are also more dynamic than rule-based ones because they can learn from borrowers' behavior. In Brazil, Nubank's AI-powered credit model (nuFormer) reduced risk by an estimated 70 percent for the same borrower populations.[a] In Kenya, Safaricom's M-PESA deployed AI-powered credit scoring on data regarding mobile money transactions and the use of airtime credits to target 18 million previously unbanked users.[b] In India, lenders were able to provide credit to more people by using machine learning algorithms to develop an alternate credit scoring based on individuals' digital presence.[c] Using AI to bring on new customers also supports the financial inclusion of previously excluded segments by reducing the time to process know-your-customer requirements from weeks to minutes—lowering compliance costs by 50–70 percent, while decreasing the rate at which customers leave.[d]

Opportunities like these will not translate into meaningful financial inclusion unless the underlying data powering AI solutions cover financial transactions conducted by women, informal workers, smallholder farmers, and MSMEs. Without proper safeguards, the use of AI in these contexts also risks entrenching exclusion rather than correcting it. For example, AI may amplify existing biases in credit scoring or exploit vulnerabilities in the behavior of prospective or current customers as financial institutions aggressively promote and offer credit.[e]

Source: WDR 2026 team.

a. Braithwaite et al. (2025).

b. Mwesigwa et al. (2026). *Airtime* refers to prepaid credits that people use to buy mobile phone services.

c. Agarwal et al. (2020).

d. Breslow et al. (2017); Verhagen et al. (2025).

e. Izaguirre et al. (2025).

AI adoption in practice: Shallow adoption and slow transformation despite rapid diffusion

Although GenAI tools are diffusing rapidly, the gap in AI adoption between high-income and low- and middle-income countries remains significant. Aggregate measures of the use of key large language models (LLMs) suggest far lower adoption rates in developing countries than in high-income countries. For example, nearly 25 percent of internet users in high-income countries had adopted ChatGPT on average by April 2025, compared with only 5.8 percent in upper-middle-income countries, 4.7 percent in lower-middle-income countries, and 0.7 percent in low-income countries (refer to figure 4.3, panel a).[18]

Figure 4.3 Developing countries still lag in adopting AI, and their lower AI exposure explains only part of the lag

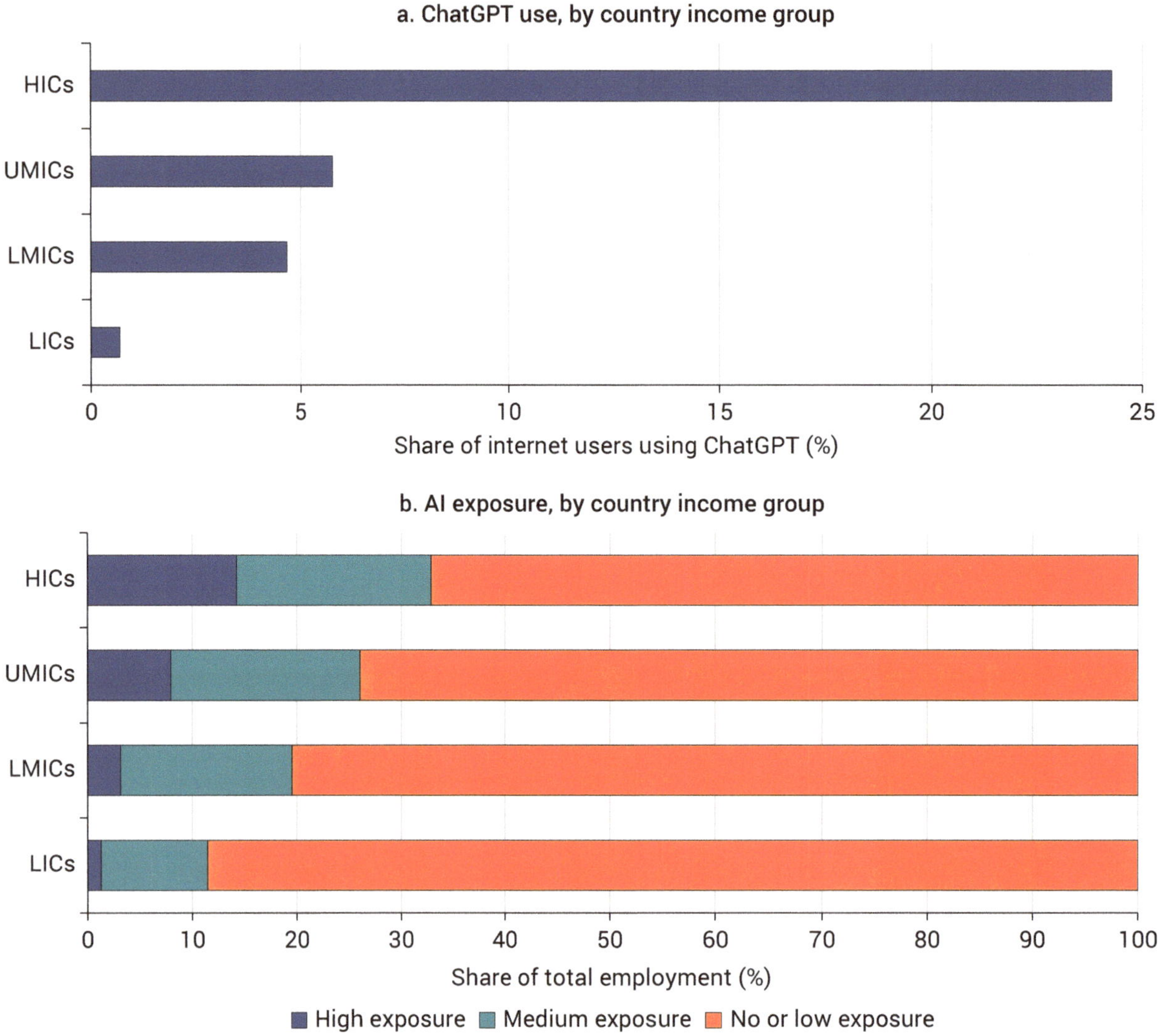

Sources: WDR 2026 team, based on Gmyrek, Viollaz, et al. 2026; Liu and Wang 2026.

Note: Panel a is based on website traffic data of Semrush (Software as a service platform), Semrush Holdings, https://www.semrush.com/. Website traffic data for China are significantly underestimated, resulting in an underestimation for upper-middle-income countries. ChatGPT users are based on unique IP (Internet Protocol) addresses and may overestimate the number of users, especially in HICs, because each individual may use ChatGPT from multiple IP addresses on different devices. Panel b displays the average score for exposure to generative AI across 137 countries (47 HICs, 38 UMICs, 35 LMICs, 17 LICs). High exposure will more likely lead to AI automating jobs, while medium exposure will more likely lead to AI complementing jobs. For details on the definitions of high exposure, medium exposure, and no or low exposure, refer to Gmyrek et al. (2026). Income classifications are for fiscal year 2027. AI = artificial intelligence; HICs = high-income countries; LICs = low-income countries; LMICs = lower-middle-income countries; MICs = middle-income countries; UMICs = upper-middle-income countries.

This adoption gap partially reflects the fact that the share of jobs that are amenable to AI use (known as *exposure*) (refer to box 4.2) is lower in low- and middle-income countries than in high-income countries. This is especially the case for GenAI (refer to figure 4.3, panel b).[19] The use of GenAI is highly concentrated in knowledge-intensive industries and relatively high-skill occupations—such as software developers, financial analysts, and marketing professionals[20]—that employ fewer people in developing countries (refer to chapter 1). However, the gap in AI adoption between high-income and developing countries is far larger than the gap in exposure to AI. In high-income countries, an internet user is 36 times more likely to use ChatGPT than in a low-income country, but exposure to AI use is only 3 times higher. This gap reflects a lower readiness among firms and people in developing countries to adopt AI in a productive manner, even for a given level of exposure to AI use.

Box 4.2 Measuring AI exposure: How amenable are jobs to AI use?

Researchers have created a number of measures of exposure to artificial intelligence (AI) to assess how relevant AI is for specific occupations. These measures generally follow a task-based approach, treating occupations as a series of tasks, with different degrees of potential for AI to perform these tasks. The measures are typically constructed using data sets such as O*NET or International Standard Classification of Occupations (ISCO) databases to identify tasks within occupations, followed by an assessment—for example, by human experts or large language models—of the extent to which each task can be performed or aided by AI. These measures are then aggregated at the occupational level.

Three common measures are those developed by Eloundou et al. (2024), Felten et al. (2023), and Gmyrek et al. (2023) and further refined by Gmyrek et al. (2025). Felten et al. (2023) use O*NET worker abilities and map these abilities to 10 AI application areas as measured by the Electronic Frontier Foundation to measure the overlap between AI capabilities and worker abilities. Eloundou et al. (2024) use O*NET worker tasks and deploy a scoring approach by both humans and AI to evaluate whether large language models can perform a task as well as a human in less than half the time. Gmyrek et al. (2025) use Poland's task-to-occupation mapping, surveys, and expert analysis to evaluate whether tasks can be performed by AI, and construct a global index of exposure. Although these approaches differ in terms of data sources and the ways in which they determine the applicability of AI at the task level, the resulting measures are highly correlated with one another (refer to figure B4.2.1).

The use of AI exposure metrics to understand labor market impacts is limited in important ways. First, exposure to AI neither equals actual use nor accounts for constraints in adopting the technology.[a] Second, these measures rely on static descriptions of current tasks.[b] As AI evolves, more tasks and therefore more occupations could be exposed to AI. Third, the measures involve some degree of subjective judgment (whether by experts or an AI tool) and may therefore suffer from measurement error.[c] Finally, the adoption of AI can create new tasks and occupations that are not captured by the exposure measures.

(Box continues next page)

Box 4.2 Measuring AI exposure: How amenable are jobs to AI use? *(continued)*

Figure B4.2.1 Most AI exposure measures are constructed similarly and are highly correlated with one another

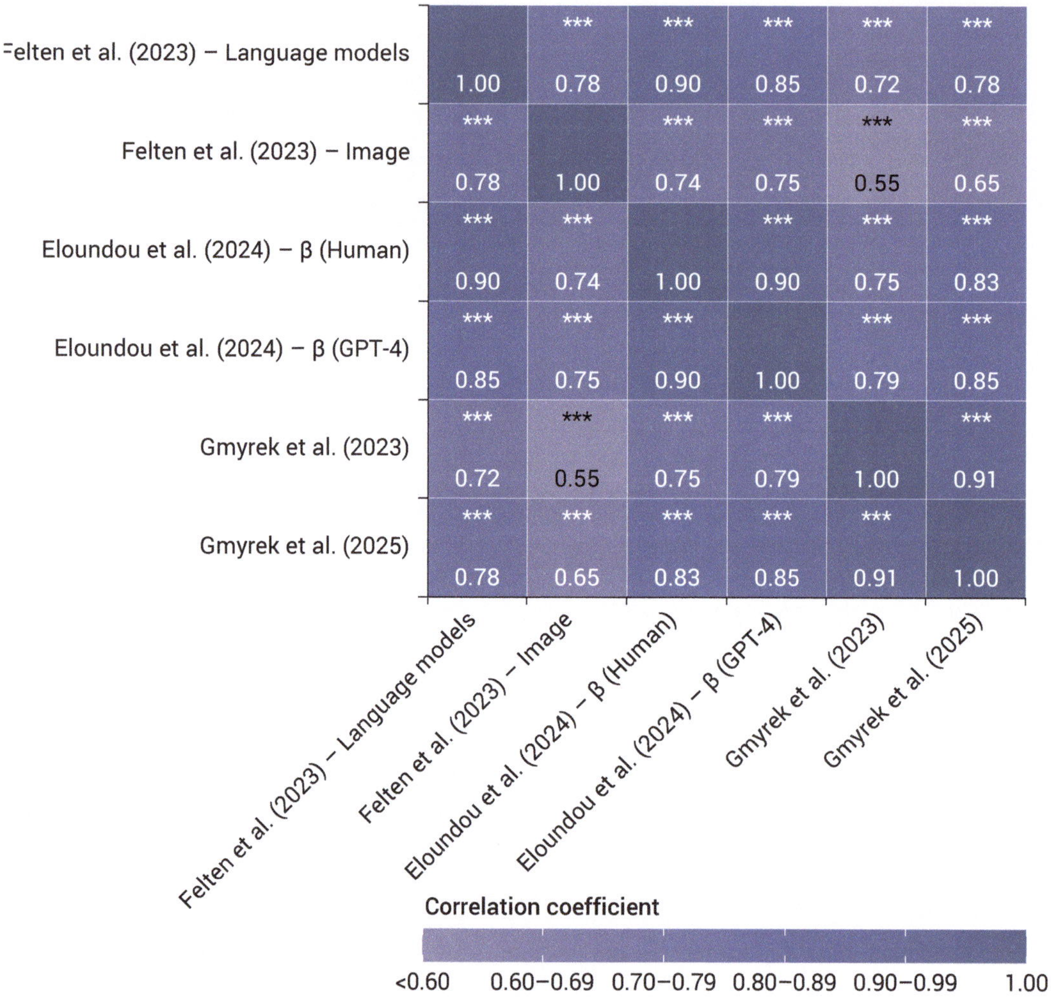

Source: WDR 2026 team, based on Eloundou et al. 2024; Felten et al. 2023; Gmyrek et al. 2023, 2025.

Note: The cells show the correlations between pairs of exposure measures. *Image* stands for the index that focuses on image recognition. *Human* stands for the index that relies on human judgment. AI = artificial intelligence; GPT = general-purpose technology.

***$p < .001$.

Source: WDR 2026 team.

a. Liu, Wang, et al. (2025); Pizzinelli et al. (2023).

b. Merola et al. (2026).

c. Yin et al. (2026).

More sophisticated uses of AI, such as using AI agents or deploying AI to automate workflows, also remain lower in developing countries (10 percent, on average, across India, Jordan, Kenya, Mexico, Nigeria, and Thailand) than in the United States (24 percent). A comprehensive measure of AI sophistication—which also takes into account the type of tasks and business functions AI is used for as well as whether the technology is sourced internally—suggests a similar large gap in AI sophistication between the United States and the surveyed low- and middle-income countries (refer to figure 4.4). These findings reflect earlier evidence on the use and adoption of technologies, highlighting that although many firms in low- and middle-income countries have access to technologies and have started using them, they deploy them less intensively than firms in high-income countries.[21]

Figure 4.4 Gaps are wider for more complex types of AI adoption and between smaller and larger firms

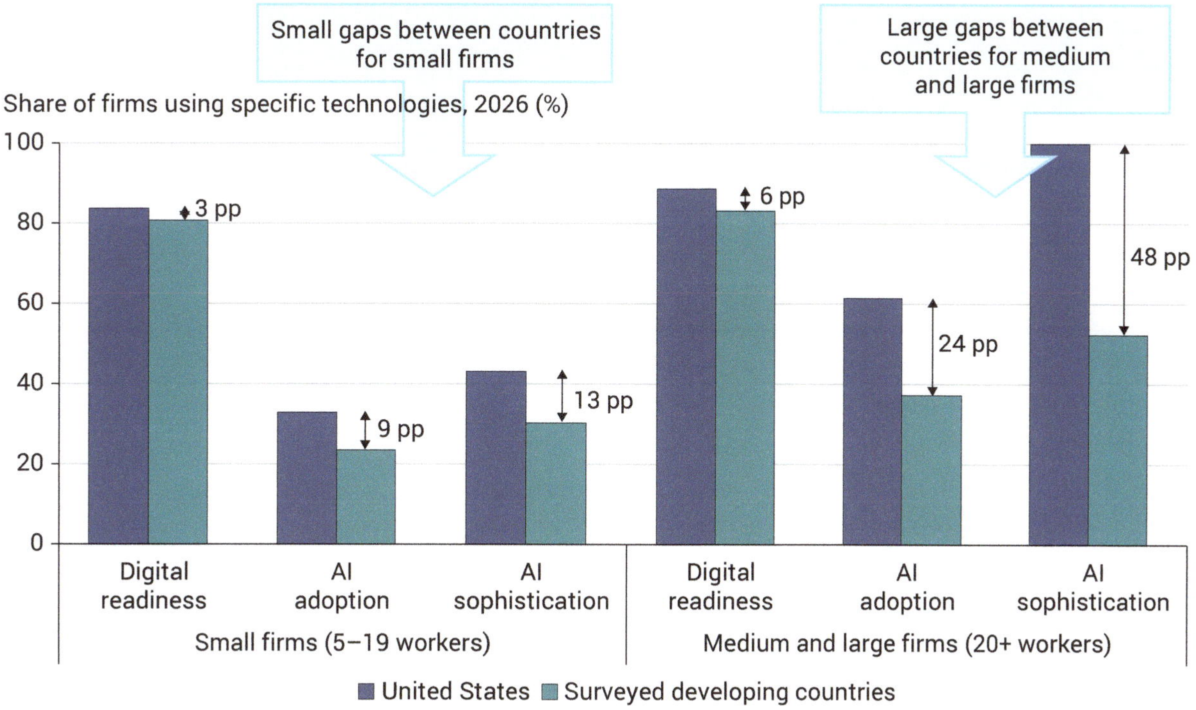

Source: WDR 2026 team, based on World Bank Enterprise Survey on AI Adoption.

Note: The figure reports data on formal firms in manufacturing, construction, and services with five or more employees. *Digital readiness* is the average of (a) the share of firms with a website, (b) the share of firms using text messenger apps, and (c) the share of firms using standardized software for business administration (such as spreadsheets). *AI adoption* is the share of firms that adopted any AI technology. *AI sophistication* is an index relative to large firms in the United States (= 100) consisting of (a) whether a firm has adopted any AI technology; (b) whether a firm, among AI technologies, adopts AI agents, AI process automation, or AI-driven robotics; (c) whether a firm uses them for more advanced tasks (such as coding) or for multiple business functions; and (d) whether a solution is customized (either internally or externally). The data for surveyed developing countries average country-level indicators, with equal weight for each country. The samples are India (1,355 firms), Jordan (358), Kenya (360), Mexico (603), Nigeria (777), Thailand (360), United States (392). Microdata are available at Enterprise Surveys (data portal), World Bank, https://www.enterprisesurveys.org/en/data. AI = artificial intelligence; GenAI = generative artificial intelligence; pp = percentage points.

Constraints within and outside the firm hold back businesses in developing countries from adopting AI

Complementary factors matter for firms' adoption of AI, driven by factors within and outside the firm. Evidence from surveys suggests that firms with stronger management capabilities (as measured by the adoption of structured managerial practices),[22] better market access (as measured by export status),[23] greater innovation activity (as measured by past product or process innovation as well as spending on research and development, R & D),[24] and higher labor productivity tend to report higher AI adoption as well as higher AI sophistication (refer to figure 4.5). For example, a firm that ranks above the median in terms of the adoption of managerial practices is 17 percent more likely to adopt an AI technology than a firm ranking below the median. Similarly, a 1 percent increase in labor productivity is associated with a 1.2 percent increase in the likelihood that the firm will adopt AI. These findings reinforce earlier evidence that firms that were more technologically sophisticated before AI use took off—in terms of their adoption of complementary technologies like cloud computing—have adopted GenAI at much higher rates than less technologically sophisticated firms.[25]

Another important complementary factor is business dynamism that supports the entry of new firms and growth of productive firms. Evidence on innovation around earlier technologies suggests that entrants and incumbents innovate differently. Entrants focus more on creating new products and services, while incumbent firms improve internal processes.[26] It is important for countries to pursue policies that enable high-growth entrepreneurship and create market conditions conducive to the growth of productive firms.[27] Foreign direct investment by multinational companies can also be leveraged to support business dynamism and technology adoption. Multinational companies are more likely to adopt AI technologies than domestic firms and diffuse this technology through their subsidiaries.[28]

Uneven AI adoption could widen productivity gaps between and within countries

AI is generating sizable productivity gains at the task level

The skewed pattern of AI adoption, both between and within countries, is likely to result in a productivity divergence between countries and within them. This is particularly the case because productivity gains at the task level can be significant. Various empirical studies evaluating the causal impacts of using AI tools on productivity for specific tasks have found gains ranging from about 6 to 88 percent, with the highest effects for coding (refer to table 4.1).[29]

Firm and economywide productivity gains from AI are projected to be higher in high-income countries

Although gains at the task level do not necessarily scale up directly to the firm level, emerging empirical evidence has found positive impacts of AI on firm-level productivity in advanced economies. A survey of 750 chief financial officers in the United States finds implied annual gains in revenue-based labor productivity from AI of 0.8 percentage points in high-skill services and finance in 2025.[30] Likewise, evidence from 12,000 European firms shows that AI adoption increased labor productivity by 4 percent on average across the European Union from 2019 to 2024.[31] A recent study of the US nonfarm business sector shows that labor productivity was 2.2 percent higher in 2026 than the January 2020 forecast due to AI.[32]

Figure 4.5 **Firm capabilities, preexisting innovation behavior, market access, and productivity all predict AI adoption and more sophisticated use of AI**

Regression coefficient on the adoption of AI technologies

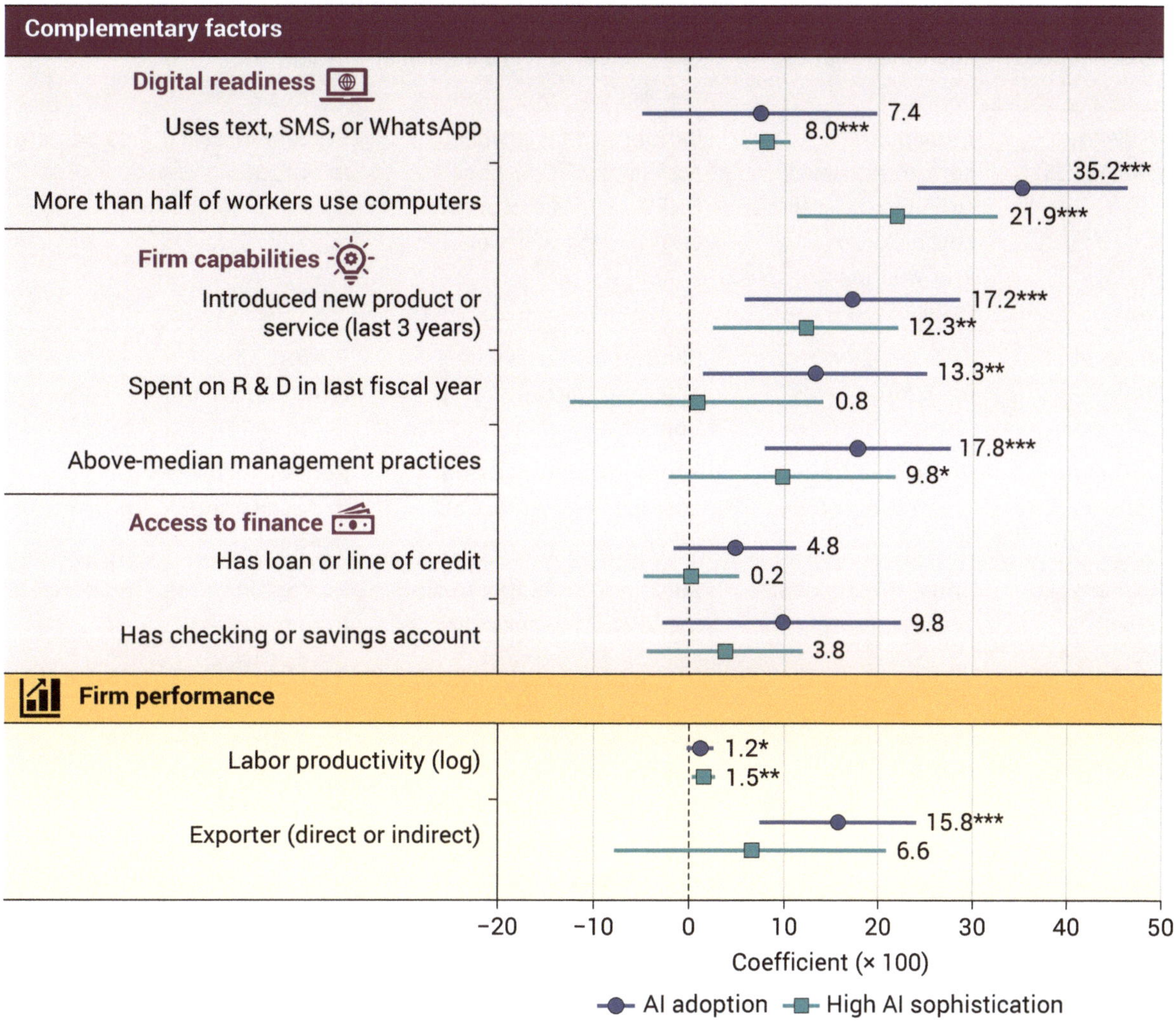

Source: WDR 2026 team, based on World Bank Enterprise Survey on AI Adoption; Davies et al. 2026.

Note: The figure presents regression coefficients (from a linear probability model) on the adoption of any AI technology, controlling for country and sector (with dummy variables), multiplied by 100. Each row corresponds to a separate regression (a regression of the predictor variable with controls). *AI adoption* refers to the adoption of any AI technology. *High AI sophistication* refers to whether a firm belongs to the top 10 percent of firms with the highest score with respect to AI sophistication, a composite measure based on (a) whether a firm has adopted any AI technology; (b) whether a firm, among AI technologies, adopts AI agents, AI process automation, or AI-driven robotics; (c) whether a firm uses them for more advanced tasks (such as coding) or for multiple business functions; and (d) whether a solution is customized (either internally or externally). Sampling weights have been applied such that each country's sum of weights equals 1. The results cover formal firms with five or more employees, pooling data across six surveyed developing countries (the United States is not included) in 2026. The samples are India (1,355 firms), Jordan (358), Kenya (360), Mexico (603), Nigeria (777), Thailand (360). Microdata are available at Enterprise Surveys (data portal), World Bank, https://www.enterprisesurveys.org/en/data. AI = artificial intelligence; R & D = research and development; SMS = short messaging service [text]. Standard errors are clustered at the strata level.

$*p < .10$ $**p < .05$ $***p < .01$.

Table 4.1 AI raises labor productivity across a wide range of white-collar tasks

Paper	Occupations and tasks	Methodology	Outcome measure	Result
Brynjolfsson, Li, et al. (2025)	Customer care agent/ customer support	Randomized trial using GPT-based conversational assistant	Percent increase in output	15 percent
Dell'Acqua et al. (2023)	Individual contributor-level consultants/realistic, complex, and knowledge-intensive tasks	Randomized trials using access to GPT-4 AI or GPT-4 AI with a prompt engineering overview	Percent increase in output	39 percent
Dillon et al. (2025)	Knowledge workers in 66 large firms	Randomized trial using access to Microsoft 365 Copilot	Percent time saved on email	12 percent
Doshi and Hauser (2024)	Writers/writing creative outputs	Randomized trial using access to GenAI tool at varying levels	Percent increase in novelty and usefulness	6–7 percent
Kalliamvakou (2024)	Software engineers/ programming	Survey of developers using the SPACE framework[a] to evaluate perceived productivity	Percent increase in perceived productivity	88 percent
Kanazawa et al. (2022)	Low-skill taxi drivers/ driving	Quasi-experimental design with fixed effects and instrumental variable analysis studying the use of AI navigation system	Productivity gap between high- and low-skill drivers	14 percent lower gap
Noy and Zhang (2023)	Range of white-collar occupations/simple writing tasks	Randomized trial using access to ChatGPT 3.5	Percent time saved per task	40 percent
Peng et al. (2023)	Software developers/ programming	Randomized trials using access to GitHub Copilot	Percent time saved per task	56 percent
Schoenegger et al. (2025)	Data forecasters (economists)/fore-casting quantified data for future events	Randomized trial in which treatment group uses frontier LLMs for forecasting	Percent improvement in prediction accuracy	24–28 percent

Source: WDR 2026 team, based on Bergeaud 2024; Filippucci et al. 2026.

Note: The table summarizes micro-level studies on the productivity impacts of generative AI tools. AI = artificial intelligence; GenAI = generative AI; GPT = general-purpose technology; LLMs = large language models; SPACE = Satisfaction, Performance, Activity, Communications and collaboration, Efficiency and flow.

a. For more on the SPACE framework, refer to Forsgren et al. (2021).

Empirical evidence on the economywide productivity gains from AI is more limited, even for high-income countries. A key approach pioneered by Acemoglu (2024) to measure aggregate productivity gains combines task-level productivity effects with the share of affected tasks in GDP. In the United States, AI adoption is estimated to provide a cumulative gain in total factor productivity (TFP) of only 0.66 percent over the next decade.[33] Other studies that use a similar approach find higher productivity gains across high-income countries under more optimistic assumptions.[34] Extending this approach to 52 countries shows that the expected productivity gains in advanced economies are more than double than in emerging market and developing economies (EMDEs) due to the higher AI exposure rates and current AI adoption rates in advanced economies (refer to figure 4.6, panel a).[35]

For advanced economies, this translates into a sizable boost to potential growth. During the 2020s, AI could increase the average annual projected potential growth rate for advanced economies from 1.2 percent to 3 percent in the most optimistic scenario (refer to figure 4.6, panel b). For EMDEs, the boost to growth is more modest, albeit still economically meaningful; AI could increase the average annual projected potential growth rate from 4.1 percent to 4.8 percent during the 2020s in the most optimistic scenario. The lower expected productivity gains in EMDEs are explained by currently lower AI adoption rates and already-higher potential growth.

Productivity gains are also concentrated in frontier industries and firms

Productivity gains are also expected to be highly concentrated in a small number of industries. Thus, the type and extent of economywide impacts will depend on patterns of structural transformation as economies adjust.[36] The projected gains mentioned assume that rates of AI adoption are even across industries. In reality, available evidence on AI adoption shows substantial variation across industries, as reported by the World Bank Enterprise Survey on AI Adoption. AI adoption has been highest in

Figure 4.6 AI's impact on productivity is expected to be much lower in emerging market and developing economies than in advanced economies, if current levels of AI exposure and adoption stay the same

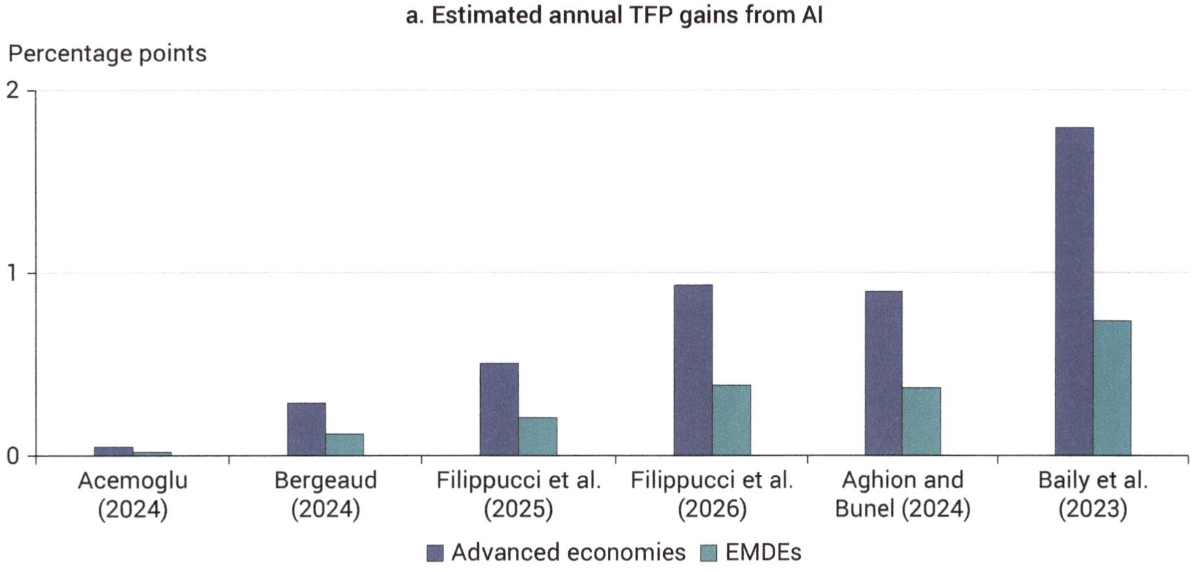

(Figure continues next page)

Figure 4.6 AI's impact on productivity is expected to be much lower in emerging market and developing economies than in advanced economies, if current levels of AI exposure and adoption stay the same *(continued)*

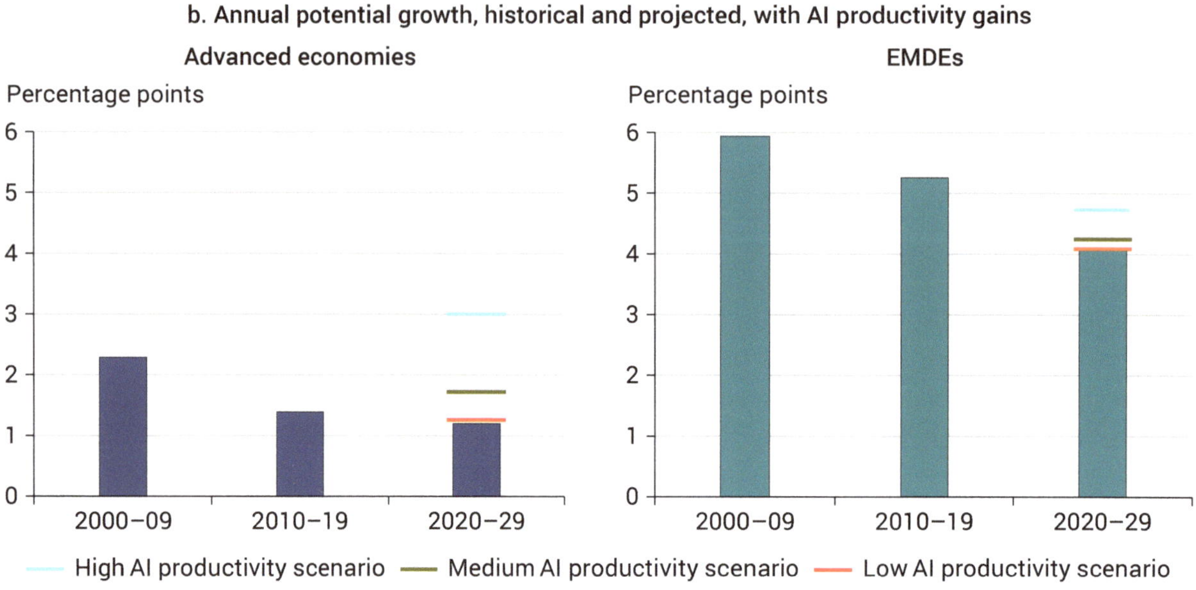

Source: WDR 2026 team, based on Acemoglu 2024; Aghion and Bunel 2024; Baily et al. 2023; Bergeaud 2024; Filippucci et al. 2025; Filippucci et al. 2026; Kose and Stamm 2026.

Note: Panel a: These measures extend the methodology of Acemoglu (2024) to 52 countries with available data by using the same occupational exposure scores and task productivity gains, but scaling the exposure scores using each country's occupation and industry wage bill composition and scaling the AI adoption measure using Anthropic's per capita usage index. The scaling of the various measures in the other studies to the country income groups assumes a constant ratio between productivity estimates, as seen in the United States. Given the lack of data on AI adoption for China, China's value is imputed as the upper-middle-income country average. Panel b: The potential growth estimates follow the methodology in Kose and Stamm (2026); the high AI scenario uses the Baily et al. (2023) estimate, the medium AI scenario uses the Filipucci et al. (2025) estimate, and the low AI scenario uses the Acemoglu (2024) estimate, for each income group. AI = artificial intelligence; EMDEs = emerging market and developing economies; TFP = total factor productivity.

information and communication technology (ICT) services and professional services. If these patterns of concentration persist, AI will likely increase productivity significantly only in a subset of economic activities, while leaving others relatively unaffected. This uneven pattern would be similar to the patterns observed in the ICT boom, when productivity gains were highly concentrated.

Within low- and middle-income countries, available evidence suggests that productivity gains are accruing disproportionately to a select group of firms. For example, in China, studies have found positive impacts of AI on firm productivity,[37] but effects have been shown to be stronger for large firms, firms with higher TFP, and firms in provinces with a larger exporting sector than other parts of China.[38] The earlier-mentioned AI-powered business mentor chatbot for small businesses in Kenya improved the performance of businesses that were already doing well before they adopted AI but lowered performance for businesses that fared worse before adoption. A main reason for this result is that small business owners with fewer business skills, and thus lower performance, were more likely to adopt "generic" advice given by the chatbot, even if that advice was not appropriate for their business, while high performers interacted with the chatbot to gather more tailored advice, which they subsequently implemented more successfully.[39] These findings underscore the critical role of complementary factors in shaping the productivity benefits of AI, both at the firm level and in the overall economy.[40]

Concentrated adoption is resulting in concentrated disruption in labor markets

Lower AI adoption in developing countries is resulting in lower job displacement effects

Lower AI adoption in low- and middle-income countries is leading to lower job losses (less labor market disruption), but also fewer job gains than in high-income countries. This dynamic effectively places an upper limit on opportunity for AI in developing countries, evidence suggests. As discussed, the net impacts of AI on labor markets are complex; both job displacement effects and job creation effects, as well as many indirect impact mechanisms, influence labor demand. Reflecting this complexity, the net impacts of AI on labor demand in advanced economies remain the subject of vigorous debate; evidence from existing studies is inconclusive. Nevertheless, several studies have documented concentrated job displacement effects for certain groups of workers, such as entry-level college-educated workers, software developers, and those working in occupations like clerical work, in which AI can readily substitute for work and workers.[41]

Evidence for low- and middle-income countries is more limited but suggests that displacement effects are lower there on average than in advanced economies, consistent with theory and findings that lower AI adoption is causing less labor market restructuring. For example, a study of the evolution of online job postings for roles that can be more easily substituted with AI found that GenAI had strong job displacement effects in high-income countries, on average, during the period after ChatGPT was released, but much smaller and statistically nonsignificant effects in low- and middle-income countries (refer to figure 4.7).[42] So far, evidence indicates, the lack of AI adoption and the absence of underlying enablers favoring adoption have lessened the displacement effects in low- and middle-income countries. Nevertheless, these findings do not rule out displacement effects in other segments of the economy, nor do they suggest such effects will remain subdued over the long term in low- and middle-income countries. The displacement effects may be concentrated in specific sectors and intensify over time, as AI continues to automate a broader range of tasks and adoption accelerates within and across developing countries. Lastly, conclusions in this area must remain tentative, given that available data are not fully representative of low- and middle-income countries.

Figure 4.7 The job displacement effect from ChatGPT has been much stronger in high-income countries than in low- and middle-income countries

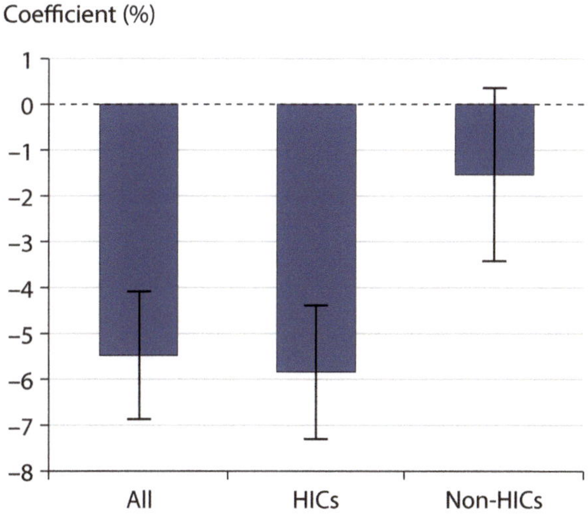

Sources: WDR 2026 team calculations; Huang et al. 2026.

Note: The effect of ChatGPT on job postings serves as a proxy for job displacement. The sample covers 84 economies (42 high-income countries, HICs) between 2021 and 2025. The bars show the estimated coefficients. Whiskers show the 90 percent confidence intervals. Non-HICs include low-income countries, lower-middle-income countries, and upper-middle-income countries.

Small and concentrated job losses may still have outsized importance in developing-country contexts

Although job losses in low- and middle-income countries may be more limited in aggregate than those in high-income countries, some concentrated displacement effects have occurred in high-skill services such as business processing outsourcing and the ICT services sector and in countries with higher AI adoption rates. A study of online job postings data from 2018 to 2024 found nontrivial displacement effects of GenAI in China, with disproportionate impacts on entry-level jobs, high-wage positions, and highly educated workers, particularly in larger and more economically advanced cities.[43] In South Asia, emerging evidence indicates that GenAI has already reduced monthly job listings by about 20 percent for the most exposed white-collar occupations that have ready substitutes [44] (refer to box 4.3).

Although concentrated, these job displacement effects are especially important in contexts in which few high-quality jobs are being created. In many low- and middle-income countries, higher-skill services sectors have been an important sector of growth in both value added and employment. For example, in Kenya, highly exposed knowledge-intensive services like ICT, professional services, and finance contributed to only 2 percent of jobs but to 19 percent of growth between 2006 and 2019.[45] Parts of the Middle East, North Africa, Afghanistan, and Pakistan (MENAAP) region are especially vulnerable. Some countries in the region have the world's highest youth unemployment rates—exceeding 25–30 percent. Unemployment is concentrated in educated young populations entering labor markets in which creation of jobs in the formal private sector is already limited. The implications of job displacement from AI could be substantial in countries like the Arab Republic of Egypt, Jordan, and Morocco, which have positioned themselves as regional service export hubs.

Overall, in low- and middle-income countries, from 2012 to 2023, employment shares increased in sectors with the highest AI exposure—even though these sectors are small. Meanwhile, employment shares declined in the sectors with the lowest AI exposure (refer to figure 4.8).

Box 4.3 GenAI is already affecting jobs in South Asia by reshaping global value chains

Data about job postings from firms in South Asia suggest that generative artificial intelligence (GenAI) is already reshaping jobs, with effects more pronounced among globally connected firms. Since 2022, South Asian firms have increased AI adoption markedly—measured by the share of job postings requiring AI skills (refer to figure B4.3.1, panel a). The introduction of GenAI has caused a measurable slowdown in hiring among South Asian firms. Job postings declined by 1.6 percent after ChatGPT was released in November 2022 (refer to figure B4.3.1, panel b). These effects are larger among more globally connected firms. The differences are consistent with a general pattern in which reshoring or labor substitution effects are stronger among firms that have greater flexibility to relocate production.[a] Multinational firms face few frictions in shifting automated tasks across borders, and suppliers of global value chains may experience some reshoring pressures, albeit to a lesser extent than other firms. The slowdown in hiring is lower among local firms. This pattern may also reflect their slower adoption of AI.

(Box continues next page)

Box 4.3 GenAI is already affecting jobs in South Asia by reshaping global value chains *(continued)*

Figure B4.3.1 GenAI is reshaping jobs in South Asia, especially among globally connected firms

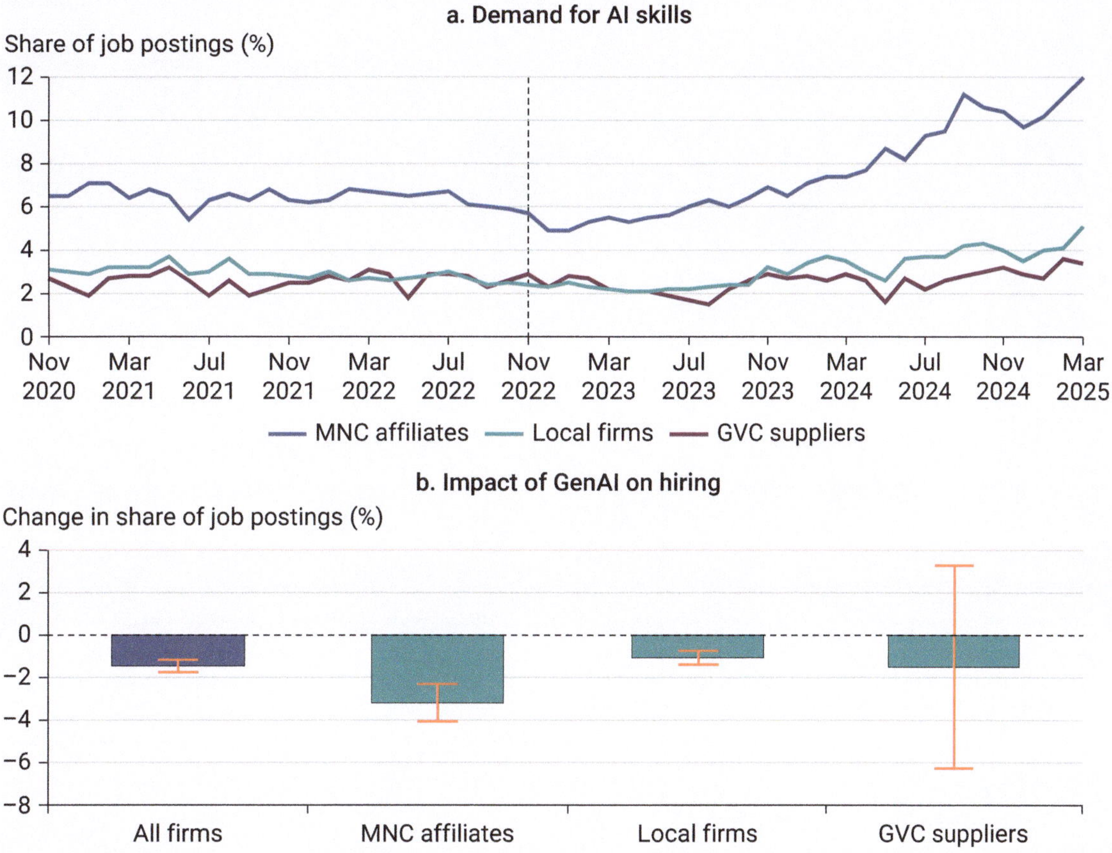

Sources: WDR 2026 team, based on 2003–25 data of FactSet Fundamentals (dashboard), FactSet Research Systems, https://www.factset.com/marketplace/catalog/product/factset-fundamentals; Felten et al. 2023; 2020–25 data of Lightcast Data (dashboard), Lightcast, https://lightcast.io/products/data/overview; World Bank 2025.

Note: Panel a: The plotted lines show the share of job postings requiring skills in AI. The dotted vertical line indicates the release of ChatGPT in November 2022. Panel b: Bars show the percent change in job postings before and after ChatGPT was released, corresponding to an interquartile range increase in AI exposure. Whiskers show the 95 percent confidence intervals from standard errors clustered at the firm level. The sample includes 196,202 firms with hiring data previous to the ChatGPT release. *MNC [multinational company] affiliates* are defined as multinational firms headquartered outside of South Asia, but operating foreign affiliates within South Asia. *Local firms* are businesses headquartered in South Asia without any foreign customers. *GVC [global value chain] suppliers* are firms that had international customers before the ChatGPT release. AI = artificial intelligence; GenAI = generative artificial intelligence.

Source: WDR 2026 team, based on World Bank 2025.

a. *Labor substitution effects* refer to the reduced demand for routine labor-intensive inputs that can be automated by GenAI.

Figure 4.8 Employment in developing countries has increased in sectors with the highest AI exposure

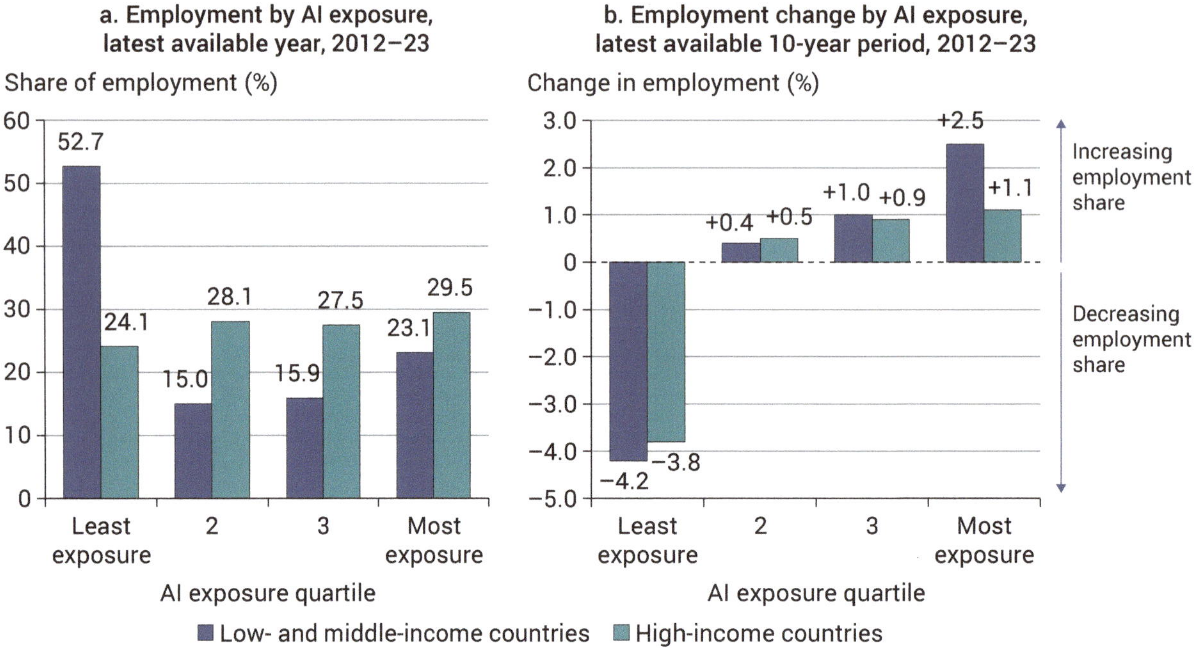

Sources: WDR 2026 team, based on Gmyrek, Viollaz, et al. 2026; 2026 data of ILOSTAT (dashboard), International Labour Organization, https://ilostat.ilo.org/.

Note: Artificial intelligence (AI) exposure levels are derived at the task level, aggregated at 2-digit International Standard Industrial Classification (ISIC) rev. 4 economic activities, based on Gmyrek, Viollaz, et al. (2026). Employment shares and employment share changes are based on country-level employment data at the 2-digit ISIC rev. 4 economic activity level from 2026 data of ILOSTAT. Quartiles are based on the average sectoral AI exposure levels in low- and middle-income countries. Employment share changes are based on the two most recent years with suitable sectoral employment data and scaled to 10-year employment change levels.

Lower AI sophistication also limits opportunities for job creation

At the same time, the creation of new skills, tasks, and occupations from AI is lower in low- and middle-income countries. New skills include AI-user skills (such as integrating GenAI applications like ChatGPT, GitHub Copilot, and DALL·E image generator into work processes), as well as AI-developer skills (such as competencies related to building and deploying AI models like Python for machine learning). Entire occupations have also emerged in response to AI, such as senior AI executives and LLM engineers.

The share of online job postings mentioning AI skills surged after 2023, following the public release of ChatGPT in late 2022, data from online job postings globally show. The share of jobs demanding AI skills was more than five times higher in high-income countries than in middle-income countries in the first half of 2025 (refer to figure 4.9, panel a). Among middle-income countries, larger upper-middle-income countries predominate, with India, Argentina, Brazil, and Colombia topping the list. Three occupations—software developers, systems analysts, and web developers—collectively accounted for 40 percent of these jobs in 2024

Figure 4.9 Demand for new AI-related skills and jobs has surged since 2023 but remains highly concentrated in a small number of advanced countries and high-skill occupations

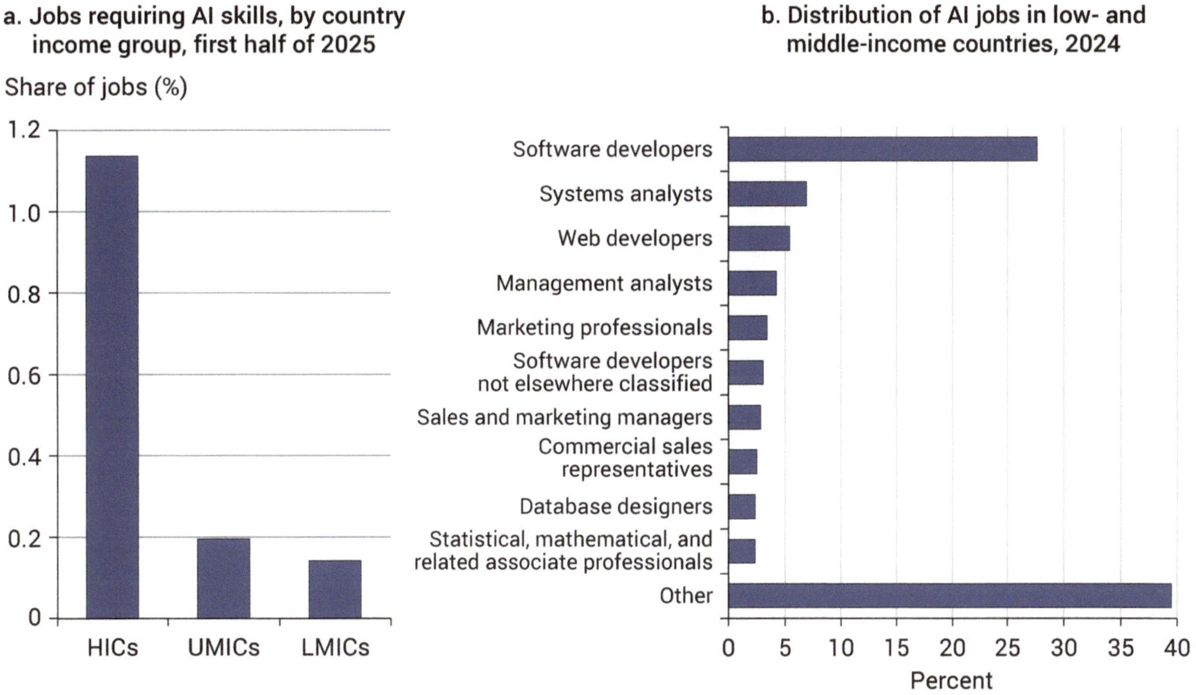

Source: WDR 2026 team, based on analysis and data of Lightcast Data (dashboard), Lightcast, https://lightcast.io/products/data/overview, covering more than 100 countries globally.

Note: Shares are weighted by the ratio of job postings to wage and salaried workers in each country to adjust for sample biases in low- and middle-income countries. AI = artificial intelligence; HICs = high-income countries; LMICs = lower-middle-income countries; UMICs = upper-middle-income countries.

(refer to figure 4.9, panel b).[46] Other major occupations include management analysts, marketing professionals, and sales and marketing managers.

Lower job creation effects from AI in low- and middle-income countries could reflect barriers to entry and limited competition (market contestability). AI-related roles tend to require advanced education in science, technology, engineering, and mathematics (STEM) fields; they also command a high wage premium, constraining hiring firms' budgets. These factors limit the pool of workers who can occupy them. Firms posting vacancies with new skills are also typically larger, younger, more innovative, less financially constrained, and more productive.[47] Job creation from AI also reflects firm-level and industry-level innovation, industry expansion, and the creation of new firms, along with the extent to which AI-enabled productivity gains lead businesses to grow. That expansion is not automatic. It requires contestable (competitive) markets, efficient reallocation, disciplined incumbents, and policies that reward firms for creating value. Many of these conditions are limited in low- and middle-income countries.

AI as an output: The AI value chain is creating growth opportunities in developing countries, but only a few firms are capturing value

Participation in the AI value chain is becoming a major source of investment and job creation in certain low- and middle-income countries even where AI adoption is modest. With the value chain spanning from commodities to manufacturing and services, the opportunities for participation are broad. Nevertheless, the value capture within the AI value chain remains highly concentrated in a small number of firms—although this pattern of concentration is likely to change as the technology matures. There is a substantial overlap between the countries experiencing the largest economic gains from the expansion of the AI value chain and those with the highest levels of AI adoption. This section explores how developing countries are participating in the AI value chain and how this participation—or lack of participation—is affecting jobs and growth.

The AI value chain offers opportunities spanning the manufacturing, services, and commodities sectors

As chapter 2 discussed, the AI value chain involves several segments including raw materials, manufacturing of electronics and semiconductors, data centers, cloud computing, and development of AI models. The AI value chain therefore affects a wider range of types of workers than those exposed to AI, including more low- and medium-skill workers in manufacturing, mining, and construction industries, as well as white-collar services industries such as software development.

The share of AI-enabling goods, as defined by the World Trade Organization (WTO), in world trade increased from about 13 percent in 2023 to nearly 17 percent by the end of 2025, driven by rising investment in the semiconductor supply chain, electronics, and data center inputs. Low- and middle-income countries accounted for about one-third of the export value of these goods, with a nearly equal split between lower- and upper-middle-income countries (refer to figure 4.10, panel a). Under a narrower definition of AI-enabling products by the US Federal Reserve, analysis for this Report finds that the share of AI-related exports from low- and middle-income countries is slightly higher (39 percent).[48] When the semiconductor supply chain is examined specifically using the definition of the Organisation for Economic Co-operation and Development (OECD), analysis for this Report estimates that just over one-third of the exports of products within the supply chain are from low- and middle-income countries.[49] China, Mexico, Malaysia, Viet Nam, and Thailand, in that order, led the list of developing countries with the highest value of exports of AI-enabling products in 2025.

Investment in AI infrastructure in low- and middle-income countries is also growing rapidly. Data centers accounted for more than one-fifth of global investment in greenfield projects in 2025, making them among the largest recipients of new, from-scratch foreign investment worldwide.[50] Although the leading recipients have been advanced economies, several middle-income countries are in the top 10 countries worldwide in terms of data center investment inflows, including Brazil, Thailand, India, and Malaysia. These investments are becoming an important source of foreign exchange and growth in these countries, even though the potential of data centers to create jobs remains a subject for debate and data centers have negative environmental externalities in terms of the water, power, and other resources they require (refer to spotlight 4).

Figure 4.10 As the AI value chain expands, exports and start-up activity are growing in low- and middle-income countries

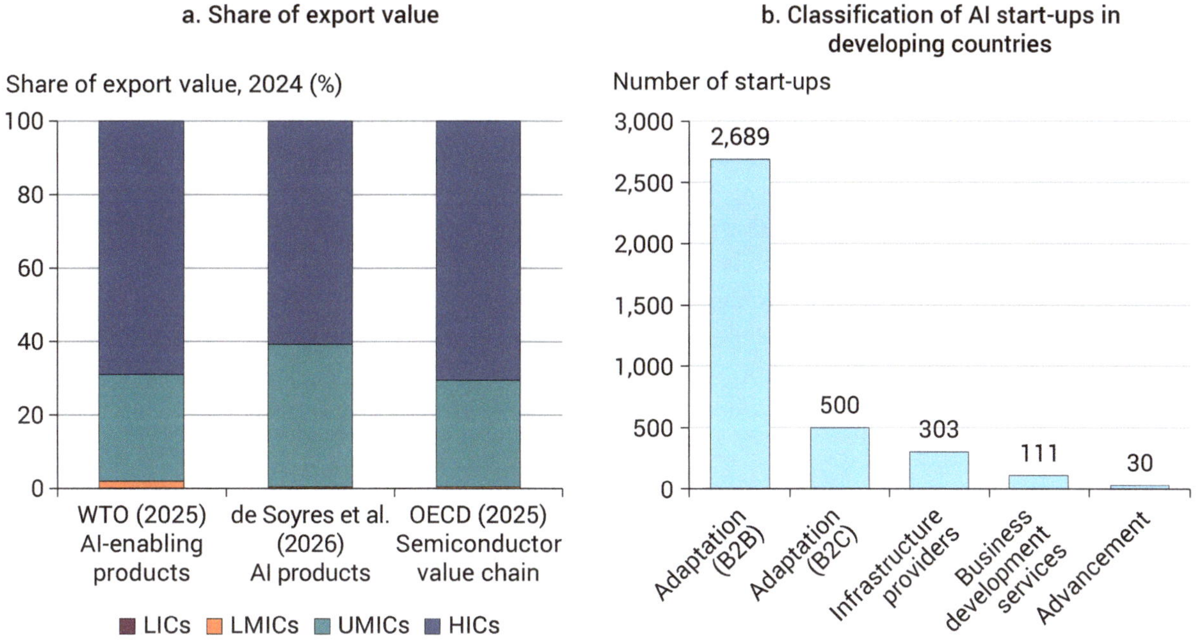

Source: WDR 2026 team, based on 2024 data of Digital Business Indicators (database), World Bank, https://www.worldbank.org/en/research/brief/digital-business-indicators; trade data of UN Comtrade Database (United Nations Commodity Trade Statistics Database), Statistics Division, Department of Economic and Social Affairs, United Nations, https://comtradeplus.un.org/; Zhu et al. 2022.

Note: Panel b shows the number of start-ups classified using a large language model based on descriptions of about 3,600 AI-related businesses in low- and middle-income countries. AI = artificial intelligence; B2B = business to business; B2C = business to customers; HICs = high-income countries; LICs = low-income countries; LMICs = lower-middle-income countries; OECD = Organisation for Economic Co-operation and Development; UMICs = upper-middle-income countries; WTO = World Trade Organization.

Data scraped from online job vacancies offer some insights into job creation along the AI value chain. The share of job postings along the AI value chain that are in medium-skill segments is higher in low- and middle-income countries—excluding China—than in high-income countries. For example, a higher share of jobs are in data entry and analysis and telecommunications, and a lower share are in cloud computing and AI development.

Growth in AI start-ups as application developers has been rapid in developing countries

Start-ups focusing on developing AI applications are also growing in low- and middle-income countries. Most of these firms focus on adapting existing technologies to build solutions that can be adopted by other businesses (72 percent) or by consumers (12 percent) (refer to figure 4.10, panel b), analysis of business descriptions of more than 3,600 AI-related start-ups in developing countries suggests. Many of these businesses build solutions targeting nondigital sectors, such as health, business management, security, finance, and education, as well as mobility services such as ride-sharing. Very few start-ups (less than 1 percent) report focusing on activities to advance AI, such as building foundational models. Another group of start-ups focuses on providing services for the wider business ecosystem, including business development services (3 percent) and providing infrastructure services (10 percent), such as data centers or producing computer components.

Although participation in AI value chains is dispersed, value creation is concentrated and overlaps with patterns of AI adoption

Although the expansion of the AI value chain is having different effects on different industries and worker groups, value creation remains highly concentrated. There is a substantial overlap between the countries with the highest rates of AI adoption and the highest revenues from the AI value chain. AI adoption rates are highest in white-collar services industries. Relatedly, the highest value added segments of the AI value chain (such as chip design) use capital, R & D, and specialized advanced skills very intensively and therefore are concentrated in a select few countries specialized in advanced manufacturing, as discussed in chapter 3. For example, of the 20 countries with the highest adoption rates of ChatGPT (measured as the number of ChatGPT users per internet user), 8 were also in the top 20 countries in terms of exports of AI-enabling products as of 2024 (refer to figure 4.11).

Figure 4.11 There is a big overlap between countries with high levels of both AI adoption and exports in the AI value chain

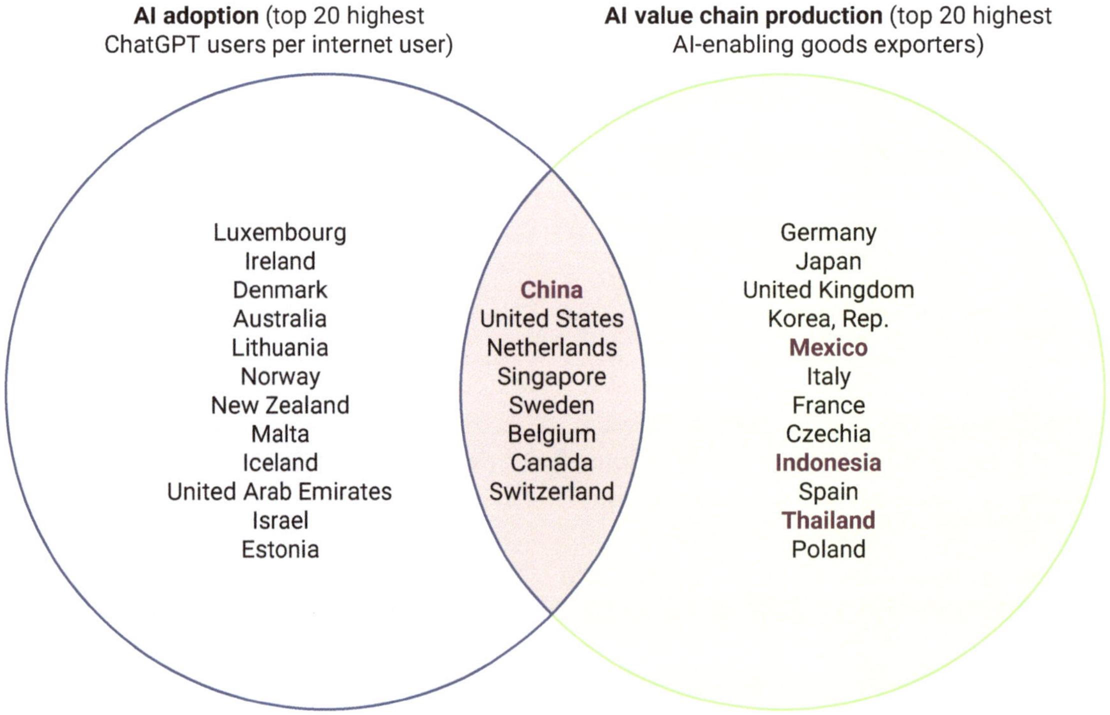

Source: WDR 2026 team calculations, based on data of Liu, Huang, et al. 2025; UN Comtrade Database (United Nations Commodity Trade Statistics Database), Statistics Division, Department of Economic and Social Affairs, United Nations, https://comtradeplus.un.org/.

Note: Low- and middle-income countries appear in red. China's value of ChatGPT users is imputed as 53 percent based upon estimates of China's adoption of other AI platforms given the low market share of ChatGPT in China. AI = artificial intelligence.

Cascading impacts: AI is also having indirect ripple effects across sectors and countries

The adoption of AI as an input and the production of AI as an output have a wide range of knock-on effects on prices, incomes, asset markets, and transaction costs. They are also changing the relative returns to capital and labor and altering patterns of trade. These impacts, in turn, are reallocating workers and capital across firms, sectors, and countries, with complex and uncertain effects.

AI-related investments are having immediate multiplier effects

The adoption of AI is expected to expand the availability and improve the quality of important services, such as education and health care, that can deliver benefits for the wider economy. There is growing evidence that this is happening in low- and middle-income countries in certain services (such as personalized tutoring, support for medical decision-making, and optimization of legal resources) for which the main obstacle (binding constraint) has historically been the cost of expert human time. This process is likely raising real incomes and welfare, which in turn could increase demand for other goods and services. The full extent of these impacts, however, has not been measured yet.

Large stimulus impacts are also occurring through capital expenditures that finance the adoption and production of AI. Meanwhile, national AI strategies are substantially increasing new public spending in sectors adjacent to AI. All of this investment could lead to further job creation through multiplier effects.

AI adoption is changing prices and the returns to capital

The boom in investment in the production of AI is having some of the most concrete near-term indirect effects of AI on prices and asset markets, with implications for a wider group of low- and middle-income countries. The large investments in data centers in many middle-income countries, including Brazil, Malaysia, India, Thailand, and China, are having immediate impacts on energy demand and prices. AI-related data centers increased electricity demand by 17 percent year on year in 2025, the International Energy Agency estimates.[51]

The production and use of AI are also raising the *capital share of income* (the share of earnings accruing to capital owners, such as investors, business owners, and landowners). Early evidence from the European Union shows that for every doubling of regional AI innovation, the *labor share of income* (the share of income paid to workers as compensation) declines by 0.6 percent to 1.6 percent, potentially reducing it by 0.20 to 0.53 percentage points from an average of 52 percent. Moreover, because of effects on job displacement and job losses, AI has a strong negative relationship with the labor share of income of high- and medium-skill workers, primarily through wage declines as the use of AI increases.[52]

AI is altering transaction costs and patterns of trade

The adoption of AI is also lowering transaction costs. AI is already reducing the costs of international trade by optimizing supply chains, automating customs clearance, reducing language barriers, and enhancing market intelligence, among other mechanisms, the WTO finds.[53] Lower trade costs can make it easier for low- and middle-income countries to integrate into foreign markets, which could, in turn, raise productivity and labor demand in these developing countries. AI could increase global trade by 34–37 percent by 2040 across different scenarios, the WTO estimates.[54] The adoption of AI is also reducing communication costs, which is likely to boost the integration of the market for services and increase the tradability of services. Notably, high-quality machine translation could expand the tradability of services, potentially enabling a development path led by services, some studies suggest.[55] The recent rapid growth in cross-border digital services appears consistent with this view, although the causal link to AI has not yet been established.

The adoption and production of AI are also shifting patterns of comparative advantage between countries (that is, a country's ability to produce a specific good or service at a lower opportunity cost than its trading partners, which is an important determinant of what countries produce and trade).[56] Because AI is capital-intensive to produce and substitutes for labor, AI is expected to shift comparative advantage in favor of economies that are abundant in capital. In addition, if AI's productivity-enhancing effects accrue mainly to high-skill workers, comparative advantage could shift in favor of countries with more abundant supplies of high-skill labor.

AI can also affect labor demand through outsourcing, with job displacement effects, job creation effects, and productivity effects that materialize across borders. The impacts of AI on the offshoring of services has been widely debated. Some studies find positive impacts of AI on offshoring of services to developing countries through productivity effects;[57] others find no measurable effects;[58] and still others find negative displacement effects of AI on outsourcing of services on online platforms.[59]

AI's impact on jobs linked to exports is expected to depend on countries' task specialization in international trade. Currently, jobs in high-income countries linked to exports tend to be more exposed to AI. Productivity gains from such jobs are expected to be larger than in other countries, which may partly offset the employment substitution impact from AI. Countries with large shares of employment in agriculture or manufacturing are currently specialized in jobs with the lowest exposure to AI. These countries, such as Ethiopia and Viet Nam, are likely to experience small productivity gains from AI that will have a relatively modest impact on employment. Countries whose employment has shifted predominantly from agriculture to low-productivity services, such as wholesale and retail services, tend to specialize in jobs linked to exports that can be augmented by AI but are less exposed to the risks of employment substitution. Employment as a result of AI is more likely to increase in these countries (including the Arab Republic of Egypt, Ghana, and Indonesia) as they undertake a moderate expansion of exports. Overall, the implications of AI for jobs linked to exports are likely to align with and reinforce countries' existing comparative advantages.[60]

Future impacts: The most important impacts of AI may be unpredictable

The future impacts of AI on low- and middle-income countries will depend on three key known unknowns: the speed and direction of technological progress, the nature and extent of the shift into knowledge-intensive services (structural transformation), and the pace of AI adoption. Beyond these factors, however, the impacts of AI will also depend on unknown unknowns, which cannot be predicted.

Known unknowns: Future AI impacts will depend more on AI adoption than technical progress

The first known unknown is the speed and direction of technological progress and the extent to which AI capabilities spread to manual tasks. There is wide agreement that the capabilities of AI are improving rapidly, but considerable uncertainty remains about AI's future capabilities, including how the performance of AI models will improve, the nature and extent of constraints on data and physical infrastructure, the application of AI to hard-to-learn tasks, and the impacts on complementary inventions.

The second factor is the pathways of structural transformation in low- and middle-income countries and whether the high-skill knowledge-intensive services industries currently most affected by AI expand substantially in these countries. Although historically countries have followed a pattern of structural transformation into high-skill services as they grow, AI is altering that path.

The third factor is the speed of AI adoption in low- and middle-income countries. As this Report discusses, AI adoption will be shaped by complementary factors at the individual, firm, market, and country levels, as well as by regulations and societal acceptance of AI. Although AI exposure is currently relatively low in many low- and middle-income countries, it could increase substantially if AI spreads to more manual tasks in manufacturing and agriculture.

Scenarios of AI progress. The share of employment in low- and middle-income countries exposed to GenAI is currently about half the share in high-income countries (that is, about one-third of employment).[61] This *World Development Report* modeled various scenarios of AI progress; figure 4.12 presents the results. Under a *moderate AI progress scenario* with 2.5 percent annual growth in exposure of currently nonexposed occupations, the share of employment exposed to AI in low- and middle-income countries is projected to reach only 25 percent in 2035 (refer to figure 4.12, panel a).

Impacts would be much larger in *an advanced AI progress scenario,* in which breakthroughs in physical AI occur. In this scenario, AI capabilities also spread to affect routine manual or routine nonmanual activities, which is where most employment is concentrated in low- and middle-income countries. In this scenario, three-quarters of occupations become exposed to AI, including many medium-skill manual occupations in manufacturing and agriculture. The share of employment exposed to AI in low- and middle-income countries is projected to exceed 50 percent.

Scenarios of structural transformation. The impacts of AI will also depend on the pace of structural transformation into the knowledge-intensive services most affected by AI. If job losses in high-skill services industries outstrip job creation, structural transformation in low- and middle-income countries could stall. If job creation outstrips job displacement in high-productivity services, structural transformation could accelerate and low- and middle-income countries could follow development pathways that focus more heavily on knowledge-intensive services. Taking the moderate AI progress scenario as a starting point, a scenario of structural transformation in which trends in the employment share of high-skill services match the trend of today's high-income countries would result in an overall AI exposure just above 30 percent (compared with 25 percent in a scenario without structural change).

Scenarios of AI adoption. The most important determinant of future AI impacts will be the pace of AI adoption. If it follows the pattern typically seen for other emerging technologies (a polynomial S-curve), AI adoption could increase more than tenfold over the next decade in low- and middle-income countries. The adoption gap with high-income countries would still widen because both the levels and growth rates of AI adoption have been lower in low- and middle-income countries than in advanced economies to date (refer to figure 4.12, panel b). If adoption rates follow an even more rapid adoption scenario, with low- and middle-income countries closing the gap with high-income countries by 2055, adoption rates by 2035 could be even higher, reaching nearly 20 times today's levels. Although a rapid scenario for technical progress would raise exposure only four times, a rapid scenario for adoption would increase it 20 times, underscoring the crucial role of the speed of AI adoption for future impacts.

Figure 4.12 The extent of AI impacts will be affected by the speed of AI adoption and whether AI capabilities spread to affect manual tasks

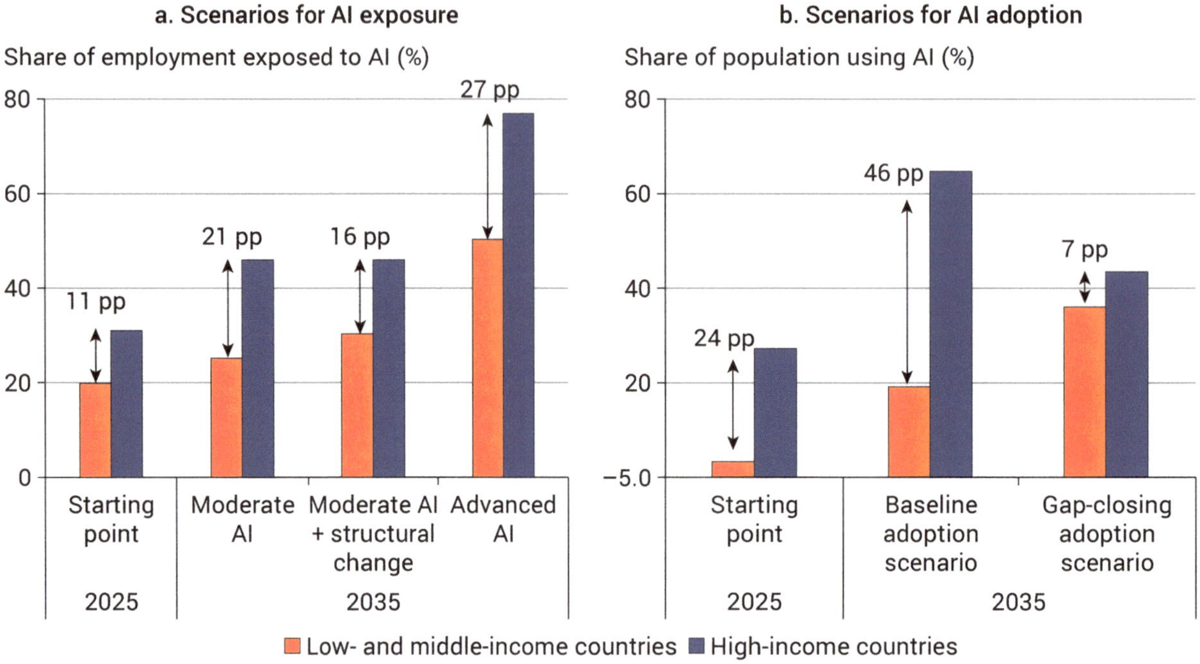

Source: WDR 2026 team, based on Gmyrek, Viollaz, et al. 2026; monthly mobile traffic data of Semrush (Software as a service platform), Semrush Holdings, https://www.semrush.com/.

Note: Panel a presents the share of employment exposed to AI under various scenarios. First, occupations are ranked by their AI exposure scores, following Gmyrek, Viollaz, et al. (2026). The moderate AI scenario assumes that, each year, 2.5 percent of the remaining occupations previously not exposed to AI become exposed, and the current employment structure remains unchanged. The advanced AI scenario assumes that, each year, 10 percent of the remaining occupations not previously exposed to AI become exposed, meaning that 75 percent of occupations will be exposed by 2035, and the current employment structure remains unchanged. The moderate AI + structural change scenario combines the moderate AI advancement scenario with shifts in employment shares whereby low- and middle-income countries are assumed to have the same employment structure (by occupation) as high-income countries within the following 40 years. Data on employment by occupation are taken from ILOSTAT (dashboard), International Labour Organization, https://ilostat.ilo.org/. Panel b presents various scenarios for the AI adoption rate. The starting point uses Semrush's monthly mobile traffic data (averaged over the calendar year) to estimate the share of the population that used ChatGPT by income group in 2025. The baseline adoption scenario assumes that the adoption rate follows a polynomial shape (similar to the diffusion pattern of the internet), reaching 95 percent in high-income countries and 75 percent in low- and middle-income countries by 2055. The gap-closing scenario assumes that the adoption rate follows a linear trendline and reaches 95 percent in both high-income countries and low- and middle-income countries by 2055. AI = artificial intelligence; pp = percentage points.

Effects on inequality. The modeled scenarios suggest there is a high probability that AI will increase inequality between countries. In the moderate AI scenario (which is the most likely scenario for technical progress), the AI exposure gap would widen. Likewise, in the baseline adoption scenario (which is the most likely scenario for AI adoption), the AI adoption gap would widen from the current level of 24 percentage points to 46 percentage points. This gap would be lower only if AI adoption growth rates in low- and middle-income countries greatly exceed rates in high-income countries, which is unlikely. Along the same line of reasoning, a recent analysis in the World Bank's *Global Economic Prospects* presents a range of illustrative scenarios for global economic growth over the next decade.[62] It shows that the growth benefits of AI are likely to vary across countries, with low- and middle-income countries at risk of falling further behind if they cannot build the right ecosystem and policy environment to adopt AI widely. Box 4.4 focuses on one economy, Poland, and explores the many offsetting factors and trends that could affect the overall impact of AI in that economy.

Box 4.4 Estimating the economywide effects of AI on growth and jobs in Poland: A general equilibrium approach

To understand the economywide effects of artificial intelligence (AI) on growth and jobs in Poland, a World Bank team developed a recursive dynamic computable general equilibrium model (MANAGE-AI).[a] The model uses an innovative approach that reorganizes production inputs into two bundles: *hardware*, comprising physical labor and capital; and *software*, consisting of cognitive (human) labor and AI or digital tools.[b]

The analysis yields three key insights. First, AI adoption could meaningfully lift Poland's GDP above its business-as-usual path, with productivity gains as the dominant driver. But the size of the growth dividend depends on how quickly action is taken: Delayed adoption forfeits gains that cannot be recovered later. Second, AI is likely to change the structure of the economy, increasing the share of digital- and knowledge-intensive activities in information and communication technology, as well as financial, professional, and technical services, while leaving the shares of manufacturing and wholesale and retail trade broadly intact. Third, employment shifts could be large, with outcomes depending on how easily workers can transition from automated tasks to new, complementary, and augmented tasks. Where workers can reallocate across sectors and occupations, the economy absorbs these shifts more readily.

AI is modeled as an intangible input that can substitute for cognitive labor within the software bundle and complement hardware across bundles. This approach allows AI automation and AI augmentation to operate at different rates across occupations and sectors, based on task-level evidence. In routine cognitive roles, AI automation can lower both employment and wages, while AI augmentation raises wages where workers retain a comparative advantage over AI. The range and type of opportunities can widen for workers who previously lacked the specialized skills to enter these roles, as AI lowers the skill threshold for entry.

Source: WDR 2026 team.

a. World Bank (2026).

b. Growiec et al. (2024).

Unknown unknowns: A wide range of uncertain outcomes

General-purpose technologies have often had the greatest impacts through the secondary inventions they have spurred. For example, the ICT revolution led not only to ATMs, which changed the jobs of bank tellers, but also spurred the invention of smartphones and their applications, which revolutionized how people access financial services. As societies adjust to general-purpose technologies, the transition dynamics are also significant. In the case of AI, macrofinancial risks are currently high, while a range of geopolitical and safety risks could have more important implications for productivity and jobs than the technology itself.

Businesses around the world acknowledge this uncertainty about the future.[63] Firms surveyed for this Report expressed a wide range of expectations about the potential impacts on their businesses in terms of productivity under different scenarios. Firms in the United States expect that a rapid development scenario for AI could result in productivity gains of about 8 percent, while a less rapid scenario would yield gains of 3 percent. Firms in the surveyed developing countries report wider ranges, with the most rapid scenario resulting in a productivity increase of 21 percent and a less rapid scenario yielding an increase of 2 percent, on average (refer to figure 4.13, panel a). In terms of impacts on labor, few firms expect the number of jobs in their own business to decrease because they adopt AI (refer to figure 4.13, panel b).

Figure 4.13 Firms expect large productivity gains from AI and positive impacts on employment

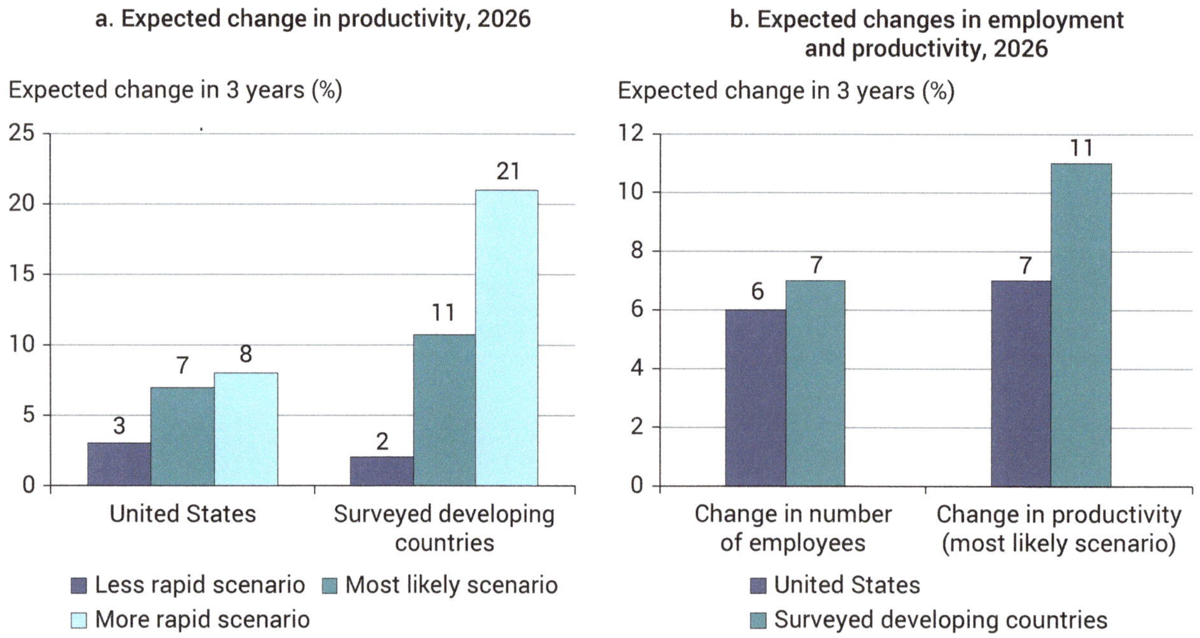

Source: WDR 2026 team, based on World Bank Enterprise Survey on AI Adoption; Davies et al. 2026.

Note: The figure presents data on formal firms in manufacturing, construction, and services with five or more employees. Expected productivity impacts are measured using the question "In three years, suppose you keep your current workforce size, what change in output do you expect due to the adoption of AI technologies?" This question was asked with respect to three scenarios (a most likely scenario, a less rapid scenario, and a more rapid scenario). The expected employment impacts were measured using the question "In three years, what change in the number of employees do you expect due to the adoption of AI technologies?" The data for the developing countries surveyed average country-level indicators, with equal weight for each country. The sample are India (1,355 firms), Jordan (358), Kenya (360), Mexico (603), Nigeria (777), Thailand (360), United States (392). Microdata are available at Enterprise Surveys (data portal), World Bank, https://www.enterprisesurveys.org/en/data. AI = artificial intelligence.

All these factors taken together indicate that the future impacts of AI in developing countries will depend most heavily on their pace of AI adoption, along with the pace of structural transformation into high-skill services and whether AI's capabilities spread to affect manual work. The future impacts of AI remain highly uncertain at this point, with history illustrating the unpredictable nature of general-purpose technologies.

Notes

1. Refer to Acemoglu and Restrepo (2019a), (2019b), (2022).
2. Acemoglu and Restrepo (2019a).
3. Autor and Thompson (2025); Gmyrek, Jimenez, et al. (2026).
4. Agrawal et al. (2026).
5. Agrawal et al. (2019); Cockburn et al. (2019).
6. For example, refer to Babina et al. (2024).
7. *Knowledge spillovers* refers to the spread of new ideas and discoveries beyond the originating firm or worker, benefiting other firms or workers who had no part in producing them. *Capital deepening* refers to an increase in the amount of capital available per worker, such as machines, equipment, and infrastructure, as well as more intangible forms of capital, such as software.
8. The *price elasticity of demand* captures the change in demand for a product following a change in price. The *income elasticity of demand* captures the change in demand for a product following a change in consumer income. As incomes rise and prices change, elasticities measure whether demand for products changes proportionally or more or less than proportionally relative to the change in price or consumer income.
9. As identified by economists Baumol and Bowen (1965), the result will be Baumol-like effects, that is, the tendency for prices in sectors that are not experiencing direct productivity impacts to increase as economywide wage and price levels change to match the higher wages and prices in sectors that are experiencing productivity impacts. This set of effects expands output in the former sectors (measured in monetary terms), even though productivity may not change.
10. Based on data of ILOSTAT (dashboard), International Labour Organization, https://ilostat.ilo.org/.
11. Nayyar et al. (2021).
12. As research for this Report, more than 4,200 firms in seven countries (India, Jordan, Kenya, Mexico, Nigeria, Thailand, the United States) were surveyed to understand the use of AI within businesses. These surveys were undertaken as a follow-up to the World Bank Enterprise Survey and covered formal establishments with five or more employees in the manufacturing sector and selected services sectors. The sample was drawn from representative listings of firms obtained from statistical agencies, business registers, and other business listings. The survey was also conducted in Malaysia and Türkiye. Data were being processed at the time of the writing of this Report. All microdata from the surveys conducted are available at Enterprise Surveys (data portal), World Bank, https://www.enterprisesurveys.org/en/data.
13. Adoption rates in the surveyed economies differ widely. Rates reported by firms in Kenya and Nigeria are similar to those reported by firms in the United States, whereas rates are lower for surveyed firms in India, Jordan, Mexico, and Thailand. Adoption rates are higher in the United States among medium and large firms (businesses with more than 20 employees) and in more highly advanced and sophisticated use cases.
14. Kim and Koning (2026).
15. Otis et al. (2024).
16. Pereira López et al. (2025).
17. Kim et al. (2026).
18. Liu and Wang (2026).
19. As defined by Gmyrek, Viollaz, et al. (2026), an occupation is deemed *exposed* to GenAI if it falls within the gradients outlined by Gmyrek et al. (2025). The GenAI exposure scores in Gmyrek et al. (2025) are based on the International Standard Classification of Occupations (ISCO) framework and provide a reliable link to internationally comparable labor force statistics across countries. The scores use a task-based approach to assess the perceived technical feasibility of automating tasks with GenAI tools, analyzing 3,123 tasks from the ISCO-08 documentation assigned to 436 occupations. The mean score and standard deviation for each occupation are then used to determine the gradients, ranging from Gradient 1 (indicating occupations with relatively low overall GenAI exposure, but significant variability across tasks) to Gradient 4 (representing occupations with the highest GenAI-driven automation exposure that is consistent across tasks).
20. Bick et al. (2026); Humlum and Vestergaard (2026).
21. The World Bank Firm-level Adoption of Technology survey measures technological use and sophistication in firms across several business functions. Evidence from the survey highlights that firms in low- and middle-income countries have increasing access to more sophisticated technologies, but that they trail firms in high-income countries in how intensively they use these technologies (Cirera, Comin, and Cruz 2026; Cirera, Comin, Cruz, et al. 2026; Cirera et al. 2022).

22. *Structured management practices* refer to formal, codified organizational practices that distinguish more well-managed firms from poorly managed firms. The practices include setting short-term and long-term objectives, monitoring achievements (and associated actions to remedy if targets are not met), and using incentives (Bloom and Van Reenen 2010).
23. This tendency may also reflect the fact that exporting firms may have better firm capabilities, driven by selection effects—that is, by greater productivity relative to firms that do not export (Melitz 2003)—and by learning through exporting (Atkin et al. 2017; De Loecker 2013).
24. Firm capabilities and innovation competencies are widely understood as important aspects of the intangible capital of businesses. For example, refer to Corrado et al. (2022). Refer also to World Bank Productivity Project (portal), World Bank, https://www.worldbank.org/en/topic/competitiveness/brief/the-world-bank-productivity-project.
25. DeStefano et al. (2026).
26. Akcigit and Kerr (2018).
27. Evidence suggests that both young firms and medium and large incumbent firms are more likely to adopt AI technologies. For example, data from venture capital firms operating in developing economies suggest that firms founded in the last decade (after 2015) are almost twice as likely to adopt AI technologies as similar, older venture capital and private equity firms (Smeets and Olarte Rodríguez 2026).
28. Calvino et al. (2026).
29. Filippucci et al. (2026).
30. Baslandze et al. (2026).
31. Aldasoro et al. (2026).
32. Brynjolfsson (2026).
33. Total factor productivity provides a measure of the amount of production relative to the inputs used. Unlike labor productivity, which represents the ratio of produced volumes (in terms of output or value added) to the amount of labor (in terms of quantity or cost), total factor productivity takes into account multiple inputs that matter in the production process, typically both capital and labor. As such, it provides a measure of how efficiently capital and labor are used jointly in the production process.
34. Refer to Aghion and Bunel (2024); Filippucci et al. (2026). A scaling of these various estimates for both advanced economies and emerging market and developing economies (EMDEs) based on their AI exposure and AI adoption levels demonstrates that there is wide variation in projected impacts but the range is smaller for EMDEs, again reflecting lower AI exposure and adoption rates at present.
35. According to the approach of Acemoglu (2024), two-thirds of the difference between high-income countries and low- and middle-income countries in productivity gains stems from lower AI adoption rates, and one-third stems from lower AI exposure.
36. *Structural transformation* refers to a process of development whereby economic activity shifts from less productive to more productive activities. At the level of an economy, the shift is typically from agriculture to industry and services. At the level of firms, the shift is usually from less productive to more productive businesses.
37. Sun and Huang (2025); Zhai and Liu (2023).
38. For example, Luo et al. (2024) use provincial-level panel data to show that AI technology innovation, measured through indexes related to patents and investment, raises aggregate TFP, but that this effect is significant only in provinces with high levels of marketization, financial development, and digital infrastructure. The effect becomes more evident at higher quantiles of the TFP distribution.
39. Otis et al. (2024).
40. Gambacorta et al. (2026).
41. Brynjolfsson, Chandar, et al. (2025); Brynjolfsson, Li, et al. (2025); Liu, Huang, et al. (2025).
42. Huang et al. (2026).
43. Liu, Wang, et al. (2025).
44. World Bank (2025).
45. World Bank (2023).
46. The top new profession in China related to AI is algorithm engineering, which, since 2022, has accounted for a notable share of the online job postings that mention AI skills (Li et al. 2026).
47. Jaumotte et al. (2026).
48. de Soyres et al. (2026).
49. OECD (2025).
50. UNCTAD (2026).
51. IEA (2025).
52. Minniti et al. (2025).
53. WTO (2025).
54. WTO (2025).
55. For example, refer to Baldwin (2020).
56. World Bank (2020).
57. For example, Stapleton and O'Kane (2021).
58. For example, Bastos and Nayyar (2026).
59. For example, Betai and Chen (2026).
60. Kruse and Yu (2026).
61. This exercise used the exposure definitions in Gmyrek, Viollaz, et al. (2026). Here, the scenarios serve as illustrations. The data on employment shares and the AI progress scenarios are conducted at the 4-digit ISCO code level. The sample covers 48 countries (including 18 high-income countries) from the latest year with available data.
62. Kose and Stamm (2026).
63. Karger et al. (2026).

References

Acemoglu, Daron. 2024. "The Simple Macroeconomics of AI." NBER Working Paper 32487, National Bureau of Economic Research. https://www.nber.org/papers/w32487.

Acemoglu, Daron, and Pascual Restrepo. 2019a. "Artificial Intelligence, Automation, and Work." In *The Economics of Artificial Intelligence: An Agenda*, edited by Ajay K. Agrawal, Joshua S. Gans, and Avi Goldfarb. National Bureau of Economic Research; University of Chicago Press. https://www.nber.org/books-and-chapters/economics-artificial-intelligence-agenda/artificial-intelligence-automation-and-work.

Acemoglu, Daron, and Pascual Restrepo. 2019b. "Automation and New Tasks: How Technology Displaces and Reinstates Labor." *Journal of Economic Perspectives* 33 (2): 3–30. https://www.aeaweb.org/articles?id=10.1257/jep.33.2.3.

Acemoglu, Daron, and Pascual Restrepo. 2022. "Tasks, Automation, and the Rise in U.S. Wage Inequality." *Econometrica* 90 (5): 1973–2016. https://doi.org/10.3982/ECTA19815.

Agarwal, Sumit, Shashwat Alok, Pulak Ghosh, and Sudip Gupta. 2020. "Financial Inclusion and Alternate Credit Scoring for the Millennials: Role of Big Data and Machine Learning in Fintech." Paper presented at the Cambridge Centre for Alternative Finance's "Fifth Annual Conference on Alternative Finance," Judge Business School, University of Cambridge, Cambridge, UK, June 29–July 1. https://www.jbs.cam.ac.uk/wp-content/uploads/2020/08/2020-06-conference-paper-agarwal-alok-ghosh-gupta.pdf.

Aghion, Philippe, and Simon Bunel. 2024. "AI and Growth: Where Do We Stand?" Working Paper (June), Federal Reserve Bank of San Francisco. https://www.frbsf.org/wp-content/uploads/AI-and-Growth-Aghion-Bunel.pdf.

Agrawal, Ajay K., Joshua S. Gans, and Avi Goldfarb, eds. 2019. *The Economics of Artificial Intelligence: An Agenda*. National Bureau of Economic Research; University of Chicago Press. https://www.nber.org/books-and-chapters/economics-artificial-intelligence-agenda.

Agrawal, Ajay K., John McHale, and Alexander Oettl. 2026. "AI in Science." NBER Working Paper 34953, National Bureau of Economic Research. https://www.nber.org/papers/w34953.

Akcigit, Ufuk, and William R. Kerr. 2018. "Growth Through Heterogeneous Innovations." *Journal of Political Economy* 126 (4): 1374–1443. https://www.journals.uchicago.edu/doi/10.1086/697901.

Aldasoro, Iñaki, Leonardo Gambacorta, Rozalia Pal, Debora Revoltella, Christoph Weiss, and Marcin Wolski. 2026. "AI Adoption, Productivity and Employment: Evidence from European Firms." EIB Economics Working Paper 2026/02, European Investment Bank. https://www.eib.org/files/publications/20250383-130126-economics-working-paper-2026-02-en.pdf.

Atkin, David Guy, Azam Chaudhry, Shamyla Chaudry, Amit Kumar Khandelwal, and Eric A. Verhoogen. 2017. "Organizational Barriers to Technology Adoption: Evidence from Soccer-Ball Producers in Pakistan." *Quarterly Journal of Economics* 132 (3): 1101–64. https://doi.org/10.1093/qje/qjx010.

Autor, David H., and Neil Thompson. 2025. "Expertise." *Journal of the European Economic Association* 23 (4): 1203–71. https://doi.org/10.1093/jeea/jvaf023.

Babina, Tania, Anastassia Fedyk, Alex He, and James Hodson. 2024. "Artificial Intelligence, Firm Growth, and Product Innovation." *Journal of Financial Economics* 151 (January): 1032745. https://www.sciencedirect.com/science/article/pii/S0304405X2300185X.

Baily, Martin Neil, Erik Brynjolfsson, and Anton Korinek. 2023. "Machines of Mind: The Case for an AI-Powered Productivity Boom." *Research* (blog), May 10. https://www.brookings.edu/articles/machines-of-mind-the-case-for-an-ai-powered-productivity-boom/.

Baldwin, Richard Edward. 2020. *The Globotics Upheaval. Globalization, Robotics, and the Future of Work*. Oxford University Press. https://global.oup.com/ushe/product/the-globotics-upheaval-9780197518618?cc=us&lang=en&.

Baslandze, Salomé, Zachary Edwards, John Graham, et al. 2026. "Artificial Intelligence, Productivity, and the Workforce: Evidence from Corporate Executives." NBER Working Paper 34984, National Bureau of Economic Research. https://www.nber.org/papers/w34984.

Bastos, Paulo, and Gaurav Nayyar. 2026. "Artificial Intelligence and International Trade in Services: Evidence from the United States." Background paper prepared for *World Development Report 2026: The Promise of Artificial Intelligence,* World Bank. https://www.worldbank.org/en/publication/wdr2026/brief/world-development-report-2026-background-papers.

Baumol, William J., and William G. Bowen. 1965. "On the Performing Arts: The Anatomy of Their Economic Problems." *American Economic Review* 55 (1/2): 495–502. http://www.jstor.org/stable/1816292.

Bergeaud, Antonin. 2024. "The Past, Present and Future of European Productivity." Paper presented at the European Central Bank's ECB Forum on Central Banking, "Monetary Policy in an Era of Transformation," Sintra, Portugal, July 1–3. https://www.ecb.europa.eu/pub/pdf/sintra/ecb.forumcentbankpub2024_Bergeaud_paper.en.pdf.

Betai, Nehai, and Maggie Chen. 2026. "Automation Without Borders: Generative AI and Cross-Border Service Outsourcing." Paper presented at the Georgetown University–World Bank Fourth Annual AI in Action (AIA) Conference, "Making AI Work: What Firms and Workers Need," Washington, DC, January 26. https://thedocs.worldbank.org/en/doc/2770aa5def57e42a6d2449c90d6cf974-0070062026/original/10-Chen.pdf.

Bick, Alexander, Adam Blandin, and David J. Deming. 2026. "The Rapid Adoption of Generative AI." *Management Science*. Published ahead of print, January 20. https://doi.org/10.1287/mnsc.2025.02523.

Bloom, Nicholas, and John Michael Van Reenen. 2010. "Why Do Management Practices Differ Across Firms and Countries?" *Journal of Economic Perspectives* 24 (1): 203–24. https://www.aeaweb.org/articles?id=10.1257/jep.24.1.203.

Braithwaite, Daniel Thomas, Misael Cavalcanti, R. Austin McEver, et al. 2025. "Your Spending Needs Attention: Modeling Financial Habits with Transformers." *arXiv:2507.23267v1 [cs.IR]*, July 31, Cornell University. https://doi.org/10.48550/arXiv.2507.23267.

Breslow, Stuart, Mikael Hagstroem, Daniel Mikkelsen, and Kate Robu. 2017. "The New Frontier in Anti–Money Laundering." *Our Insights* (blog), November 7. https://www.mckinsey.com/capabilities/risk-and-resilience/our-insights/the-new-frontier-in-anti-money-laundering.

Brynjolfsson, Erik. 2026. "The AI Productivity Take-Off Is Finally Visible." *Opinion: Artificial Intelligence* (blog), February 15. https://www.ft.com/content/4b51d0b4-bbfe-4f05-b50a-1d485d419dc5?countryCode=USA.

Brynjolfsson, Erik, Bharat Chandar, and Ruyu Chen. 2025. "Canaries in the Coal Mine? Six Facts About the Recent Employment Effects of Artificial Intelligence." Working Paper, Stanford Digital Economy Lab, Stanford University. https://digitaleconomy.stanford.edu/publication/canaries-in-the-coal-mine-six-facts-about-the-recent-employment-effects-of-artificial-intelligence/.

Brynjolfsson, Erik, Danielle Li, and Lindsey R. Raymond. 2025. "Generative AI at Work." *Quarterly Journal of Economics* 140 (2): 889–942. https://doi.org/10.1093/qje/qjae044.

Calvino, Flavio, Chiara Criscuolo, Timothy DeStefano, Jonathan David Timmis, and Antonio Ughi. 2026. "AI Diffusion Within Multinationals." Paper presented at the World Bank–Georgetown University Zoom conference, "Making AI Work: What Firms and Workers Need," Washington, DC, January 26. https://thedocs.worldbank.org/en/doc/84a308f46cca26eb8dadaf4f6fccdb06-0070062026/original/8-Criscuolo.pdf.

Cirera, Xavier, Diego A. Comin, and Marcio Jose Vargas da Cruz. 2022. *Bridging the Technological Divide: Technology Adoption by Firms in Developing Countries*. World Bank. https://hdl.handle.net/10986/37527.

Cirera, Xavier, Diego A. Comin, and Marcio Jose Vargas da Cruz. 2026. "Technology Sophistication Across Establishments." *Quarterly Journal of Economics* 141 (3): 2025–85. https://doi.org/10.1093/qje/qjag018.

Cirera, Xavier, Diego A. Comin, Marcio Jose Vargas da Cruz, and Kyungmin Lee. 2026. "The Impact of AI in Developing Countries: Lessons from the Adoption of Advanced Digital Technologies." Background paper prepared for *World Development Report 2026: The Promise of Artificial Intelligence,* World Bank. https://www.worldbank.org/en/publication/wdr2026/brief/world-development-report-2026-background-papers.

Cockburn, Iain M., Rebecca Henderson, and Scott Stern. 2019. "The Impact of Artificial Intelligence on Innovation: An Exploratory Analysis." In *The Economics of Artificial Intelligence: An Agenda*, edited by Ajay K. Agrawal, Joshua S. Gans, and Avi Goldfarb. National Bureau of Economic Research; University of Chicago Press. https://www.nber.org/books-and-chapters/economics-artificial-intelligence-agenda/impact-artificial-intelligence-innovation-exploratory-analysis.

Corrado, Carol, Jonathan Haskel, Cecilia Jona-Lasinio, and Massimiliano Iommi. 2022. "Intangible Capital and Modern Economies." *Journal of Economic Perspectives* 36 (3): 3–28. https://www.aeaweb.org/articles?id=10.1257/jep.36.3.3.

Davies, Elwyn, David Francis, Filip Jolevski, Gaurav Nayyar, Katherine Stapleton, and Shu Yu. 2026. "Adopting Fast and Slow: Cross-Country Evidence on Business Adoption of AI." Background paper prepared for *World Development Report 2026: The Promise of Artificial Intelligence,* World Bank. https://www.worldbank.org/en/publication/wdr2026/brief/world-development-report-2026-background-papers.

De Loecker, Jan K. 2013. "Detecting Learning by Exporting." *American Economic Journal: Microeconomics* 5 (3): 1–21. https://www.aeaweb.org/articles?id=10.1257/mic.5.3.1.

de Soyres, François, Alex Haag, Mike Liu, and Eva Van Leemput. 2026. "The Global Trade Effects of the AI Infrastructure Boom." FEDS Notes, February 13, Board of Governors of the Federal Reserve System. https://www.federalreserve.gov/econres/notes/feds-notes/the-global-trade-effects-of-the-ai-infrastructure-boom-20260213.html.

Dell'Acqua, Fabrizio, Edward McFowland III, Ethan Mollick, et al. 2023. "Navigating the Jagged Technological Frontier: Field Experimental Evidence of the Effects of Artificial Intelligence on Knowledge Worker Productivity and Quality." HBS Working Paper 24-013, Harvard Business School, Harvard University. https://www.hbs.edu/faculty/Pages/item.aspx?num=64700.

DeStefano, Timothy, Manuel Hofmann, Mattthew Murtagh-White, Katherine Stapleton, and Jonathan David Timmis. 2026. "Generative AI Around the World: The Role of Complementary Technologies." Background paper prepared for *World Development Report 2026: The Promise of Artificial Intelligence,* World Bank. https://www.worldbank.org/en/publication/wdr2026/brief/world-development-report-2026-background-papers.

Dillon, Eleanor W., Sonia Jaffe, Nicole Immorlica, and Christopher T. Stanton. 2025. "Shifting Work Patterns with Generative AI." NBER Working Paper 33795, National Bureau of Economic Research. https://www.nber.org/papers/w33795.

Doshi, Anil R., and Oliver P. Hauser. 2024. "Generative AI Enhances Individual Creativity but Reduces the Collective Diversity of Novel Content." *Science Advances* 10 (28): eadn5290. https://www.science.org/doi/10.1126/sciadv.adn5290.

Eloundou, Tyna, Sam Manning, Pamela Mishkin, and Daniel Rock. 2024. "GPTs are GPTs: Labor Market

Impact Potential of LLMs." *Science* 384 (6702): 1306–08. https://doi.org/10.1126/science.adj0998.
Felten, Edward W., Manav Raj, and Robert Seamans. 2023. "How Will Language Modelers Like ChatGPT Affect Occupations and Industries?" *arXiv:2303.01157v2 [econ.GN]*, March 18, Cornell University. https://doi.org/10.48550/arXiv.2303.01157.
Filippucci, Francesco, Peter N. Gal, Katharina Laengle, and Matthias Schief. 2025. "Macroeconomic Productivity Gains from Artificial Intelligence in G7 Economies." OECD Artificial Intelligence Paper 41, Organisation for Economic Co-operation and Development, Paris. https://www.oecd.org/en/publications/macroeconomic-productivity-gains-from-artificial-intelligence-in-g7-economies_a5319ab5-en.html.
Filippucci, Francesco, Peter N. Gal, and Matthias Schief. 2026. "Aggregate Productivity Gains from Artificial Intelligence: A Sectoral Perspective." *AEA Papers and Proceedings* 116 (May): 31–35. https://www.aeaweb.org/articles?id=10.1257/pandp.20261035.
Forsgren, Nicole, Margaret-Anne Storey, Chandra Maddila, Thomas Zimmermann, Brian Houck, and Jenna Butler. 2021. "The SPACE of Developer Productivity." *acmqueue* 19 (1) (March 6). https://queue.acm.org/detail.cfm?id=3454124.
Gambacorta, Leonardo, Enisse Kharroubi, Aditya Mehrotra, and Tommaso Oliviero. 2026. "Artificial Intelligence and Growth in Advanced and Emerging Economies: Short-Run Impact." BIS Working Paper 1321, rev., Monetary and Economic Department, Bank for International Settlements. https://www.bis.org/publ/work1321.pdf.
Gmyrek, Pawel, Janine Marie Berg, and David Bescond. 2023. "Generative AI and Jobs: A Global Analysis of Potential Effects on Job Quantity and Quality." ILO Working Paper 96, International Labour Organization. https://www.ilo.org/sites/default/files/2024-07/WP96_web.pdf.
Gmyrek, Pawel, Janine Marie Berg, Karol Kamiński, et al. 2025. "Generative AI and Jobs: A Refined Global Index of Occupational Exposure." ILO Working Paper 140, International Labour Organization. https://www.ilo.org/sites/default/files/2025-05/WP140_web.pdf.
Gmyrek, Pawel, Hector Daniel Segura Jimenez, Hernán Jorge Winkler, and Shu Yu. 2026. "Generative AI and Global Redistribution of Expertise." Background paper prepared for *World Development Report 2026: The Promise of Artificial Intelligence,* World Bank. https://www.worldbank.org/en/publication/wdr2026/brief/world-development-report-2026-background-papers.
Gmyrek, Pawel, Mariana Viollaz, and Hernán Jorge Winkler. 2026. "Disruption Without Dividend? How the Digital Divide and Task Differences Split GenAI's Global Impact." Policy Research Working Paper 11328 and background paper prepared for *World Development Report 2026: The Promise of Artificial Intelligence,* World Bank. https://www.worldbank.org/en/publication/wdr2026/brief/world-development-report-2026-background-papers.
Growiec, Jakub, Julia Jabłońska, and Aleksandra Parteka. 2024. "Hardware and Software: A New Perspective on the Past and Future of Economic Growth." Working Paper, Brookings Center on Regulation and Markets, Brookings Institution. https://www.brookings.edu/wp-content/uploads/2024/07/Hardware-and-software-A-new-perspective-on-the-past-and-future-or-economic-growth.pdf.
Huang, Jingyun, Yan Liu, He Wang, and Shu Yu. 2026. "Who Takes the Hit? The Uneven Impacts of Generative AI on Labor Demand Across Countries." Background paper prepared for *World Development Report 2026: The Promise of Artificial Intelligence,* World Bank. https://www.worldbank.org/en/publication/wdr2026/brief/world-development-report-2026-background-papers.
Humlum, Anders, and Emilie Vestergaard. 2026. "Still Waters, Rapid Currents: Early Labor Market Transformation Under Generative AI." NBER Working Paper 33777, rev., National Bureau of Economic Research. https://www.nber.org/papers/w33777.
IEA (International Energy Agency). 2025. *Energy and AI.* World Energy Outlook Special Report. IEA. https://www.iea.org/reports/energy-and-ai.
Izaguirre, Juan Carlos, Sonia Arenaza, Patrick Meagher, and Myra Valenzuela. 2025. *Responsible Digital Credit: Frontier Solutions for Authorities and Providers.* Technical Guide. Consultative Group to Assist the Poor. https://www.cgap.org/sites/default/files/publications/Tech%20Guide_Responsible%20Digital%20Credit_v5.pdf.
Jaumotte, Florence, Jaden Kim, David Koll, et al. 2026. "Bridging Skill Gaps for the Future: New Jobs Creation in the AI Age." IMF Staff Discussion Note 26/001, International Monetary Fund. https://www.imf.org/-/media/files/publications/sdn/2026/english/sdnea2026001.pdf.
Kalliamvakou, Eirini. 2024. "Research: Quantifying GitHub Copilot's Impact on Developer Productivity and Happiness." *Research* (blog), updated May 21. https://github.blog/news-insights/research/research-quantifying-github-copilots-impact-on-developer-productivity-and-happiness/.
Kanazawa, Kyogo, Daiji Kawaguchi, Hitoshi Shigeoka, and Yasutora Watanabe. 2022. "AI, Skill, and Productivity: The Case of Taxi Drivers." NBER Working Paper 30612, National Bureau of Economic Research. https://www.nber.org/papers/w30612.
Karger, Ezra, Otto Kuusela, Jason Abaluck, et al. 2026. "Forecasting the Economic Effects of AI." Working Paper, rev., Forecasting Research Institute. https://forecastingresearch.org/research/economic-effects-of-ai.
Kim, Hyunjin, Dahyeon Kim, and Rembrand Koning. 2026. "Mapping AI into Production: A Field Experiment on Firm Performance." INSEAD Working Paper 2026/20/STR, INSEAD. https://doi.org/10.2139/ssrn.6513481.
Kim, Hyunjin, and Rembrand Koning. 2026. "AI-Native Firms." Harvard Business School Working Paper 26-090, Harvard Business School, Harvard University. https://www.hbs.edu/ris/Publication%20Files/26-090_96f92aa0-37d9-4789-beaa-5c0cb87a4032.pdf.

Kose, M. Ayhan, and Kersten Stamm. 2026. "Box 1.1: How Much Will AI Affect Global Growth?" In *Global Economic Prospects, June 2026*, 8–13. World Bank. https://thedocs.worldbank.org/en/doc/2b672b3b0415d6b66c45b66579db4ef5-0050012026/related/GEP-Jun-2026-Box-1-1.pdf.

Kruse, Hagen, and Shu Yu. 2026. "The AI Exposure of Export-Linked Jobs." Background paper prepared for *World Development Report 2026: The Promise of Artificial Intelligence,* World Bank. https://www.worldbank.org/en/publication/wdr2026/brief/world-development-report-2026-background-papers.

Li, Lixing, Zhencen Liu, Anqi Wang, He Wang, and Shu Yu. 2026. "Now Hiring: Firm-Level Adoption of Generative AI in China." Background paper prepared for *World Development Report 2026: The Promise of Artificial Intelligence,* World Bank. https://www.worldbank.org/en/publication/wdr2026/brief/world-development-report-2026-background-papers.

Liu, Yan, Jingyun Huang, and He Wang. 2025. "Who on Earth Is Using Generative AI? Global Trends and Shifts in 2025." Policy Research Working Paper 11231 and background paper prepared for *World Development Report 2026: The Promise of Artificial Intelligence*, World Bank. https://www.worldbank.org/en/publication/wdr2026/brief/world-development-report-2026-background-papers.

Liu, Yan, and He Wang. 2026. "Who on Earth Is Using Generative AI?" *World Development* 199 (March): 107260. https://doi.org/10.1016/j.worlddev.2025.107260.

Liu, Yan, He Wang, and Shu Yu. 2025. "Labor Demand in the Age of Generative AI: Early Evidence from the U.S. Job Posting Data." Policy Research Working Paper 11263 and background paper prepared for *World Development Report 2026: The Promise of Artificial Intelligence,* World Bank. https://www.worldbank.org/en/publication/wdr2026/brief/world-development-report-2026-background-papers.

Luo, Shuang, Wenting Lei, and Peng Hou. 2024. "Impact of Artificial Intelligence Technology Innovation on Total Factor Productivity: An Empirical Study Based on Provincial Panel Data in China." *National Accounting Review* 6 (2): 172–94. https://www.aimspress.com/article/doi/10.3934/NAR.2024008.

Melitz, Marc J. 2003. "The Impact of Trade on Intra-Industry Reallocations and Aggregate Industry Productivity." *Econometrica* 71 (6): 1695–1725. https://onlinelibrary.wiley.com/doi/abs/10.1111/1468-0262.00467.

Merola, Rossana, Ekkehard Ernst, Daniel Samaan, Maria del Rio-Chanona, and Ole Teutloff. 2026. "Workers' Exposure to AI: What Indicators Tell Us, and What They Don't." ILO Brief (February), International Labour Organization. https://www.ilo.org/sites/default/files/2026-05/Research%20Brief_Workers%20exposure%20to%20AI_updated.pdf.

Minniti, Antonio, Klaus Prettner, and Francesco Venturini. 2025. "AI Innovation and the Labor Share in European Regions." *European Economic Review* 177 (August): 105043. https://www.sciencedirect.com/science/article/pii/S0014292125000935.

Mwesigwa, Daniel, Steven J. Jackson, and Christopher Csikszentmihalyi. 2026. "Risk, Data, Alignment: Making Credit Scoring Work in Kenya." *arXiv:2602.01824v1 [cs.HC]*, February 2, Cornell University. https://doi.org/10.48550/arXiv.2602.01824.

Nayyar, Gaurav, Mary Hallward-Driemeier, and Elwyn Davies. 2021. *At Your Service? The Promise of Services-Led Development*. World Bank. https://hdl.handle.net/10986/35599.

Noy, Shakked, and Whitney Zhang. 2023. "Experimental Evidence on the Productivity Effects of Generative Artificial Intelligence." *Science* 381 (6654): 187–92. https://www.science.org/doi/10.1126/science.adh2586.

OECD (Organisation for Economic Co-operation and Development). 2025. "Mapping the Semiconductor Value Chain: Working Towards Identifying Dependencies and Vulnerabilities." OECD Science, Technology and Industry Policy Paper 182, OECD. https://doi.org/10.1787/4154cdbf-en.

Otis, Nicholas G., Rowan Clarke, Solène Delecourt, David Holtz, and Rembrand Koning. 2024. "The Uneven Impact of Generative AI on Entrepreneurial Performance: Evidence from a Field Experiment in Kenya." Working Paper 24-042, Harvard Business School, Harvard University. https://www.hbs.edu/ris/Publication%20Files/24-042_567db548-5b24-4182-b703-9d5ef1328043.pdf.

Peng, Sida, Eirini Kalliamvakou, Peter Cihon, and Mert Demirer. 2023. "The Impact of AI on Developer Productivity: Evidence from GitHub Copilot." *arXiv:2302.06590v1 [cs.SE]*, February 13, Cornell University. https://doi.org/10.48550/arXiv.2302.06590.

Pereira López, Mariana De La Paz, Stephen J. Anderson, Leonardo Iacovone, Andreas Menzel, Florian Anselm Münch, and Rahul Suhag. 2025. *Creating Ecosystems for Innovation in a Post-Coal Region: Evidence from an RCT in the Czech Republic*. Strengthening Monitoring and Evaluation of Innovation Programs in the EU Series, June 18. World Bank. https://documents1.worldbank.org/curated/en/099062725130041014/pdf/P171223-48a49632-7dc2-41ab-8161-8c1e8e4f67c1.pdf.

Pizzinelli, Carlo, Augustus J. Panton, Marina Mendes Tavares, Mauro Cazzaniga, and Longji Li. 2023. "Labor Market Exposure to AI: Cross-Country Differences and Distributional Implications." IMF Working Paper 23/216, International Monetary Fund. https://doi.org/10.5089/9798400254802.001.

Schoenegger, Philipp, Peter S. Park, Ezra Karger, Sean Trott, and Philip E. Tetlock. 2025. "AI-Augmented Predictions: LLM Assistants Improve Human Forecasting Accuracy." *ACM Transactions on Interactive Intelligent Systems* 15 (1), art. 4. https://doi.org/10.1145/3707649.

Smeets, Eveline, and Liliana Olarte Rodríguez. 2026. "AI Adoption Among Frontier Firms in Emerging Markets." Background paper prepared for *World Development Report 2026: The Promise of Artificial Intelligence,* World Bank. https://www.worldbank.org/en/publication/wdr2026/brief/world-development-report-2026-background-papers.

Stapleton, Katherine, and Layla O'Kane. 2021. "Artificial Intelligence and Services Offshoring." https://drive.google.com/file/d/1evN3SdPqfuPzFsJTRopmvqBWuN9UNVvw/view.

Sun, Quan, and Minjie Huang. 2025. "Firm-Level Evidence on AI-Driven Output Expansion and Productivity in China." *Socio-Economic Planning Sciences* 103 (February): 102389. https://doi.org/10.1016/j.seps.2025.102389.

UNCTAD (UN Trade and Development). 2026. "Data Centres Are Reshaping the Global Investment Landscape." *News* (blog), January 22. https://unctad.org/news/data-centres-are-reshaping-global-investment-landscape.

Verhagen, Alexander, Angela Luget, Vasiliki Stergiou, Debanjan Banerjee, and Olivia Conjeaud. 2025. "How Agentic AI Can Change the Way Banks Fight Financial Crime." *Our Insights* (blog), August 7. https://www.mckinsey.com/capabilities/risk-and-resilience/our-insights/how-agentic-ai-can-change-the-way-banks-fight-financial-crime.

World Bank. 2020. *World Development Report 2020: Trading for Development in the Age of Global Value Chains*. World Bank. https://www.worldbank.org/en/publication/wdr2020.

World Bank. 2023. *Kenya Country Economic Memorandum: Seizing Kenya's Services Momentum*. World Bank. https://documents1.worldbank.org/curated/en/099072623125529056/pdf/P177156008ee600bc0bf75078832b97b48f.pdf.

World Bank. 2025. *Jobs, AI, and Trade*. South Asia Development Update, October. World Bank. https://doi.org/10.1596/978-1-4648-2291-9.

World Bank. 2026. "Navigating the Age of AI, Implications for Poland's Economy: What AI Means for Growth, Firms, and Jobs." World Bank. http://documents.worldbank.org/curated/en/099061826172092709.

WTO (World Trade Organization). 2025. *World Trade Report 2025: Making Trade and AI Work Together to the Benefit of All*. WTO. https://www.wto.org/english/res_e/booksp_e/wtr25_e.pdf.

Yin, Michelle, Hoa Vu, and Claudia Persico. 2026. "How (un)Stable Are LLM Occupational Exposure Scores? Evidence from Multi-Model Replication." NBER Working Paper 35110, National Bureau of Economic Research. https://www.nber.org/papers/w35110.

Zhai, Shaoxuan, and Zhenpeng Liu. 2023. "Artificial Intelligence Technology Innovation and Firm Productivity: Evidence from China." *Finance Research Letters* 58 (Part B, December): 104437. https://doi.org/10.1016/j.frl.2023.104437.

Zhu, Tingting Juni, Philip Grinsted, Hangyul Song, and Malathi Velamuri. 2022. *A Spiky Digital Business Landscape: What Can Developing Countries Do?* October. World Bank. https://hdl.handle.net/10986/39437.

2 Spotlight 2

The Power of AI to Enhance Agricultural Advisory and Extension Services

Research-based agronomic knowledge, market information, and access to financial and input services have traditionally reached farming households through agricultural extension services. In most low- and middle-income countries, the critical system through which this is accomplished is often severely strained.[1] The planning guidelines of the Food and Agriculture Organization of the United Nations (FAO) for agricultural extension services specify one agent for every 500–2,000 rural inhabitants, depending on a country's production systems and the density of its population.[2] But the reality on the ground falls short. Recent estimates indicate that in Nigeria, for example, a single public extension agent may serve anywhere from 5,000 to 10,000 farmers.[3] In India, which has one of the largest public extension systems in the world, with about 120,000 extension professionals[4]—the ratio of extension workers to farmers is about 1 to 5,000, far below the ratio suggested by the national staffing guidelines (about 1:400 in hilly areas and between about 1:750 and 1:1,100 in irrigated and rainfed regions).[5]

A gap in service delivery is evident not only in the number of extension agents available to farmers, but also in the quality and responsiveness of the advice they provide. Public extension advice tends to be structurally generic (designed for an average farmer in an average season), asymmetric (information flows from the institution to farmers and rarely the other way around), and reactive (based on fixed seasonal calendars meant to guide a typical season, rather than real-time data that could anticipate problems before a loss in yields occurs). Furthermore, it does not account for the many modes of data and information needed to diagnose problems thoroughly at the farm level. For example, leaf discoloration, unusual pests, and soil degradation are visual and spatial problems that farmers cannot communicate adequately using text-only or voice-only channels. Early digital services such as bulk SMS (text messaging), interactive voice response alerts, and radio broadcasts have reached more farmers than nondigital means, but they have limitations similar to those of public extension advice. These services are pushed by a single agent to many farmers and are generic. They provide no predictive or diagnostic capability at the level of the individual farm, which is where farmers earn their living.

Agricultural advisory services driven by artificial intelligence (AI) can address some of the gap in service delivery. Such services are not new. What is new is their speed, scope, lower cost, and greater accessibility. Although this spotlight focuses on advisory services, AI applications extend across the entire agrifood value chain, from supply chain logistics and reducing the amount of food lost between harvest and sale to market access and food safety monitoring.[6]

A first generation of AI tools for agricultural advisory services applied statistical and machine learning models to predict crop yields, model pest risk, and forecast weather.[7] For instance, the International Crops Research Institute for the Semi-Arid Tropics, in collaboration with Microsoft, developed an AI-powered sowing application and personalized village advisory dashboard to generate recommendations at the village level on optimal windows for sowing and fertilizer application rates, tailored to crop, soil, and seasonal conditions.[8] The institute's Meghdoot application, developed in collaboration with the India Meteorological Department, the Indian Institute of Tropical Meteorology, and the Indian Council of Agricultural Research, provides farmers with district-level meteorological data along with advice on crop management derived from machine learning models.[9] However, these first-generation tools were designed within certain constraints: Responses are typically scripted or template-based rather than tailored to a specific farmer's context, user interfaces assume a level of literacy and smartphone ownership that excludes many smallholders, and individual tools tend to operate in isolation, with weather, pest, and agronomic guidance rarely integrated into a single coherent system.

Generative AI has the potential to address each of these constraints. Unlike scripted systems, a large language model produces responses tailored to farmers' specific contexts, including their crops, locations, and soil conditions and their precise questions. Farmers' interaction with advisory platforms are now conversations that can accommodate follow-up questions, images of diseased crops, or requests for simpler explanations and can take place in farmers' own language or dialect through voice on a basic feature phone. For the first time, the interface itself ceases to be a barrier. Figure S2.1 depicts the technical architecture that links the capabilities needed to provide these advantages.

Productivity, income, efficiency, and farm-level outcomes

Early deployments across diverse geographies and farming systems demonstrate that personalization of AI advisory services leads to substantial gains in productivity (though the strength of evidence varies by study design), specifically, in crop yield, efficiency of inputs, and generated income, among other things. iSDA's Virtual Agronomist, operating in Ghana, Kenya, Malawi, Rwanda, Tanzania, Uganda, and Zambia, expanded to 200,000 farm plots within the first year of its launch.[10] Users had average yields 1.4–1.9 times greater than those of neighboring nonusers, and yields among sunflower farmers in Tanzania increased by up to 70 percent.[11] In addition, early assessments indicated that profits were 2.7 to 4.7 times greater than before the AI model was used, with the increases driven by better timing on when inputs such as fertilizers and pesticides should be applied, improved selection of varieties planted, and better pest management.[12] The income effect was greatest where the shift from generic-based advice to plot-level advice was most pronounced. Estimates of the program's impact are subject to selection bias, because voluntary adoption is unlikely to be random; farmers who opt into AI advisory platforms may differ from nonadopters on unobservable characteristics—such as managerial ability, risk tolerance, or access to complementary inputs—that independently drive productivity gains.

The NextGen Agroadvisory program of CGIAR (formerly the Consultative Group on International Agricultural Research) replaced decades of standardized fertilizer recommendations with plot-specific guidance to more than 50,000 smallholder farmers in Ethiopia, resulting in a 38 percent increase in wheat yields: the clearest available illustration of how large the difference between generic and farm-level advice is in regard to its effect on productivity.[13] Income effects (gains in income) also compound, not only through gains in yield, but also through improved efficiency as to when inputs are applied. Farmers receiving personalized advice tend to apply inputs such as fertilizer, pesticide, and irrigation at the right time and in the right quantities, reducing waste and cost while improving output.

Figure S2.1 Illustrative architecture of a generative AI agricultural advisory platform

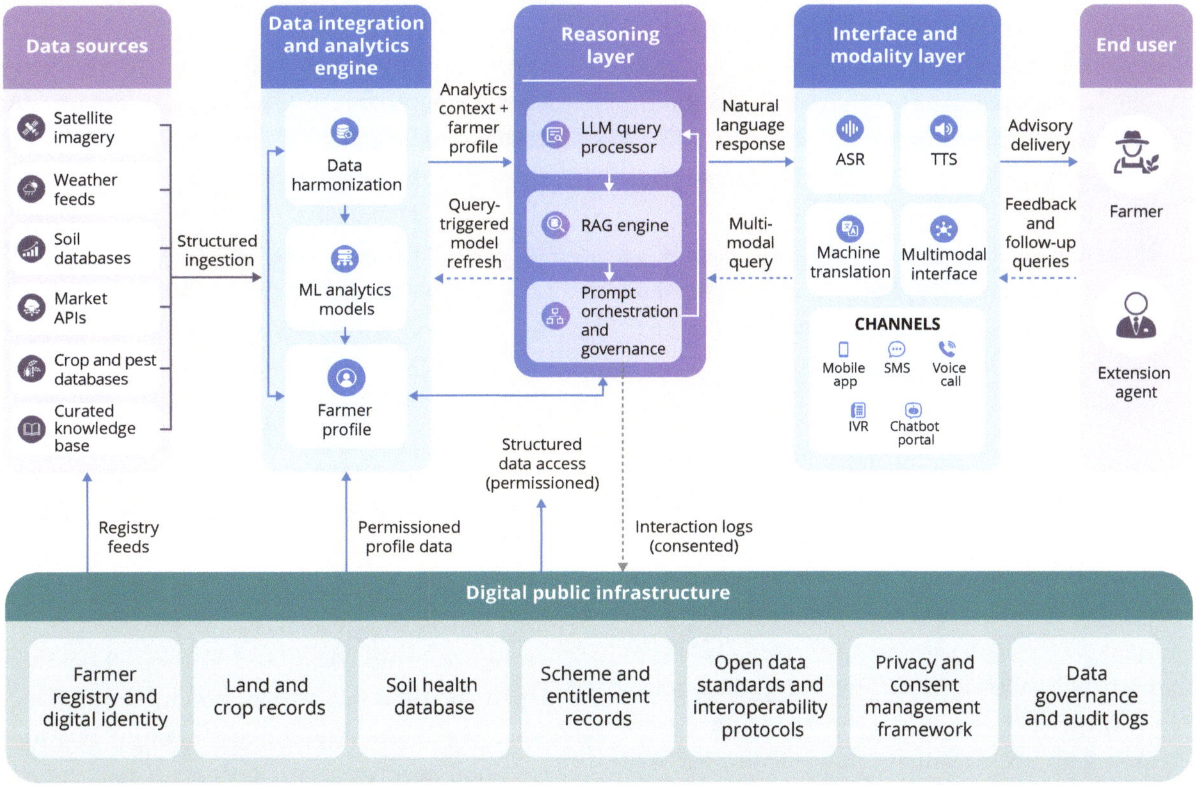

Source: WDR 2026 team.

Note: Permissioned indicates that the data are accessed or shared only with the explicit consent or authorization of the data owner, ensuring that privacy and data protection safeguards govern farmer information and institutional records. AI = artificial intelligence; APIs = application programming interfaces; ASR = automatic speech recognition; IVR = interactive voice response; LLM = large language model; ML = machine learning; RAG = retrieval-augmented generation; TTS = text to speech.

This dual effect of digital advisory services on cost and income drives the outsized benefit-cost ratios observed in early evaluations and explains why adoption of such services has accelerated. An example is Ama Krushi, which was launched in the state of Odisha, India, in 2018, later integrated AI-powered advisory capabilities, and now operates as Krushi Samruddhi. Originally developed under a build-operate-transfer model, Ama Krushi was transitioned to full government ownership in 2022, when it served approximately 3 million farmers.[14] As the service demonstrated that better-timed, lower-cost advice could raise both harvests and income, uptake continued to spread: under government operation, the service has since scaled to more than 7 million farmers.[15] A randomized evaluation in 2025 found that the service improved farming practices, boosted harvests, and reduced severe crop loss, with benefit-cost ratios ranging from 9:1 to 15:1 at scale.[16]

The volume of queries submitted to AI chatbots is even more telling. Kisan e-Mitra, a grievance redress chatbot launched by India's Ministry of Agriculture and Farmers Welfare in September 2023 and enhanced with advanced AI capabilities in February 2024, provides immediate answers in 11 Indic languages to farmer queries related to India's Pradhan Mantri Kisan Samman Nidhi income support initiative. Within 186 days of AI integration, the chatbot handled approximately 2.7 million queries, nearly seven times the volume that traditional manual processing could have managed in the same period.[17] Although the chatbot addresses inquiries related to the initiative rather than dispensing agronomic advice, its rapid adoption suggests that farmers are willing and able to engage with conversational AI interfaces when the services that such interfaces provide meet a real need.

In addition, the cost of delivering agricultural advisory services has fallen dramatically across successive generations of technology. Evaluations of traditional public extension systems and early video-based programs suggest that conventional in-person advisory services can cost $30–$35 per farmer annually after staffing, travel, and training overhead costs are fully accounted for. Large-scale randomized evaluations of video-mediated group extension models show that digitizing content and using group screenings can reduce the cost of delivering advisory services to about $3.50 per farmer while still generating significant gains in the adoption of improved practices, in knowledge, and in yields.[18] Later waves of advisory services based on phone and interactive voice response, such as Ama Krushi, demonstrate that once advice is delivered through low-cost mobile channels, annual costs of delivery can fall to as little as $0.15 per farmer, with benefit-cost ratios of 9:1 or higher at scale.[19] More recently, advisory systems enabled by generative AI indicate the potential for a further reduction in the cost of delivery, with early estimates suggesting costs could fall by another tenfold from previous digital models[20] and implied costs of less than $1 per interaction when conversational AI is deployed at scale on top of existing digital infrastructure.

Managing the risks of automated advisory

The same properties that make generative AI advisory powerful—its fluency, confidence, and capacity to respond to almost any query—also introduce risks that require active governance. The most serious risk is model *hallucination:* the tendency of probabilistic language models to generate plausible-sounding but factually incorrect responses. In most AI applications, hallucination poses a problem in regard to quality of output, but in agricultural advisory services, it can also raise safety concerns. For example, implementing advice that involves an incorrect pesticide concentration, an incorrect fertilizer dosage, or a mistimed recommendation regarding planting can cause farmers to suffer losses in crop yields, financial harm, chemical contamination, or health risks, and for households that depend on their own production for food, a failed harvest can directly threaten family nutrition and food security. Such outcomes risk eroding trust among rural communities that have limited prior experience with digital services. The need for AI applications to generate agronomic advice that is highly specific to context compounds the problem. For example, what is considered to be sound guidance in Kenya's Great Rift Valley may be actively harmful in the alluvial plains in Bihar, India, a situation that researchers have coined *contextual hallucination*[21] in general-purpose models that are deployed without being grounded in regional contexts.

Typically, three methods are used to mitigate the risks posed by automated advisory models. *Retrieval-augmented-generation-based grounding* connects AI models to external, trusted sources of data, such as internal documents, databases, or live websites, to ensure that AI-generated responses are accurate, current, and verifiable. It acts as an "anchor" for models that use it, forcing them to use specific, provided facts rather than relying solely on their training data. *Red teaming* is a systematic adversarial simulation performed before an AI model is deployed in which data security professionals act as attackers—using real-world techniques like social engineering and network infiltration—to test some of the highest risks of the model, such as its potential to generate harmful advice on pesticides, incorrect fertilizer or pesticide dosage calculations, recommendations that ignore local crop calendars or regional pest pressures, and demographic bias in the quality of advice delivered to women farmers or marginalized communities. *Human-in-the-loop validation* is an approach in which human expertise is integrated into an AI model to verify, correct, and improve its output, particularly in regard to complex or high-risk queries. However, trust gaps and limited digital literacy mean that human intermediaries remain essential complements, as illustrated by Rwanda's Digital Ambassadors Program,[22] which embeds community facilitators in rural communities to support farmer uptake of digital advisory services. Studies confirm that validation by humans with the required expertise significantly improves the quality of AI model outputs and that farmer trust increases when the advice such models provide is grounded in verified, expert-curated sources.[23]

Extending the reach of agronomic knowledge

Although generative AI does not replace human extension agents, it does extend the reach of agronomic knowledge beyond what any human workforce could achieve, delivering advice that is personalized and specific to context to farmers who have never had access to a trained agronomist. Increasing the number of agents alone cannot address the structural barriers that have defined extension systems for decades: understaffing, generic advice, and information that flows only one way. These barriers require a different architecture entirely.

Evidence from early deployments suggests that such architectural options now exist. But their effectiveness is contingent on having the required foundational infrastructure, which remains underdeveloped in many low- and middle-income countries. For example, adopting AI agricultural advisory services is possible only with good digital public infrastructure, including farmer and land registries, soil health databases, and a unified digital identity system. An AI application that cannot identify who farmers are, what they grow, or where their land is located would be unable to deliver advice that is more meaningful than what they would receive through a generic bulletin. Narrowing the gap between what is currently possible and what could potentially be delivered will require coordinated investment—from governments, development institutions, and the research community—in the data architecture that makes such personalization possible.

The convergence of falling AI costs, increasing mobile connectivity, growing curated agricultural knowledge bases, and maturing governance frameworks means that the conditions for scaling AI-powered extension are more favorable now than at any prior point. The question is no longer whether generative AI can deliver the right advice to smallholder producers, but rather whether institutional investment will be at sufficient levels, data infrastructure and the needed governance architecture will be built quickly enough, and the necessary protections will be put in place to service the hundreds of millions of farmers today who still farm without reliable advisory support.

Notes

1. Swanson (2008).
2. Blum and Szonyi (2014).
3. Piserchia and Edimu (2025).
4. Nandi and Nedumaran (2019).
5. Pathak (2025).
6. World Bank (2025).
7. Jabed and Azmi Murad (2024).
8. Dhulipala et al. (2021).
9. CGIAR (2024).
10. iSDA (2025).
11. Shepherd et al. (2025).
12. iSDA (2025).
13. Mesfin et al. (2023).
14. Vaidya and Keshaw (2022).
15. Konnect Team (2025).
16. Cole et al. (2025); Zhu and Harigaya (2025).
17. Gorke (2025).
18. IDinsight (2023).
19. Cole et al. (2025).
20. Digital Green Uses OpenAI to Increase Farmer Income (web page), OpenAI, https://openai.com/index/digital-green/.
21. Fanuel et al. (2025).
22. The Digital Ambassadors Program (DAP) was built specifically because digital/e-service adoption stalled due to barriers related to trust and literacy rather than access. Digital Ambassadors provided digital skills training to nearly 42,000 youth, women, and rural populations across 12 districts, and more than 75 percent of citizens trained reported that their skills and use of mobile technology had improved significantly, with 75 percent of women reporting greater motivation and confidence to use digital technology. For further details, refer to DAP (web page), Ministry of ICT and Innovation, Rwanda, https://www.minict.gov.rw/projects/digital-ambassadors-programme.
23. Singh et al. (2024).

References

Blum, Magdalena L., and Judit Szonyi. 2014. "Investment Requirements in Extension to Achieve Zero Hunger and Adapt to Climate Change." *Journal of Agricultural Science and Technology* A 4 (7): 552–62. https://www.davidpublisher.com/Public/uploads/Contribute/550257098ca2e.pdf.

CGIAR. 2024. "Inside Meghdoot, the App Delivering Weather-Based Agricultural Advice to Farmers Across India." *News*, May 15. https://www.cgiar.org/news-events/news/inside-meghdoot-the-app-delivering-weather-based-agricultural-advice-to-farmers-across-india.

Cole, Shawn Allen, Jessica Goldberg, Tomoko Harigaya, and Jessica Zhu. 2025. "The Impact of Digital Agricultural Extension Service: Experimental Evidence from Rice Farmers in India." PxD Working Paper (May 27), Precision Development. https://precisiondev.org/wp-content/uploads/2025/05/Odisha_RCT_05272025.pdf.

Dhulipala, Ram Kiran, Pranuthi Gogumalla, Rao Karuturi, et al. 2021. "Meghdoot: A Mobile App to Access Location-Specific Weather-Based Agro-Advisories Pan India." CCAFS Working Paper 370, CGIAR Research Program on Climate Change, Agriculture, and Food Security, Wageningen University. https://oar.icrisat.org/11917/1/WP370.pdf.

Fanuel, Mesafint, Mahmoud Nabil Mahmoud, Crystal Cook Marshall, et al. 2025. "AgriRegion: Region-Aware Retrieval for High-Fidelity Agricultural Advice." *arXiv:2512.10114v1 [cs.AI]* December 10, Cornell University. https://arxiv.org/pdf/2512.10114.

Gorke, Nishtha. 2025. "Empowering Millions of Indian Farmers with Instant AI Chatbot Support." *Wadhwani AI* (blog), November 6. https://www.wadhwaniai.org/empowering-millions-of-indian-farmers-with-instant-ai-chatbot-support/.

IDinsight. 2023. "Summary of Evidence Review of Digital Green's Video-Mediated Farmer Extension Approach: Technical Report Presented to Digital Green." DG Evidence Paper, September 19, Digital Green.

iSDA. 2025. "200,000 Plots and Counting: Celebrating One Year of Our Virtual Agronomist AI Advisory Service." *Posts* (blog), March 21. https://www.isda-africa.com/posts/virtual-agronomist-one-year/.

Jabed, Md. Abu, and Masrah Azrifah Azmi Murad. 2024. "Crop Yield Prediction in Agriculture: A Comprehensive Review of Machine Learning and Deep Learning Approaches, with Insights for Future Research and Sustainability." *Heliyon* 10 (24): e40836. https://doi.org/10.1016/j.heliyon.2024.e40836.

Konnect Team. 2025. "Amrit Series #12: Transforming Agricultural Extension in Odisha." *samagragovernance.in* (blog), January 18. https://samagragovernance.in/blog/2025-01-21-krushi-samruddhi-case-study-blog/.

Mesfin, Tewodros, Feyera Liben, Mohammed Ebrahim, et al. 2023. "Empowering Smallholder Wheat Farmers with NextGen Agroadvisory in Ethiopia: A Tailored, Season-Smart, and Scalable Approach." Summary Report (November), Alliance of Bioversity International and International Center for Tropical Agriculture, CGIAR. https://cgspace.cgiar.org/server/api/core/bitstreams/a3344f4b-8781-4854-8f88-002b794c646c/content.

Nandi, Ravi, and Swamikannu Nedumaran. 2019. "Agriculture Extension System in India: A Meta-Analysis." *Research Journal of Agricultural Sciences* 10 (3): 473–79. https://oar.icrisat.org/11401/1/Agriculture-Extension-System-in-India-A-Meta-analysis.pdf.

Pathak, Himanshu. 2025. "Strengthening Agri-Extension for a Strong Farm Sector." *Institutional News: India* (blog), November 1. https://pressroom.icrisat.org/strengthening-agri-extension-for-a-strong-farm-sector.

Piserchia, Ochuko, and David Edimu. 2025. "Enhancing Agricultural Extension Services in Nigeria Leveraging Digital Technology." EasyChair Preprint 15786, EasyChair. https://easychair.org/publications/preprint/SLr3/open/.

Shepherd, Keith D., Matthew A. E. Miller, Bruce Kisitu, et al. 2025. "Virtual Agronomist: An AI-Assisted Chatbot for Guiding Crop Management Decisions of Smallholder Farmers in Africa." *agriRxiv* (May 31). https://doi.org/10.31220/agriRxiv.2025.00332.

Singh, Namita, Jacqueline Wang'ombe, Nereah Okanga, et al. 2024. "Farmer.Chat: Scaling AI-Powered Agricultural Services for Smallholder Farmers." *arXiv:2409.08916v2 [cs.ET]*, October 8, Cornell University. https://doi.org/10.48550/arXiv.2409.08916.

Swanson, Burton E. 2008. "Global Review of Good Agricultural Extension and Advisory Service Practices." Food and Agriculture Organization of the United Nations. https://www.fao.org/4/i0261e/i0261e00.pdf.

Vaidya, Revati, and Vineet Keshaw. 2022. "Befriending the Farmer: Reflections on Building and Transitioning the Ama Krushi Service." *Insights* (blog), August 30. https://precisiondev.org/befriending-the-farmer-reflections-on-transitioning-ama-krushi/.

World Bank. 2025. "Harnessing Artificial Intelligence for Agricultural Transformation." World Bank. http://hdl.handle.net/10986/43990.

Zhu, Jessica, and Tomoko Harigaya. 2025. "Customized Digital Advice Can Help Farmers Reduce Crop Loss and Manage Weather Shocks: A Summary (or as Much as We Can Summarize!)." *Insights* (blog), February 26. https://precisiondev.org/customized-digital-advice-can-help-farmers-reduce-crop-loss-and-manage-weather-shocks-a-summary-or-as-much-as-we-can-summarize/.

5

AI's Social Impact: Improving Public Service Delivery

Main messages

- **AI can improve public services where skilled workers are scarce**
  Use evidence-backed tools, such as AI-supported medical imaging and weather forecasts, to support professionals and reach more people.
- **Predictive AI in back offices offers governments the fastest payoff**
  Prioritize predictive AI for forecasting, early-warning systems, tax enforcement, monitoring, and oversight, using administrative and satellite data.
- **AI can help governments deliver public services to more citizens**
  Scale up proven tools for teachers, health care providers, and case workers by adapting them to local languages and investing in devices, connectivity, and training.
- **Unproven AI tools can put frontline services at risk**
  Require rigorous testing and strong evidence that AI tools are accurate, fair, and suited to local needs before deploying them.

Introduction

Clifford Ogutu, a court assistant in Kenya, has worked in court-annexed mediation for many years. Kenya's court system introduced this type of mediation in 2016 to deal with large backlogs in court cases and give Kenyans better access to justice.[1] Before the advent of artificial intelligence (AI), court officers scheduled mediators by phone and kept records using unwieldy Excel spreadsheets. Finding a mediator for a new case could take up to 10 days. Today, the Kenyan judiciary's platform for digital mediation management, Cadaster, handles thousands of cases per year. A newly deployed customized algorithm instantly suggests a mediator for each case, based on mediators' accreditation and availability and the outcomes of their past cases. Most cases are assigned within one day, and caseloads are more evenly distributed among mediators. Over time, the algorithm is expected to increase case resolution rates by up to 8 percent.[2] "We are still doing sensitization with

A reproducibility package is available for this book in the Reproducible Research Repository at https://reproducibility.worldbank.org/catalog/624.

our mediators. It boils down to a culture change," Ogutu says. "But our new system has improved communications, and case assignments are more transparent and fairer. This is something I know other agencies would be interested in, too."[3]

Meanwhile in Brazil, schoolteacher Patricia faces a challenge known to millions of educators across the world. Each of her students has different gaps in subject knowledge and learns at a different pace. Planning activities that benefit all students takes time and energy. Recently, however, she started using ChatGPT to create lesson plans and devise additional pedagogical activities. "I have students with different backgrounds. ChatGPT helps me prepare activities that account for their differences." She often has to adjust the advice and materials ChatGPT suggests, using her pedagogical judgment and experience, but she embraces AI as a new paradigm. To her, AI cannot replace face-to-face contact or substitute for the relationship between teacher and student; instead, it makes administrative, clerical, and planning tasks easier and allows her to focus on the aspects of teaching that only she can do.[4]

As these examples show, AI holds considerable potential to improve the services governments in low- and middle-income countries provide, precisely because it can help them overcome the constraints they face. At the citizen-facing "front end" of public service delivery, primarily in education and health, governments often must carry out vital functions with a critical shortage of skilled personnel. Frontline providers like Patricia are often overburdened. In such contexts, AI can expand the reach and improve the quality and efficiency of basic services. At the "back end," public administration tasks rely on processing large quantities of information to, for example, make allocation decisions or carry out due diligence. AI systems perform such activities particularly well and can create considerable value by harnessing underused administrative data, as the earlier example from Kenya's court system shows.

This chapter aims to ground the conversation about AI in government in concrete, evidence-based use cases across both the decentralized front end and the less prominent but highly influential administrative back end of public administration in developing countries. The chapter discusses many areas of application for AI where the evidence is encouraging, but also provides examples where the anticipated benefits do not yet justify the risks. The chapter also emphasizes how the context in which AI will be deployed shapes considerations about introducing AI into service delivery. The many ways in which AI as an input can improve public services warrants subdividing applications further into what this chapter terms *front-end* and *back-end* AI (refer to figure 5.1).

Providing front-end AI tools to thousands or even millions of users poses challenges of scale and may require significant complementary investments, all while the evidence on impacts and cost-effectiveness is still in flux. Even so, there is already strong support for adoption at scale in areas such as AI-based academic tutoring and sharing of personalized information with citizens, as well as in medical imaging. AI is an even better fit with the back end of government, the main focus for early efforts at adopting AI. Procurement records across countries show that 88.7 percent of AI systems have been built for internal functions of government and 78.5 percent have used more traditional predictive and optimization AI models, whereas only 7.6 percent have used generative AI, mostly in front-end applications.[5] In typical back-end use cases, a small team of specialists deploys AI to handle systemwide forecasting, targeting, or enforcement tasks with data from centralized systems. This chapter presents various examples that demonstrate the substantial potential for AI in this setting.

The promise of AI in government should not obscure challenges. Compared with the private sector, public administrations lag in their technical capacity to implement AI. The limited evidence on AI impacts makes it difficult for

Figure 5.1 AI differs by tasks, users, capacity requirements, and costs depending on whether it is used in the front end or back end of government

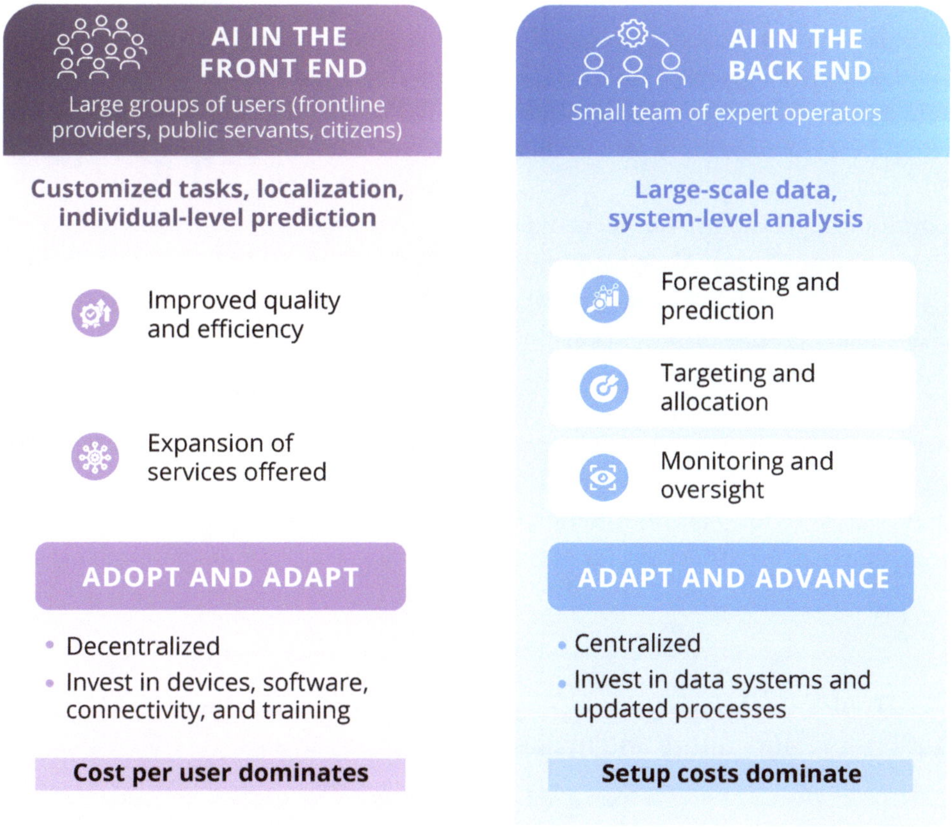

Source: WDR 2026 team.
Note: AI = artificial intelligence.

governments to accurately weigh benefits against potential risk of harm, and citizens cannot typically choose to "opt out." Understanding how AI systems work in government and what factors can lead to their failure, carefully considering how market factors shape government procurement of AI, and anticipating institutional and political economy constraints can prepare governments to integrate AI safely and successfully into their delivery of public services. As further explored in chapter 8, governments can shape how AI develops and diffuses in alignment with public values through thoughtful and selective adoption of AI and complementary investments in data systems, evaluation mechanisms, and procurement standards.

In the front end of government, evidence-backed AI applications can increase the quality of public services and expand access

The front-end versus back-end typology for AI used in this chapter aligns mostly—although not perfectly—with what might be thought of as external- versus internal-facing functions of government. The purpose here is not to classify tasks performed by government but to highlight the implications of different types of uses for costs and for decisions about AI adoption, adaptation, or advancement.

Uses of AI in government's front end involve decentralized applications that have thousands or millions of users, including applications supporting public servants in their duties as well as uses in public health care and education. Low- and lower-middle-income countries procure front-end AI mainly for early warning systems, smart agriculture, intelligent transportation, and biometric identification. The most prevalent types of AI procured are predictive AI and optimization, but chatbots and virtual assistants, as well as speech and document processing, increasingly use generative AI (refer to figure 5.2).

The core value added of front-end AI is to generate context-specific, customized outputs that improve users' access to relevant information or help them accomplish specific tasks. Front-end AI implementations can have two important roles in enhancing government service delivery. The first is *augmentation*: improving the quality of services delivered by human providers. The second is *automation* or *task shifting*: expanding access by using AI to provide services to citizens directly or reallocate tasks to lower-skill workers.

At the front end, the *last-mile* challenge of reaching remote, marginalized, or low-income populations requires complementary investments in accessibility and connectivity, in technologies that can work offline and on a wide range of devices, and in internal training and *change management*—structured processes to guide staff through the transition—to implement AI. To meet the related engineering and design challenges, governments

Figure 5.2 Front-end AI deployments in government focus on the environment, transportation, and agriculture and mainly involve predictive AI

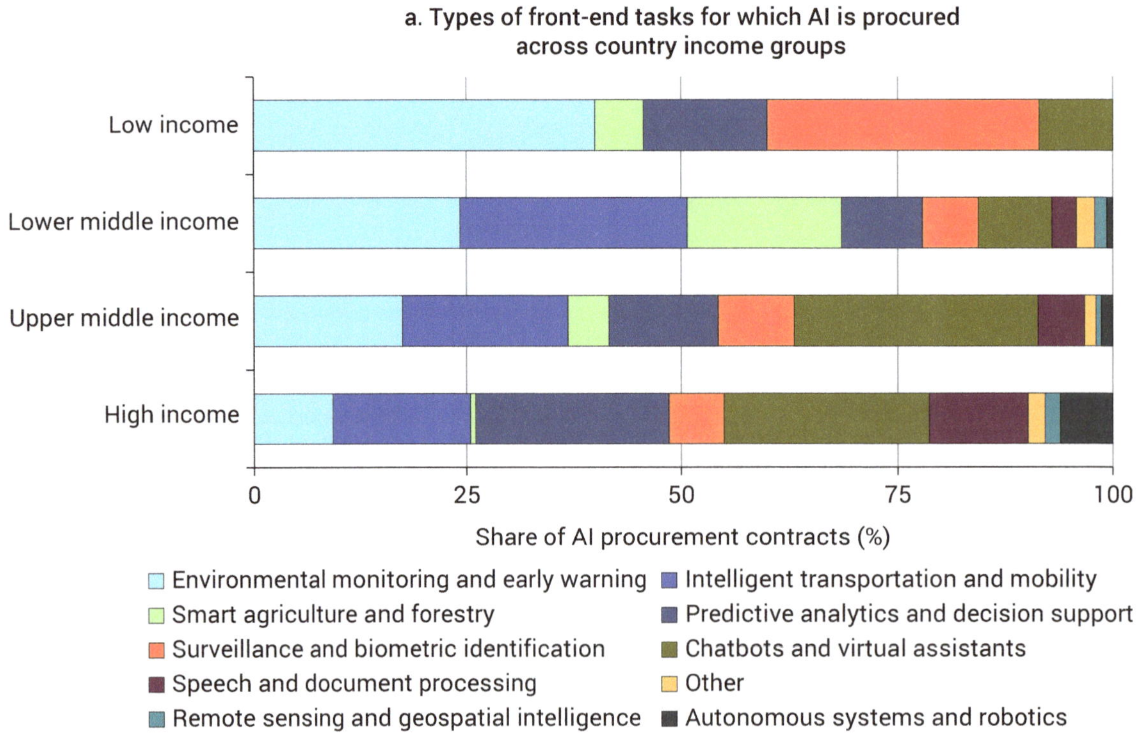

(Figure continues next page)

Figure 5.2 Front-end AI deployments in government focus on the environment, transportation, and agriculture and mainly involve predictive AI *(continued)*

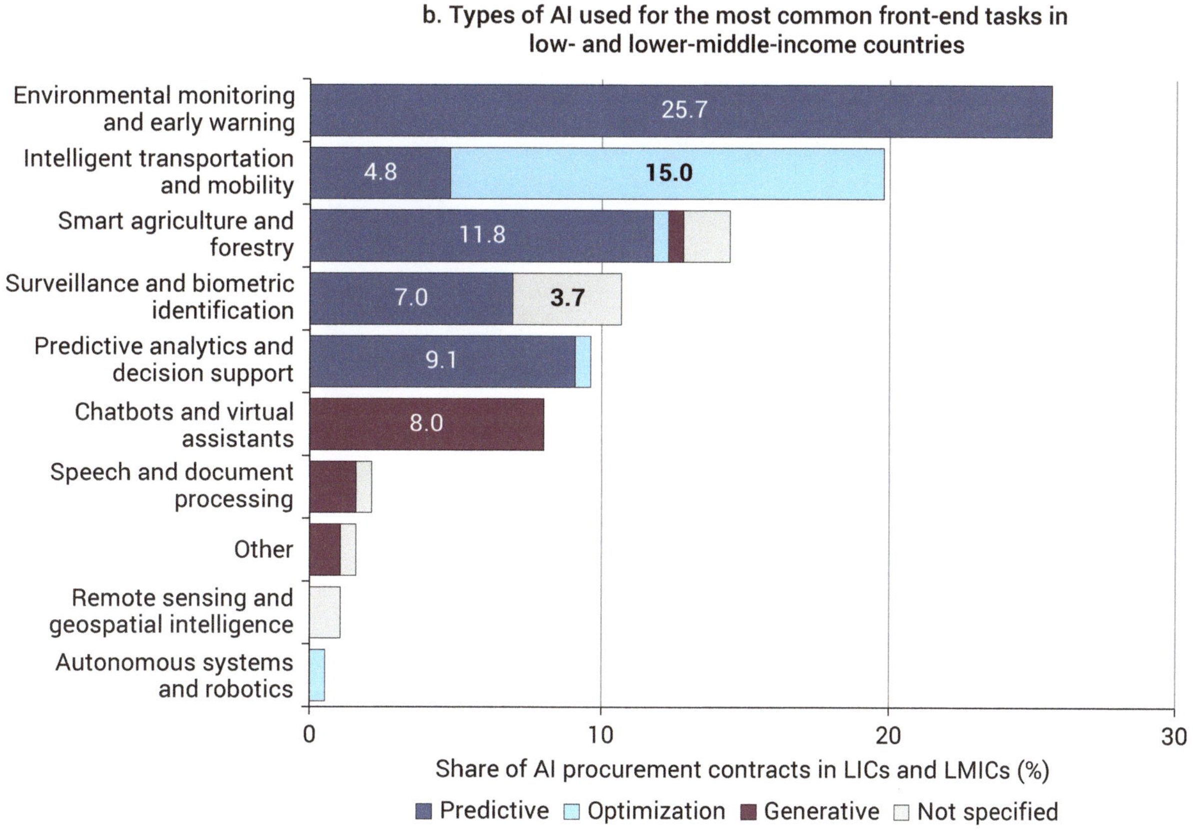

Source: WDR 2026 team, based on analysis of procurement contracts.

Note: GPT-5 was used to classify 6,127,564 procurement contracts from Tenders Electronic Daily, EU Tenders, Publications Office of the European Union, https://ted.europa.eu/en/; the Open Contracting Partnership; and the World Bank. Panel b focuses on the 10 most frequent task categories in procurement contracts classified as front end in low- and lower-middle-income countries (one of which is "Other"). The sample includes 15 low-income countries (36 contracts), 31 lower-middle-income countries (149 contracts), 25 upper-middle-income countries (146 contracts), and 34 high-income countries (1,443 contracts). Procurement contracts may not capture all possible uses of AI in government. AI = artificial intelligence; LICs = low-income countries; LMICs = lower-middle-income countries.

tend to adopt or adapt commercial solutions. Yet, across the vast range of front-end tasks governments perform, the maturity of AI applications varies considerably. In many areas, a full understanding of the benefits and risks associated with these AI applications is in the very early stages. These factors add significant costs and uncertainty to government efforts to adopt or adapt specific AI solutions and create challenges for government deployment at scale.

Improving the quality and efficiency of work by frontline providers of public services and public servants

Generative AI as a tool to enhance the productivity of public workforces

Much of the civil service is built around tasks that use text and information intensively, such as drafting documents, searching records, and applying rules to individual cases. As a result, the public sector has more tasks amenable to automation or augmentation by generative AI (that is, its *AI exposure* is higher) than other parts of the economy, especially in low- and lower-middle-income countries (refer to figure 5.3). Thus, the potential productivity gains are large. For instance, civil servants in the UK central government conduct approximately 1 billion citizen-facing transactions every year; saving just one minute per transaction that could be automated could save an estimated 1,200 person-years annually.[6] Various studies have shown that generative AI has increased the quality and speed of the work of government employees in high-income countries.[7] The latest generative AI models have enough versatility to take on vastly different tasks. This is even true increasingly in regard to low-resource languages, from automating various stages of legal case analysis in Brazil to screening media for news items relevant to conservation issues in Nepal to grading job application essays by candidates for jobs as teachers in Ghana.[8]

Figure 5.3 Public administration has more tasks that are amenable to automation and augmentation by generative AI than other sectors, particularly in low- and lower-middle-income countries

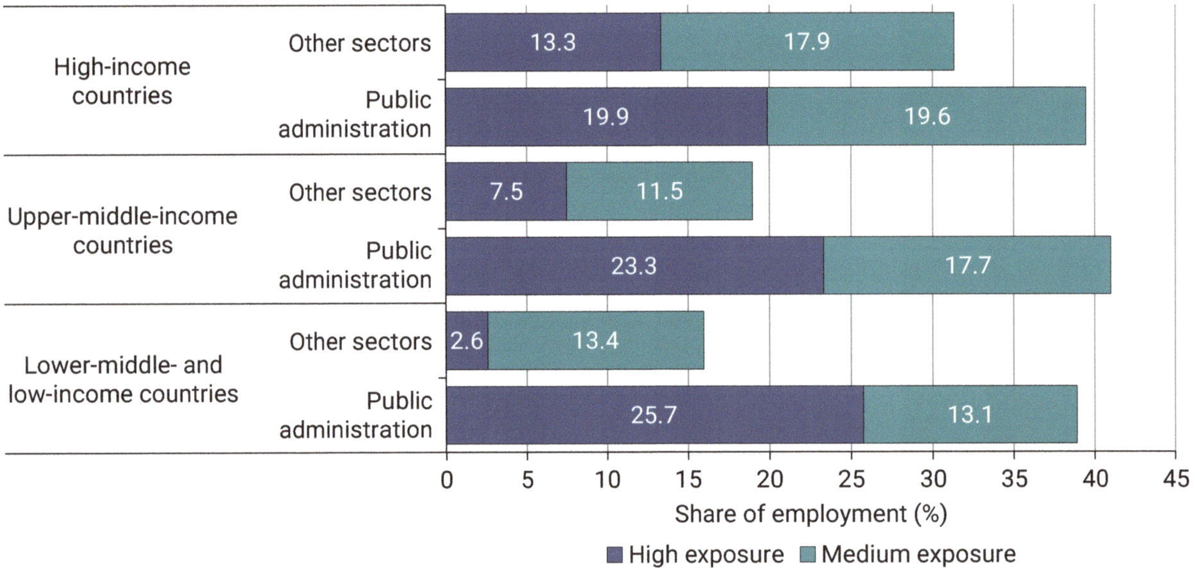

Source: WDR 2026 team, based on data and analysis of Gmyrek et al. 2026.

Note: Exposure refers to a job's potential for automation or augmentation by generative AI at the task level. Jobs with *medium exposure* are in occupations in which a moderate share of tasks could be automated with generative AI and the task-level exposure within the same occupation varies (exposure gradients 1–2 in Gmyrek et al. 2026). Jobs with *high exposure* are in occupations with a consistently high share of task-level exposure (exposure gradients 3–4 in Gmyrek et al. 2026). Jobs with *minimal exposure* (not shown) are in occupations in which only a small share of tasks have potential to be automated.

Support from large language models to help principals and teachers refocus on classroom instruction

A prime example of a government job highly exposed to AI is that of a public school principal. In Africa, Asia, and Latin America, principals report spending 30–35 percent of their time on administrative tasks and budgeting.[9] They experience high levels of stress on the job, driven by administrative burdens. Yet evidence shows that what matters for student outcomes is principals' instructional leadership.[10] Generative AI tools that automate reporting, draft communications, and generate timetables can free principals from paperwork so they can reallocate their time to tasks supporting instruction.[11]

Beyond supporting their bosses, generative AI can also support teachers by performing administrative tasks and providing access to knowledge. Many teachers in low- and middle-income countries begin their careers with gaps in subject knowledge or pedagogical training and balance their core teaching duties with a heavy load of administrative tasks. Survey evidence suggests that two in five teachers and school leaders around the world are already using AI tools.[12] As one of the aspects of teaching that demands the most time and energy, lesson preparation has particularly strong potential for AI augmentation. Generative AI can support lesson planning and tailor learning materials to students' individual skill levels. For instance, teachers in Sierra Leone preferred an AI-based assistant accessed through WhatsApp over standard searches on the web because they consider the material to be more accurate and more relevant to their queries and because AI responses consume less mobile data.[13]

AI can also provide quicker feedback, flag common learning gaps, and target instruction more precisely. In a field experiment on writing instruction in Brazil, teachers used technologies that automated grading and feedback on student essays.[14] Teachers spent more time on higher-value activities that require human judgment and interaction, such as discussing essay structure, argumentation, and clarity with students, and improved student performance on a high-stakes college entrance exam. Following this success, researchers developed a small AI approach to automating grading for the Brazilian context that does not require additional infrastructure, reliable internet access, or advanced digital skills.[15]

The available evidence indicates that the promise of AI in education is in freeing teachers to focus on what matters most: explaining difficult concepts, motivating students, and responding to individual student needs. Even in low-resource settings, this shift in how teachers spend their time can make a meaningful difference.[16]

Large language models in the provision of frontline health care: Not yet a priority

Another high-profile front-end application of AI is the use of large language models (LLMs) in primary health care. The astonishing capabilities of these models to answer clinical questions correctly, structure patient records, and ace medical exams have inspired hope that LLMs could support decision-making by health workers in low-resource contexts.[17] As early as 2024, the diagnostic performance of LLMs in simulated patient cases (vignettes) rivaled that of general physicians. In contexts involving minimal medical record keeping, a key advantage for scalability is that LLMs, unlike comparable predictive models, do not need to be trained on large volumes of context-specific patient data.[18] Correspondingly, the philanthropic and tech communities are pouring resources into this area of work.[19]

However, as of early 2026, the empirical evidence on deployment of LLM-based clinical decision support in low- and lower-middle-income contexts is mixed. In a clinical trial in Kenya, an LLM that created alerts and gave feedback to providers improved patient documentation and adherence to guidelines, such as those for drug choice or dosage, but did not significantly improve clinical outcomes.[20] In a study in Nigeria, the LLM did not reliably identify missed diagnoses, a major source of low quality of care. Although the health workers who used the LLM application judged the feedback it provided to be helpful, they were not effective at distinguishing good from bad advice.[21] The application's mixed performance may stem in part from the fact that the information the LLM can access is mediated by the health worker's initial record for the patient and lacks localized and seasonal information on epidemiology and risk factors. In addition to these problems, last-mile challenges loom large. A study in Rwanda that tested whether LLMs could make accurate referral decisions based on real-time background recordings of patient consultations found that nearly one-quarter of recordings were inaudible or incomplete.[22]

Context-specific information from predictive AI to increase the efficiency and quality of public services

Predictive AI and machine learning are not getting the same attention as generative AI, but they have significant potential to improve the quality of delivery of front-end public services, and they are often more mature. Across seemingly disparate areas, the powers of AI-based perception and prediction help process information at the individual level and provide outputs geared to specific individuals and contexts. Predictive AI applications in the front end range from improving patient triage to relieve pressure on medical staff[23] to helping maintenance technicians interpret measurements of truck engines.[24]

A compelling application is the AI-based verification of individuals' eligibility for benefits, which can be embedded in front-end services to improve monitoring services without adding undue burden. For example, subsidies for malaria drugs are difficult to sustain because they encourage recipients to overuse medications.[25] A computer vision application deployed in drug shops and pharmacies in Kenya can automatically verify the results of malaria tests and support targeted incentives for malaria care for infected patients.[26] The program significantly increased adherence to malaria testing and lowered the cost of treatment per person who tested positive for malaria.[27]

Helping governments offer services for which human capacity is scarce

Beyond improving the *quality* of services by augmenting existing staff and service providers, AI can also expand the *quantity* of services that can be offered, through direct AI support to citizens or through automation and task shifting, that is, increasing the skills of providers of lower-level services through the use of AI-based tools. In settings with a critical shortage of skilled human providers of certain public services, AI may be the only realistic strategy for providing these services at scale.

AI assistants and chatbots to help citizens make better use of what government offers

When designed well, AI-based tools can deliver tailored, context-specific information to far more people than human-mediated outreach, significantly increasing access to public services. For example, lack of information about options for further schooling perpetuates inequities in educational attainment[28] and distorts students' decisions about how much effort to invest in their education.[29] The choice of college and major has significant consequences for lifetime earnings,[30] but small errors on college applications can derail it. ConsiliumBots in Chile addresses this problem by providing personalized advice to students as they complete applications to college programs. The tool has helped 44 percent more students go to college and increased placement into higher-ranked programs by 20 percent.[31] Another example with high returns in the area of health care is chatbots that provide information on vaccines, which can significantly increase uptake.[32]

Within the public sector, tax authorities are among the savviest users of AI. By 2023, 62 percent of revenue agencies around the world were using AI and 56 percent reported using virtual assistants for citizens, including nearly 30 percent of low- and lower-middle-income countries (refer to figure 5.4). For instance, the Inland Revenue Authority of Singapore provides taxpayers with access to an agentic chatbot that allows them to check outstanding balances, view or modify payment plans, and make payments; it saved taxpayers an estimated 11,666 hours in 2024.[33] In South Africa, an automated assessment system completed 5.8 million assessments of tax returns in 2025 and disbursed more than $580 million in refunds within 72 hours.[34]

Figure 5.4 Tax authorities are savvy AI adopters of both front-end virtual assistants for citizens and back-end enforcement functions for auditors

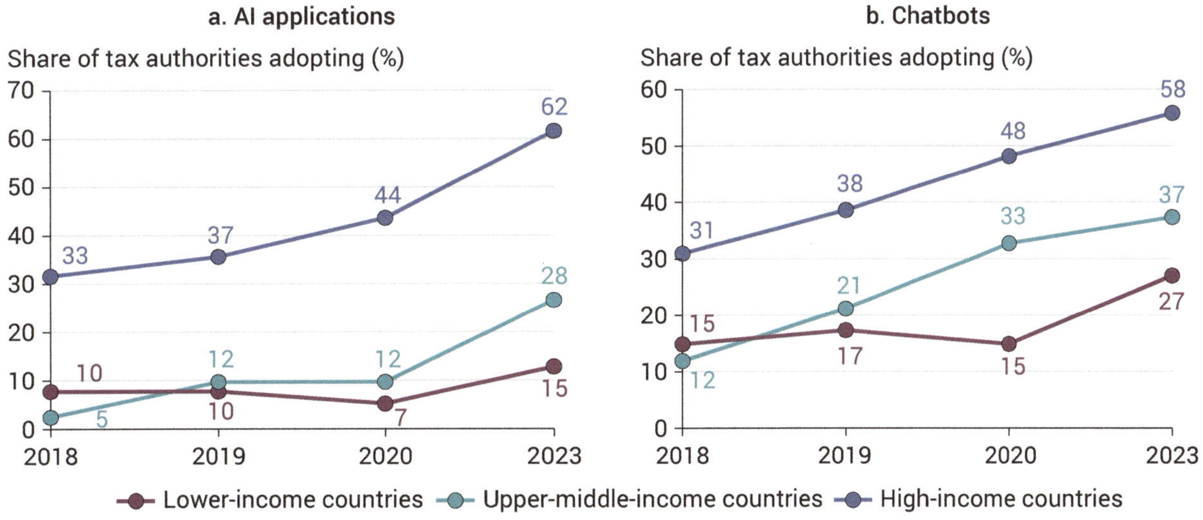

Source: WDR 2026 team, based on 2023 data of International Survey on Revenue Administration (ISORA) (dashboard), International Monetary Fund, https://ISORADATA.ORG.

Note: The sample includes responses from 41 lower-income countries, 43 upper-middle-income countries, and 52 high-income countries. The lower-income countries group includes both low- and lower-middle-income countries. AI = artificial intelligence.

Medical-imaging AI for low-resource contexts

One area in which the use of AI is well developed and becoming fully commercialized is medical imaging. This progress stems partly from the maturity of computer vision as a field and the standardization of imaging applications. As a result, algorithms now often match the performance of, or even outperform, human specialists in detecting anomalies in medical images that can cause illness.[35] This active area of AI advancement is also a response to the severe worldwide shortage of radiologists. There are only 44 radiologists per million people worldwide, less than half the level considered adequate (refer to figure 5.5, panel a). Dramatic geographic inequities exacerbate the problem: Fewer than 1,000 radiologists serve low-income countries as a group (refer to the thin yellow band in figure 5.5, panel b).

Modern computer-aided detection for medical scans or video uses deep learning algorithms to flag abnormalities. Research validating these tools has focused on implementations or procedures that are primarily relevant for medical specialties and in high-resource contexts, such as AI-aided diagnostics and real-time video annotation for colonoscopies.[36] However, some AI-assisted medical imaging screening or triage applications are emerging that work with portable devices or require only basic X-ray and ultrasound technologies, which are more widely available and cost-effective. If regulatory hurdles can be overcome, AI-supported imaging for medical screening tasks could vastly expand access to such screening by enabling task shifting and decentralization, resulting in earlier detection of abnormalities and improving patient outcomes.

Figure 5.5 The global shortage of radiologists affects low- and lower-middle-income countries the most

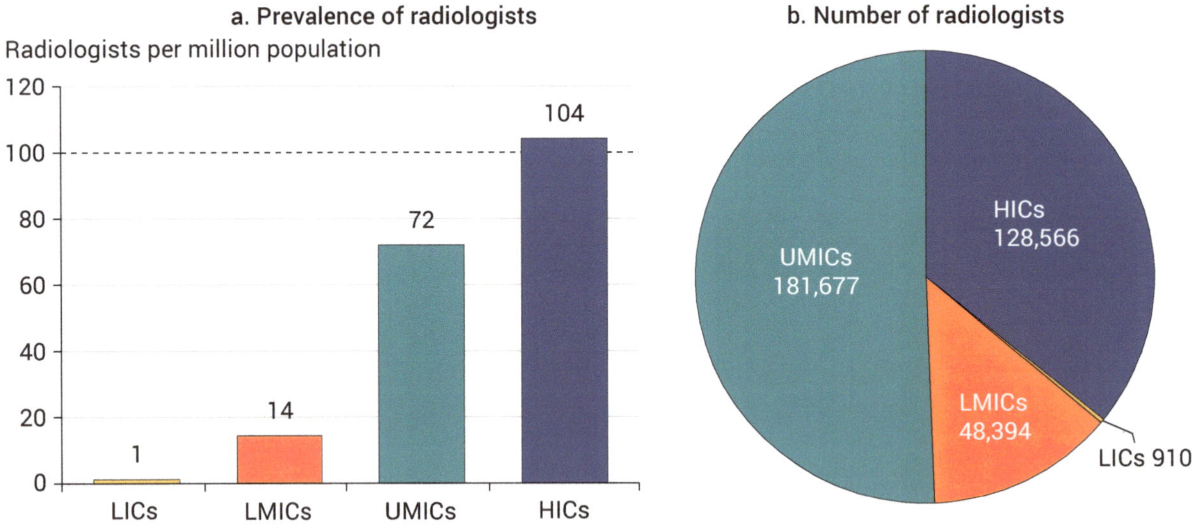

Source: WDR 2026 team, based on data of IAEA Medical Imaging and Nuclear Medicine Global Resources Database (IMAGINE), International Atomic Energy Agency, https://www.iaea.org/resources/hhc/nuclear-medicine/databases/imagine.

Note: The minimum adequate coverage for radiologists is considered to be 100 per million people; see the dotted line in panel a (Sarkodie et al. 2023). HICs = high-income countries; LICs = low-income countries; LMICs = lower-middle-income countries; UMICs = upper-middle-income countries.

An example backed by strong evidence is screening for diabetic retinopathy. This condition is a common complication of diabetes and a leading cause of preventable blindness in the working population, projected to affect 160 million adults worldwide by 2045.[37] Access to AI-based screening in clinics in Bangladesh increased the number of patients screened per day by 39.5 percent.[38] In Rwanda, AI-generated image grading—via the free nonprofit platform Cybersight—increased patients' adherence to referrals by 30.1 percent compared with delayed human grading of the retinal images.[39] India's Tamil Nadu state has rolled out large-scale screening for diabetic retinopathy using AI.[40]

Another mature and evidence-backed AI application is screening for tuberculosis using chest X-rays. In 2021, the World Health Organization (WHO) recommended computer-aided detection as a reliable method for tuberculosis screening. By 2025, multiple commercially available AI solutions had passed independent WHO tests.[41] A trial in Malawi demonstrated the benefits of computer-aided screening for initiating tuberculosis treatment.[42] Computer-aided detection is one of the most accurate methods of screening for tuberculosis.[43] It can detect cases that are asymptomatic (that is, those that do not or do not yet show the cough, fever, and weight loss typical of tuberculosis) and can help diagnose other lung conditions. However, both the screening software and the devices needed to use that software are expensive. Thus, screening for tuberculosis using computer-aided detection is a case study of the trade-offs in at-scale adoption of AI (refer to box 5.1).

Box 5.1 The trade-offs between cost-effectiveness and ability to scale: The case of AI-assisted screening for tuberculosis

Systematic analyses of the cost-effectiveness of medical artificial intelligence (AI) are an important factor for making decisions about whether to adopt the technology in developing countries. Yet such analyses are rare. An exception is the analysis of Qure.ai's qXR software for AI-assisted screening for tuberculosis (TB).

Background. Tuberculosis is preventable and curable, yet it kills more than 1 million people every year.[a] Systematic screening of susceptible populations is a central strategy for improving early diagnosis and reducing the prevalence of the disease in communities. The World Health Organization has recommended computer-aided detection (CAD) as an alternative to human reading of chest X-rays, but with explicit caveats about cost, infrastructure requirements, and equity considerations.[b] Two important drivers of the cost-effectiveness of AI imaging are its sensitivity (the share of true cases correctly flagged) and specificity (the share of true negatives correctly classified): higher sensitivity increases a population's health benefits from screening, whereas higher specificity saves time and cost at the diagnosis stage.

The cost-effectiveness of AI imaging depends on the alternative. A health technology assessment by the government of India compared CAD with standard-of-care readings of X-ray images by radiologists at clinics in Maharashtra. The assessment found that not only was computer-aided detection more accurate in screening for tuberculosis than human readers,

(Box continues next page)

Box 5.1 The trade-offs between cost-effectiveness and ability to scale: The case of AI-assisted screening for tuberculosis *(continued)*

but qXR was also less expensive than those readers.[c] By contrast, an assessment of the use of portable AI-assisted X-ray machines in lung health camps in Nigeria found that both the devices and software licenses were major cost factors. Adding a computer-aided detection screen to a symptom screen detected only eight additional TB cases but raised screening costs significantly.[d]

Beyond cost: AI-enabled X-ray screening as a path to eradicating TB? From a cost perspective, tuberculosis screening that employs CAD screening is most attractive when X-rays are already being used for such screening. But, from a public health perspective, CAD offers two key advantages in the fight to eradicate TB. First, it can identify asymptomatic cases, which is key for preventing the spread of the disease and facilitating early access to treatment.[e] Second, like a radiologist, it can typically flag a range of lung anomalies besides TB, but in doing so it does not rely on scarce radiologist time, thus removing a prohibitive capacity barrier and opening up the possibility of screening populations much more broadly.

Source: WDR 2026 team.

a. WHO (2026).

b. WHO (2021, 2025a).

c. Raval et al. (2025).

d. Garg et al. (2025).

e. Garg et al. (2025).

Access to other services for which skilled professional providers do not exist

AI applications have the potential to significantly increase access to services in other areas in which expertise is scarce, including agricultural extension (discussed in detail in spotlight 2) and mental health. Although mental health conditions affect millions of people worldwide[44] and account for a sizable share of the global burden of disease, trained professionals are in critically short supply. Evidence from Mexico suggests that an AI chatbot that guides users through exercises based on cognitive behavioral therapy can improve mental health outcomes at low cost.[45]

Another area in which AI has great potential for increasing access to services is personalized tutoring. Targeted instruction matched to students' learning level can deliver large learning gains,[46] especially in systems with overcrowded classrooms and wide variations in students' preparedness. AI can help scale this high-intensity intervention (refer to box 5.2). Evidence from

AI-powered tutoring for students shows that the most successful models of AI-supported learning keep teachers actively engaged with students.[47] These tutoring models work best when teachers receive appropriate training, including training in AI literacy, and can guide how the tools are used.[48] Such models support scale while keeping human tutors involved, because one teacher can oversee AI-based personalized tutoring for a large group of students.

Box 5.2 AI-powered tutoring and its potential to address learning gaps

High-impact tutoring—high-frequency, sustained tutoring in small groups[a]—requires trained personnel and sustained funding, resources that are often scarce in low-capacity education systems. Digital technologies can help overcome these barriers. For example, virtual tutoring programs have delivered learning gains even in difficult circumstances.[b] If both in-person and virtual tutoring work, the question becomes whether AI-powered tools can push personalization even further.

Results from a recent synthesis of randomized experiments evaluating AI-powered tutoring programs implemented in China, Ghana, Nigeria, Türkiye, and the United States are encouraging.[c] On average, 30 sessions of AI-powered tutoring produce meaningful improvements in student learning, which are equivalent to 0.12 standard deviations or at least 0.56 years of schooling (refer to figure B5.2.1).[d]

Additional lessons emerge from the evidence. First, AI-powered tutoring works best as a complement to teachers, not a substitute for them. Second, program design matters. The strongest results come from tutoring models embedded in a broader instructional strategy, with clear objectives, alignment with the curriculum, and safeguards against misuse. Third, training and support are essential. Teachers and students need guidance to use AI tools responsibly and effectively. When students are given unrestricted access to AI tools, many use them to shortcut learning during practice sessions, which undermines their acquisition of skills. This behavior parallels effects from unsupervised adoption of generative AI outside the classroom (refer to spotlight 3).[e] It is therefore essential that AI-powered tutoring systems be designed to incorporate teacher supervision, integrate well into broader education systems, and align the incentives of students and educators.

The evidence base on AI-powered tutoring is still evolving. More rigorous studies from low- and middle-income countries are needed to assess whether the impacts of AI-powered tutoring can be generalized and how to mitigate the potential negative effects of such tutoring. Given the small set of pilot studies to date, published findings may overstate average effects.[f] As additional evidence with larger samples accumulates, it will enhance understanding of how these programs work, for whom, and under what conditions.

(Box continues next page)

Box 5.2 AI-powered tutoring and its potential to address learning gaps *(continued)*

Figure B5.2.1 AI-powered tutoring programs have yielded meaningful improvements in student learning and skills in a number of countries

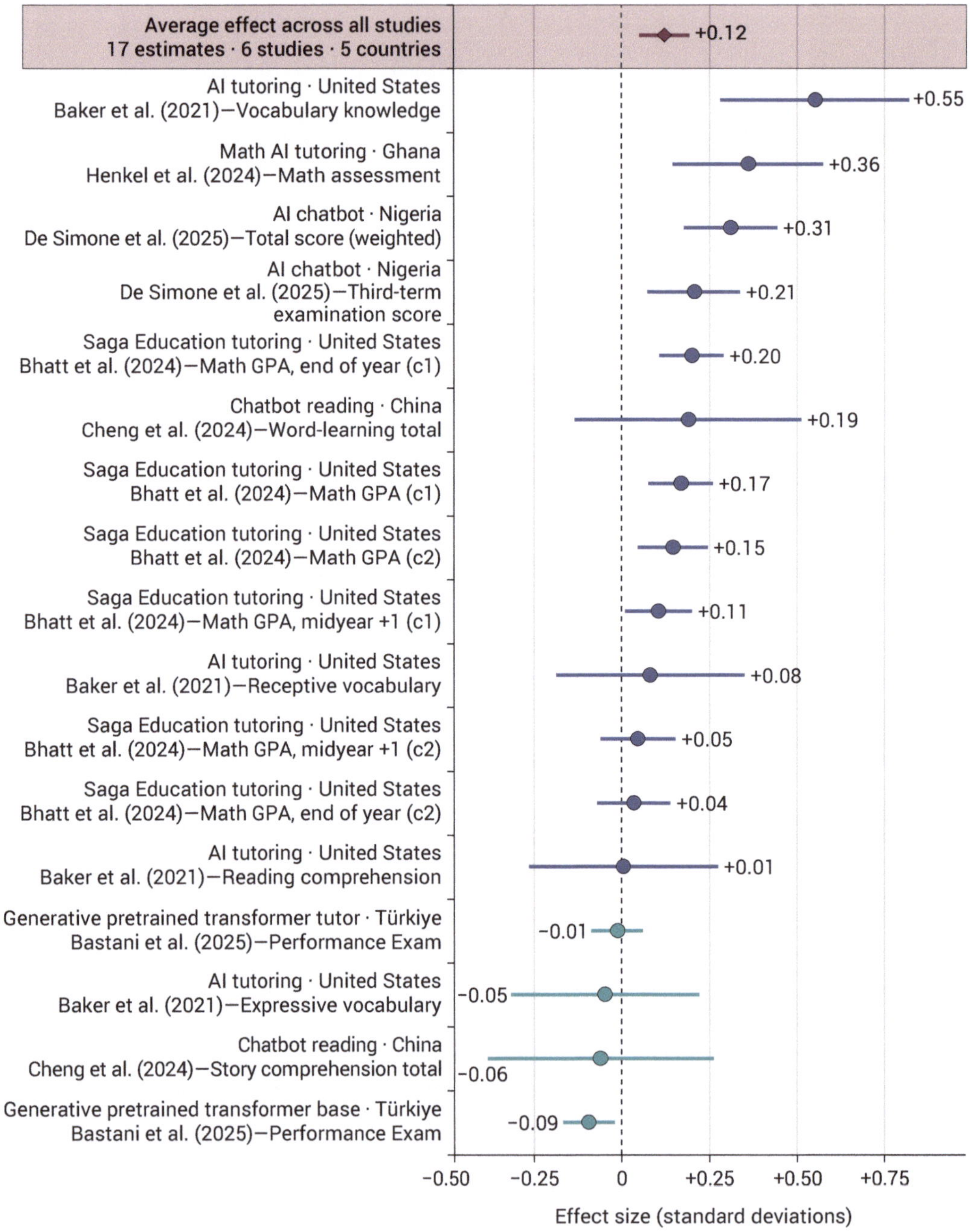

(Box continues next page)

Box 5.2 AI-powered tutoring and its potential to address learning gaps *(continued)*

Source: Burneo et al. 2026.

Note: The dots in the figure denote the estimated average value, and the bars represent the margin of error (the 95% confidence interval, which provides the range in which the true average value most likely falls). Saga Education tutoring was developed by the nonprofit Saga Education. It alternates in-person tutoring with working on a computer-assisted learning platform. The notation +1 following midyear represents the effects on midyear outcomes in the year following treatment. Word learning total and story comprehension total refer to the total index scores composed of several sub-scores for the respective skill. AI = artificial intelligence; c1 = cohort 1, academic year 2018/19; c2 = cohort 2, academic year 2019/20; GPA = grade point average.

Source: WDR 2026 team.

a. *High-impact tutoring* refers to a structured, evidence-based approach for rapid learning acceleration. It requires 3–5 sessions of at least 30–60 minutes per week over 10 weeks or more, with four or fewer students (Robinson et al. 2021).

b. Carlana and La Ferrara (2025); Dinarte-Díaz et al. (2025); Gortazar et al. (2023).

c. Burneo et al. (2026).

d. Based on Evans and Yuan (2019), one standard deviation of learning is equivalent to at least 4.7 years of business-as-usual schooling in low- and middle-income countries. An effect of 0.12 standard deviations therefore corresponds to roughly 0.56 years (about half a school year) of learning.

e. Bastani et al. (2025); Strömberg et al. (2026). For example, Bastani et al. (2025) compare a generative AI tutor that mimics a standard ChatGPT interface ("GPT base") with one designed to safeguard learning ("GPT tutor"). Results show that both AI tutors improved short-term performance but that, when access to the tutors is taken away, students using the GPT base perform worse than those who have never had access; these negative effects are mitigated by the safeguards in GPT tutor.

f. DellaVigna and Linos (2022).

Scaling AI for the front end of government: Uncertainty about impacts and the high cost of adoption as main barriers

While front-end applications show clear promise, the challenge to successful implementation is scaling safely and affordably. Many applications, particularly those in health care, pose significant risk of harm, and the wider impacts of AI use, such as its impacts on cognitive development (refer to spotlight 3), are still understudied. Moreover, the costs can accumulate, given dependencies on infrastructure and a reliance on the private sector to supply front-end AI tools.

The challenge of identifying high-value applications

The evidence on the impacts of AI for most application areas is still emerging, especially for low-resource contexts. Even if the performance of a particular AI model for a given task is well validated—not always a given—many other factors beyond the model's performance determine the success of an AI tool. For example, impediments to adopting the tool and integrating it into workflows must be removed. Especially vulnerable populations may distrust digital and AI solutions, as well as government institutions more generally (refer to chapter 9).

Frontline workers may perceive AI tools as an added burden or as opening their activities up to surveillance.[49] Human biases can prevent users from integrating AI recommendations in an optimal way.[50]

Very little is also known about the system-wide impacts of implementing AI tools. For example, if such tools decrease job satisfaction or limit employment prospects for radiologists or teachers, they may ultimately worsen shortages of needed experts and professionals, threatening service capacity as well as governments' ability to monitor and improve AI-based systems. Expanding access by using AI tools at one level could also lead to downstream bottlenecks in areas in which services delivery is extremely constrained, such as public health care systems.

Despite a flood of research, many capabilities of AI have been tested only in simulations or with model cases (refer to box 5.3). Developing countries must also consider whether a system was built for them and their citizens. The risk that those with no representation in the data, such as ethnic minorities, will be overlooked or poorly served is well known and documented.[51] These issues are amplified for generative AI. More than 75 percent of low- and lower-middle-income economies responding to the AI and Data for Better Governance Survey conducted for this Report cited limited AI capabilities in local languages as an important barrier to the adoption of AI.[52] Furthermore, LLMs may *hallucinate*, that is, present incorrect information as factual or aggregate conflicting information inaccurately; however, it is difficult to design safeguards because the models constantly change and their behavior varies to a surprising degree.

Box 5.3 AI evidence relevant for policy in low- and middle-income countries is still scarce: The case of AI in frontline health care

A recent study[a] screened more than 280,000 papers from scientific databases in March 2026, assisted by GPT-5. Nearly 10,000 studies concerned health interventions based on artificial intelligence (AI). However, less than 1 percent of these interventions (1) provided support to frontline providers in triage, prevention, screening, or primary care; (2) were empirically tested with the intended providers and with data from actual patients; and (3) were conducted in low-resource settings or in low- and middle-income countries. Among the 57 studies that met all three of these criteria, only 17 measured causal impacts on patient outcomes, health care quantity or quality, or cost of health care; that is, only 17 provided the type of evidence that is most relevant for policy decisions about the allocation of health care resources in low- and middle-income countries (refer to figure B5.3.1).

(Box continues next page)

Box 5.3 AI evidence relevant for policy in low- and middle-income countries is still scarce: The case of AI in frontline health care *(continued)*

Figure B5.3.1 Only 0.2 percent of articles on AI use in health care measure the impact of AI on patient health or on quality or efficiency of health care provision

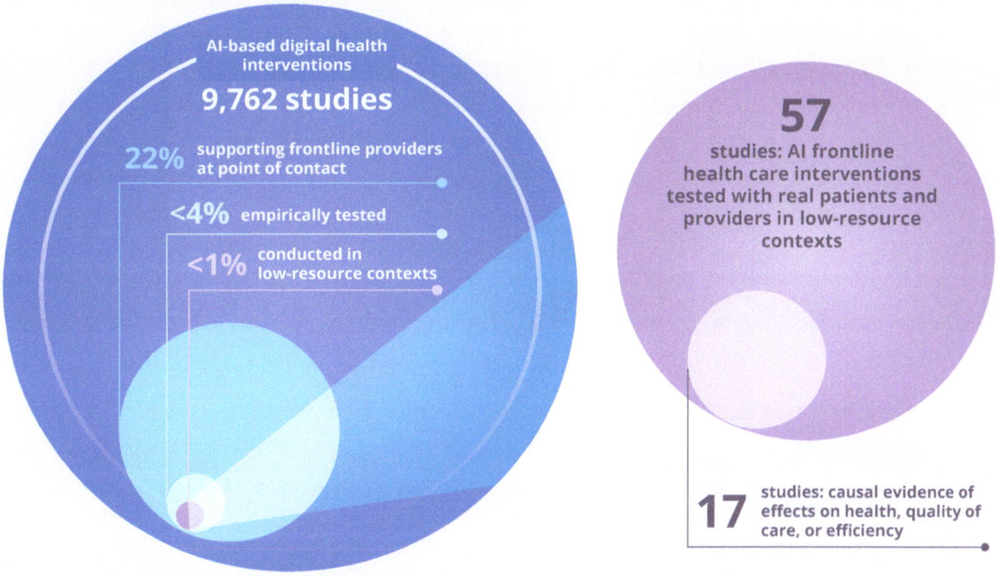

Source: Sautmann and Weinert 2026.

Note: Low-resource contexts refer to contexts in low- and middle-income countries, as well as low-resource settings in high-income countries. AI = artificial intelligence.

Source: WDR 2026 team, based on Sautmann and Weinert 2026.

a. Sautmann and Weinert (2026).

Software and complementary investments as cost drivers

Front-end AI systems depend critically on basic last-mile reliability factors such as adequate electricity and connectivity, as well as affordable costs of data and sufficient capacity of devices. These factors can be more important for sustaining use of AI than the power and sophistication of the underlying technology.[53] Digital identification, data exchange, and payment systems are needed to allow AI tools to interact with public records and services. The AI application may also need specialized devices, such as portable X-ray machines, and, in the case of medical applications, require regulatory approvals.

Ensuring equitable access for low-literacy or differently abled populations or linguistic minorities requires dedicated investments (for example, in voice and local language options).[54] In addition to lack of support for local languages, government officials cite lack of skills or training as a major barrier, with low- and lower-middle-income economies particularly vulnerable (refer to figure 5.6).[55] For example, a 2024 study found that teachers in Sierra Leone needed guidance and support to become comfortable using AI tools, even those with familiar platforms and formats, such as a chat on a messaging app.[56] Without investments in training and accessibility, AI could perpetuate inequities and deepen the digital divide.

Provided these multiple barriers are not prohibitive outright, these requirements make it more likely that governments will adopt or adapt front-end AI tools developed by the private sector. Technology companies have experience with portability and user interface design, as well as with engineering tasks such as keeping applications running reliably across diverse devices, operating systems, and network conditions and building small applications that load quickly on weak networks, work on basic devices, and remain usable when a user's internet connection drops.

Figure 5.6 **Skill, connectivity, and support for local languages are central barriers to adoption of front-end AI, especially in low- and lower-middle-income economies**

Survey question: "To what extent do the following constraints prevent or limit your government's use of AI in the delivery of front-facing public services?"

Share of economies identifying a barrier as major or moderate (%)

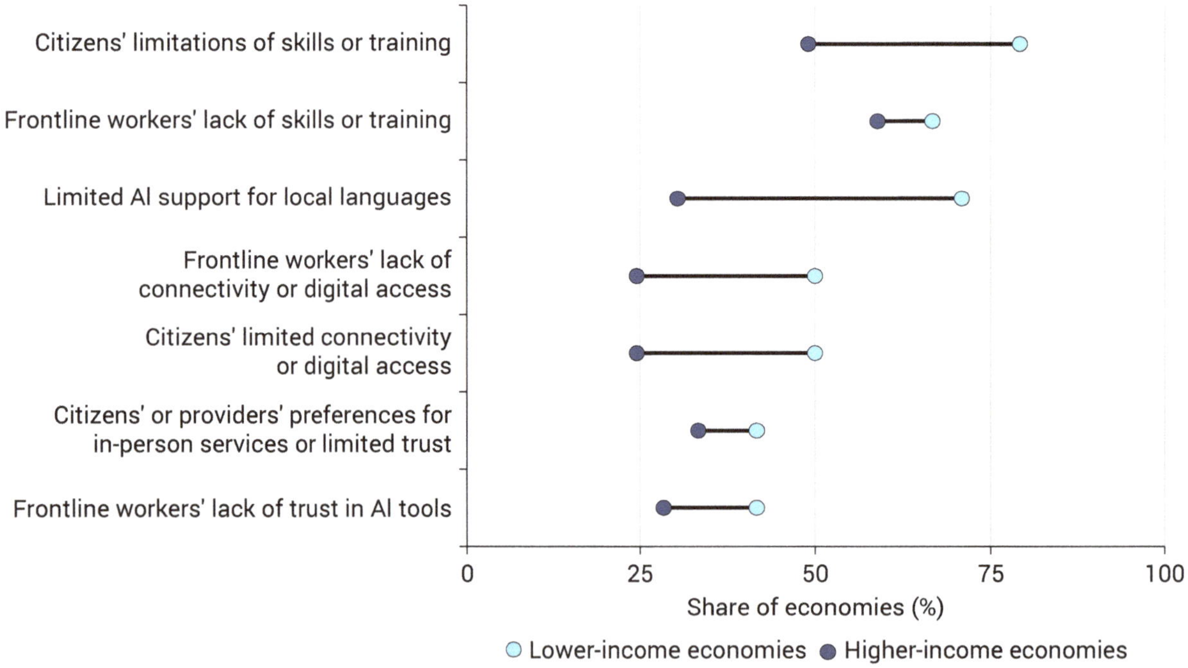

Source: WDR 2026 team, based on the AI and Data for Better Governance Survey, World Bank.

Note: The sample includes 12 low-income and 12 lower-middle-income economies (lower-income group) and 16 upper-middle-income economies and 17 high-income economies (higher-income group). AI = artificial intelligence.

All these factors—from complementary investments to dedicated devices to user training and adoption of commercial AI tools through software subscriptions or licensing—can increase costs per use or per user. Assistants based on large language models are particularly expensive to run at scale. Although fees have been falling, it is not clear how long this trend will last. Firms are currently operating below cost to gain market share.[57]

Verification gaps and lock-in risks: Why AI is difficult to buy

Adoption of AI solutions purchased from the private sector typically means less control over the capabilities of the technology and less transparency about their performance. This creates challenges for public organizations that lack the technical capacity to evaluate claims by private vendors about the performance of their products or to anticipate risks, or for those whose procurement rules restrict access to system details needed to scrutinize performance.[58] Exiting commercial systems also becomes more costly as systems absorb organizational data and workflows become entangled. Providers reinforce this process through free pilots, exclusive contracts, and bundled features.[59] Outdated procurement rules that do not protect governments' right to retain all information and data needed to switch between providers of AI services can further limit the ability of government users to change models or components.[60] In this context, the initial price quote may matter less than the buyer's long-term bargaining position.[61]

The high cost of front-end AI, combined with uncertainty and a current lack of evidence, makes it challenging to decide whether and where to invest in AI tools, or which AI tools to incorporate. Governments need to critically evaluate not only how an AI model performs but also how an AI tool changes user behaviors and affects relevant outcomes, including whether there are any unintended consequences. The complementary inputs required for front-end AI mean realistically that, for many countries, investments will be highly selective and focused on a narrow set of applications that are supported by strong evidence and reliable analysis of their cost-effectiveness. Chapter 8 provides guidance on how to choose where to invest in AI and how to resolve the tradeoffs between external versus internal development based on preexisting capacity. Together with spotlight 6, the chapter also discusses relevant considerations for the monitoring and evaluation of AI solutions. It also lays out concrete steps governments can take to assess these solutions before and after they have been adopted to understand the value they add and safeguard against any potential negative effects. Finally, chapter 8 discusses effective procurement processes that can ensure that AI solutions do not create unforeseen cost hikes or lock-in to a single vendor.

In the back end of government, AI can solve problems at scale to make public administration more effective, efficient, and precise

Compared with front-end systems, back-end AI systems must overcome fewer barriers to access and usability and may therefore be more feasible for governments to deploy in the near term. Back-end AI can augment the capacity of overstretched experts in specialized agencies such as tax agencies, meteorological institutes, traffic administration agencies, and agencies overseeing pension funds. The technology is typically operated by a small number of specialized users and takes advantage of the centralized nature of many government tasks, as well as the higher digitization rate in public administration than in the rest of the economy.

Deployments of back-end AI in government in low- and lower-middle-income countries focus on predictive analysis and decision support, remote sensing and geospatial intelligence, and monitoring and early warning systems. They overwhelmingly use predictive AI (refer to figure 5.7). Predictive AI can help fill gaps in capacity and data in critical back-end functions by doing more with sparse information through, for example, sophisticated statistical inference, integration of novel data sources such as satellite imagery, or algorithms for reinforcement learning (automated learning through trial and error). It can also distill the extensive administrative records that governments often hold (such as tax returns, procurement contracts, health insurance information, and school transcripts) into insights and action.

Figure 5.7 Back-end AI deployments in government focus on decision support, geospatial intelligence, and early warning systems, and mainly use predictive AI

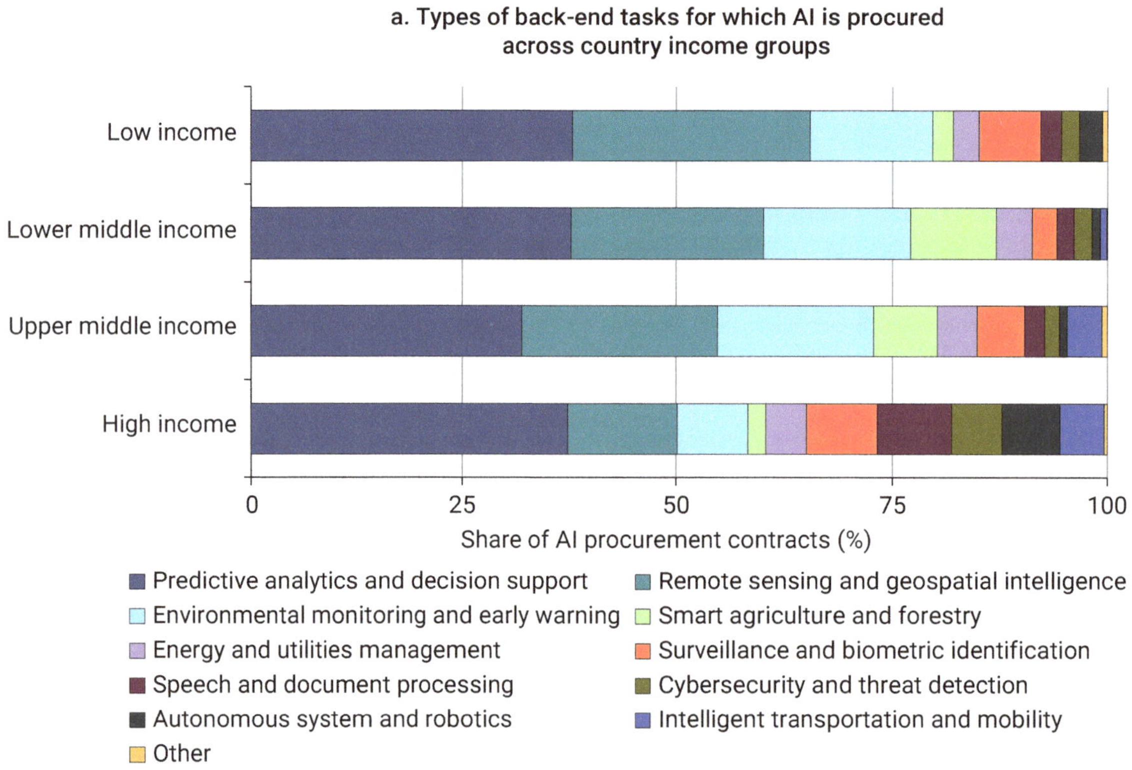

(Figure continues next page)

Figure 5.7 Back-end AI deployments in government focus on decision support, geospatial intelligence, and early warning systems, and mainly use predictive AI *(continued)*

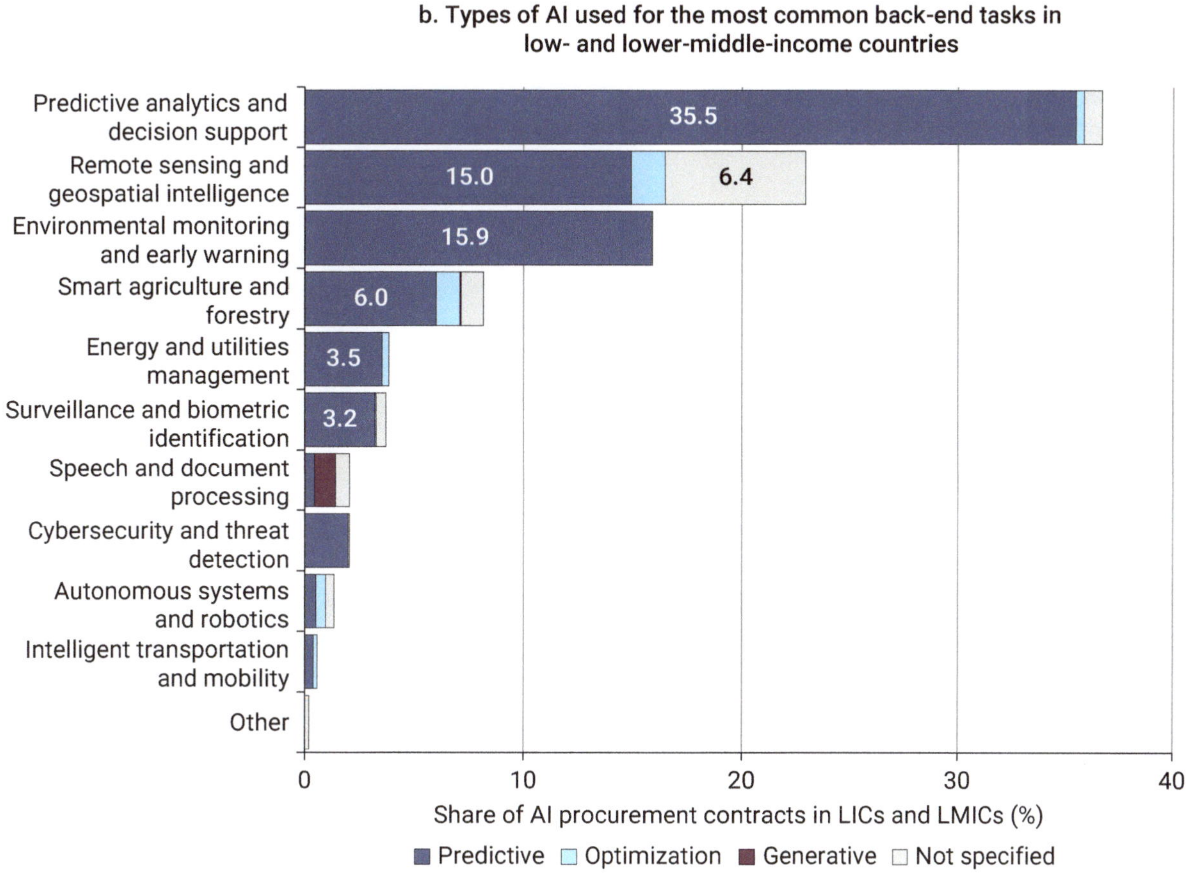

Source: WDR 2026 team, based on analysis of data on procurement contracts from Open Contracting Partnership 2025; Tenders Electronic Daily, EU Tenders, Publications Office of the European Union, https://ted.europa.eu/en/; World Bank.

Note: GPT-5 was used to classify 6,127,564 procurement contracts. Panel b focuses on the 10 most frequent categories of tasks in procurement contracts classified as back end in low- and lower-middle-income countries. The sample of procurements of AI for back-end government services includes contracts from 19 low-income countries (338 contracts), 48 lower-middle-income countries (1,302 contracts), 43 upper-middle-income countries (1,190 contracts), and 40 high-income countries (11,156 contracts). Procurement contracts may not capture all possible uses of AI in government. AI = artificial intelligence; LICs = low-income countries; LMICs = lower-middle-income countries.

Back-end tasks are determined by the needs and processes of government agencies as well as the specifics of their data, and fulfill critical functions that require close oversight. Therefore, most back-end AI tends to be customized for the purpose at hand. Governments may customize a machine learning algorithm or model using their own data and optimize and validate the model for a specific purpose. In instances in which institutional capacity is sufficient, governments may even build or enable AI with new capacities—for example, in weather forecasting—often in close collaboration with nonprofit institutions and researchers that provide the AI expertise. Back-end applications of AI are an area of adaptation and advancement in which governments and public sector functions can significantly contribute to AI innovation, as the examples in this section showcase.

Providing better forecasts and predictions of risks for the public

Forecasts and predictions of risks are an important centralized and highly specialized *information public good* that governments provide. Climate- and weather-related risks pose a particular threat to low-income populations, but many governments in developing countries have limited capabilities to forecast weather and provide early warnings, given the demands of conventional numerical modeling in terms of technology and infrastructure. AI can significantly reduce the need for input data on physical variables such as thermodynamics or atmospheric motion. Although training AI-based systems for weather prediction requires significant computational resources, running them may not require anything more than a laptop computer.

AI-based weather forecasting systems are already being piloted in several African countries.[62] The advances in this area are remarkable. For example, Google's Flood Hub AI can forecast extreme river events without needing long-range data gathered from stream gauges—previously a major obstacle to reliable warning systems. Consequently, 80 countries, many of them developing countries, have free access to flood forecasting that is comparable to what is available in Europe.[63] A study in Telangana, India, demonstrated the value of these public goods: simply giving farmers access to monsoon forecasts yielded benefits more than half as large as those from large-scale irrigation schemes.[64]

Beyond climate forecasting, enhanced predictive methods can be used in many domains to identify risks before they escalate into emergencies. For example, AI can provide earlier and faster detection of outbreaks of infectious diseases and more accurate predictions of case numbers by processing large quantities of data from diverse sources—such as medical records, but also social media and traffic data—for early warning systems.[65] A model developed by the Wadhwani Institute for Artificial Intelligence that forecast cases of COVID-19 helped the city of Mumbai increase the capacity of its intensive care units by more than 1,200 beds to match peak hospitalization rates.[66]

Improving the allocation of scarce resources

Government has an important role in allocating goods and services to citizens, notably where markets do not function well or do not exist, creating exceedingly complex allocation problems. The case study on the assignment of mediators to court cases that opened this chapter illustrates this complexity. The algorithm behind Cadaster currently assigns more than 10,000 cases per year to more than 1,500 mediators all over Kenya, accounting for a complex set of conditions. Finding an allocation that makes optimal use of the capacities of participating mediators would challenge any human decision-maker but poses no difficulty for the AI tool.[67] Similar allocation problems for large systems are ubiquitous in the delivery of public services, from distributing supplies to clinics to assigning children to spots in public schools.

Augmenting digital platforms with algorithmic assignment

Industries such as energy management, transportation, and cloud computing are already using AI frequently to manage resources efficiently. Governments are increasingly applying these optimization methods to problems involving delivery of services.[68] Machine learning methods provide heuristics for choosing the best allocation out of a very large set of possibilities or integrate predictive models into optimization loops.[69] In contexts in which information is incomplete, techniques such as reinforcement learning can further improve allocations over time. Innovations of this type are possible partly because central digital platforms have begun to handle the collection and management of data. Returning to the earlier example, after Kenya's judiciary introduced Cadaster to help manage mediation, data analysis revealed that manual case assignment was resulting in capacity bottlenecks and inefficiencies. At that point, the judiciary partnered with researchers to find ways to improve capacities, assign cases more equitably, and increase the rate of successful mediation proceedings. The resulting system is explicitly built to learn about new mediators without making any assumptions based on personal characteristics, and human court officers make all final decisions regarding assignments.[70]

Directing scarce public health resources

Although governments still rarely use sophisticated optimization techniques in low-resource service contexts, some compelling recent examples from health care illustrate how governments and nonprofits have collaborated with computer scientists and operations researchers.[71] In Sierra Leone, a machine learning tool for supply chain management increased access to essential medicines by 19 percent.[72] Similar applications could help optimize inventories and reduce pharmaceuticals shortages elsewhere. In Oyo, Nigeria, the AI Driven Vaccination Optimization assistant (ADVISER)—deployed by a local health nongovernmental organization, HelpMum, in cooperation with the government—allocates a series of interventions aimed at getting children vaccinated. ADVISER is formulated to find the most effective intervention for each child, from call reminders about vaccination appointments to pickup services for those appointments, while optimizing HelpMum's very limited resources. It combines multiple technical innovations into a practical deployment package. For example, it makes sure that children are vaccinated within the appropriate time window for vaccination and optimizes routes of vehicles picking up children and families for vaccinations.[73]

Leveraging new data sources for emergency social protection

One of the most difficult tasks for governments in low- and middle-income countries is to provide timely assistance in emergencies when there are no comprehensive registries that help identify beneficiaries. The potential of AI to leverage nontraditional data sources has attracted a lot of attention. During the COVID-19 pandemic, for example, Togo needed to distribute emergency cash fast, without direct human contact. Researchers working with the country's government combined mobile phone metadata with satellite imagery to infer which households in the country were most in need of assistance. The country's cash transfer program Novissi scored every mobile subscriber nationwide, then transferred aid via mobile money to those individuals predicted to be poorest. Compared with simple geographic targeting, the approach reduced exclusion errors (missing poor people) by 421 percent.[74]

The success of the Novissi program raised hopes that AI plus mobile phone data could be used permanently to undertake the expensive task of finding poor people for social protection, freeing up resources for distributing benefits. However, the approach had more mixed results in Afghanistan[75] and arguably failed in Bangladesh (refer to box 5.4). The experience in Bangladesh highlights the potential risks in deploying AI for high-stakes allocation tasks: even excellent data and careful model training do not guarantee perfect predictions for use in allocation decisions, and people who do not appear in the data—often the most vulnerable populations—are at risk of being excluded from the allocations entirely.

Box 5.4 Not yet a solution for identifying poor people for assistance: Shortcomings in using algorithms based on mobile phone data in Bangladesh

Can poverty targeting be improved by combining machine learning methods with a novel data source: namely, metadata from phone records? A recent study of a cash transfer program in Bangladesh illustrates how the benefits of artificial intelligence (AI) are closely tied to the performance of the model deployed.[a]

The difficult task of identifying poor people. The focus of the study is a cash transfer program aimed at the poorest 21 percent of the population in Bangladesh, implemented by the national government in collaboration with GiveDirectly, a nonprofit organization that distributes donor funds directly to poor recipients. The program was designed to compare two (very different) ways of estimating which households are poor: the novel method of phone-based targeting (PBT) and an established method, proxy-means testing (PMT).[b] In contexts in which employment and housing are often informal, identifying poor households requires considerable resources and is subject to high degrees of error. PMT asset surveys, in particular, consume significant resources and time, yet their ability to find truly poor people—their *recall*, in machine-learning speak—is often shockingly low. Some studies have found that about half of poor households identified by such surveys were not receiving benefits.[c]

Comparing prediction methods. Both PBT and PMT approaches in the program built on a "ground truth" survey in which all 5,000 surveyed households were visited to measure household consumption. The consumption data collected in this survey were then linked with either information on asset ownership from the same survey (for PMT) or with the phone records of survey household members (for PBT) to build models that could predict household consumption, and therefore poverty, for all 106,000 households that were potential beneficiaries under the program. PMT uses a very simple model, based in AI, that maps assets owned into consumption levels, whereas for phone-based targeting, researchers trained a gradient-boosting machine learning model that uses more than 1,500 features in the phone use data.

Unfortunately phone use patterns in the survey population were not well correlated with poverty. PBT had an estimated recall of only 32 percent—meaning that 68 percent of poor people did not receive benefits, and 68 percent of program funds went to ineligible households—compared with 52 percent for PMT. For comparison, random distribution of funds would have had a recall of 21 percent. One challenge for PBT is that not all poor households own phones that have SIM cards (without which, phone data cannot be collected), and, if they do, they may change phone numbers often; overall, 6 percent of households in the study could not be linked to phone use records. Not surprisingly, households were largely dissatisfied with phone-based targeting, and only 45 percent perceived it as fair.

(Box continues next page)

Box 5.4 Not yet a solution for identifying poor people for assistance: Shortcomings in using algorithms based on mobile phone data in Bangladesh *(continued)*

Does it save money? The costs of PMT-based targeting are high because every household must be visited to record its assets. The authors of the study argue that PBT saves money that could instead be used for transfers (at least as long as phone data are freely available and individual phone lines in mobile operator data can be linked to targeted households).[d] The authors make the valid point that the costs of acquiring data for making predictions with the trained machine learning model—that is, collecting information on assets from every household for PMT versus the costs of obtaining information on households' phone usage for PBT—can be an important and sometimes overlooked factor in cost-benefit calculations of poverty assistance. Even so, it stands to reason that targeting accuracy needs to improve to justify using PBT over other methods.

Source: WDR 2026 team.

a. Aiken et al. (2025).

b. The researchers also tested community-based targeting, but this method is not a focus here.

c. Alatas et al. (2012); AusAID (2011).

d. Okamura et al. (2024).

Spotting patterns in big data to improve monitoring and oversight

Machine learning has shown particular promise in strengthening state functions that depend on enforcement capacity, from customs to environmental protection. Government agencies often hold extensive and detailed records but can investigate only a small share of relevant cases. This creates scope for machine learning systems trained on historical data to improve the effectiveness of enforcement by identifying candidates for auditing. In high-income countries, for example, agencies are already routinely using advanced machine learning techniques to support functions in the area of health care financing such as reviewing claims and detecting fraud. Although these approaches are still less common in developing countries, some scaled deployments have been notable. For example, studies indicate that the introduction of machine learning solutions into claims management in the Philippines has helped detect and deter fraud.[76]

Weak state capacity particularly curtails the collection of taxes, limiting government revenues available to fund the delivery of public services. In response, tax administrations in many countries have invested in digital case management systems. These databases now support the deployment of AI to strengthen tax enforcement. In France, starting in 2021, the Foncier Innovant project analyzed aerial imagery using AI to detect undeclared swimming pools and recovered approximately €10 million in property taxes. By 2023, the system had been expanded nationwide and broadened to target other undeclared construction, generating €40 million in additional local tax revenue (and exceeding the program's estimated cost) within two years.[77]

Research indicates significant potential for such approaches in other domains. In Malaysia, the Protection Assistant for Wildlife Security (PAWS) algorithm optimizes patrol routes rangers take to deter poaching in protected areas.[78] Machine learning models trained on municipal audit data in Brazil can predict which local governments face elevated risk of corruption,[79] and, in the area of occupational safety, predictive models can identify firms with high risks of workplace injury,[80] although these approaches have not yet been implemented for enforcement purposes. The common thread is a government agency with limited inspection capacity, a large population of potential targets, and administrative data that can be used to predict where enforcement efforts are most likely to pay off. A typical challenge is that, even if AI predictions are very accurate, they have limited impact when the tools are not appropriately integrated into workflows or legal and institutional mechanisms of enforcement are underresourced. Examples where this tension persists can be found across contexts, from the identification of fictitious firms registered for tax evasion purposes to the satellite-based detection of illegal deforestation in the Amazon.[81]

Deploying AI in the back end: Data systems and capacity for AI adaptation and oversight as main challenges

In contrast with front-end applications which may be used by thousands or even millions of people, back-end applications require less change management or smaller investments in devices and connectivity. The centralized nature of back-end AI, which makes it easy to scale back-end AI applications quickly, can justify high up-front investments; running a trained model typically involves comparatively low day-to-day costs. However, there are other barriers: the legitimacy and long-term viability of back-end AI depends critically on clear frameworks to govern accountability, as well as strong data infrastructure, backed by institutional and human capacity.

Data quality, capacity for oversight, and data security as critical capacity gaps

Typical back-end applications based on predictive AI or machine learning depend heavily on strong data systems. Such systems require not only shared standards, clear institutional mandates, and secure mechanisms through which agencies can exchange data, but also targeted improvements in the quality of the data. Many administrative registries are incomplete and hampered by delays in reporting data, which weaken the data used to train, test, and monitor AI and machine learning models.

Converting government knowledge and administrative practice into usable (training) data is an important and often underrated foundational step. For predictive AI, this means translating administrative judgment into labels to classify cases or data points. For generative AI, it requires codifying rules, procedures, and regulatory exceptions into documentation that can be reliably retrieved and applied. In many governments, these inputs are scattered across multiple sources: PDF manuals, fragmented legal texts, legacy systems, or institutional memory and staff experience.

Failures of back-end AI may affect broad swaths of a country's population, with serious negative consequences.[82] Between 2015 and 2019, an automated system that the Dutch Tax Administration used to detect welfare fraud wrongly flagged more than 26,000 individuals, disproportionately from migrant backgrounds, in some cases leading to unemployment, bankruptcies, and divorces.[83] A parliamentary inquiry faulted systemic bias and the opaqueness of the system, and the resulting public outcry led the prime minister and cabinet to resign in 2021.[84] These types of risks are compounded in contexts with weaker institutional capacity, where mistakes may take longer to identify or address. Citizens may also have fewer avenues to contest such decisions effectively.

A related risk is cybersecurity. Although privacy and security concerns often lead to calls for "sovereignty" of AI systems and localization of data,[85] locally hosted infrastructure may in practice be less secure if governments lack the ability to maintain systems, monitor intrusions into them, manage responses to incidents, or operate redundant infrastructure. Well-managed international cloud services can often provide stronger protection than domestic systems, but legal barriers may prevent governments from using them. The experience of Ukraine underscores this point. In 2022, Ukraine's parliament reversed a prohibition on storing government data in the cloud, and more than 100 state registries migrated to international cloud providers. This allowed services to continue operating even as physical infrastructure was destroyed.[86]

Beyond cybersecurity, AI in government creates additional risks of misuse and deliberate manipulation, including the use of mass surveillance (discussed in detail in chapter 6). Addressing these risks goes beyond technical considerations and may require explicit political decisions. Governments may benefit from defining clear red lines on which uses of AI they will and will not permit and being transparent about the action plans they put in place to uphold those positions. In contexts already characterized by weak institutions, opaqueness, or corruption, these risks can further erode the perceived legitimacy of public services and raise additional barriers to legal redress, compounding preexisting governance challenges. Robust accountability mechanisms are therefore essential to ensure that adopting a particular AI system reinforces legitimacy and public trust, rather than eroding them (refer to chapters 8 and 9 for further discussion).

Challenges in determining accountability for decisions supported by AI

AI-supported government activities can lack clear pathways for accountability. The law is built on doctrines focused on human conduct, such as intent and causation.[87] When an algorithm makes a flawed decision, is the algorithm's developer, the vendor that provided it, the agency that procured and deployed it, or the frontline official who used it responsible? The diffusion of responsibility can create new challenges for the implementation of AI solutions in government.[88]

Additionally, administrative law and due process often require that individuals affected by adverse decisions receive sufficient information to understand and contest them. However, many AI tools function as black boxes, producing outputs through processes that neither users nor developers fully understand. As AI systems are updated, retrained, or exposed to new data, their behavior can shift in ways that alter outcomes, even without any intended policy change.

Governments can support strong data systems, strengthen accountability frameworks, and improve oversight of such systems to guard against system failures. However, each of these actions also imposes additional requirements for internal capacity. These requirements tend to be higher for back-end systems that are customized for a given agency or policy process. Experience suggests that governments are prone to deploying AI they cannot govern and sustain.[89] The mismatch is greater in lower-income settings, where infrastructure gaps, fragmented data, and staffing constraints strain management.[90]

Chapter 8 discusses how to build internal capacity and meet the data needs of modern AI. It also sets out a framework for matching approaches to deploy AI to institutional capacity. Chapter 9 emphasizes the importance of maintaining the public's trust in the government with regard to the use of AI and citizens' data, and explores how to close accountability gaps by strengthening governance and regulatory frameworks, building capacity of regulatory bodies, and using other tools.

AI can be successfully integrated into the public sector by prioritizing accountability, oversight, and procurement that fits government capacities

The emerging evidence suggests that AI could significantly expand government capacities and ultimately improve the well-being of citizens in many ways. The demand exists: citizens in developing countries express greater willingness to use AI-mediated public services than their counterparts in wealthier nations.[91] AI may effectively be stepping into the role of community intermediaries such as cybercafé workers and local brokers in navigating government procedures.[92]

This chapter showcases innovative, evidence-backed AI applications that can yield benefits even today. At the front end, these include medical-imaging AI to support task shifting from scarce specialists to lower-level providers; AI tools for academic tutoring that adapt learning levels to individual students; and AI-powered information systems that help users through high-stakes decisions or processes, such as college applications. At the back end, AI can vastly improve local forecasting and support a wide range of enforcement and monitoring functions of the government. However, given their constraints with respect to infrastructure, data, and resources, governments in developing countries need to carefully weigh costs and benefits and pick and choose where to invest. Especially for front-end AI, without the complementary investments necessary to guarantee broad access, AI adoption risks perpetuating the digital divide and preexisting inequities.

When governments are considering whether to adopt AI and machine learning, especially in sensitive and high-impact functions such as health, law enforcement, and social protection, they have a heightened responsibility to verify that these applications do not cause harm, and that the benefits they provide justify the costs. The public expects government to be accountable for its use of AI, given the government's outsized influence on people's lives[93] and given that the technology is at a very early stage, with new risks potentially materializing over time that are not anticipated today. Chapter 8 discusses in detail how governments can adopt AI responsibly in the near term by choosing AI projects that are well matched with governments' existing capacity and infrastructure, building internal skills, designing good procurement processes, and monitoring outcomes carefully. In addition, chapter 8 points to high-value investments in data systems and infrastructure and in impact evaluations that can expand the evidence base on AI in the public sector.

The public sector is likely to adopt or adapt existing AI models for most applications, especially in the near term. But governments in low- and middle-income countries can, and do, undertake targeted investments to advance AI in high-value use cases (refer to chapter 8 for examples). Such uses will often involve less resource-intensive AI applications (such as predictive models or optimization algorithms used in back-end data systems) or applications that high-income countries consider to be less of a priority (such as regional forecasting systems or developing large language models for low-resource languages). The BHASHINI initiative in India, for instance, provides open access to more than 350 AI models for speech recognition, translation, and text-to-speech conversion across 22 languages.[94] Governments may also choose to invest in AI solutions that can work with intermittent connectivity or on basic devices.

Through their decisions to adopt, adapt, or advance AI, governments shape what kind of AI is built and how it affects countries' economies as a whole. Government spending averages 32 percent of GDP in emerging markets.[95] In low-income countries, the state can account for up to 60 percent of formal jobs.[96] It would therefore be costly to leave AI-driven productivity gains on the table. Moreover, government standards for interoperability and auditability, rights to the data on which they train and which they use to operate, and portability diffuse beyond uses in the public sector. In France, for example, a 2012 regulation requiring agencies to favor open-source software increased open-source contributions by more than 1.1 million per year, spurred adoption by private firms, and grew start-ups.[97]

Adoption by public agencies signals which uses of AI are considered safe and aligned with public values; conversely, high-profile failures can slow beneficial adoption across both the public and private sectors. Through thoughtful choices, governments can manage the risks while reaping the benefits of AI for more competent, efficient, and accessible public administration. Chapter 8 covers key considerations for realizing this promise. Chapter 9 treats the complementary topic of how to effectively regulate the public sector to protect citizens from risk while leaving room for beneficial innovation and technology adoption.

Notes

1. World Bank (2017).
2. Farabi et al. (2026).
3. Personal communication, Clifford Ogutu, May 2026.
4. Based on focus group discussions conducted by World Bank staff members in Brazil in April 2026.
5. Based on WDR 2026 team analysis of procurement contracts.
6. Straub et al. (2024).
7. Fitzpatrick et al. (2025); GDS (2025); Maršál and Perkowski (2025).
8. Refer to Awuah et al. (2025) on Ghana; Jain et al. (2024) on Brazil; Pereira et al. (2024) on Nepal.
9. GSL (2024).
10. Robinson et al. (2008).
11. For example, the AI assistant El Director LIBRE is designed to reduce the administrative and bureaucratic workload of school principals in Latin America, thereby allowing the principals to focus on teaching and learning. Refer to Molina et al. (2025).
12. GSL (2024); OECD (2025a).
13. Björkegren et al. (2025).
14. Ferman et al. (2021).
15. Isotani et al. (2023).
16. Muralidharan et al. (2019).
17. For evidence, refer to Armitage (2025) on performance on medical exams; Fernández-Pichel et al. (2025) on clinical questions; Huang et al. (2024) on structuring patient records.
18. Li et al. (2022).
19. Refer to Google.org Impact Challenge: AI for Government Innovation (dashboard), Google, https://google.org/impact-challenges/ai-government-innovation; OpenAI (2026).
20. Agweyu et al. (2026); Korom et al. (2025).
21. Abaluck et al. (2026).
22. Shimelash et al. (2026).
23. Gellert et al. (2024); Li et al. (2022); Liang et al. (2019); Taylor et al. (2025).
24. Harris and Yellen (2024).
25. López et al. (2022).
26. Refer to Maisha Meds (homepage), https://maishameds.org/; Skjefte et al. (2024).
27. Dieci et al. (2024).
28. Larroucau et al. (2025).
29. Jensen (2010); López (2025).
30. Altonji et al. (2014).
31. Larroucau et al. (2025).
32. Hou et al. (2025); Wang et al. (2025).
33. OECD (2025b).
34. SARS (2025).
35. Sabri et al. (2025); Salinas et al. (2024).
36. For example, refer to Han et al. (2024).
37. Teo et al. (2021).
38. Abramoff et al. (2023).
39. Refer to Cybersight (website), Orbis International, https://cybersight.org/about/; Mathenge et al. (2022); Whitestone et al. (2024).
40. Brant et al. (2025).
41. WHO (2026).
42. MacPherson et al. (2021).
43. Qin et al. (2019).
44. WHO (2025b).
45. Angelucci et al. (2026).
46. Guryan et al. (2023); Nickow et al. (2024).
47. Burneo et al. (2026).
48. De Simone et al. (2025); LearnLM and Fab AI (2026).
49. Borges do Nascimento et al. (2023); Shaw et al. (2018).

50. Agarwal et al. (2023); Koçak et al. (2024).
51. Buolamwini and Gebru (2018); Seyyed-Kalantari et al. (2021).
52. World Bank (2026).
53. Borges do Nascimento et al. (2023); Whitehead et al. (2023).
54. Naggirinya et al. (2024); Sondaal et al. (2016); Whitehead et al. (2023).
55. This chapter presents the findings from the AI and Data for Better Governance Survey of governments conducted by the World Bank for this Report. The survey's findings focus on the use of, barriers to use of, and governance of AI, highlighting key differences across countries according to income level. The survey included a core module for digital agencies (or ministries of digital transformation or the equivalent), as well as two modules each for the following sectors: health, education, tax, public finance, civil service, and procurement. The survey was sent to relevant authorities in 129 economies. Respondents in 60 economies completed at least one of the modules, with 57 economies responding to the core module.
56. Choi et al. (2024).
57. Korinek and Vipra (2024); Schmid et al. (2024).
58. Hickok (2024); Johnson et al. (2025).
59. Open Contracting Partnership (2025).
60. Hagiu and Wright (2025); OECD (2025b).
61. Hagiu and Wright (2025); OECD (2025b).
62. Okoth (2024); WMO (2025).
63. Refer to Flood Forecasting (dashboard), Google, https://sites.research.google/gr/floodforecasting/.
64. Burlig et al. (2025).
65. Villanueva-Miranda et al. (2025).
66. Jain et al. (2022).
67. Analysis of mediation data by the WDR 2026 team, based on Farabi et al. (2026).
68. Esnaashari et al. (2023).
69. *Optimization loops* are iterative mathematical processes for finding optimal solutions. AI predictions can be fed into a decision-making algorithm that then iterates over alternatives to compute the best action. Bengio et al. (2021); Hady et al. (2025).
70. Farabi et al. (2026).
71. For example, refer to Dasgupta et al. (2025); Mate et al. (2022); Pal et al. (2024).
72. Chung et al. (2026).
73. Kehinde et al. (2024); Nair et al. (2022).
74. Aiken et al. (2022).
75. Aiken et al. (2023).
76. Mathauer and Oranje (2024); WHO (2024).
77. DGFiP (2024).
78. Fang et al. (2016).
79. Ash et al. (2025).
80. Johnson et al. (2023).
81. Assunção et al. (2023); Barwahwala et al. (2024); Coelho-Junior et al. (2022).
82. Alon-Barkat and Busuioc (2023); Busuioc (2021).
83. Henley (2021).
84. Heikkilä (2022).
85. Chander (2020).
86. Gelvanovska-Garcia et al. (2024).
87. Bathaee (2018).
88. Busuioc (2021); Yuan and Chen (2025).
89. Hashim and Piatti-Fünfkirchen (2018); Pahlka (2023).
90. Syed et al. (2023).
91. PEARL and SRI (2024).
92. Hoefsloot et al. (2025).
93. OECD (2025b).
94. Kumar et al. (2025).
95. IMF (2025).
96. World Bank (2026).
97. Nagle (2023).

References

Abaluck, Jason, Robert Pless, Nirmal Ravi, Anja Sautmann, and Aaron Schwartz. 2026. "Does LLM Assistance Improve Healthcare Delivery? An Evaluation Using On-Site Physicians and Laboratory Tests." NBER Working Paper 34660, National Bureau of Economic Research. https://www.nber.org/papers/w34660.

Abramoff, Michael D., Noelle Whitestone, Jennifer L. Patnaik, et al. 2023. "Autonomous Artificial Intelligence Increases Real-World Specialist Clinic Productivity in a Cluster-Randomized Trial." *npj Digital Medicine* 6 (October): 184. https://doi.org/10.1038/s41746-023-00931-7.

Agarwal, Nikhil, Alex Moehring, Pranav Rajpurkar, and Tobias Salz. 2023. "Combining Human Expertise with Artificial Intelligence: Experimental Evidence from Radiology." NBER Working Paper 31422, National Bureau of Economic Research. https://doi.org/10.3386/w31422.

Agweyu, Ambrose, Paul Mwaniki, Vaishnavi Menon, et al. 2026. "Generative-AI Enabled Clinical Decision Support System in Primary Care: A Pragmatic, Cluster Randomized Trial." *Nature Medicine*, Open Access (June 26). https://doi.org/10.1038/s41591-026-04503-6.

Aiken, Emily L., Anik Ashraf, Joshua Evan Blumenstock, Raymond Guiteras, and Ahmed Mushfiq Mobarak. 2025. "Scalable Targeting of Social Protection: When Do Algorithms Out-Perform Surveys and Community Knowledge?" NBER Working Paper 33919, National Bureau of Economic Research. https://www.nber.org/papers/w33919.

Aiken, Emily L., Guadalupe Bedoya, Joshua Evan Blumenstock, and Aidan Coville. 2023. "Program Targeting with Machine Learning and Mobile Phone Data: Evidence from an Anti-Poverty Intervention in Afghanistan." *Journal of Development Economics* 161 (March): 103016. https://doi.org/10.1016/j.jdeveco.2022.103016.

Aiken, Emily L., Suzanne Bellue, Dean S. Karlan, Christopher R. Udry, and Joshua Evan Blumenstock. 2022. "Machine Learning and Phone Data Can Improve Targeting of Humanitarian Aid." *Nature* 603 (7903): 864–70. https://doi.org/10.1038/s41586-022-04484-9.

Alatas, Vivi, Abhijit Banerjee, Rema Hanna, Benjamin A. Olken, and Julia Tobias. 2012. "Targeting the Poor: Evidence from a Field Experiment in Indonesia." *American Economic Review* 102 (4): 1206–40. https://doi.org/10.1257/aer.102.4.1206.

Alon-Barkat, Saar, and Madalina Busuioc. 2023. "Human–AI Interactions in Public Sector Decision Making: 'Automation Bias' and 'Selective Adherence' to Algorithmic Advice." *Journal of Public Administration Research and Theory* 33 (1): 153–69. https://doi.org/10.1093/jopart/muac007.

Altonji, Joseph G., Lisa B. Kahn, and Jamin D. Speer. 2014. "Trends in Earnings Differentials Across College Majors and the Changing Task Composition of Jobs." *American Economic Review* 104 (5): 387–93. https://doi.org/10.1257/aer.104.5.387.

Angelucci, Manuela, Raissa Fábregas, and Antonia Vazquez. 2026. "The Well-Being Effects of Digital Mental Health Care." IZA Discussion Paper 18538, Institute of Labor Economics. https://docs.iza.org/dp18538.pdf.

Armitage, Richard. 2025. "Performance of Leading Large Language Models in May 2025 in Membership of the Royal College of General Practitioners-Style Examination Questions: A Cross-Sectional Analysis." *arXiv:2506.02987v1 [cs.CL]*, June 3, Cornell University. https://doi.org/10.48550/ARXIV.2506.02987.

Ash, Elliott, Sergio Galletta, and Tommaso Giommoni. 2025. "A Machine Learning Approach to Analyze and Support Anticorruption Policy." *American Economic Journal: Economic Policy* 17 (2): 162–93. https://doi.org/10.1257/pol.20210618.

Assunção, Juliano, Clarissa Gandour, and Romero Rocha. 2023. "DETER-ing Deforestation in the Amazon: Environmental Monitoring and Law Enforcement." *American Economic Journal: Applied Economics* 15 (2): 125–56. https://doi.org/10.1257/app.20200196.

AusAID (Australian Agency for International Development). 2011. "Targeting the Poorest: An Assessment of the Proxy Means Test Methodology." September, AusAID. https://www.dfat.gov.au/sites/default/files/targeting-poorest.pdf.

Awuah, Kobbina, Urša Krenk, and David Yanagizawa-Drott. 2025. "Augment or Automate? An Early Field Experiment with Generative AI in Hiring." Working Paper, University of Zurich. https://ursakrenk.com/docs/AKY_GenAI_Automation.pdf.

Baker, Doris Luft, Hao Ma, Paul Polanco, et al. 2021. "Development and Promise of a Vocabulary Intelligent Tutoring System for Second-Grade Latinx English Learners." *Journal of Research on Technology in Education* 53 (2): 223–47. https://doi.org/10.1080/15391523.2020.1762519.

Barwahwala, Taha, Aprajit Mahajan, Shekhar Mittal, and Ofir Reich. 2024. "Is Model Accuracy Enough? A Field Evaluation of a Machine Learning Model to Catch Bogus Firms." NBER Working Paper 32705, National Bureau of Economic Research. https://doi.org/10.3386/w32705.

Bastani, Hamsa, Osbert Bastani, Alp Sungu, Haosen Ge, Özge Kabakcı, and Rei Mariman. 2025. "Generative AI Without Guardrails Can Harm Learning: Evidence from High School Mathematics." *PNAS, Proceedings of the National Academy of Sciences* 122 (26): e2422633122. https://doi.org/10.1073/pnas.2422633122.

Bathaee, Yavar. 2018. "The Artificial Intelligence Black Box and the Failure of Intent and Causation." *Harvard Journal of Law and Technology* 31 (2): 890–938. https://jolt.law.harvard.edu/assets/articlePDFs/v31/The-Artificial-Intelligence-Black-Box-and-the-Failure-of-Intent-and-Causation-Yavar-Bathaee.pdf.

Bengio, Yoshua, Andrea Lodi, and Antoine Prouvost. 2021. "Machine Learning for Combinatorial Optimization: A Methodological Tour d'horizon." *European Journal of Operational Research* 290 (2): 405–21. https://doi.org/10.1016/j.ejor.2020.07.063.

Bhatt, Monica P., Jonathan Guryan, Salman A. Khan, Michael LaForest-Tucker, and Bhavya Mishra. 2024. "Can Technology Facilitate Scale? Evidence from a Randomized Evaluation of High Dosage Tutoring." NBER Working Paper 32510, National Bureau of Economic Research. https://doi.org/10.3386/w32510.

Björkegren, Daniel, Jun Ho Choi, Divya Budihal, Dominic Sobhani, Oliver Garrod, and Paul Atherton. 2025. "Could AI Leapfrog the Web? Evidence from Teachers in Sierra Leone." *arXiv:2502.12397v3 [cs CY]*, December 2, Cornell University. https://doi.org/10.48550/arXiv.2502.12397.

Borges do Nascimento, Israel Júnior, Hebatullah Abdulazeem, Lenny Thinagaran Vasanthan, et al. 2023. "Barriers and Facilitators to Utilizing Digital Health Technologies by Healthcare Professionals." *npj Digital Medicine* 6 (September): 161. https://doi.org/10.1038/s41746-023-00899-4.

Brant, Arthur, Preeti Singh, Xiang Yin, et al. 2025. "Performance of a Deep Learning Diabetic Retinopathy Algorithm in India." *JAMA Network Open* 8 (3): e250984. https://doi.org/10.1001/jamanetworkopen.2025.0984.

Buolamwini, Joy, and Timnit Gebru. 2018. "Gender Shades: Intersectional Accuracy Disparities in Commercial Gender Classification." In *PMLR, Proceedings of Machine Learning Research*, vol. 81, *FAT 2018, Conference on Fairness, Accountability, and Transparency, 23–24 February 2018, New York, NY, USA*, edited by Sorelle A. Friedler and Christo Wilson. MIT Press. https://dam-prod.media.mit.edu/x/2018/02/06/Gender%20Shades%20Intersectional%20Accuracy%20Disparities.pdf.

Burlig, Fiona, Amir Jina, Erin M. Kelley, Gregory Lane, and Harshil Saha. 2025. "Beliefs, Forecasts, and Investments: Experimental Evidence from India." Working Paper, Agricultural Technology Adoption Initiative, Abdul Latif Jameel Poverty Action Lab, Massachusetts Institute of Technology; Center for Effective Global Action, University of California, Berkeley. https://www.atai-research.org/the-value-of-forecasts-experimental-evidence-from-india/.

Burneo, Alegria, Lelys Ileana Dinarte-Díaz, Carolina Lopez, and Ezequiel Molina. 2026. "Can EdTech Close Learning Gaps? Global Evidence from Digital Interventions." Background paper prepared for *World Development Report 2026: The Promise of Artificial Intelligence,* World Bank. https://www.worldbank.org/en/publication/wdr2026/brief/world-development-report-2026-background-papers.

Busuioc, Madalina. 2021. "Accountable Artificial Intelligence: Holding Algorithms to Account." *Public Administration Review* 81 (5): 825–36. https://doi.org/10.1111/puar.13293.

Carlana, Michela, and Eliana La Ferrara. 2025. "Apart but Connected: Online Tutoring, Cognitive Outcomes, and Soft Skills." *American Economic Review* 115 (10): 3487–513. https://doi.org/10.1257/aer.20240401.

Chander, Anupam. 2020. "Is Data Localization a Solution for Schrems II?" *Journal of International Economic Law* 23 (3): 771–84. https://doi.org/10.1093/jiel/jgaa024.

Cheng, Xi, Li Yin, Chaochao Lin, et al. 2024. "Chatbot Dialogic Reading Boosts Comprehension for Chinese Kindergarteners with Higher Language Skills." *Journal of Experimental Child Psychology* 240 (April): 105842. https://doi.org/10.1093/jiel/jgaa024.

Choi, Jun Ho, Oliver Garrod, Paul Atherton, Andrew Joyce-Gibbons, Miriam Mason-Sesay, and Daniel Björkegren. 2024. "Are LLMs Useful in the Poorest Schools? TheTeacher.AI in Sierra Leone." *arXiv:2310.02982v2 [cs.CY]*, February 1, Cornell University. https://doi.org/10.48550/arXiv.2310.02982.

Chung, Angel Tsai-Hsuan, Jatu Abdulai, Patrick Bayoh, et al. 2026. "Improving Access to Essential Medicines via Decision-Aware Machine Learning." *Nature* 653 (8116): 1178–83. https://doi.org/10.1038/s41586-026-10433-7.

Coelho-Junior, Marcondes G., Ana P. Valdiones, Julia Z. Shimbo, et al. 2022. "Unmasking the Impunity of Illegal Deforestation in the Brazilian Amazon: A Call for Enforcement and Accountability." *Environmental Research Letters* 17: 041001. https://doi.org/10.1088/1748-9326/ac5193.

Dasgupta, Arpan, Mizhaan Maniyar, Awadhesh Srivastava, et al. 2025. "Learning to Call: A Field Trial of a Collaborative Bandit Algorithm for Improved Message Delivery in Mobile Maternal Health." *arXiv:2507.16356v2 [cs.AI]*, November 24, Cornell University. https://doi.org/10.48550/arXiv.2507.16356.

DellaVigna, Stefano, and Elizabeth Linos. 2022. "RCTs to Scale: Comprehensive Evidence from Two Nudge Units." *Econometrica* 90 (1): 81–116. https://doi.org/10.3982/ECTA18709.

De Simone, Martín Elias, Federico Hernan Tiberti, Maria Rebeca Barron Rodriguez, Federico Alfredo Manolio, Wuraola Mosuro, and Eliot Jolomi Dikoru. 2025. "From Chalkboards to Chatbots: Evaluating the Impact of Generative AI on Learning Outcomes in Nigeria." Policy Research Working Paper 11125, World Bank. https://documents.worldbank.org/en/publication/documents-reports/documentdetail/099548105192529324.

DGFiP (Direction générale des Finances publiques, Public Finances Directorate General, France). 2024. "The DGFiP, At the Heart of Government, Working for All, Nationwide: Annual Report 2023." June, DGFiP. https://www.economie.gouv.fr/files/files/directions_services/dgfip/Rapport/2023/ra_2023_en.pdf.

Dieci, Maria, Paul J. Gertler, Jonathan Kolstad, and Carlos Paramo. 2024. "Using Diagnosis Contingent Incentives to Improve Malaria Treatment." Working Paper, Institute for Business and Social Impact, Haas School of Business, University of California, Berkeley. https://haas.berkeley.edu/ibsi/research/using-diagnosis-conditional-incentives-to-improve-malaria-treatment/.

Dinarte-Díaz, Lelys Ileana, James Gresham, Renata Freitas Lemos, Harry Anthony Patrinos, and Rony Rodriguez-Ramirez. 2025. "Investing in Human Capital During Wartime: Experimental Evidence from Ukraine." Policy Research Working Paper 11196, World Bank. https://documents.worldbank.org/en/publication/documents-reports/documentdetail/099918209022550719.

Esnaashari, Saba, Jonathan Bright, John Francis, Youmna Hashem, Vincent Straub, and Deborah Morgan. 2023. "Approaches to the Algorithmic Allocation of Public Resources: A Cross-Disciplinary Review." *arXiv:2310.06475v1 [cs.CY]*, October 10, Cornell University. https://doi.org/10.48550/arXiv.2310.06475.

Evans, David, and Fei Yuan. 2019. "Equivalent Years of Schooling: A Metric to Communicate Learning Gains in Concrete Terms." Policy Research Working Paper 8752, World Bank. http://documents.worldbank.org/curated/en/123371-550594320297/Equivalent-Years-of-Schooling-A-Metric-to-Communicate-Learning-Gains-in-Concrete-Terms.

Fang, Fei, Thanh H. Nguyen, Rob Pickles, et al. 2016. "Deploying PAWS: Field Optimization of the Protection Assistant for Wildlife Security." *Proceedings of the Twenty-Eighth Conference on Innovative Applications of Artificial Intelligence* 30 (2): 3966–73. https://doi.org/10.1609/aaai.v30i2.19070.

Farabi, Shafkat, Didac Marti Pinto, Wei Lu, et al. 2026. "SMaRT: Online Reusable Resource Assignment and an Application to Mediation in the Kenyan Judiciary." *arXiv:2602.18431v2 [cs.CY]*, June 26, Cornell University. https://doi.org/10.48550/arXiv.2602.18431.

Ferman, Bruno, Lycia Lima, and Flávio Riva. 2021. "Artificial Intelligence, Teacher Tasks and Individualized Pedagogy." *SocArXiv*, Paper qw249 (February 17), Center for Open Science. https://osf.io/download/602bcf2338d719006674552a/.

Fernández-Pichel, Marcos, Juan C. Pichel, and David E. Losada. 2025. "Evaluating Search Engines and Large Language Models for Answering Health Questions." *npj Digital Medicine* 8 (March): 153. https://www.nature.com/articles/s41746-025-01546-w.

Fitzpatrick, Trevor, Seamus Kelly, Patrick Carey, David Walsh, and Ruairi Nugent. 2025. "Assessing Generative AI Value in a Public Sector Context: Evidence from a Field Experiment." *arXiv:2502.09479v1 [q-fin.GN]*, February 13, Cornell University. https://doi.org/10.48550/arXiv.2502.09479.

Garg, Tushar, Stephen John, Suraj Abdulkarim, et al. 2025. "Implementation Costs and Cost-Effectiveness of

Ultraportable Chest X-Ray with Artificial Intelligence in Active Case Finding for Tuberculosis in Nigeria." *PLOS Digital Health* 4 (6): e0000894. https://doi.org/10.1371/journal.pdig.0000894.

GDS (Government Digital Service, United Kingdom). 2025. "Microsoft 365 Copilot Experiment: Cross-Government Findings Report." GDS, Department for Science, Innovation and Technology. https://www.gov.uk/government/publications/microsoft-365-copilot-experiment-cross-government-findings-report.

Gellert, George A., Paula Galvão, Sandra Maria Gomes, et al. 2024. "Impact of Integrated Virtual and Live Nurse Triage on Patient Care Seeking and Health Care Delivery Effectiveness and Efficiency." *Telemedicine Reports* 5 (1): tmr.2024.0054. https://doi.org/10.1089/tmr.2024.0054.

Gelvanovska-Garcia, Natalija, Vaiva Mačiulė, and Carlo Maria Rossotto. 2024. *Advancing Cloud and Data Infrastructure Markets: Strategic Directions for Low- and Middle-Income Countries*. Sustainable Infrastructure Series. World Bank. https://doi.org/10.1596/978-1-4648-2065-6.

Gmyrek, Pawel, Mariana Viollaz, and Hernán Jorge Winkler. 2026. "Disruption Without Dividend? How the Digital Divide and Task Differences Split GenAI's Global Impact." Policy Research Working Paper 11328 and background paper prepared for *World Development Report 2026: The Promise of Artificial Intelligence,* World Bank. https://www.worldbank.org/en/publication/wdr2026/brief/world-development-report-2026-background-papers.

Gortazar, Lucas, Claudia Hupkau, and Antonio Roldán. 2023. "Online Tutoring Works: Experimental Evidence from a Program with Vulnerable Children." EdWorkingPaper 23-743, Annenberg Institute, Brown University. https://doi.org/10.26300/TPXJ-QS08.

GSL (Global School Leaders). 2024. "PULS Survey Report 2024: Promoting Understanding of Leadership in Schools (PULS)." GSL. https://drive.google.com/file/d/1n0oXZhQE2H91ocYUWB96CPhTf8BMdshU/view.

Guryan, Jonathan, Jens Ludwig, Monica P. Bhatt, et al. 2023. "Not Too Late: Improving Academic Outcomes Among Adolescents." *American Economic Review* 113 (3): 738–65. https://doi.org/10.1257/aer.20210434.

Hady, Mohamad A., Siyi Hu, Mahardhika Pratama, Zehong Cao, and Ryszard Kowalczyk. 2025. "Multi-Agent Reinforcement Learning for Resources Allocation Optimization: A Survey." *Artificial Intelligence Review* 58 (11): 354. https://doi.org/10.1007/s10462-025-11340-5.

Hagiu, Andrei, and Julian Wright. 2025. "Artificial Intelligence and Competition Policy." *International Journal of Industrial Organization* 103 (Part A, December): 103134. https://doi.org/10.1016/j.ijindorg.2025.103134.

Han, Ryan, Julián N. Acosta, Zahra Shakeri, John P. A. Ioannidis, Eric J. Topol, and Pranav Rajpurkar. 2024. "Randomised Controlled Trials Evaluating Artificial Intelligence in Clinical Practice: A Scoping Review." *Lancet Digital Health* 6 (5): e367–e373. https://doi.org/10.1016/S2589-7500(24)00047-5.

Harris, Adam S., and Maggie B. Yellen. 2024. "Decision-Making with Machine Prediction: Evidence from Predictive Maintenance in Trucking." Paper presented at the National Bureau of Economic Research "Economics of Transportation in the 21st Century, Spring 2024" Zoom conference, May 3. https://adamharris380.github.io/files/HarrisYellen-JMP.pdf.

Hashim, Ali, and Moritz Piatti-Fünfkirchen. 2018. "Lessons from Reforming Financial Management Information Systems: A Review of the Evidence." Policy Research Working Paper 8312, World Bank. https://doi.org/10.1596/1813-9450-8312.

Heikkilä, Melissa. 2022. "Dutch Scandal Serves as a Warning for Europe over Risks of Using Algorithms." *Technology* (blog), March 29. https://www.politico.eu/article/dutch-scandal-serves-as-a-warning-for-europe-over-risks-of-using-algorithms/.

Henkel, Owen, Hannah Horne-Robinson, Nessie Kozhakhmetova, and Amanda Lee. 2024. "Effective and Scalable Math Support: Experimental Evidence on the Impact of an AI-Math Tutor in Ghana." In *Artificial Intelligence in Education: Proceedings of the 25th International Conference on Artificial Intelligence in Education (AIED 2024)*, edited by Andrew M. Olney, Irene-Angelica Chounta, Zitao Liu, Olga C. Santos, and Ig Ibert Bittencourt. Communications in Computer and Information Science Series, vol. 2150. Springer Nature. https://link.springer.com/chapter/10.1007/978-3-031-64315-6_34.

Henley, Jon. 2021. "Dutch Government Resigns over Child Benefits Scandal." *World* (blog), January 15. https://www.theguardian.com/world/2021/jan/15/dutch-government-resigns-over-child-benefits-scandal.

Hickok, Merve. 2024. "Public Procurement of Artificial Intelligence Systems: New Risks and Future Proofing." *AI and Society* 39 (3): 1213–27. https://doi.org/10.1007/s00146-022-01572-2.

Hoefsloot, Fenna Imara, Neha Gupta, Dennis Mbugua Muthama, and José de Jesús Flores Durán. 2025. "Broker Bureaucracies: The Subsidiary Offices of the Digitalizing State." *Digital Geography and Society* 8 (June): 100112. https://doi.org/10.1016/j.diggeo.2025.100112.

Hou, Zhiyuan, Zhengdong Wu, Zhiqiang Qu, et al. 2025. "A Vaccine Chatbot Intervention for Parents to Improve HPV Vaccination Uptake Among Middle School Girls: A Cluster Randomized Trial." *Nature Medicine* 31 (6): 1855–62. https://doi.org/10.1038/s41591-025-03618-6.

Huang, Ting-Yun, Pei Hsing Hsieh, and Yung-Chun Chang. 2024. "Performance Comparison of Junior Residents and ChatGPT in the Objective Structured Clinical Examination (OSCE) for Medical History Taking and Documentation of Medical Records: Development and Usability Study." *JMIR Medical Education* 10 (November): e59902. https://doi.org/10.2196/59902.

IMF (International Monetary Fund). 2025. *Fiscal Monitor: Spending Smarter—How Efficient and Well-Allocated Public Spending Can Boost*

Economic Growth. October. IMF. https://www.imf.org/en/publications/fm/issues/2025/10/07/fiscal-monitor-october-2025.

Isotani, Seiji, Ig Ibert Bittencourt, Geiser C. Challco, Diego Dermeval, and Rafael F. Mello. 2023. "AIED Unplugged: Leapfrogging the Digital Divide to Reach the Underserved." In *Artificial Intelligence in Education: 24th International Conference, AIED 2023, Tokyo, Japan, July 3–7, 2023, Proceedings*, edited by Ning Wang, Genaro Rebolledo-Mendez, Vania Dimitrova, Noboru Matsuda, and Olga C. Santos. Communications in Computer and Information Science Series, vol. 1831. Springer Nature. https://link.springer.com/chapter/10.1007/978-3-031-36336-8_118.

Jain, Sameer, Sedrick Scott Keh, Shova Chhetri, et al. 2024. "Where It Really Matters: Few-Shot Environmental Conservation Media Monitoring for Low-Resource Languages." *Proceedings of the 38th AAAI Conference on Artificial Intelligence* 38 (20): 22141–49. https://ojs.aaai.org/index.php/AAAI/article/view/30218.

Jain, Sansiddh, Avtansh Tiwari, Nayana Bannur, et al. 2022. "Deploying COVID-19 Case Forecasting Models in the Developing World." In *AI for Social Impact*, online textbook edited by Milind Tambe, Fei Fang, and Bryan Wilder. https://ai4sibook.org/covid-19-case-forecasting/.

Jensen, Robert T. 2010. "The (Perceived) Returns to Education and the Demand for Schooling." *Quarterly Journal of Economics* 125 (2): 515–48. https://doi.org/10.1162/qjec.2010.125.2.515.

Johnson, Matthew S., David I. Levine, and Michael W. Toffel. 2023. "Improving Regulatory Effectiveness Through Better Targeting: Evidence from OSHA." *American Economic Journal: Applied Economics* 15 (4): 30–67. https://doi.org/10.1257/app.20200659.

Johnson, Nari, Elise Silva, Harrison Leon, Motahhare Eslami, Beth Schwanke, Ravit Dotan, and Hoda Heidari. 2025. "Legacy Procurement Practices Shape How U.S. Cities Govern AI: Understanding Government Employees' Practices, Challenges, and Needs." *arXiv:2411.04994v3 [cs.CY]*, May 13, Cornell University. https://doi.org/10.48550/arXiv.2411.04994.

Kehinde, Opadele, Ruth Abdul, Bose Afolabi, et al. 2024. "Deploying ADVISER: Impact and Lessons from Using Artificial Intelligence for Child Vaccination Uptake in Nigeria." *Proceedings of the 38th AAAI Conference on Artificial Intelligence* 38 (20): 22185–92. https://doi.org/10.1609/aaai.v38i20.30223.

Koçak, Burak, Andrea Ponsiglione, Arnaldo Stanzione, et al. 2024. "Bias in Artificial Intelligence for Medical Imaging: Fundamentals, Detection, Avoidance, Mitigation, Challenges, Ethics, and Prospects." *Diagnostic and Interventional Radiology*, ahead of print, July 2. https://doi.org/10.4274/dir.2024.242854.

Korinek, Anton, and Jai Vipra. 2024. "Concentrating Intelligence: Scaling and Market Structure in Artificial Intelligence." NBER Working Paper 33139, National Bureau of Economic Research. https://doi.org/10.3386/w33139.

Korom, Robert, Sarah Kiptinness, Najib Adan, et al. 2025. "AI-Based Clinical Decision Support for Primary Care: A Real-World Study." *arXiv:2507.16947v1 [cs.CL]*, July 22, Cornell University. https://doi.org/10.48550/arXiv.2507.16947.

Kumar, Santosh, Gouri Sarin, and Rishita Aggarwal. 2025. "BHASHINI: Transforming Maha Kumbh Through Multilingual Innovation." January 16, Research Unit, Press Information Bureau, India. https://static.pib.gov.in/WriteReadData/specificdocs/documents/2025/jan/doc2025116486101.pdf.

Larroucau, Tomás, Ignacio A. Rios, Anaïs Fabre, and Christopher Neilson. 2025. "College Application Mistakes and the Design of Information Policies at Scale." NBER Working Paper 34164, National Bureau of Economic Research. https://www.nber.org/papers/w34164.

LearnLM and Fab AI. 2026. "Teaching with Gemini: Measuring the Impact of Guided Learning on Student Mathematics Progress in Sierra Leone." May 15, LearnLM, Google. http://goo.gle/LearnLM-SierraLeone-May26.

Li, Xiaoqing, Dan Tian, Weihua Li, et al. 2022. "Using Artificial Intelligence to Reduce Queuing Time and Improve Satisfaction in Pediatric Outpatient Service: A Randomized Clinical Trial." *Frontiers in Pediatrics* 10 (August): 929834. https://doi.org/10.3389/fped.2022.929834.

Liang, Huiying, Brian Y. Tsui, Hao Ni, et al. 2019. "Evaluation and Accurate Diagnoses of Pediatric Diseases Using Artificial Intelligence." *Nature Medicine* 25 (3): 433–38. https://doi.org/10.1038/s41591-018-0335-9.

López, Carolina. 2025. "Tripping at the Finish Line: Experimental Evidence on the Role of Misperceptions on Secondary School Completion." Working Paper, Development Research Group, World Bank. https://papers.jcarolinalopez.com/Misperceptions_Secondary_School_Completion_CL.pdf.

López, Carolina, Anja Sautmann, and Simone Schaner. 2022. "Does Patient Demand Contribute to the Overuse of Prescription Drugs?" *American Economic Journal: Applied Economics* 14 (1): 225–60. https://doi.org/10.1257/app.20190722.

MacPherson, Peter, Emily L. Webb, Wala Kamchedzera, et al. 2021. "Computer-Aided X-Ray Screening for Tuberculosis and HIV Testing Among Adults with Cough in Malawi (the PROSPECT Study): A Randomised Trial and Cost-Effectiveness Analysis." *PLOS Medicine* 18 (9): e1003752. https://doi.org/10.1371/journal.pmed.1003752.

Maršál, Aleš, and Patryk Perkowski. 2025. "Task-Based Returns to Generative AI: Evidence from a Central Bank." *VoxEU Column: Artificial Intelligence* (blog), July 31. https://cepr.org/voxeu/columns/task-based-returns-generative-ai-evidence-central-bank.

Mate, Aditya, Lovish Madaan, Aparna Taneja, et al. 2022. "Field Study in Deploying Restless Multi-Armed Bandits: Assisting Non-Profits in Improving Maternal and Child Health." *Proceedings of the 36th AAAI Conference on Artificial Intelligence* 36 (11): 12017–25. https://doi.org/10.1609/aaai.v36i11.21460.

Mathauer, Inke, and Maarten Oranje. 2024. "Machine Learning in Health Financing: Benefits, Risks and Regulatory Needs." *Bulletin of the World Health Organization* 102 (3): 216–24. https://doi.org/10.2471/BLT.23.290333.

Mathenge, Wanjiku, Noelle Whitestone, John Nkurikiye, et al. 2022. "Impact of Artificial Intelligence Assessment of Diabetic Retinopathy on Referral Service Uptake in a Low-Resource Setting: The RAIDERS Randomized Trial." *Ophthalmology Science* 2 (4): 100168. https://doi.org/10.1016/j.xops.2022.100168.

Molina, Ezequiel, Carolina Lopez, Octavio Lizama, and Paul Bambrick-Santoyo. 2025. *El Director LIBRE: El método de IA que libera horas de papeleo para liderar el aprendizaje*. World Bank. https://documents1.worldbank.org/curated/en/099731109172514920/pdf/IDU-86373363-2741-4f78-a1cb-be22662e4459.pdf.

Muralidharan, Karthik, Abhijeet Singh, and Alejandro J. Ganimian. 2019. "Disrupting Education? Experimental Evidence on Technology-Aided Instruction in India." *American Economic Review* 109 (4): 1426–60. https://doi.org/10.1257/aer.20171112.

Naggirinya, Agnes Bwanika, David B. Meya, Maria Sarah Nabaggala, et al. 2024. "Effectiveness of Interactive Voice Response-Call for Life mHealth Tool on Adherence to Anti-Retroviral Therapy Among Young People Living with HIV: A Randomized Trial in Uganda." *PLOS One* 19 (11): e0308923. https://doi.org/10.1371/journal.pone.0308923.

Nagle, Frank. 2023. "Government IT Procurement Policy and Firm Behavior: Evidence from a French Open Source Software Policy." *Academy of Management Proceedings* 2023 (1): 13046. https://doi.org/10.5465/AMPROC.2023.13046abstract.

Nair, Vineet, Kritika Prakash, Michael Wilbur, et al. 2022. "ADVISER: AI-Driven Vaccination Intervention Optimiser for Increasing Vaccine Uptake in Nigeria." *arXiv:2204.13663 [cs.AI]*, July 5, Cornell University. https://doi.org/10.48550/arXiv.2204.13663.

Nickow, Andre, Philip Oreopoulos, and Vincent Quan. 2024. "The Promise of Tutoring for PreK–12 Learning: A Systematic Review and Meta-Analysis of the Experimental Evidence." *American Educational Research Journal* 61 (1): 74–107. https://doi.org/10.3102/00028312231208687.

OECD (Organisation for Economic Co-operation and Development). 2025a. *Results from TALIS 2024: The State of Teaching*. December. OECD. https://www.oecd.org/content/dam/oecd/en/publications/reports/2025/10/results-from-talis-2024_28fbde1d/90df6235-en.pdf.

OECD (Organisation for Economic Co-operation and Development). 2025b. *Tax Administration 2025: Comparative Information on OECD and Other Advanced and Emerging Economies*. OECD. https://www.oecd.org/content/dam/oecd/en/publications/reports/2025/11/tax-administration-2025_6360fad8/cc015ce8-en.pdf.

Okamura, Yuko, Tim Ohlenburg, and Emil Tesliuc. 2024. "Scaling Up Social Assistance Where Data Is Scarce: Opportunities and Limits of Novel Data and AI." Social Protection and Jobs Discussion Paper 2402, World Bank. https://documents1.worldbank.org/curated/en/099050724145524418/pdf/P171913-1f545ae0-ad05-4e97-b3db-7f9d6820d240.pdf.

Okoth, Dann. 2024. "AI Forecasting Equips East Africa for Extreme Weather." *News* (blog), August 2. https://www.scidev.net/global/news/ai-forecasting-equips-east-africa-for-extreme-weather/.

OpenAI. 2026. "Horizon 1000: Advancing AI for Primary Healthcare." Global Affairs (blog), January 20. https://openai.com/index/horizon-1000/.

Open Contracting Partnership. 2025. "Buying AI: Tips and Tools for Public Procurement." Open Contracting Partnership. https://www.open-contracting.org/resources/buying-ai-tips-and-tools-for-public-procurement/.

Pahlka, Jennifer. 2023. *Recoding America: Why Government Is Failing in the Digital Age and How We Can Do Better*. Macmillan. https://us.macmillan.com/books/9781250266774/recodingamerica/.

Pal, Soumyabrata, Milind Tambe, Arun Suggala, Karthikeyan Shanmugam, and Aparna Taneja. 2024. "Improving Mobile Maternal and Child Health Care Programs: Collaborative Bandits for Time Slot Selection." In *AAMAS '24: Proceedings of the 23rd International Conference on Autonomous Agents and Multiagent Systems*, edited by Natasha Alechina, Virginia Dignum, Mehdi Dastani, and Jaime Sichman. International Foundation for Autonomous Agents and Multiagent Systems. https://dl.acm.org/doi/proceedings/10.5555/3635637.

PEARL (Policy, Elections and Representation Lab) and SRI (Schwartz Reisman Institute for Technology and Society). 2024. *Global Public Opinion on Artificial Intelligence (GPO-AI)*. May 16. PEARL, Munk School of Global Affairs and Public Policy, Department of Political Science, University of Toronto; SRI, University of Toronto. https://srinstitute.utoronto.ca/public-opinion-ai.

Pereira, Jayr, Andre Assumpcao, Julio Trecenti, et al. 2024. "INACIA: Integrating Large Language Models in Brazilian Audit Courts: Opportunities and Challenges." *arXiv:2401.05273v3 [cs.CL]*, February 26, Cornell University. https://doi.org/10.48550/arXiv.2401.05273.

Qin, Zhi Zhen, Melissa S. Sander, Bishwa Rai, et al. 2019. "Using Artificial Intelligence to Read Chest Radiographs for Tuberculosis Detection: A Multi-Site Evaluation of the Diagnostic Accuracy of Three Deep Learning Systems." *Scientific Reports* 9 (October): 15000. https://doi.org/10.1038/s41598-019-51503-3.

Raval, Devang, Dhaval Parmar, Somen Saha, et al. 2025. "Cost-Effectiveness Analysis of AI-Assisted Chest X-Ray Interpretation Tools for TB Screening: A Rapid HTA." *Frontiers in Digital Health* 7 (December): 1629127. https://doi.org/10.3389/fdgth.2025.1629127.

Robinson, Carly, Matt Kraft, Susanne Loeb, and Beth Schueler. 2021. "Design Principles for Accelerating Student Learning with High-Impact Tutoring." Ed Research for Action Research Brief #16. Brown University and Results for America. https://annenberg.brown.edu/sites/default/files/EdResearch_for_Recovery_Design_Principles_1.pdf.

Robinson, Viviane M. J., Claire A. Lloyd, and Kenneth J. Rowe. 2008. "The Impact of Leadership on Student Outcomes: An Analysis of the Differential Effects of Leadership Types." *Educational Administration Quarterly* 44 (5): 635–74. https://doi.org/10.1177/0013161X08321509.

Sabri, Omar, Bassam Al-Shargabi, and Abdelrahman Abuarqoub. 2025. "The Role of Artificial Intelligence in Improving Diagnostic Accuracy in Medical Imaging: A Review." *Computers, Materials and Continua* 85 (2): 2443–86. https://doi.org/10.32604/cmc.2025.066987.

Salinas, Maria Paz, Javiera Sepúlveda, Leonel Hidalgo, et al. 2024. "A Systematic Review and Meta-Analysis of Artificial Intelligence Versus Clinicians for Skin Cancer Diagnosis." *npj Digital Medicine* 7 (1): 125. https://doi.org/10.1038/s41746-024-01103-x.

Sarkodie, Benjamin Dabo, Benard Ohene-Botwe, Yaw B. Mensah, et al. 2023. "Density and Regional Distribution of Radiologists in a Low-Income Country: The Ghana Situation." *Chinese Journal of Academic Radiology* 6 (4): 188–95. https://doi.org/10.1007/s42058-023-00130-z.

SARS (South African Revenue Service). 2025. *Annual Report 2024/2025*. SARS. https://www.sars.gov.za/wp-content/uploads/Docs/StratAnnualPerfplans/SARS-AR-30-Annual-Report-2024-2025.pdf.

Sautmann, Anja, and Jonas Weinert. 2026. "Artificial Intelligence Interventions to Support Frontline Healthcare Workers in Low-Resource Settings: A Review." Background paper prepared for *World Development Report 2026: The Promise of Artificial Intelligence,* World Bank. https://www.worldbank.org/en/publication/wdr2026/brief/world-development-report-2026-background-papers.

Schmid, Jon, Tobias Sytsma, and Anton Shenk. 2024. "Evaluating Natural Monopoly Conditions in the AI Foundation Model Market." Research Report, RAND Corporation. https://doi.org/10.7249/RRA3415-1.

Seyyed-Kalantari, Laleh, Haoran Zhang, Matthew B. A. McDermott, Irene Y. Chen, and Marzyeh Ghassemi. 2021. "Underdiagnosis Bias of Artificial Intelligence Algorithms Applied to Chest Radiographs in Under-Served Patient Populations." *Nature Medicine* 27 (December): 2176–82. https://doi.org/10.1038/s41591-021-01595-0.

Shaw, James, Payal Agarwal, Laura Desveaux, et al. 2018. "Beyond 'Implementation': Digital Health Innovation and Service Design." *npj Digital Medicine* 1 (September): 48. https://doi.org/10.1038/s41746-018-0059-8.

Shimelash, Natnael, Samuel Rutunda, Vaishnavi Menon, et al. 2026. "A 'Silent Trial' Assessing the Accuracy of Large Language Models for Assisting Community Health Workers in Low-Resource Settings." *medRxiv* (February 17). https://www.medrxiv.org/content/10.64898/2026.02.16.26346409v1.full-text.

Skjefte, Malia, Shawna Cooper, Stephen Poyer, et al. 2024. "Use of a Health Worker-Targeted Smartphone App to Support Quality Malaria RDT Implementation in Busia County, Kenya: A Feasibility and Acceptability Study." *PLOS ONE* 19 (3): e0295049. https://doi.org/10.1371/journal.pone.0295049.

Sondaal, Stephanie Felicie Victoria, Joyce Linda Browne, Mary Amoakoh-Coleman, et al. 2016. "Assessing the Effect of mHealth Interventions in Improving Maternal and Neonatal Care in Low- and Middle-Income Countries: A Systematic Review." *PlOS One* 11 (5): e0154664. https://doi.org/10.1371/journal.pone.0154664.

Straub, Vincent J., Youmna Hashem, Jonathan Bright, et al. 2024. "AI for Bureaucratic Productivity: Measuring the Potential of AI to Help Automate 143 Million UK Government Transactions." *arXiv:2403.14712v1 [cs.CY]*, March 18, Cornell University. https://doi.org/10.48550/arXiv.2403.14712.

Strömberg, David, Victor Lei, and Yanhui Wu. 2026. "The Generative AI Learning Penalty: Evidence from Chinese Secondary Education." CEPR Discussion Paper DP21577, Center for Economic Policy Research. https://cepr.org/publications/dp21577.

Syed, Rehan, Wasana Bandara, and Rebekah Eden. 2023. "Public Sector Digital Transformation Barriers: A Developing Country Experience." *Information Polity* 28 (1): 5–27. https://doi.org/10.3233/IP-220017.

Taylor, R. Andrew, Chris Chmura, Jeremiah Hinson, et al. 2025. "Impact of Artificial Intelligence–Based Triage Decision Support on Emergency Department Care." *NEJM AI* 2 (3): AIoa2400296. https://doi.org/10.1056/AIoa2400296.

Teo, Zhen Ling, Yih-Chung Tham, Marco Yu, et al. 2021. "Global Prevalence of Diabetic Retinopathy and Projection of Burden Through 2045: Systematic Review and Meta-Analysis." *Ophthalmology* 128 (11): 1580–91. https://doi.org/10.1016/j.ophtha.2021.04.027.

Villanueva-Miranda, Ismael, Guanghua Xiao, and Yang Xie. 2025. "Artificial Intelligence in Early Warning Systems for Infectious Disease Surveillance: A Systematic Review." *Frontiers in Public Health* 13 (June):1609615. https://doi.org/10.3389/fpubh.2025.1609615.

Wang, Zixin, Siyu Chen, Josiah Poon, et al. 2025. "A Hybrid Chatbot to Promote Pneumococcal Vaccination Among Older Adults: A Randomized Clinical Trial." *JAMA Network Open* 8 (10): e2535813. https://doi.org/10.1001/jamanetworkopen.2025.35813.

Whitehead, Lara, Jason Talevski, Farhad Fatehi, and Alison Beauchamp. 2023. "Barriers to and Facilitators of Digital Health Among Culturally and Linguistically Diverse Populations: Qualitative Systematic Review." *Journal of Medical Internet Research* 25 (February): e42719. https://doi.org/10.2196/42719.

Whitestone, Noelle, John Nkurikiye, Jennifer L. Patnaik, et al. 2024. "Feasibility and Acceptance of Artificial Intelligence-Based Diabetic Retinopathy Screening in Rwanda." *British Journal of Ophthalmology* 108 (6): 840–45. https://doi.org/10.1136/bjo-2022-322683.

WHO (World Health Organization). 2021. "WHO Consolidated Guidelines on Tuberculosis, Module 2: Screening; Systematic Screening for Tuberculosis Disease." WHO. https://iris.who.int/handle/10665/340255.

WHO (World Health Organization). 2024. "Use of Machine Learning for Fraud Detection Within the Claims Management Process in the Philippines: Insights from the National Health Insurance Scheme PhilHealth." Country Studies Series on Digital Technologies for Health Financing. WHO. https://www.who.int/publications/i/item/9789240101333.

WHO (World Health Organization). 2025a. "Use of Computer-Aided Detection Software for Tuberculosis Screening: WHO Policy Statement." WHO. https://www.who.int/publications/i/item/9789240110373.

WHO (World Health Organization). 2025b. "World Mental Health Today: Latest Data." WHO. https://www.who.int/publications/i/item/9789240113817.

WHO (World Health Organization). 2026. "Tuberculosis." Fact Sheet, March 24, WHO. https://www.who.int/news-room/fact-sheets/detail/tuberculosis.

WMO (World Meteorological Organization). 2025. "WMO Supports Artificial Intelligence Forecasting Pilot in Africa." *News* (blog), June 30. https://wmo.int/media/news/wmo-supports-artificial-intelligence-forecasting-pilot-africa.

World Bank. 2017. "Court Annexed Mediation Offers Alternative to Delayed Justice for Kenyans." *Feature Story* (blog), October 5. https://www.worldbank.org/en/news/feature/2017/10/05/court-annexed-mediation-offers-alternative-to-delayed-justice-for-kenyans.

World Bank. 2026. *Public Workforce Performance and Prosperity*. World Bank. https://www.worldbank.org/en/publication/public-workforce-performance-and-prosperity.

Yuan, Qianli, and Tzuhao Chen. 2025. "Holding AI-Based Systems Accountable in the Public Sector: A Systematic Review." *Public Performance and Management Review* 48 (6): 1389–422. https://doi.org/10.1080/15309576.2025.2469784.

3 Spotlight 3

Generative AI and the Erosion of Knowledge, Learning, and Human Skills

Generative artificial intelligence (AI) has the potential to expand human capabilities. Whereas chapter 1 outlines how human capital is a critical complement to AI and chapter 5 discusses how generative AI can support learning by providing immediate feedback or guidance through formal tutoring,[1] this spotlight examines a different but related question: Can excessive reliance on AI erode the processes that build human skills—inside the classroom, but more important, in undirected and unrestricted uses of AI outside the classroom and at work? If generative AI routinely substitutes for skills that require cognitive abilities, it may weaken the acquisition and retention of these skills, lower workers' productivity, and hamper innovation in a range of settings, from academic institutions to workplaces. Fortunately, lessons from the past can guide the adoption of policies that can help humans reduce these risks while realizing the benefits from generative AI. In low- and middle-income countries, the slower pace at which AI is being adopted could provide a window of opportunity to learn from early adopters and proactively prepare for the impacts of AI.

The use of generative AI can reduce cognitive abilities and intrinsic motivation to learn by doing

Although much of the existing evidence on the impact of using large language models on cognition is limited and based primarily on small, short-term experiments in high-income education settings, some patterns are emerging. First, the unstructured use of AI tools like ChatGPT reduces the level of engagement with cognitive tasks. For example, study participants researching a question with the help of large language models had lower cognitive load and produced weaker reasoning in their final answers.[2] In another study, measured brain activity during essay writing was found to be reduced when participants used large language models.[3] An analysis of multiple ChatGPT studies found that mental effort generally declined when the tool was used, even as the quality of the output increased.[4] In two studies, students who were given unrestricted access to large language models bypassed "desirable difficulty" during learning—that is, creating challenges, such as varying the conditions of practice, that enhance retention and comprehension[5]—and afterwards performed worse than students who never had access.[6] This pattern of cognitive off-loading resembles the "Google effect": When people expect to be able to access learned information again, they tend to not remember the information itself, only where to find it.[7]

A second, related effect of using large language models is that it may undermine intrinsic motivation, that is, the drive to engage in an activity because it is personally rewarding rather than for any external reward.[8] This impact suggests that the pervasive use of generative AI could diminish both the opportunities and motivation for "learning by doing."

Generative AI is reshaping secondary and tertiary education

Generative AI is rapidly becoming an integral part of how students complete coursework in secondary and tertiary education. More than 80 percent of undergraduate students in the United Kingdom[9] and secondary school and university students in the United States reported using AI for schoolwork in 2025.[10] Furthermore, in that same year, students at a US university reported using AI to "augment" their learning experience, such as by requesting explanations or feedback, but also to "automate" tasks such as generating essays.[11] Between 40 percent and 50 percent of the students included in these studies relied on generative AI to complete assigned tasks intended to develop their own skills such as brainstorming, summarizing, structuring thoughts, and suggesting research ideas. In addition, more than half of these students professed to using AI simply to save time.[12]

A recent study of generative AI adoption among students in grades 7–12 in China confirms these patterns of AI use and suggests detrimental effects on knowledge acquisition.[13] From 2022 to 2025, self-reported AI use among the study sample rose from nearly zero to approximately 80 percent. Over six months following first use, homework scores improved gradually by 18 percent, even though students spent much less time on their assignments. Meanwhile, however, grades in monthly in-class exams dropped by 20 percent. Crucially, students who continued to spend similar amounts of time on homework—indicating continued effort—saw less impact on their exam performance. While these results are not yet peer-reviewed and come from the very early adoption phase, the implications are serious enough to warrant attention. Students who had ever used AI scored on average 5 to 7 percent lower in senior high school and college entrance exams, with the negative effects compounding with the length of exposure.

In addition to affecting knowledge acquisition and retention, teachers are also concerned that the use of AI reinforces learning that is either incorrect or misleading. More than 80 percent of teachers surveyed across 51 high- and middle-income countries report that AI can generate inappropriate or inaccurate recommendations, and 65 percent note that AI can amplify biases that reinforce misconceptions (refer to figure S3.1).[14] These reservations are less pronounced in lower-middle-income countries than in upper-middle- or high-income countries, which may reflect different levels of exposure to AI. But the difference also raises concerns about whether students in lower-middle-income countries are being adequately prepared to use AI tools critically.

If students use AI to complete their homework, or if teachers no longer assign work because of the difficulty of evaluating it, the "productive struggle" central to learning disappears. The prevalent use of AI in education may result in weaker foundational skills, particularly in reasoning and writing, or in students' never acquiring them at all. The risk is compounded by overreliance on AI-generated content that may be inaccurate.

Figure S3.1 Teachers, especially those in higher-income countries, are concerned about the risks of using AI in education

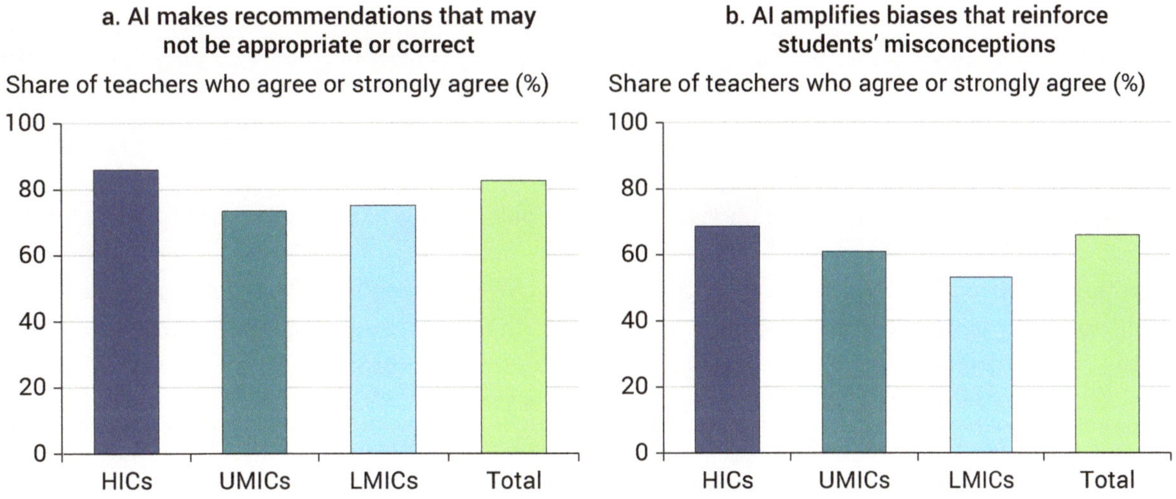

Source: WDR 2026 team, based on data from TALIS [Teaching and Learning International Survey] 2024 Database (dashboard), Organisation for Economic Co-operation and Development, https://www.oecd.org/en/data/datasets/talis-2024-database.html.

Note: The sample includes 37 high-income countries (HICs), 11 upper-middle-income countries (UMICs), and 3 lower-middle-income countries (LMICs). Low-income countries are not included in the survey. AI = artificial intelligence.

Established methods for evaluating job qualifications become less reliable

The widespread use of AI in schools and universities makes it more challenging to evaluate the work of students fairly. In the United States, school principals report growing concerns about academic integrity. Instructors and students, along with the AI tools they use, seem locked in an "arms race" between AI-assisted plagiarism and detection of it.[15] In 2025, one-quarter of students in the United Kingdom reported submitting text in assessments that was partly or fully written by a large language model.[16] More than 80 percent of teachers surveyed in the 2024 Teaching and Learning International Survey reported that AI enables students to present the work of others as their own more easily, although these concerns are less prevalent in lower-middle-income countries, where approximately half of the teachers reported having them.[17]

For employers, pervasive unchecked use of AI in education contexts presents new challenges. Students' grades on written assignments may no longer reflect the mastery of specific topics or broader reasoning skills that are also relevant in the workplace. In addition, substantial assignments such as the writing of a thesis are no longer reliable signals of a student's ability to sustain effort over extended periods of time, a socioemotional skill that is also relevant for the labor market. The informational value of written application materials is similarly diluted. Just months after the launch of ChatGPT in November 2022, a detection software flagged at least one application essay as AI-generated for 60 percent of applicants for a teaching fellowship in Ghana. Teachers tasked with reviewing these applications still assigned higher scores to high-quality essays, but they reduced the "quality bonus" when they suspected applicants used AI. This trend indicates lower levels of trust in the notion that high-quality written work still accurately reflects a candidate's teaching ability when AI is involved.[18]

In developing economies, job applicants often already struggle to signal their skills credibly to employers, and the qualifications of employees are typically poorly matched to the jobs they are undertaking.[19] Academic performance may therefore matter less when hiring relies on informal networks or tasks that can be observed directly anyway. But when formal credentials play a key role, AI may erode their informational value. As the signaling of skills weakens, so do incentives: If acquiring knowledge no longer reliably improves young people's job prospects or salaries, their motivation to learn will erode even more than just from the use of AI itself.

Overreliance on AI erodes organizational capacity

Like students, workers who have access to generative AI are increasingly delegating tasks to it that demand high levels of cognitive ability, sometimes with explicit encouragement from employers, changing how work is done. In an experiment with experienced programmers, access to GitHub Copilot led workers to spend less time coding, reading, or searching for information and more time waiting for AI-generated outputs.[20] By outsourcing cognitive tasks, from coding to interpreting medical images, workers may slowly forget—or never learn—how to properly perform them. Over time, fewer experts may be available who can spot errors in AI outputs or take on those tasks that AI cannot do.

The use of AI may lead organizations to invest less in human capacity internally. There is evidence that in the US software and service sectors, exposure to AI has disproportionately reduced the demand for entry-level workers.[21] This trend is consistent with AI's substituting for codified knowledge acquired in schools and universities, while complementing experience-based knowledge that large language models do not yet provide, such as project management, people skills, or exercising judgment in ambiguous contexts. Because this latter type of "tacit" knowledge develops from years of "learning by doing," the availability of these experience-based skills could decrease over time if entry-level workers are replaced by AI.[22] This potential long-term effect on capacity would create a detrimental externality, because firms might not want to shoulder the cost of maintaining opportunities to learn on the job for junior workers when the benefits accrue largely to workers themselves, to other employers, or to the economy more broadly. Together, these impacts could mean that firms and public administrations become overly reliant on AI, both through overdelegating to the point of losing control and through underinvesting in "learning on the job." This raises important questions about how firms and governments should respond (for a broader discussion of training and labor market policies, refer to chapters 4 and 7).

Substituting AI for human effort may hamper innovation and productivity in the long term

Over the long term, substituting generative AI for human effort may affect how knowledge is created if AI reduces overall learning rather than redirects it. If fewer individuals acquire the more advanced skills that can develop only through sustained deep engagement, innovation may be hampered, especially if AI-generated outputs become increasingly homogenized.

In addition, some observers have suggested that agentic and generative AI may decrease the accumulation of collective knowledge or even lead to a "knowledge collapse."[23] Acemoglu and coauthors (2026) argue that humans learn in order to address needs tied to specific contexts (such as choosing a pension portfolio), with general knowledge (such as how financial markets work) emerging as a by-product. If AI can generate context-specific advice that is accurate enough for most purposes, individuals may stop investing in learning, slowing the accumulation of general knowledge.[24]

Policies can safeguard learning and knowledge in the age of AI

In a knowledge collapse scenario, both general and specific knowledge could eventually become predominantly "AI knowledge" rather than "human knowledge." Without deliberate policy approaches, low-income countries may struggle to transition toward high-skill, knowledge-based economies and instead become highly reliant on externally developed technologies, with limited capacity for internal innovation.

Although such a scenario highlights risks that require close monitoring, whether these risks materialize depends on how AI is designed and used. Generative AI tools that adhere to a pedagogical design can foster learning rather than displace it, such as when an AI tool provides hints in response to queries rather than ready-made answers.[25] For example, in a 2026 study, interaction with a chatbot built with guardrails and adaptive, personalized problem sequencing was found to produce substantial learning gains, particularly among disadvantaged students, compared with students who lacked access to the chatbot.[26] In addition, users can be taught to engage with generative AI in ways that promote deep engagement and critical thinking.[27] For example, providing students with explicit guidance on shifting from answer-seeking to tutor-style engagement when using AI tools increased their examination scores and passing rates in two separate 2026 studies.[28]

Some users of generative AI have the ability to identify productive patterns on their own, such as requesting explanations or asking high-level conceptual questions.[29] The aforementioned study on AI adoption among grade 7–12 students in China found that the effects on monthly exam scores were strongest among early adopters (who used AI by October 2022) after approximately six months of use. Subsequent cohorts did not experience the same large effect, and at the same time, the performance of the early adopters partially recovered. These patterns suggest that students (or teachers and parents) may be able to adapt to reduce the negative impacts of AI use.

To ensure that AI complements rather than replaces cognitive abilities, policy makers can draw on decades of research on "desirable difficulty" in learning environments[30] and on well-researched best practices that emerge from the educational technology literature.[31] When curriculum and assessments are adapted to it and teachers are trained to use it, AI can be designed in ways that enhance learning in classrooms and workplaces.

Similarly, even before the arrival of AI, the hiring and retention of young workers often entailed a net cost to employers. Firms, sectors, and countries have devised strategies to remedy this. Imperfect labor markets, in which workers cannot easily signal their skills to outsiders, paradoxically encourage firms to invest more in training entry-level workers.[32]

The debate around the erosion of knowledge through AI reinforces the fact that general knowledge, in the sense of shared, generalizable knowledge that does not (only) inform a specific context, is an important public good. Because individual contributions benefit many, optimal levels are achieved only when individual efforts are encouraged through policies such as subsidies for R & D, patenting systems, and research funding. Many countries are already investing heavily in public education and foundational research, but these investments will become more salient with the increasing use of AI.

In short, AI can augment human capabilities, but it must not replace the processes through which more advanced skills are acquired. Achieving the needed balance will be central to sustaining human capital and long-term productivity. It will require careful thought about AI design and coordinated policy action across education sectors, labor markets, and workplaces (refer to chapter 7).

Notes

1. Burneo et al. (2026).
2. Stadler et al. (2024).
3. Refer to Kosmyna et al. (2025). The more drastic conclusions on long-term deterioration in this study have attracted a lot of attention, but the relevant experimental condition relies on a sample of only 18 participants, and the study has not yet been peer reviewed.
4. Deng et al. (2025).
5. Bjork and Bjork (2011).
6. Barcaui (2025); Bastani et al. (2025).
7. Sparrow et al. (2011).
8. Wu et al. (2025).
9. Freeman (2025).
10. Adair et al. (2025); Flaherty (2025).
11. Contractor and Reyes (2025).
12. Adair et al. (2025); Flaherty (2025); Freeman (2025).
13. Strömberg et al. (2026).
14. Data from TALIS [Teaching and Learning International Survey] 2024 Database (dashboard), Organisation for Economic Co-operation and Development, https://www.oecd.org/en/data/datasets/talis-2024-database.html.
15. Gewirtz (2025).
16. Freeman (2025).
17. Data from TALIS [Teaching and Learning International Survey] 2024 Database (dashboard), Organisation for Economic Co-operation and Development, https://www.oecd.org/en/data/datasets/talis-2024-database.html.
18. Awuah et al. (2025).
19. Breza and Kaur (2025).
20. Becker et al. (2025).
21. Brynjolfsson et al. (2025, 2026); Hosseini and Lichtinger (2025).
22. Gans (2025).
23. Acemoglu et al. (2026).
24. Acemoglu et al. (2026) describe *general knowledge* as knowledge that makes context-specific evidence interpretable and valuable. By its nature, general knowledge can be shared, implying that most of the general knowledge an individual generates is an externality that he or she does not internalize. When more general knowledge exists, the same amount of effort is more beneficial for understanding and usefully acting on an individual's specific context. Thus general knowledge is complementary to human learning effort.
25. Bastani et al. (2025).
26. Chung et al. (2026).
27. Gerlich (2025).
28. Burneo et al. (2026); Gallegos (2026).
29. Shen and Tamkin (2026).
30. Bjork and Bjork (2011).
31. For example, refer to the World Bank EdTech [Educational Technology] Strategy (Hawkins et al. 2020).
32. Acemoglu and Pischke (1998).

References

Acemoglu, Daron, Dingwen Kong, and Asuman Ozdaglar. 2026. "AI, Human Cognition and Knowledge Collapse." NBER Working Paper 34910, National Bureau of Economic Research. https://doi.org/10.3386/w34910.

Acemoglu, Daron, and Jörn-Steffen Pischke. 1998. "Beyond Becker: Training in Imperfect Labor Markets." NBER Working Paper 6740, National Bureau of Economic Research. https://doi.org/10.3386/w6740.

Adair, Alexandra, Jessica Howell, Amanda Jacklin, and Alexandria Walton Radford. 2025. "U.S. High School Students' Use of Generative Artificial Intelligence: New Evidence from High School Students, Parents, and Educators." October, College Board. https://research.collegeboard.org/media/pdf/ai-research-brief-1_vf.pdf.

Awuah, Kobbina, Urša Krenk, and David Yanagizawa-Drott. 2025. "Automation with Generative AI? Evidence from a Teacher Hiring Pipeline." BREAD Working Paper 643, Bureau for Research and Economic Analysis of Development, Brown University. https://yanagizawadrott.com/wp-content/uploads/2025/07/GenAI_Automation.pdf.

Barcaui, André. 2025. "ChatGPT as a Cognitive Crutch: Evidence from a Randomized Controlled Trial on Knowledge Retention." *Social Sciences and Humanities Open* 12 (November): 102287. https://doi.org/10.1016/j.ssaho.2025.102287.

Bastani, Hamsa, Osbert Bastani, Alp Sungu, Haosen Ge, Özge Kabakcı, and Rei Mariman. 2025. "Generative AI Without Guardrails Can Harm Learning: Evidence from High School Mathematics." *PNAS: Proceedings of the National Academy of Sciences* 122 (26): e2422633122. https://doi.org/10.1073/pnas.2422633122.

Becker, Joel, Nate Rush, Elizabeth Barnes, and David Rein. 2025. "Measuring the Impact of Early-2025 AI on Experienced Open-Source Developer Productivity." *arXiv:2507.09089v2 [cs.AI]*, July 25, Cornell University. https://doi.org/10.48550/arXiv.2507.09089.

Bjork, Elizabeth Ligon, and Robert A. Bjork. 2011. "Making Things Hard on Yourself, but in a Good Way: Creating Desirable Difficulties to Enhance Learning." In *Psychology and the Real World: Essays Illustrating Fundamental Contributions to Society,* edited by Morton Ann Gernsbacher, Richard W. Pew, Leaetta M. Hough, and James R. Pomerantz. Worth Publishers.

https://bjorklab.psych.ucla.edu/wp-content/uploads/sites/13/2016/04/EBjork_RBjork_2011.pdf.
Breza, Emily, and Supreet Kaur. 2025. "Labor Markets in Developing Countries." *Annual Review of Economics* 17 (August): 747–76. https://doi.org/10.1146/annurev-economics-091124-051650.
Brynjolfsson, Erik, Bharat Chandar, and Ruyu Chen. 2025. "Canaries in the Coal Mine? Six Facts About the Recent Employment Effects of Artificial Intelligence." Working paper, Stanford Digital Economy Lab, Stanford University. https://digitaleconomy.stanford.edu/publication/canaries-in-the-coal-mine-six-facts-about-the-recent-employment-effects-of-artificial-intelligence/.
Brynjolfsson, Erik, Bharat Chandar, and Ruyu Chen. 2026. "Canaries, Interest Rates, and Timing: More on the Recent Drivers of Employment Changes for Young Workers." *News* (blog), February 9. https://digitaleconomy.stanford.edu/news/canaries-interest-rates-and-timinga-more-on-recent-drivers-of-employment-changes-for-young-workers/.
Burneo, Alegría, Lelys Dinarte-Diaz, Carolina Lopez, and Ezequiel Molina. 2026. "Can EdTech Close Learning Gaps? Global Evidence from Digital Interventions." Background paper prepared for *World Development Report 2026: The Promise of Artificial Intelligence*, World Bank. https://www.worldbank.org/en/publication/wdr2026/brief/world-development-report-2026-background-papers.
Chung, Angel Tsai-Hsuan, Botong Zhang, Ling-Chieh Kung, Hamsa Bastani, and Osbert Bastani. 2026. "Effective Personalized AI Tutors via LLM-Guided Reinforcement Learning." Wharton School Research Paper, Wharton School, University of Pennsylvania. http://dx.doi.org/10.2139/ssrn.6423358.
Contractor, Zara, and Germán Reyes. 2025. "Generative AI in Higher Education: Evidence from an Elite College." IZA Discussion Paper 18055, Institute of Labor Economics. https://docs.iza.org/dp18055.pdf.
Deng, Ruiqi, Maoli Jiang, Xinlu Yu, Yuyan Lu, and Shasha Liu. 2025. "Does ChatGPT Enhance Student Learning? A Systematic Review and Meta-Analysis of Experimental Studies." *Computers and Education* 227 (April): 105224. https://doi.org/10.1016/j.compedu.2024.105224.
Flaherty, Colleen. 2025. "How AI Is Changing, Not 'Killing,' College." *Academics* (blog), August 29. https://www.insidehighered.com/news/students/academics/2025/08/29/survey-college-students-views-ai.
Freeman, Josh. 2025. "Student Generative AI Survey 2025." HEPI Policy Note 61, Higher Education Policy Institute. https://www.hepi.ac.uk/reports/student-generative-ai-survey-2025/.
Gallegos, Sebastian. 2026. "Guidance over Adoption: Experimental Evidence on AI-Assisted Learning in Higher Education." Research report, Business School, Adolfo Ibáñez University. http://dx.doi.org/10.2139/ssrn.6536142.
Gans, Joshua. 2025. "If AI and Workers Were Strong Complements, What Would We See?" *Mess and Magic* (blog), August 30. https://joshuagans.substack.com/p/if-ai-and-workers-were-strong-complements.
Gerlich, Michael. 2025. "From Offloading to Engagement: An Experimental Study on Structured Prompting and Critical Reasoning with Generative AI." *Data* 10 (11): 172. https://doi.org/10.3390/data10110172.
Gewirtz, David. 2025. "I've Been Testing AI Content Detectors for Years: These Are Your Best Options in 2025." *ZDNET* (blog), October 29. https://www.zdnet.com/article/ive-been-testing-ai-content-detectors-for-years-these-are-your-best-options-in-2025/.
Hawkins, Robert J., Michael Trucano, Juan Cristóbal Cobo Romani, Alex Twinomugisha, and Iñaki Alejandro Sánchez Ciarrusta. 2020. "Reimagining Human Connections: Technology and Innovation in Education at the World Bank." World Bank. https://documents1.worldbank.org/curated/en/829491606860379513/pdf/Reimagining-Human-Connections-Technology-and-Innovation-in-Education-at-the-World-Bank.pdf.
Hosseini, Seyed Mahdi, and Guy Lichtinger. 2025. "Generative AI as Seniority-Biased Technological Change: Evidence from U.S. Résumé and Job Posting Data." DEL Seminar Series, Stanford Digital Economy Lab, Stanford University, September 22. https://digitaleconomy.stanford.edu/event/seyed-m-hosseini-and-guy-lichtinger-generative-ai-as-seniority-biased-technological-change-evidence-from-u-s-resume-and-job-posting-data/.
Kosmyna, Nataliya, Eugene Hauptmann, Ye Tong Yuan, et al. 2025. "Your Brain on ChatGPT: Accumulation of Cognitive Debt When Using an AI Assistant for Essay Writing Task." *arXiv:2506.08872v2 [cs.AI]*, December 31, Cornell University. https://doi.org/10.48550/arXiv.2506.08872.
Shen, Judy Hanwen, and Alex Tamkin. 2026. "How AI Impacts Skill Formation." *arXiv:2601.20245v2 [cs.CY]*, February 1, Cornell University. https://doi.org/10.48550/arXiv.2601.20245.
Sparrow, Betsy, Jenny Liu, and Daniel M. Wegner. 2011. "Google Effects on Memory: Cognitive Consequences of Having Information at Our Fingertips." *Science* 333 (6043): 776–78. https://doi.org/10.1126/science.1207745.
Stadler, Matthias, Maria Bannert, and Michael Sailer. 2024. "Cognitive Ease at a Cost: LLMs Reduce Mental Effort but Compromise Depth in Student Scientific Inquiry." *Computers in Human Behavior* 160 (November): 108386. https://doi.org/10.1016/j.chb.2024.108386.
Strömberg, David, Victor Lei, and Yanhu Wu. 2026. "The Generative AI Learning Penalty: Evidence from Chinese Secondary Education." CEPR Discussion Paper 21577, Centre for Economic Policy Research, June 2. https://cepr.org/publications/dp21577.
Wu, Suqing, Yukun Liu, Mengqi Ruan, Siyu Chen, and Xiao-Yun Xie. 2025. "Human-Generative AI Collaboration Enhances Task Performance but Undermines Human's Intrinsic Motivation." *Scientific Reports* 15 (1): 15105. https://doi.org/10.1038/s41598-025-98385-2.

6

AI's Political Impact: Reshaping Power Within and Across Countries

Main messages

- **AI dependence and AI sovereignty are both costly**
  Diversify AI suppliers, ensure systems work together, use open models, and join with similarly situated countries to strengthen bargaining power.
- **Governments can become too dependent on the AI firms they regulate**
  Use regulation and procurement to shape AI markets while avoiding excessive reliance on the firms being regulated or accommodating them with overly generous incentives.
- **Dominant AI firms can lock in users and their data**
  Use collective data governance, open public infrastructure, data portability, and competition policy to prevent dominant firms from locking in users and their data.
- **Algorithms can give dominant firms unchecked power over workers**
  Require transparency, meaningful avenues for appeal, and labor protections whenever automated systems shape employment decisions.
- **AI can intensify surveillance and information manipulation**
  Limit mass surveillance and the spread of propaganda by supporting fact-checking, transparency, civic oversight, and informed public debate.

Introduction

In a quiet office in the capital of a developing country, Minister Maya faces a decision that will shape her country's technological future. Two proposals written by her advisers sit on her desk. One involves acquiring the latest artificial intelligence (AI) chips, the leading models, and cloud services from a small group of leading AI economies. The other involves her country building its own chips, models, and data centers. The first proposal enables her country to quickly acquire the capabilities of AI but risks her country becoming overly dependent on foreign providers.

A reproducibility package is available for this book in the Reproducible Research Repository at https://reproducibility.worldbank.org/catalog/624.

The second proposal reduces dependence but may be prohibitively expensive. Choosing either proposal entails trade-offs.

A few miles away, Samuel, a resident of the capital city, walks past a new array of AI-powered cameras. At first, he welcomed them; they promised to reduce traffic congestion and speed up emergency response. But during a recent peaceful protest over rising living costs, the cameras were used to identify and track participants, turning a tool for public safety into an instrument of surveillance.

These scenes illustrate two of the four axes along which AI is changing power dynamics: between countries, between governments and corporations, between corporations and individuals, and between citizens and states. Although AI presents developing countries with an opportunity to transform their economies, power and politics will determine whether this opportunity is realized. The opportunity can be lost in three ways. Countries may *fail to access layers of the AI stack* because of geopolitics.[1] They may *waste the opportunity* because of misaligned incentives between governments and corporations, as well as between corporations and individuals. And governments may *misuse the opportunity* in their relationship with citizens.

What can go wrong along each axis depends on where power lies. Between countries, power stems from control over key inputs in the AI value chain: semiconductors, data centers, cloud networks, data, and critical minerals. Between corporations and governments, power arises from firms' control over frontier technologies and governments' authority over markets, regulation, and procurement. Between corporations and individuals, power reflects market structures that produce concentration, leaving users and workers with limited ability to push back on the terms companies set. Between states and citizens, power stems from the state's capacity to surveil, influence, and shape public discourse. Across all four axes, structural incentives can lead outcomes to diverge from the public interest.

AI does not determine political outcomes on its own. It expands the range of possibilities for surveillance as well as transparency, for manipulation as well as mobilization, and for concentration as well as diffusion of power. The outcomes depend on who controls the technology, who sets the rules for its use, and who has the capacity to contest those rules. Where institutions are weak and civic space is constrained, AI is more likely to amplify authoritarian tendencies; where the rule of law is robust and civil society is active, it can strengthen democratic accountability. This challenge places many developing countries in a difficult situation. They need AI to improve public services and accelerate economic growth but lack the resources to build domestic AI capacity and often have a weak regulatory environment to govern its use. This leaves them vulnerable to both state overreach and unfavorable terms of engagement with global technology firms, while limiting their influence over the rules being written.

This chapter examines how AI is reshaping these four axes of power, with particular attention to developing-country contexts. These four dimensions are neither exhaustive nor independent. They intersect and reinforce one another in ways that shape development outcomes. The chapter draws on evidence where such evidence exists and identifies gaps where the evidence is limited (or nonexistent).

Dynamics between countries: A technology with geopolitical stakes

States have long competed for control over transformative technologies. Naval power shaped imperial rivalry in the early modern period. Nuclear weapons and space technology became critical arenas of competition during the Cold War. Today, governments increasingly view AI as a foundational technology that shapes economic activity, social and political structures, national security, and global influence.[2] This dynamic will have significant repercussions for whether and how developing countries can access AI.

Since 2018, the United States has introduced export controls on advanced semiconductor chips and related supply chains, with exports to restricted entities requiring approval by the government.[3] Meanwhile, China has leveraged its control over critical raw materials by announcing a ban on the export of technologies to process rare earths, as well as export controls on the rare earth elements themselves.[4] China's latest measures also target technological know-how and foreign products made with Chinese inputs. However, several of the latest measures have been suspended until November 2026.[5]

Key layers of the AI stack can function as strategic "choke points": Control at each layer constrains who can participate in the AI value chain and acquire the capabilities of AI. Although open-source and open-weight models provide developing countries with access to models,[6] running models at scale requires either domestic data centers, which would have to be built on chips controlled by major powers, or commercial cloud providers based in some of these countries. Countries may seek to reduce dependence in several ways. One approach is to source different layers of the AI stack from different countries, choosing the best available technology for each layer. However, because AI systems depend on these layers working together, this strategy can create interoperability problems and expose countries to conflicting regulations tied to technologies from different jurisdictions. Pursuing "AI sovereignty" is an alternative approach, but as will be discussed, it is often a costly and ineffective one. Part 1 argued that AI offers developing countries an opportunity to ease shortfalls in skilled capabilities. Mishandling such trade-offs could cost developing economies access to this very technology.

Incentives and asymmetric dependence shape technology choices

Why do the major powers promote the use of their AI technology? The first reason relates to scale. As discussed in part 1, AI benefits from economies of scale at many layers of the stack. The second reason involves influence. Having control over the AI infrastructure determines whose rules become the dominant global standard. More than 80 percent of the world's population lives in developing countries. Every additional country whose infrastructure, developers, and users are tied to a given technological ecosystem contributes to scale economies, strengthening the influence of the leading powers.

Notably, these powers often use incentives to promote their technology through financing and market access. The American AI Exports Program, launched under a US executive order in July 2025, promotes exporting US-developed "full-stack" AI technologies consisting of hardware, software, and services to allies to secure global technology leadership.[7] China's Digital Silk Road, launched in 2015 as part of the Belt and Road Initiative, aims to build crucial infrastructure in developing countries, including 5G networks, undersea cables, AI laboratories, data centers, and smart cities.[8]

Beyond incentives, asymmetric dependencies can also influence a country's technology choices. One common form of asymmetric dependency is that of trade.[9] Developing countries often rely heavily on a single major economy for trade (refer to figure 6.1). For example, developing countries in Latin America export a disproportionate share of their goods to the United States compared with other major powers, while those in East Asia and Pacific export an approximately equal share of goods to China and the United States—suggesting the presence of asymmetric dependencies with not just one but both countries.

Figure 6.1 Developing countries depend heavily on a few major economies as export destinations

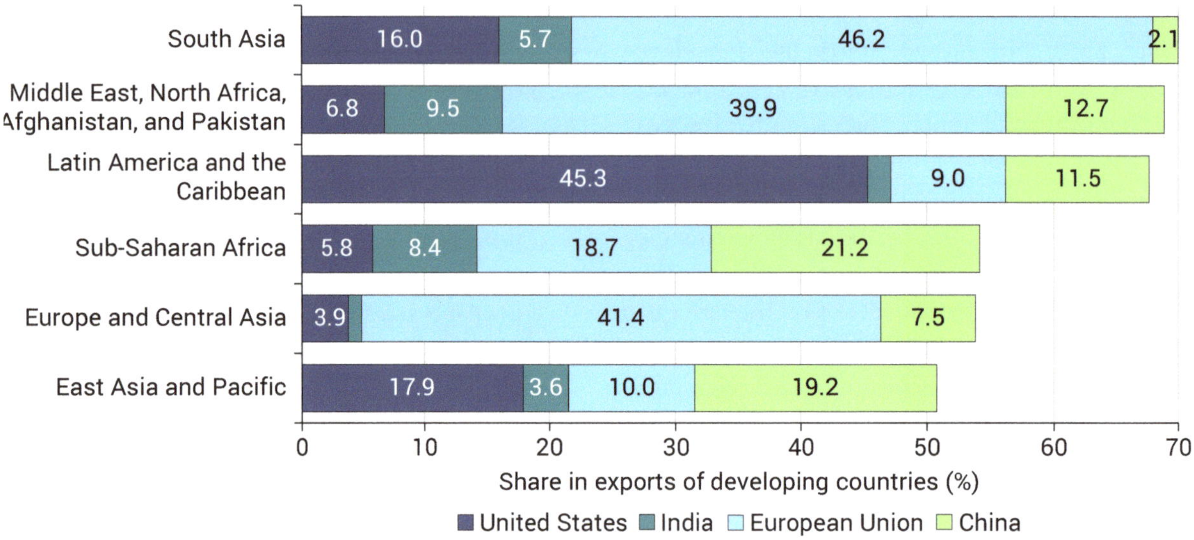

Source: WDR 2026 team, based on data of the CEPII-BACI (Centre d'études prospectives et d'informations internationales/Center for Prospective Studies and International Information–Base pour l'Analyse du Commerce International/Database for International Trade Analysis) Dataset, CEPII, https://www.cepii.fr/DATA_DOWNLOAD/baci/doc/baci_webpage.html.

Note: The bars use 2024 data. *Developing countries* are defined as low-income, lower-middle-income, and upper-middle-income countries based on the World Bank fiscal year 2027 income classification. (Refer to Metreau et al. 2026; World Bank Country and Lending Groups [dashboard], World Bank, https://datahelpdesk.worldbank.org/knowledgebase/articles/906519-world-bank-country-and-lending-groups.) China and India are excluded from the export share data even though they belong to the regions of East Asia and Pacific and South Asia, respectively. This is done to avoid mixing their role as both a source and a destination country. The United States and all European Union member countries are classified as high-income countries and are therefore also excluded from the export share data.

Trade dependencies, as well as dependencies in other domains such as security and financial systems, can reinforce one another. Crucially, the power arising from such imbalances need not be exercised or even articulated to be effective. Where one country is materially dependent on another across many domains, the mere existence of such asymmetric dependencies can shape the technology choices countries make.[10] The choices developing countries faced in the late 1990s regarding technologies related to genetic modification provide an instructive parallel. States with closer ties to the European Union were more likely to ratify the Cartagena Protocol on Biosafety early, whereas those closer to the United States were slower to support it or did not support it at all.[11]

In the case of AI, similar dynamics surrounding dependencies can be observed in the signing of the Pax Silica Declaration. Launched by the United States in 2025, the Pax Silica Initiative spans the entire AI stack and aims to reduce coercive dependencies, secure global technology supply chains, address AI supply chain opportunities and vulnerabilities, and explore joint investment, as well as protect sensitive technologies and build trusted digital infrastructure.[12] At the time of writing, signatories to the declaration include Australia, Finland, Greece, India,

Israel, Japan, the Republic of Korea, Norway, the Philippines, Qatar, Singapore, Sweden, the United Arab Emirates, and the United Kingdom. These signatory countries tend to rely on the United States for defense and trade, even as the United States depends less on them as export destinations (refer to figure 6.2). Other strategic factors, such as the opportunity to be a partner in deploying capital and building infrastructure to accelerate national AI objectives, may also explain why some countries have chosen to participate. Although few of the participants are developing countries, the role that such dependencies may play in influencing their decisions makes it pertinent for developing economies.

Raw materials and data are rarely sufficient to rebalance the dependency that developing countries have on the major AI powers

A striking feature of the AI ecosystem is that, while control over the highest-value segments of the AI stack is concentrated in a few leading economies, several raw materials essential to this stack are geographically concentrated in developing economies (for further details, refer to chapter 2). In principle, control over these critical raw materials could give developing countries an opportunity to rebalance their interactions with leading economies. However, extraction alone

Figure 6.2 Pax Silica Declaration signatories share strong defense, economic, and trade ties with the United States

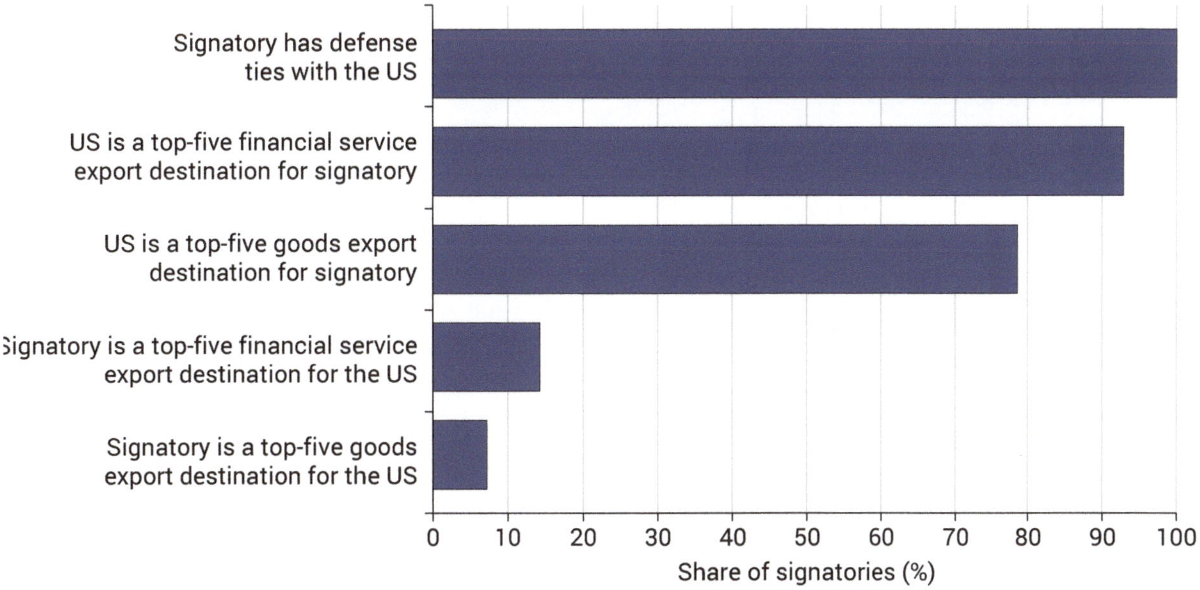

Source: WDR 2026 team, based on data of the CEPII-BACI (Centre d'études prospectives et d'informations internationales/ Center for Prospective Studies and International Information–Base pour l'Analyse du Commerce International/Database for International Trade Analysis) Dataset, CEPII, https://www.cepii.fr/DATA_DOWNLOAD/baci/doc/baci_webpage.html, and WTO-OECD (World Trade Organization-Organisation for Economic Co-operation and Development) Balanced Trade in Services dataset, https://www.wto.org/english/res_e/statis_e/gstdh_batis_e.htm

Note: A country is considered to have defense ties with the United States if it hosts or provides access to a US military base, has a framework agreement with the United States for defense cooperation, or has a defense pact with the United States. Financial service exports include the categories *financial services* and *insurance and pension services*. Goods export values are calculated by aggregating all products between each exporter-importer pair.

rarely translates into bargaining power without downstream processing capacity, which most developing countries lack. Discovered mineral reserves cannot always be extracted in a commercially viable way.

Data can be another potential counterbalancing force. Many developing countries generate large volumes of data that remain relatively untapped. For the major powers, access to such data is attractive for model development and market access alike. However, data in many developing countries are highly fragmented[13]—scattered across informal systems and government agencies and divided among dozens or hundreds of language communities, often too small individually to justify building specialized AI models.

The pursuit of AI sovereignty risks becoming a development trap

Faced with concerns about overdependence, many governments have started to adopt strategies to reduce dependence by securing ownership or control of the key physical resources that power AI. Although these strategies may also serve economic objectives, they are often framed as efforts to achieve AI sovereignty. Measures to achieve this include developing local models and capabilities to manufacture semiconductors, subsidizing domestic computing infrastructure,[14] and localizing data. From a national standpoint, AI sovereignty measures are rational if the objective is reduced dependence; they may also help countries move up the AI value chain. However, these measures often fail to deliver the promised sovereignty or a sustainable economic path for developing economies.[15]

First, AI sovereignty measures frequently fail to achieve their intended goals, especially if the goals involve complete self-sufficiency. Data localization can be complicated by the extraterritorial reach of a cloud provider's home-country laws, which may be triggered in situations such as serious criminal investigations.[16] Domestic semiconductor initiatives often struggle to match the scale economies of established incumbents. Even countries with a local data center may not be able to avoid upstream dependencies on hardware and software from major foreign providers.[17]

Second, AI sovereignty strategies commit governments to building at home, and this can generate domestic political costs. AI infrastructure is resource-intensive. As a result, AI sovereignty strategies bring to the forefront of political discourse concerns about the siting of such infrastructure, especially data centers.[18] In Malaysia, the state of Johor, which is the fastest-growing data center hub in Southeast Asia, is facing community backlash over the rapid expansion of data centers.[19] Similar opposition has emerged in other developing countries such as Brazil and Mexico.[20] Unlike a commercial developer that can relocate to another country if blocked in one, a government that has staked a sovereignty claim on building data centers cannot. It faces the political liabilities of public backlash as well as absorbing the fiscal cost of the abandoned or delayed project—often for an unmet goal.

Third, AI sovereignty imposes an aggregate cost through fragmentation. AI benefits from scale. Integrated global markets lower costs in many layers of the stack, such as those for training models, manufacturing chips, and building applications. Excessive fragmentation into duplicative country-level stacks reverses these scale economies. What emerges is a form of a self-reinforcing "fragmentation doom loop,"[21] which can create a development trap. Efforts to duplicate resources are already prohibitively expensive. Yet the more countries fragment, the more expensive it is for them to build their own AI stacks, adding strain to already-weak fiscal balances and diverting resources from pressing needs in health, education, or other infrastructure. Smaller developing countries bear a greater burden because they are unable to replicate at the national level the scale economies that they once accessed globally. By contrast, incumbent firms from the major powers continue to benefit by providing the AI stack and selling to the fragmented markets.

For developing countries, neither overdependence nor excessive fragmentation offers a sustainable path. Most countries cannot afford to build every layer from scratch. Thus, for most countries, the middle path between sovereignty and dependence is a more viable strategy. This entails, where possible, diversifying suppliers within each layer to reduce the risk of choke points while ensuring interoperability. It also involves targeted steps to reduce dependence, such as using open-source and open-weight models, establishing strong data governance, engaging in standards setting, and forming coalitions with like-minded countries to boost collective bargaining power. Part 3 of the Report builds upon such initiatives. This approach accepts that there will be trade-offs. Some choke points will persist, but this approach maintains access to economies of scale and frontier performance that outright sovereignty strategies would forgo.

Dynamics between governments and corporations: Entanglements could impede development

Within a country, the relationship between governments and corporations affects whether the gains from AI are broad based, wasted, or concentrated in the hands of existing power holders. Governments can lean too far toward accommodating firms, offering preferential terms to attract investment, at the expense of public funds. At times, governments may exercise their regulatory and enforcement powers in an unanticipated way, creating uncertainty for firms. In some instances, the relationship can settle into arrangements that are too cooperative, entrenching the interests of both through government-backed contracts flowing to connected firms and firms aiding in the extension of state power over citizens.

Each of these phenomena can be partly attributed to the same underlying cause of many imbalances of power between firms and governments. Firms lobby at scale.[22] The number of firms lobbying in the United States on AI-related issues nearly doubled between 2019 and 2025,[23] even as lobbying activity concerning issues such as immigration remained relatively constant during this period (refer to figure 6.3).[24] Active industry engagement in the European Union led to a shift in regulatory approach toward innovation and competitiveness.[25] An extensive investigation by the Centro Latinoamericano de Investigación Periodística and various partners documented nearly 3,000 lobbying actions across multiple economies between 2012 and 2025, with such activity rising rapidly in Latin America.[26]

Even without lobbying, these companies wield significant influence stemming from their position across the AI stack.[27] Moreover, because throughout the AI ecosystem switching costs are substantial, the possibility that a firm may reduce operations or withdraw owing to unfavorable regulations is credible, even without explicit threats. In some instances, because the technology is evolving so quickly, as government officials and agencies formulate policies and regulations, they may rely on the very corporations that they are tasked with regulating to explain the technology's abilities and potential risks.

Governments are not powerless. They retain significant levers such as export controls,[28] regulating access to domestic markets,[29] designations of supply chain risk,[30] and procurement rules (refer to chapter 8), as well as acquiring stakes in companies.[31] However, it is not easy to strike the right balance in using these levers. When used too readily, they can create uncertainty for firms, but when used too sparingly, governments may become too accommodative to firms or settle into arrangements that are too cooperative.

Figure 6.3 Since the launch of GPT-1 in 2018, the number of firms engaged in AI-related lobbying in the United States has rapidly increased

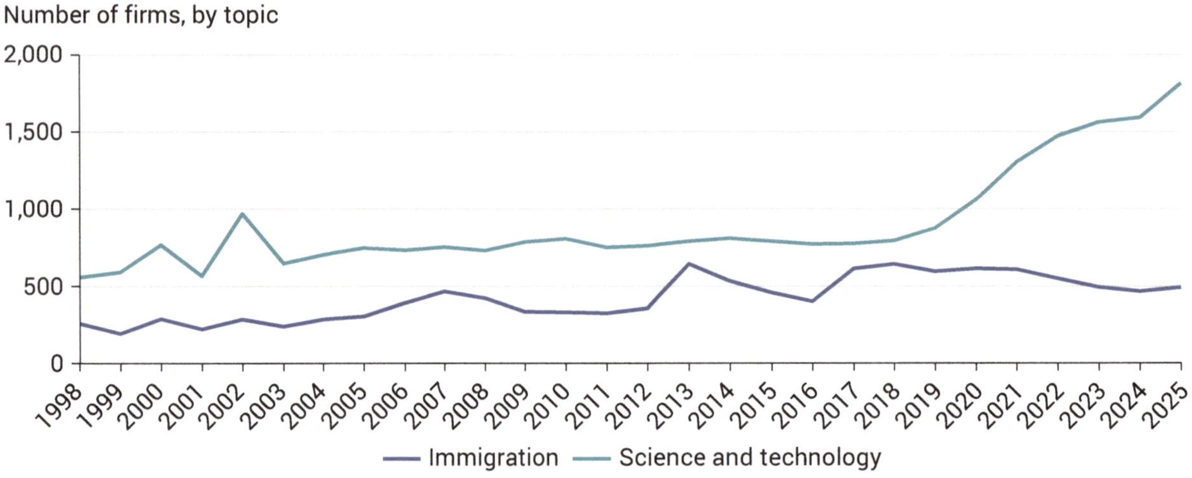

Source: WDR 2026 team, based on data of Top Issues (dashboard), OpenSecrets, https://www.opensecrets.org/federal-lobbying/top-issues.

Note: The year 2018 corresponds to the launch of the first OpenAI large language model, Generative Pre-trained Transformer 1 (GPT-1). The plotted lines show the total number of firms engaged in lobbying by issue. The AI-related category *science and technology* is the combined total of *science and technology, computers and information technology, and manufacturing*. Lobbying on *immigration* is shown separately. If a firm lobbies on more than one issue, it is counted multiple times in the data. AI = artificial intelligence.

In developing countries, the power imbalance between firms and governments is often exacerbated by weak state capacity. This implies that even for countries that navigate the geopolitics well and can secure access to various layers of the AI stack, the opportunities for AI to transform their economies can still be wasted because of the ways in which domestic governments engage with AI firms. Three outcomes are highlighted next. Each lets the opportunity slip away in different ways: straining government finances, foreclosing the investment that is needed, or channeling the gains to those who already hold power.

Competition to attract AI investment strains government finances and maneuver room

When firms are able to secure significant concessions from governments, competition among countries to attract AI-related investments may lead some countries to commit significant fiscal resources. Examples of fiscal commitments abound. In Uzbekistan, the government has introduced policies to attract investment in AI and data centers through tax exemptions and discounted electricity rates.[32] India has announced a 20-year tax holiday until 2047 for foreign providers of cloud services and data center operators.[33]

While these arrangements may incentivize AI investments, if entered into excessively, they may place a disproportionate share of the financial and technological risks on the public while allowing firms to capture a significant share of the economic returns. Fiscal balances in many developing countries are already deteriorating while pressure from rising debt is growing.[34] Such policies risk creating a race to the bottom in which countries undercut one another in offering incentives to attract investments, further straining fiscal space.

Fiscal commitments can also stimulate overinvestment in AI-related sectors, contributing to macroeconomic instability through boom-bust cycles. Episodes from history suggest that booms in technology are highly susceptible to such cycles, even in advanced economies (refer to box 6.1).

Unanticipated application of state power deters investment, while cozy arrangements between governments and firms could lead to rent seeking and weakened institutions

When firms cannot anticipate how state power will be applied, they factor this uncertainty into their choices by seeking higher returns, shortening investment commitments, or opting out entirely. Crucially, the fear is not regulation itself, given that firms routinely invest in heavily regulated environments, but rather sudden rule changes. The risk of unanticipated policy is compounded because much of the AI infrastructure, such as data centers and chip fabrication plants, requires large investments tied to specific locations. Once the investment is completed and the capital becomes sunk, the firm's ability to relocate declines. This shifts greater bargaining power to the host government, in a dynamic known as the "obsolescing bargain."[35] Governments can now raise preferential tax rates agreed upon before the investment was made, renegotiate access to land or power, introduce data localization requirements, and in extreme cases, expropriate the assets. Thus, reflecting the political risk, firms may make investments that have shorter commitments, limit transfers of capabilities, and create less local value.

Box 6.1 Boom, bang, bust in technology investments: Does history repeat itself?

Developments in artificial intelligence (AI) in the United States share certain characteristics with historical episodes like the railroads boom in the 1800s and the telecommunications boom of the late 1990s, in which the early promises of technological breakthroughs generated waves of exuberant expectations, massive leveraged investment, and eventual financial distress. Importantly, these episodes did not reflect technological failure but overinvestment based on overly optimistic forecasts. Although demand eventually caught up, the adjustment path was costly. Understanding how AI developments play out among firms in the United States matters because they are one of the dominant builders of the global AI infrastructure, including in developing countries. Whether a crash happens depends crucially on whether demand matches the high levels of investment.

High expectations of rapid growth. Past technology booms, like today's AI wave, have been marked by expectations of rapid growth in demand. A 1998 report by the US Department of Commerce claimed that internet traffic was doubling every 100 days—a figure later credited to WorldCom, a leading telecommunications company at the time.[a] This expectation underpinned a massive build-out of network infrastructure, even as growth rates slowed in subsequent years.[b] Similar expectations can be observed today and have been used to justify

(Box continues next page)

Box 6.1 Boom, bang, bust in technology investments: Does history repeat itself? *(continued)*

building ahead to meet anticipated demand. An analysis from 2018 shows that demand for compute has been doubling every 3.4 months[c]—a figure that is remarkably close to the 100-day doubling cited in the early days of the internet.

Elevated levels of capital investment. In anticipation of future demand, in past technology booms as well as the current AI wave, levels of capital investment have soared. The belief that the use of railroads and the internet would grow exponentially led to frenzied building of infrastructure. Between 1868 and 1871, rail companies in the United States built 33,000 miles of tracks, often in remote areas.[d] During the telecommunications boom, capital investment by publicly traded telecommunications service companies nearly tripled from $47 billion in 1995 to a peak of $121 billion in 2000.[e] The increase was so great that only 2.7 percent of fiber-optic lines were being used in 2002 when the sector crashed.[f] Strikingly, capital spending on AI by hyperscalers in the United States is expected to be about 2 percent of GDP in 2026, more than double the figure at the height of the telecommunications boom[g] and about the same as that on railroads in the 1860s.[h]

High level of debt. Elevated levels of capital investment that were mainly funded by debt have characterized past technology booms and the current AI wave. When financial crisis in Europe led to investors selling off railroad bonds in the 1870s, the market was flooded with more bonds than buyers were willing to absorb.[i] Telecommunications firms had run up total debts of about $1 trillion at the time of the crash.[j] Twenty-three telecommunications companies went bankrupt in a wave capped off by the collapse of WorldCom in 2002, the single largest bankruptcy in the history of the United States at that time.[k] Today, concerns are growing that AI hyperscalers are taking on excessive debt, as seen in their increasing share in the public investment-grade bond index and the increasingly complex structures of deals between AI companies.[l]

Source: WDR 2026 team.

a. *Economist* (2002b).
b. Couper et al. (2003).
c. OpenAI (2018). *Compute* is defined in this article as petaflop/s-days. A petaflop/s-day consists of performing 10^{15} neural net operations per second for one day, or a total of about 10^{20} operations.
d. Wooldridge (2025).
e. Doms (2004).
f. Dreazen (2002).
g. Slok et al. (2026).
h. Wooldridge (2025).
i. Refer to "Financial Panic of 1873" (web page), US Department of the Treasury, https://home.treasury.gov/about/history/freedmans-bank-building/financial-panic-of-1873.
j. *Economist* (2002a).
k. Starr (2002).
l. Sam et al. (2026).

Besides holding the power to change rules suddenly, governments control access to a range of valuable resources. Past experience suggests these resources can be allocated in ways that reflect political favoritism rather than competitive allocation.[36] As a result, capital, labor, and public funds can be directed toward firms that are politically connected rather than those that create the greatest economic value, weakening institutions in the process.[37]

A recent example is Indonesia's Pusat Data Nasional Sementara (Temporary National Data Center) project. Investigators found that a small group of opportunistic officials misused their contracting power to rig the tender process to benefit Lintasarta, a subsidiary of Indosat Ooredoo Hutchison group, in exchange for kickbacks. As a result, the state lost an estimated 140.8 billion rupiah.[38] Checks and balances held, however, and the officials were held accountable. The example provides a cautionary tale; if checks and balances fail and transparency is lacking, such conduct may evolve into systemic rent-seeking dynamics. Research from several countries has shown that politically connected firms tend to survive, yet industries with a higher share of such firms exhibit lower growth and productivity.[39] Over time, such misallocation reduces market dynamism, crowding out firms that would have generated more value. This process could diminish the broad-based gains AI could have generated and could concentrate the greatest gains in the hands of those who already hold power.

Beyond resource allocation, there is also the risk of firms being drawn into the exercise of state power. Many technology companies collect large volumes of personal information; governments increasingly request access to such data.[40] Although there may be legitimate security or law enforcement reasons for such requests and companies have safeguards in place, the rising frequency of these requests normalizes this access mechanism—which may be exploited to further the state's power over its citizens. Ultimately, the safeguards rely on mutual restraint—with companies pushing back on overreach and governments using such access judiciously. This equilibrium can easily go either way when there is a change in corporate policy or government.

Although the three outcomes discussed are distinct, they all stem in part from the imbalance of power between corporations (which supply the technology) and states (which depend on these technologies but are responsible for regulating them). Reducing or eliminating this imbalance is crucial to ensuring that countries do not let the opportunities for AI to deliver positive outcomes for their economies slip away. Part 3 of this Report discusses policies to avoid such outcomes.

Dynamics between corporations and individuals: Market structure determines who gains from AI

Unlike competition between states or contested bargains between governments and firms, the power imbalances between firms and individuals in the AI economy emerge from features of the AI value chain itself, such as large up-front investments, network effects, data feedback loops, and spillover effects that standard market mechanisms cannot address.[41] These characteristics lead to market concentration that benefits capital owners more than users and workers. Treating this concentration as a well-understood market failure rather than an inherent characteristic of the AI value chain helps clarify which policy tools can address it.

Data advantages lead to durable market power that benefits AI capital owners more than users

AI systems improve with use. Each user interaction generates data that can be used to train better models; better models attract more users; more users generate more data. This feedback loop makes it harder for new entrants to catch up once a leader has emerged. Moreover, users may find it costly to switch between providers. It is difficult for a business that has built workflows around one AI provider to move to another or for individuals to move their data and history between platforms. Other markets, such as those for operating systems and search engines, are characterized by similar tendencies for data advantages that compound concentration.

Data concentration is harder to address through standard competition tools than concentration in other inputs because of data externalities; that is, a single user's data are nearly redundant for predicting that user's own behavior, but useful for predicting the behavior of similar users.[42] This pattern has significant policy implications. Giving individuals property rights over their own data does little to prevent the concentration of AI's predictive capability. Even if many users withheld their data, firms holding the largest existing data sets would retain their advantage. Data externalities of this kind require collective governance arrangements rather than specific provisions of individual contracts between AI providers and users alone.

Beyond data concentration, individuals in many developing countries face significant challenges in understanding what happens to their data because minimal safeguards are in place. As of 2026, only 73 percent of developing countries have enacted data protection legislation, compared with 98 percent of advanced economies.[43] Even where such laws exist, they are rarely enforced. This concern has become increasingly important because data collected for one purpose are often repurposed to train models for entirely different applications, making it difficult to trace where the training data come from. Furthermore, documentation regarding the origin of training data, whether user consent was obtained, and the authenticity of the data remains insufficient.[44]

Several policy approaches are emerging to address these market failures. India's digital public infrastructure, built before the current AI wave, shows how public alternatives can prevent the concentration that AI is likely to intensify. The Unified Payments Interface is a government-provided payment system accounting for about 70 percent of India's digital payment volume as of fiscal year 2023–24. It processed more than 12 billion transactions in the single month of December 2023.[45] The interface is open and works with many systems, allowing any private company to build on it. This feature prevents the platform lock-in that often happens with payment systems in other countries. Meanwhile, India's Data Empowerment and Protection Architecture expands this model by giving individuals control over their data through consent managers and by enabling data portability.[46] While implementation challenges remain, the model has attracted interest from several countries.

Data cooperatives offer an alternative approach in which individuals pool their data to gain collective bargaining power that they lack individually, aggregating decisions that individual users cannot make effectively on their own and thus addressing the externality problem. Small-scale pilots in India and Kenya are testing this approach for gig workers and others in the informal sector, though evidence on their effectiveness at scale is limited.

These asymmetries are not new to AI; they characterize the platform economy more broadly, in which users generate the data that firms convert into commercial advantage. What AI changes is their intensity. When user interactions train the models that are a firm's main asset, data become more valuable to capture, one user's data reveal more about others, and switching providers gets harder. Individuals are left with limited means to bargain over how their data are used or to share in the returns they generate. Whether digital public infrastructure, open-weight models, data cooperatives, and competition policy enforcement can achieve sufficient coordination to shift these structural dynamics will depend on whether countries adopt and enforce the required policies and on effective international coordination that does not yet exist.

AI can concentrate power in the hands of capital owners at the expense of workers

The development of AI systems has created new employment opportunities for millions of relatively low-skill workers in developing countries—from data labeling for AI training to content moderation. These opportunities share a common feature that economists recognize as a source of market failure: A few large companies are the main source of jobs for many workers in the AI industry, giving these employers extra power over determining pay and working conditions. This phenomenon is what economists call a *monopsony*. Meanwhile, workers are being managed by algorithms; human managers are absent, for the most part. This type of algorithmic management at scale, combined with the monopsony powers of employers, results in AI companies paying wages below workers' additional contribution to total value,[47] working conditions that workers have little ability to negotiate, and a structural difficulty in workers organizing collectively.

The data labeling industry is a clear example. A few companies, such as Scale AI, Sama, CloudFactory, and Appen, hire workers from a large global pool of workers. High global labor supply combined with concentrated buyer-side demand drives down wages. A 2023 investigation in Kenya found that some data labelers earned between $1.32 and $2.00 per hour, barely above Kenya's minimum wage of about $1.20 per hour, for psychologically and emotionally challenging work that included reviewing graphic content.[48] In addition to low wages, workers must contend with sudden shutdowns of the platform, late or withheld payments, restrictions on workers organizing, and contracts designed to place legal liability in jurisdictions that favor the platforms. Fairwork Cloudwork Ratings, which evaluates platforms on five areas of fair work, found that none of the 16 platforms reviewed met basic standards of fair pay, working conditions, contracts, management, or worker representation.

The same AI systems that require labeled data to operate also depend on humans to filter out the most disturbing content. Content moderators and data workers who screen for disturbing content carry psychological costs that are well documented. A 2023 lawsuit by Kenyan content moderators against Meta and Sama found diagnoses of posttraumatic stress disorder (PTSD), depression, and anxiety among workers exposed to traumatic content without proper psychological support.[49] Much of this work is outsourced to developing countries,[50] where workers typically lack access to mental health services and other protections that are necessary for such disturbing work. This situation poses a difficult labor market problem: In a competitive market with sufficient information and bargaining power, workers taking on such risks would receive higher wages and structured psychological support. The combination of monopsony, a large global labor supply, and outsourcing through jurisdictions with weak labor protections has prevented those conditions from emerging. They persist, at least in part, because AI companies can shift the offshore locations for this work across countries at a relatively low cost.

Beyond the firms that are involved in the value chain of AI, businesses across the economy can potentially deploy AI to exercise greater control over workers. Algorithmic management is not inherently worse than human management; in some respects it can be fairer because consistent rules applied uniformly are easier to scrutinize than the discretionary and sometimes arbitrary decisions of a human supervisor.[51] The concern is not the algorithm itself but the conditions under which it operates: Workers cannot observe how decisions are made, have limited means to contest those decisions, and often face a single buyer with little ability to switch employers.

Under these conditions, the consistency that could make algorithmic management fairer instead entrenches the firm's advantage. Machine learning systems can monitor worker performance, tracking outputs, time allocation, and patterns as workers complete tasks extremely closely. Firms have always had advantages over workers in terms of information, but AI greatly reduces the cost of acting on those advantages at scale.[52]

This dynamic is most apparent in platform companies in which algorithms can make automated decisions about task assignment, pricing, and account status with limited human oversight. They can also remove workers' access to the platform, with limited options for appeal. Dynamic pricing that modifies prices constantly depending on supply and demand and other conditions shifts income variability from the platform onto the worker. Platform communication structures are often one-sided: Firms can reach individual workers directly, but workers cannot easily communicate with one another through the platform, making it harder to organize collectively. Box 6.2 highlights how these mechanisms play out in ride-hailing platforms and how courts and regulators have begun to respond in high-income countries.

In developing countries, most existing employment is in the informal sector. In Sub-Saharan Africa, informal employment accounts for 85 percent of total employment.[53] When algorithmic management enters informal sectors in these countries through apps for taxi drivers, delivery workers, or domestic workers, among others, it formalizes some aspects of work without bringing the protections traditionally associated with formalization, such as employment contracts, social security, and grievance mechanisms.

Box 6.2 How AI amplifies the market power of ride-hailing and delivery platforms

Ride-hailing platforms have become the most litigated case of algorithmic labor management. Uber uses artificial intelligence (AI) algorithms to manage approximately 9 million drivers worldwide, controlling every aspect of the job, including who gets which rides, how much the fare is, and whether a driver's account remains active. The platform modifies prices constantly by using machine learning algorithms to forecast demand. Drivers have no information about how these decisions are made, how the drivers themselves are rated, or why they are offered particular rides at specific prices. Each driver only sees their own transactions, but the platform tracks every transaction for every driver.

This information advantage translates into leverage for the platform. Drivers have no control over the algorithms. Drivers must maintain scores above a certain threshold to avoid deactivation under Uber's rating system. The platform continuously tracks acceptance and cancelation rates, response times, driving habits, and location. Algorithms adjust fares in real time. Performance categories determine which drivers get priority access to trips, creating what a Dutch court described as "a financial incentive and a disciplining and instructing effect."[a]

(Box continues next page)

Box 6.2 How AI amplifies the market power of ride-hailing and delivery platforms *(continued)*

Several countries have pushed back. In 2021, the United Kingdom Supreme Court declared that Uber drivers are "workers" entitled to minimum wage and paid leave. That same year, a Dutch court ruled that algorithmic management constituted a "modern relationship of authority" and deemed Uber an employer. Spain's Rider Law compels delivery platforms to treat couriers as employees and establishes worker rights regarding algorithmic management and labor protections.

Platforms have responded in three ways. Some exit markets when confronted with employment classification, as Deliveroo did in Spain following the passage of the Rider Law in 2021. Others switch to subcontracting models that preserve algorithmic control while avoiding direct employment. A third group lobbies for intermediate legal categories that retain flexibility without granting full employment rights. Proposition 22 in California is the most prominent example.

What distinguishes this dynamic from conventional employment disputes is AI's ability to scale and automate control. Algorithms can monitor thousands of workers simultaneously, adjust pricing across entire cities in seconds, and enforce performance standards with no human oversight. This shifts the balance of power in ways that individual workers cannot counter. A driver cannot negotiate with an algorithm, appeal to its discretion, or organize fellow drivers when the platform controls who sees which messages. Although AI is not the only source of monopsony power,[b] it makes exercising the powers held by employers cheaper, faster, and harder to contest.

Source: WDR 2026 team.

a. Refer to ruling from Court of Amsterdam, 8937120 CV EXPL 20-22882, September 13, 2021, https://www.courthousenews.com/wp-content/uploads/2021/09/amsterdam-uber-ruling.pdf.

b. *Monopsony* refers to a market in which there is a single buyer or a small group of dominant buyers: in the context of this box, employer.

Dynamics between citizens and the state: AI strengthens the state's hand, for better or worse

AI is changing the relationship between states and their citizens in two opposing directions. While AI can improve the delivery of public services (refer to chapter 5), it can also facilitate widespread surveillance, polarize public discourse, and sway voter behavior. Public perceptions of AI in developing countries reflect this dichotomy. Among surveyed low- and middle-income countries, levels of concern are highest in Brazil and Argentina (and similar to those in the United States and Europe), and lowest in Nigeria and India (refer to figure 6.4). These differences show that attitudes concerning AI are influenced by the context of the country, not only its income level.

Figure 6.4 Attitudes toward AI vary widely across countries

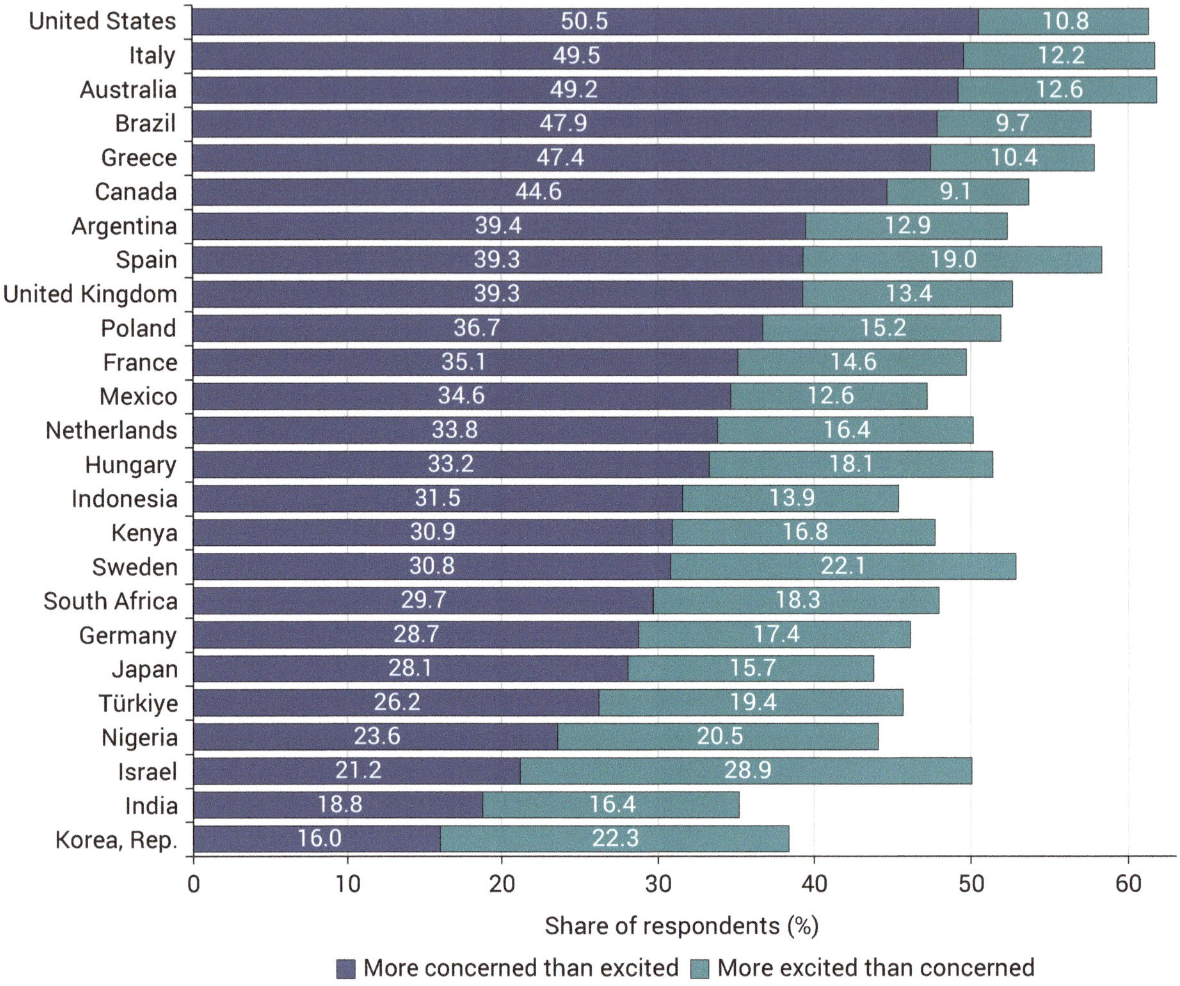

Sources: Poushter et al. 2025. Data for the United States are from the American Trends Panel Wave 152, Pew Research Center, https://www.pewresearch.org/dataset/american-trends-panel-wave-152/.

Note: The data are from the Global Attitudes Survey, Spring 2025 edition, Pew Research Center (Poushter et al. 2025). For each country, the bars show only the "more concerned than excited" and "more excited than concerned" responses and hence do not total 100 percent. The remaining share comprises respondents who did not answer or responded with "equally concerned and excited." AI = artificial intelligence.

AI makes surveillance cheap and scalable

Surveillance by government is not new. What AI changes is its scale, precision, and cost. Facial recognition can identify individuals in crowds in real time. Predictive analytics can flag potential targets before they act. Natural language processing can scan millions of messages for keywords or sentiment. These capabilities can transform surveillance from a targeted activity requiring significant resources into a persistent, scalable one.

Autocracies and weak democracies are more likely to import surveillance technologies, such as facial recognition AI, especially following episodes or periods of domestic political unrest; the technologies, once deployed, in turn suppress subsequent unrest.[54] The scope of AI surveillance extends beyond physical monitoring to include analysis of online behavior, social networks, and communication patterns. At least 75 countries were using AI surveillance technologies as of 2019, and adoption was increasing in all regions, the Carnegie Endowment's AI Global Surveillance Index reports.[55] This figure is likely a lower bound given the improvements in performance of recent AI models.

Many low- and middle-income countries have weak rule of law, limited checks on executive power, and constrained civic space. In such contexts, AI surveillance technologies can shift the balance between the state and citizens. In the absence of robust data protection laws, independent judiciaries, and effective oversight mechanisms, misuses of AI face few institutional constraints.

The use of AI for surveillance or predictive policing can also result in mistargeting and disproportionate enforcement among marginalized groups due to preexisting biases in policing data that get encoded in AI algorithms.[56] This problem extends to judicial decision-making, in which algorithmic tools used to inform bail, sentencing, and parole decisions can reproduce racial and socioeconomic disparities.[57] These problems may be compounded in developing countries, where training data are scarcer and populations may be more diverse. The underlying issue is that supervised learning methods reproduce the patterns present in their training data, including discriminatory ones.

Another concern is that AI surveillance could constrain civic space even without formal repression as people change their behavior because they know they are being monitored (so-called chilling effects). The extent to which this dynamic operates in low- and middle-income countries is an empirical question that warrants further research.

AI surveillance systems also raise concerns about due process. Unlike traditional surveillance, which typically requires warrants and documentation, AI systems can flag individuals automatically and trigger investigations without human review. The opacity of these systems means that individuals may be unable to contest their classification, even when it is based on flawed data.

An additional concern is that technologies deployed for legitimate governance objectives can be repurposed for surveillance. During the COVID-19 pandemic, Israel repurposed phone-tracking technology originally developed to combat terrorism for contact tracing to identify, notify, and monitor individuals who may have been exposed to the virus, prompting legal challenges.[58] Developing countries often lack the institutional checks, such as independent courts, privacy regulators, and active civil society, needed to prevent such function creep. The global diffusion of surveillance capabilities raises questions about the responsibility of the countries and firms that export these technologies.[59] Without international norms governing the export of surveillance technologies, these tools will continue to reach governments with weak accountability mechanisms.

AI can also enable citizen oversight of government. In Ukraine, for instance, the nongovernmental organization Transparency International Ukraine runs DOZORRO, which applies machine learning to the government's e-procurement system and ProZorro, the public electronic procurement system, to flag irregularities and routes citizen and civil society complaints to regulators and law enforcement bodies.[60] Since 2017, the project has reviewed thousands of risky tenders and has helped save Ukraine billions of dollars in public funds.[61] Whether AI strengthens accountability or surveillance depends on the institutional context and the distribution of technical capacity between the state and civil society.

Synthetic content erodes shared facts

Generative AI has substantially reduced the cost of producing convincing synthetic content like fake images, videos, and text. At least 16 countries had used generative AI to influence public debate, and at least 47 governments had deployed commentators to manipulate online discussions, as of 2023;[62] the number has probably grown since then. Deepfake videos of political candidates have appeared in many recent elections in many countries.[63] The implications for public deliberation are significant given that social media has increasingly become the primary source of information on current events[64] and individuals are largely incapable of distinguishing between AI- and human-generated text.[65]

AI-generated disinformation can erode the shared foundations of information necessary for democratic deliberation and undermine trust in electoral processes. These challenges are amplified in developing countries for several reasons. Media and information literacy tends to be lower. Fact-checking infrastructure remains limited: As of 2025, Africa had 66 active fact-checking organizations serving 1.5 billion people, compared with 139 in Europe serving 750 million.[66] Electoral management bodies often lack the technical capacity and resources to detect AI-enabled disinformation at scale.

The proliferation of synthetic content also makes it possible to dismiss authentic evidence as fabricated,[67] threatening accountability mechanisms that are central to governance quality.[68] When citizens cannot trust evidence of official misconduct, demanding explanations becomes futile and accountability breaks down.

AI systems can also analyze behavioral data to identify persuadable voters and deliver tailored messages. Large language models can test thousands of message variants and optimize for engagement in real time. Recent research finds that large language models can be highly persuasive using factual arguments, even when those arguments include misinformation.[69]

AI also creates possibilities for improving the integrity of information. Platforms using natural language processing allow citizens to report corruption or failures of public service delivery in local languages. AI-powered analysis of government budgets can help civil society organizations track public spending. Whether these applications can keep pace with the manipulative uses of the same technologies remains to be seen.

AI polarizes public discourse

Beyond direct manipulation, AI is also reshaping public discourse. Social media platforms use AI to personalize content and target ads. These AI algorithms analyze user behavior to predict what content will maximize engagement, creating feedback loops that reinforce emotional content over informational content. Research demonstrates that moral and emotional language in social media content increases the spread of these media through online networks; outrage is particularly contagious online.[70] This is the mechanism through which AI contributes to polarization: By systematically prioritizing content that triggers strong emotional reactions, algorithmic curation amplifies divisive messages while suppressing more measured discourse.

Internal research from Meta, disclosed in the Facebook Papers, showed that its engagement-maximizing algorithms have disproportionately promoted divisive content because such content has generated more engagement.[71] While this research focused on high-income countries, the dynamics operate globally. For example, in Myanmar, Facebook's algorithms helped amplify hate speech against Rohingya Muslims, contributing to what United Nations investigators described as potential genocide.[72] In Ethiopia, platform algorithms have been implicated in spreading inflammatory content during ethnic conflicts.[73]

Although the causal relationship between exposure to algorithmically curated content and changes in political attitudes or behavior is not fully established, algorithmic curation appears to exacerbate existing polarization in societies with weak institutions, limited media literacy, and deep ethnic or religious cleavages. Even if platforms do not create these divisions, they can intensify them by making emotionally charged content more visible than content encouraging compromise or mutual understanding.

Algorithmic curation is not the only way AI shapes public discourse. As citizens, journalists, civil servants, and analysts increasingly draft, summarize, and reason with the same chatbots—most of them trained abroad—the range of positions people express may narrow toward whatever those models treat as default. Controlled experiments show that exposure to opinionated language models can shift users' own expressed views,[74] that groups writing with a shared model produce less diverse text,[75] and that the same flattening appears in creative output.[76] These are short-term effects measured in experiments; whether they aggregate into societywide homogenization is not established. But the possibility matters most where pluralism, rather than consensus, is what holds a fragile political settlement together. In such settings, homogenization is a risk distinct from disinformation, and addressing it points toward supporting a plurality of models so that no single foreign-trained system becomes the default voice in a national public sphere.

These challenges are especially salient in lower-income countries because platforms have made limited investments in content moderation. For instance, Meta provides content moderation for only a fraction of the world's 7,000 languages.[77] When AI systems trained predominantly on high-resource languages make decisions about content in more regional or local languages like Amharic, Burmese, or Swahili, the error rates are predictably higher and result in both underdetection of hate speech and overflagging of legitimate discourse.

Polarization limits citizens' willingness to process information that contradicts their group identity.[78] Consequently, in contexts with significant societal divisions, algorithmically amplified polarization can make cooperation across groups even more difficult; weaken institutional accountability; and erode trust in government, media, and expertise. However, recent evidence suggests that low-cost interventions can reduce susceptibility to misinformation. In South Africa, biweekly fact-checks delivered via WhatsApp over six months improved citizens' ability to identify new misinformation, particularly when they received financial incentives to review those fact-checks.[79] In Mexico, simply providing voters with accurate information about local government performance during the COVID-19 pandemic backfired: Providing voters with unfavorable information about relative COVID-19 cases and deaths increased the vote share of incumbent candidates.[80] A short antipolarization message delivered alongside the same information reversed the backlash, restoring the link between performance and electoral accountability.

If governments can identify which citizens are susceptible to which messages, they can target disinformation and curtail it instead of disseminating it. Conversely, governments can use concerns about disinformation to justify expanded surveillance. This interaction means that the individual dynamics described earlier may compound in contexts in which institutional checks on both surveillance and information manipulation are weak. But even when governments are well intentioned, cybersecurity risks may pose challenges to their efforts, which can perpetuate mistrust in AI.

The evidence reviewed in this section suggests that deliberate policy choices—such as fact-checking, algorithmic transparency, and opportunities for citizens to deliberate—can counter the default trajectory. The investments required are not prohibitive. The main challenge may be the lack of institutional capacity and political will.

Policy choices will shape power imbalances among governments, corporations, and individuals

Power has always been about access and control, whether to land, capital, markets, or information. What distinguishes AI is the speed and scale at which it can redistribute access, often in ways invisible to those most affected. The governance challenge may be more fundamental than simply writing better rules or investing more resources. It may require rethinking what sovereignty means when essential infrastructure is privately owned and globally distributed, what accountability means when decisions are made by systems too complex for even their designers to fully explain, and what consent means when the costs of refusing to participate are too high for most people to bear.

A broader consideration is whether the current patterns shaping AI align with the needs of most of the world's population. Most people live in developing countries, work in informal sectors, speak languages other than English, and interact with institutions limited by capacity constraints. Yet AI systems are predominantly designed by and for populations in high-income countries—a relatively small fraction of humanity.

History shows that outcomes depend on choices about regulation, public investment, labor protections, and international cooperation. For developing countries, the path forward involves building governance capacity, making strategic investments in areas of comparative advantage, and coordinating with other countries to shape international norms. The technology does not determine outcomes; governance choices do.

Notes

1. The *AI stack*, as discussed in chapter 2, consists of five interdependent layers: applications, AI models, data, infrastructure, and hardware.
2. Allen and Chan (2017).
3. Sutter (2025).
4. Baskaran (2024); Szczepański (2025).
5. Szczepański (2025).
6. *Open-source models* provide transparency and customization, allowing those that build AI applications to access the model weights, architecture, training data, and source code, with minimal licensing restrictions. Examples include AI Singapore's Southeast Asian Languages in One Network (SEA-LION), Allen Institute for AI's Olmo models, BigScience Large Open-science Open-Access Multilingual (BLOOM) Language Model, EleutherAI's GPT-NeoX, Google's Bidirectional Encoder Representations from Transformers (BERT) models, and the Swiss AI Initiative's Apertus. *Open-weight models* allow developers to access the model weights, but restrict access to other areas. Examples include Chile's National Center for Artificial Intelligence's Latam-GPT, DeepSeek's models, Google's Gemma models, Lelapa AI's InkubaLM, and Meta's Llama models (although they are sometimes marketed as open source). A couple of OpenAI's GPT models also fall into this category.
7. United States, White House (2025).
8. As of 2019, China had reportedly spent $79 billion on projects related to the Digital Silk Road and, by 2020, had signed cooperation agreements or provided related investments to at least 16 countries (Kurlantzick 2020). The actual numbers are likely to be higher because many of these agreements are unreported.
9. Liu and Yang (2025).
10. Clayton et al. (2025).
11. Schneider and Urpelainen (2013).
12. Refer to Pax Silica (dashboard), Under Secretary for Economic Affairs, US Department of State, https://www.state.gov/pax-silica.
13. Kaushik et al. (2025); Marivate (2026).
14. *Computing infrastructure* refers to the hardware needed to train and run AI models, including specialized chips, networking and storage

equipment, along with the cooling and power systems that support them. Such infrastructure is often housed in data centers and can be accessed through cloud providers.

15. *AI sovereignty* is an ambiguous concept, with definitions ranging from the most ambitious form of complete self-sufficiency to more calibrated approaches involving control over certain parts of the AI value chain. Anthony (2025); Pava et al. (2026); Tanner et al. (2026).
16. Daskal (2018); Schwartz (2018). In part to address concerns surrounding data localization, cloud providers now offer various approaches with different degrees of sovereignty. Such approaches range from software-based controls, to clouds operated by domestic entities using the hyperscalers' technologies, to standalone environments deployed on premises or within secure facilities. For more information, refer to Meinhardt et al. (2026).
17. Narratives around AI sovereignty are often driven by foreign technological companies that operate under the laws of their own countries and benefit greatly from the demand that sovereignty generates. NVIDIA has been among its most visible proponents. Jensen Huang, NVIDIA's chief executive officer, declared that "every country needs sovereign AI" (Yew et al. 2025). Leading hyperscalers have developed specialized sovereign cloud solutions. For example, Amazon Web Services now provides the European Sovereign Cloud offering.
18. Regardless of whether it is built for economic or sovereign reasons, a data center tends to generate domestic political costs wherever it is built. The clearest illustration is in the United States, where the build-out has not been to reduce foreign dependence. Nonetheless, the building of data centers has mobilized considerable opposition across political lines and in many types of communities. In 2025, at least 48 data center projects, worth more than $156 billion, were blocked or delayed amid local opposition (DePillis 2026, citing research by Data Center Watch). Commonly cited concerns include rising utility bills, noise, and strain on grid capacity. In some cases, opposition has led to county- or statewide moratoriums, as well as suspensions of tax incentives. This pattern is not unique to the United States. Because of intense local opposition, Meta's planned 166-hectare data center in the Netherlands was halted in 2022, and so was Google's planned $1.1 billion data center in Luxembourg (Roach and Krukowska 2022). Media coverage in 2026 indicates that planning for Google's data center in Luxembourg is advancing despite opposition (Monaghan 2026).
19. Anand and Mookerjee (2026).
20. Mozur et al. (2025); Pooler (2026).
21. Clayton et al. (2025).
22. For example, refer to Bertrand et al. (2014); Blanes i Vidal et al. (2012); Blanga-Gubbay et al. (2025); Kang (2016).
23. 2025 data of Issue Profile: Science and Technology (dashboard), OpenSecrets, https://www.opensecrets.org/federal-lobbying/issues/summary?cycle=2025&id=SCI.
24. Despite the dramatic rise, only about 4 percent to 5 percent of firms participating in lobbying were lobbying on AI-related issues.
25. Csernatoni (2025); Jones (2023); Mukherjee and Chee (2025).
26. Agência Pública and CLIP (2025).
27. Narechania and Sitaraman (2024).
28. Since 2018, the United States has imposed a number of export controls on advanced semiconductor chips and the associated supply chain. The measures have compelled AI companies based in the United States, such as Advanced Micro Devices (AMD) and NVIDIA, to halt or modify sales to major Chinese customers, illustrating how state authority can override market incentives in strategically important sectors (Sutter 2025).
29. For example, in 2021, the Nigerian government indefinitely suspended Twitter's operations in response to disputes concerning content moderation and political expression (Olurounbi 2021). The ban persisted for seven months and was lifted only when the company largely agreed to the government's demands (BBC 2022).
30. A notable example is the disagreements between Anthropic and the US government in 2026 over the company's refusal to relax AI safety guardrails for military use, specifically on autonomous weapons and mass surveillance. As a result, Anthropic was classified as a supply chain risk (Shalal et al. 2026).
31. For instance, in 2025, the US government agreed to purchase 433.3 million primary shares of Intel common stock at a discounted price of $20.47 per share, equivalent to a 9.9 percent stake in the company (Intel Corporation 2025). In recent years, state-owned entities in China have acquired golden shares in subsidiaries of major Chinese firms, such as Alibaba, ByteDance, and Tencent.
32. Reuters (2025).
33. Phartiyal (2026).
34. World Bank (2026).
35. Kobrin (1984); Vernon (1971).
36. Artunç and Saleh (2025); Faccio (2006); Fisman (2001).
37. *Rent seeking* refers to the practice of manipulating public policy or economic conditions as a strategy to increase profits.
38. *Jakarta Post* (2026).
39. Akcigit et al. (2023).
40. Refer to Government Requests for User Data (graphic), Meta, https://transparency.meta.com/reports/government-data-requests/.
41. *Network effects* refer to a phenomenon in which the value of a product or service increases exponentially as more people use it. As the user base grows, the service becomes more useful, secure, or valuable, creating a self-reinforcing loop that drives widespread adoption. *Data feedback loops*

refer to cyclical processes in which the output of a system is captured as data and fed back into the system as input to automatically trigger modifications, optimizations, or learning.
42. Kasy (2025).
43. UNCTAD (2026).
44. Longpre et al. (2024).
45. India, PIB (2024); Product Statistics: UPI (data page), National Payments Corporation of India, https://www.npci.org.in/product/upi/product-statistics.
46. India, NITI Aayog (2020).
47. Azar and Marinescu (2024); Dube et al. (2020).
48. Perrigo (2023).
49. Espada (2023).
50. Roberts (2019).
51. Ludwig and Mullainathan (2021).
52. Jarrahi et al. (2021); Kellogg et al. (2020).
53. ILO (2018).
54. Beraja et al. (2023).
55. Based on the latest available reliable information from Feldstein (2019).
56. Dressel and Farid (2018); Lee et al. (2024); Richardson et al. (2019).
57. Arnold et al. (2021); Dobbie et al. (2018).
58. Shwartz Altshuler and Hershkowitz (2020).
59. Hill (2021).
60. For details, refer to Nestulia et al. (2019).
61. Kelman and Yukins (2022).
62. Funk et al. (2023).
63. Bond (2024).
64. UNESCO (2025).
65. Kreps et al. (2022).
66. Ryan (2025).
67. Chesney and Citron (2019).
68. Larreguy et al. (2020); Pande (2011).
69. Hackenburg et al. (2025).
70. Brady et al. (2020).
71. Merrill and Oremus (2021).
72. UNHRC (2018).
73. BBC (2021); Hale and Peralta (2021).
74. Jakesch et al. (2023).
75. Anderson et al. (2024); Padmakumar and He (2024).
76. Doshi and Hauser (2024).
77. Merrill and Oremus (2021).
78. Larreguy and Raffler (2025).
79. Bowles et al. (2025).
80. Enríquez et al. (2025).

References

Agência Pública and CLIP (Centro Latinoamericano de Investigación Periodística, Latin American Center for Investigative Journalism). 2025. "The Invisible Hand of Big Tech." September 9, Agência Pública; CLIP. https://www.elclip.org/la-mano-invisible-de-las-big-tech/.

Akcigit, Ufuk, Salomé Baslandze, and Francesca Lotti. 2023. "Connecting to Power: Political Connections, Innovation, and Firm Dynamics." *Econometrica* 91 (2): 529–64. https://doi.org/10.3982/ECTA18338.

Allen, Greg, and Taniel Chan. 2017. *Artificial Intelligence and National Security*. Belfer Center Study. Belfer Center for Science and International Affairs, Harvard Kennedy School. https://www.belfercenter.org/sites/default/files/2024-10/Artificial percent20Intelligence percent20and percent20National percent20Security.pdf.

Anand, Ram, and Ishika Mookerjee. 2026. "Malaysia Draws First Data Center Protest over Pollution and Water." *Technology* (blog), February 7. https://www.bloomberg.com/news/articles/2026-02-07/malaysia-draws-first-data-center-protest-over-pollution-water.

Anderson, Barrett R., Jash Hemant Shah, and Max Kreminski. 2024. "Homogenization Effects of Large Language Models on Human Creative Ideation." In *C&C '24: Proceedings of the 16th Conference on Creativity and Cognition*. Association for Computing Machinery. https://doi.org/10.1145/3635636.3656204.

Anthony, Aubra. 2025. "On the Path to AI Sovereignty, AI Agency Offers a Shortcut." *Foreign Relations and International Law* (blog), May 20. https://www.lawfaremedia.org/article/on-the-path-to-ai-sovereignty--ai-agency-offers-a-shortcut.

Arnold, David, Will Dobbie, and Peter Hull. 2021. "Measuring Racial Discrimination in Algorithms." *American Economic Review: Papers and Proceedings* 111 (May): 49–54. https://www.aeaweb.org/articles?id=10.1257/pandp.20211080.

Artunç, Cihan, and Mohamed Saleh. 2025. "Connected National Capital: Corporations in Colonial and Independent Egypt." *Journal of Development Economics* 180 (March): 103697. https://doi.org/10.1016/j.jdeveco.2025.103697.

Azar, José, and Ioana Marinescu. 2024. "Monopsony Power in the Labor Market: From Theory to Policy." *Annual Review of Economics* 16 (August): 491–518. https://doi.org/10.1146/annurev-economics-072823-030431.

Baskaran, Gracelin. 2024. "What China's Ban on Rare Earths Processing Technology Exports Means." *Commentary* (blog), January 8. https://www.csis.org/analysis/what-chinas-ban-rare-earths-processing-technology-exports-means.

BBC (British Broadcasting Corporation). 2021. "Explainer: Ethiopia's Polarised Social Media Scene Amplifies Conflict." *Insight* (blog), December 9. https://monitoring.bbc.co.uk/product/c2033f3s.

BBC (British Broadcasting Corporation). 2022. "Twitter Agrees to Nigeria's Demands to End Seven-Month Ban." *News* (blog), January 13. https://www.bbc.com/news/world-africa-59958417.

Beraja, Martin, Andrew Kao, David Y. Yang, and Noam Yuchtman. 2023. "AI-tocracy." *Quarterly Journal of Economics* 138 (3): 1349–1402. https://doi.org/10.1093/qje/qjad012.

Bertrand, Marianne, Matilde Bombardini, and Francesco Trebbi. 2014. "Is It Whom You Know or What You Know? An Empirical Assessment of the Lobbying Process." *American Economic Review* 104 (12): 3885–920. https://www.aeaweb.org/articles?id=10.1257/aer.104.12.3885.

Blanes i Vidal, Jordi, Mirko Draca, and Christian Fons-Rosen. 2012. "Revolving Door Lobbyists." *American Economic Review* 102 (7): 3731–48. https://www.aeaweb.org/articles?id=10.1257/aer.102.7.3731.

Blanga-Gubbay, Michael, Paola Conconi, and Mathieu Parenti. 2025. "Lobbying for Globalisation." *Economic Journal* 135 (666): 487–518. https://doi.org/10.1093/ej/ueae082.

Bond, Shannon. 2024. "How AI Deepfakes Polluted Elections in 2024." *Heard on* All Things Considered (blog), December 21. https://www.npr.org/2024/12/21/nx-s1-5220301/deepfakes-memes-artificial-intelligence-elections.

Bowles, Jeremy, Kevin Croke, Horacio Larreguy, Shelley Liu, and John Marshall. 2025. "Sustaining Exposure to Fact-Checks: Misinformation Discernment, Media Consumption, and Its Political Implications." *American Political Science Review* 119 (4): 1864–87. https://doi.org/10.1017/S0003055424001394.

Brady, William J., Molly J. Crockett, and Jay J. Van Bavel. 2020. "The MAD Model of Moral Contagion: The Role of Motivation, Attention, and Design in the Spread of Moralized Content Online." *Perspectives on Psychological Science* 15 (4): 978–1010. https://doi.org/10.1177/1745691620917336.

Chesney, Robert, and Danielle Citron. 2019. "Deep Fakes: A Looming Challenge for Privacy, Democracy, and National Security." *California Law Review* 107 (6): 1753–820. https://www.californialawreview.org/print/deep-fakes-a-looming-challenge-for-privacy-democracy-and-national-security.

Clayton, Christopher, Matteo Maggiori, and Jesse Schreger. 2025. "A Theory of Economic Coercion and Fragmentation." NBER Working Paper 33309, National Bureau of Economic Research. https://www.nber.org/papers/w33309.

Couper, Elise A., John P. Hejkal, and Alexander L. Wolman. 2003. "Boom and Bust in Telecommunications." *Federal Reserve Bank of Richmond Economic Quarterly* 89 (4): 1–24. https://www.richmondfed.org/publications/research/economic_quarterly/2003/fall/couperhejkalwolman.

Csernatoni, Raluca. 2025. "The EU's AI Power Play: Between Deregulation and Innovation." Carnegie Europe. https://carnegieendowment.org/research/2025/05/the-eus-ai-power-play-between-deregulation-and-innovation.

Daskal, Jennifer. 2018. "Borders and Bits." *Vanderbilt Law Review* 71 (1): 179–240. https://scholarship.law.vanderbilt.edu/cgi/viewcontent.cgi?article=1011&context=vlr.

DePillis, Lydia. 2026. "Local Opposition Is Slowing A.I. Data Centers: Wall Street Has Noticed." *Artificial Intelligence* (blog), March 26. https://www.nytimes.com/2026/03/26/business/economy/ai-data-centers-construction-local-opposition.html.

Dobbie, Will, Jacob Goldin, and Crystal S. Yang. 2018. "The Effects of Pretrial Detention on Conviction, Future Crime, and Employment: Evidence from Randomly Assigned Judges." *American Economic Review* 108 (2): 201–40. https://www.aeaweb.org/articles?id=10.1257/aer.20161503.

Doms, Mark E. 2004. "The Boom and Bust in Information Technology Investment." *FRBSF Economic Review* 2004: 19–34. https://www.frbsf.org/wp-content/uploads/er19-34bk.pdf.

Doshi, Anil R., and Oliver P. Hauser. 2024. "Generative AI Enhances Individual Creativity but Reduces the Collective Diversity of Novel Content." *Science Advances* 10 (28): eadn5290. https://www.science.org/doi/10.1126/sciadv.adn5290.

Dreazen, Yochi J. 2002. "Wildly Optimistic Data Drove Telecoms to Build Fiber Glut." *Wall Street Journal* (blog), September 26. https://www.wsj.com/articles/SB1032982764442483713.

Dressel, Julia, and Hany Farid. 2018. "The Accuracy, Fairness, and Limits of Predicting Recidivism." *Science Advances* 4 (1): eaao5580. https://doi.org/10.1126/sciadv.aao5580.

Dube, Arindrajit, Jeff Jacobs, Suresh Naidu, and Siddharth Suri. 2020. "Monopsony in Online Labor Markets." *American Economic Review: Insights* 2 (1): 33–46. https://doi.org/10.1257/aeri.20180150.

Economist. 2002a. "The Great Telecoms Crash." *Leaders: Telecoms* (blog), July 18. https://www.economist.com/leaders/2002/07/18/the-great-telecoms-crash.

Economist. 2002b. "The Power of WorldCom's Puff." *Special Report: Internet Traffic* (blog), July 18. https://www.economist.com/special-report/2002/07/18/the-power-of-worldcoms-puff.

Enríquez, José Ramón, Horacio Larreguy, John Marshall, and Alberto Simpser. 2025. "Accountability Under Polarization." Working Paper, Stanford Digital Economy Lab, Stanford University. https://digitaleconomy.stanford.edu/publication/accountability-under-polarization/.

Espada, Mariah. 2023. "Facebook Content Moderators Sue Meta over Layoffs in Kenya." *Time* (blog), March 20. https://time.com/6264621/facebook-content-moderators-lawsuit-kenya/.

Faccio, Mara. 2006. "Politically Connected Firms." *American Economic Review* 96 (1): 369–86. https://www.aeaweb.org/articles?id=10.1257/000282806776157704.

Feldstein, Steven. 2019. "The Global Expansion of AI Surveillance." Working Paper, Carnegie Endowment for International Peace. https://carnegieendowment.org/research/2019/09/the-global-expansion-of-ai-surveillance.

Fisman, Raymond. 2001. "Estimating the Value of Political Connections." *American Economic Review* 91 (4): 1095–102. https://www.aeaweb.org/articles?id=10.1257/aer.91.4.1095.

Funk, Allie, Adrian Shahbaz, and Kian Vesteinsson. 2023. "Freedom on the Net 2023: The Repressive Power of Artificial Intelligence." Freedom House. https://freedomhouse.org/sites/default/files/2024-10/FOTN2023Final24.pdf.

Hackenburg, Kobi, Ben M. Tappin, Luke Hewitt, et al. 2025. "The Levers of Political Persuasion with Conversational Artificial Intelligence." *Science* 390 (6777): eaea3884. https://www.science.org/doi/10.1126/science.aea3884.

Hale, Lee, and Eyder Peralta. 2021. "Social Media Misinformation Stokes a Worsening Civil War in Ethiopia." *Africa* (blog), October 15. https://www.npr.org/2021/10/15/1046106922/social-media-misinformation-stokes-a-worsening-civil-war-in-ethiopia.

Hill, Kashmir. 2021. "The Secretive Company That Might End Privacy as We Know It." *Technology* (blog), updated, November 2. https://www.nytimes.com/2020/01/18/technology/clearview-privacy-facial-recognition.html.

ILO (International Labour Organization). 2018. *Women and Men in the Informal Economy: A Statistical Picture*, 3rd ed. ILO. https://www.ilo.org/sites/default/files/2024-04/Women_men_informal_economy_statistical_picture.pdf.

India, NITI Aayog (National Institution for Transforming India). 2020. "Data Empowerment and Protection Architecture, Draft for Discussion: A Secure Consent-Based Data Sharing Framework to Accelerate Financial Inclusion." August, NITI Aayog. https://www.niti.gov.in/sites/default/files/2023-03/Data-Empowerment-and-Protection-Architecture-A-Secure-Consent-Based.pdf.

India, PIB (Press Information Bureau). 2024. "DFS Drives Expansion of Digital Payments in India and Abroad." Press Release 2057013, September 25. https://www.pib.gov.in/PressReleaseIframePage.aspx?PRID=2057013&reg=3&lang=2.

Intel Corporation. 2025. "Intel and Trump Administration Reach Historic Agreement to Accelerate American Technology and Manufacturing Leadership." Press Release, August 22. https://www.intc.com/news-events/press-releases/detail/1748/intel-and-trump-administration-reach-historic-agreement-to.

Jakarta Post. 2026. "Ex-Communications Ministry Officials Jailed in Data Center Graft Case." *Indonesia: Politics* (blog), March 11. https://www.thejakartapost.com/indonesia/2026/03/11/ex-communications-ministry-officials-jailed-in-data-center-graft-case.html.

Jakesch, Maurice, Advait Bhat, Daniel Buschek, Lior Zalmanson, and Mor Naaman. 2023. "Co-Writing with Opinionated Language Models Affects Users' Views." In *CHI '23: Proceedings of the 2023 CHI Conference on Human Factors in Computing Systems*, edited by Albrecht Schmidt, Kaisa Väänänen, Tesh Goyal, Per Ola Kristensson, Anicia Peters, Stefanie Mueller, Julie R. Williamson, and Max L. Wilson. Association for Computing Machinery. https://doi.org/10.1145/3544548.3581196.

Jarrahi, Mohammad Hossein, Gemma Newlands, Min Kyung Lee, Christine T. Wolf, Eliscia Kinder, and Will Sutherland. 2021. "Algorithmic Management in a Work Context." *Big Data and Society* 8 (2): PAR 10303797. https://doi.org/10.1177/20539517211020332.

Jones, Emily. 2023. "Digital Disruption: Artificial Intelligence and International Trade Policy." *Oxford Review of Economic Policy* 39 (1): 70–84. https://doi.org/10.1093/oxrep/grac049.

Kang, Karam. 2016. "Policy Influence and Private Returns from Lobbying in the Energy Sector." *Review of Economic Studies* 83 (1): 269–305. https://doi.org/10.1093/restud/rdv029.

Kasy, Maximilian. 2025. *The Means of Prediction: How AI Really Works (and Who Benefits)*. University of Chicago Press. https://press.uchicago.edu/ucp/books/book/chicago/M/bo255887145.html.

Kaushik, Aprajita, Capucine Barcellona, Nikita Kanumoory Mandyam, Si Ying Tan, and Jasper Tromp. 2025. "Challenges and Opportunities for Data Sharing Related to Artificial Intelligence Tools in Health Care in Low- and Middle-Income Countries: Systematic Review and Case Study from Thailand." *Journal of Medical Internet Research* 27 (February 4): e58338. https://www.jmir.org/2025/1/e58338/.

Kellogg, Katherine C., Melissa A. Valentine, and Angèle Christin. 2020. "Algorithms at Work: The New Contested Terrain of Control." *Academy of Management Annals* 14 (1): 366–410. https://doi.org/10.5465/annals.2018.0174.

Kelman, Steven, and Christopher R. Yukins. 2022. "Overcoming Corruption and War: Lessons from Ukraine's ProZorro Procurement System." GW Paper Series 2022-60, NCMA Contract Management Magazine July: 22–27. https://scholarship.law.gwu.edu/cgi/viewcontent.cgi?article=2887&context=faculty_publications.

Kobrin, Stephen J. 1984. "Expropriation as an Attempt to Control Foreign Firms in LDCs: Trends from 1960 to 1979." *International Studies Quarterly* 28 (3): 329–48. https://doi.org/10.2307/2600634.

Kreps, Sarah, R. Miles McCain, and Miles Brundage. 2022. "All the News That's Fit to Fabricate: AI-Generated Text as a Tool of Media Misinformation." *Journal of Experimental Political Science* 9 (1): 104–17. https://doi.org/10.1017/XPS.2020.37.

Kurlantzick, Joshua. 2020. "Assessing China's Digital Silk Road Initiative: A Transformative Approach to Technology Financing or a Danger to Freedoms?" December 18, Council on Foreign Relations. https://www.cfr.org/china-digital-silk-road/.

Larreguy, Horacio A., John Marshall, and James M. Snyder, Jr. 2020. "Publicising Malfeasance: When the Local Media Structure Facilitates Electoral Accountability in Mexico." *Economic Journal* 130 (631): 2291–327. https://doi.org/10.1093/ej/ueaa046.

Larreguy, Horacio A., and Pia J. Raffler. 2025. "Accountability in Developing Democracies: The Impact of the Internet, Social Media, and Polarization." *Annual Review of Political Science* 28 (June): 413–34. https://doi.org/10.1146/annurev-polisci-033123-015559.

Lee, Youngsub, Ben Bradford, and Krisztian Posch. 2024. "The Effectiveness of Big Data-Driven Predictive Policing: Systematic Review." *Justice Evaluation Journal* 7 (2): 127–60. doi:10.1080/24751979.2024.2371781.

Liu, Ernest, and David Y. Yang. 2025. "International Power." NBER Working Paper 34006, National Bureau of Economic Research. https://www.nber.org/papers/w34006.

Longpre, Shayne, Robert Mahari, Naana Obeng-Marnu, et al. 2024. "Position: Data Authenticity, Consent, and Provenance for AI Are All Broken: What Will It Take to Fix Them?" *arXiv:2404.12691v2 [cs.AI]*, August 30, Cornell University. https://doi.org/10.48550/arXiv.2404.12691.

Ludwig, Jens, and Sendhil Mullainathan. 2021. "Fragile Algorithms and Fallible Decision-Makers: Lessons from the Justice System." *Journal of Economic Perspectives* 35 (4): 71–96. https://www.aeaweb.org/articles?id=10.1257/jep.35.4.71.

Marivate, Vukosi. 2026. "The Annotation Scarcity Paradox in Low-Resource NLP Evaluation: A Decade of Acceleration and Emerging Constraints." *arXiv:2605.19066v1 [cs.CL]*, May 18, Cornell University. https://doi.org/10.48550/arXiv.2605.19066.

Meinhardt, Caroline, Juan N. Pava, Caroline Yee, and James A. Landay. 2026. "The Commercial Landscape of AI Sovereignty Offerings." *Issue Brief: HAI Policy & Society* (July), Stanford University. https://hai.stanford.edu/policy/the-commercial-landscape-of-ai-sovereignty-offerings.

Merrill, Jeremy B., and Will Oremus. 2021. "Five Points for Anger, One for a 'Like': How Facebook's Formula Fostered Rage and Misinformation." *Technology* (blog), October 26. https://www.washingtonpost.com/technology/2021/10/26/facebook-angry-emoji-algorithm/.

Metreau, Eric, Kathryn Elizabeth Young, and Shwetha Grace Eapen. 2026. "Who Moves Up and Why? A Closer Look at the 2026–2027 Release of the World Bank Group Country Income Classifications." *Data Blog* (blog), July 1. https://blogs.worldbank.org/en/opendata/who-moves-up-and-why--a-closer-look-at-the-new-world-bank-group-/.

Monaghan, John. 2026. "Environmental Group Files Appeal Against Google's Luxembourg Data Centre Plan." *Google* (blog), March 30. https://www.luxtimes.lu/luxembourg/environmental-group-files-appeal-against-googles-luxembourg-data-centre-plan/144806337.html.

Mozur, Paul, Adam Satariano, and Emiliano Rodríguez Mega. 2025. "From Mexico to Ireland, Fury Mounts over a Global A.I. Frenzy." *Technology* (blog), October 20. https://www.nytimes.com/2025/10/20/technology/ai-data-center-backlash-mexico-ireland.html.

Mukherjee, Supantha, and Foo Yun Chee. 2025. "EU Eases AI, Privacy Rules as Critics Warn of Caving to Big Tech." *Sustainability* (blog), November 19. https://www.reuters.com/sustainability/boards-policy-regulation/eu-ease-ai-privacy-rules-critics-warn-caving-big-tech-trump-2025-11-19/.

Narechania, Tejas N., and Ganesh Sitaraman. 2024. "An Antimonopoly Approach to Governing Artificial Intelligence." *Yale Law and Policy Review* 43 (1): 95–170. https://yalelawandpolicy.org/antimonopoly-approach-governing-artificial-intelligence.

Nestulia, Viktor, Ivan Lakhtionov, Anastasiya Mazurok, Marta Hohol, and Sergii Pavliuk. 2019. "DOZORRO Story: From an Idea of a Platform to the Biggest Monitoring Community in Ukraine." April 12, Transparency International Ukraine. https://oecd-opsi.org/wp-content/uploads/2019/04/DOZORRO-STORY-ENG.pdf.

Olurounbi, Ruth. 2021. "Twitter Shuttered in Nigeria After Removing President's Post." *Technology* (blog), June 5. https://www.bloomberg.com/news/articles/2021-06-05/twitter-shuttered-in-nigeria-after-removing-president-s-tweet.

OpenAI. 2018. "AI and Compute." *Conclusion* (blog), May 16. https://openai.com/index/ai-and-compute/.

Padmakumar, Vishakh, and He He. 2024. "Does Writing with Language Models Reduce Content Diversity?" In *Proceedings of the Twelfth International Conference on Learning Representations (ICLR 2024)*, edited by B. Kim, Y. Yue, S. Chaudhuri, K. Fragkiadaki, M. Khan, and Y Sun. ICLR. https://proceedings.iclr.cc/paper_files/paper/2024/hash/02dec8877fb7c6aa9a79f81661baca7c-Abstract-Conference.html.

Pande, Rohini P. 2011. "Can Informed Voters Enforce Better Governance? Experiments in Low-Income Democracies." *Annual Review of Economics* 3 (1): 215–37. https://doi.org/10.1146/annurev-economics-061109-080154.

Pava, Juan N., Caroline Meinhardt, Elena Cryst, and James Landay. 2026. "AI Sovereignty's Definitional Dilemma." *HAI: News* (blog), February 17. https://hai.stanford.edu/news/ai-sovereigntys-definitional-dilemma.

Perrigo, Billy. 2023. "Exclusive: OpenAI Used Kenyan Workers on Less Than $2 per Hour to Make ChatGPT Less Toxic." *Time* (blog), January 18. https://time.com/6247678/openai-chatgpt-kenya-workers/.

Phartiyal, Sankalp. 2026. "India Unveils 20-Year Tax Break to Woo Global Data Centers." *Technology* (blog), February 1. https://www.bloomberg.com/news/articles/2026-02-01/india-unveils-20-year-tax-break-to-woo-global-data-centers.

Pooler, Michael. 2026. "Why Isn't the Energy Used by People? China's Global AI Push Hits Resistance." *Brazilian Economy* (blog), April 21. https://www.ft.com/content/001dec5b-9e13-4a23-9dc5-dda537a47ae3.

Poushter, Jacob, Moira Fagan, and Manolo Corichi. 2025. "How People Around the World View AI." Pew Research Center *Report* (blog), October 15. https://www.pewresearch.org/global/2025/10/15/how-people-around-the-world-view-ai/.

Reuters. 2025. "Uzbekistan Sets Up Tax-Free Zone for AI to Attract Foreign Investors." *World* (blog), November 7. https://www.reuters.com/world/asia-pacific/uzbekistan-sets-up-tax-free-zone-ai-attract-foreign-investors-2025-11-07/.

Richardson, Rashida, Jason M. Schultz, and Kate Crawford. 2019. "Dirty Data, Bad Predictions: How Civil Rights Violations Impact Police Data, Predictive Policing Systems, and Justice." *New York University Law Review* 94 (May): 15–55. https://www.nyulawreview.org/wp-content/uploads/2019/04/NYULawReview-94-Richardson_etal-FIN.pdf.

Roach, April, and Ewa Krukowska. 2022. "Big Tech Gets Caught Up in Europe's Energy Politics." *Green Energy Crisis* (blog), June 23. https://www.bloomberg.com/news/articles/2022-06-23/google-facebook-data-centers-face-europe-political-snags-over-in-energy-crisis.

Roberts, Sarah T. 2019. *Behind the Screen: Content Moderation in the Shadows of Social Media*. Yale University Press. https://yalebooks.yale.edu/book/9780300261479/behind-the-screen/.

Ryan, Erica. 2025. "2025 Census: Fact-Checkers Persevere as Politicians, Platforms Turn Up Heat." *Fact-Checking News* (blog), June 19. https://reporterslab.org/latest-news/.

Sam, Cedric, Rachael Dottle, Agnee Ghosh, and Kyle Kim. 2026. "A Guide to the Circular Deals Underpinning the AI Boom." *Technology: Explainer* (blog), January 22. https://www.bloomberg.com/graphics/2026-ai-circular-deals/.

Schneider, Christina J., and Johannes Urpelainen. 2013. "Distributional Conflict Between Powerful States and International Treaty Ratification." *International Studies Quarterly* 57 (1): 13–27. https://www.jstor.org/stable/pdf/41804843.pdf.

Schwartz, Paul M. 2018. "Legal Access to the Global Cloud." *Columbia Law Review* 18 (6): 1681–762. https://www.jstor.org/stable/26511248.

Shalal, Andrea, Jeffrey Dastin, and Ryan Patrick Jones. 2026. "Trump Directs US Agencies to Toss Anthropic's AI as Pentagon Calls Startup a Supply Risk." *World* (blog), February 28. https://www.reuters.com/world/us/trump-says-he-is-directing-federal-agencies-cease-use-anthropic-technology-2026-02-27/.

Shwartz Altshuler, Tehilla, and Rachel Aridor Hershkowitz. 2020. "How Israel's COVID-19 Mass Surveillance Operation Works." *Commentary* (blog), May 6. https://www.brookings.edu/articles/how-israels-covid-19-mass-surveillance-operation-works/.

Slok, Torsten, Rajvi Shah, and Shruti Galwankar. 2026. "Putting the Total Amount of Hyperscaler Capex into Perspective." Apollo Global Management, February. https://www.apolloacademy.com/wp-content/uploads/2026/02/Hyperscaler-capex-022226_v2.pdf.

Starr, Paul. 2002. "The Great Telecom Implosion." *American Prospect: Features* (blog), August 19. https://prospect.org/2002/08/19/great-telecom-implosion/.

Sutter, Karen M. 2025. "U.S. Export Controls and China: Advanced Semiconductors." CRS Report R48642, Congressional Research Service. https://www.congress.gov/crs-product/R48642.

Szczepański, Marcin. 2025. "China's Rare-Earth Export Restrictions." *At a Glance*, November 24, European Parliamentary Research Service, European Union. https://www.europarl.europa.eu/RegData/etudes/ATAG/2025/779220/EPRS_ATA(2025)779220_EN.pdf.

Tanner, Brooke, Cameron F. Kerry, Andrew W. Wyckoff, Nicoleta Kyosovska, Andrea Renda, and Elham Tabassi. 2026. "Is AI Sovereignty Possible? Balancing Autonomy and Interdependence." *Research* (blog), February 17. https://www.brookings.edu/articles/is-ai-sovereignty-possible-balancing-autonomy-and-interdependence/.

UNCTAD (UN Trade and Development). 2026. "Global Cyberlaw Tracker: Data Protection and Privacy." Updated June 24, United Nations. https://unctad.org/topic/ecommerce-and-digital-economy/ecommerce-law-reform/summary-adoption-e-commerce-legislation-worldwide#.

UNESCO (United Nations Educational, Scientific and Cultural Organization). 2025. *World Trends in Freedom of Expression and Media Development: Global Report 2022/2025; Journalism: Shaping a World at Peace*. UNESCO. https://www.unesco.org/en/world-media-trends.

UNHRC (United Nations Human Rights Council). 2018. "Report of the Independent International Fact-Finding Mission on Myanmar." Document A/HRC/39/64 (September 12), United Nations. https://www.ohchr.org/sites/default/files/Documents/HRBodies/HRCouncil/FFM-Myanmar/A_HRC_39_64.pdf.

United States, White House. 2025. "Promoting the Export of the American AI Technology Stack." Executive Order 14320 (July 23), White House. https://www.whitehouse.gov/presidential-actions/2025/07/promoting-the-export-of-the-american-ai-technology-stack/.

Vernon, Raymond. 1971. *Sovereignty at Bay: The Multinational Spread of U.S. Enterprises*. Harvard Multinational Enterprise Series. Basic Books. https://archive.org/details/sovereigntyatbay0000raym/page/n5/mode/2up.

Wooldridge, Adrian. 2025. "AI's Future May Be Written in Railroads' Past." *Opinion* (blog), December 5. https://www.bloomberg.com/opinion/articles/2025-12-05/ai-future-may-be-written-in-railroads-past.

World Bank. 2026. *Global Economic Prospects, June 2026*. World Bank. https://www.worldbank.org/en/publication/global-economic-prospects.

Yew, Rui-Jie, Kate Elizabeth Creasey, and Suresh Venkatasubramanian. 2025. "'Sovereignty' Myth-Making in the AI Race." *Perspectives* (blog), July 7. https://www.techpolicy.press/sovereignty-myth-making-in-the-ai-race/.

4 Spotlight 4

AI and the Environment

Artificial intelligence (AI) imposes significant environmental costs that are likely to increase rapidly in the absence of more stringent regulation and environmentally conscious policies. Environmental harms occur across the technology life cycle of AI, from the extraction of the raw materials used for the development of AI infrastructure to the operation and disposal of it. Developing countries are particularly vulnerable to these environmental harms, but improved governance and innovative policies can substantially mitigate them. Even as governments must work to curtail the environmental harm of the technology, AI presents new opportunities to address environmental challenges, such as by improving the efficiency of energy and transportation systems and strengthening climate resilience.

Environmental costs along the AI value chain

Mining and e-waste

Rare earth minerals are an integral component of the AI value chain, but mining communities are exposed to environmental risks.[1] These risks are particularly high in low-income settings, where regulatory oversight is weak. Environmental risks also tend to be higher for extraction of critical minerals than for other forms of mining.[2] For instance, rates of deforestation are three times higher around mines extracting critical minerals than around those for other materials.[3] As AI drives up prices for critical minerals, incentives to profit at the expense of the local environment will become stronger, making effective regulation more difficult in settings with low capacity to enforce environmental safeguards. Addressing the harms arising from extraction of critical minerals will be crucial, however, given that recycling efforts currently meet only 1 percent of the demand for rare earth minerals.[4]

On the other end of the product life cycle, the electronic waste (e-waste) produced by generative AI is expected to increase nearly fivefold, from 1.2 million tons to 5.0 million tons, between 2020 and 2030, to make up more than 6 percent of global e-waste by 2030.[5] The *Global E-Waste Monitor 2024* reports that only one-fifth of e-waste was recycled as of 2022, with recycling rates reaching only 12 percent in Asia and 1 percent in Africa.[6] In addition, the report estimates that 65 percent of e-waste that crosses borders does so from high-income to low- and middle-income countries; this pattern increases the risk that the environmental and human costs of AI's life cycle will fall disproportionately on developing countries. The combination of intensive mineral extraction and inadequate e-waste management creates a cycle of persistent environmental and health vulnerabilities that are likely to be most concentrated in low- and middle-income countries.

Energy use

Once the hardware for AI has been built, the primary environmental risks AI presents stem from the use of energy and water resources.

The total electricity consumption of data centers (of which 15 percent is estimated to stem from AI) increased by about 12 percent per year from 2017 to 2024: more than four times faster than the growth in total electricity consumption from all other sectors.[7] It is estimated that electricity consumption by data centers will more than double by 2030, driven by projected growth in China and the United States (refer to figure S4.1).[8] In addition, the energy consumption from the use of AI models can be 25 times greater than the consumption from developing them, indicating that demand for energy stemming from AI will likely soar in coming years.[9]

Figure S4.1 Electricity consumption in global data centers is projected to double by 2030

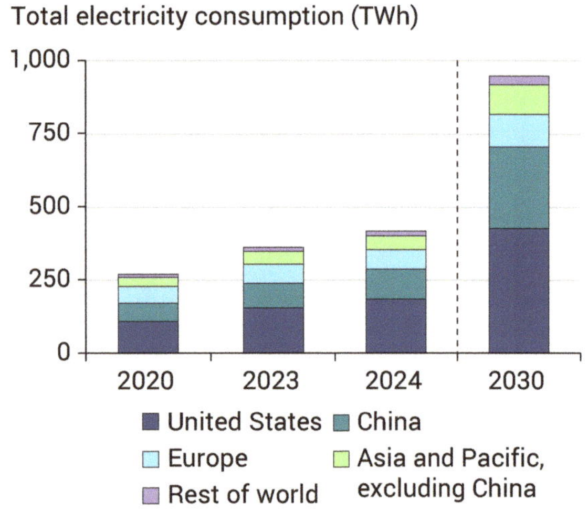

Source: WDR 2026 team, based on data of IEA 2025, table A.4.

Note: Europe comprises member states of the European Union, as well as Albania, Belarus, Bosnia and Herzegovina, Gibraltar, Iceland, Israel, Kosovo, Moldova, Montenegro, North Macedonia, Norway, Serbia, Switzerland, Türkiye, Ukraine, and the United Kingdom. *Asia and Pacific* comprises countries in Southeast Asia, as well as Australia, Bangladesh, the Democratic People's Republic of Korea, India, Japan, Mongolia, Nepal, New Zealand, Pakistan, the Republic of Korea, Sri Lanka, and other Asia Pacific countries and territories. TWh = terawatt-hours.

Although electricity grids, particularly those in high-income countries, are increasingly shifting to renewable sources of energy, the rapid growth in the demand for energy stemming from AI may still lead to an increase in global emissions of greenhouse gases. Recent estimates show that under current energy policies, global emissions will increase by 1.2 percent by 2030. Policies promoting renewables could reduce this increase to 0.9 percent and help mitigate potential increases in electricity prices but cannot offset either entirely.[10] Several large technology companies—including Amazon, Google, and Microsoft—are investing heavily in nuclear power to achieve their internal target of using only emissions-free power by 2030.[11] Such actions suggest that the combination of public pressure and risks from stricter climate regulations in the future may limit the growth in emissions of greenhouse gases from AI. However, the use of nuclear power in markets like the United States remains uncertain; it is unclear at what pace nuclear plants could be approved and become operational and at what cost and risk.[12]

The high demand for energy from AI also raises concerns about economic equity. Households that share electricity grids with data centers bear a substantial proportion of the costs incurred to serve these data centers.[13] Traditionally, regulators have allowed utility providers to charge prices that cover their costs and earn a reasonable return on investment. Therefore, providers have typically set prices for a given group of consumers by estimating the cost that the provider incurs to serve those consumers, a process that is usually public and subject to contestation. This process can increase costs for consumers through two channels.[14] First, if utility providers sell energy to data centers at concessional prices, they must recover the difference by increasing prices for other customers. Second, consumers may bear the cost of the infrastructure investments required to serve data centers, given that the distribution of such costs among different groups of customers is often not transparent. Individuals living in places with weak consumer protections are particularly vulnerable to inequitable electricity-pricing practices. As with the environmental costs of mining and e-waste, those that profit from the infrastructure for AI may not bear the cost of building and maintaining it.

Water use

Data centers' water use poses another environmental concern, especially given competing demands and dwindling supplies of water in many places. Global consumption of water for data centers is projected to more than double from about 560 billion liters per year currently to about 1,200 billion liters per year in 2030.[15] In 2023, about two-thirds of global water consumption for data centers was associated with primary energy supply and electricity generation, one-quarter with direct cooling, and the remainder with the manufacturing of semiconductors and microchips.[16]

Data centers are also a growing concern in regard to water use because factors such as the availability of energy resources and favorable regulations, rather than the availability of abundant water resources, increasingly determine where these centers are located. As of 2022, 72 percent of China's computing capacity was located in regions facing severe water scarcity.[17] And in the United States since 2022, about two-thirds of data centers have been built in areas facing high levels of strain on water resources.[18] The siting of data centers in areas subject to water shortages places additional pressure on already-scarce resources and threatens the supply of water for local communities.

Effective policy choices

Policy choices can help mitigate the pressures related to these environmental costs. A number of countries—including Australia, China, France, and Germany—have already begun adopting measures to manage the growing energy demand of data centers. One approach is to make access to the electricity grid conditional on greater operational flexibility. Under this approach, data centers that receive new connections to the grid may be required to reduce consumption during periods of peak demand, shift computing tasks that are not urgent to off-peak hours, or install on-site battery storage and backup capacity. Because data centers can be large consumers but are also flexible in regard to the time at which they use electricity, these measures can ease the strain on power systems and reduce the need for costly new generation capacity. In the United States, such demand-response measures cut investment in new natural gas combined-capacity by 10–50 percent in modeled scenarios, as coordinating time of use offsets the need for power plants that can quickly ramp up and down. This could generate systemwide savings of $40 billion–$150 billion over the next decade.[19]

A second policy choice involves siting. A data center connected to a corridor where renewable energy can be readily tapped under a power purchase agreement tied to new generation based on renewables can help expand cleaner capacity, reducing the strain on congested networks and averting large increases in emissions. By contrast, a facility added to a grid that is dependent on fossil fuel or already constrained may increase emissions, worsen congestion, and increase the cost of local electricity. Dedicated gas-to-power generation may seem like a solution, but it requires substantial overbuilding of capacity, which raises concerns about the availability of timely supply given the long waiting times for new turbines.[20] These considerations are already shaping global patterns in investment for data centers. Brazil and Malaysia are emerging as preferred destinations for hyperscaling operations, whereas South Africa's chronic load shedding and Viet Nam's 2023 power shortages illustrate how grid constraints can deter large-scale investment in AI and limit the potential dividends for its development.[21]

Improving the management of environmental resources

Although its environmental costs pose many challenges, AI also presents opportunities to improve the management of environmental and natural resources. A few examples from different sectors follow.

Electricity grid management

AI can help manage complex, dynamic processes such as those involved in the management of electricity grids. In Zambia, which is subject to severe power shortages, telecommunications and utility operators have developed an AI solution that allows the country's mobile telephone network to operate for a longer period during power outages.[22] The solution dynamically prioritizes critical functions such as maintaining communication networks so that essential infrastructure remains powered during major load-shedding episodes. In India, Tata Power is working with BluWave-ai to generate accurate day-ahead and intraday plans for dispatching electricity that incorporate real-time data on weather and grid constraints into historical information on power plant output. These tools have significantly improved the accuracy of electricity scheduling, improving quality of service.[23]

City planning and transportation

City planners can leverage AI for sustainable urban development to increase the data available for making decisions about key urban challenges, including energy efficiency, environmental monitoring, and infrastructure resilience.[24] For example, machine learning and deep learning approaches can improve accuracy in the monitoring and prediction of air pollution, leading to better-informed public health warnings and urban policy decisions.[25] In the transportation sector, AI can help drive the reduction of emissions in the freight logistics industry by optimizing routes and managing assets, by improving the use of space in vehicles to minimize empty capacity, and by identifying more carbon-efficient modes of transportation that the industry can switch to. It is estimated that these levers can reduce total emissions from freight logistics by 10–15 percent.[26]

Climate resilience

AI is rapidly changing the field of weather forecasting. Machine learning is enabling meteorologists to generate forecasts more quickly and, in specific contexts, predicting weather events more accurately than traditional models.[27] Although machine learning forecasts still have limitations, the field of weather forecasting is increasingly moving toward hybrid approaches that integrate machine learning systems with physics-based numerical weather prediction.[28] The combination of more accurate and more timely predictions can allow governments, businesses, and households to better prepare for extreme weather events, lowering potential damages from climate impacts. AI can also enable faster and more efficient response and assessment after natural disasters. For example, in the United States, an AI system using drone imagery was deployed after two recent hurricanes, assessing the damage to more than 400 buildings in rural locations within 18 minutes.[29] To use these technologies, however, developing countries must strengthen local capacity. The World Bank has been investing in training local-government staff members and stakeholders in Dominica, for example, to manage large-scale geospatial data sets and operate drones, enabling the use of AI models to support more timely assessments following a disaster.[30]

Transparent measurement and regulation as a path forward

Given the multiple uses of AI for environmental management, the net environmental effects remain unclear. Some of the environmental risks arising from AI pose opportunities. For example, as noted earlier, technology firms that are facing public pressure to cut emissions have been investing heavily in expanding zero-emission generation of electricity. In addition, the increasing demand for rare earth minerals may accelerate innovation in e-waste recycling efforts. However, market forces alone are unlikely to deliver adequate environmental protection. The transparent measurement and documentation of the environmental impacts of specific AI activities will be critical in enabling firms to make environmentally conscious trade-offs, in allowing policy makers to focus their efforts on mitigating the most environmentally damaging activities, and in helping consumers make informed decisions about which AI tools they choose to use. If policy makers focus on ensuring that the measurement of the environmental impact and regulation of AI catch up with its rapid development, they may be able to help ensure that AI is a net benefit for the environment rather than a net cost.

Notes

1. Berthelot et al. (2025); Waelen and van Wynsberghe (2025). There is relatively little evidence that directly quantifies the impact that AI has on the demand for *rare earth minerals,* a group of 17 chemically similar metallic elements so named because they are rarely found in concentrated, economically viable deposits. Extraction of these minerals is therefore difficult and costly.
2. *Critical minerals* are nonfuel metallic or nonmetallic elements that are essential to a country's economy or national security and that are associated with supply chains that are highly vulnerable to disruption.
3. Damania et al. (2025).
4. Baldé et al. (2024).
5. Wang et al. (2024).
6. Baldé et al. (2024).
7. IEA (2025).
8. IEA (2025).
9. Chien et al. (2023).
10. Bogmans et al. (2025).
11. Penn and Weise (2024).
12. Penn and Weise (2024).
13. Martin and Peskoe (2025).
14. Martin and Peskoe (2025).
15. IEA (2025).
16. IEA (2025).
17. Jiang et al. (2025).
18. Nicoletti et al. (2025).
19. Ross and Ewing (2026).
20. IEA (2026).
21. Aykut et al. (2026). *Load shedding* is the intentional, temporary switching off of the supply of electricity to specific areas to prevent a total collapse of the power grid.
22. *Energize* (2025).
23. Tata Power (2024).
24. Salhi et al. (2025).
25. Chadalavada et al. (2025).
26. WEF (2025).
27. Price et al. (2025).
28. Rabier et al. (2026).
29. Manzini et al. (2025).
30. Tingzon et al. (2023).

References

Aykut, Dilek, Selcuk Ozyurt, K. Jung, and Estefania Vergara Cobos. 2026. "Data Center and AI Investment in EMDEs: Risks and Opportunities." DEC Private Markets–IFC, Infrastructure, Chief Economist Office, World Bank.

Baldé, Cornelis P., Ruediger Kuehr, Tales Yamamoto, et al. 2024. *Global E-Waste Monitor 2024*, 2nd ed. International Telecommunication Union and United Nations Institute for Training and Research. https://ewastemonitor.info/wp-content/uploads/2024/12/GEM_2024_EN_11_NOV-web.pdf.

Berthelot, Adrien, Eddy Caron, Mathilde Jay, and Laurent Lefèvre. 2025. "Understanding the Environmental Impact of Generative AI Services." *Communications of the ACM* 68 (7): 46–53. https://doi.org/10.1145/3725984.

Bogmans, Christian, Patricia Gomez-Gonzalez, Ganchimeg Ganpurev, Giovanni Melina, Andrea Pescatori, and Sneha D. Thube. 2025. "Power Hungry: How AI Will Drive Energy Demand." IMF Working Paper 25/81, International Monetary Fund. https://doi.org/10.5089/9798229007207.001.

Chadalavada, Sreeni, Oliver Faust, Massimo Salvi, et al. 2025. "Application of Artificial Intelligence in Air Pollution Monitoring and Forecasting: A Systematic Review." *Environmental Modelling and Software* 185 (February): 106312. https://doi.org/10.1016/j.envsoft.2024.106312.

Chien, Andrew A., Liuzixuan Lin, Hai Nguyen, Varsha Rao, Tristan Sharma, and Rajini Wijayawardana. 2023. "Reducing the Carbon Impact of Generative AI Inference (Today and in 2035)." In *HotCarbon*

2023: Proceedings of the 2nd Workshop on Sustainable Computer Systems, edited by George Porter, Tom Anderson, Andrew A. Chien, Tamar Eilam, Colleen Josephson, and Jonggyu Park. Association for Computing Machinery. https://dl.acm.org/doi/10.1145/3604930.3605705.

Damania, Richard, Ebad Ebadi, Kentaro Mayr, Jason Russ, and Esha Zaveri. 2025. *Reboot Development: The Economics of a Livable Planet*. World Bank. https://hdl.handle.net/10986/43522.

Energize. 2025. "MTN Zambia and Huawei Launch the World's First AI-Powered Power Backup for Resilient Networks." *Energize*, November 18. https://www.energize.co.za/article/mtn-zambia-and-huawei-launch-the-worlds-first-ai-powered-power-backup-for-resilient.

IEA (International Energy Agency). 2025. *Energy and AI*. World Energy Outlook Special Report. IEA. https://iea.blob.core.windows.net/assets/dd7c2387-2f60-4b60-8c5f-6563b6aa1e4c/EnergyandAI.pdf.

IEA (International Energy Agency). 2026. *Key Questions on Energy and AI*. World Energy Outlook Special Report. IEA. https://www.iea.org/reports/key-questions-on-energy-and-ai.

Jiang, Feng, Cuncun Duan, and Bin Chen. 2025. "Facility-Level Energy-Driven Water Footprint and Scarcity Implications of Chinese Data Centers: A Bottom-Up Analysis and Scenario-Based Projection." *Applied Energy* 399 (December): 126522. https://doi.org/10.1016/j.apenergy.2025.126522.

Manzini, Thomas, Priyankari Perali, and Robin R. Murphy. 2025. "Deploying Rapid Damage Assessments from sUAS Imagery for Disaster Response." *arXiv:2511.03132v3 [cs.CV]*, Cornell University. https://arxiv.org/abs/2511.03132.

Martin, Eliza, and Ari Peskoe. 2025. "Extracting Profits from the Public: How Utility Ratepayers Are Paying for Big Tech's Power." Environmental and Energy Law Program, Harvard Law School. https://eelp.law.harvard.edu/wp-content/uploads/2025/03/Harvard-ELI-Extracting-Profits-from-the-Public.pdf.

Nicoletti, Leonardo, Michelle Ma, and Dina Bass. 2025. "AI Is Draining Water from Areas That Need It Most." *Bloomberg Technology + Green*, May 8. https://www.bloomberg.com/graphics/2025-ai-impacts-data-centers-water-data/.

Penn, Ivan, and Karen Weise. 2024. "Hungry for Energy, Amazon, Google, and Microsoft Turn to Nuclear Power." *Energy and Environment* (blog), October 16. https://www.nytimes.com/2024/10/16/business/energy-environment/amazon-google-microsoft-nuclear-energy.html.

Price, Ilan, Alvaro Sanchez-Gonzalez, Ferran Alet, et al. 2025. "Probabilistic Weather Forecasting with Machine Learning." *Nature* 637 (8044): 84–90. https://doi.org/10.1038/s41586-024-08252-9.

Rabier, Florence, Andrew Brown, Matthew Chantry, and Florian Pappenberger. 2026. "Weather Forecasting in a Changing Climate: The Rise of AI and Machine Learning?" *Journal of the European Meteorological Society* 4 (June): 100040. https://doi.org/10.1016/j.jemets.2026.100040.

Ross, Martin T., and John Jackson Ewing. 2026. "Data Centers and Generation Capacity over the Next Decade: Potential Benefits of Flexibility." Report NI 26-04, Nicholas Institute for Energy, Environment and Sustainability, Duke University. https://nicholasinstitute.duke.edu/sites/default/files/publications/data-centers-generation-capacity-over-next-decade.pdf.

Salhi, Amina, Fahad Algarni, Rayan Alshamrani, Ashrf Althbiti, Atef Ismail, and Basma M. Hassan. 2025. "Leveraging Artificial Intelligence to Enable Sustainable Urban Development Through the Creation of Smart and Environmentally Friendly Carbon-Free Cities." *Scientific Reports* 15 (October): 35791. https://doi.org/10.1038/s41598-025-16801-z.

Tata Power. 2024. "How Real-Time Data Is Reinventing India's Power Grid." *tatapower.com* (blog), August 6. https://www.tatapower.com/blogs/how-real-time-data-is-reinventing-india-s-power-grid.

Tingzon, Isabelle, Nuala Margaret Cowan, and Pierre Chrzanowski. 2023. "Can AI Help Build Climate Resilience in the Caribbean? Let's Look at Housing." *Sustainable Cities* (blog), October 2. https://blogs.worldbank.org/en/sustainablecities/can-ai-help-build-climate-resilience-caribbean-lets-look-housing.

Waelen, Rosalie, and Aimee van Wynsberghe. 2025. "Considering the Social and Economic Sustainability of AI." *Science and Engineering Ethics* 31 (July): 19. https://doi.org/10.1007/s11948-025-00544-1.

Wang, Peng, Ling-Yu Zhang, Asaf Tzachor, and Wei-Qiang Chen. 2024. "E-Waste Challenges of Generative Artificial Intelligence." *Nature Computational Science* 4 (11): 818–23. https://doi.org/10.1038/s43588-024-00712-6.

WEF (World Economic Forum). 2025. "Intelligent Transport, Greener Future: AI as a Catalyst to Decarbonize Global Logistics." White Paper, WEF. https://reports.weforum.org/docs/WEF_Intelligent_Transport_Greener_Future_2025.pdf.

Part 3

Shaping AI: Governments as Enablers, Users, and Regulators

Part 2 analyzed the promise and peril of artificial intelligence (AI) through its economic, social, and political impacts on development. Part 3 discusses how governments, in tandem with markets, can shape AI's impacts on development through policy actions that aim to leverage AI's potential and guard against AI's risks across the three pathways of AI adoption, adaptation, and advancement (refer to figure P3.1).

Chapter 7 discusses the role of governments as enablers of AI in shaping economic impacts. The focus here is on establishing the analog and digital complements, such as infrastructure, data, skills, and institutions, that enable the adoption, adaptation, and advancement of AI by countries' private sectors. This starts with establishing the analog complements for the productive adoption of AI: foundational skills, infrastructure, and information. For those who lose jobs or livelihoods because of AI, governments can upgrade social protection, as discussed in spotlight 5. Governments should also support local firms' ability to access key digital and analog complements—compute, training data, and AI talent—for AI adaptation and for AI advancement at a later stage.

Chapter 8 discusses the role of governments as users of AI in shaping social impacts. The focus here is on leveraging governments' buying power to enable AI adaptation and potential advancement across use cases—such as those in education, health, and the legal system—in which local contexts are paramount. Governments should spur the development of AI solutions fit to context by making public administrative data AI-ready. Governments should also establish frameworks for testing, procuring, and evaluating AI solutions in public services to move from pilots to large-scale deployment. Spotlight 6 examines issues in monitoring and evaluating AI solutions. Government procurement can also crowd in local AI solutions if those developed elsewhere are either less effective or even harmful in high-stakes applications, such as health care. All of this will require investments in staff capacity.

Figure P3.1 Governments as enablers, users, and regulators of AI can shape its development impacts through the pathways of adopting, adapting, and advancing AI

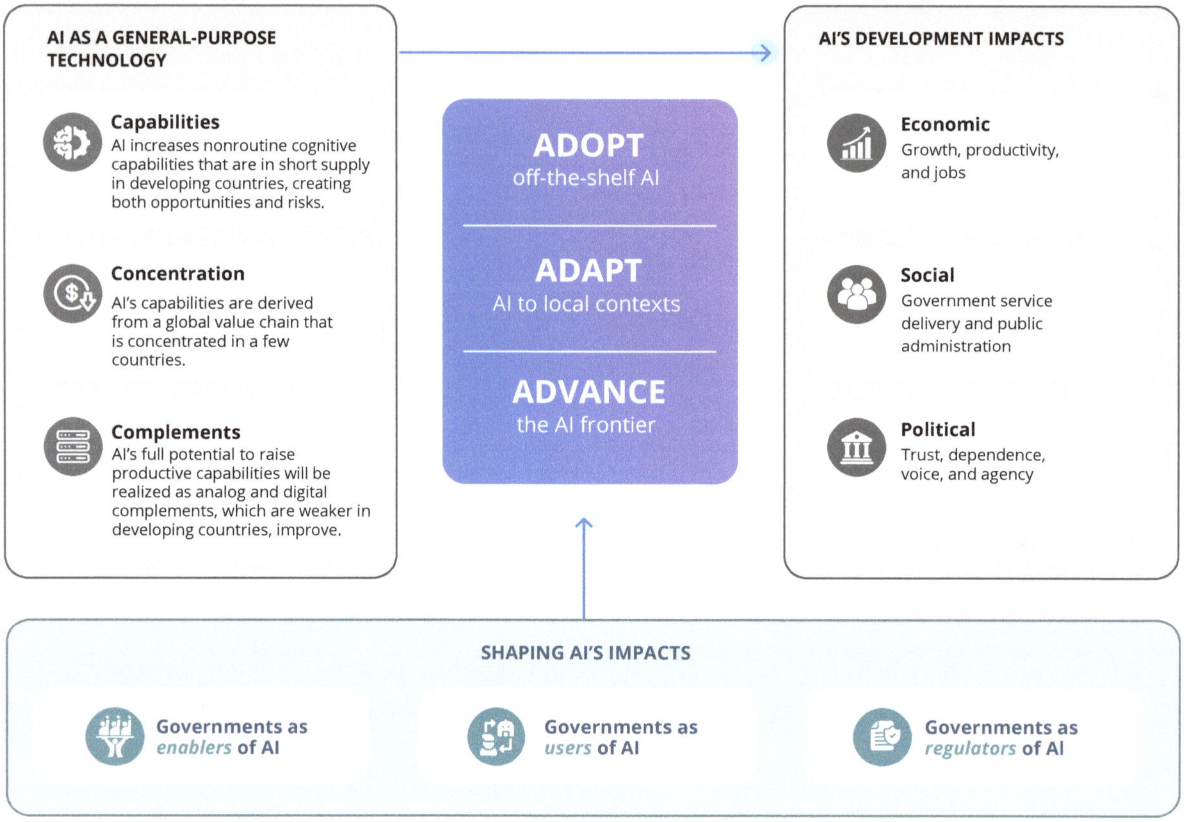

Source: WDR 2026 team.
Note: AI = artificial intelligence.

Chapter 9 discusses the role of governments as regulators of AI in shaping political impacts. The focus here is on using voluntary standards as a starting point to build trustworthy AI. Where market forces are not aligned with the responsible adoption, adaptation, and advancement of AI solutions, governments should use existing legal instruments to address social harms (such as discrimination against certain social groups, violations of privacy, and cybersecurity failures). Over time, to develop an AI governance framework, governments should assess the current landscape of regulations, identify and address regulatory gaps, and build enforcement and compliance capacity. The process of framework development should emphasize interagency coordination within governments, a topic discussed in spotlight 7. It should also emphasize international cooperation that guards against fragmentation of regulations across countries.

The roles of government as enablers, users, and regulators of AI are not mutually exclusive. Overstepping in one role might mean impinging on another. For example, by overregulating AI use, governments will hamper efforts to enable the private sector to innovate with AI. In each of its roles, government should leverage market solutions where appropriate.

7

Governments as Enablers: Establishing the Analog and Digital Complements of AI

Main messages

- **Without basic infrastructure and skills, AI adoption will stall**
  Expand reliable electricity, affordable internet, access to digital devices, foundational learning, and basic AI literacy.
- **Firms need help finding and using the right AI tools**
  Share information about the use of AI solutions, connect businesses with suitable AI providers, and strengthen the organizational capabilities needed to use AI productively.
- **Local AI solutions need local data, affordable computing, and skilled workers**
  Invest in open local language data, ensure affordable access to computing infrastructure, and align technical training with industry needs.
- **Adapting AI requires local firms that can experiment and grow**
  Improve access to finance, establish links between industry and universities, and simplify requirements in government procurement so firms can turn local AI solutions into viable products.
- **AI policies work best as a coherent system**
  Sequence and coordinate investments in infrastructure, data, computing, skills, and the business environment around the biggest constraints in adopting and adapting AI.

A reproducibility package is available for this book in the Reproducible Research Repository at https://reproducibility.worldbank.org/catalog/624.

Introduction

In San Salvador, Jorge runs JD Smart Code, a software firm with six employees that builds cloud solutions, sets up platforms such as Salesforce, and develops customized artificial intelligence (AI) solutions for its clients. JD Smart Code is an example of the many small, ambitious companies that are increasingly driving digital transformation across Central America and other developing regions and doing so with limited resources. For a firm of this size, gaining or losing a client often comes down to how well the business understands the client's problem and how fast it can deliver the solution. AI has made it easier for Jorge's company to achieve both speed and depth in terms of services delivered. Jorge describes AI as a "capability enabler," that is, a tool that can explore unfamiliar technical areas, examine complex problems from several angles at once, and address client requests more quickly.[1]

But Jorge is clear-eyed about what the larger ecosystem still lacks. As someone who both uses and builds AI-powered solutions, he identifies a constraint that tools cannot resolve: finding people who understand what AI can and cannot do for a given task. This lack of talent is the main bottleneck for small firms competing with much larger players. Jorge's experience illustrates the central issue that this chapter addresses. Although AI is becoming increasingly available to firms and workers across developing countries, access to AI does not always equate to the productive use of AI. Whether AI delivers on its promise for development will depend on whether the conditions are in place that allow firms and workers to use AI well and that allow domestic firms to build AI solutions that are customized to the local context.

For most firms and workers in low- and middle-income countries, AI is an *input* that can improve productivity if deployed well. The myriad uses range from a smallholder farmer using an AI-powered crop advisory application (app), to a shopkeeper adopting automated inventory management, to a community health worker using a diagnostic support tool. The main barriers to *adopting* AI relate to the basic conditions for use—foundational infrastructure that powers the reliable supply of electricity and affordable internet connectivity, the availability of digital devices, foundational skills, and a regulatory and legal environment that supports investment and start-ups.

A smaller set of firms—providers of AI solutions, including the more sophisticated frontier firms—create AI as *output* or a product they develop, customize, and sell. Again, the range is myriad: an agritech start-up building a pest-detection AI model trained on local crop varieties, a fintech firm developing credit-scoring algorithms using data about mobile money, or a health tech firm creating triage tools for district hospitals. The constraints that these firms face in *adapting* and *advancing* AI center on their lack of access to key inputs: scarcity of data that are locally relevant; expensive or unavailable compute (the hardware and processing power needed to train and run AI models); limited supply of technical capabilities required to build and maintain AI systems; and weak entrepreneurship ecosystems that foster innovation and bring AI solutions to market. The disparities in accessing key inputs relative to large technology companies can limit competition in the development of AI solutions. Frontier firms looking to advance AI face even steeper barriers: insufficient compute for frontier workloads, gaps in large-scale training data, and limited AI research talent.

Adopting and adapting AI should not be understood as fixed sequential pathways but as mutually reinforcing. Adaptation can enable adoption by making AI tools more affordable, more relevant to local needs, and more usable in local languages. Countries can move through these categories at different speeds and from different starting points. For example, where many people still lack reliable electricity and internet access, governments should balance support for next-level data centers that enable AI adaptation with investments in the foundational infrastructure that is necessary for widespread AI adoption. AI advancement requires substantially higher investments in complementary foundations, including computing infrastructure, data, and skills, and can build on the foundation of successful AI adaptation. This chapter argues that getting the sequence right, and recognizing the interdependence between policy domains within each pathway, matters.

Moreover, the rationale for policy intervention rests on a common foundation: left to themselves, markets underprovide the complementary inputs that firms and workers need to adopt and adapt AI. The role of policy is to correct these market failures, not to substitute for markets where they function well.

Adopting AI: The analog foundations must be in place

Firms and workers cannot use AI productively unless the basic conditions for adoption in three policy domains are in place: infrastructure, business environment, and workforce skills. Gaps in any of these domains stall adoption.

Improving the physical infrastructure layer of AI adoption

Electricity, internet, and digital devices are essential for adopting AI. Although policy makers have long been addressing barriers in these areas, the emergence of AI makes removing these barriers more pressing and changes which barriers matter most.

Ensuring adequate, affordable, and reliable electricity and internet services: Where AI adoption begins

Less than half the population in low-income countries had access to electricity as of 2023, whereas nearly everyone does in high- and middle-income countries (refer to figure 7.1, panel a). Similarly, only about one-quarter of people in low-income countries and about half of the population in lower-middle-income countries used the internet in 2024, compared with 93 percent in high-income countries (refer to figure 7.1, panel b).

The quality and reliability of electricity and internet are also uneven across countries. Half of firms in Latin America and the Caribbean and South Asia and about three-quarters in Sub-Saharan Africa report experiencing electrical outages.[2] Internet speeds are less than 25 megabits per second in low-income and lower-middle-income countries, but exceed 300 megabits per second in high-income countries.[3] Affordability of the internet also varies. In low-income countries, a limited (5 gigabyte) fixed broadband subscription is 30 times more expensive than in high-income countries in relative terms, consuming 29 percent of the average monthly income.[4] The types of AI applications that can be used across countries depend on filling these wide gaps in access to affordable, reliable electricity and internet services.

For broadband infrastructure, countries should prioritize creating conditions that attract private investment, including liberalizing restrictions on foreign direct investment, enforcing fair competition, and ensuring that regulations are consistently enforced. India's progressive opening of its telecom sector—culminating in 100 percent foreign direct investment—spurred competition and the rollouts of large-scale networks, which rapidly increased the uptake of the internet nationwide.[5] In situations where private investment alone cannot deliver internet coverage at a reasonable cost, infrastructure sharing in fiber-optic networks, shared deployment plans, and financial incentives can ease the burden on any single provider, though the governance risks need to be carefully managed.[6]

Satellites can bring internet to places where fixed and mobile networks do not reach. For example, Bangladesh, Brazil, Nigeria, and Rwanda have opened their markets to providers like Starlink, OneWeb, and SpaceSail, thus avoiding licensing "red tape" to speed up the process.[7]

Figure 7.1 Access to electricity and internet varies significantly across countries

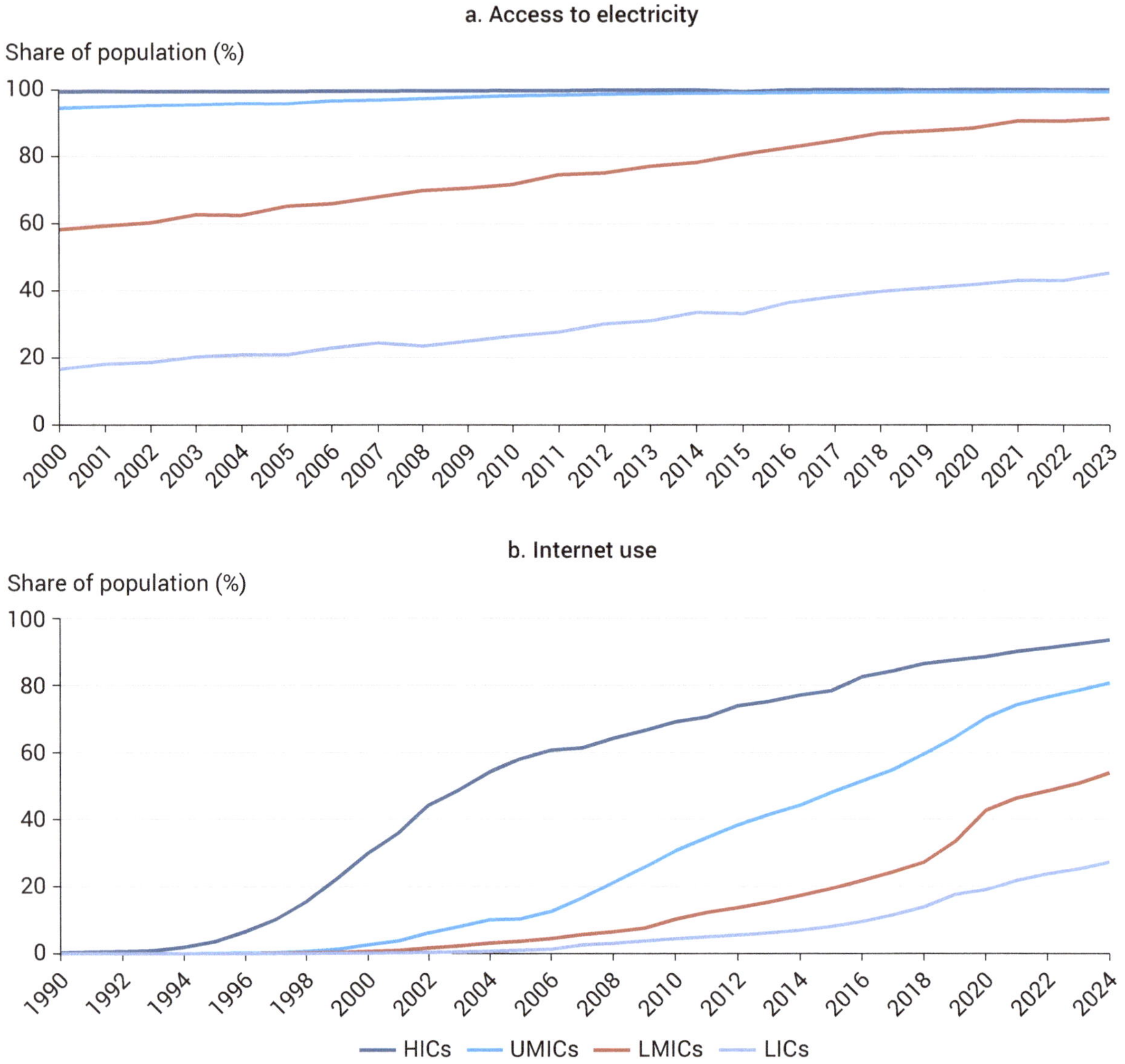

Sources: Panel a: WDR 2026 team, based on 2000–23 data of World Development Indicators (DataBank), World Bank, https://databank.worldbank.org/source/world-development-indicators. Panel b: WDR 2026 team, based on 1990–2024 data of DataHub (portal), International Telecommunication Union, https://datahub.itu.int/.

Note: HICs = high-income countries; LICs = low-income countries; LMICs = lower-middle-income countries; UMICs = upper-middle-income countries.

Lowering the price to buy and use devices: The access layer between workers and AI

Digital devices are the point of entry to AI, but their affordability remains a major obstacle. In low-income countries, only 63 percent of adults own a mobile phone, compared with 95 percent in upper-middle-income and high-income countries (refer to figure 7.2, panel a).[8] A typical smartphone costs about 60 percent of monthly income in low-income countries, compared with about 4 percent in high-income countries (refer to figure 7.2, panel b).[9]

Figure 7.2 Mobile phone ownership remains limited in low-income countries

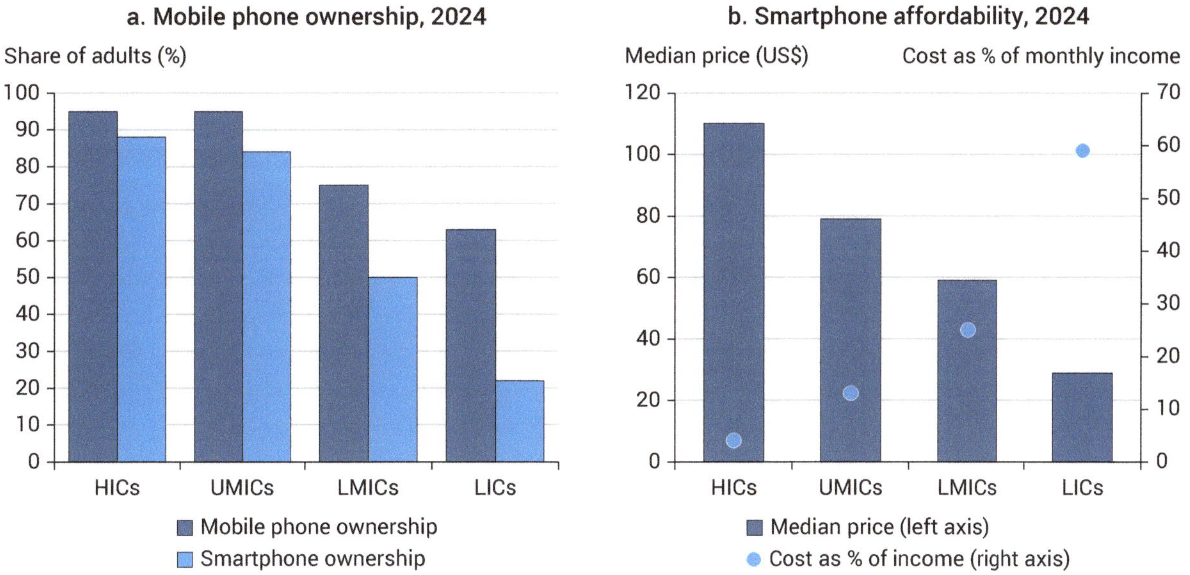

Source: WDR 2026 team, based on Klapper et al. 2025 (panel a) and GDIP 2024 (panel b).

Note: The figure shows, by country income group, the share of the population ages 15 and above that owns a mobile phone and a smartphone. Data are as of 2024. HICs = high-income countries; LICs = low-income countries; LMICs = lower-middle-income countries; UMICs = upper-middle-income countries.

Several approaches can help improve access to digital devices. Shared internet access points, pay-as-you-go financing, and lower taxes on digital devices can all reduce the cost of access. In Kenya, the removal of the 16 percent value added tax on mobile handsets led to more than a 200 percent increase in handset purchases and a 50–70 percent increase in penetration rates.[10] Pay-as-you-go models offered by service providers are increasingly popular for increasing the ownership of devices. Access to such financing is estimated to be equivalent to a 3.4–6.0 percent increase in annual income for the average user in developing countries.[11]

Reforming the business environment for AI adoption

Although access to infrastructure is necessary for AI adoption, it is not sufficient in the absence of a good regulatory environment that promotes firm entry, growth, and investment or without addressing important information gaps that firms might have about the use of AI solutions.

Clearing the regulatory path for AI investment

The productive use of AI requires firms to reconfigure how they work—redeveloping workflows, reassigning workers and tasks, and making other necessary investments. Regulatory uncertainty and high compliance costs around licensing, taxation, and import and export procedures can deter such actions. In Bangladesh, for instance, firms cite regulatory compliance costs as one of the top obstacles to adopting new hardware or software, especially among large firms.[12] Restrictions on accessing foreign technologies create further barriers. For example, firms may struggle to obtain foreign currency or use credit cards to buy tokens from foreign providers to use application programming interfaces (APIs). Although frontier firms can often work around these barriers, smaller firms cannot.[13]At the same time, governments in developing countries should ensure that taxes and other regulations do not distort the incentives for firms to buy AI software at the expense of hiring or retaining workers.[14]

Regulation can also shape AI adoption by allowing new firms with disruptive models to enter and productive incumbents to grow.[15] For entrants, policies should aim to lower barriers to firm entry. Start-ups are among the most likely adopters of AI, but regulations often work against their interests. Business registration, licensing, tax compliance, and rules and regulations around digital use (such as regulations concerning data transfers) can all create significant hurdles. In Ethiopia, new firms must provide proof of a lease for a physical office in order to obtain a tax identification number, which effectively excludes any digital businesses that operate from the owner's home.[16]

Some countries have tried to address these barriers for start-ups. Tunisia's Startup Act provides eligible firms with exemptions from taxes and social security contributions, easier access to foreign exchange, and simplified customs procedures. Eligible firms were 18 percentage points more likely to survive and increased their workforce by 2 workers on average, compared with 1.8 workers in noneligible firms.[17] Firms that are backed by venture capital face a separate challenge. Venture capital funds are typically structured as limited partnerships, but not all legal systems recognize this form or enable it fully, which limits the supply of early-stage risk capital.

For productive incumbents seeking to grow, policies should ensure a level playing field. Regulations that protect certain firms (such as investment restrictions that benefit domestic firms), direct state involvement in markets (such as state ownership stakes in private entities), and weak enforcement of competition policies dampen the competitive pressures that push firms to invest in technologies that enhance productivity, including AI.[18]

Connecting AI solutions to the firms that can use them

Incomplete information is another challenge to adopting AI solutions. Lack of knowledge about AI solutions is among the main reasons surveyed businesses in India, Jordan, Kenya, Mexico, Nigeria, and Thailand cite for not adopting AI or for not increasing its use (refer to figure 7.3). Governments can address the gap in awareness by compiling and offering provider listings and sector-specific registries, and providing more intensive brokerage between providers and potential adopters.[19] Firms' experiences with earlier technologies is illustrative. In Nigeria, when the government worked with a marketplace platform that provided quality ratings for professional business service providers, purchasing firms shifted their preferences toward providers with higher ratings.[20] This matchmaking role especially matters in sectors where AI applications are emerging but are not yet widely known. For example, a small agricultural cooperative may be unaware that AI-powered soil analysis services exist.

Equipping workers and firms to use AI productively

The capabilities of firms and workers determine whether AI adoption leads to productive use.

Generative AI tools can be used without specialized training, but the real challenge is learning to evaluate their advice. Farmers using an AI-based advisory tool still need to know the microclimate well enough to judge whether an AI-based recommendation fits the conditions of their specific farms. The same logic applies to firms: the adoption of AI can pay off only when managerial practices, organizational routines, and absorptive capacity are in place. No simplification of an AI interface can eliminate these demands for foundational skills.

Moreover, women tend to use AI less than men. They are also more exposed to job loss through AI than men, and thus need training to find other jobs. Box 7.1 addresses these issues.

Closing foundational learning gaps so workers can engage with AI

Foundational skills such as literacy, numeracy, basic reasoning, and learning habits are largely developed

Figure 7.3 Firms report lack of knowledge and high costs as the main reasons for not adopting AI

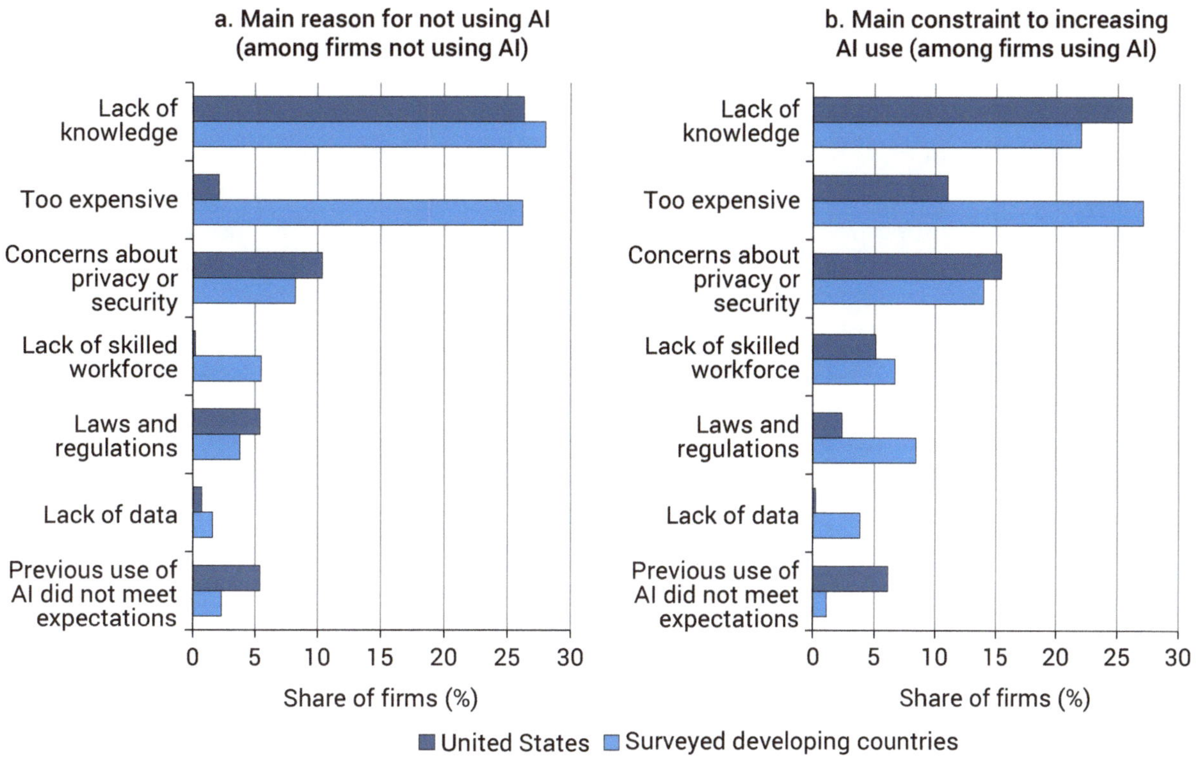

Sources: WDR 2026 team, based on World Bank Enterprise Survey on AI Adoption; Davies et al. 2026.

Note: Firms could select only one option. The figure covers formal firms with five or more employees, pooling data across all countries (averaging country-level indicators). The data for surveyed developing countries average country-level indicators, with equal weight for each country. The sample sizes are as follows: India (1,355 firms); Jordan (358); Kenya (360); Mexico (603); Nigeria (777); Thailand (360); United States (392). Microdata are available at Enterprise Surveys (data portal), World Bank, https://www.enterprisesurveys.org/en/data. AI = artificial intelligence.

during early childhood and primary school. Investing in AI-specific training during adulthood, when foundations have not been developed, may yield limited returns.[21] The current gap in these skills is large and unequal. An estimated 70 percent of 10-year-olds worldwide could not read and understand a simple text as of 2022, but in Sub-Saharan Africa that figure exceeded 89 percent.[22]

Narrowing these gaps requires well-established policies that educational systems in low- and middle-income countries have long understood but failed to deliver consistently. High-impact interventions that are feasible in low-capacity settings include structured pedagogy programs,[23] targeted instruction that groups students by learning level rather than age,[24] early childhood development programs,[25] and policies reducing barriers to school attendance such as fees and distance. AI tutoring and adaptive learning tools[26] can help students master foundational learning—the basic literary, numeracy, and socioemotional skills that matter for lifelong learning, personal development, and societal participation—by delivering personalized feedback at scale (refer to chapter 5). But overreliance on such initiatives can undercut the foundational learning that they are meant to support (refer to spotlight 3).[27] Countries should prioritize supporting teachers to remain actively involved in how students use AI tools.[28]

Box 7.1 Bridging the AI gender divide

Women use artificial intelligence (AI) less than men do. A systematic review of 76 studies from more than 100 countries finds that the adoption of generative AI tools was about 16 percent higher for men than for women in 2025.[a] This can limit opportunities to realize AI's benefit, for example, through AI tutors that deliver personalized instruction to girls unable to attend school regularly.[b] Closing the gender gap in access to digital devices and connectivity is an important starting point to bridge this AI divide. In low- and middle-income countries, women are 12 percent less likely than men to use mobile internet and 13 percent less likely to own a smartphone.[c]

Many women also work in jobs where AI is more likely to replace people. Across 88 countries, female-dominated occupations are five times more likely to be automated by generative AI than male-dominated ones (16 percent versus 3 percent).[d] This disparity reflects the large numbers of women working in clerical and administrative roles, where tasks are routine and codifiable—precisely the tasks for which generative AI performs best. Establishing pipelines for science, technology, engineering, and mathematics fields can expand women's participation in jobs where the demand for AI-related skills is increasing.[e]

AI systems may also reproduce the gender bias prevalent in society, as reflected in the underlying training data.[f] Simulations using data from a fintech lender serving emerging markets show that credit-scoring models discriminate against women.[g] AI-powered facial recognition systems that are increasingly used in digital identification have misclassified darker-skinned women at rates up to 34.7 percent, compared with 0.8 percent for lighter-skinned men.[h] Large language models systematically associate women with home and family and men with business and leadership, and about one in five responses to gender-primed sentence completions returns sexist or misogynistic content.[i] Investing in open data matters—the lack of gender-disaggregated data can make algorithmic discrimination harder to detect and correct.[j] Institutional safeguards, such as algorithmic audits, can also reduce gender bias. For example, commercial providers of AI solutions publicly named for bias in such audits substantially reduced their errors within months, whereas unaudited competitors did not.[k]

Source: WDR 2026 team.

a. Cranney et al. (2026).
b. Angrist et al. (2022).
c. GSMA (2026).
d. ILO (2026).
e. Smith and Rustagi (2021).
f. Smith and Rustagi (2021).
g. Kelley et al. (2022).
h. Buolamwini and Gebru (2018).
i. UN Women (2026).
j. Kelley et al. (2022).
k. Raji and Buolamwini (2019).

Strengthening teacher capacity to integrate AI in the classroom

About 41 percent of teachers globally reported using AI for teaching in the past year as of 2024. Although 65 percent of teachers cited a high need for AI-related training, only 41 percent received such training (refer to table 7.1). This gap between use and preparedness risks misuse of AI by teachers (refer to chapter 5). And teachers matter most when it comes to student learning.[29]

Teachers need training that helps them understand how AI tools can be well integrated into teaching practice, testing, and assessment tools, and why those tools can yield incorrect results. They also need practical experience in using AI for lesson planning and assessment.[30] Programs that combine structured training with coaching and peer learning are most likely to change classroom behavior, as Uruguay's Ceibal program and Ghana's mentorship-based approaches demonstrate. The Youth Coding Initiative—under the United Nations Educational, Scientific and Cultural Organization (UNESCO) and CODEMAO—has adopted a similar approach across Africa and Asia, providing certification training to teachers in the Republic of Congo, Kenya, Namibia, and Thailand, who then return to train peers and students.[31] Teachers' perceptions of AI's trustworthiness also matter. Thus, engaging teacher unions early can build trust.

Embedding AI literacy across the curriculum

AI literacy does not require coding or knowledge of machine learning algorithms. It means understanding that these systems generate probabilistic outputs that can appear to be accurate and still be incorrect, developing the habit of verifying AI outputs, and using these tools ethically. Some countries are already implementing AI literacy programs. Singapore has rolled out a national AI curriculum focused on ethics and safe use. The United Arab Emirates has embedded AI literacy into its national competency framework,[32] and Rwanda is piloting AI modules in secondary schools.[33] In countries with constrained resources, the most realistic approach is to embed AI literacy into subjects that are already being taught, such as discussing misinformation produced by AI in a social studies class, or examining AI-powered tools in a science lesson.

Table 7.1 Demand for AI training for teaching and learning support is high, but supply is limited

	High-income countries	Upper-middle-income countries	Lower-middle-income countries	All countries
Used AI in their teaching during the last 12 months (%)	39.5	45.3	51.0	41.4
Training for using AI for teaching is highly needed (%)	64.4	65.4	77.2	65.3
Use of AI for teaching was part of their training during the last 12 months (%)	40.4	42.3	43.1	41.0

Source: OECD 2025b.

Note: Percentages indicate the share of teachers who reported a high or moderate level of need for AI training or that they had received AI training in the previous year. The sample includes 34 high-income countries, 12 upper-middle-income countries, and 5 lower-income countries. The study excludes low-income countries. AI = artificial intelligence.

Building firm capabilities for productive AI use

Capabilities matter for firms, as they do for workers. Managerial skills and organizational practices shape whether AI tools translate into productivity gains. Firms with more structured management practices are more likely to adopt AI.[34] A trial of a GPT-4 business assistant with small business owners in Kenya illustrates the asymmetry: the tool raised the performance of businesses that were already performing well but lowered the performance of firms that lacked the practices needed to use AI well.[35]

Although evidence on interventions that build firms' capabilities to adopt AI is limited, early results are encouraging. Providing participants of a three-month global capacity-building program for young businesses with workshops showcasing how AI-native businesses organized their workflows and processes increased the amount of AI use cases within firms by 44 percent, increased task completion by 12 percent, and increased revenue by 1.9 times.[36] In Czechia, the AI Klub program, which combines training, peer-to-peer learning, and linkages between participating firms, increased the rate of AI adoption by 26 percent and increased the sales and profits of participating firms more than it did for similar firms that did not complete the program.[37] These results align with broader evidence on building firms' capabilities. Among the very smallest firms that operate in the informal sector, providing training in business skills and entrepreneurial mindset has led to adoption of better business practices and improved performance.[38] Among medium and large firms, offering business advisory services, including consulting and peer learning, can drive the adoption of structured managerial practices and sustained gains in performance.[39]

From adopting AI to adapting AI and advancing AI: The analog and digital foundations must be in place

The main goal of most countries is to strengthen the conditions that allow firms and workers to use AI productively. But a subset of countries, and within those countries a subset of firms, has the capabilities to go beyond only adopting AI to building applications, adapting models to local languages, and, in an even smaller number of cases, advancing the AI frontier.

The transition from adopting AI to adapting and advancing AI changes the conditions that are needed. Firms and entrepreneurs building AI models must have access to training *data* and *compute*. *Skills* must extend beyond AI literacy to the more advanced technical capabilities required to build, deploy, and maintain AI systems. The *business environment* and *innovation ecosystem* must function well enough to allow ideas to be turned into products that can compete in both the domestic and global markets. And public procurement systems must be redesigned to create demand that local providers can meet.

Policies that support AI adaptation and advancement are best understood as a continuum, with the requirements being higher for the latter across each policy domain described earlier. All five domains operate within a market structure where local AI firms may be unable to compete against leading technology companies because of disparities in access to key inputs across the AI value chain—such as semiconductors, data centers, high-quality training data, and specialized technical talent (refer to box 7.2).

Box 7.2 Keeping AI markets competitive: From chips to cloud to models

A handful of companies in a handful of economies dominate the market for artificial intelligence (AI) foundation models, graphics processing units, chip production, and cloud services. This reliance on a small number of providers can affect cost, terms of access, and terms of use, deterring AI adaptation and adoption.[a] Dominant providers can maintain their position through multiple, reinforcing mechanisms (refer to figure B7.2.1).[b] For example, companies can impose licensing terms that restrict the customization of AI models, the reuse of data, or the development of complementary applications. Even when access to AI is free, this arrangement can reinforce dominance because providers can derive value by accumulating user data that allow them to fine-tune models and "lock in" customers to a specific platform, and potentially later charge fees for access.[c]

The policy objective for governments is not to limit access to foreign technologies, which are often at the frontier, but to guarantee equitable access to a wide range of AI providers—and maintain the ability to switch between them.[d] Governments can do so in several ways. The first is regulation: rules that prevent bundling, restrictive licensing, or discriminatory access; interoperability requirements that allow AI models to connect with a wide range of services; and rules on data portability that allow users to switch between providers. An example of this approach is the European Union's Digital Markets Act, which requires designated "gatekeeper" platforms to make their products interoperable with third parties and limits the combining of user data across platforms under common ownership.[e]

The acquisition of local AI start-ups by foreign incumbents deserves particular attention. Although the prospect of a profitable takeover could encourage the creation of local start-ups and innovation, such deals can absorb the most promising domestic capabilities before they have had the chance to mature. Competition policies must strike a balance between preventing conduct that would hamper complementary innovation and allowing for the scale required for advanced research and development.

Governments can also use their procurement of AI solutions and licensing to negotiate better terms that are beyond the reach of individual firms and set standards for contracts, including control over outputs and transparency around the ability to audit AI systems.

(Box continues next page)

Box 7.2 Keeping AI markets competitive: From chips to cloud to models *(continued)*

Figure B7.2.1 Dominant market positions can reinforce market power in AI

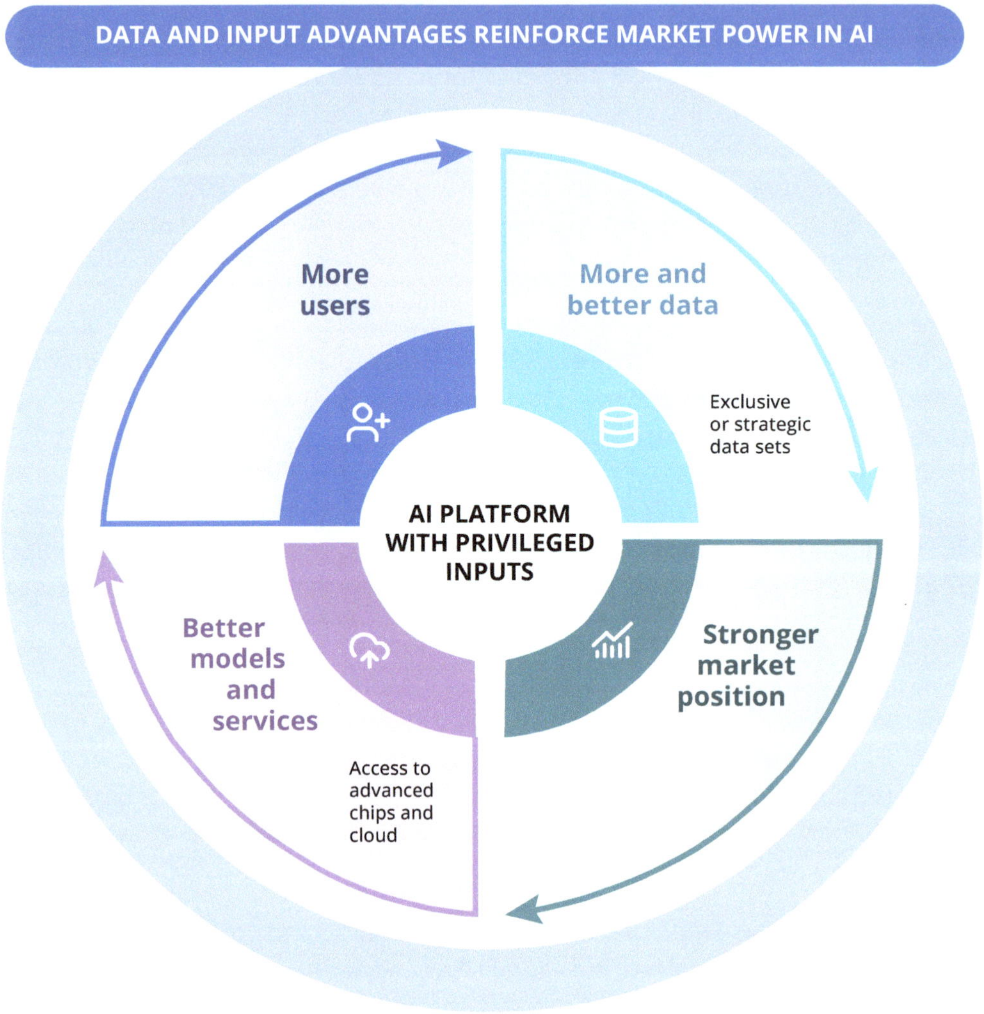

Source: Phumpiu Chang et al. 2026.
Note: AI = artificial intelligence.

Source: WDR 2026 team.

a. Athey and Morton (2025).
b. Phumpiu Chang et al. (2026).
c. Agrawal et al. (2019).
d. Jones (2023).
e. Article 5(2) of the European Union's Digital Markets Act.

Supporting the data ecosystems behind AI adaptation

The adaptation of AI requires data that are high quality and relevant to the local context, but such data are scarce in most developing countries. The sectors that drive these economies, such as agriculture and small-scale retail, have a very limited amount of digitized data available, especially in local languages. Public data also often tend to be in paper format and fragmented. As for online content generated by users around the world, much of it is controlled by global platforms that are headquartered in advanced economies.[40] Moreover, both data and AI models themselves reflect systematic biases against women, as discussed in box 7.1.

Market failures such as unintended consequences from the use of data, unclear intellectual property rights, difficulties in determining the market value of data, and privacy concerns pose additional challenges that can deter private companies, particularly smaller ones in developing countries, from investing in generating more data.[41]

Making public data AI-ready

In countries with weak private data ecosystems, the public sector can play an outsized role in providing high-quality data by digitizing and publishing administrative records such as court rulings, land registries, health statistics, and business registries that others can build on (refer to chapter 8). For providers of AI solutions in developing countries, digitized public data serve as the foundation for building applications in health, agriculture, finance, and other sectors that are relevant to the local context.[42]

Ensuring that such data are useful for AI requires going beyond making the data machine-readable. Machines need to be able to understand these data sets, which entails providing metadata for each data set that are context-specific and organized into standard, interpretable formats.[43] India's digital initiatives—such as DigiLocker, the e-Courts Mission Mode Project, and the National Judicial Data Grid—are good examples.[44]

Building local data ecosystems for domestic AI models

Although high-quality data and adopting data governance frameworks are necessary, they are not sufficient. Developing countries seeking to build AI solutions that are relevant to the local context must also invest in the creation of new data, particularly data in local languages and sector-specific data sets, and in financial and institutional support that enables firms and researchers to use data effectively.

Open data collaboratives and data commons, where public institutions, firms, and civil society contribute data sets under clear governance frameworks, offer a promising model. Community-led efforts have been crucial to producing data sets in languages and contexts that digital data have largely ignored (refer to box 7.3). However, sustaining such efforts poses a challenge. Most are operated by volunteers and have limited funding that is not predictable in the long term. In addition, such initiatives often lack formal institutional support from governments, universities, or other organizations.

Box 7.3 Unlocking AI for low-resource languages

As artificial intelligence (AI) spreads globally, many languages and sectors remain underrepresented in the digital data sets these systems are built on. The shortfall is especially acute for low-resource languages that lack annotated data sets, native speakers, computational tools, or other linguistic resources needed to develop natural language processing models. Most African languages have fewer than 10 hours of clearly licensed and usable audio available[a]—far below the level needed for models robust enough to handle various accents, background noise, and domain-specific vocabulary. In response to this deficit, community-driven initiatives led by researchers, start-ups, and volunteer networks are creating open data sets and tools to support the development of AI in diverse languages and contexts.

The Masakhane Research Foundation, a pan-African research community focused on natural language processing for African languages, convenes hundreds of researchers, linguists, and engineers to develop open data sets, benchmarks, and models. Since its founding, the foundation has produced multilingual data sets covering dozens of African languages, enabling researchers and start-ups to build AI systems in languages that were previously underrepresented in digital data sets. Similarly, Universal Dependencies, a global open-science collaboration, creates standardized annotated linguistic data sets used to train natural language processing systems, covering over 100 languages.

In Malawi, the National Language Data Trust—a partnership between the World Bank's Development Data Partnership and the Malawi Research and Education Network—uses content licensing agreements with media houses and government agencies to unlock language content. Through 15 signed agreements, available high-quality audio data in the Chichewa language expanded from approximately 35 hours to more than 10,000 hours at a preliminary estimated cost of less than $10 per hour across audio, text, and video combined.[b] Data are made available to researchers under noncommercial terms. A commercial subscription pathway, developed with a local law firm, would ensure that content creators receive compensation and that revenues help offset the steward's operating costs. The model thus offers a path by which language communities retain control over their linguistic assets as AI development accelerates around them.

Source: WDR 2026 team.
Note: A *low-resource language* is a human language that lacks the digital data, tools, and written texts needed to build accurate computer programs such as translation apps or smart assistants.

a. Imam et al. (2025).
b. Refer to the Development Data Partnership, Low Resource Language Catalog, https://datapartnership.org/lrl-catalog/.

Governments can support such initiatives by providing grants, tax deductions, and competitions (such as innovation challenges). These types of support can incentivize firms and research institutions to create annotated data sets that they may not otherwise have invested in. In India, the BHASHINI initiative is building open language resources across dozens of linguistic communities,[45] and Mozilla's Common Voice has proven that crowdsourcing data collection can work on a large scale.[46]

Firms also need funding support to enable them to do more with data they already have. The European Union's Horizon 2020 program has funded thousands of AI-related projects. Firms that participated experienced levels of job growth that were 20 percent higher than firms that did not participate, and gains in assets and revenues that were 30 percent higher.[47] The Republic of Korea has used a data voucher program targeted specifically to small and medium enterprises (SMEs) and start-ups.[48]

Synthetic data (artificially generated data that mimic real-world patterns) offer an alternative where actual data are too scarce or too sensitive to use in some use cases.[49] Some African universities are already exploring this solution. Kwame Nkrumah University of Science and Technology in Ghana, for instance, is investigating the use of synthetic data for AI applications in the health care and agriculture sectors.[50]

Expanding capabilities of and access to compute

Access to compute is critical for adapting AI, but supply is concentrated among a handful of chip producers, hyperscalers, and foundation model providers because up-front investments are so large. For most firms, access through the cloud remains the practical pathway. A smaller set of countries with mature digital economies and emerging AI ecosystems may need to decide whether to build local data centers, how to position themselves in globally concentrated markets, and how to do so without overcommitting their fiscal resources.

Making cloud-delivered AI affordable and accessible

Cloud platforms and *application programming interfaces* (sets of rules and protocols that allow different software applications to communicate and exchange data with one another) are the means that build modern AI, making access rather than ownership the most important limitation for many firms.

Governments can aggregate demand. Shared cloud access programs—where governments negotiate bulk agreements with cloud providers to supply discounted resources to governments, technology parks, or research networks—allow small users to benefit from scale that they cannot achieve alone. Government partnerships with providers such as NVIDIA, Google, and Microsoft have provided cloud-based access to graphics processing units and development tools to start-up ecosystems in multiple countries.

As a temporary measure, governments can also reduce up-front costs of accessing cloud-delivered AI services to foster the development of AI solutions that directly consider the local context. For example, Singapore's Enterprise Compute Initiative allows SMEs, start-ups, and researchers to access compute credits from approved providers through vouchers. In multiple cities in China, governments at the local level provide computing vouchers worth \$140,000–\$280,000 to subsidize AI start-ups.

Last, governments can reduce the uncertainty of the regulatory environment, especially around procuring AI solutions, by clarifying data regulations and fostering the adoption of interoperable standards to lower the barriers that prevent firms—and government agencies themselves—from moving to the cloud. Simplifying the public procurement process can also spur demand for compute from local firms.

Data centers: A requirement for frontier AI, not AI adoption

Data centers are concentrated in developed countries (refer to map 7.1). Local data centers can reduce time delays (latency),[51] create jobs, and catalyze domestic AI ecosystems.[52] But complementary factors need to be in place to realize the benefits, including an AI talent pool, a start-up ecosystem, and an affordable energy supply. Where these are absent, local computing risks becoming stranded infrastructure that is not used productively.

Governments can help build local computing capacity by attracting private investment. India has granted infrastructure status to data centers, opening up financing channels that were typically reserved for more traditional infrastructure such as roads and utilities.[53] Malaysia and Thailand have attracted hyperscaler investments through greater regulatory clarity and coherence.[54] Saudi Arabia, which is among the top 10 countries in terms of global private AI investment, combines tax incentives with special economic zones.[55] In fragile and conflict-affected situations, investment guarantees can support the establishment of infrastructure (refer to box 7.4).

Map 7.1 Data centers are concentrated in developed countries

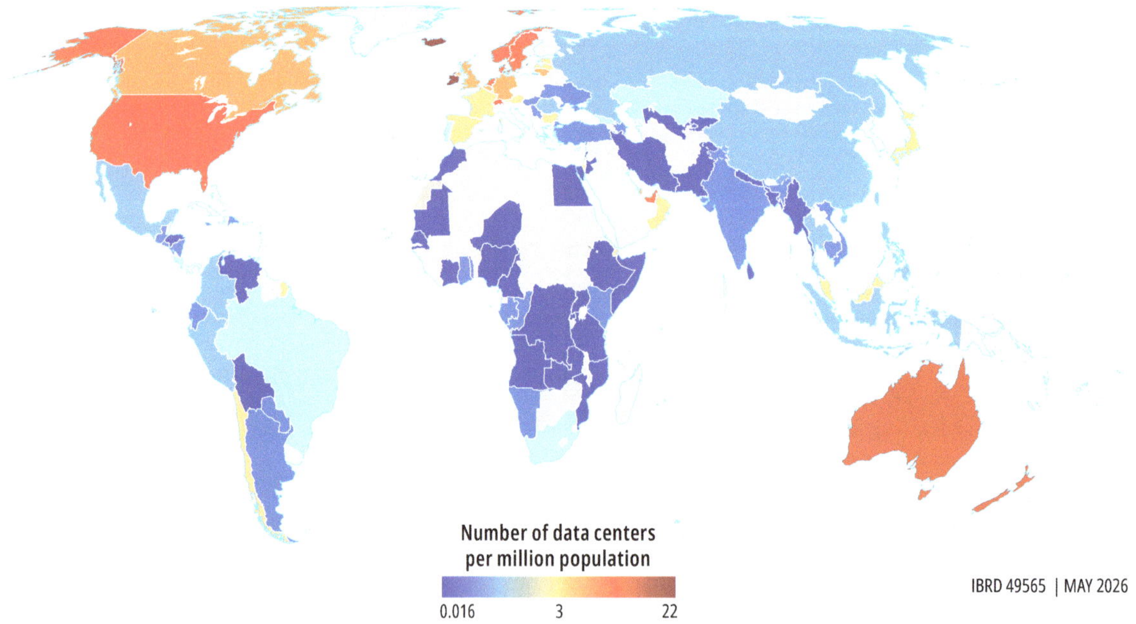

Source: Straub et al. 2026.

Note: The color gradient shows the number of data centers per one million inhabitants (with red indicating the highest concentration and dark blue showing the lowest concentration). Gray indicates countries with data not available. The data are from the latest year available at the time of publication.

Box 7.4 Investment guarantees and AI-related infrastructure in fragile and conflict-affected situations

Investments in infrastructure related to artificial intelligence (AI)—including data centers, broadband networks, and electricity generation—are particularly exposed to political risk because of their profile of large sunk costs, long horizons, and geographic concentration.[a] As such infrastructure has become increasingly concentrated and economically valuable, it has become a target in armed conflict—which adds another layer of political risk.

The Ukrainian government relocated core public sector data to overseas cloud providers in the first days of the invasion, as Russian missile and drone strikes caused recurring disruption to data centers, internet exchange points, and the electricity supply that sustained them.[b] In March 2026, Iranian drone strikes caused structural damage to hyperscale cloud facilities in the Gulf, prompting insurers, governments, and investors to reassess the gaps in standard infrastructure coverage that exclude coverage for losses caused by war, armed conflict, or related hostile acts.[c] In fragile and conflict-affected settings—precisely the markets where AI infrastructure investment is already most constrained—this emerging source of risk further narrows the conditions under which private capital can be mobilized and insured.[d]

A long-standing toolkit of noncommercial risk insurance and investment guarantees administered by multilateral institutions—designed precisely to absorb the risks that private insurers will not price and that sovereign guarantees alone cannot make bankable—can reduce the political risk of AI-related investments. War and civil disturbance accounted for 75 percent of multilateral political risk insurance issued in fragile and conflict-affected situations between 2010 and 2021.[e] In Ukraine, an unprecedented multilateral mobilization of political risk insurance—comprising insurance and guarantees from multilateral development banks, regional development banks, and national development finance institutions—enabled foreign direct investment to continue in an active conflict zone.[f]

Source: WDR 2026 team, based on Dahan et al. 2026.

a. Henisz (2000); Moran (2011); Wells and Ahmed (2007).
b. Bateman (2022); Smith (2022).
c. Harding (2026).
d. Aykut et al. (2026).
e. World Bank (2022).
f. Refer to Support for Ukraine's Reconstruction and Economy Trust Fund (web page), Multilateral Investment Guarantee Agency, World Bank Group, https://www.miga.org/support-ukraines-reconstruction-and-economy-trust-fund-sure-tf.

The benefits of local compute must also be weighed against its costs. Data centers can increase electricity, land, and housing prices; strain household and agricultural water consumption; and generate noise and e-waste[56] (for further details, refer to spotlight 4). Reliance on international providers can also challenge sovereignty, even when the infrastructure is installed locally. Therefore, governments need to conduct cost-benefit analyses to weigh these trade-offs.

Pooling compute across borders to make AI adaptation affordable

For smaller economies, regional approaches can expand access to compute by harmonizing rules on data governance, privacy, and cross-border flows to attract private investment. The African Union's Data Policy Framework and the ASEAN Framework on Cross-Border Cloud Computing in Southeast Asia—both of which introduce trusted data corridors where participating members adopt shared rules—are good examples of how regional cooperation can lower barriers to accessing compute.

When small countries cannot afford to build data center capacity, cross-border arrangements can also offer an alternative. One such model is data embassies—where countries store critical data abroad while retaining legal control. Estonia's data embassy, located in Luxembourg, enjoys the rights of a conventional embassy and serves as a backup for digital services and critical data sets.[57] Countries like Monaco and small island states in the Pacific have adopted similar setups. Such arrangements require strong governance, mutual trust, and clear agreements on sovereignty and cost sharing.[58]

Developing the skills that AI demands and keeping them current

When countries transition from adopting off-the-shelf AI tools to adapting them, the level of skills required increases significantly. Adapting AI tools requires professionals with highly specialized skills, such as data engineers, machine learning practitioners, cloud architects, and other specialists who understand both the technology and the industry it applies to. Unlike past digital tools that remained stable for years, AI capabilities are evolving rapidly. Ensuring that a country creates and sustains a capable workforce requires not only better training institutions but also systems designed for steady adaptation.

Training the workforce for AI-related technical skills

AI is reshaping the profiles of jobs more quickly than any academic program can keep up with. But higher education and technical and vocational education and training (TVET) programs, especially in developing countries, are typically not well aligned to the changing demands of the labor market.[59] The curriculums are often five to ten years out of date, the links between programs and industry are weak or nonexistent, and classroom instruction favors teaching theoretical concepts at the expense of hands-on learning.[60] Only 31 percent of universities in Africa offer dedicated AI programs.[61]

Three types of policies can help address the challenges faced by higher-education and TVET systems in the AI era. The first policy is strengthening the links between educational institutions and industry through apprenticeships and industry-led instruction so that training reflects the AI workflows that employers use.[62] The second policy is upgrading teaching capacity by upskilling faculty, incorporating blended learning combining classroom instruction and on-the-job experience, and adding open educational resources (materials that have been released into the public domain or are under a Creative Commons license). In Kenya, for example, faculty skilling programs have supported university curriculum reviews. More than 78,000 TVET learners have achieved "AI fluency" through bootcamps.[63] The third policy is to help adult learners upskill and reskill through recognition of prior learning, transferable credentials, and new financing mechanisms such as individual learning accounts.

Reforming formal institutions takes time. Private platforms often move faster than public providers in offering training that responds to labor market demands. For example, ALX South Africa—a technology training provider that equips young South Africans with high-demand technical and professional skills for the digital economy—has helped 85 percent of its graduates find employment after completing the program.[64] Although such platforms have a wide reach, they operate outside of formal qualification systems. Therefore, the challenge for public training systems is to move faster and expand the type of programs they offer, while ensuring that the credentials issued by private providers are recognized in the labor market and that they lead to career advancement.[65]

Supporting adult learning systems for workers as AI reshapes occupations

Upskilling and reskilling programs for employed workers need to be accessible, affordable, and flexible. Modular credentials (qualifications broken into small, stackable units, for example, a short certified course in a specific technical skill), such as those taking shape in Brazil, Estonia, and Mexico, allow workers to build relevant skills gradually and reenter formal training programs without starting over.[66] In Kenya, workforce transition initiatives combine different forms of learning for workers. Ajira Digital offers courses that are customized to workers in the informal sector and gig economy. Training-data company Sama combines training in digital skills with job referrals.[67] Microsoft's Mesh platform reaches more than one million Kenyan microentrepreneurs monthly with AI-focused learning opportunities.[68]

What workers learn is just as relevant as *how* they learn it. In the United States, workers who learn skills that can be transferred across jobs earn significantly more than workers who learn skills aimed at occupations that are AI-intensive.[69] Retraining initiatives should be designed around the capacity to learn and adapt as the landscape shifts, rather than around specialization.[70]

Public subsidies can be more effective in lowering the costs of reskilling when tied to skills in demand in the labor market. "Skill India" and Brazil's Serviço Nacional de Aprendizagem Industrial both link public financing to skills that are relevant to the industry and have achieved higher employment rates.[71] But expanding reskilling programs remains a challenge. High-income countries spend up to 0.35 percent of their GDP on labor market programs,[72] whereas upper-middle-income countries spend less than 0.10 percent, and the percentage is even lower in lower-middle-income countries.[73]

Focusing on firm-based training: Where most AI skills are actually built

Many skills relevant to AI are best learned on the job, where training corresponds to actual needs of the production process of firms. Employers remain the primary source of adult learning in most countries (refer to figure 7.4), and 74 percent of workers across Brazil, India, the United Kingdom, and the United States prefer to learn through their employers.[74] Because AI tools evolve quickly and their application varies across sectors, on-the-job training offers direct engagement with the specific AI tools that workers will actually use.

Sector-based models offer a practical complement to government programs. Brazil's Serviço Nacional de Aprendizagem Industrial codesigns curriculums with industry and enrolls 2.2 million students annually. In South Africa, sector education and training authorities, which are undergoing a reform process, are funded through levies on employers. In Morocco, industry federations develop sector-specific programs tied to emerging technologies, including AI.[75]

Governments can enhance firm-based training programs. Although large firms may voluntarily

Figure 7.4 Most midcareer training is funded by the employer or the learner personally

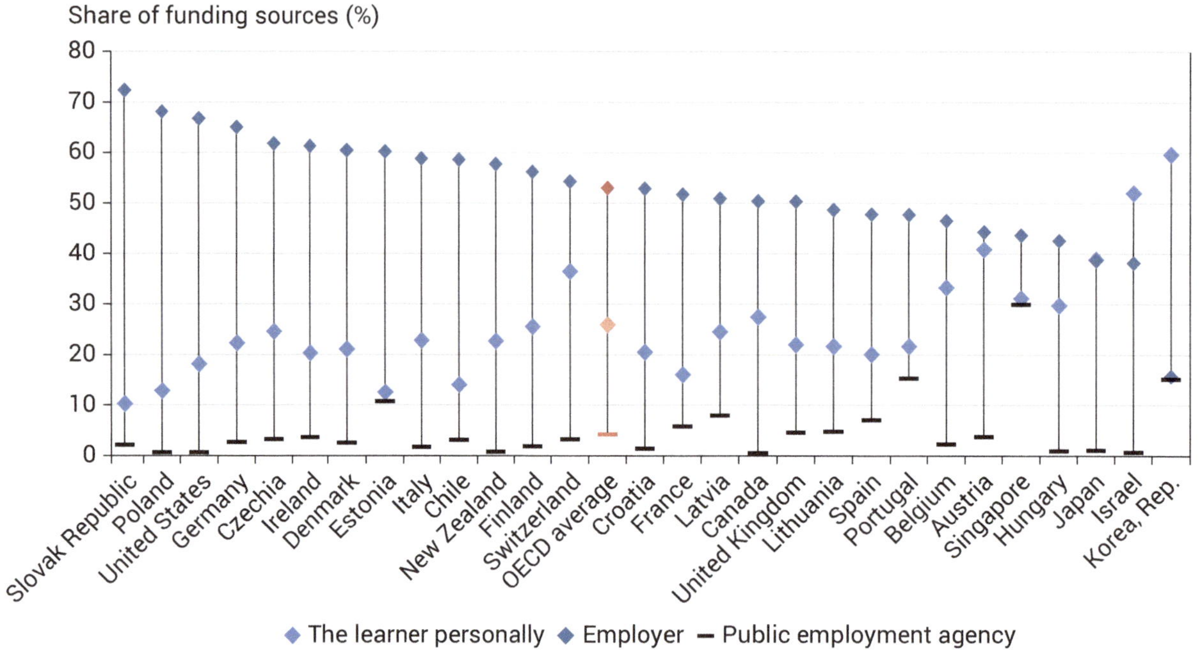

Source: OECD 2024.

Note: The figure shows the percentage of 35- to 44-year-olds whose training was funded by each type of sponsor. Financial support is defined as support that covers some or all of the expenses for learning, including tuition fees, course materials, travel, and accommodation. AI = artificial intelligence; OECD = Organisation for Economic Co-operation and Development.

train their employees, they tend to train them on capabilities that are specific to the firm rather than on capabilities that can be transferred across jobs. In economies with high turnover, firms underinvest in training for fear of losing their workers. Governments can mitigate this risk through tax credits, matching grants, and cofinancing instruments, especially for SMEs.

Providing information about needed skills: From employer surveys to labor market forecasts

Workers need information about which skills are worth investing in. Firms need to anticipate what type of skills they may need. Skills forecasting infrastructure offers guidance by combining information about the current and anticipated needs of employers, the availability of skills, and training outcomes.

High-income countries have already invested in this type of infrastructure. Denmark's system combines statistical forecasts of labor supply and demand, an assessment of productive sectors, employer surveys, and coordination across ministries and social partners into practical guidance for education providers and workers.[76] Middle-income countries are building similar capabilities. Colombia links vacancy data with opportunities for training by its Servicio Nacional de Aprendizaje. South Africa determines training priorities through sectoral skills plans developed by its Sector Education and Training Authorities—statutory bodies governed jointly by employers, unions, and government.[77] Low-income countries can start by conducting regular employer surveys, analyzing job postings, and collecting information on interactions between training providers and industry. Without such skills forecasting infrastructure, workers risk investing in skills that may already be outdated by the time they finish training.

Turning AI ideas into products: The innovation ecosystem

Building local AI capabilities, rather than simply consuming AI, requires firms that can transition from adopting AI to customizing and developing it. This, in turn, requires an ecosystem of financiers, researchers, incubators, and policy makers that support these firms.[78] This nexus is particularly important for AI because it is a technology that builds on other technologies. Governments can support this ecosystem by strengthening the inputs required for innovation, such as the capability of firms that are developing AI, their access to financing, the universities that produce talent and ideas, and the cross-border flows of people and investment that connect domestic ecosystems to global ones. Policies need to take into account that both existing firms (incumbents) and new entrants play important—but sometimes distinct—roles in driving innovation.

Fostering the innovation and entrepreneurship ecosystem that AI depends on

To foster innovation within existing firms and new firms, business development services, technology extension services, and financial support can help address gaps in information and coordination failures that limit firm-level investment in AI. Take-up of these programs is often low because firms undervalue advisory services, and the impacts can vary greatly, making targeting of beneficiaries difficult.[79] For AI, more specific instruments include credits that subsidize access to cloud-based technologies, programs to access data sets that allow firms to build on public or shared data, and regulatory sandboxes.

For new firms, incubators and accelerators, which offer mentoring and networking opportunities as well as technical assistance, can play an important role. For example, Start-Up Chile provides funding, coworking space, and entrepreneurial training to firms, and participating firms have been more likely to raise capital and recruit employees.[80]

The gap in financing is particularly acute. The process of developing AI is long and capital-intensive, and venture capital markets in low- and middle-income countries are weak, particularly for ventures that go beyond basic applications into more technical work. Public coinvestment, blended finance combining public and private monies, and partial credit guarantees can help firms operate for a longer period of time. Without an ongoing stream of capital, even start-ups that are technically capable may not be able to scale up.

In Korea, the AX-Sprint program provides financing to cover demonstration, scale-up production, and certification costs for AI products close to commercialization, and requires at least 30 percent private co-investment.[81] Selected products are then fast-tracked into public procurement processes.

Beyond financing, ecosystems require viable markets for producers to sell what they produce. Policy makers play a crucial convening role for the many actors involved—by linking start-ups to corporate buyers and international networks, and by being a buyer of services through procurement.

Bridging the gap between universities and firms

Universities educate the talent that firms hire, which in turn becomes the next generation of entrepreneurs.[82] Beyond talent, universities and firms exchange knowledge through sponsored research, spinoffs (whereby a company creates a separate, independent business entity from one of its existing divisions to enhance its strategic focus), licensing, and joint initiatives such as the MIT-IBM Watson AI Lab. These links help diffuse knowledge and increase the applicability of academic research, but the new endeavors can face challenges, such as differing time horizons, incentive structures, and unresolved questions about intellectual property when university contributions are publicly funded. Policies can help address these challenges through technology transfer offices (academic or commercial entities that facilitate intellectual property rights management and technology transfer), science and technology parks that act as a home for both knowledge institutions and firms, and collaboration grants.

A specific challenge for universities is retaining faculty because salaries in the private sector are typically higher. This gap is often even wider in low- and middle-income countries. The implications for entrepreneurship depend on where the departing faculty members go. If they leave the country, it is a clear loss to the domestic talent pool. However, if the departing faculty members move into the local private sector or fund their own companies, it can strengthen or deplete the local innovation base. Evidence from North America shows one aspect of this trade-off: students at universities where faculty members left for industry were less likely to set up AI businesses—probably because they had less access to the departing faculty member's specialized knowledge.[83] Industry increasingly attracts the top AI researchers; the top 1 percent of industry scientists who publish in academic journals now earn $1.5 million more annually than comparable academics, a fivefold increase since 2001.[84]

Supporting the flow of knowledge and capital across borders

Domestic innovation ecosystems do not develop in isolation. They draw on talent, capital, and ideas from other countries. Policies can either facilitate or impede those flows. Streamlined visa regimes for highly skilled workers can help increase the talent pool, particularly in AI engineering, machine learning operations, and sector-specific model development.[85] The United Arab Emirates offered long-term residency incentives for AI experts to strengthen the national AI ecosystem.[86] Leveraging diaspora networks offers a parallel channel. Citizens who have migrated to another country to pursue opportunities there can mentor domestic start-ups in their country of origin, invest in early-stage ventures, host distributed research collaborations, and, in some cases, return when domestic conditions improve.[87] India's information technology sector grew partly through links between citizens in Bangalore and Hyderabad and its diaspora.

Foreign direct investment can also help boost the domestic ecosystem. Multinational enterprises have played an important role in encouraging the adoption of technologies and best practices across subsidiaries[88] and can function as bridges between locations: successful piloting of an AI technology in one location of a multinational firm is often replicated in other locations.[89] Spillovers further extend the parent company's reach across borders through demonstration effects, market linkages, and labor mobility, allowing local firms to absorb practices first introduced by foreign entrants.

Using public procurement as a catalyst for AI markets

The viability of building AI solutions depends on the demand for such solutions. In most low- and middle-income countries, governments are among the largest purchasers of goods and services, making public procurement a powerful lever for the demand of AI solutions, including those delivered by local suppliers.

Opening government contracts to AI start-ups and smaller firms

Procurement systems in most developing countries are designed to purchase standardized goods from established vendors rather than innovative AI-enabled services delivered by small firms or new firms. They favor lowest-cost bidding, require lengthy approval processes, and impose minimum size, certification, or other compliance requirements that start-ups cannot easily meet. Reducing requirements and the size of contracts can help attract more small firms to bid for contracts. Smaller contract sizes can also facilitate piloting. Testing AI applications in public service delivery on a small scale, such as an AI diagnostic tool in a district health system or automated document processing in a tax office, can inform later procurement decisions on a larger scale.

Setting standards that shape the market

Public procurement also sets standards that can shape the wider market. When governments procure AI systems, they can establish requirements that increase competition, such as comprehensive documentation that supports third-party integration to avoid vendor lock-in or mechanisms for auditing bias and performance. They can also adopt clear policies on the reuse of data. Bidders must adhere to these criteria, raising the baseline expectations in the market and improving the bargaining position of domestic firms that seek comparable standards. Smaller economies can strengthen their position further through international coordination on shared procurement, technical standards, and unified positions in dealings with global vendors.

From buying AI to building AI markets: Treating procurement as ecosystem policy

Government procurement can also support the development of the local AI solution ecosystem, by lowering entry barriers for smaller and innovative firms to bid for contracts. The United Kingdom's GovTech Catalyst program invited firms to propose solutions to challenges that are specific to the public sector through challenge-based competitions, and provided development funding before full procurement (through precommercial procurement). India's Government e-Marketplace has reduced its minimum turnover and experience requirements to allow start-ups to compete for public contracts. Framework agreements that allow multiple providers to serve a sector can play a similar role, sustaining competition and decreasing the risk of being locked into a single vendor.

Sequencing AI policy for firms and workers: Not everything can happen at once

This chapter has outlined an extensive policy agenda to empower workers and firms to use AI as an input and build it as a product. No country can pursue all of these policies simultaneously. Countries need to decide which policies to pursue first. The answer depends on the current conditions and gaps, that is, where a country starts.

Treating AI policy for workers and firms as a coherent system, not a menu

The pathways of AI adoption, adaptation, and advancement establish a natural sequence. Within each pathway, the policy domains are tightly linked. They are not a menu from which governments choose their preferred items. Instead, their effectiveness depends on how they interact with one another.

At the adoption stage, an AI literacy program will be of little benefit if schools lack access to electricity and connectivity. Similarly, business environment reforms that enable the entry of new firms may fail if the workforce lacks the skills to use the tools that these new firms create. At the adaptation and advancement stages, a country that builds data centers without investing in the development of skills required from their employees, or that trains AI engineers without addressing the barriers to entry that prevent entrepreneurship, will see limited returns on either investment. The most effective strategies calibrate the combination of policies to whichever constraints are the most limiting.

Choosing what comes first at each stage: The priority matrix

Table 7.2 maps the policy priorities introduced across this chapter by the pathways of AI adoption, adaptation, and advancement, and by policy domain. Three features of the matrix are worth

Table 7.2 The AI policy matrix: Priorities for adoption, adaptation, and advancement of AI

	STAGE		
	Adopt	Adapt	Advance
FOUNDATIONS			
Infrastructure	• Low-cost electrification • Broadband and satellite connectivity • Priority access for schools and public hubs • Measures for accessing affordable devices	• Grid modernization and renewables • High-speed, low-latency infrastructure • Regional infrastructure agreements	• Large-scale clean power for AI • Ultra-low latency networks • Fiber-optic densification
Data	• Digitizing public records • Metadata standards • Foundational data governance	• Open-data collaboratives and commons • Grants and incentives for data sets • Data vouchers for SMEs • Language- and sector-specific data sets • Supplementing real data with synthetic data	• Mature data ecosystems • Frontier research data sets • International data infrastructure
Compute	*Not applicable*	• Cloud vouchers and bulk purchase • Regulatory clarity for adoption of cloud services and solutions • Shared high-performance computing • Regional approaches and data embassies • Targeted tax incentives	• Domestic data centers for frontier workloads • Competition policy to deal with concentration
ENVIRONMENT FOR FIRMS AND INNOVATIONS			
Business environment	• Streamlined registration and licensing • Legal frameworks targeted to start-ups • FDI and access to foreign exchange • Matchmaking platforms and facilitation	*Same as under adopt*	*Same as under adopt*

(Table continues next page)

Table 7.2 The AI policy matrix: Priorities for adoption, adaptation, and advancement of AI *(continued)*

	STAGE		
	Adopt	Adapt	Advance
Innovation ecosystem	*Not applicable*	• R & D grants and tax incentives • Improve R & D and innovation legal frameworks • Incubators and accelerators • University-industry linkages • Talent visa regimes • FDI for knowledge spillovers • Procurement reform to enable inclusion of local suppliers	• Frontier R & D consortiums • International research partnerships • Researcher mobility programs
WORKFORCE SKILLS			
Foundational skills	• Structured pedagogy and early childhood programs • Teacher training integrating AI • AI literacy across the curriculum • AI-powered learning with safeguards • Firm capability-building	• AI literacy for adult and informal workers • Continuous curriculum updating • Firm capability programs with peer learning	*Same as under adapt*
Advanced skills	*Not applicable*	• TVET and higher education reform • Lifelong reskilling for adaptability • Subsidized reskilling for vulnerable workers • Firm-based training with public incentives • Infrastructure to forecast needed skills	• AI-powered skills forecasting • Frontier AI research programs • Deep specialization in priority sectors

Source: WDR 2026 team.

Note: AI = artificial intelligence; FDI = foreign direct investment; R & D = research and development; SMEs = small and medium enterprises; TVET = technical and vocational education and training.

highlighting. First, many of the policy actions in the domains of infrastructure, business environment, and skills should be undertaken for the AI adoption stage. For most low- and lower-middle-income countries, these actions are not optional. They should comprise most of their effort in the short term to medium term.

Second, certain policy domains either (1) do not yet apply for that pathway or (2) involve the same instruments listed for a prior pathway rather than new ones. For example, reforming the business environment is concentrated in the adoption stage because the frictions it removes (registration, licensing, access to foreign direct investment, and matchmaking) are the same regardless of whether businesses are looking to adopt or adapt AI solutions. Policies for compute, advanced skills, and the innovation ecosystem are absent at the adoption stage because firms using prebuilt AI tools do not yet need local compute, AI engineers, or a frontier research and development ecosystem. These domains become critical only when countries transition from adopting AI to adapting or advancing it.

Third, policy priorities in countries traverse the pathways of AI adoption, adaptation, and advancement because of differences between types of firms and workers. For example, a country that is mainly in the adoption stage may still have firms or people (such as a national agricultural advisory service or a fintech cluster) that are already working at the adaptation stage.

Pursuing other agendas that AI policy depends on

Three other agendas not covered by this chapter could determine whether a country's policy recommendations succeed. First, the disruption in the labor market driven by AI adoption requires social protection and transition support to workers, including informal and self-employed workers, who are often the least able to absorb income shocks or finance retraining on their own (for further details, refer to spotlight 5). Second, governments themselves are among the largest users of AI for both public service delivery and public administration (for further details, including on redesigning procurement systems, refer to chapter 8). Third, the data governance frameworks examined in this chapter are based on a larger architecture—rules on data protection, algorithmic accountability, cross-border cooperation, and the governance of foundation models (for further details, refer to chapter 9).

Notes

1. Personal communication, Jorge Jimenez, May 2026.
2. Based on data of Enterprise Surveys (data portal), World Bank, https://www.enterprisesurveys.org/en/data.
3. World Bank (2025).
4. World Bank (2025).
5. Refer to Telecom (dashboard), Invest India, https://www.investindia.gov.in/sector/telecom; UNCTAD (2021).
6. Strusani and Houngbonon (2020).
7. Nicas (2024).
8. Klapper et al. (2025).
9. GDIP (2024).
10. Deloitte and GSMA (2011).
11. Gertler et al. (2025). By contrast, programs that subsidize the purchase of devices may not work without complementary investments in incentives for retention and user support. In Tanzania, distributing smartphones to women increased household consumption, but most women either sold their devices or lost them within the first year they owned them (Roessler et al. 2021).
12. Gu et al. (2021).
13. Many online AI platforms restrict the purchase of API tokens to users with a credit or debit card. In 2024, only 8.5 percent of the population in low-income countries (with suitable data) owned a debit card, and 1.8 percent owned a credit card (Klapper et al. 2025).
14. In the United States, businesses pay a tax of less than 5 percent on the purchase of automation equipment or software. In contrast, businesses have paid an average rate of 25 percent over the last four decades in payroll and federal income taxes on the hiring of workers for the same tasks (Acemoglu and Johnson 2023).
15. World Bank (2024b).

16. Ethiopia's recently adopted Startup Proclamation (No. 1396/2025) includes provisions that address this limitation, but, as of March 2026, the corresponding directives had not been issued.
17. Ali et al. (2025).
18. In many low- and middle-income countries, the failure of productive firms to expand is a major source of weak productivity growth overall (Cusolito and Maloney 2018; Restuccia and Rogerson 2017; Vostroknutova et al. 2025; World Bank 2024b).
19. Cirera et al. (2020).
20. Anderson and McKenzie (2021).
21. Heckman (2008).
22. World Bank et al. (2022).
23. Piper et al. (2018); Snilstveit et al. (2015).
24. Banerjee et al. (2016).
25. Heckman (2008).
26. *Adaptive learning* uses data analytics, computer algorithms, and AI to interact with learners and deliver customized resources and learning activities to address the unique needs of each learner.
27. Strömberg et al. (2026) present evidence from China illustrating this risk. They find that generative AI use among students in grades 7–12 was associated with higher scores on homework but lower performance on in-class exams, suggesting that AI may improve students' completion of assignments while weakening their acquisition of knowledge when it substitutes for student effort.
28. Burns et al. (2026).
29. Chetty et al. (2014); Rivkin et al. (2005).
30. UNESCO (2023).
31. UNESCO (2026).
32. UNESCO (2025).
33. Rwanda, Ministry of Education (2026).
34. World Bank (2025).
35. Otis et al. (2024).
36. Kim et al. (2026).
37. Pereira López et al. (2025).
38. McKenzie and Woodruff (2025).
39. Bloom et al. (2020); Iacovone et al. (2026).
40. World Bank (2025).
41. World Bank (2021).
42. For details on how governments can use this body of data more effectively for their own functioning, refer to chapter 8.
43. Wise et al. (2024).
44. Refer to NJDG (National Judicial Data Grid) (dashboard), District Court of India, E-Committee, Supreme Court of India, https://njdg.ecourts.gov.in/njdg_v3//?p=home; PIB (2026).
45. PIB (2022).
46. Refer to Common Voice (portal), Mozilla Foundation, https://commonvoice.mozilla.org/.
47. Mitra and Niakaros (2023).
48. World Bank (2024a).
49. Liu et al. (2024).
50. Muinde (2025); Mwigereri et al. (2025).
51. *Latency* is the time delay between a user action (sending a request) and the network's response. Lower latency provides a smoother, more responsive internet experience.
52. World Bank (2025).
53. MeitY (2020).
54. Fourteau (2025); Maverick Consulting Group (2026).
55. Vanderbilt (2026).
56. World Bank (2025).
57. Meyer (2022).
58. Sharwood (2024).
59. Cima et al. (2022); Criscuolo et al. (2021).
60. World Bank et al. (2023).
61. World Bank (2025).
62. Examples include recent reforms of the Servicio Nacional de Aprendizaje in Colombia, the TVET system in Rwanda, and the Office of Vocational Training and Employment Promotion in Morocco.
63. Microsoft (2025).
64. Another example is Zindi, a professional network and AI competition platform dedicated to data scientists and AI builders in Africa and emerging markets. Zindi has engaged more than 90,000 data scientists through hackathons (Mutandiro 2024).
65. This is especially important for informal and self-employed workers, who often lack both employer support and funding to undertake training on their own. For these workers, governments may need to subsidize participation in modular TVET and short-cycle programs.
66. OECD (2025a).
67. Atkin et al. (2021).
68. Microsoft (2025). Some examples in high-income countries include Singapore's SkillsFuture credits and France's Compte Personnel de Formation, which give workers control over short periods of training in skills relevant to current or future jobs.
69. Hyman et al. (2026).
70. New Organisation for Economic Co-operation and Development data provide a population-level measure of adaptability, covering adaptive problem solving in 30 countries. Defined as the ability to pursue goals in dynamic situations without an obvious solution method, adaptive problem solving is highly correlated with literacy and numeracy (Demombynes 2026).
71. Barría and Klasen (2016); MSDE (2024).
72. Public spending on labor market programs refers to government expenditure on policies aimed at supporting jobseekers and improving labor market outcomes. It includes spending on public employment services, training (classroom-based and on-the-job learning), employment incentives (such as hiring subsidies and job creation), and out-of-work income maintenance (such as unemployment benefits).
73. Public Spending on Labour Markets (graphic), Organisation for Economic Co-operation and Development, https://www.oecd.org/en/data/indicators/public-spending-on-labour-markets.html.
74. Pearson (2023).
75. CGEM (2025).

76. WEF (2017).
77. Refer to Government Gazette (1998); SENA (Servicio Nacional de Aprendizaje, National Learning Service, Colombia) (homepage), https://ape.sena.edu.co.
78. Cruz and Zhu (2023).
79. McKenzie and Sansone (2019).
80. Gonzalez-Uribe and Leatherbee (2018).
81. Smart City Korea (2026).
82. Akcigit et al. (2025).
83. Gofman and Jin (2024).
84. Akcigit et al. (2026).
85. Skilled workers also consider other factors while deciding whether to migrate, including the acceptance of foreign documents, the availability of English-language work environments, and the competitive treatment of stock options and taxes.
86. BusinessDubai (2026).
87. World Bank (2023).
88. Bloom et al. (2012).
89. Calvino et al. (2026).

References

Acemoglu, Daron, and Simon Johnson. 2023. *Power and Progress: Our Thousand-Year Struggle over Technology and Prosperity*. PublicAffairs. https://www.hachettebookgroup.com/titles/daron-acemoglu/power-and-progress/9781541702547/?lens=publicaffairs.

Agrawal, Ajay K., Joshua S. Gans, and Avi Goldfarb. 2019. "Economic Policy for Artificial Intelligence." *Innovation Policy and the Economy* 19 (January): 139–59. https://doi.org/10.1086/699935.

Akcigit, Ufuk, Craig A. Chikis, Emin Dinlersoz, and Nathan Goldschlag. 2026. "Attention (and Money) Is All You Need: Why Universities Are Struggling to Keep AI Talent." NBER Working Paper 34964 (March), National Bureau of Economic Research. https://www.nber.org/papers/w34964.

Akcigit, Ufuk, Jeremy G. Pearce, and Marta Prato. 2025. "Tapping into Talent: Coupling Education and Innovation Policies for Economic Growth." *Review of Economic Studies* 92 (2): 696–736. https://doi.org/10.1093/restud/rdae047.

Ali, Nadia, Massimiliano Cali, and Bob Rijkers. 2025. "Promoting Innovative Startups: Quasi-Experimental Evidence from Tunisia." *Journal of Development Economics* 177 (October): 103539. https://doi.org/10.1016/j.jdeveco.2025.103539.

Anderson, Stephen J., and David J. McKenzie. 2021. "What Prevents More Small Firms from Using Professional Business Services? An Information and Quality-Rating Experiment in Nigeria." Policy Research Working Paper 9614, World Bank. https://doi.org/10.1596/1813-9450-9614.

Angrist, Noam, Peter Bergman, and Moitshepi Matsheng. 2022. "Experimental Evidence on Learning Using Low-Tech When School Is Out." *Nature Human Behaviour* 6 (7): 941–50.

Athey, Susan Carleton, and Fiona Scott Morton. 2025. "Artificial Intelligence, Competition, and Welfare." NBER Working Paper 34444 (November), National Bureau of Economic Research. https://www.nber.org/papers/w34444.

Atkin, David Guy, Antoinette Schoar, and Kiara Wahnschafft. 2021. "Evaluating Sama's Training and Job Programs in Nairobi, Kenya." Research paper, May 7, Abdul Latif Jameel Poverty Action Lab, Massachusetts Institute of Technology. https://www.povertyactionlab.org/media/file-research-paper/evaluating-samas-training-and-job-programs-nairobi-kenya.

Aykut, Dilek, Selcuk Ozyurt, K. Jung, and Estefania Vergara Cobos. 2026. "Data Center and AI Investment in EMDEs: Risks and Opportunities." DEC Private Markets–IFC, Infrastructure, Chief Economist Office, World Bank.

Banerjee, Abhijit Vinayak, Rukmini Banerji, James Berry, et al. 2016. "Mainstreaming an Effective Intervention: Evidence from Randomized Evaluations of 'Teaching at the Right Level' in India." NBER Working Paper 22746 (October), National Bureau of Economic Research. https://doi.org/10.3386/w22746.

Barría, Carlos Villalobos, and Stephan Klasen. 2016. "The Impact of SENAI's Vocational Training Program on Employment, Wages, and Mobility in Brazil: Lessons for Sub Saharan Africa?" *Quarterly Review of Economics and Finance* 62 (November): 74-96. https://doi.org/10.1016/j.qref.2016.07.010.

Bateman, Jon. 2022. "Russia's Wartime Cyber Operations in Ukraine: Military Impacts, Influences, and Implications." Working Paper, December, Cyber Conflict in the Russia-Ukraine War Series, Carnegie Endowment for International Peace. https://carnegieendowment.org/research/2022/12/russias-wartime-cyber-operations-in-ukraine-military-impacts-influences-and-implications.

Bloom, Nicholas, Aprajit Mahajan, David J. McKenzie, and John Roberts. 2020. "Do Management Interventions Last? Evidence from India." *American Economic Journal: Applied Economics* 12 (2): 198–219. https://doi.org/10.1257/app.20180369.

Bloom, Nicholas, Raffaella Sadun, and John Michael Van Reenen. 2012. "Americans Do IT Better: US Multinationals and the Productivity Miracle." *American Economic Review* 102 (1): 167–201. https://www.aeaweb.org/articles?id=10.1257/aer.102.1.167.

Buolamwini, Joy, and Timnit Gebru. 2018. "Gender Shades: Intersectional Accuracy Disparities in Commercial Gender Classification." *Proceedings of Machine Learning Research* 81: 1–15. 2018 Conference on Fairness, Accountability, and Transparency.

Burns, Mary, Rebecca Winthrop, Natasha Luther, Emma Venetis, and Rida Karim. 2026. "A New Direction for Students in an AI World: Prosper, Prepare, Protect." Report (January), Center for Universal Education, Brookings Institution. https://www.brookings.edu/articles/a-new-direction-for-students-in-an-ai-world-prosper-prepare-protect/.

BusinessDubai. 2026. "AI Specialist Visa UAE: New 3-Year Renewable Category 2026." *BusinessDubai* (blog), June 1. https://www.businessdubai.ae/blogs/ai-specialist-visa-uae.
Calvino, Flavio, Chiara Criscuolo, Timothy DeStefano, Jonathan Timmis, and Antonio Ughi. 2026. "AI Diffusion Within Multinationals." Paper presented at the World Bank–Georgetown University Zoom conference, Making AI Work: What Firms and Workers Need, January 26. https://thedocs.worldbank.org/en/doc/84a308f46cca26eb8dadaf4f6fccdb06-0070062026/original/8-Criscuolo.pdf.
CGEM (General Confederation of Moroccan Enterprises). 2025. "Launch of the AI Xcelerate Morocco Program." *Activities* (blog), December 9. https://cgem.ma/en/activites/launch-of-the-ai-xcelerate-morocco-program/.
Chetty, Raj, John N. Friedman, and Jonah E. Rockoff. 2014. "Measuring the Impacts of Teachers II: Teacher Value-Added and Student Outcomes in Adulthood." *American Economic Review* 104 (9): 2633–79. https://doi.org/10.1257/aer.104.9.2633.
Cima, Joana Ferreira, Ana Catarina Pimenta, Miguel Portela, and Marta Silva. 2022. "Workforce Skills and Firm Productivity." *Banco de Portugal Economic Studies* 8 (1): 77–99. https://www.bportugal.pt/sites/default/files/anexos/papers/re202204_en.pdf.
Cirera, Xavier, Marcio Jose Vargas Da Cruz, Elwyn Adriaan Robin Davies, et al. 2020. "Policies to Support Businesses Through the COVID-19 Shock: A Firm-Level Perspective." Policy Research Working Paper 9506, World Bank. https://documents1.worldbank.org/curated/en/188461610547807479/pdf/Policies-to-Support-Businesses-through-the-COVID-19-Shock-A-Firm-Level-Perspective.pdf.
Cranney, Katelyn, Solène Delecourt, and Rembrand Koning. 2026. "Global Evidence on Gender Gaps and Generative AI Over Time." Working Paper 25-023, Harvard Business School, Harvard University. htpps:/www.hbs.edu/ris/Publication%20Files/25-023_be8fb517-3dd5-40aa-97f9-4e42e1c8e6ff.pdf.
Criscuolo, Chiara, Peter N. Gal, Timo Leidecker, and Giuseppe Nicoletti. 2021. "The Human Side of Productivity: Uncovering the Role of Skills and Diversity for Firm Productivity." OECD Productivity Working Paper 29 (December), Organisation for Economic Co-operation and Development. https://doi.org/10.1787/5f391ba9-en.
Cruz, Marcio, and Tingting Juni Zhu. 2023. *Developing Entrepreneurial Ecosystems for Digital Businesses and Beyond: A Diagnostic Toolkit*. International Development in Practice Series. World Bank. https://openknowledge.worldbank.org/server/api/core/bitstreams/343b62c3-f6b5-4000-a1e4-5c973f97a235/content.
Cusolito, Ana Paula, and William F. Maloney. 2018. *Productivity Revisited: Shifting Paradigms in Analysis and Policy*. World Bank. https://doi.org/10.1596/978-1-4648-1334-4.
Dahan, Mariana, Junaid K. Ahmad, and David Savage. 2026. "De-Risking the Digital Foundations of AI." Background paper prepared for *World Development Report 2026: The Promise of Artificial Intelligence*, World Bank. https://www.worldbank.org/en/publication/wdr2026/brief/world-development-report-2026-background-papers.
Davies, Elwyn, David Francis, Filip Jolevski, Gaurav Nayyar, Katherine Stapleton, and Shu Yu. 2026. "Adopting Fast and Slow: Cross-Country Evidence on Business Adoption of AI." Background paper prepared for *World Development Report 2026: The Promise of Artificial Intelligence*, World Bank. https://www.worldbank.org/en/publication/wdr2026/brief/world-development-report-2026-background-papers.
Deloitte and GSMA. 2011. "Mobile Telephony and Taxation in Kenya." Deloitte LLP and GSMA. https://www.gsma.com/solutions-and-impact/connectivity-for-good/public-policy/wp-content/uploads/2012/03/mobiletelephoneandtaxationinkenya.pdf.
Demombynes, Gabriel. 2026. "How Can We Equip People to Ride the AI Wave." *Protect and Invest in People* (blog), June 11. https://blogs.worldbank.org/en/investinpeople/how-can-we-equip-people-to-ride-the-ai-wave.
European Union. 2022. European Union Regulation (EU) 2022/1925 of the European Parliament and of the Council of 14 September 2022 on contestable and fair markets in the digital sector (Digital Markets Act), *Official Journal of the European Union*, L 265, October 12, 2022, 1–66, europa.eu.
Fourteau, Tim. 2025. "What Is Propelling Malaysia's Data Centre Boom?" *Insights* (blog), October 17. https://www.whitecase.com/insight-our-thinking/what-propelling-malaysias-data-centre-boom.
GDIP (Global Digital Inclusion Partnership). 2024. "The Price of the World in Your Pocket: A Price Only Some Can Afford, 2024 Device Pricing." September, GDIP. https://globaldigitalinclusion.org/wp-content/uploads/2024/09/GDIP-The-price-of-the-world-in-your-pocket-a-price-only-some-can-afford.pdf.
Gertler, Paul J., Brett Green, Renping Li, and David Sraer. 2025. "The Welfare Benefits of Pay-As-You-Go Financing." NBER Working Paper 33484 (February), National Bureau of Economic Research. https://www.nber.org/papers/w33484.
Gofman, Michael, and Zhao Jin. 2024. "Artificial Intelligence, Education, and Entrepreneurship." *Journal of Finance* 79 (1): 631–67. https://doi.org/10.1111/jofi.13302.
Gonzalez-Uribe, Juanita, and Michael Leatherbee. 2018. "The Effects of Business Accelerators on Venture Performance: Evidence from Start-Up Chile." *Review of Financial Studies* 31 (4): 1566–1603. https://doi.org/10.1093/rfs/hhx103.
Government Gazette, South Africa. 1998. "Skills Development Act, Act No. 97, of 1998." *Government Gazette* 401 (19420), November 2. https://www.gov.za/sites/default/files/gcis_document/201409/a97-98.pdf.
GSMA. 2026. *The Mobile Gender Gap Report 2026*. GSMA.
Gu, Yunfan, Gaurav Nayyar, and Siddharth Sharma. 2021. "Gearing Up for the Future of Manufacturing in Bangladesh." World Bank. https://doi.org/10.1596/35879.
Harding, Emily. 2026. "Data Is Now the Front Line of Warfare." *Commentary* (blog), March 19. https://www.csis.org/analysis/data-now-front-line-warfare.

Heckman, James J. 2008. "Schools, Skills, and Synapses." *Economic Inquiry* 46 (3): 289–324. https://doi.org/10.1111/j.1465-7295.2008.00163.x.
Henisz, Witold J. 2000. "The Institutional Environment for Multinational Investment." *Journal of Law, Economics, and Organization* 16 (2): 334–64. https://doi.org/10.1093/jleo/16.2.334.
Hyman, Benjamin Gabriel, Benjamin Lahey, Karen Ni, and Laura Pilossoph. 2026. "How Retrainable Are AI-Exposed Workers?" NBER Working Paper 34174, rev. (May), National Bureau of Economic Research. https://www.nber.org/papers/w34174.
Iacovone, Leonardo, David J. McKenzie, and William F. Maloney. 2026. "Group Consulting Continues to Benefit Firms After a Decade: Experimental Evidence from Colombian Auto Parts Firms." Policy Research Working Paper 11278, World Bank. https://doi.org/10.1596/1813-9450-11278.
ILO (International Labour Organization). 2026. *Gen AI, Occupational Segregation and Gender Equality in the World of Work*. Research Brief. ILO. doi: https://doi.org/10.54394/00033798.
Imam, Sukairaj Hafiz, Babangida Sani, Dawit Ketema Gete, et al. 2025. "Automatic Speech Recognition for African Low-Resource Languages: Challenges and Future Directions." In *Proceedings of the Sixth Workshop on African Natural Language Processing (AfricaNLP 2025)*, edited by Constantine Lignos, Idris Abdulmumin, and David Adelani. Association for Computational Linguistics. https://aclanthology.org/2025.africanlp-1.13.pdf.
Jones, Emily. 2023. "Digital Disruption: Artificial Intelligence and International Trade Policy." *Oxford Review of Economic Policy* 39 (1): 70–84. https://doi.org/10.1093/oxrep/grac049.
Kelley, Stephanie, Anton Ovchinnikov, David R. Hardoon, and Adrienne Heinrich. 2022. "Antidiscrimination Laws, Artificial Intelligence, and Gender Bias: A Case Study in Nonmortgage Fintech Lending." *Manufacturing & Service Operations Management* 24 (6): 3039–59.
Kim, Hyunjin, Dahyeon Kim, and Rembrand Koning. 2026. "Mapping AI into Production: A Field Experiment on Firm Performance." INSEAD Working Paper 2026/20/STR (March 30), INSEAD. https://doi.org/10.2139/ssrn.6513481.
Klapper, Leora F., Dorothe Singer, Laura Starita, and Alexandra Norris. 2025. *The Global Findex Database 2025: Connectivity and Financial Inclusion in the Digital Economy*. World Bank. http://hdl.handle.net/10986/43438.
Liu, Ruibo, Jerry Wei, Fangyu Liu, et al. 2024. "Best Practices and Lessons Learned on Synthetic Data." *arXiv:2404.07503v2 [cs.CL]*, August 10, Cornell University. https://doi.org/10.48550/arXiv.2404.07503.
Maverick Consulting Group. 2026. "Thailand's Data Centre Moment in a Shifting Global Landscape." *Insights* (blog), March 22. https://www.mcg-asia.com/featured-insights//thailand-data-centre-investment-geopolitical-risk.
McKenzie, David J., and Dario Sansone. 2019. "Predicting Entrepreneurial Success Is Hard: Evidence from a Business Plan Competition in Nigeria." *Journal of Development Economics* 141 (November): 102369. https://doi.org/10.1016/j.jdeveco.2019.07.002.
McKenzie, David J., and Christopher M. Woodruff. 2025. *Training Entrepreneurs* 1 (4). https://voxdev.org/voxdevlit/training-entrepreneurs.
MeitY (Ministry of Electronics and Information Technology, India). 2020. "Draft for Discussion: Data Center Policy 2020." e-Governance Division, MeitY. https://www.nitiforstates.gov.in/public-assets/Policy/policy_files/PNC510C000384.pdf.
Meyer, Thiébaut. 2022. "Data Embassies: Strengthening Resiliency with Sovereignty." *Security and Identity* (blog), November 11. https://cloud.google.com/blog/products/identity-security/data-embassies-strengthening-resiliency-with-sovereignty.
Microsoft. 2025. "Tapping into Africa's 230-Million AI-Powered Jobs Opportunity." *Source EMEA* (blog), October 21. https://news.microsoft.com/source/emea/features/tapping-into-africas-230-million-ai-powered-jobs-opportunity/.
Mitra, Alessio, and Konstantinos Niakaros. 2023. "The Horizon Effect: A Counterfactual Analysis of EU Research and Innovation Grants." Working Paper 2023/08, R&I Paper Series, Directorate-General for Research and Innovation, European Commission. https://data.europa.eu/doi/10.2777/584781.
Moran, Theodore Harvey. 2011. *Foreign Direct Investment and Development: Launching a Second Generation of Policy Research*. Peterson Institute for International Economics. https://www.piie.com/bookstore/foreign-direct-investment-and-development-launching-second-generation-policy-research.
MSDE (Ministry of Skill Development and Entrepreneurship, India). 2024. *Annual Report 2023–2024*. MSDE. https://www.msde.gov.in/static/uploads/2024/11/4f71465f72e9f90ff079f76ca2e374a9.pdf.
Muinde, Ezra. 2025. "Synthetic Data: What It Means for Africa." *Medium* (blog), January 8. https://medium.com/@ezra.muinde/synthetic-data-what-it-means-for-africa-1802d7cedcd3.
Mutandiro, Kimberly. 2024. "African Universities Are Failing to Prepare Tech Graduates for Jobs in AI." *Rest of World* (blog), April 29. https://restofworld.org/2024/ai-skills-training-africa/.
Mwigereri, Dorcas G., Nigel T. Kamotho, Akbar K. Waljee, et al. 2025. "Synthetic Data Generation of Health and Demographic Surveillance Systems Data: A Case Study in a Low- and Middle-Income Country." *JAMIA Open* 8 (6): ooaf137. https://doi.org/10.1093/jamiaopen/ooaf137.
Nicas, Jack. 2024. "The Internet's Final Frontier: Remote Amazon Tribes." *New York Times*, June 2. https://www.nytimes.com/2024/06/02/world/americas/starlink-internet-elon-musk-brazil-amazon.html.
OECD (Organisation for Economic Co-operation and Development). 2024. *Do Adults Have the Skills They Need to Thrive in a Changing World? Survey of Adult Skills 2023*. OECD Skills Studies Series. OECD. https://doi.org/10.1787/b263dc5d-en.
OECD (Organisation for Economic Co-operation and Development). 2025a. *Education Policy Outlook 2025: Nurturing Engaged and Resilient Lifelong Learners in*

a World of Digital Transformation. OECD. https://doi.org/10.1787/c3f402ba-en.

OECD (Organisation for Economic Co-operation and Development). 2025b. *Results from TALIS 2024: The State of Teaching*. December. OECD. https://www.oecd.org/content/dam/oecd/en/publications/reports/2025/10/results-from-talis-2024_28fbde1d/90df6235-en.pdf.

Otis, Nicholas G., Rowan Clarke, Solène Delecourt, David Holtz, and Rembrand Koning. 2024. "The Uneven Impact of Generative AI on Entrepreneurial Performance: Evidence from a Field Experiment in Kenya." Working Paper 24-042, Harvard Business School, Harvard University. https://www.hbs.edu/ris/Publication%20Files/24-042_567db548-5b24-4182-b703-9d5ef1328043.pdf.

Pearson. 2023. "Pearson Skills Outlook Shows Employees are Preparing for a Tech Focused World by Sharpening Their Human Skills." *News* (blog), April 20. https://plc.pearson.com/en-GB/news-and-insights/news/pearson-skills-outlook-shows-employees-are-preparing-tech-focused-world.

Pereira López, Mariana De La Paz, Stephen J. Anderson, Leonardo Iacovone, Andreas Menzel, Florian Anselm Münch, and Rahul Suhag. 2025. *Creating Ecosystems for Innovation in a Post-Coal Region: Evidence from an RCT in the Czech Republic*. Strengthening Monitoring and Evaluation of Innovation Programs in the EU Series, June 18. World Bank. https://documents1.worldbank.org/curated/en/099062725130041014/pdf/P171223-48a49632-7dc2-41ab-8161-8c1e8e4f67c1.pdf.

Phumpiu Chang, Paul Fernando, Jan Orlowski, and Yauheni Rahetsen. 2026. "Competition in AI Markets." Background paper prepared for *World Development Report 2026: The Promise of Artificial Intelligence*, World Bank. https://www.worldbank.org/en/publication/wdr2026/brief/world-development-report-2026-background-papers.

PIB (Press Information Bureau, India). 2022. "Bhashini: National Language Translation Mission." FactSheet RU-39-02-0167-260822, August 26. https://static.pib.gov.in/WriteReadData/specificdocs/documents/2022/aug/doc202282696201.pdf.

PIB (Press Information Bureau, India). 2026. "E-Courts Mission Mode Project." Press Release, March 12. https://www.pib.gov.in/PressReleasePage.aspx?PRID=2238787&reg=48&lang=2.

Piper, Benjamin, Stephanie Simmons Zuilkowski, Margaret Dubeck, Evelyn Jepkemei, and Simon J. King. 2018. "Identifying the Essential Ingredients to Literacy and Numeracy Improvement: Teacher Professional Development and Coaching, Student Textbooks, and Structured Teachers' Guides." *World Development* 106 (June): 324–36. https://doi.org/10.1016/j.worlddev.2018.01.018.

Raji, Inioluwa Deborah, and Joy Buolamwini. 2019. "Actionable Auditing: Investigating the Impact of Publicly Naming Biased Performance Results of Commercial AI Products." In *Proceedings of the 2019 AAAI/ACM Conference on AI, Ethics, and Society*, 429–35. ACM.

Restuccia, Diego, and Richard Rogerson. 2017. "The Causes and Costs of Misallocation." *Journal of Economic Perspectives* 31 (3): 151–74. https://doi.org/10.1257/jep.31.3.151.

Rivkin, Steven G., Eric Alan Hanushek, and John F. Kain. 2005. "Teachers, Schools, and Academic Achievement." *Econometrica* 73 (2): 417–58. https://onlinelibrary.wiley.com/doi/abs/10.1111/j.1468-0262.2005.00584.x.

Roessler, Philip, Peter Carroll, Flora Myamba, Cornel Jahari, Blandina Kilama, and Daniel Nielson. 2021. "The Economic Impact of Mobile Phone Ownership: Results from a Randomized Controlled Trial in Tanzania." CSAE Working Paper WPS/2021-05 (April 9), Centre for the Study of African Economies, Department of Economics, University of Oxford. https://ora.ox.ac.uk/objects/uuid:2877ad95-64e5-4309-bbd5-40f862f62187/files/skh04dq40v.

Rwanda, Ministry of Education. 2026. "Rwanda Achieves Major AI Education Milestone: First Round of National Day of AI Training Reaches 5,000 Teachers." February 11.https://www.mineduc.gov.rw/news-detail/in-rwanda-first-round-of-national-day-of-ai-training-reaches-5000-teachers.

Sharwood, Simon. 2024. "'Data Embassies' Promise Bubbles of Digital Sovereignty, but India Just Cooled on the Idea." *Public Sector* (blog), July 24. https://www.theregister.com/2024/07/24/data_embassies/.

Smart City Korea. 2026. "7,540 Billion Won in Support for Development of 246 AI Application Products ... AX-Sprint Launched in Full Swing." March 18, Smart City Korea. https://smartcity.go.kr/en/2026/03/18/246%EA%B0%9C-ai-%EC%9D%91%EC%9A%A9%EC%A0%9C%ED%92%88-%EA%B0%9C%EB%B0%9C%EC%97%90-7540%EC%96%B5%EC%9B%90-%EC%A7%80%EC%9B%90-ax-sprint%EC%A0%84%EB%A0%A5%EC%A7%88%EC%A3%BC-%EB%B3%B8%EA%B2%A9/.

Smith, Brad. 2022. "Defending Ukraine: Early Lessons from the Cyber War." *Microsoft On the Issues* (blog), June 22. https://blogs.microsoft.com/on-the-issues/2022/06/22/defending-ukraine-early-lessons-from-the-cyber-war/.

Smith, Genevieve, and Ishita Rustagi. 2021. "When Good Algorithms Go Sexist: Why and How to Advance AI Gender Equity." *Stanford Social Innovation Review*, March 31.

Snilstveit, Birte, Jennifer Stevenson, Daniel Phillips, et al. 2015. *The Impact of Education Programmes on Learning and School Participation in Low- and Middle-Income Countries: A Systematic Review*. 3ie Systematic Review 24 (December). International Initiative for Impact Evaluation. https://www.3ieimpact.org/sites/default/files/2019-05/SR24-education-review_2.pdf.

Straub, Stéphane, He He, Yue Li, et al. 2026. *Infrastructure Foundations: From Current Assets to Future Growth*. Sustainable Infrastructure Series. World Bank. https://openknowledge.worldbank.org/server/api/core/bitstreams/064573b1-0bff-4594-b756-ef76eba1ad06/content.

Strömberg, David, Victor Lei, and Yanhui Wu. 2026. "The Generative AI Learning Penalty: Evidence from Chinese Secondary Education." CEPR Discussion Paper DP21577 (June 2), Center for Economic Policy Research. https://cepr.org/publications/dp21577.

Strusani, Davide, and Georges Vivien Houngbonon. 2020. "Accelerating Digital Connectivity Through Infrastructure Sharing." EM Compass Note 79 (February), International Finance Corporation. https://doi.org/10.1596/33616.

UNCTAD (United Nations Trade and Development). 2021. "India: 100% Foreign Participation in the Telecoms Sector Now Allowed via the Automatic Route." *Investment Policy Monitor* (blog), October 6. https://investmentpolicy.unctad.org/investment-policy-monitor/measures/3746/india-100-foreign-participation-in-the-telecoms-sector-now-allowed-via-the-automatic-route.

UNESCO (United Nations Educational, Scientific and Cultural Organization). 2023. "Guidance for Generative AI in Education and Research." Global Education 2030 Agenda, UNESCO. https://unesdoc.unesco.org/ark:/48223/pf0000386693.

UNESCO (United Nations Educational, Scientific and Cultural Organization). 2025. "National Educators Competency Framework and AI-Enabled Assessment Initiative in the UAE: Good Practice in Using Evidence for Education Policy and Practice." UNESCO. https://media.unesco.org/sites/default/files/webform/ed3002/9-ministry-of-education-professional-development-sector-uae.pdf.

UNESCO (United Nations Educational, Scientific and Cultural Organization). 2026. "UNESCO-CODEMAO 'Youth Coding Initiative.'" Updated, April 7, UNESCO. https://www.unesco.org/en/articles/unesco-codemao-youth-coding-initiative.

UN Women. 2026. "AI Is Already Rewriting Reality for Billions of People. It Is Getting Women Wrong." Media advisory, June 22. UN Women.

Vanderbilt, Donovan. 2026. "Cloud and Data Center Investment." *Investment* (blog), April 18. https://vision2030.ai/investment/guides/cloud-data-center/.

Vostroknutova, Ekaterina, James Robert Sampi, Charl Jooste, and Jorge Thompson Araujo. 2025. *Competition and Productivity Growth in Latin America and the Caribbean*. World Bank. https://doi.org/10.1596/978-1-4648-2081-6.

WEF (World Economic Forum). 2017. "Accelerating Workforce Reskilling for the Fourth Industrial Revolution: An Agenda for Leaders to Shape the Future of Education, Gender and Work." White Paper, July, WEF. https://www.weforum.org/publications/accelerating-workforce-reskilling-for-the-fourth-industrial-revolution/.

Wells, Louis T., and Rafiq Ahmed. 2007. *Making Foreign Investment Safe: Property Rights and National Sovereignty*. Oxford University Press. https://global.oup.com/academic/product/making-foreign-investment-safe-9780195310627.

Wise, Oliver, Sallie Ann Keller, and Victoria Houed. 2024. "Preparing Open Data for the Age of AI." *News* (blog), January 18. https://www.commerce.gov/news/blog/2024/01/preparing-open-data-age-ai.

World Bank. 2021. *World Development Report 2021: Data for Better Lives.* World Bank. https://wdr2021.worldbank.org.

World Bank. 2022. *The International Finance Corporation's and Multilateral Investment Guarantee Agency's Support for Private Investment in Fragile and Conflict-Affected Situations, Fiscal Years 2010–21: An Independent Evaluation*. World Bank. https://ieg.worldbankgroup.org/sites/default/files/Data/Evaluation/files/IFC_MIGA_FCS.pdf.

World Bank. 2023. *World Development Report 2023: Migrants, Refugees, and Societies.* World Bank. https://www.worldbank.org/en/publication/wdr2023.

World Bank. 2024a. "Data Vouchers: Korea Case Study for Revitalizing the Data Ecosystem." Korea Office Innovation and Technology Note Series 12 (June), World Bank. https://documents1.worldbank.org/curated/en/099624206122421867/pdf/IDU-23deed99-62a0-45c6-98fe-bcf6de4d5868.pdf.

World Bank. 2024b. *World Development Report 2024: The Middle-Income Trap.* World Bank. https://www.worldbank.org/en/publication/wdr2024.

World Bank. 2025. *Digital Progress and Trends Report 2025: Strengthening AI Foundations*. World Bank. https://openknowledge.worldbank.org/server/api/core/bitstreams/f2509a0f-7153-4f32-b180-bc11e90c4940/content.

World Bank, UNESCO (United Nations Educational, Scientific and Cultural Organization), and ILO (International Labour Organization). 2023. *Building Better Formal TVET Systems: Principles and Practice in Low- and Middle-Income Countries*. World Bank; UNESCO; ILO. https://documents.worldbank.org/en/publication/documents-reports/documentdetail/099071123130516870.

World Bank, UNESCO (United Nations Educational, Scientific and Cultural Organization), UNICEF (United Nations Children's Fund), FCDO (Foreign, Commonwealth, and Development Office, UK), USAID (United States Agency for International Development), and BMGF (Bill and Melinda Gates Foundation). 2022. "The State of Global Learning Poverty: 2022 Update." Conference Edition, June 23, World Bank. https://thedocs.worldbank.org/en/doc/34035a49acb5700ce8b118aeda81a5cb-0510022023/original/TheStateOfLearningPoverty-Feb2023Update-03-08-23.pdf.

5 Spotlight 5

Upgrading Social Safety Nets as AI Transforms the Nature of Work

Disruptions driven by artificial intelligence (AI) will not affect all workers and firms equally. Workers and firms that are highly exposed to AI but lack the capacity to use it well account for about 10 percent of employment in low- and middle-income countries, comprising about 43 million workers concentrated in the business and professional services sector, the retail sector, and the customer and legal services sectors (refer to chapter 4).[1] AI has had and will likely continue to have the greatest negative effects on employment among workers who have fewer skills that can be transferred to other jobs and a weaker ability to adapt.[2]

The existing social safety nets, such as unemployment benefits, pensions, and health care benefits, for these types of workers were adopted under a different labor market structure. Most social protection systems in low- and middle-income countries are targeted toward stable employment in the formal sector, an employment category that covers a minority of the workforce in these countries. Three out of four people in low-income countries receive no social protection benefits if they lose their job, and 1.6 billion workers across low- and middle-income countries are not covered under any social protection scheme. For another 400 million workers, the benefits they receive after losing their jobs are too small to help lift them out of poverty or mitigate the shocks caused by job loss.[3] Although this mismatch between benefits and needs precedes AI's emergence, AI has made the effects more pronounced. As jobs become more fragmented and task based and rely increasingly on technology-based platforms, systems that tie benefits to a single employer and assume that career paths will be predictable will leave the most vulnerable workers stranded precisely when they need help most.

Keep workers covered, even when jobs change

In most low- and middle-income countries, social protection benefits such as pensions, health care coverage, and paid leave are linked to a particular job. If workers lose their jobs, they also lose these benefits. Although such an arrangement may suit an environment in which careers are stable, it is far from an ideal arrangement in an environment in which AI can reorganize the structure of the tasks within an entire occupation in a matter of months.

An alternative arrangement is to provide benefits to workers through individual accounts that can be carried over across employers, platforms, jobs, and retraining periods. When they move with workers rather than staying behind with employers, social benefits can support the mobility of workers rather than trapping them in jobs that may be on the decline. More broadly, the direction that needs to be taken is to delink social protection from specific jobs, even if the institutional form this takes varies across countries. In some cases, it may involve moving toward a guaranteed minimum level of assistance, adapted to country circumstances.[4]

A good example is Rwanda's EjoHeza, a voluntary long-term savings program established in 2017 and linked to national digital IDs and accessible by mobile phone. Under the program, participants do not have to make a minimum contribution, an important factor in an economy in which earnings are irregular. By 2023, millions of workers from the informal sector had enrolled in the scheme. The government pays all the operating costs, allowing workers to save their contributions in full. A worker who changes jobs—say, a taxi worker who goes to work in a shop—or moves to another district maintains the same account, the same balance, and the same benefits. Chile's unemployment insurance system adopts a different approach, combining individual savings accounts with a solidarity fund that allows workers to maintain their unemployment benefits across jobs.[5]

Bring workers into the system before AI leaves them further behind

Allowing workers to maintain their social benefits across jobs may address one problem but does not address a larger one: protecting workers who have no benefits at all. In many low- and middle-income countries, 60–80 percent of workers are not part of the formal social insurance scheme (refer to figure S5.1). Globally, 70 percent of workers employed in the formal sector contribute to at least one social protection program, but only 37 percent of informal workers do so. This gap worsens as work becomes more fragmented and platform based.

Coverage of social benefits should be expanded gradually to workers who have none, starting where administrative capacity is strongest—among formal employees, larger firms, and major platforms—followed by focusing on the most exposed workers as coverage broadens. Governments might distribute subsidies first to workers who are at the highest risk of AI-induced job displacement and gradually reduce these subsidies as workers' incomes from their replacement jobs increase or as those jobs become more stable. Such support should also have clear sunset clauses so that temporary assistance does not become a permanent substitute for work. The aim is to help workers manage the transition while labor markets adjust to the effects of AI.

Rules for contributing to pension plans need to match how people actually earn. For example, gig workers, self-employed workers, and platform workers need simple enrollment processes, the ability to make contributions that reflect irregular incomes, and start-up subsidies. Several countries are already implementing schemes that incorporate such elements. China's rural pension system has enrolled hundreds of millions of workers in the country's informal sector. Costa Rica covers part of pension contributions for self-employed workers. Thailand subsidizes premiums for workers in the informal sector who join a pension system aimed at low-income individuals.

Although none of these systems is perfect, all have put infrastructure in place that can be built on before disruptions—such as the ones caused by AI—squeeze workers' income or jobs or benefits further. The COVID-19 pandemic emphasized this point: Countries that had already invested in systems that delivered social benefits responded far better than those that tried to establish them very quickly after the pandemic started.[6] Building this type of infrastructure typically takes years, not months. For example, EjoHeza took five years to reach 3 million savers in Rwanda, and Togo could deploy Novissi—an innovative, fully digital emergency cash transfer program launched in April 2020 to support informal workers affected by the pandemic—rapidly only because the country already had a widespread mobile money system. Countries without such programs should start implementing them as a priority.

Figure S5.1 Social insurance coverage in developing countries is generally low

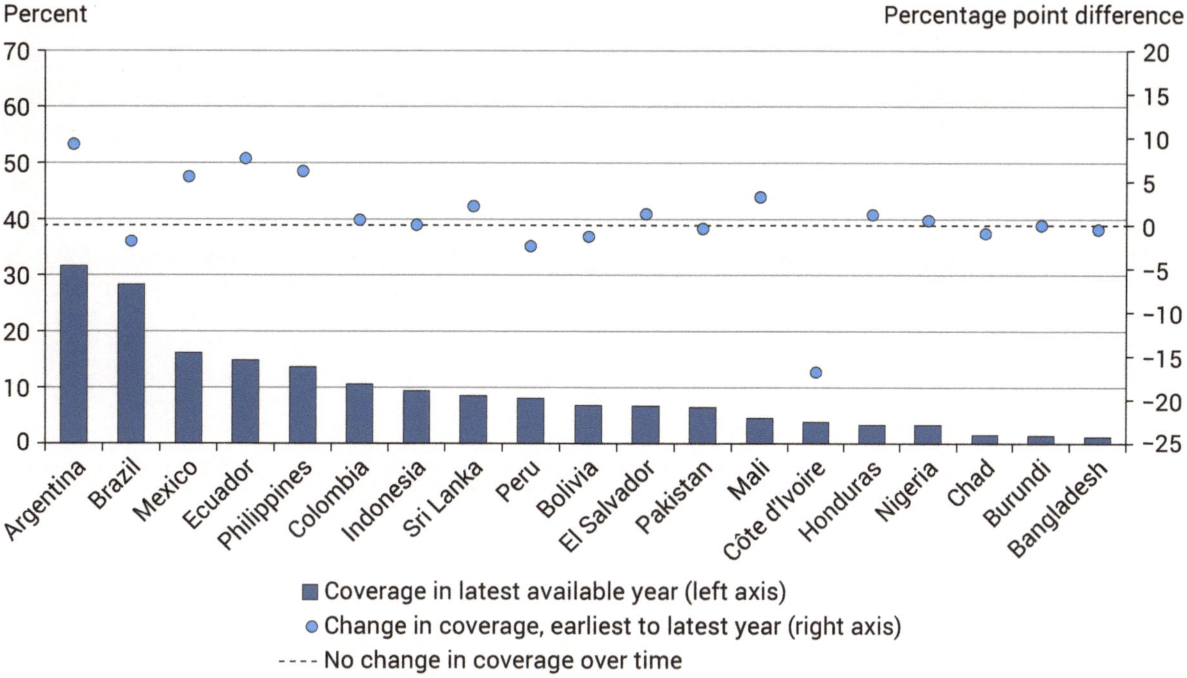

Source: Atlas of Social Protection Indicators of Resilience and Equity (ASPIRE) (dashboard), World Bank, https://www.worldbank.org/en/data/datatopics/aspire.

Note: The figure shows data for the indicator on coverage of social insurance programs, which reflects the percentage of population participating in programs that provide old age contributory pensions (including survivors and disability) and social security and health insurance benefits (including occupational injury benefits, paid sick leave, maternity and other social insurance). Estimates include both direct and indirect beneficiaries. Data are as of the last year available (ranging from 2018 to 2022).

Design adaptive systems that automatically activate benefits based on triggers

Having a social protection system that covers a wide range of workers is not enough to protect them from AI-driven disruptions if the system only delivers benefits *well after* workers lose their jobs. Traditional safety nets are reactive, scaling up only after disruption is well under way. Adaptive systems rely on real-time monitoring and pre-established triggers to expand support automatically. For disruptions driven by AI, triggers can include sharp increases in unemployment claims within specific occupations, reductions in sectoral employment that exceed historical norms, or real-time indicators of adoption of automated processes in industries with particular exposures to AI-related job losses.

Some social protection systems in other contexts already use trigger-based activation mechanisms. The World Bank's Sahel Adaptive Social Protection Program links early-warning indicators to rapid cash transfers during climate shocks. In Niger, timely support under the program has been found to improve consumption, income, and well-being.[7] Applying the same logic to addressing disruptions in labor markets means investing in occupational databases, systems supporting skills assessments, and digital platforms that match workers to jobs: infrastructure that costs far less to build before a shock occurs than while one is under way or after one has subsided.

Once a trigger activates a support or social protection program, what matters is what workers actually receive and what they have to do to receive it. Call center agents who have lost their jobs, for example, should not have to navigate three agencies to receive the social protection benefits they need. A single package can combine short-term income support with accelerated training in skills that are in demand and assistance related to direct placement. Support should focus on enabling workers to move into new roles and sectors, not on making it easier for them to leave the labor market entirely.

Turn AI into a tool for better targeting and delivery of safety nets

The same technology that is displacing workers in some sectors can improve the systems protecting these workers. Globally, the reach and resources of systems for delivering social benefits remain limited. For example, labor market programs cover only about 5 percent of the population, on average, and only 0.25 percent of GDP is spent on such programs.[8] AI tools, layered on top of digital public infrastructure, can improve the targeting of social benefits, increase the speed of distributing payments, and reach workers that conventional systems may overlook.

The Nigeria Social Register and Brazil's Cadastro Único (Single Registry) offer examples of how centralized registries can connect households to multiple programs. Kenya's M-PESA network enables government-to-person payments where bank branches do not exist. AI can also sharpen early-warning triggers: Real-time analysis of vacancy postings, platform work records, and administrative data can spot displacement patterns months before household surveys do.[9]

But experience in several African countries has shown what can go wrong when digital and AI-based systems are deployed without proper safeguards in place. Remote communities can lose access to social benefits when there is no network coverage,[10] when registration platforms default to English over local languages, and when algorithmic errors go uncorrected.[11] The value of AI in social protection lies in helping governments identify problems faster, target better, and respond earlier, not in replacing the rules and human judgment that keep social protection systems fair.

Don't forget the public sector

In many emerging market and developing economies, the public sector accounts for 15–30 percent of employment in the formal sector.[12] Much of public sector employment entails tasks with high degrees of exposure to AI, such as data entry, records management, routine compliance checks, and document drafting. AI typically reorganizes such tasks rather than eliminating the jobs of those who perform them, but only if retraining is available and job descriptions are updated. A tax officer whose data entry task becomes automated, for example, can move into audit analysis; without that bridge, however, the tax officer role itself becomes unnecessary. India's Mission Karmayogi is working to integrate the acquisition of digital and AI skills into the professional development of civil servants (refer to chapter 8).

Procurement contracts should specify requirements for government contractors, who typically lack the benefits offered to public sector employees, whose responsibilities are reshaped by AI to transition to other positions. How governments handle their own workforces will signal whether the gains of AI will be broadly shared.

Move from pilots to permanent systems

In emerging markets, 1.2 billion young people will reach working age in the next decade, but only about 420 million jobs are expected to be created.[13] Social protection systems that are still at the pilot stage will not be able to cope with the resulting demand, particularly on this scale. Meeting it will require moving from pilots to permanent systems. And with tight budgets, sequencing matters. Governments should prioritize investing in the assistance that offers the greatest immediate payoff to the workers who are most exposed to job losses or phasing out of their skills—expanding digital registries, enrolling workers in the informal sector in basic portable accounts, and building trigger infrastructure—rather than attempting all reforms simultaneously.

The fiscal challenge involved in expanding social protection along these lines is real but manageable. Low-income countries spend 1.6 percent of their GDP on social protection benefits, compared with 3.7 percent in lower-middle-income countries and 6.4 percent in upper-middle-income countries.[14] By comparison, 8 percent of GDP globally is spent on subsidies for fossil fuel, agriculture, and fisheries.[15] Shifting even a portion of these subsidies and broadening progressive tax bases would change the picture substantially. Platforms and large firms that benefit from productivity gains driven by AI can contribute through dedicated fees tied to reskilling. Where domestic resources fall short, concessional finance from international sources can cover up-front costs, with domestic resources increasing over time.

Clear rules build trust. Workers participate in contribution schemes when they can see what their contributions buy, and firms comply with requirements when their obligations are predictable. Shifts of the kind mentioned earlier face resistance—from employers wary of new levies, from bureaucracies built around established programs, and from existing firms (incumbents) in sectors that are already subsidized. Countries that have made progress, such as Rwanda and Togo, have typically started with executive-level commitment and used early, visible results to build broader support.

Although public social protection schemes must be the backbone for protecting workers, such schemes cannot be the only mechanism. Large firms and platforms that benefit from AI can help smooth workers' transitions between jobs by providing early notice to workers of a firm's plan to automate tasks, providing internal reskilling opportunities, and offering support for job placement. Both voluntary efforts from the private sector and public policy efforts can go hand in hand: The government sets the rules, and others help carry them out.

Upgrades to social safety nets should embed rigorous evaluation from the start so that governments can test which approaches work, for whom, and under what conditions and subsequently shift resources toward them. One way to achieve this is by linking social protection records to employment and training data to identify which programs actually yield results. Togo is investing in a data lab for policy evaluation, and Rwanda tracks EjoHeza's enrollment patterns to fine-tune the design of the fund's incentives for workers to contribute to it. The goal is not to design the perfect policy on the first attempt, but to build systems that can learn and adapt by eliminating approaches that do not work.

AI will disrupt labor markets in developing countries against a backdrop of weak safety nets, widespread informality, and tight fiscal resources. Over the past decade, social protection schemes have expanded to cover 4.7 billion workers across low- and middle-income countries, an unprecedented achievement.[16] The practical path forward builds on what exists, step by step, with digital infrastructure as the connective thread. The more difficult aspect is dealing with the political landscape: turning promising experiments into permanent, funded, accountable institutions before disruption makes the cost of waiting too high to bear.

Notes

1. Refer to Global Trends at a Glance (graphic), ILO Modelled Estimates Database, International Labour Organization, https://datawrapper.dwcdn.net/S4doK/8/.
2. Demirci et al. (2025); Hui et al. (2024); Teutloff et al. (2025).
3. World Bank (2025).
4. Packard et al. (2019).
5. van Ours et al. (2010).
6. World Bank (2025).
7. Bossuroy et al. (2022).
8. World Bank (2025).
9. Aiken et al. (2025).
10. Faith et al. (2024).
11. Khene et al. (2025).
12. World Bank (2021).
13. World Bank (2025).
14. World Bank (2025).
15. Damania et al. (2023).
16. World Bank (2025).

References

Aiken, Emily L., Anik Ashraf, Joshua Evan Blumenstock, Raymond Guiteras, and Ahmed Mushfiq Mobarak. 2025. "Scalable Targeting of Social Protection: When Do Algorithms Out-Perform Surveys and Community Knowledge?" NBER Working Paper 33919, National Bureau of Economic Research. https://www.nber.org/papers/w33919.

Bossuroy, Thomas, Markus P. Goldstein, Bassirou Karimou, et al. 2022. "Tackling Psychosocial and Capital Constraints to Alleviate Poverty." *Nature* 605 (7909): 291–97. https://doi.org/10.1038/s41586-022-04647-8.

Damania, Richard, Esteban Balseca, Charlotte de Fontaubert, et al. 2023. *Detox Development: Repurposing Environmentally Harmful Subsidies*. World Bank. https://openknowledge.worldbank.org/server/api/core/bitstreams/61d04aca-1b95-4c06-8199-3c4a423cb7fe/content.

Demirci, Ozge, Jonas Hannane, and Xinrong Zhu. 2025. "Who Is AI Replacing? The Impact of Generative AI on Online Freelancing Platforms." *Management Science* 71 (10): 8097–108. https://doi.org/10.1287/mnsc.2024.05420.

Faith, Becky, Tony Roberts, and Laura Alfers, eds. 2024. "The Digitalisation of Social Protection in Africa: The Perspective of Marginalised Workers." IDS Research Report 90, Institute of Development Studies. https://www.doi.org/10.19088/IDS.2024.022.

Hui, Xiang, Oren Reshef, and Luofeng Zhou. 2024. "The Short-Term Effects of Generative Artificial Intelligence on Employment: Evidence from an Online Labor Market." *Organization Science* 35 (6): 1977–89. https://doi.org/10.1287/orsc.2023.18441.

Khene, Caroline, Hafeni Mthoko, Gugulethu Baduza, and Carolina Holland-Szyp. 2025. "Beyond Digital Displacement: Accountability in South Africa's Digitalised South Protection System." IDS Working Paper 627, Institute of Development Studies. https://doi.org/10.19088/IDS.2025.097.

Packard, Truman G., Ugo Gentilini, Margaret E. Grosh, et al. 2019. *Protecting All: Risk Sharing for a Diverse and Diversifying World of Work*. Human Development Perspectives Series. World Bank. https://documents1.worldbank.org/curated/en/997741568048792164/pdf/Protecting-All-Risk-Sharing-for-a-Diverse-and-Diversifying-World-of-Work.pdf.

Teutloff, Ole, Johanna Einsiedler, Otto Kässi, Fabian Braesemann, Pamela Mishkin, and R. Maria del Rio-Chanona. 2025. "Winners and Losers of Generative AI: Early Evidence of Shifts in Freelancer Demand." *Journal of Economic Behavior and Organization* 235 (July): 106845. https://doi.org/10.1016/j.jebo.2024.106845.

van Ours, Jan C., Milan Vodopivec, and Gonzalo Reyes. 2010. "Incentive Effects of Unemployment Insurance Savings Accounts: Evidence from Chile." CEPR Discussion Paper DP 7632, Centre for Economic Policy Research. https://cepr.org/publications/dp7632.

World Bank. 2021. "Public Sector Employment and Compensation: A Framework 6." World Bank. https://documents1.worldbank.org/curated/en/710421625760208867/pdf/Public-Sector-Employment-and-Compensation-A-Framework-6.pdf.

World Bank. 2025. *State of Social Protection Report 2025: The 2-Billion-Person Challenge*. World Bank. https://openknowledge.worldbank.org/server/api/core/bitstreams/3a191516-270b-40c9-acdf-79e3f382c708/content.

8

Governments as Users: Enhancing Capabilities to Deploy AI

Main messages

- **AI is not the right answer to every public problem**
  Start with the problem, compare the AI option with simpler alternatives, and select AI solutions where they fit best.
- **AI from private vendors still requires government capacity to improve public services**
  Match the ambition to deploy AI solutions in public services with readiness on data, budget, and institutional capacity to integrate them into workflows.
- **Government AI tools are only as reliable as the data feeding them**
  Digitize administrative records, improve management information systems, connect data across agencies, and strengthen digital public infrastructure and data safeguards.
- **AI tools cannot simply be imported and expected to work**
  Make them accessible and easy to use, integrate them into real workflows, and measure whether they improve public services.
- **One-off AI contracts can leave governments in a costly bind**
  Make it possible to change suppliers, retain control of government data, and build an in-house team to maintain and oversee the system.

A reproducibility package is available for this book in the Reproducible Research Repository at https://reproducibility.worldbank.org/catalog/624.

Introduction

Governments around the world are asking a deceptively simple question: Should we invest in AI? And if so, where? Ministers of finance, health, or education are being told that AI (artificial intelligence) could strengthen the delivery of public services by improving the allocation of public resources, enhancing the productivity of civil servants and frontline staff, and reducing administrative inefficiencies. Yet policy makers also must contend with tight budgets, competing priorities, and limited capacity to evaluate whether new technologies are worth the investment—particularly with technologies that change as quickly as AI. In this context, the core policy question is whether AI is the right solution for a specific problem, given the budget, digital infrastructure, and institutional capacity available.

This uncertainty can be dealt with through a sequence of practical decisions. Before committing scarce resources, governments need to determine whether AI is the right solution or whether the problem can be addressed better through other means. If AI is appropriate, governments must assess whether the foundations to enable the technology to add value are in place (data, operational capacity, procurement expertise) and whether the AI solutions will perform well in their local context and language. Even a government that clears those hurdles still faces choices about how to procure AI responsibly, avoid vendor lock-in, and monitor performance over time.

Governments do not start from a blank slate. They hold large administrative data sets, perform tasks well aligned with AI's capabilities, and operate under a mandate to improve services that are often of poor quality, scarce, or overwhelmed. AI can enhance both the front end of government, where services are delivered but skilled personnel are in short supply, and the back end, where much of government management happens (refer to chapter 5). But that potential is conditional. Basic components of government capacity—data, budgets, and talent—are the most common barriers to AI reported by low- and middle-income countries in the World Bank's AI and Data for Better Governance Survey.[1] This chapter helps governments facing these constraints make better decisions today: where to start, what to build first, how to buy AI without losing control, and how to know whether any of it is working (refer to figure 8.1). Governments that navigate these issues well will be positioned to use AI in ways that genuinely improve public services and to sustain the public trust that makes those improvements last.

Figure 8.1 A practical road map for AI in government

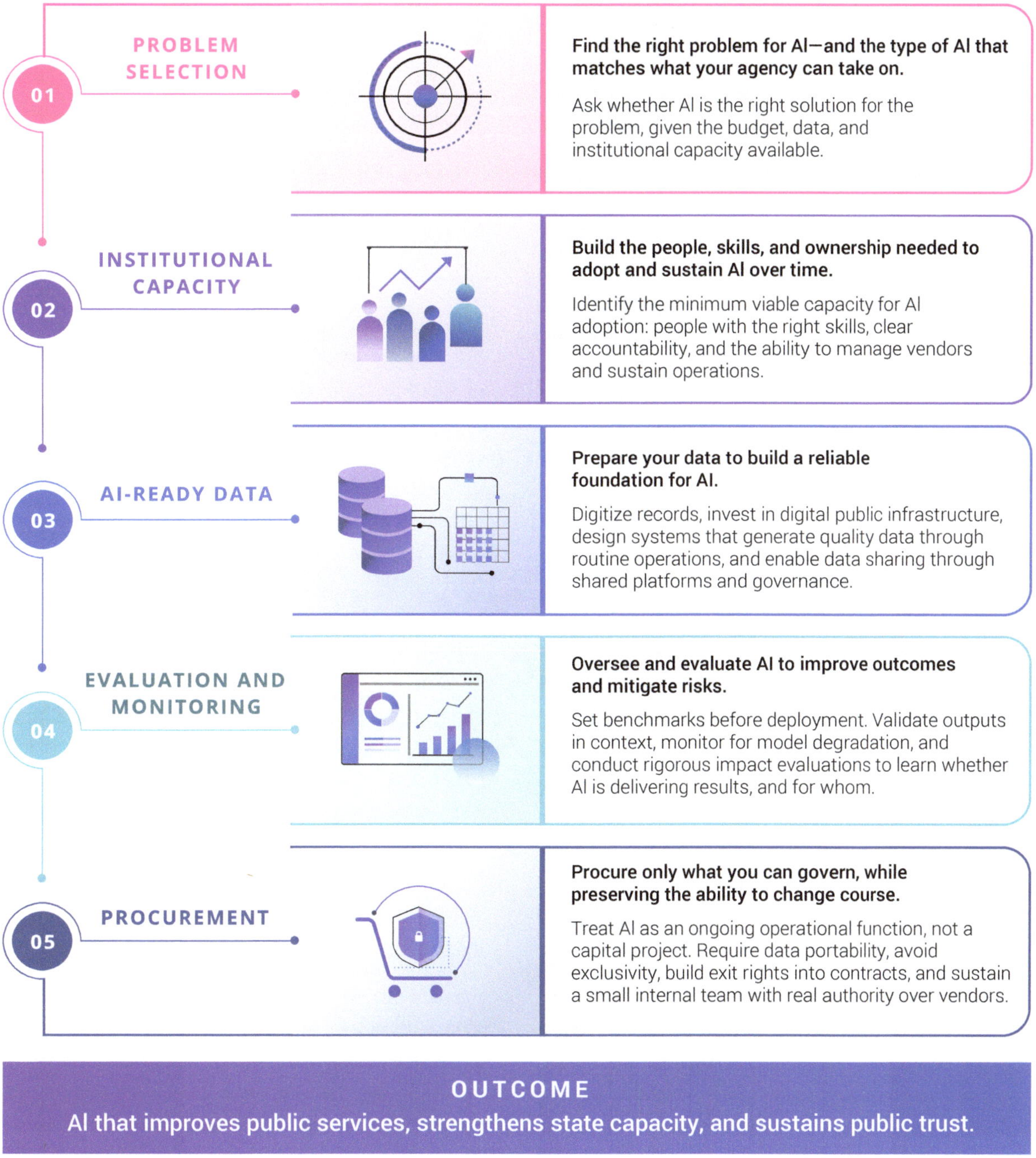

Source: WDR 2026 team.

Note: AI = artificial intelligence.

Getting AI right starts with matching it to the problem and the agency's capacity to sustain it

Starting with the operational problem

The first question for governments is which operational problem AI can help solve. As chapter 5 shows, AI can strengthen both back-end administration and front-end delivery; however, not every problem can be handled with the same AI tools, and some do not benefit from AI at all. Moreover, deploying AI on top of poorly designed processes automates inefficiencies rather than resolving them.

Thus, the biggest barrier is often identifying *where* AI creates value and *what* complementary changes are needed to realize it. This is essentially a *mapping problem*. A recent study of the private sector found that prompting firms to search across a broader range of business functions for AI uses led them to identify more applications and improve their performance.[2] Governments face the same challenge. They must identify potential applications and then weigh their expected benefits against their costs and against alternative interventions. This mapping exercise can also help pool demand for AI applications common to many agencies—areas in which joint procurement can reduce costs.

The right opportunity also depends on which type of AI is being considered. Predictive models suit agencies that have large, structured data sets.[3] For example, the national water utility in the Republic of Korea has deployed predictive AI across more than 40 water treatment plants, including for energy management and predictive equipment maintenance.[4] Similarly, revenue authorities in several countries have used historical data on tax returns to uncover compliance risks that manual audits missed. Generative tools can be applied across both internal tasks (such as drafting or translating documents) and external ones (such as supporting the decisions of frontline service providers). Agentic systems, which initiate tasks and act across multiple steps without continuous oversight, place the highest demands on AI deployment, requiring authorization frameworks, audit trails, and protocols in case of failure to be specified in advance, rather than retrofitted afterward.[5]

Matching the technology to what your agency can sustain

The choice of adopting, adapting, and advancing AI is guided by a government agency's level of readiness in terms of data quality, human capital, systems infrastructure, and governance capacity (refer to table 8.1).[6] At early stages of digital maturity, *adopting AI* can address operational bottlenecks without requiring new talent pipelines. For instance, agencies can train and equip staff members to use general-purpose AI tools for low-risk tasks (such as drafting, summarizing, or translating documents) under clear guidelines or procure proven solutions for specific workflows (such as processing tax returns or medical imaging). These approaches can help build the evidence base for further AI investment by revealing which data sets need structuring, which performance benchmarks matter for local conditions, and where additional investment in technical capacity or data infrastructure is most likely to produce measurable returns.

For government agencies that have established data capabilities and can provide oversight, uses expand to *adapting AI*. Agencies can customize, train, or fine-tune an externally developed language model or an established machine learning method based on government data and fit the AI system to local workflows. Examples include retrieval-augmented-generation (RAG) systems that allow civil servants to systematically search, sort, and interpret documentation about government policies, risk-scoring for tax audits, and customs checks built on top of off-the-shelf machine learning libraries.

Table 8.1 A government agency's readiness determines the most appropriate approach to deploying AI

Stage of AI readiness	Strategies: Adopt AI	Strategies: Adapt AI	Strategies: Advance AI
Early digital government	★	⚠	✗
Limited digital capability, partially paper-based systems, weak implementation and oversight.	Priority starting point	Targeted pilots	Not recommended
Connected digital government	✓	★	⚠
Moderate digital capability, established administrative systems, functioning e-government platforms. Some capacity for oversight and model use.	Feasible	Priority starting point	Rare, strong case
Advanced digital government	✓	✓	★
Broad digital skills; interoperable, well-governed data ecosystems; mature platforms. Robust legal, institutional, and technical controls.	Feasible	Default for many high-value uses	Only for selective strategic investment

Source: WDR 2026 team.
Note: AI = artificial intelligence.

Only in select cases and when digital maturity is advanced should government agencies consider *advancing AI* by building complex AI models from scratch. Examples include developing bespoke systems for use cases in which no external model is fit for purpose (such as a national language model).[7] Line departments and executive agencies do not typically have sufficient capacity to advance AI in-house. Instead, they might partner with government-funded scientific agencies or research institutes, nongovernmental research and academic institutions, nonprofits, and private AI labs—whether domestic or international. The internal capacity requirements remain high, because frontier AI models must be monitored and maintained, input data must be correctly preprocessed, risks must be assessed correctly, and outputs must be used appropriately. The government agency's direct role is usually to define the objectives and operational requirements, commit substantial resources, and test the AI system on government tasks.

Avoiding systemic pressure to pursue unrealistic strategies

Governments often might be willing or have incentives to skip stages. Advancing national language models, dedicated compute infrastructure,[8] and locally trained predictive systems generate political visibility more readily than the slower work of building capable teams and improving data quality. But political visibility is not the same as public value. A more durable path is to start small and adapt AI as the landscape evolves. Singapore's experience with Southeast Asian Languages in One Network (SEA-LION)—an initiative developed by AI Singapore to build large language models for Southeast Asian languages—demonstrates this process. At first, the initiative aimed to acquire in-house capability to train models from scratch. However, as better open models became available, the initiative shifted to customizing existing models—an approach better suited to the constraints of data, talent, and cost.[9] This example shows that modest early investments can preserve strategic options for exiting an approach that may not survive the next shift in AI capabilities.

Overall, getting the match between problem and technology right is only the first step. After finding the right technology for a problem, deployment can fail if the government lacks the institutional and technical capacity to execute it, the data to do so reliably, systems to evaluate and monitor operations, and the contractual protections to keep government in control if things go wrong when procuring AI solutions. The four sections that follow address each of these factors, starting with the institutional capacity needed to make an AI solution effective and sustainable.

Investing in staff capacity is essential to make AI work and last

General-purpose technologies are more likely to generate returns when organizations possess the complementary capabilities required to deploy them effectively.[10] For digital transformation in the public sector, those complements are not only technical, but also organizational: teams capable of understanding user needs, redesigning workflows, evaluating vendors, deciding when to build versus buy, and maintaining systems as operational conditions change.[11]

Three complementary strategies can strengthen governments' capability to choose, deploy, maintain, and improve AI systems over time without requiring large increases in head count or wholesale institutional redesign: recruiting for the specific skills public administrations most need, empowering digital teams and expanding their capacity, and building AI literacy across the broader civil service.

Recruiting the right talent and skills

Governments identify shortages of digital talent as one of the most significant barriers to AI adoption.[12] The shortage is real, but frequently misdiagnosed. Public employers cannot compete with private firms in terms of salaries for frontier AI researchers and rarely need to do so. The capabilities most needed in government are not training models or developing algorithms. They are the ability to understand user workflows, identify where AI reduces administrative friction, evaluate vendor claims, and ensure systems evolve as policies change.

Before any AI system goes live, whether in-house or outsourced, governments should define the minimum internal skill set required to own it and enable it to evolve. Adequate staffing includes product management capacity that translates user needs into technical requirements; the ability to evaluate AI outputs; and enough technical expertise to understand how the model, data, and interface connect. If these components can be replaced separately, governments retain greater flexibility; if they are tightly bundled, changing any part may require replacing the entire system, increasing the risk of vendor lock-in. These capabilities matter especially for AI because operating conditions, data, and regulations change over time, and a system that performs accurately at the time of deployment may not continue to do so unless it is continuously measured and adjusted.[13]

The talent profile required broadens across the AI use spectrum as the government takes on greater ownership of the process. For *adopting* AI, the critical gap is product management. Without staff members who can evaluate vendor claims and specify requirements to hold suppliers accountable, governments may be subject to cost overruns, dependence on a single vendor, and systems that cannot adapt when needs change. For *adapting* AI, product managers remain essential, but the necessary additions are data engineers and systems integrators who connect government data to AI tools, structure data for retrieval and risk scoring, and manage the privacy and security obligations when sensitive data feed external systems. For *advancing AI* in-house, government departments also need domain experts and infrastructure specialists who can collaborate with scientists and machine learning engineers from specialized government agencies, universities, and nonprofits to build, retrain, and maintain the AI solutions deployed.

An agency's ability to recruit and retain staff members with these profiles is often constrained by the structure of civil service systems, including rigid job classifications, slow recruitment, entry rules, and compressed pay scales. Governments that have built digital capacity have therefore combined civil service reform with targeted flexibilities: establishing autonomous digital agencies that sit outside the general civil service statute; opening routes through which experienced practitioners can enter laterally or through contractual arrangements; and using partnerships with research institutes, universities, and the private sector to gain access to skills while developing in-house capability to sustain the system over time.

Empowering digital teams and expanding their capacity through AI

Attracting the right talent is only part of the challenge. Governments that recruit capable digital staff members but do not involve these professionals in making decisions about AI procurement, the architecture of AI systems, and budgets can undermine the digital capacity they sought to build in the first place.[14] Brazil's gov.br platform shows what stronger internal ownership in the hands of qualified in-house digital teams makes possible. The platform has brought thousands of federal services onto a common infrastructure. More than 156 million users have registered, and more than 4,000 digital public services are available.[15] The United Arab Emirates has established AI executives within federal entities and a unified federal authority for AI, data, and digital government.[16]

Beyond recruiting technical talent and giving them authority, governments must also expand what existing teams can do. The most productive place to begin deploying AI is often with the teams that already build, maintain, or improve digital services. These teams have the technical grounding to extract value from AI tools faster and recognize when outputs should not be trusted. Recent experience supports this sequencing. In the United Kingdom, a randomized controlled trial of the use of AI coding assistants by technical staff in the public sector reported average savings of 56 minutes per working day[17]—more than twice as much as the 26 minutes per day reported by another randomized controlled trial that investigated the use of Microsoft 365 Copilot by more than 20,000 civil servants throughout government.[18] Brazil's federal government saw similar gains with AI coding tools supporting digital teams in accelerating delivery across 53 projects.[19]

This insight has two implications for sequencing. First, governments may realize faster and safer gains by deploying AI tools within existing digital teams before rolling them out across the civil service. Second, doing so creates a learning channel within the institution. Early use by technically grounded teams generates practical evidence on failure modes, quality assurance, procurement needs, and workflow redesign. It also creates an internal cadre of experienced users who can support and train others as access expands.

Building digital and AI skills across the civil service

Beyond central digital teams, successful deployment of AI systems depends on the capabilities of the broader public workforce. Three layers of capability are often conflated: *basic digital literacy* (routine use of digital tools and data systems), *AI literacy* (understanding what AI can and cannot do, when its use is appropriate, and how to interpret its outputs), and *task-specific operational competence* (integrating AI into particular workflows, verifying outputs against domain knowledge, and knowing when to override the AI or escalate the decision to a qualified human). Not every civil servant needs to understand how models are trained. But many would benefit from either the second or the third layer, and neither is likely to succeed when the first is absent.

Governments increasingly recognize this constraint. In the World Bank's AI and Data for Better Governance Survey, most participating economies reported that training and capacity building would make the biggest difference for adopting AI responsibly in their government.[20] Civil servants themselves are asking for this training. In Malaysia, civil servants have consistently demanded a higher level of advanced digital and data skills training than what they received. Interest in generative AI is particularly strong.[21] Several countries are moving toward more structured training. India has built the iGOT Karmayogi platform into one of the largest government e-learning systems in the world, offering more than 4,000 courses in 16 languages. It has more than 15 million registered users, and more than 1.3 million learners have completed AI-related courses.[22] Course completion is linked to annual performance appraisals, incentivizing participation. Kenya's emerging model pairs free AI skilling with virtual and in-person delivery and includes an Africa Centre of Competence for Digital and Artificial Intelligence Skilling, cocreated by the United Nations Development Programme (UNDP) Kenya and Microsoft, designed around modular, cohort-based learning and mentorship.[23]

Beyond foundational digital and AI literacy for all staff members, deeper technical training for technical staff members is essential—particularly for those who will redesign workflows, procure AI tools, oversee vendors, or use AI in higher-stakes settings. Training leaders also matters. A randomized controlled trial in Pakistan, for example, found that AI training for deputy ministers increased support for AI in policy making and made them more likely to allocate funds for digitalization. Importantly, this training for leaders also led to greater support for AI among subordinate staff members who had never been trained themselves.[24]

As governments invest in expanding training on AI, it is important to ensure that the training is effective. However, evidence on the training of civil servants remains limited, especially in regard to which delivery models work best. Instructor coaching, stronger delivery, and train-the-trainer approaches can improve training quality,[25] while linking learning to on-the-job performance is essential for evaluating whether training changes behavior.

The broader institutional environment can also support or undermine the effectiveness of AI adoption. Leadership support, communities of practice, and opportunities to apply new skills on the job can help efforts to integrate AI responsibly. Furthermore, whether civil servants are allowed to have access to AI tools, and whether guidance exists on appropriate use, shapes whether learning translates into practice. Box 8.1 examines the current state of AI licenses and guidelines across country income groups[26] and how their absence may lead to unsanctioned use of AI.

Box 8.1 Generative AI licenses, guidelines, and the limits of compliance

For public officials to use artificial intelligence (AI) appropriately and effectively, AI licenses and guidelines are essential. However, only 33 percent of digital agencies in lower-middle-income economies reported that they had enterprise licenses in early 2026, according to the World Bank's AI and Data for Better Governance Survey.[a] No low-income economy had any, and only 17 percent of low- and lower-middle-income economies had formal AI guidelines, with 48 percent still drafting them (refer to figure B8.1.1).

(Box continues next page)

Box 8.1 Generative AI licenses, guidelines, and the limits of compliance *(continued)*

Figure B8.1.1 Government guidelines and licenses for generative AI are rare in low- and lower-middle-income economies

Survey question: "Does your government provide licenses or official access to generative AI tools for civil servants?"

Survey question: "Has your government issued guidelines or policies regarding the use of generative AI tools by civil servants?"

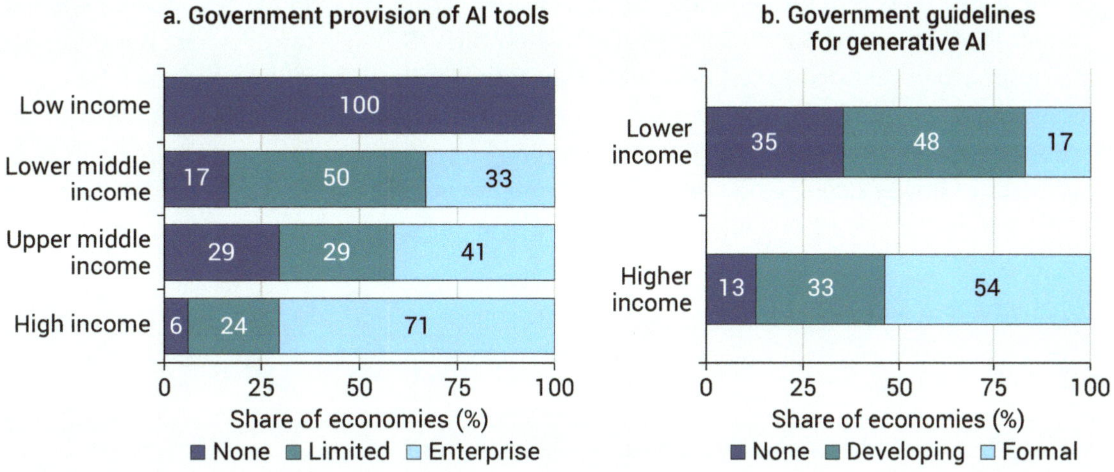

Source: WDR 2026 team, based on AI and Data for Better Governance Survey, World Bank.

Note: The sample includes 12 low-income and 12 lower-middle-income economies (lower-income group), as well as 16 upper-middle-income economies and 17 high-income economies (higher-income group). AI = artificial intelligence.

This gap in guidance and licensing increases the likelihood of unsanctioned use of AI (also known as *shadow AI*). A survey of 560 judicial workers across 96 countries found that 44 percent had used AI tools in their work, yet only 9 percent had received guidance on appropriate use.[b] A study of more than 32,000 employees across 47 countries found that nearly 70 percent prefer free, public AI tools over employer-provided solutions, and almost half had uploaded sensitive organizational data onto public platforms.[c] In the public sector, this practice can expose highly sensitive citizen data such as tax records, law enforcement histories, or case files to unvetted consumer tools with no audit trail, risking data leakages.

Even when licenses exist, shadow AI does not necessarily disappear. When approved tools are harder to use, workers often circumvent them. Common responses such as repeated system warnings and mandatory acknowledgment screens have had limited impact because users habituate to alerts that interrupt routine tasks.[d] Thus, governments should treat guidelines

(Box continues next page)

Box 8.1 Generative AI licenses, guidelines, and the limits of compliance *(continued)*

as behavioral interventions to be continuously evaluated—not as safeguards whose mere existence confers protection.

For governments that have not yet formalized guidelines or procured solutions, learning from shadow usage can identify security risks, reveal the needs that vetted tools must meet, and surface spontaneous uses already occurring. To spur adoption of internal AI tools, licenses can be allocated competitively under a use-it-or-lose-it rule, making access a scarce and visible signal of active use. Banco Bilbao Vizcaya Argentaria (BBVA), a large private bank, applied this approach by instructing business area leaders to distribute its initial licenses to their most motivated and committed employees, not necessarily the most senior. The bank scaled enterprise AI from 3,000 to 11,000 users in about a year, leveraging peer-to-peer diffusion through networks of power users, who were deeply familiar with the technology from frequent and sustained use, provided valuable feedback, and acted as champions with new users.[e]

Source: WDR 2026 team.

a. Lundy et al. (2026).

b. UNESCO (2024).

c. Gillespie et al. (2025).

d. Dang-Pham et al. (2025); van Acken et al. (2024); Vance et al. (2019).

e. Alfaro et al. (2026).

Building AI-ready data requires targeted investments in digitization and digital public infrastructure

AI systems are only as reliable as the data pipelines feeding them. In governments, the stakes concerning data are particularly high because small errors can scale into large harms. Governments are, in many respects, the original data collection machines, through censuses, tax registers, property cadasters, and military levies.[27] In recent years, the digitization of core management information systems (MIS) has generated vast amounts of data in functions related to public services, such as taxation, social benefits, health and education, legal proceedings, and civil registration, among others. Through regulatory and research functions, governments also often have access to data generated by private markets, such as phone or satellite data, which expands the opportunities to use AI.

Despite this progress, government data are frequently fragmented across agencies, partly stored in formats that are not machine readable, inconsistently classified, and institutionally difficult to reuse on account of unclear mandates and low levels of cooperation among agencies. For instance, two-thirds of surveyed experts in Latin America and the Caribbean report that government MIS remain only partially digitized, and only a minority report the presence of systematic data quality frameworks.[28] More generally, governments around the world report data quality

Figure 8.2 The most common barriers to AI use in government are data quality and availability

Survey question: "To what extent do the following constraints prevent or limit your government's internal use of AI tools?"

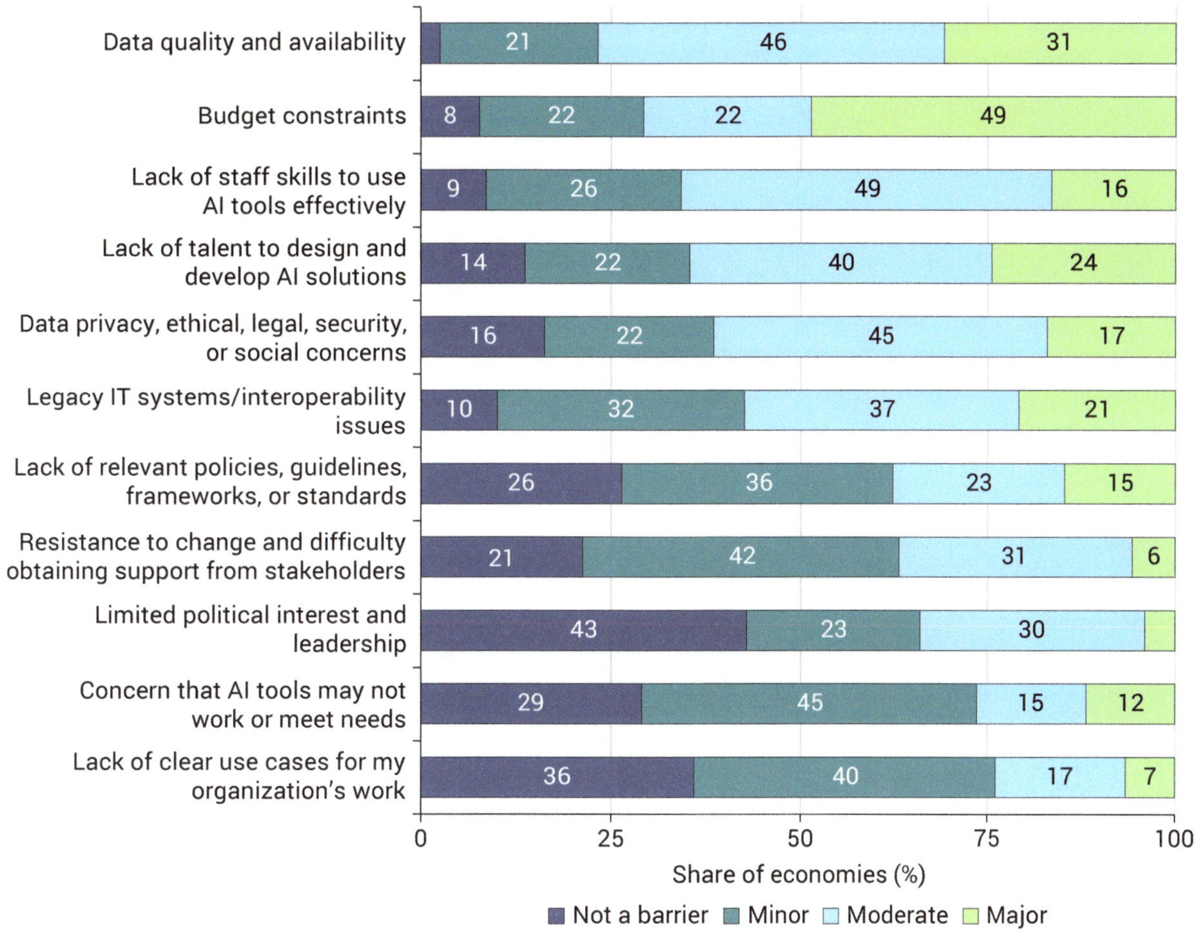

Source: WDR 2026 team, based on AI and Data for Better Governance Survey, World Bank.

Note: The sample includes 12 low-income and 12 lower-middle-income economies, as well as 16 upper-middle-income and 17 high-income economies. AI = artificial intelligence; IT = information technology.

and availability to be the most common barrier to using AI (refer to figure 8.2).

Building an AI-ready data pipeline

Governments can take targeted action to build an AI-ready data pipeline. Steps include digitizing the records that governments already hold, improving the data their routine operations generate, and connecting data across agencies through digital public infrastructure.

Digitizing existing records

Data that have accumulated from civil registries, land records, court archives, and policy documents often reside on paper, in scanned images, or in proprietary formats. Converting this body of data into structured, machine-readable data is a prerequisite for AI applications. For example, building on a pipeline that converts scanned legal documents into machine-readable text, an AI tool for the Brazilian Supreme Federal Court now analyzes whether an appeal to the court has general repercussions, doing in 5 seconds what a civil servant used to take 40 minutes to do.[29]

Advances in AI are dramatically reducing the cost of this digitization effort. Newer generative AI models can extract information directly from unlabeled scanned pages without task-specific model training, and these models achieve higher accuracy out of the box, reducing the amount of time needed for review and correction.[30] A recent study found that this approach makes digitization of large-scale tables 50 times less expensive than traditional outsourcing while reducing the share of tables with structural errors from 61.4 percent to 0.35 percent.[31] Generative AI can also create structured data in table form from free-form text. In some cases, large language models perform as well as, or even better than, human annotators, while working much faster and at a fraction of the cost.[32] A hybrid approach can use human expert review of AI-generated labels. Over successive rounds, this approach can progressively improve training data sets, accelerating the development of task-specific AI.

For low-resource languages (languages underrepresented in AI training data), this digitization effort takes on additional significance. Governments may be the only actor with both the mandate and the incentive to produce high-quality collections of local-language data. Digitized records in local languages can serve as public goods that enhance not only public service delivery but also the capacity of private sector innovators to adapt AI tools for local markets, thus addressing an existing market failure. The value of this type of data will compound as governments can use such data to support the training of local-language AI models and power their own AI tools. Where appropriate, they can also publish the data to help improve search engines and AI assistants, thereby expanding citizens' access to public information.

Generating better data from routine operations

The long-term path to AI-ready government lies in designing digital systems that produce structured, reliable data as a by-product of routine operations. In well-designed MIS and on well-designed online platforms, each transaction generates a record with standardized fields, unique identifiers, time stamps, and outcome codes, so that downstream analytics and AI can learn from comparable events. MIS platforms are increasingly available in countries across all levels of per capita income (refer to figure 8.3). However, even where such platforms exist, inconsistent usage and low data quality remain common challenges, introducing systematic bias into any AI system trained on their outputs.

Administrative data reflect the workflows that generate them, not necessarily the underlying phenomena policy makers seek to measure. In government MIS, uneven uptake across offices or staff members (including parallel paper processes, partial completion of forms, discretionary recording of data and information, or inconsistent coding) creates patterns of missing data that are not random. If AI is trained on such data, it risks learning who gets measured rather than the phenomenon of interest. A related risk arises when the variable being measured is a poor proxy for the outcome of interest. For instance, in criminal justice, arrest data are commonly used as a proxy for tracking offenses, but because arrests depend on the locations where police are deployed, police can be repeatedly sent to the same areas regardless of true crime rates,[33] potentially leading to disparities across groups.[34]

Figure 8.3 In countries across all income levels, management information systems are widespread although AI is not

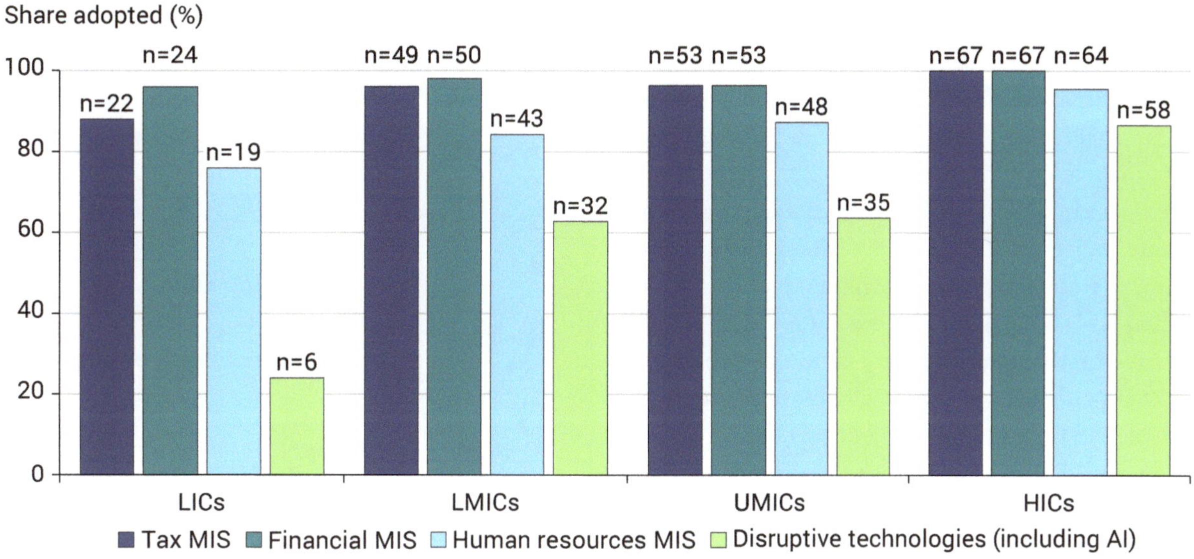

Source: WDR 2026 team, based on GovTech Dataset (GovTech Maturity Index Dataset) (December 2025), Data Catalog, World Bank, https://datacatalog.worldbank.org/search/dataset/0037889/govtech-dataset.

Note: The sample number appears above each corresponding sector bar. AI = artificial intelligence; HICs = high-income countries; LICs = low-income countries; LMICs = lower-middle-income countries; MIS = management information system; UMICs = upper-middle-income countries.

Reducing these risks requires ensuring that training data are representative and their quality is monitored continuously rather than assessed ex post. Data work must be built into operational workflows by, among other things, embedding validation rules, mandatory fields, and automated consistency checks in digital systems; creating incentives for recording data accurately and mechanisms for correcting records; monitoring the completeness and consistency of data by office, user, and case type so that uneven usage is detected early; and closing feedback loops so that frontline staff can see how the data they enter are actually used. Before data are used to train or evaluate AI models, domain experts can review and verify training samples manually as additional safeguards. For instance, inspecting a representative subset of records can help identify labeling errors or quality gaps that automated checks might have overlooked.

Connecting data through digital public infrastructure and data exchange platforms

Even after records are digitized and routine systems are well designed, data often remain trapped in institutional silos. They tend to be isolated within individual agencies or departments with weak interoperability standards and stranded by unclear legal mandates, lack of incentives, or lack of trust for sharing across organizations. For many AI applications, the value lies not in any single data set but in the ability to link and cross-reference records across systems, such as connecting health data with education data to identify vulnerable children, or combining procurement records with company registries to detect conflicts of interest.

Digital public infrastructure (DPI) provides critical support in the process of connecting data across government units. DPI comprises a set of reusable, interoperable building blocks that any agency or service can use to participate in a unified data ecosystem: digital identity, e-signatures, e-payments, data exchange, base registries, and verifiable credentials (which enable AI agents to prove their authority to act on a citizen's behalf).[35] Some DPI components are already widely deployed. India's Aadhaar identity layer, Brazil's Pix payment system, and Estonia's X-Road data exchange illustrate the possibilities. DPI enables a shift from an AI system making recommendations—which then have to be manually executed by a civil servant—to a system that can execute by verifying a citizen's identity, checking eligibility across registries, and triggering a payment through a national system.[36] DPI allows AI to be both powerful and accountable.[37] However, it is much less utilized in lower-income countries than in higher-income countries (refer figure 8.4).

Among the DPI building blocks, data exchange is crucial for ensuring that an AI model has all the data it needs to be effective, yet governments typically underinvest in it. Building it well requires two layers of investment. The first layer is technical infrastructure: application programming interfaces (APIs) that let systems communicate, common identifiers that allow records to be matched across registries, and catalogs that make data sets discoverable and interpretable. For example, in Saudi Arabia, the platform operated by the Saudi Data & AI Authority (SDAIA) integrates data from more than 60 public agencies[38] while maintaining data within its own systems.[39]

The second layer of investment is data governance. Data-sharing agreements define what can be shared, with whom, and under what conditions. By contrast, agreements negotiated case by case are harder to scale. A shared consent layer, such as India's Data Empowerment and Protection Architecture consent manager model, standardizes how individuals grant and revoke permission for specific data flows, so that any provider and any authorized service can connect through a common mechanism rather than needing to do so through burdensome ad hoc data exchange agreements across institutions. Together, the technical and governance layers turn data exchange into a permanent infrastructure that can function with clear rules and dedicated institutional capacity.

Figure 8.4 Lower-income economies are less likely to leverage digital public infrastructure in their AI projects than higher-income economies

Survey question: "Are there any AI projects in your government that leverage any of the following?"

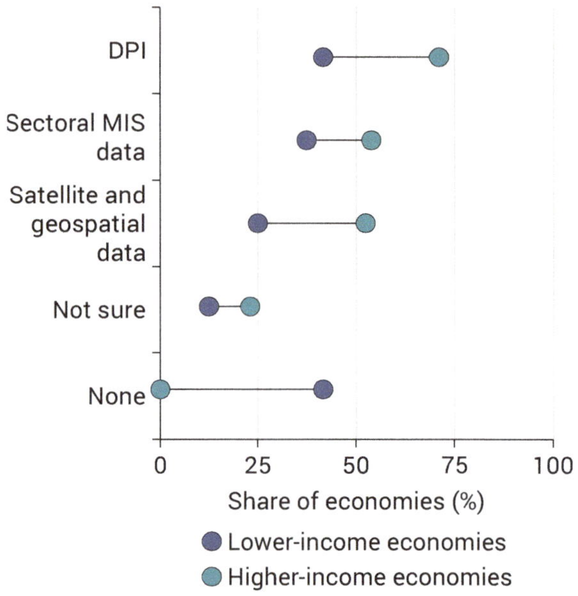

Source: WDR 2026 team, based on AI and Data for Better Governance Survey, World Bank.

Note: Digital public infrastructure (DPI) includes digital ID, data exchange, and digital payments. The sample includes 12 low-income and 12 lower-middle-income economies (lower-income group), as well as 16 upper-middle-income and 17 high-income economies (higher-income group). AI = artificial intelligence; MIS = management information system.

Governing the use of data

Governments occupy a unique position in the data ecosystem. Unlike private firms, they collect data under conditions in which citizens often have no choice, such as in taxation, justice, or civil registration. This relationship increases responsibility and introduces a fundamental tension between leveraging data for improving AI-driven public services and minimizing the risks of data misuse or reuse without consent. This tension is heightened by data protection frameworks modeled on the European Union's General Data Protection Regulation, with principles such as purpose limitation and data minimization that constrain how freely government data can be combined and reused. Overly restrictive interpretations can paralyze governments in regard to beneficial uses of data, including AI-driven solutions; overly permissive regulations can erode trust and expose populations to surveillance risks.

Some jurisdictions are beginning to manage this tension through trusted data environments and privacy-enhancing technologies. Synthetic data, in combination with differential privacy (which limits what analytical outputs reveal about any specific individual), can be used to gain insights or train AI models without exposing the underlying data. Other approaches enable organizations to collaborate without pooling their raw data. Federated learning trains models across multiple decentralized devices or data repositories, and secure multiparty computation enables multiple parties to compute joint analysis without revealing the inputs to one another. Both approaches permit data to remain under the control of their original holders.[40]

Many AI applications also require data that governments do not hold internally. For instance, telecom records proxy for mobility, satellite imagery supports land monitoring, and data on financial transactions enhance fraud detection. Negotiating access to these external sources poses a variety of issues, including privacy concerns, asymmetric bargaining power against large platforms, and the risk of dependency on proprietary sources. Establishing clear, fair frameworks for public-private data partnerships is a core condition of AI readiness. The choices governments make now with regard to data governance will shape their AI readiness for years (for details, refer to chapter 9).

Looking ahead, the AI systems that citizens already use to navigate their lives will increasingly interact with government systems directly—large language models and AI agents querying registries, checking eligibility, and possibly initiating transactions on citizens' behalf (refer to box 8.2). Public infrastructure will be used by private AI providers whether governments plan for it or not. Adjusting to this new reality will require new governance and technical arrangements, such as authenticating agents through verifiable credentials, defining what actions they are authorized to take on behalf of citizens or institutions, and recording those actions in a form that can be audited.[41] Governments that design for secure, authorized machine-to-machine interaction will set the terms of that access; those that do not will leave private providers to shape how citizens interact with the state.

Box 8.2 When AI and its agents come knocking at the door of public services, are governments ready?

Governments must ensure that their information and services are accessible through the artificial intelligence (AI) systems citizens increasingly rely on. When a citizen asks a chatbot a question (how to renew an ID, apply for benefits, or register a business), the chatbot should provide correct, country-specific guidance based on official sources. Moreover, as AI agents begin to act on users' behalf (searching websites, following links, and potentially completing tasks), they must be able to navigate government portals.

Analysis for this Report tested both scenarios across 166 countries. Four frontier large language models (LLMs) were evaluated on citizen-style questions regarding 20 public services from taxation to public safety. Each service was tested through a short exchange covering details on the service (the *chat mode*). In addition, automated agents were asked to navigate government portals (the *agent mode*).

Two results stand out. First, a country's scores on the United Nations E-Government Development Index are highly predictive of its chat mode scores, confirming that an LLM's information about a country is largely consistent with its overall digital maturity. In contrast, the agent mode scores are far less predictable, meaning that specific choices about the ways in which government portals are engineered drive most of the variation in the agent's performance.

Second, there is a clear advantage for English-speaking countries in LLM conversations about public services. Countries where English is the primary official language score 0.2–0.4 points higher on chat scores, on average, after GDP per capita and other metrics of government readiness are controlled for (refer to figure B8.2.1). This gap might reflect the composition of AI training data more than the quality of government services.

Many of the fixes governments can implement are low-cost, no-regret measures that also overlap with good web accessibility practices. Clear official pages, stable links, step-by-step procedures, and consistently organized information make public services easier for people and AI tools to navigate. Publishing official content in crawlable, text-accessible formats—that is, on open web pages whose text can be read automatically, rather than as scanned images or behind logins—can also increase the amount of reliable local-language information available to retrieval systems and for inclusion in future training corpora, contributing over time to better model performance in underrepresented languages. Website security should also avoid inadvertently blocking legitimate AI tools.

(Box continues next page)

Box 8.2 When AI and its agents come knocking at the door of public services, are governments ready? *(continued)*

Figure B8.2.1 AI performs better on public service queries in English-speaking countries, even after considering their income level

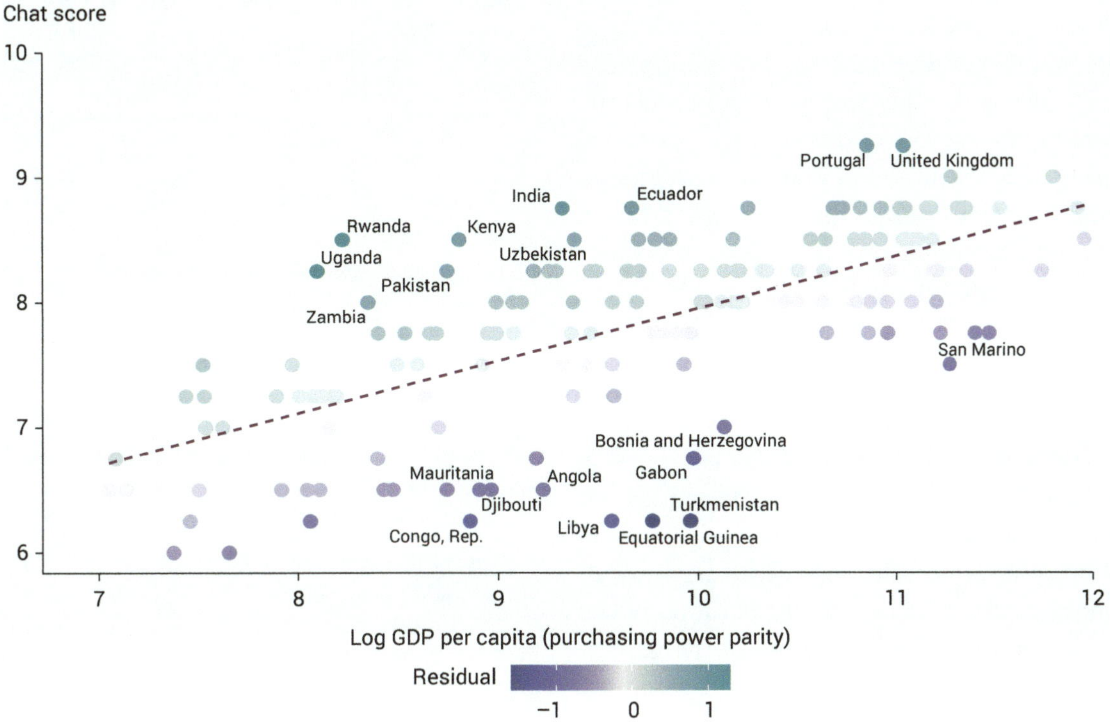

Source: Jordan et al. 2026.

Note: The figure includes ratings from four large language models across services. Green dots indicate higher scores relative to country income level, and purple dots indicate lower scores. The top 10 overperforming countries in chat scores (relative to GDP per capita) are labeled at the top, and the bottom 10 underperformers are labeled at the bottom. Overperformers are more likely to be English-speaking countries (even though not all of them are overperformers). In separate regression results, the relation between higher chat scores and English-speaking countries is statistically significant after GDP per capita, population, or access to the internet is controlled for. AI = artificial intelligence.

Source: WDR 2026 team, based on Jordan et al. 2026.

Evaluating and monitoring performance ensures that AI improves services

Institutional capacity and data are essential foundations, yet they alone do not ensure that AI fulfills its purpose and serves the public interest. Governments have a heightened responsibility to deploy AI that works for the people it was designed for. At the same time, governments in low- and lower-middle-income countries have constrained capacities to monitor and evaluate AI solutions, and 80 percent of these countries report having no or only basic mechanisms in place to evaluate AI performance (refer to figure 8.5).

Governments need to consider how to establish effective evaluation and monitoring mechanisms given their constrained budgets and technical capacities (refer to spotlight 6 for key steps in evaluating and monitoring AI). Most often, AI will not be built in-house, but procured from for-profit firms or codeveloped with academic or nonprofit partners. The interests of these entities may not always align with those of the government and need to be managed: for example, by using standardized tools to create transparency, building internal capacity, and setting standards for oversight functionalities as part of AI procurement. The discussion that follows highlights a number of practical considerations for this task. Documenting AI performance carefully and transparently will not only make government more effective but will also help foster public trust and accelerate the adoption of successful approaches by others.

Figure 8.5 Capabilities for AI evaluation in low- and lower-middle-income economies are limited, and more than half of agencies surveyed have no performance evaluation mechanisms in place

Survey question: "How do you (or relevant bodies) evaluate the performance of AI investments in government?"

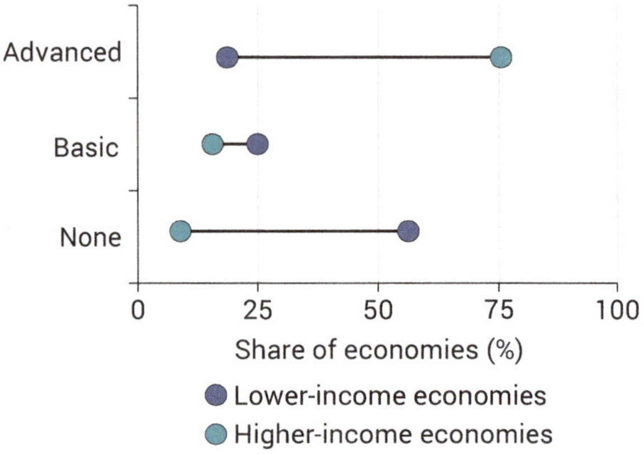

Source: WDR 2026 team, based on AI and Data for Better Governance Survey, World Bank.

Note: "Advanced" methods include assessments of service quality, cost-benefit analyses, independent audits, or other methods. "Basic" methods refer to basic monitoring of implementation and AI usage statistics. The sample includes 12 low-income and 12 lower-middle-income economies (lower-income group), as well as 16 upper-middle-income economies, and 17 high-income economies (higher-income group). AI = artificial intelligence.

Setting benchmarks and validating AI outputs

The stakes for performance are especially high in public service delivery in situations in which AI decisions can directly affect citizens' entitlements and rights. AI systems that are opaque or cannot be audited create serious accountability risks. Managing such risks requires setting clear performance standards before AI is deployed, verifying that those standards are met in the local context, and sustaining oversight throughout the system's operational life. The steps that follow provide an overview of this process.

Identifying the benchmark. To assess an AI model, the parameters that constitute acceptable performance must be made clear. Knowing how (and how well) the task is currently performed without AI can guide decisions and serve as justification for any requirements and standards that define acceptable AI performance parameters for use in government functions. As the case study of tuberculosis screening in box 5.1 illustrates, determining the cost-effectiveness of AI imaging depends on the alternative: Analysts considered other screening methods, such as symptom-based screening in lung health camps versus X-ray interpretation by humans in public clinics, and examined their sensitivity and specificity in regard to detecting tuberculosis.

Learning how the model was built and what data were used. The first step in understanding an AI product is to know how it was made, what it is optimizing, and for whom it is likely to work well. Academic researchers often publish detailed, albeit highly technical, information about their models, but in nonacademic contexts, model details are not always publicly shared. Governments can build transparency requirements into licensing and contracting. A *model card* is a voluntary transparency tool aimed at standardizing key information about an AI or machine learning model,[42] akin to a nutrition label for the AI. Basic model information should include the sample used in training; its composition, size, and properties; and any preprocessing the data underwent. A complementary tool is the *algorithmic impact assessment* (AIA), which uses structured exercises to understand risks and societal impacts of automating decision-making.[43] Mandatory disclosure of this kind is especially valuable in situations in which government agencies lack the in-house expertise to evaluate proprietary vendor systems. The method shifts the burden of explanation onto suppliers.

Making performance verification a part of procurement and deployment. All models require *validation* before being deployed: that is, testing how the model performs with data from the context in which it will be deployed. Testing can be done in-house or built into the contract. Validation should assess not only average accuracy, but also performance across relevant groups, regions, facilities, or case types, particularly in cases in which model biases may have consequences for the relative distribution of benefits, harms, and risks. In addition, regular revalidation should be embedded in the AI system itself to monitor model drift and inform future improvements. A challenge is that creating "ground truth" data is demanding. For example, one approach is to compare manual and AI-based decisions for a sample of cases, but this approach requires considerable time and strong subject matter expertise.

Ideally, manual review processes are automatically triggered, the set of cases is randomly sampled, and review results are tracked over time in visual dashboards to spot any changes in patterns early. For example, the system can track the share of all firms flagged for fraud, or the proportion of patient cases suspected of tuberculosis, and trigger alerts when these numbers change significantly. Combined with the predeployment documentation described earlier and a clear fallback plan if performance deteriorates, these monitoring practices reduce the risk of catastrophic failure.

Tracking intermediate outcomes and directing complementary investments. In addition to recording model performance, the AI system should also track *intermediate outcomes* such as usage analytics or adherence of humans to AI recommendations (refer to spotlight 6). Intermediate outcomes help the implementer spot bottlenecks that in many cases can be addressed with auxiliary measures, such as upgrading hardware, providing additional training and opportunities for users to give feedback, improving the user interface, or putting suitable incentives in place for adoption and use. It is important to plan the appropriate budget and sufficient time for these activities.

Tallying all costs. Tracking the costs of AI solutions—both fixed costs (for development and deployment) and variable costs (from continued training to software subscriptions)—enables governments to conduct cost-effectiveness analyses. To expand access among rural and underserved populations, governments may choose to prioritize voice and short message service (text-based) tools with offline capabilities that make fewer demands on devices and connectivity. Although these features can add adaptation costs up front, they may improve inclusion and lower the cost of additional users at scale. Careful comparisons of costs and impacts can appropriately factor in the trade-offs involved.

Answering the "big questions" with impact evaluation

Even when a given AI application has passed model validation and usability tests, it is uncertain what the effects on final outcomes (such as human well-being and productivity) will be and whether the solution is cost-effective relative to other options. Impact evaluations can establish whether the AI tool achieves improvements in development outcomes and what the costs are.

Answering the impact question requires more rigorous methods, which in turn typically require collaborations with academic or other research partners as well as external funding. In return, research can inform decisions about which types of AI interventions governments and funders should prioritize, how AI use might affect future capacity or resource needs, and where other interventions might have more impact. As spotlight 6 illustrates, impact evaluations can assess the risk of unintended consequences and systemwide effects. They can help yield deeper insights about how humans respond to AI and how such responses diminish or enhance final outcomes. They can also be used to investigate more fundamental systemwide impacts. For example, as AI changes the nature and content of work, it will also affect *who* will do the work and how well they do it; these shifts will have downstream effects—positive or negative—on final outcomes, such as the quality of public education and health care. In this context, it is important to formulate a clear understanding of the status quo or counterfactual. For impact evaluation purposes, an AI solution should be compared with the best available human or technical alternative; the goal is not a perfect system but to enable AI that produces net positive outcomes in regard to citizens' well-being.

Instituting operational oversight and integrity safeguards

Beyond technical performance, AI systems in public services require ongoing operational oversight to protect against integrity failures in which systems, software, or data are compromised, allowing unauthorized changes, tampering, or corruption that undermine trust and reliability. Transparency and oversight requirements must also extend to the users and operators of the system. Automated interactions can help reduce discretion; however, they may also introduce opportunities for manipulation by insiders who can override or alter AI outputs. Audit trails; access controls that determine who can access specific system components and under what conditions; immutable logging that creates tamper-proof, cryptographically secured records of system events that cannot be altered, deleted, or rewritten; and tamper detection mechanisms are part of a well-designed system and prevent diversion of benefits, manipulation, or distortions of performance metrics. Regular ex post reviews by trained human supervisors can detect anomalies in both the AI's outputs and the way these outputs are processed, used, communicated, and implemented, and can trigger corrective action.

A baseline governance architecture incorporates documented human review mechanisms, incident reporting and monitoring requirements, appeal and grievance channels, auditability and recordkeeping, and credible fallback or exit procedures when systems fail or drift. These principles and procedures create legitimacy, foster trust in public sector AI deployments and give the public levers for addressing integrity considerations.

Procuring AI effectively involves keeping control and oversight

A government or agency that has matched its ambition to deploy AI with its institutional readiness, structured its data for reliable use, and built the monitoring capacity needed to detect when things go wrong has done the hard internal work. What remains is procurement: how to acquire systems without losing the ability to act on new information, whether it is to require improvements, switch providers, or terminate contracts.

Procuring only what can be governed

Procurement choices depend on the level of government readiness for AI solutions (refer to table 8.1). An agency with basic infrastructure and weak procurement capacity that acquires a bespoke AI model to be built from scratch creates an implementation gap that it does not have the capacity to close. When system complexity exceeds operational capacity, one in six information technology projects ends in cost overruns of about 200 percent, studies indicate.[44] These mismatches are greater in countries where infrastructure gaps, fragmented data, and staffing constraints make it difficult to continue managing the process effectively (refer to box 8.3).[45]

Box 8.3 Why governments keep paying more for technology that keeps getting worse

Governments fund technology as if it were static, following a *project model* that is both expensive and more prone to failure.[a] The arc is familiar: identification of requirements, procurement, a large team of contractors, a brief internal sign-off that replaces thorough testing with real users, and handover to an underfunded phase of operations and maintenance. The system then deteriorates until a modernization cycle restarts the process at a higher price. Each cycle is larger than the last, as illustrated in figure B8.3.1. Users are consulted at the end, if at all, and knowledge walks out with the vendor.

Artificial intelligence (AI) intensifies this mismatch. The dominant costs are ongoing, not up-front; however, the project model funds the launch as if it were the largest cost. Systems adequately funded at launch become chronically underfunded in operation, when governance requirements are highest. And AI systems that are not actively maintained degrade over time. Model versions deteriorate, performance drifts, and security vulnerabilities accumulate.

(Box continues next page)

Box 8.3 Why governments keep paying more for technology that keeps getting worse *(continued)*

Figure B8.3.1 The traditional project model for funding AI produces poor results with rising costs

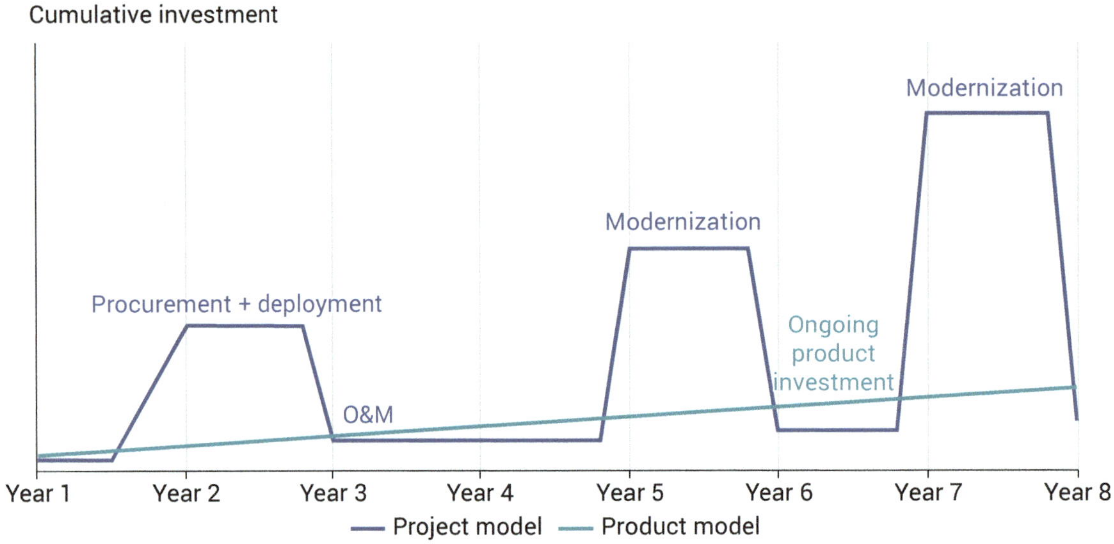

Source: Adapted from Pahlka 2024.
Note: AI = artificial intelligence; O&M = operations and maintenance.

The *product model* is the alternative: A small internal team holds ownership across the system's life, working with vendors on smaller contracts that can be switched to other vendors, iterating on feedback from real users, and adjusting as models and policy evolve. Experienced practitioners observe that most government technology could deliver 85 percent of required functionality at 10 percent of typical project cost if governments started smaller and improved continuously rather than attempting completeness up front.[b] Sustainable AI deployment requires a stable budget line, a permanent internal team, and a mandate that does not expire when the contract is signed.

Source: WDR 2026 team.
a. Pahlka (2024).
b. Pahlka (2023).

Early AI adoption patterns reflect this pattern. Off-the-shelf AI is a feasible entry point and dominates initial use across country income levels for such tasks such as drafting, classifying, and managing documents.[46] Even then, governments must define requirements, test performance, and keep exit options open.[47] There is a risk of lock-in even before any of that happens. Low-cost pilots, vendor partnerships, and donor-funded packages let a system accumulate the interaction logs, configurations, and integrations that make it useful, and the more such connections it accumulates, the harder it is to leave. None of this activity passes through regular procurement channels, so by the time a formal contract is signed the vendor has been chosen in all but name. Governing AI therefore means extending procurement discipline to those early engagements rather than reserving it for the contract at the end.[48]

The procurement stakes only intensify as governments move from adopting off-the-shelf tools toward adapting proven solutions for use with government data or even toward building bespoke models. At the adaptation stage, pricing is based on usage. At the advancement stage, the government becomes the system operator and must make large up-front investments.[49] For most governments, bespoke model development should be reserved for strategic uses with no adequate alternative—and undertaken only once operational capacity is in place. Most government activity will therefore occur at the adoption and adaptation stages.

Designing contracts to preserve agency

Outsourcing shifts the locus of responsibility, but it does not eliminate it. Contracts are the main instrument for protecting future options. Preserving agency is crucial. Three principles of contracts to preserve agency follow.

First, *data and context must be portable.* An AI system's value over time depends on the institutional knowledge (context) it accumulates: interaction logs, administrative decisions and operational manuals, and ongoing configuration choices. If none of this can be exported when the contract ends, a government that switches providers starts from zero: years of records, corrections, and refinements stay behind with the old vendor. Contracts should therefore state that this context belongs to the government and must be stored in formats that can be moved.

Second, *contracts should assume a future in which different AI models are used.* No frontier model performs best across all tasks, and a model's relative performance and costs change over time. Organizations already route workloads across models based on capability, reliability, and cost.[50] Locking an administration into one platform forecloses the option to adopt better tools as they evolve and encourages shadow usage. Contracts should require interoperable interfaces, avoid exclusivity clauses, and include migration paths with safeguards against price escalations and the right to engage in new contracts (retender).

Third, *lock-in should never be the default.* For high-impact uses such as identity verification, eligibility decisions, and security systems, the cost of lock-in and of failure is far higher than for low-stakes tasks like drafting, so these functions must remain switchable: context exportable, interfaces interoperable, and contracts open to retender, so that a replacement vendor or model can be substituted without having to rebuild the surrounding system.

Shaping AI markets through procurement

Procurement is one of governments' most powerful levers for shaping AI markets. Its terms determine which design decisions get embedded in public functions, what standards vendors must meet, and what accountability survives deployment.[51] The monetary value of public procurement averages 12.7 percent of GDP in member countries of the Organisation for Economic Co-operation and Development (OECD)[52] and even more (15–22 percent of GDP) in many developing countries.[53] When that share of national demand requires interoperability, auditability, data rights, and portability, suppliers build toward those specifications, and standards diffuse beyond government.

Procurement can also influence who participates in digital markets. France's decision to favor open-source software in public procurement created a demand shock that increased open-source contributions, expanded software entrepreneurship, and grew employment in the country's digital sector.[54] Some governments use procurement even more directly to build domestic capabilities. Rwanda's Public Procurement for Innovation framework allows agencies to procure solutions to public problems rather than predefined technical specifications. Firms compete through staged milestones while retaining intellectual property rights over what they build, creating an entry point for start-ups and local innovators that might otherwise be crowded out by large international vendors. For governments in lower-income countries with limited bargaining power against global AI providers, this way of shaping demand through procurement may be the most practical lever available.

Two mechanisms can extend that lever. Advance market commitments let buyers precommit to purchasing products that meet specified requirements, giving suppliers a reason to build toward those requirements rather than wait for demand to emerge.[55] A single government can use this mechanism domestically, or several governments can use it together. Pooling demand across borders aggregates many small buyers into one: GAVI, the Vaccine Alliance, has helped transform access to vaccines by aggregating demand across low- and middle-income countries. Pooled ownership does the same for digital infrastructure: Estonia, Finland, and Iceland jointly own and operate the X-Road data exchange platform through the Nordic Institute for Interoperability Solutions.[56] The same approach could be applied to AI. Governments could jointly commit to procuring AI tools that meet common standards for portability, interoperability, auditability, and public sector data rights, making these design features worth building.

Treating AI as an ongoing operational function of government requires different ways of thinking and funding

Governments generate value from AI when they select problems carefully, match their ambition to deploy the technology with their readiness level, invest in data and digital infrastructure, evaluate performance continuously, and procure systems in ways that preserve public control. AI systems are not finished when they are launched. Their performance depends on whether the model continues to fit the data, rules, and needs of the environment in which it operates. As those conditions change, performance can degrade quietly; the system may keep approving, denying, classifying, or recommending, but with declining reliability. Trustworthy AI systems therefore require continuous monitoring, periodic updating, active vendor management, and sufficient in-house technical capacity to detect problems and correct course.

A government that treats AI in public services as an operational function—with an expert team, a stable budget for data and evaluation, and clear authority over vendors—can keep it working and adjust as conditions change. Conversely, government administrations that implement AI as a one-time, fixed-duration project built around delivery milestones risk paying twice: first to build the system, and again to repair or replace it once it has drifted beyond their control.

The practical implication is straightforward. Instead of asking how much AI they can buy, governments should ask which problems they can leverage AI for; which digital public infrastructure, data, and teams are needed to sustain it; and which contracts preserve their ability to change course. The contracts being signed now, the effort made today to make data AI-ready, and the budget lines being approved in this cycle will determine whether governments remain able to direct these systems or become dependent on systems they no longer fully understand or control. The next generation of public service delivery will not be shaped by who adopts AI fastest, but by who builds the digital and institutional capacity to govern it.

Notes

1. This chapter presents the findings from a survey of governments conducted by the World Bank for *World Development Report 2026*. The survey findings focus on the use of, barriers to use of, and governance of AI, highlighting key differences across economies according to income level. The survey included a core module for digital agencies (or ministries of digital transformation or the equivalent), as well as two modules each for the following sectors: health, education, tax, public finance, civil service, and procurement. The survey was sent to relevant authorities in 129 economies. Respondents in 60 economies completed at least one of the modules, with 57 economies responding to the core module.
2. Kim et al. (2026).
3. *Structured data* refer to information organized according to a predefined, standardized format, allowing the data to be stored and processed systematically. In contrast, *unstructured data* do not follow a predefined scheme or tabular format and often include free text, images, audio, video, and documents.
4. For further details, refer to https://www.kwater.or.kr/web/eng/download/tech/ai_water_plant_en.pdf.
5. Ilves et al. (2025).
6. Readiness should not be assessed at the level of government in the aggregate. Tax administrations, for instance, tend to have richer data and more mature infrastructure available relative to local services offices or primary care systems.
7. A *national language model* is a large language model funded, built, or endorsed by a government or public institution to reflect a country's specific language, culture, legal frameworks, and societal priorities.
8. *Compute infrastructure* refers to the hardware and processing power needed to train and run AI models, from specialized chips to the energy that powers them. It provides the processing capacity required for training and inference, while software directs the ways in which the capacity is applied.
9. Lu et al. (2026).
10. Brynjolfsson and Hitt (2000); Brynjolfsson et al. (2021).
11. Clarke (2020); Greenway et al. (2018); Mergel et al. (2019).
12. Lundy et al. (2026).
13. Olsson and Bosch (2025).
14. Forsgren et al. (2018); Pahlka (2024).
15. Venson et al. (2024). For details, refer to Digital Government (portal), Ministry of Management and Innovation in Public Services, https://www.gov.br/governodigital/pt-br/home.
16. Aldane (2026).
17. United Kingdom, GDS (2025a).
18. United Kingdom, GDS (2025b).
19. For details, refer to Serpro (Serviço Federal de Processamento de Dados, Federal Data Processing Service) (homepage), https://www.serpro.gov.br/.
20. Lundy et al. (2026).
21. World Bank (2025b).
22. For details, refer to CBC (Capacity Building Commission) (web page), https://cbc.gov.in/about-cbc.
23. Refer to Africa Centre of Competence for Digital and Artificial Intelligence Skilling (dashboard), United Nations Development Programme, Kenya Country Office, https://www.undp.org/kenya/africa-centre-competence-digital-and-artificial-intelligence-skilling.
24. Mehmood et al. (2024).
25. Silveira et al. (2025).
26. *AI licenses* refer to government-provided access to approved AI tools, often through secure, enterprise-level accounts with appropriate privacy and data protections. *AI guidelines* set out how officials should use these tools responsibly, including what information may be entered, how outputs should be verified, and when human oversight may be required.
27. Monge (2025).
28. Santini et al. (2024).
29. Becker and Ferrari (2020).
30. Li et al. (2022); Xu et al. (2020).
31. Bäcker-Peral et al. (2026).
32. Gilardi et al. (2023).
33. Ensign et al. (2017).
34. Neil and Zanger-Tishler (2025).
35. World Bank (2025a).
36. Velmet (2026).
37. Nagar and Eaves (2024).
38. Saudi Arabia, SPA (2024).

39. This arrangement works if technical capacity is broadly distributed. If capacity is uneven across agencies, a centralized design that concentrates the technical burden on one capable team may be more advisable (refer to spotlight 7). The choice depends on the context and should therefore be determined case by case.
40. OECD (2025b).
41. Ilves et al. (2025).
42. Mitchell et al. (2019).
43. This assessment is based on a structured questionnaire in which the deploying agency describes the decisions that are being automated, the populations that are affected, the foreseeable risks, and the planned mitigations (Government of Canada 2025).
44. Flyvbjerg and Budzier (2011); Flyvbjerg et al. (2022).
45. Hashim and Piatti-Fünfkirchen (2018); Syed et al. (2023).
46. Frauscher and Sklar (2025).
47. Zick et al. (2024).
48. Hickok (2024).
49. Cottier et al. (2025); Lu et al. (2026). Some sources estimate that the actual costs of development run 1.2 to 4.0 times the published model training costs.
50. Aubakirova et al. (2025).
51. Mulligan and Bamberger (2019).
52. OECD (2025a).
53. Refer to https://www.worldbank.org/en/topic/procurement-for-development.
54. Nagle (2023).
55. Kremer et al. (2022).
56. ITS Rio (2024).

References

Aldane, Jack. 2026. "UAE Creates Dedicated Artificial Intelligence and Data Authority to 'Build Government of the Future.'" Global Government Forum. https://www.globalgovernmentforum.com/uae-creates-dedicated-artificial-intelligence-and-data-authority-to-build-government-of-the-future/.

Alfaro, Elena, Antonio Cabrales, José Elías Durán Roa, et al. 2026. "The Hidden Demand for AI Inside Your Company." *Enterprise Computing* (blog), April 14. https://hbr.org/2026/04/the-hidden-demand-for-ai-inside-your-company.

Aubakirova, Malika, Alex Atallah, Chris Clark, Justin Summerville, and Anjney Midha. 2025. "State of AI: An Empirical 100 Trillion Token Study with OpenRouter." December, OpenRouter. https://openrouter.ai/state-of-ai.

Bäcker-Peral, Verónica, Vitaly Meursault, and Christopher Severen. 2026. "Can LLMs Credibly Transform the Creation of Panel Data from Diverse Historical Tables?" *arXiv preprint arXiv:2505.11599*, version 2, July 1, 2026. https://arxiv.org/html/2505.11599v2.

Becker, Daniel P., and Isabela Ferrari. 2020. "VICTOR, the Brazilian Supreme Court's Artificial Intelligence: A Beauty or a Beast?" In *Regulação 4.0: Desafios da Regulação Diante de Um Novo Paradigma Científico*, vol. 2, edited by Daniel P. Becker and Isabela Ferrari. Editora Revista dos Tribunais. https://www.jusbrasil.com.br/doutrina/secao/victor-the-brazilian-supreme-court-s-artificial-intelligence-a-beauty-or-a-beast-regulacao-40-desafios-da-regulacao-diante-de-um-novo-paradigma-cientifico/1198075998.

Brynjolfsson, Erik, and Lorin Moultrie Hitt. 2000. "Beyond Computation: Information Technology, Organizational Transformation, and Business Performance." *Journal of Economic Perspectives* 14 (4): 23–48. https://doi.org/10.1257/jep.14.4.23.

Brynjolfsson, Erik, Daniel Rock, and Chad Syverson. 2021. "The Productivity J-Curve: How Intangibles Complement General Purpose Technologies." *American Economic Journal: Macroeconomics* 13 (1): 333–72. https://doi.org/10.1257/mac.20180386.

Clarke, Amanda. 2020. "Digital Government Units: What Are They, and What Do They Mean for Digital Era Public Management Renewal?" *International Public Management Journal* 23 (3): 358–79. https://doi.org/10.1080/10967494.2019.1686447.

Cottier, Ben, Robi Rahman, Loredana Fattorini, Nestor Maslej, Tamay Besiroglu, and David Owen. 2025. "The Rising Costs of Training Frontier AI Models." *arXiv:2405.21015v2 [cs.CY]*, February 7, Cornell University. https://doi.org/10.48550/ARXIV.2405.21015.

Dang-Pham, Duy, Nik Thompson, Atif Ahmad, and Sean Maynard. 2025. "Shadow Information Security Practices in Organizations: The Role of Information Security Transparency, Overload, and Psychological Empowerment." *Computers and Security* 156 (September): 104538. https://doi.org/10.1016/j.cose.2025.104538.

Ensign, Danielle, Sorelle A. Friedler, Scott Neville, Carlos Scheidegger, and Suresh Venkatasubramanian. 2017. "Runaway Feedback Loops in Predictive Policing." *arXiv:1706.09847v3 [cs.CY]*, December 22, Cornell University. https://doi.org/10.48550/ARXIV.1706.09847.

Flyvbjerg, Bent, and Alexander Budzier. 2011. "Why Your IT Project May Be Riskier Than You Think." *Harvard Business Review* 89 (9): 601–03. https://hbr.org/2011/09/why-your-it-project-may-be-riskier-than-you-think.

Flyvbjerg, Bent, Alexander Budzier, Jong Seok Lee, Mark Keil, Daniel Lunn, and Dirk W. Bester. 2022. "The Empirical Reality of IT Project Cost Overruns: Discovering A Power-Law Distribution." *arXiv:2210.01573v1 [physics.soc-ph]*, September 30, Cornell University. https://doi.org/10.48550/ARXIV.2210.01573.

Forsgren, Nicole, Jez Humble, and Gene Kim. 2018. *Accelerate: The Science of Lean Software and DevOps; Building and Scaling High Performing Technology Organizations*. IT Revolution. https://itrevolution.com/product/accelerate/.

Frauscher, Kathrin, and Kaye Sklar. 2025. "The Surprising Shifts in How the Public Sector Is Buying AI, and What

Policymakers Can Do About It." *AI Blog*, November 10. https://www.open-contracting.org/2025/11/10/the-surprising-shifts-in-how-the-public-sector-is-buying-ai-and-what-policymakers-can-do-about-it/.

Gilardi, Fabrizio, Meysam Alizadeh, and Maël Kubli. 2023. "ChatGPT Outperforms Crowd Workers for Text-Annotation Tasks." *PNAS: Proceedings of the National Academy of Sciences* 120 (30): e2305016120. https://doi.org/10.1073/pnas.2305016120.

Gillespie, Nicole, Steven Lockey, Tabi Ward, Alexandria Macdade, and Gerard Hassed. 2025. *Trust, Attitudes and Use of Artificial Intelligence: A Global Study 2025*. University of Melbourne; KPMG International. https://doi.org/10.26188/28822919.

Government of Canada. 2025. "Algorithmic Impact Assessment." Version 1.0.1 (October 3), Open Government, Government of Canada. https://canada-ca.github.io/aia-eia-js/.

Greenway, Andrew, Ben Terrett, Mike Bracken, and Tom Loosemore. 2018. *Digital Transformation at Scale: Why the Strategy Is Delivery*. Perspectives Series. London Publishing Partnership. https://www.andrewgreenway.com/book.

Hashim, Ali, and Moritz Piatti-Fünfkirchen. 2018. "Lessons from Reforming Financial Management Information Systems: A Review of the Evidence." Policy Research Working Paper 8312, World Bank. https://doi.org/10.1596/1813-9450-8312.

Hickok, Merve. 2024. "Public Procurement of Artificial Intelligence Systems: New Risks and Future Proofing." *AI and Society* 39 (3): 1213–27. https://doi.org/10.1007/s00146-022-01572-2.

Ilves, Luukas, Manuel Kilian, Simone Maria Parazzoli, Tiago C. Peixoto, and Ott Velsberg. 2025. "The Agentic State: Rethinking Government for the Era of Agentic AI." Vision Paper, Global Government Technology Centre Berlin and World Bank. https://agenticstate.org/paper.html.

ITS Rio (Instituto de Tecnologia & Sociedade, Institute for Technology & Society). 2024. "Building a Global Alliance for Compute Power: Lessons from GAVI's History, Governance Structure, and Funding Strategies." Draft version, ITS Rio. https://itsrio.org/wp-content/uploads/2016/12/Building-a-Global-Alliance-for-Compute-Power.pdf.

Jordan, Luke, Manuel Ramos-Maqueda, and Tiago C. Peixoto. 2026. "RADAR: Benchmarking AI-Mediated Access to Government Services." World Bank. https://manuelramosmaqueda.com/wp-content/uploads/2026/07/radar_arxiv_preprint.pdf.

Kim, Hyunjin, Dahyeon Kim, and Rembrand Koning. 2026. "Mapping AI into Production: A Field Experiment on Firm Performance." INSEAD Working Paper 2026/20/STR, INSEAD. https://doi.org/10.2139/ssrn.6513481.

Kremer, Michael Robert, Jonathan Levin, and Christopher M. Snyder. 2022. "Designing Advance Market Commitments for New Vaccines." *Management Science* 68 (7): 4786–814. https://doi.org/10.1287/mnsc.2021.4163.

Li, Minghao, Tengchao Lv, Jingye Chen, et al. 2022. "TrOCR: Transformer-Based Optical Character Recognition with Pre-Trained Models." *arXiv:2109.10282v5 [cs.CL]*, September 6, Cornell University. https://doi.org/10.48550/ARXIV.2109.10282.

Lu, Jiahao, Ziwei Xu, William Tjhi, et al. 2026. "Buy Versus Build an LLM: A Decision Framework for Governments." *arXiv:2602.13033v2 [cs.CY]*, February 23, Cornell University. https://doi.org/10.48550/ARXIV.2602.13033.

Lundy, Timothy, Shyam Jayanti Patel, Manuel Ramos-Maqueda, Daniel Rogger, Flavia Sacco Capurro, and Josefina Silva Fuentealba. 2026. "How Is Government Using AI?" Background paper prepared for *World Development Report 2026: The Promise of Artificial Intelligence*, World Bank. https://www.worldbank.org/en/publication/wdr2026/brief/world-development-report-2026-background-papers.

Mehmood, Sultan, Shaheen Naseer, and Daniel Chen. 2024. "AI Education as State Capacity: Experimental Evidence from Pakistan." National Bureau of Economic Research. https://users.nber.org/~dlchen/papers/Transmitting_AI_Training.pdf.

Mergel, Ines, Noella Edelmann, and Nathalie Haug. 2019. "Defining Digital Transformation: Results from Expert Interviews." *Government Information Quarterly* 36 (4): 101385. https://doi.org/10.1016/j.giq.2019.06.002.

Mitchell, Margaret, Simone Wu, Andrew Zaldivar, et al. 2019. "Model Cards for Model Reporting." In *FAT* '19: Proceedings of the 2019 Conference on Fairness, Accountability, and Transparency*, edited by Danah Boyd and Jamie Morgenstern. Association for Computing Machinery. https://doi.org/10.1145/3287560.3287596.

Monge, Fernando. 2025. "Data For Sale: When Governments Become Data Buyers." *Datapolis* (blog), October 19. https://fermonge.substack.com/p/data-for-sale-when-governments-become?r=p5o68&utm_campaign=post&utm_medium=web&triedRedirect=true.

Mulligan, Deirdre K., and Kenneth A. Bamberger. 2019. "Procurement as Policy: Administrative Process for Machine Learning." *Berkeley Technology Law Journal* 34 (3): 773–851. https://doi.org/10.15779/Z38RN30793.

Nagar, Sarosh, and David Eaves. 2024. "Interactions Between Artificial Intelligence and Digital Public Infrastructure: Concepts, Benefits, and Challenges." *arXiv:2412.05761v1 [cs.CY]*, December 7, Cornell University. https://doi.org/10.48550/ARXIV.2412.05761.

Nagle, Frank. 2023. "Government IT Procurement Policy & Firm Behavior: Evidence from a French Open Source Software Policy." *Academy of Management Proceedings* 2023 (1): 13046. https://doi.org/10.5465/AMPROC.2023.13046abstract.

Neil, Roland, and Michael Zanger-Tishler. 2025. "Algorithmic Bias in Criminal Risk Assessment: The Consequences of Racial Differences in Arrest as a Measure of Crime." *Annual Review of Criminology* 8 (January): 97–119. https://doi.org/10.1146/annurev-criminol-022422-125019.

OECD (Organisation for Economic Co-operation and Development). 2025a. *Government at a Glance 2025*. OECD. https://www.oecd.org/en/publications/2025/06/government-at-a-glance-2025_70e14c6c/full-report/size-of-public-procurement_6979cd47.html#indicator-d1e18876-94cb3dc3a1.

OECD (Organisation for Economic Co-operation and Development). 2025b. "Sharing Trustworthy AI Models with Privacy-Enhancing Technologies." OECD Artificial Intelligence Paper 38, OECD. https://www.oecd.org/content/dam/oecd/en/publications/reports/2025/06/sharing-trustworthy-ai-models-with-privacy-enhancing-technologies_5df6fd05/a266160b-en.pdf.

Olsson, Helena Holmström, and Jan Bosch. 2025. "Strategic Digital Product Management: Nine Approaches." *Information and Software Technology* 177 (January): 107594. https://doi.org/10.1016/j.infsof.2024.107594.

Pahlka, Jennifer. 2024. "Project vs Product Funding." *Eating Policy*, June 3. https://www.eatingpolicy.com/p/project-vs-product-funding.

Santini, Juan Francisco, Flavia Sacco Capurro, Daniel Oliver Rogger, et al. 2024. *Data for Better Governance: Building Government Analytics Ecosystems in Latin America and the Caribbean*. World Bank. https://doi.org/10.1596/978-1-4648-2159-2.

Saudi Arabia, SPA (Saudi Press Agency). 2024. "SDAIA Report: Saudi Arabia Leads the Way in Global AI Innovation." Press Release, September 6. https://www.spa.gov.sa/en/N2201971.

Silveira, Bernardo, Daniel L. Chen, and Manuel Ramos-Maqueda. 2025. "Bureaucratic Training and State Capacity: Experimental Evidence from Peru's Judiciary." Paper presented at Georgetown Law's Conference on Empirical Legal Studies, Georgetown University, Washington, DC, October 24–25. http://www.bernardosilveira.net/resources/Peru_Training_AMAG.pdf.

Syed, Rehan, Wasana Bandara, and Rebekah Eden. 2023. "Public Sector Digital Transformation Barriers: A Developing Country Experience." *Information Polity* 28 (1): 5–27. https://doi.org/10.3233/IP-220017.

UNESCO (United Nations Educational, Scientific and Cultural Organization). 2024. "UNESCO Global Judges' Initiative: Survey on the Use of AI Systems by Judicial Operators." UNESCO. https://unesdoc.unesco.org/ark:/48223/pf0000389786.

United Kingdom, GDS (Government Digital Service). 2025a. "AI Coding Assistant Trial: UK Public Sector Findings Report." September 12, GDS, Department for Science, Innovation and Technology. https://www.gov.uk/government/publications/ai-coding-assistant-trial/ai-coding-assistant-trial-uk-public-sector-findings-report.

United Kingdom, GDS (Government Digital Service). 2025b. "Microsoft 365 Copilot Experiment: Cross-Government Findings Report." June 2, GDS, Department for Science, Innovation and Technology. https://assets.publishing.service.gov.uk/media/683db42bd23a62e5d32680d0/M365_Copilot_Experiment_Findings_Report.pdf.

van Acken, Jan-Philip, Floris Jansen, Slinger Jansen, and Katsiaryna Labunets. 2024. "Who Is the IT Department Anyway: An Evaluative Case Study of Shadow IT Mindsets Among Corporate Employees." In *SOUPS '24: Proceedings of the Twentieth USENIX Conference on Usable Privacy and Security*, edited by Patrick Gage Kelley and Apu Kapadia. USENIX Association. https://www.usenix.org/system/files/soups2024-van-acken.pdf.

Vance, Anthony, David Eargle, Jeffrey L. Jenkins, C. Brock Kirwan, and Bonnie Brinton Anderson. 2019. "The Fog of Warnings: How Non-Essential Notifications Blur with Security Warnings." In *SOUPS'19: Proceedings of the Fifteenth USENIX Conference on Usable Privacy and Security*, edited by Heather Richter Lipford. USENIX Association.

Velmet, Aro. 2026. "Database Politics: Informational Infrastructure and Network Utopias in Soviet and Post-Soviet Estonia." *Internet Histories* 10 (1–2): 45–64. https://doi.org/10.1080/24701475.2026.2639221.

Venson, Elaine, Rejane Maria da Costa Figueiredo, and Edna Dias Canedo. 2024. "Leveraging a Startup-Based Approach for Digital Transformation in the Public Sector: A Case Study of Brazil's Startup Gov.Br Program." *Government Information Quarterly* 41 (3): 101943. https://doi.org/10.1016/j.giq.2024.101943.

World Bank. 2025a. "Digital Public Infrastructure and Development: A World Bank Group Approach." Digital Transformation White Paper, vol. 1, World Bank. https://doi.org/10.1596/42935.

World Bank. 2025b. *From Bytes to Benefits: Digital Transformation as a Catalyst for Public Sector Productivity*. Malaysia Economic Monitor (October). World Bank. https://doi.org/10.1596/43809.

Xu, Yiheng, Minghao Li, Lei Cui, Shaohan Huang, Furu Wei, and Ming Zhou. 2020. "LayoutLM: Pre-Training of Text and Layout for Document Image Understanding." In *KDD '20: Proceedings of the 26th ACM SIGKDD International Conference on Knowledge Discovery and Data Mining*, edited by Rajesh Gupta, Yan Liu, Mohak Shah, Suju Rajan, Jiliang Tang, and B. Aditya Prakash. Association for Computing Machinery. https://doi.org/10.1145/3394486.3403172.

Zick, Tom, Mason Kortz, David Eaves, and Finale Doshi-Velez. 2024. "AI Procurement Checklists: Revisiting Implementation in the Age of AI Governance." *arXiv:2404.14660v1 [cs.CY]*, April 23, Cornell University. https://doi.org/10.48550/arXiv.2404.14660.

6 Spotlight 6

Evaluating and Monitoring the Performance of AI Solutions

This Report provides many examples of how artificial intelligence (AI) and machine learning models may increase productivity across sectors and promote development and human well-being. For these gains to materialize, however, four evaluation steps that build on one another must be undertaken: defining objectives and establishing minimal performance requirements for the AI or machine learning model; validating that the model performs well with real-world data; ensuring that users can access tools based on the model easily and use them in the intended manner; and ultimately, verifying that the tools achieve the desired outcomes and do not cause harm while remaining cost-effective. Figure S6.1 illustrates these four steps.

This spotlight discusses considerations for evaluating the performance and impact of an AI or machine learning application. Akin to a theory of change, the steps outlined provide organizations planning to use AI in their work with an introductory framework for anticipating risks and potential failure points and implementing good practices. They also serve as a guide for asking the right questions about how the model underlying an application has been trained and what monitoring functions are in place for adopting AI systems built by others.

Monitoring and evaluation are relevant for both decentralized "front-end" AI applications for large numbers of users and centralized "back-end" AI systems. Each may use predictive AI, optimization algorithms, or generative AI (for more information, refer to chapter 5). Readers interested specifically in front-end generative AI applications may find the *Generative AI Evaluation Playbook* useful.[1] The playbook, a living document, has parallels to the theory-of-change framework used here and delves more deeply into technical methods for validating and evaluating generative AI tools.

Model validation against a performance benchmark

An important prerequisite in ensuring that an AI model delivers positive impacts is that it fulfills its intended objectives and produces accurate outputs. Does the model predict the onset of monsoon season accurately, for example? Are chat questions answered with relevant information and in the right tone? *Validation* uses real-world inputs and compares model-generated outputs with independently created validation data to assess AI model performance.

Figure S6.1 Evaluating and monitoring the performance and impacts of AI applications to promote development

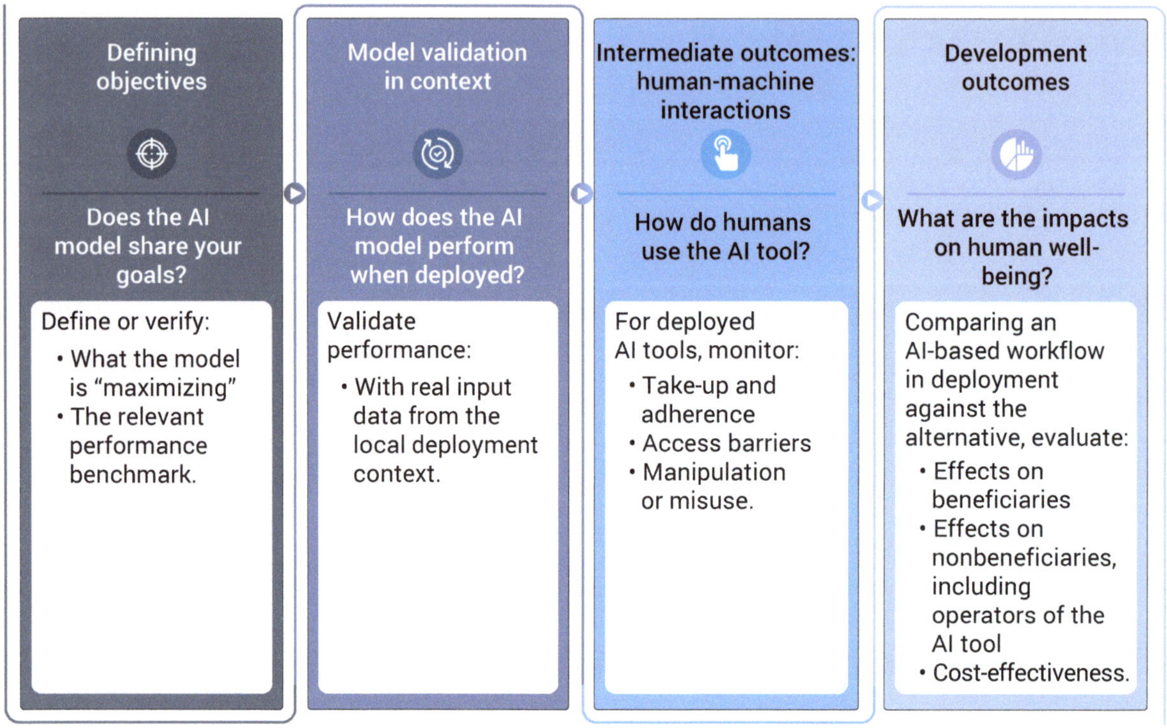

Source: WDR 2026 team.

Note: Adherence refers to the extent to which users of an AI tool follow its recommendations. It includes the possibility of selective adherence (that is, users may follow only some of the tool's recommendations and perhaps in a biased way). AI = artificial intelligence.

Model validation should always be part of model training. For example, a study on the benefits of applying machine learning to phone records to improve poverty targeting in Bangladesh collected detailed data on 5,000 households that identified which families were truly poor.[2] Researchers then separated the sample into two parts, using one subsample to train the model and the other to measure how well the trained model identified the poorest households (refer to box 5.4 in chapter 5). Using data held out in this manner for validation is a best practice and ensures that the model has not just "memorized" the training sample.

However, validation in the training context is only the first step. AI and machine learning models can perform much worse when deployed than they did under the original training and testing conditions. The risk increases if a model has been built using data from a very different context than the one in which it has been deployed or if the original training and validation sample was too small or biased toward specific populations. This is because the model may have learned patterns that do not apply to the population where the model is being deployed.

Models must therefore also be validated using data from the local context, and those that do not pass such validation should not be deployed. What counts as passing should, ideally, be defined in advance of the validation process. Setting *benchmarks* or *minimal performance requirements* provides a path for governments and international organizations to influence AI or machine learning development. Benchmarks may build on expert human performance, outcomes under the status quo, or normative decision-making. For example, the error rate of the machine learning model for poverty targeting in the Bangladesh study discussed earlier was about 20 percent higher than that of a more conventional proxy means test. A high error rate of this type could be a basis for deciding against deploying the AI tool (refer to box 5.4).

Even if their performance is initially strong, AI models may also "drift" over time as the contexts in which they are deployed shift. Regular repeated validation exercises should therefore be built into any deployment. For example, for a model used to identify poor households, a social protection agency could periodically conduct a survey among a representative sample of the population to confirm that the recipients the AI model has selected to receive benefits are indeed poor and nonrecipients are not.

Tools based on *generative AI* typically adapt existing foundational large language or multimodal models rather than training a new model from scratch, but such adapted models carry risks similar to those of other AI models, and the methods for evaluating their performance are similar. For validation purposes, text generated by a generative AI model can, for example, be compared with an "ideal" response, fact-checked by an expert, or scored under relevant criteria, sometimes using another large language model. Just as with a classical machine learning model, a large language model may not perform well when deployed in a particular local context if the inputs used in training the model are not representative of the local context or if a small sample has been overused to adapt the model to that context.

Generative AI behaviors add to the challenge of controlling the outputs of generative AI models and verifying their performance. Generative AI outputs are not deterministic and may be "jagged": That is, they may succeed at one task but fail at another seemingly similar task.[3] Even consecutive versions of the same generative AI model can respond to the same prompts differently, and small variations in how the model is instructed or used can affect outputs, sometimes dramatically.[4] Fine-tuning a large language model can unravel built-in protections and increase the risk of harmful outputs, such as violent, defamatory, or illegal content.[5] Any specific use of a large language model should therefore be validated using inputs that resemble as closely as possible the real-world context in which the model will be deployed. Additional stress-testing techniques, such as "red teaming," in which another large language model agent systematically searches for vulnerabilities in a large language model being tested, can reveal safety risks, such as divulging personal information that was inadvertently included in the model's training data.[6]

Human-machine interactions and intermediate outcomes

Many times, the model on which an AI tool is based is only a small factor in whether the tool ultimately achieves the desired outcomes. Do struggling students use an AI tutoring app regularly, for instance? Do audit patterns change based on AI-generated fraud flags? Are messages with automated weather alerts successfully delivered to farmers' phones? Accessibility, usability, and integration with actual workflows are key factors in the success of an AI tool, particularly in front-end AI applications. For example, for public servants who are accustomed to performing paper-based tasks, AI tools that accommodate this habit (such as enabling AI-generated maps to be printed and allowing space for paper-based signatures) can greatly increase acceptance.[7]

For an AI tool to improve development outcomes, adoption, acceptance, and appropriate use of the tool are necessary steps. *Intermediate outcome metrics* for AI systems measure whether and how AI tools are used. These metrics include user expectations; trust in and satisfaction with the tools; usage analytics such as click rates or the rates at which users manually override AI recommendations; and measures of basic functioning, such as server downtime or the number of help desk requests. Many intermediate outcomes are by-products of deployment and should be monitored day to day, but measures of these outputs can also come from pilots or test sessions. A key advantage of digital systems, including AI systems, is that intermediate outcomes from such systems can be continuously tracked and used to make iterative improvements using, for example, *A/B testing* (short experiments comparing user responses under different implementation choices).

Impact evaluation to scale successful interventions

Intermediate outcome measures capture what happens while an AI tool is deployed, but not what would have happened without the tool. *Impact evaluations* establish the *overall effect of using an AI system compared with a counterfactual,* such as maintaining the status quo or investing the funds used to develop the AI tool elsewhere. Accurate estimates of impact are a key ingredient in measuring *cost-effectiveness* (the per unit cost of improvements to an outcome of interest). They also help inform the allocation of resources both within a country and at the global level. Impact evaluations are especially valuable given the thin evidence base concerning AI interventions in low- and middle-income countries, but such evaluations require time, resources, and technical capacity. International institutions and donors should therefor make funding impact evaluations a priority for investment.

Questions that an impact evaluation can answer

Key questions about the impact of an intervention involving an AI tool must include the potential for unintended consequences from the intervention, the effects on populations or outcomes that were not the target of the intervention, systemwide impacts that change the environment in which the tool is deployed, and human responses to the tool. Measuring such impacts typically requires substantial research expertise. Unless such capacity exists in-house, evaluations of the impact of AI tools are best conducted in collaboration with an external partner.

Unanticipated effects on targeted outcomes

AI may affect—or not affect—targeted outcomes in unexpected ways. For example, the burden of collecting data as inputs into the algorithm may fall on the same frontline service providers who are already struggling to carry out their day-to-day work consistently and at high quality. Nisar et al. (2022) coin the term "counterproductive computing" to describe algorithmic solutions that distract overstretched and underpaid bureaucrats to the point that their implementation adversely affects these workers' core responsibilities. Or take the hypothetical example of a chatbot that helps community health workers identify high-risk pregnancies. If a lack of transport options prevents pregnant women at risk from traveling to a clinic where appropriate medical action can be initiated, the chatbot may work as expected yet have no impact on pregnancy outcomes. An impact evaluation can measure the net effect of factors such as these.

Effects on nonbeneficiaries and systemwide impacts

A complete evaluation of the impact of an AI tool must include everyone the tool could affect. For example, if an AI model is used to determine the allocation of resources, it is important to understand the impact on those who are not included in the data used as inputs for the model. AI use by some can also have indirect effects on nonusers. Such effects are well-known in the context of labor market programs to improve job placement, in which program beneficiaries often displace other job seekers.[8] These types of system-level effects can crop up in many forms. For example, clinics or schools equipped with AI tools might attract higher-quality staff, leaving patients or students in institutions that are not equipped with such tools at a double disadvantage.

Human responses to AI

Evidence is limited regarding how human biases in interpreting AI outputs affect and how these biases play out in low- and middle-income contexts. Over time, research can improve understanding of what forms of collaboration between humans and AI are most effective. Incentives are another important factor to consider. In cases in which AI models inform decisions about the allocation of resources, for example, potential beneficiaries may intentionally modify their behavior to influence the algorithms underlying the models. Some machine learning design choices can protect against manipulation (such as using incoming calls rather than outgoing calls in phone data, which the phone user can less easily affect).[9] In general, the economic literature has shown that strategic attempts to influence allocation decisions can sometimes be prevented only with artificial restrictions that can have negative impacts on well-being, such as imposing onerous conditions or requiring copious paperwork to access these benefits. Impact evaluations can measure these side effects of AI.

Challenges for conducting impact evaluations

Conducting rigorous impact evaluations of AI-based interventions poses some challenges. For one thing, it can be difficult to create comparable intervention and control groups that truly reflect outcomes with and without an AI system. The groups can influence each other as a result of, among other things, systemwide effects described earlier. So-called network effects, in which the value of adopting a particular AI tool increases when many people have already adopted it, may also be a factor. For example, the success of ride-sharing apps depends on having a large enough number of drivers and riders for the app to function.[10] AI often adds the most value when applied to large data sets and complex, interconnected systems. For instance, a tool for optimizing supply chains that centrally manages medication deliveries to rural clinics cannot operate at its best when applied to only a small subset of facilities. These types of effects can mean that a control group is tempted to adopt an AI tool on its own, but also that rolling out the same tool in only a small group does not capture all of the tool's benefits.

A second challenge is that markets are evolving extremely rapidly along many dimensions, from the technological capabilities of AI to market structure, prices, and broad diffusion. For example, an evaluation of the impact of a policy intervention involving an AI model that is "frozen" at the start will measure the effects of the intervention *conditional* on the performance of the model (as validated in an earlier step in the evaluation process). Researchers may attempt to extrapolate the impact of "the AI of tomorrow" from the effects of "the AI of today,"[11] although this adds uncertainty. Alternatively, a research design can track both evolving model performance and impacts across the evaluation period and measure how they are related. Thoughtful research design choices can help address such issues.

Notes

1. CGD et al. (2026).
2. Aiken et al. (2025).
3. Gans (2026); Mollick (2023).
4. Chen et al. (2023).
5. Qi et al. (2023).
6. Perez et al. (2022).
7. Nisar et al. (2022).
8. Crépon et al. (2013).
9. Refer to Björkegren et al. (2026).
10. Chen (2021).
11. Björkegren (2025).

References

Aiken, Emily L., Anik Ashraf, Joshua Evan Blumenstock, Raymond Guiteras, and Ahmed Mushfiq Mobarak. 2025. "Scalable Targeting of Social Protection: When Do Algorithms Out-Perform Surveys and Community Knowledge?" NBER Working Paper 33919, National Bureau of Economic Research. https://doi.org/10.3386/w33919.

Björkegren, Daniel. 2025. "AI Is Transforming the Economy: Understanding Its Impact Requires Both Data and Imagination." *Nature* 648 (8094): 535–37. https://doi.org/10.1038/d41586-025-04053-w.

Björkegren, Daniel, Joshua Evan Blumenstock, and Samsun Knight. 2026. "Manipulation-Robust Prediction." *American Economic Review*. Preview published ahead of print. https://www.aeaweb.org/articles?id=10.1257/aer.20241087&&from=f.

CGD (Center for Global Development), The Agency Fund, and IDinsight. 2026. *Generative AI Evaluation Playbook for the Development Sector*. CGD, The Agency Fund, and IDinsight. https://eval.playbook.org.ai/.

Chen, Andrew. 2021. *The Cold Start Problem: How to Start and Scale Network Effects*. Harper Business. https://andrewchen.com/wp-content/uploads/2022/01/ColdStartProb_9780062969743_AS0928_cc20_Final.pdf.

Chen, Lingjiao, Matei Zaharia, and James Zou. 2023. "How Is ChatGPT's Behavior Changing over Time?" *arXiv:2307.09009v3 [cs.CL]*, October 31, Cornell University. https://arxiv.org/abs/2307.09009.

Crépon, Bruno, Esther Duflo, Marc Gurgand, Roland Rathelot, and Philippe Zamora. 2013. "Do Labor Market Policies Have Displacement Effects? Evidence from a Clustered Randomized Experiment." *Quarterly Journal of Economics* 128 (2): 531–80. https://doi.org/10.1093/qje/qjt001.

Gans, Joshua S. 2026. "Artificial Jagged Intelligence: When AI Benchmarks Misstate Deployment Value." NBER Working Paper 34712, National Bureau of Economic Research. https://doi.org/10.3386/w34712.

Mollick, Ethan. 2023. "Centaurs and Cyborgs on the Jagged Frontier." *One Useful Thing* (blog), September 16. https://www.oneusefulthing.org/p/centaurs-and-cyborgs-on-the-jagged.

Nisar, Harsh, Deepak Gupta, Pankaj Kumar, Srinivasa Rao Murapaka, A. V. Rajesh, and Alka Upadhyaya. 2022. "Algorithmic Rural Road Planning in India: Constrained Capacities and Choices in Public Sector." In *Proceedings of 2022 ACM Conference on Equity and Access in Algorithms, Mechanisms, and Optimization (EAAMO '22)*, Article 14. Association for Computing Machinery. https://doi.org/10.1145/3551624.3555299.

Perez, Ethan, Saffron Huang, Francis Song, et al. 2022. "Red Teaming Language Models with Language Models." *arXiv:2202.03286v1 [cs.CL]*, February 7, Cornell University. https://doi.org/10.48550/ARXIV.2202.03286.

Qi, Xiangyu, Yi Zeng, Tinghao Xie, et al. 2023. "Fine-Tuning Aligned Language Models Compromises Safety, Even When Users Do Not Intend To!" *arXiv:2310.03693v1 [cs.CL]*, October 5, Cornell University. https://doi.org/10.48550/ARXIV.2310.03693.

9

Governments as Regulators: Ensuring Trustworthy AI to Manage the Concentration of Power

Main messages

- **Unclear AI rules can erode trust and slow adoption**
  Start with voluntary standards, but back them with regulation when such standards alone do not ensure rights, safety, and the public interest.
- **One-size-fits-all AI laws may not suit local needs**
  Review existing laws that may apply to AI, identify gaps, test approaches, improve transparency, and consult widely.
- **Existing rules may not cover AI's new and amplified risks**
  Clarify or extend protections for training data, privacy, transparency, discrimination, surveillance, and cybersecurity.
- **Regulators and AI providers may lack the capacity to make AI requirements work**
  Provide adequate budgets, strengthen technical expertise, and help AI providers meet compliance requirements.
- **Developing economies risk having global AI rules written without them**
  Participate in international forums and standards-setting bodies, promote globally compatible rules, and cooperate across borders to enforce them.

A reproducibility package is available for this book in the Reproducible Research Repository at https://reproducibility.worldbank.org/catalog/624.

Introduction

An artificial intelligence (AI) system deployed by a government denied a 67-year-old widow her legal entitlement to subsidized food grain because it mistook her late husband, a street vendor, for an unrelated restaurant owner who shared part of his name. Investigations by journalists and civil society later revealed that thousands of such exclusions stemmed from flawed algorithmic decisions facilitated by an AI system the government deployed with the aim of providing a more transparent and accountable method of identifying beneficiaries than an earlier system based on officials' discretion.

This story illustrates how power imbalances among people, firms, and governments outlined in chapter 6 converge in practice. Information asymmetries allow firms to determine the conditions under which their AI systems can be scrutinized: Private vendors may not be required to provide open access to the system's source code or relevant data, preventing civil society actors from independently auditing the system. The decision of governments to prematurely integrate AI technologies at scale can have serious negative effects on rights and safety, because citizens have few formal avenues for challenging government decisions that are enabled by AI.

Evidence of the immediacy, scale, and magnitude of the harms that AI can cause, particularly in developing countries, is rapidly emerging.[1] Whereas the benefits of AI take time to materialize as complementary factors—infrastructure, skills, and institutions—evolve, harm to rights and safety can spread quickly when AI is integrated at scale into existing systems for delivering services. For example, cyberthreats such as deepfakes and large-scale phishing attacks propagate quickly in developing countries as a result of existing cybersecurity vulnerabilities, weak enforcement of regulations, and corruption in technology procurement.[2]

Visible failures in areas that can have severe consequences erode societal trust much faster than successful deployments build it. If AI is adopted widely in a country with few guardrails and a large-scale disaster occurs, trust may collapse in ways that are difficult to reverse, reducing the rate at which the country will adopt AI across economic sectors in the long run.[3] Conversely, when countries gradually introduce well-governed AI into society, optimism regarding AI should increase over time as trust builds and adoption increases.[4] The fragile nature of trust, and the speed and scope with which harm can spread, indicate the need for a precautionary approach, ensuring that safeguards are in place from the outset before widespread harms occur that cannot be easily remedied.[5] As the *World Development Report 2025* notes, "history shows that standards sometimes arrive only after serious harm has occurred: a risky path given the scale of today's technological and planetary challenges."[6]

This chapter discusses a governance framework—created through policies, regulatory frameworks, institutional arrangements, and technical standards—that governments can use to ensure that AI systems are developed and deployed in a safe, transparent, accountable, and trustworthy manner.

Trust is needed to ensure AI lives up to its promise

Trust in AI matters for political, social, and economic reasons. If communities do not trust that AI will be developed and used in a way that respects their rights and protects their interests, they will resist its adoption, undermining the potential of the technology to deliver the benefits highlighted elsewhere in this Report.[7] A survey of 48,000 people across 47 countries found that only 46 percent of people globally are willing to trust AI systems, and 70 percent believe that greater regulation of such systems is needed.[8]

Ensuring trust, however, is not a matter of persuading citizens to accept AI. It rests on making AI demonstrably trustworthy, which places the burden on firms and governments that build and deploy AI tools rather than on the public. The good news, in regard to AI's potential in developing countries, is that people in those countries are generally more trusting of AI than people in high-income countries.[9] However, this trust needs to be earned—and cannot be taken for granted.

People and communities globally have already begun resisting AI when this societal trust is broken. In the Philippines, for example, call center workers have pushed back against AI tools being used to make call center work more demanding as well as to surveil and discipline workers.[10] In China, a voice actress won a $34,000 lawsuit when she discovered a commercial AI voice generator had used her data without her consent.[11] In Brazil, the O Panóptico project has mapped 535 projects in which public security systems are using facial recognition, creating risks of surveillance.[12] In Uruguay, protests erupted in 2023 over Google's plans to build a large, water-intensive data center in the midst of a multiyear drought.[13] Once societal trust is broken, it can be difficult to rebuild it without incurring significant institutional and political costs. This was the case in the Netherlands, where AI-driven false allegations of child-benefits fraud affected 26,000 parents and led to the resignation of the government in power (refer to chapter 5).

Governance done well enables AI adoption, rather than putting a brake on it

Trust is not just about public perception; it is about creating a framework of safety, accountability, and predictability around AI systems so that all societal stakeholders can reasonably rely on AI. Low trust in AI creates *missed uses*: instances of forgone development benefits because of local pushback.[14] Stable, predictable governance frameworks are essential for enabling the private sector to build, invest, and rely on AI with confidence; and uncertainty around how to measure, mitigate, and govern AI risks hampers investment, innovation, and adoption by the public sector in particular.[15] In a survey conducted for this Report, senior officials in government agencies across 58 economies in varying income groups consistently identified ethical and legal concerns around AI as a major barrier to the responsible use of AI. About 43 percent of respondents in low- and lower-middle-income economies cited the absence of relevant policies, frameworks, and standards as a key constraint (refer to figure 9.1).[16]

Figure 9.1 **Legal and ethical concerns, as well as a lack of relevant frameworks and standards for managing those concerns, are key barriers to AI adoption**

Survey question: "To what extent do the following constraints prevent or limit your government's internal use of AI tools?"

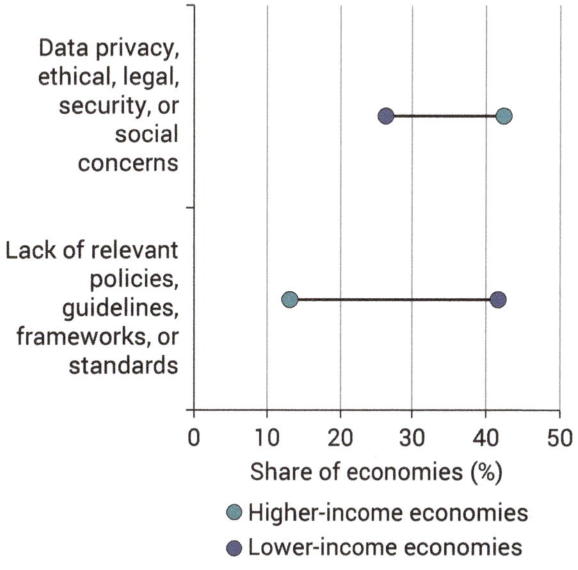

Source: WDR 2026 team, based on AI and Data for Better Governance Survey, World Bank.

Note: The sample includes 12 low-income and 12 lower-middle-income economies (lower-income group) and 16 upper-middle-income and 17 high-income economies (higher-income group). AI = artificial intelligence.

Voluntary standards are a powerful starting point to build trustworthy AI, but market forces alone may not be enough

To respond to uncertainty around how to measure, mitigate, and govern AI risks, as well as growing market demand for standardized practices relating to compliance and assurance, voluntary standards development organizations have begun developing international standards for AI governance. More than 800 voluntary AI-related standards have been published or are under development,[17] providing organizations with guidance on how to adopt a system for managing AI risks, how to conduct an impact assessment in regard to AI, and how to measure and test levels of transparency.[18]

Voluntary standards are a powerful tool for *coregulation* of AI systems because they are driven by expertise of technical stakeholders that are involved in developing, using, and shaping the technology. Unlike high-level ethical principles for AI, such as the Organisation for Economic Co-operation and Development (OECD) AI Principles or the United Nations Educational, Scientific and Cultural Organization (UNESCO) Recommendation on the Ethics of Artificial Intelligence, standards can shape how principles like transparency and fairness are implemented, measured, and audited in practice.[19] Critically, standards are forward-looking tools, seeking to ensure that appropriate levels of quality, safety, and protection are embedded within AI systems before harm occurs. Because of the potentially global reach of certain AI systems, a small group of AI providers makes choices that have a disproportionate impact on rights and safety protections around the world.

At the same time, policy makers should be mindful that standards setting is not a value-neutral exercise: It requires participants to decide on value-laden terms like *fairness, safety,* and *risk*.[20] Voluntary standards are often shaped by a handful of technical experts and companies that may not have a background in fundamental rights or safety issues.[21] More broadly, stakeholders that have less resources, such as civil society organizations and policy makers based in developing countries, face barriers to participation in developing standards for AI, including the significant time commitment required, opacity of the processes involved in standards development, and dominance of industry voices in those processes.[22]

Standards development organizations have been responsive to these concerns. In December 2025, the International Electrotechnical Commission (IEC), the International Organization for Standardization (ISO), and the International Telecommunication Union issued the Seoul Statement, committing themselves to deepening their understanding of the relationship between international standards and human rights, incorporating sociotechnical dimensions into the development of standards, and strengthening the multistakeholder community for developing and applying AI standards.

Market forces alone will not create trust; governments need a new social contract for AI

As the *World Development Report 2025* notes, “most standards start as voluntary efforts, but governments make them count.”[23] Voluntary standards clearly have a critical role to play in governing AI, but governments need to amplify them by embedding critical voluntary standards into regulation when rights and public safety are at stake.

AI governance should not be left to market forces alone. Most AI providers are private sector actors largely driven by profit incentives that do not consider the social and political costs of AI. Anthropic cofounder Christopher Olah has acknowledged that AI companies can often be swayed by "a set of incentives and constraints that can sometimes conflict with doing the right thing."[24] Research shows that this can create an environment in which the direction of innovation can become "systematically distorted" toward disproportionately harmful AI systems.[25] Leaving governance solely to voluntary standards risks making private standards misaligned with public goals.[26] A purely voluntary framework can increase the risk of *ethics washing*, in which companies develop standards on paper but do not apply concrete guardrails in reality.[27]

If market forces alone cannot produce trustworthy AI, and if uncertainty surrounding AI governance is slowing adoption, then governments need a new *social contract* for AI that minimizes its harms and maximizes its social benefits to sustain trust as AI diffuses across developing economies.[28] Such a social contract can be created by using the full toolbox of AI governance, combining voluntary standards and ethical and strategic frameworks with regulation. Regulations alone cannot specify every technical detail involved in compliance with them.[29] Laws should be written to specify key outcomes society cares about: protecting rights, ensuring safety, and promoting accountability.[30] Voluntary standards are one way of defining how to achieve these outcomes, leveraging global good practices. The remainder of this chapter discusses how to build frameworks for AI governance.

There is no single best-practice approach to AI governance

Currently, there is no single best-practice governance instrument for comprehensively regulating AI. Because AI is a general-purpose technology diffusing rapidly across economic sectors, every country already has a mix of sectoral and technology-neutral regulations that can apply to AI, from authorization processes for the use of AI in medical devices to rights-based protections against surveillance and intrusions into privacy. The framework of existing governance instruments that can apply to AI, and the gaps in that framework, vary greatly from country to country. In this context, blanket prescriptions are difficult to make.

Several jurisdictions around the world have now enacted *horizontal AI laws* that aim to regulate AI across all economic sectors, often modeled on the risk-based approach of the EU Artificial Intelligence Act. These laws represent ambitious attempts to classify AI systems based on different tiers of risk and apply to AI developers and deployers obligations that are proportionate to those tiers of risk. At the same time, evidence on the implementation of these laws is limited and preliminary, especially because the ongoing European Union (EU) Digital Omnibus process has delayed enforcement of most of the obligations regarding high-risk AI systems under the EU AI Act (refer to box 9.1). Even attempts to estimate the costs of complying with the act have become contentious.[31] Given that evidence is still emerging, even in regard to high-income jurisdictions, it is too early to say whether horizontal AI laws are the best-practice approach for all developing countries. Policy makers should continue to study the evidence on the effect of these laws as they begin to be implemented.

Box 9.1 Crosscutting laws for governing AI are increasingly popular, but evidence regarding their effectiveness is still emerging

The most comprehensive law to date that aims to govern all artificial intelligence (AI) systems, regardless of the economic sector (a *horizontal law*), is the EU Artificial Intelligence Act, adopted in May 2024. It establishes tiered obligations based on risk, from outright prohibitions on unacceptable uses of AI such as real-time biometric surveillance (which can identify and surveil individuals in public spaces without their consent) and subliminal manipulation to mandatory safeguards for certain high-risk systems in health, finance, employment, and law enforcement. Academic debates have emerged around whether the act will become a template for AI laws around the world through the Brussels effect,[a] mirroring the effect of the EU's General Data Protection Regulation on global data protection regulations.[b]

Evidence on the global diffusion of the EU AI Act is still emerging. Six economies outside of the EU have now enacted horizontal AI legislation, five (Japan; Kazakhstan; the Republic of Korea; Taiwan, China; and Viet Nam) in 2025 and the sixth (Uzbekistan) in 2026. Similar proposals are under debate in Argentina, Brazil, Chile, and Nigeria.

Among these laws, Japan's Act on the Promotion of Research and Development, and Utilization of Artificial Intelligence-related Technology, adopted in May 2025, is an outlier in deliberately employing a light touch. It imposes no penalties and relies on name-and-shame enforcement alongside existing sectoral laws.[c] In contrast, Kazakhstan, Korea, and Viet Nam have adopted a risk-based tiered framework similar to that of the EU AI Act, imposing differentiated obligations depending on whether an AI system poses unacceptable, high, or low or minimal risk. However, even within this group, legislation varies. For example, Korea's Framework Act on the Development of Artificial Intelligence and Establishment of Trust adopts obligations similar to those in the EU AI Act for AI deployed in high-risk economic sectors such as health and critical infrastructure but does not prohibit unacceptable uses of AI systems. Kazakhstan's AI law, in contrast, functionally adopts the same tiers of risk as the EU AI Act while overlaying a new autonomy-based classification, with additional obligations for highly autonomous systems.

Importantly, there is little information regarding enforcement of these legal frameworks, given how recent they are. The EU is still in the process of implementing the EU AI Act, with most obligations regarding high-risk uses of AI not entering into effect until December 2027. The start date for implementation of these obligations was delayed as part of the EU's Digital Omnibus, a package of reforms that aims to streamline and simplify digital regulations. In June 2026, the Council of the European Union formally approved amendments to the EU AI Act to postpone to December 2027 compliance deadlines for stand-alone high-risk AI systems and to August 2028 those for high-risk systems embedded in products. Obligations to comply with transparency requirements for deployers of AI systems remain in effect, however, starting in August 2026.

Many simplifications to the EU AI Act as part of the Digital Omnibus process have been driven by discussions around competitiveness and pressure from industry, along with delays to delegated guidance and technical standards and the complexity of implementing the act at the

(Box continues next page)

Box 9.1 Crosscutting laws for governing AI are increasingly popular, but evidence regarding their effectiveness is still emerging *(continued)*

national level.[d] More than 40 civil society organizations issued a joint statement criticizing the Digital Omnibus over concerns around the weakening of protections for fundamental rights and insufficient public consultation.[e]

Source: WDR 2026 team.

a. The *Brussels effect* refers to two phenomena. The *de jure Brussels effect* occurs when countries adopt laws that look similar to those of the EU, for political or market access reasons. The *de facto Brussels effect* refers to the phenomenon in which multinational companies voluntarily extend EU compliance practices across their global businesses. Because of the cost of running parallel compliance regimes for the same product, some companies adopt the highest standard required (often the EU standard) and then apply it uniformly across their entire business (Bradford 2020).

b. Crum (2025); Siegmann and Anderljung (2022).

c. Habuka (2025); Paulger (2025).

d. Corporate Europe Observatory (2026).

e. Article 19 (2026).

Policy makers should create AI governance frameworks using an iterative, continuous process

There is no fixed list of laws, rules, and regulations for countries to use to govern AI, and the global regulatory landscape is changing daily. Countries seeking to govern AI face a *pacing problem*.[32] Laws, rules, and regulations take time to design, draft, and implement, whereas AI is being developed and deployed at breakneck speed, with relevant harms scaling rapidly as well.[33] Therefore, what matters is that countries create and enforce AI governance frameworks[34] through a trusted, continuously updated process (refer to figure 9.2 and box 9.2). Importantly, governance is most effective when it influences upstream choices made by AI providers and deployers around optimization objectives, acceptable error rates, and representativeness of data sets. These are deeply political choices that have social and distributive consequences; meaningful governance means creating incentives to address these questions up front, rather than waiting until path-dependent decisions are fixed.

Such a *governance life cycle*—assessing the landscape; identifying gaps; making laws, rules, and regulations; and building capacity for enforcement (among regulators) and regulatory compliance (among firms and the public sector)—remains the same regardless of whether a country's priorities are to adopt, adapt, or advance AI. Instead, the emphasis placed on the different stages of this life cycle depends more on countries' regulatory capacities. Most of the cycle is within reach of countries with high regulatory capacity, and they should prioritize extending or making new policy instruments and strengthening enforcement and compliance capacity. In countries with low regulatory capacity, the realistic entry points sit early in the cycle. Those countries should use existing laws, rules, and regulations and assess where they fall short, but also leverage international voluntary standards to build compliance capacity around key good practices, such as human rights impact assessments. The rest of this chapter discusses the different stages of the AI governance life cycle, complemented by a process of monitoring and adaptation. International cooperation can bolster actions along the stages of the cycle.

Figure 9.2 The AI governance life cycle

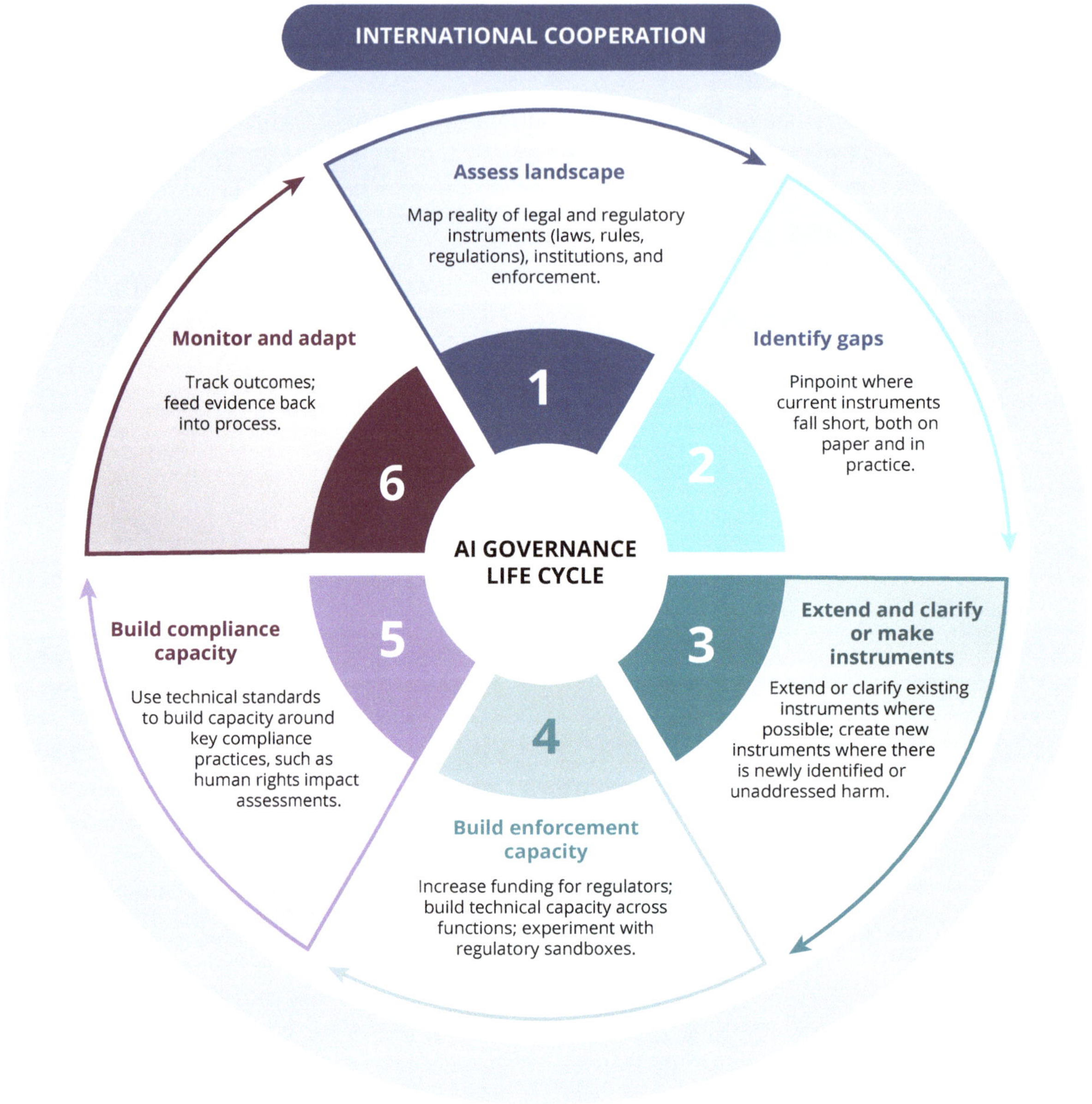

Source: WDR 2026 team, based on World Bank 2025a.

Note: Regulatory sandboxes are time-limited, supervised environments in which artificial intelligence (AI) providers test products against regulatory requirements in close collaboration with relevant authorities.

Box 9.2 Design principles for building and sustaining a robust framework for AI governance

Four design principles in particular can help countries build and sustain a robust framework for governing artificial intelligence (AI), regardless of which laws, standards, and voluntary instruments they adopt:

- *Experiment.* Because no single gold standard has yet emerged, policy makers should treat AI governance as an ongoing experiment.[a] Developing countries can act as *fast followers,* examining evidence of what works (and what does not) before selectively adapting certain practices and tools to fit their local contexts.
- *Reinforce.* Where policy tools have proven to be effective, countries should invest in capacity to enforce these policies. This approach avoids *isomorphic mimicry*: adopting best practices from other countries without the underlying capacity to enforce them in practice.[b]
- *Codesign.* Civil society, affected communities, industry, and academia should be involved in *shaping* instruments from the start, not consulted after the fact. Marginalized groups need to be meaningfully represented in this codesign process. Because larger AI providers often have far greater lobbying resources than civil society organizations, the research community, and smaller firms, governments can fund participation for underresourced stakeholders and support institutional structures that promote the voices of all groups. Countries including Bangladesh, Canada, and France have created multistakeholder external advisory councils to ensure the perspectives of these groups are included in their national AI policies. The Africa AI Council established by Smart Africa plays a similar role at the regional level.[c]
- *Disclose.* Transparency about who is shaping rules and why is essential to public trust. Published consultation records, public debate, clear rationales for policy choices, and lobbying disclosures allow early flagging of capture by influential groups to serve their own narrow interests.

These are standard principles of good regulation, but the pace of AI, its opacity, and the concentration of expertise in a few firms make each principle harder to sustain.

Source: Adapted from World Bank 2024.

a. Crum (2025); Sabel and Zeitlin (2008).

b. Andrews et al. (2017).

c. Smart Africa is a regional alliance of 42 countries and other partners, including the African Development Bank, African Union, GSMA, International Telecommunication Union, Internet Corporation for Assigned Names and Numbers, United Nations Economic Commission for Africa, World Bank, and private sector representatives.

AI governance begins with an assessment of existing laws, rules, and regulations

AI is not being deployed in a vacuum; it is a general-purpose technology embedded within products, services, and processes subject to a variety of existing laws, rules, and regulations in areas including data protection, cybercrime, consumer protection, and rules for various economic sectors, from health to finance regulation. Among the 121 economies included in the World Bank's Digital Trade Regulatory Readiness Database, almost all have a data protection law, and 43 now require that individuals be informed when they are subject to an automated decision.[35]

The starting point for any country in developing a framework for governing AI is taking stock of the laws that already apply to AI. Countries that want to conduct a stocktaking exercise can look to the example of the United Kingdom's white paper on AI regulation, published in 2023, which required existing regulators to evaluate their regulatory frameworks and assess how they could implement five key cross-sectoral principles of AI governance, identifying any relevant gaps.[36]

The section that follows includes examples of regulatory areas that such a stocktaking exercise could examine, as well as case studies of how laws, rules, and regulations governing AI have been applied across different countries to regulate the harms caused by AI.

Many existing laws already apply to AI

Data protection laws protect people from violations of privacy rights caused by the development or use of AI. For instance, in 2023, Senegal's Commission for Personal Data Protection rejected a company's application to use facial recognition to monitor its employees, citing significant privacy risks, and subsequently issued a directive limiting the use of biometric data in the workplace.[37] In that same year, Kenya's Data Protection Commissioner suspended the operations of Worldcoin, a product that scanned the irises of data subjects for digital identification, because of concerns regarding data protection.[38]

Cybercrime laws protect people against the malicious misuse of AI. In January 2026, the Philippines Department of Information and Communications Technology blocked xAI's AI assistant Grok under the Cybercrime Prevention Act of 2012, citing its association with the nonconsensual generation of sexually explicit content. The ban was lifted five days later after xAI implemented enhanced safeguards.[39]

Environmental laws protect communities against harms created by hyperscale data centers (for further details, refer to spotlight 4). In February 2024, Chile's Second Environmental Court revoked part of a 2020 permit issued to Google to build a $200 million data center project in a region plagued by a megadrought for more than 15 years after local communities objected to the data center's high consumption of water resources. The court ordered an environmental impact assessment and mandated that the company reevaluate its water-intensive cooling. Later that year, in September, Google withdrew the original application for the permit and committed to a redesign that would make the center air cooled rather than water cooled.[40]

Human rights law and constitutional law give people ways to challenge government decisions that violate their economic and social rights. A group of activists filed a case earlier this year in the High Court of Kenya arguing that the rapid deployment of AI without adequate safeguards threatens constitutional and fundamental rights including privacy, equality, and freedom of expression.[41] In August 2024, the

Constitutional Court of Colombia issued a ruling setting out guiding principles for the use of generative AI in judicial decision-making, requiring transparency, verifiability, and preservation of judicial independence.[42] Following the ruling, Colombia's Superior Council of the Judicature issued guiding principles for the use of AI across the country's judiciary.[43]

The biggest obstacle to governing AI is often enforcement on the ground

When looking at the regulatory landscape governing AI, a country's policy makers should assess not only the laws, rules, and regulations on the books (de jure), but also assess gaps in their actual (de facto) enforcement and implementation.

Evidence points to a significant gap between the two. Although many developing countries can draft data protection and consumer protection laws that reflect good international practices, effective enforcement remains a persistent challenge, one often driven by a lack of financial resources, low institutional capacity, and coordination challenges (refer to figure 9.3).[44] The large asymmetries in resources and knowledge between industry and regulators means this is also a problem for developed countries. A €20 million fine issued in 2023 by the Italian data protection regulator against Clearview AI, a US company that was found to have unlawfully processed personal data (including biometric and geolocation data) of people in Italy, remains unenforced, and the unlawfully processed data have yet to be deleted.[45]

Figure 9.3 Countries across income groups struggle to implement and enforce data protection regulations in practice, even where legal frameworks are robust on paper

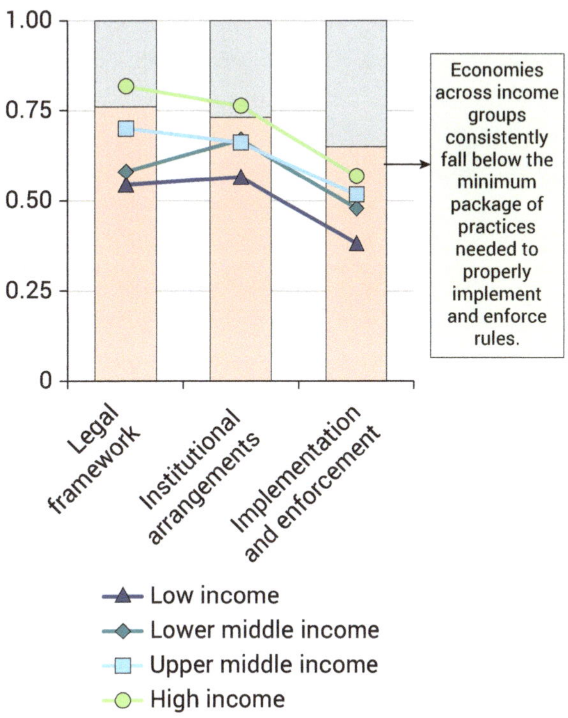

Source: World Bank 2025a.

Note: Global Regulations, Institutional Development, and Market Authorities Perspective (GRIDMAP) toolkit assessment results are based on an evaluation, using information collected through a survey-based tool completed by relevant regulatory authorities, of country practices against a minimum package needed for safe and trustworthy markets. Tan areas in the figure's three bars indicate the minimum package of practices needed. The first wave of the assessment, conducted in 2025, covered 53 economies, concentrated in Europe and Central Asia, Latin America and the Caribbean, and Sub-Saharan Africa.

Closing governance gaps involves addressing harms of AI

Once a country has mapped its existing landscape for AI governance, its next step is to identify and close gaps in governance that the mapping has identified. Policy makers should look at potential harms across AI's operational life cycle, from inputs to processes and outputs. AI's *input layer* comprises critical technical inputs across the AI value chain, including data, human labor, and environmental resources. Its *process layer* covers how those inputs are developed into a functioning AI system, including decisions around model training and whether an AI model's reasoning can be explained or audited. Its *output layer* includes recommendations, predictions, and other outputs of AI that affect people, communities, and institutions.

AI poses a range of new challenges across these layers that existing regulations may not be able to address. In regard to the input layer, data on which AI systems are trained are often extracted without meaningful consent from local communities. Companies are often able to ignore data protection laws because of a lack of transparency.[46] Importantly, data protection laws oriented toward individual consent are often ineffective at giving communities greater agency over how their data are used;[47] consent becomes an exercise in checking boxes rather than meaningful control over practices regarding extraction of data. With respect to the process layer, the black box nature of AI's development presents real challenges for regulators in regard to auditing or enforcing compliance with existing laws. Regarding the output layer, AI's capacity to evolve over time, as well as the scale and potential reach of algorithmic systems, poses challenges for frameworks often designed for backward-looking accountability, that is, accountability once harm has already occurred.

The discussion that follows examines how countries have sought to create, update, and clarify laws, rules, and regulations on AI to address these new challenges.[48] Importantly, these should be taken as a starting point for experimentation and not as a fixed list of best practices, because many of the instruments outlined are emerging in higher-income countries, and both their success in those countries and their applicability for contexts in developing countries remain to be seen.

Addressing harms from AI-related inputs

Transparency of training data for AI models

One of the key drivers of the aggregation of power by larger corporations is their practices regarding large-scale data collection conducted without transparency.[49] In many cases, AI providers do not disclose details around how they have obtained data sets used for training AI models. This lack of disclosure can facilitate mass collection of data in ways that violate data protection and intellectual property rights.[50] These practices can increase information asymmetries and power imbalances between people and corporations (for further details, refer to chapter 6).

Some jurisdictions are now addressing this issue. The California AI Transparency Act requires generative AI developers to publish on their websites documentation on the sources, ownership, and intellectual property status of training data.[51] These kinds of disclosures can also facilitate compliance with existing laws by surfacing cases in which data have been collected in clear breach of laws.

Community-level data governance

AI products are often created using data extracted from local communities, without compensation and without providing these communities with agency over how their data are used (for further discussion on this topic, refer to chapter 6). One area of ongoing experimentation by local communities, policy makers, and the development community is the use of *social licensing frameworks*.[52]

Several social licensing frameworks are now emerging around the world. In New Zealand, crowdsourced labeled speech samples provided by more than 2,500 Māori community members have been used, under the community-developed Kaitiakitanga License, to build an automatic speech recognition tool for the *te reo* language.[53] The license requires the tool's developer to use the samples only for the benefit of the Māori people and prohibits surveillance, tracking, and discrimination. It also limits the building of Māori data sets or natural language processing models by other actors. The World Bank, supported by the Gates Foundation, is piloting a national language library for low-resource languages, in collaboration with the government of Malawi and local media houses (for more information on this pilot, refer to chapter 7).[54]

A key principle of community-level data governance is equitable but differentiated access, meaning that the licenses granted for accessing and using the data often do not make the data uniformly *open* (that is, available to all users with no restrictions on use) or publicly available, to protect against extractive practices. At the same time, community-level approaches to data governance are part of an ongoing debate around the appropriate level of openness of data in the context of existing power imbalances in the AI ecosystem (refer to box 9.3).

Box 9.3 Efforts to give communities in developing countries more control over their data

The Nwulite Obodo Open Data License (NOODL) is an approach that seeks to address power dynamics between data communities in developing countries and providers of artificial intelligence (AI) models. Its creators argue that standard open licenses for data access and use do not mesh well with African data realities in three ways:

- *Power imbalances.* Unrestricted open licensing can enable well-resourced actors to harvest data from African (and other lower-middle-income-country) sources without fair compensation or recognition of original creators.
- *Attribution.* Open licenses often require attribution for data that are used, which can be difficult given that African data sets are often developed collaboratively, with input from multiple stakeholders.
- *Cultural and community rights.* Because open data licenses by definition are designed to include few or no limitations on access and reuse of data, they can undermine local communities' agency and local norms over how cultural materials are shared and reused.

To address these realities, NOODL applies different terms to different categories of data users. Users from Africa and developing countries can reuse and distribute data within those regions and must release under the same license any data sets they have modified;

(Box continues next page)

Box 9.3 Efforts to give communities in developing countries more control over their data *(continued)*

commercial use is restricted to markets outside Africa or developing countries. Users from other regions must comply with the same terms but are also required to provide royalty payments or other benefits to the providers of African data sets.

NOODL reflects a broader debate about whether open data are unambiguously beneficial when there are sizable power asymmetries in regard to capacity to extract value from the commons. Open data are a powerful tool for preventing centralization of power, and traditional open data licenses have been widely celebrated for enabling innovation and downstream reuse of data. At the same time, the use of open licenses without modifications may expose local communities and marginalized groups to extractive practices from actors with greater resources than those communities and groups, especially given that most advanced AI models have been largely trained on data extracted from sources on the internet without regard to existing licensing terms or copyright interests.

NOODL is one of many approaches to governing and licensing language data. For example, the Mozilla Data Collective allows communities to upload and govern data sets on their own terms. Data set creators on the platform currently use a range of existing open-source licenses such as Apache 2.0 alongside newer licenses such as NOODL, showing that a range of licensing approaches can be compatible with a more community-centric form of data governance. The CC Signals project, led by Creative Commons, allows holders of data sets to signal their preferences regarding how AI companies can reuse the holders' content based on a set of limited options shaped by public interest considerations.

Sources: Adapted from Fisher and Streinz 2022; Koros and Ogonjo 2025; Okorie and Omino 2025.

Labor regulation

As discussed in chapter 6, labor markets in the AI industry are often characterized by one or a small number of buyers (the company or companies) and many sellers (the workers). This can give some AI companies disproportionate leverage over their workers. Some jurisdictions have begun updating their labor regulations to address the harms created by such imbalances. For example, in 2024 Mexico updated its Federal Labor Law to protect those who work on digital platforms, requiring businesses to inform such workers when algorithms are used for decision-making in the workplace, adopt a policy for managing such algorithms, and provide workers with access to mechanisms for human-led reviews.[55] Chapter 7 and spotlight 5 discuss broader policy responses to potential AI-caused disruptions to labor markets, including strengthening social safety nets.

Safe reuse of sensitive public sector data

Governments hold high-value data—health, statistical, administrative—that are difficult to make publicly available owing to legal limitations (such as those relating to confidentiality, trade secrets, intellectual property rights, or privacy concerns). The EU Data Governance Act, enacted in 2023, aims to address these concerns by clarifying the legal framework permitting the regulated reuse of such data, subject to safeguards such as secure processing environments (for example, secure spaces used to house privileged or confidential data). Policy makers should ensure baseline safeguards for data protection are operating effectively before opening new channels for reusing data.[56]

Addressing harms from AI-related processes and outputs

Procurement guardrails for high-impact AI

The public sector's ability to spend or withhold spending on public goods and services is one of the most direct tools governments have to influence the behavior of private sector AI providers. In the United States, for instance, in 2025, the Office of Management and Budget issued guidance to executive agencies that procure certain kinds of "high-impact" AI,[57] where outputs have an impact on rights or safety. The guidance mandates continuous impact assessments, human oversight of AI systems, and appeal mechanisms for persons whose rights or safety are adversely impacted by AI systems.

Cybersecurity obligations for high-risk AI

Cyberharms deserve particular attention because AI both scales up existing cyberattacks and creates new vulnerabilities when it becomes embedded within existing systems. Article 15 of the EU AI Act requires high-risk AI systems to achieve certain levels of accuracy, robustness, and cybersecurity; the European Commission has submitted a request to the European standardization organizations to further define how accuracy, robustness, and cybersecurity are specified in practice. Article 55 applies additional cybersecurity obligations to general-purpose AI models that pose systemic risks. Peru's AI law[58] and AI decree[59] adopt a similar approach for public administration entities that use AI, mandating regular digital-security audits to identify and correct vulnerabilities and biases. The AI decree mandates that public administration entities use technical standards to design and implement appropriate information security controls.

Red lines on unacceptable uses of AI

Some jurisdictions are creating new prohibitions on certain clearly unacceptable uses of AI that concentrate power in ways that violate rights. For example, Brazil's pending national AI bill proposes prohibitions on manipulative systems, social scoring, and real-time biometric identification.[60] In the United States, although no federal legislation yet exists regarding AI, the Texas Responsible Artificial Intelligence Governance Act prohibits AI systems that discriminate against protected classes or enable biometric identification without consent.[61]

Sectoral regulation

Some countries have begun to update their existing regulatory frameworks to account for new challenges raised by the integration of AI into products, services, and systems across a range of economic sectors. In the health sector, Singapore's Health Sciences Authority revised its Regulatory Guidelines for Software Medical Devices in 2025 to address machine learning in medical software, within the legal framework of the country's Health Products Act 2007.

Governments need strong enforcement and compliance capacity to avoid having rules that govern on paper without providing safeguards in practice

Commit financial resources for regulators

Most consumer protection and data protection authorities around the world report having insufficient financial resources to carry out their mandates. The differences are particularly stark by country income level, with 43 percent of data protection authorities in low-income countries stating that they strongly disagree that their budgets are adequate, compared with just 15 percent in high-income countries (refer to figure 9.4).

To address this challenge, policy makers need to ensure that the funding for regulators is sufficient to fulfill their mandates and is insulated from changes in political will and from private influence. They can do this by creating appropriate procedures for proposing and approving dedicated budgets and providing funding on a multiyear basis rather than annually to increase financial stability.[62] To ensure the impartiality of public institutions and maintain public trust in them, it is important to support financial (and other forms of) independence of regulators, particularly where rule of law or institutional accountability is generally weak.

Figure 9.4 Regulators in low-income countries identify inadequate budgets as a barrier to fulfilling their mandate much more often than those in high-income countries

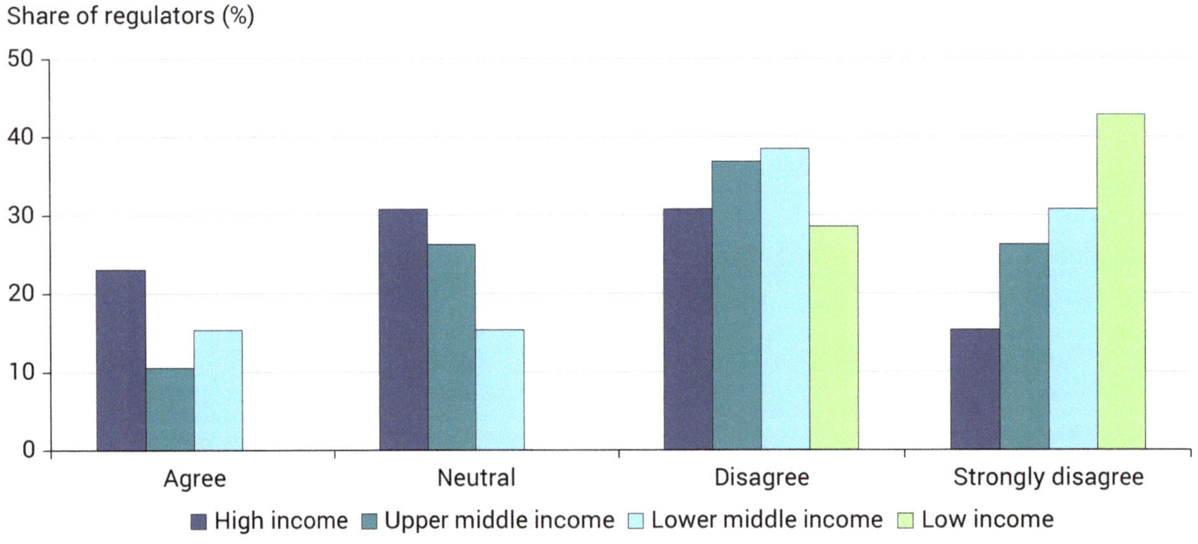

Source: World Bank 2025b.

Note: The figure shows the share of respondents from each country income group selecting responses to the following question: "Do you agree with the following: The Authority has sufficient budget to carry out the activities associated with handling complaints, investigations, hiring staff, and delivering training programs?"

Build the capacity of regulators to share knowledge and collaborate across disciplines

Regulators who need to grapple with the harms AI can cause are likely to be at an early stage of their understanding of the technology, even in high-income countries. The Alan Turing Institute independently studied AI regulators in the United Kingdom and found that a range of regulators in a variety of economic sectors, including competition, health, finance, and communications, all faced similar challenges: limitations in AI-specific knowledge and skills, insufficient coordination among regulatory bodies, and issues of management in response to the challenges posed by AI.[63]

Given the number of regulatory bodies in a country that will likely be working to regulate AI, it may not be feasible or practical to build in-house AI expertise in all of them. Options for developing AI expertise in such situations include building common hubs of regulatory expertise on AI, facilitating greater collaboration among regulators across economic sectors, providing opportunities for training, and building shared AI tools for regulators to use. Policy makers should also consolidate existing initiatives.[64] Spotlight 7 discusses the need to create horizontal coordination between existing sectoral or vertical regulatory bodies and other institutions.[65]

Pilot regulatory sandboxes to help build capacity in real time

Regulatory sandboxes—time-limited, supervised environments in which AI providers test products against regulatory requirements in close collaboration with relevant authorities—are one tool policy makers can use both to generate evidence and to build regulatory capacity simultaneously.[66] An analysis of six AI sandboxes in Brazil, Colombia, Mauritius, Mexico, Rwanda, and Thailand found that sandboxes are most useful as tools for learning and capacity building.[67] By participating in these sandboxes, regulators and policy makers acquire hands-on knowledge of how AI systems are built and used. Such knowledge can inform choices regarding where to build regulatory capacity, where to provide legal flexibility for promising AI applications, and where to extend or adapt existing rules or create new ones. Throughout the sandbox process, companies receive hands-on guidance on how to comply with regulations and how to send a credible signal to the market that their products are safe and trustworthy.

However, sandboxes are not a turnkey solution for building capacity. When deciding to conduct a sandbox, policy makers need to assess whether the regulatory questions in which they are interested can be answered through experimentation, whether the sandbox experiment is worth its opportunity cost, and whether the state has sufficient capacity to deploy the sandbox successfully.[68] Evidence from fintech sandboxes suggests that operating costs range from about $25,000 to more than $1 million each.[69] Sandboxes also require sustained multistakeholder coordination; technical expertise that many regulators are still building; and clear eligibility, testing, and exit criteria, without which sandboxes can divert capacity needed for core supervisory functions.[70] Sandboxes in which supervisory authorities play a passive role can become vehicles for regulatory privatization in practice, with private actors shaping the rules of the game more than governments do.[71]

Build compliance capacity with AI providers and deployers using voluntary standards

Governments around the world are coalescing around a handful of assurance practices to ensure they deploy AI responsibly and demonstrate their compliance with regulations (refer to figure 9.5). However, lower-income economies generally lag behind higher-income economies in their adoption of these tools. Impact assessments, audit frameworks, and testing protocols play a critical role in translating legal obligations into concrete system-level outcomes.

Figure 9.5 Government users of AI across country income groups are engaging in a number of assurance practices to ensure AI is implemented responsibly

Survey question: "For AI systems deployed or piloted by your government, which of the following practices are used?"

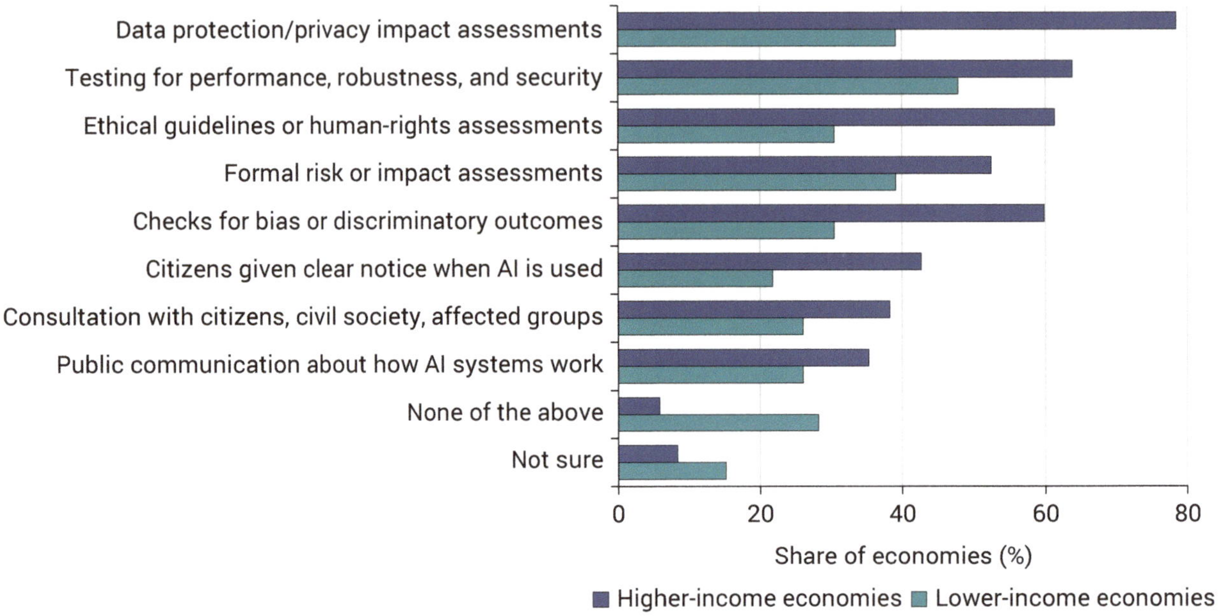

Source: WDR 2026 team, based on the AI and Data for Better Governance Survey, World Bank.
Note: The sample includes 12 low-income and 12 lower-middle-income economies (lower-income group) and 16 upper-middle-income and 17 high-income economies (higher-income group). AI = artificial intelligence.

One approach countries can take to link standards with regulation is to permit those deploying AI to use voluntary standards as a way of demonstrating their compliance with legal instruments. This approach is already gaining traction in high-income countries. In the United States, for example, state laws in Colorado[72] and Texas[73] allow AI deployers to use compliance with the National Institute of Standards and Technology's Artificial Intelligence Management Framework as a shield from legal liability.[74] Similarly, the EU AI Act sets binding requirements for high-risk systems around key issues such as data governance, accuracy, and cybersecurity, while using voluntary standards developed by European standardization organizations[75] as one route for AI providers to take to demonstrate compliance with regulatory requirements. Another approach is to use certification systems to reinforce existing governance systems. Many data protection laws around the world reference voluntary certification schemes as tools for promoting cross-border data transfers between trusted, accredited parties.[76]

International cooperation gives developing countries greater leverage when acting alone is not enough

Developing countries have largely been absent from shaping global multistakeholder AI governance processes. An analysis of seven key frameworks and initiatives developed by organizations that were not part of the United Nations (UN) system[77] found that only seven countries, all high income, were parties to all initiatives,[78] and 118 countries (mostly from the developing world) were not party to any of them (refer to figure 9.6).[79] Among significant initiatives

Figure 9.6 Developing countries are systematically underrepresented in non-UN global AI governance initiatives

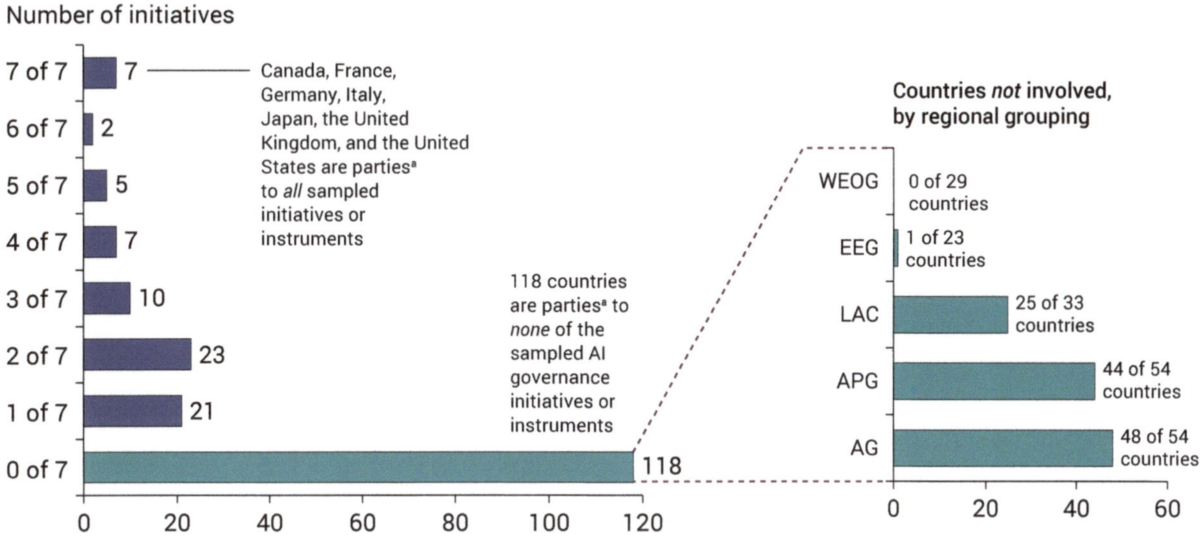

Source: United Nations High-Level Advisory Body on Artificial Intelligence 2024.

Note: The sample includes interregional initiatives only and excludes regional initiatives. It includes the OECD AI Principles (2019); G20 AI Principles (2019); GPAI Minister's Declaration 2022; Hiroshima AI Process G7 Digital & Tech Ministers' Statement (2023); Council of Europe's Framework Convention on Artificial Intelligence and Human Rights, Democracy and the Rule of Law (2024); and Seoul Declaration for Safe, Innovative, and Inclusive AI (2024). AG = African Group; AI = artificial intelligence; APG = Asia and the Pacific Group; EEG = Eastern European Group; G20 = Group of 20; G7 = Group of Seven; GPAI = Global Partnership on Artificial Intelligence; LAC = Latin America and the Caribbean; OECD = Organisation for Economic Co-operation and Development; UN = United Nations; WEOG = Western Europe and Others Group.

a. According to endorsement of relevant intergovernmental issuances. Countries are not considered involved in a plurilateral initiative solely because they are members of the African Union or the European Union.

in this area, only UNESCO's Recommendation on the Ethics of AI was developed with broad participation from developing countries.

Reimagining global multistakeholder cooperation

Global cooperation on AI governance often seems challenging given today's fragmented geopolitics.[80] However, without greater global cooperation, developing countries looking to govern AI systems will continue to face three challenges.

First, if the international community does not agree on a floor for AI safeguards, developing countries may be pressured into a race to the bottom in which countries remove essential guardrails to encourage foreign investment.[81] Second, although experimentation is a key pillar of the governance approach outlined earlier, a lack of interoperability between national regulations will increase costs for AI providers that sell their products in multiple markets.[82] Third, without cross-border collaboration on enforcement of regulatory frameworks, developing countries will struggle to apply the laws, standards, and policies they have on the books. In 2025, when Nigeria's Federal Competition and Consumer Protection Tribunal upheld a $220 million fine against Meta for violating local consumer, data protection, and privacy laws, Meta subsequently stated that it might withdraw from the Nigerian market to mitigate the risk of being subjected to enforcement measures.[83]

Countries looking to create AI governance frameworks will find that going alone is not an option. This is because AI governance does not simply occur at the national level: It is shaped by international law (such as international human rights law), international principles (such as the OECD AI Principles and UNESCO Recommendation on the Ethics of AI), and international standards (such as those set by the ISO/IEC). Policy makers that rely solely on national instruments to govern AI risk overlooking valuable channels for shaping global norms. For countries faced with these challenges, participating in global governance processes and standards development provides an important avenue for expanding their leverage.

Countries can take a number of steps to promote international cooperation, leveraging existing mechanisms wherever possible rather than creating parallel processes.

First, countries should participate in existing high-level multistakeholder dialogues that seek to create consensus on AI governance. Forums such as the UN Global Dialogue on AI Governance provide governments, civil society, the private sector, and the scientific community with important avenues for discussing the most pressing AI governance issues on equal footing. Importantly, the UN provides a forum that includes voices from developing countries by design. Stakeholders should also participate in other multistakeholder forums, such as the AI summits that have been held in France, India, the Republic of Korea, and the United Kingdom.[84]

Importantly, global dialogue should aim for regulatory pluralism—allowing countries to shape national governance frameworks in ways that match local communities' needs—as its goal, but underpinned by a shared *AI governance floor*, where countries agree to ensure a common level of human rights protection and interoperability of different governance regimes.[85]

Evidence of global convergence is emerging. For example, a number of countries now require mandatory impact assessments for certain high-risk AI systems before they can be deployed.[86] It is often assumed that regulatory consensus among China, the EU, and the United States, which offer the largest markets for AI technology and thus exert the greatest regulatory clout, is difficult to reach because of the opposing regulatory philosophies the three economies hold.[87] However, this is not necessarily the case in practice. Notably, convergence around the need for AI governance is increasing among many of the leading jurisdictions in which advanced AI providers are based, as illustrated by the examples of the US state of California and of China (refer to box 9.4).

Policy makers should also continue engaging with both global and regional multilateral development banks and international financial institutions, which have a critical role to play in disseminating AI governance norms and building state capacity to govern AI through both their lending projects and their policy advice to developing countries.[88]

Box 9.4 Beyond narratives of regulatory competition: California and China as leaders in both innovation and regulation

One popular model for understanding regulatory competition in the governance of artificial intelligence (AI) argues that China, the European Union (EU), and the United States compete to promote their own models for regulating AI and digital technology.[a] This model argues that the United States is promoting a largely market-driven model with minimal government

(Box continues next page)

Box 9.4 Beyond narratives of regulatory competition: California and China as leaders in both innovation and regulation *(continued)*

regulatory intervention, China is promoting a state-driven model focusing on maximizing the country's technological advantage, and the EU is embracing a rights-driven model that focuses on safeguarding individual rights and the rule of law.

However, this narrative of regulatory competition misses the fact that leading jurisdictions for the development of AI, such as the US state of California and China, have more common ground than initially meets the eye. California and China lead the way in private investment in AI, filings for AI-related patents, and production of notable advanced AI models.[b] At the same time, these jurisdictions are also advancing the frontier of AI governance.

Although the United States currently lacks federal legislation on AI governance or data protection, California has long led the way in technology regulation. In 2018, it became the first US state to pass a comprehensive law regarding data protection, and it is leading the way on the regulation of AI. In 2025 alone, it enacted 13 bills related to AI, covering safety and transparency obligations for AI companies, child safety measures, data rights, and consumer protection. Notably, California's legislative process is transparent and participatory—featuring open hearings, multistakeholder expert testimony from civil society and the private sector, and iterative revision—which increases the legitimacy of the entire process.

China has also played a leading role in AI governance. It was one of the first countries to introduce binding legislation governing AI systems, and it has been particularly agile in responding to the risks posed by generative AI. It currently has separate laws regulating recommendation algorithms, *deep-synthesis technologies* (a subset of generative AI technologies that includes deepfakes and digital simulation models), and generative AI services.

The cases of California and China show that two jurisdictions can take different legal approaches to governing AI while still sharing the common philosophy that binding regulation is needed to ensure AI is safe, trustworthy, and rights-respecting. The specific regulatory frameworks adopted by California and China will not work for all countries, however. Both jurisdictions have benefited from a mix of available and specialized talent, large and deep pools of funding for AI ecosystems, and enabling policies that have allowed them to thrive as hubs for development of advanced AI. However, lessons from these jurisdictions suggest that, for developing countries, the choice is less about which regulatory model (market based, rights based, or state based) and more about finding common ground with other countries around the need for good governance to promote responsible innovation.

Source: WDR 2026 team, based on Bradford 2023; Randolph 2025; Rotenberg 2025; White & Case 2025.

a. Bradford (2023).

b. "Notable" models here are based on Epoch AI's (2026) definition: "models that were state-of-the-art when released, have over 1,000 citations, one million monthly active users, or an equivalent level of historical significance."

Second, countries should look to collaborate with regional neighbors to develop common policy approaches, searching for avenues where harmonization is possible. In August 2024, 17 countries from Latin America and the Caribbean adopted the Cartagena de Indias Declaration for Governance, the Construction of AI Ecosystems and the Promotion of AI Education in an Ethical and Responsible Manner in Latin America and the Caribbean, committing to coordinated action to promote the ethical, responsible, and inclusive use of the technology. In April 2025, at the Global AI Summit on Africa in Kigali, Rwanda, 49 African countries and the African Union endorsed the Africa Declaration on Artificial Intelligence, emphasizing the need for safeguards for AI deployment to protect human dignity, rights, freedoms, and environmental sustainability. These instruments are largely strategic rather than binding but reflect regional consensus around the need for clear guardrails for AI. They may provide important regional forums for coordinating national policy reform.

Third, countries should observe and join existing multilateral frameworks. The Council of Europe[89] Framework Convention on AI is one example. The convention is the first binding international treaty on AI, with signatory countries committing to ensuring that AI-related activities are compatible with human rights and are not used to undermine democratic processes and the rule of law. Though the convention is a legally binding instrument under international law, it also provides countries with the autonomy to choose how best to update their national frameworks for AI governance.[90]

Although developed under the auspices of the Council of Europe, the convention has begun to gain wider traction. A number of countries outside of Europe have signed the convention, including Canada, Israel, Japan, Mexico, Peru, the United States, and Uruguay. Notably, other countries, such as Bangladesh, have signaled their intention to ratify the convention in their national AI strategies. Several developing countries that are not members of the Council of Europe are observers to its AI processes, including Brazil, Cabo Verde, Cameroon, Costa Rica, Ecuador, the Arab Republic of Egypt, and Ghana. Developing countries can become observers to the Council of Europe AI processes and use outcome-based tools like the convention to orient their domestic policy around the protection of human rights while retaining the freedom to continue experimenting with different domestic regulatory frameworks that achieve that goal.

Countries should also ensure that their international commitments facilitate, rather than preempt, domestic regulatory oversight. For example, digital trade agreements increasingly include strong protections against requirements for disclosure of source code and algorithms.[91] These protections can restrict the ability of governments to access, review, or audit proprietary algorithms, creating barriers to regulation and accountability.[92] Policy makers negotiating digital trade agreements should ensure that these agreements preserve rather than undermine regulatory freedom, for example, by ensuring that the agreements permit requirements for source code disclosure if the requirements relate to compliance with or enforcement of laws. Policy makers should also make sure that agreements exempt government procurement from any prohibitions on requirements for source code disclosure.[93]

At the same time, policy makers have also recognized that many preexisting international commitments, such as international human rights law, are aligned with domestic governance. Article 1 of Korea's Framework Act on the Development of Artificial Intelligence and Establishment of Trust states that the act's purpose is to protect the "rights and interests" of people, and Brazil's proposed national AI bill also takes an explicitly rights-based approach.

Fourth, policy makers and regulators need to join forces across countries and continents to ensure regulatory cooperation and enforcement across borders, holding AI providers accountable regardless of where they are based. Promising examples exist for established systems like those for data protection. In 2021, the Global Privacy Assembly, which coordinates the work of more than 130 data protection authorities around the world, established the International Enforcement Cooperation Working Group. The first meeting of the group resulted in a joint investigation by the Australian and UK data protection authorities of Clearview AI, a US-based facial recognition company sanctioned in the EU for extracting, without their consent, individuals' selfies from the internet to create a database of 10 billion faces it then used to power an identity-matching service that it sold to law enforcement agencies.[94]

Finally, policy makers should engage in international standards development processes. Such engagement is important because international standards provide a key bridge for AI providers looking to sell their products in multiple markets, allowing them to demonstrate *trustworthiness by design* by adhering to internationally recognized good practices.[95]

Importantly, standards are not neutral guardrails. A wide range of entities can develop standards, from international standards development bodies like the ISO and IEC with global multistakeholder participation to national standards bodies, private consortiums, and even single companies. Whoever writes these standards determines the definitions of value-laden terms like *fairness, safety,* and *risk*.[96] To ensure international standards reflect the interests of all countries and stakeholders rather than those of only a few countries or incumbent AI providers, policy makers can take two key actions.[97]

First, policy makers should participate in standards development processes, so that the standards that are developed reflect the interests of all countries. To ensure that their policy makers can participate actively and effectively in these processes, developing countries need to build their capacity to do so. Currently, only one-third of the members of ISO and IEC's standards development committee for AI are from developing countries. Strengthening genuine participation by countries from all income groups will reinforce the legitimacy of international standards developed through multistakeholder consensus.

Second, policy makers should work to broaden the types of stakeholders involved in the development of AI standards. Technical standards are strongest when they reflect a sociotechnical approach, recognizing that the impacts of AI are shaped not only by technical design, but also by real-world choices relating to existing processes, cultures, data, and other systems.[98] Multiple international initiatives[99] recognize that standards need to reflect participation from civil society, legal experts, and diverse economic groups to prevent capture and ensure standards serve all whom AI may affect.

Collectively, countries can tip the scales toward social good

Policy makers should not underestimate the challenges posed by the task of governing AI: Limited regulatory capacity, a fragmented geopolitical landscape, and the speed and opacity of advanced AI development all pose serious challenges to traditional regulatory processes. The stakes are high: Failure to govern AI adequately can lead to irreversible harms to people and communities that will undermine trust in AI and hinder the ability of the technology to improve development outcomes. Going it alone is not a viable option for most developing countries, nor is waiting for a perfect global framework that fragmented geopolitics will not deliver. The pragmatic path is to act on both fronts at once: build domestic capacity to govern AI in ways that fit the local context, and use every available channel—multilateral, regional, treaty based, and standards driven—to shape the international rules of the game while they are still being written.

Notes

1. Refer to chapter 6 as well as Acemoglu (2024).
2. Schipper (2025).
3. Acemoglu and Lensman (2024).
4. Acemoglu and Lensman (2024).
5. Acemoglu and Lensman (2024). The *World Development Report 2025* also notes that, "for transformative technologies such as AI, which carry risks that are poorly understood and evolving faster than regulatory systems can adapt, it is sensible to follow the precautionary principle: If serious harm is possible, take preventive measures even if there is not yet full scientific evidence that confirms these risks. . . . In short, it is sensible to implement standards before harm becomes irreversible" (World Bank 2025c, 371).
6. World Bank (2025c, 348).
7. Acemoglu (2024); World Bank (2025c). Refer also to Leslie et al. (2022) and Mantelero and Esposito (2021) for a discussion of the irreversibility of harms caused by AI.
8. Gillespie et al. (2025). The survey was conducted in late 2024 and early 2025 by researchers at KPMG International and the University of Melbourne.
9. Gillespie et al. (2025) find notable differences in public trust between advanced economies and emerging markets. For example, they find that people in advanced economies are less trusting (39 percent versus 57 percent) and accepting (65 percent versus 84 percent) of AI when compared with those in emerging markets. Nevertheless, in all economies across all income groups (except India), a majority of people agreed that regulation of AI is needed.
10. Beltran (2025).
11. Cao (2024).
12. Refer to Monitor de Novas Tecnologias na Segurança Pública do Brasil (Monitor of New Technologies in Public Security in Brazil) (dashboard), Panóptico, Centro de Estudo de Segurança e Cidadania (Center for Studies on Security and Citizenship), https://www.opanoptico.com.br/.
13. Livingstone (2024).
14. United Nations High-Level Advisory Body on Artificial Intelligence (2024).
15. Tomei et al. (2025); World Bank (2025a).
16. These findings are based on the AI and Data for Better Governance Survey of governments conducted by the World Bank for this Report. The survey's findings focus on the use of, barriers to use of, and governance of AI, highlighting key differences across countries according to income level. The survey included a core module for digital agencies (or ministries of digital transformation or the equivalent), as well as two modules each for the following sectors: health, education, tax, public finance, civil service, and procurement. The survey was sent to relevant authorities in 129 economies. Respondents in 60 economies completed at least one of the modules, with 57 economies responding to the core module.
17. Hennessy et al. (2026).
18. For managing AI risks: the US National Institute of Standards and Technology's NIST-AI-600-1, Artificial Intelligence Management Framework, and the International Organization for Standardization and International Electrotechnical Commission's ISO/IEC 42001:2023, Artificial Intelligence Management System; for assessing the impact of AI: the International Organization for Standardization and International Electrotechnical Commission's ISO/IEC 42005:2025, AI System Impact Assessment; and for measuring and testing levels of transparency: the Institute of Electrical and Electronics Engineers' IEEE 7001-2021, IEEE Standard for Transparency of Autonomous Systems.
19. World Bank (2025a).
20. Hennessy et al. (2026); Solow-Niederman (2023).
21. Hennessy et al. (2026); Smuha and Yeung (2025).
22. Galvagna (2023).
23. World Bank (2025c, xxiii).
24. Rich et al. (2026). Olah delivered his comments at the launch of a papal encyclical issued by Pope Leo XIV in May 2026 warning leaders to safeguard people from the most disruptive harms of AI.
25. Acemoglu (2023).
26. Roberts et al. (2024). Refer also to the discussion in World Bank (2025c).
27. Veale et al. (2023). Refer also to World Bank (2025a) on the risk of ethics washing in AI governance.
28. This recommendation builds on the concept of the new social contract for data, advocated in the *World Development Report 2021* (World Bank 2021).
29. World Bank (2025c).
30. World Bank (2025c).
31. For example, a policy paper by the Centre for Data Innovation (CDI) argued that compliance with the act could cost the EU economy €31 billion. However, the Centre for European Policy Studies (CEPS), which authored the original compliance cost study as part of the European Commission's Impact Assessment for the AI Act in late 2020, has questioned the accuracy of these figures. The CEPS argued that the CDI had extrapolated costs based on factually incorrect assumptions and had recompiled statistics from the original study in a misleading way (Laurer et al. 2021).
32. The pacing problem is not unique to AI: It is a common problem facing all policy makers seeking to govern emerging technologies, for which evidence is often limited and still being gathered.
33. Bennett Moses (2017); Marchant et al. (2011). The United Nations' *Preliminary Report of the Independent International Scientific Panel on Artificial Intelligence* (composed of 40 independent scientists and experts from all five UN regions), released in July 2026, recognizes this evidence dilemma: Policy makers need evidence to make consequential governance decisions; however, by the time the evidence emerges, it may be too late to act (United Nations 2026).

34. Throughout the chapter, the terms *instruments* and *laws, rules, and regulations* are used interchangeably.
35. World Bank (2025a).
36. DSIT (2023). The principles are safety, security, and robustness; appropriate transparency and explainability; fairness; accountability and governance; and contestability and redress.
37. Tsebee and Oloyede (2024).
38. Tsebee and Oloyede (2024).
39. Trajano (2026).
40. Tironi and Albornoz (2025).
41. Mumbi (2026).
42. Constitutional Court (2024).
43. Oxford Institute of Technology and Justice (2026). Colombia is the first country to implement the UNESCO Guidelines for the Use of AI Systems in Courts and Tribunals.
44. World Bank (2025b).
45. Andrews (2025).
46. Lu (2022); Ng (2025a).
47. Viljoen (2021).
48. The final section of this chapter, on international cooperation, discusses power imbalances among governments.
49. Although many countries now have provisions in their data protection laws that require people to be informed if they are the subject of an automated decision (World Bank 2025a), the requirements in these provisions focus on transparency with respect to users. They do not address fundamental questions around how AI providers collect and use training and evaluation data, even though the literature has long identified these questions as a key foundation for responsible AI (Gebru et al. 2021).
50. Lu (2022); Ng (2025a).
51. California Legislative Information (2024).
52. Social licensing frameworks are license-based frameworks for governance structures that aim to give communities formal mechanisms for defining how their collective data are used and how they share in the returns (Gordon-Tapiero et al. 2023; Verhulst et al. 2025; Viljoen 2021). These frameworks are innovative because they focus on collective agreement rather than individual-based consent, aiming to shift power back to local communities (Verhulst et al. 2025).
53. Lee (2024).
54. Lee et al. (2025).
55. Morales et al. (2024).
56. Ruohonen and Mickelsson (2023).
57. OMB (2025).
58. Refer to *El Peruano* (2023).
59. Refer to *El Peruano* (2025).
60. Projeto de Lei n° 2338, de 2023 (Bill No. 2338 of 2023) (dashboard), Atividade Legislativa, Federal Senate, https://www25.senado.leg.br/web/atividade/materias/-/materia/157233.
61. The act also prohibits certain uses that are not explicitly targeted against government uses of AI, such as explicit deepfakes and AI that encourages self-harm.
62. World Bank (2021).
63. Aitken et al. (2022).
64. Aitken et al. (2022).
65. For a general discussion of building technical capacity on AI in government, refer to chapter 8.
66. World Bank (2024). It is worth distinguishing regulatory sandboxes from other kinds of product-focused AI or data sandboxes, because the two are often conflated. A regulatory sandbox is oriented toward regulatory learning—testing how a product performs against rules and building capacity to supervise it—whereas, in a product-focused AI or data sandbox, researchers, start-ups, and public agencies access anonymized or synthetic data to develop and train AI models.
67. Guio Español and Konig (2025).
68. World Bank (2025a).
69. Appaya and Jenik (2019).
70. OECD (2023); World Bank (2024).
71. Guio Español and König (2025).
72. Colorado General Assembly (2024).
73. Texas Legislature Online (2025).
74. Fryc (2026).
75. These organizations are the European Committee for Standardization and European Committee for Electrotechnical Standardization.
76. For example, the Global Cross-Border Privacy Rules are an accountability-based certification framework in which third-party accountability agents assess and certify organizations' privacy policies, practices, and data governance against a set of key standards derived from the Asia-Pacific Economic Cooperation's Cross-border Privacy Enforcement Arrangement. Certain national laws, such as Singapore's Personal Data Protection Act 2012, then recognize the certification, eliminating additional compliance requirements for cross-border data transfers (Aw et al. 2025).
77. The seven initiatives are the OECD AI Principles (2019); G20 [Group of Twenty] AI Principles (2019); GPAI [Global Partnership on Artificial Intelligence] Minister's Declaration 2022; Hiroshima AI Process G7 Digital & Tech Ministers' Statement (2023); Bletchley Declaration by Countries Attending the AI Safety Summit, 1–2 November 2023; Council of Europe's Framework Convention on Artificial Intelligence and Human Rights, Democracy and the Rule of Law (2024); and Seoul Declaration for Safe, Innovative, and Inclusive AI (2024).
78. These countries are Canada, France, Germany, Italy, Japan, the United Kingdom, and the United States.
79. This analysis does not consider countries to be involved in an initiative solely through membership in the African Union or the European Union, the former of which has endorsed the G20 AI Principles.
80. Refer to the discussion of the fragmentation doom loop in chapter 6, as well as to Radu (2026).
81. United Nations High-Level Advisory Body on Artificial Intelligence (2024); Veale et al. (2023).
82. In the most extreme cases of global fragmentation, companies may lose so much scale by having

to adapt AI systems to many different local requirements that they may pull out of smaller markets altogether (Lancieri et al. 2024).

83. Enendu (2025).
84. The AI Safety Summit 2023, the first of its kind, held in the United Kingdom in November 2023, culminated in the Bletchley Declaration, which emphasized the urgency of governing frontier AI and the need for international coordination. The declaration led to the establishment of a wave of AI safety institutes in Japan, Singapore, the United Kingdom, and the United States. Subsequent summits were held in Korea (AI Seoul Summit 2024) and France (AI Action Summit 2025). The India AI Impact Summit 2026, the first of these summits hosted by a developing country, resulted in the New Delhi Declaration 2026, which gained 89 signatures.
85. Refer to the Ada Lovelace Institute's proposal for a "global AI governance floor" as an organizing concept for the Global Dialogue on AI Governance (Schüür et al. 2026), as well as the discussion of benign forms of fragmentation in Lancieri et al. (2024).
86. They are Brazil (articles 14 and 18 of the proposed national AI bill, Bill 2338/2023), Chile (proposed AI Systems Regulation, articles 7–8), the European Union, and Korea, as well as the US state of Colorado (Consumer Protections for Artificial Intelligence). Refer also to the US Office of Management and Budget memorandum "Accelerating Federal Use of AI Through Innovation, Governance, and Public Trust" (OMB 2025) (which applies only to use of AI by US federal agencies).
87. Bradford (2023).
88. Ng (2025b).
89. The Council of Europe should not be confused with the European Union. The Council of Europe, founded in 1949, is a wider intergovernmental organization focused on human rights, democracy, and the rule of law; it has 46 member states (including non-EU countries such as Türkiye, Ukraine, and the United Kingdom). The European Union, by contrast, is a deeper political and economic union of 27 member states with its own legislative bodies, single market, common currency (for most members), and binding law that takes precedence over national law. The two bodies share no formal institutional relationship, though all member states of the EU are also members of the Council of Europe.
90. The convention was created through a multiyear negotiation process that involved the participation of 68 representatives of civil society, industry, and academia as observers. Some civil society actors have criticized the convention for taking an excessively vague approach because it allows countries to determine whether they will apply obligations under the convention to private sector actors or instead implement "other appropriate measures" (Amnesty International 2024). At the same time, other civil society actors have endorsed the convention as a "major milestone" and "historic." For details, refer to Council of Europe AI Treaty (dashboard), Center for AI and Digital Policy, https://www.caidp.org/resources/coe-ai-treaty/.
91. Examples include the United States–Mexico–Canada Agreement, the Japan-Mongolia Economic Partnership Agreement, the Indonesia-Australia Comprehensive Economic Partnership Agreement, and the Comprehensive and Progressive Agreement for Trans-Pacific Partnership.
92. Dorobantu et al. (2021); Jones (2023).
93. For example, article 24 of the Protocol to the African Continental Free Trade Area on Digital Trade preserves the ability of regulatory bodies to inspect and audit algorithms when required for public interest reasons, subject to safeguards against unauthorized disclosure. For a detailed discussion of carve outs related to prohibitions on requirements for disclosing source code in digital trade agreements, refer to Dorobantu et al. (2021). Refer also to the discussion on retaining developmental freedom in Fisher and Streinz (2022).
94. IEWG (2021).
95. ISO (2025).
96. Hennessy et al. (2026); Solow-Niederman (2023).
97. The next two paragraphs are adapted from content authored by Philip Grinsted and Cindy Parokkil.
98. ISO (2025).
99. Including the 2025 Seoul Statement (issued by IEC, ISO, and International Telecommunication Union), the UN Global Digital Compact, and the Council of Europe Framework Convention.

References

Acemoglu, Daron. 2023. "Distorted Innovation: Does the Market Get the Direction of Technology Right?" *AEA Papers and Proceedings* 113 (May): 1–28. https://doi.org/10.1257/pandp.20231000.

Acemoglu, Daron. 2024. "Harms of AI." In *The Oxford Handbook of AI Governance*, edited by Justin B. Bullock, Yu-Che Chen, Johannes Himmelreich, Valerie M. Hudson, Anton Korinek, Matthew M. Young, and Baobao Zhang. Oxford University Press. https://doi.org/10.1093/oxfordhb/9780197579329.013.65.

Acemoglu, Daron, and Todd Lensman. 2024. "Regulating Transformative Technologies." *American Economic Review: Insights* 6 (3): 359–76. https://doi.org/10.1257/aeri.20230353.

Aitken, Mhairi, David Leslie, Florian Ostmann, Jacob Pratt, Helen Margetts, and Cosmina Dorobantu. 2022. *Common Regulatory Capacity for AI*. Alan Turing Institute. https://doi.org/10.5281/ZENODO.6838946.

Amnesty International. 2024. "Council of Europe: Amnesty International's Recommendations on the Draft Framework Convention on Artificial Intelligence, Human Rights, Democracy and the Rule of Law." *Statements and Reports* (blog), April 11. https://www.amnesty.eu/news/council-of-europe-amnesty/-internationals-recommendations-on-the-draft-framework-convention-on-artificial-intelligence-human-rights-democracy-and-the-rule-of-law/.

Andrews, Caitlin. 2025. "GPS 2025: How 3 AI Regulators View Cross-Border Regulation." *News* (blog), April 24. https://iapp.org/news/a/gps-2025-how-three-ai-regulators-view-cross-border-regulation.

Andrews, Matt J., Lant H. Pritchett, and Michael Woolcock. 2017. *Building State Capability: Evidence, Analysis, Action*. Oxford University Press. https://academic.oup.com/book/26994.

Appaya, Sharmista, and Ivo Jenik. 2019. "Running a Sandbox May Cost over $1M, Survey Shows." *Regulatory Sandboxes: What Have We Learned So Far?* (blog), August 1. https://www.cgap.org/blog/running-sandbox-may-cost-over-1m-survey-shows.

Article 19. 2026. "EU: Safeguard the AI Act." *Digital* (blog), April 15. https://www.article19.org/resources/eu-safeguard-the-ai-act/.

Aw, Charmain, Guillermo Larrea, Scott Loughlin, and Eduardo Ustanan. 2025. "The Global Cross-Border Privacy Rules: A New Paradigm in Data Protection." *News* (blog), May 29. https://www.hoganlovells.com/en/publications/the-global-cross-border-privacy-rules-a-new-paradigm-in-data-protection.

Beltran, Michael. 2025. "Filipino Tech Workers Demand Protections in AI Bill After Rest of World Report." *Labor* (blog), January 28. https://restofworld.org/2025/code-ai-filipino-tech-workers/.

Bennett Moses, Lyria. 2017. "Regulating in the Face of Sociotechnical Change." In *The Oxford Handbook of Law, Regulation and Technology*, edited by Roger Brownsword, Eloise Scotford, and Karen Yeung. Oxford University Press. https://doi.org/10.1093/oxfordhb/9780199680832.013.49.

Bradford, Anu. 2020. *The Brussels Effect: How the European Union Rules the World*. Oxford University Press. https://doi.org/10.1093/oso/9780190088583.001.0001.

Bradford, Anu. 2023. *Digital Empires: The Global Battle to Regulate Technology*. Oxford University Press. https://doi.org/10.1093/oso/9780197649268.001.0001.

California Legislative Information. 2024. "AB-2013 Generative Artificial Intelligence: Training Data Transparency." Assembly Bill 2013, September 30, Office of Legislative Counsel, State of California. https://leginfo.legislature.ca.gov/faces/billTextClient.xhtml?bill_id=202320240AB2013.

Cao, Yin. 2024. "AI-Generated Voice Mimicry Infringes on Rights." *Society* (blog), April 24. https://global.chinadaily.com.cn/a/202404/24/WS66286719a31082fc043c3acf.html.

Colorado General Assembly. 2024. "Consumer Protections for Artificial Intelligence." Bill SB24-205, 2024 Regular Session, 75th General Assembly, Colorado General Assembly. https://leg.colorado.gov/bills/sb24-205.

Constitutional Court, Colombia. 2024. "Right to Due Process: Guiding Criteria for the Proper Use of Artificial Intelligence (AI)." Judgment T-323/24, Bogotá, August 2. https://www.corteconstitucional.gov.co/relatoria/2024/t-323-24.htm.

Corporate Europe Observatory. 2026. "Article by Article, How Big Tech Shaped the EU's Roll-Back of Digital Rights." *Tech* (blog), January 14. https://corporateeurope.org/en/2026/01/article-article-how-big-tech-shaped-eus-roll-back-digital-rights.

Crum, Ben. 2025. "Brussels Effect or Experimentalism? The EU AI Act and Global Standard-Setting." *Internet Policy Review* 14 (3): 1–21. https://doi.org/10.14763/2025.3.2032.

Dorobantu, Cosmina, Florian Ostmann, and Christina Hitrova. 2021. "Source Code Disclosure: A Primer for Trade Negotiators." In *Addressing Impediments to Digital Trade*, edited by Ingo Borchert and L. Alan Winters. CEPR Press. https://www.turing.ac.uk/sites/default/files/2021-06/dorobantu_ostmann_hitrova_2021_1.pdf.

DSIT (Department for Science, Innovation, and Technology). 2023. "A Pro-Innovation Approach to AI Regulation." Command Paper CP 815 (March), DSIT. https://www.gov.uk/government/publications/ai-regulation-a-pro-innovation-approach.

El Peruano. 2023. "Ley N. 31814: Ley que promueve el uso de la inteligencia artificial en favor del desarrollo económico y social del país" [Law 31814: Law that promotes the use of artificial intelligence in favor of the economic and social development of the country]. [In Spanish.] *Normas Legales* July 5: 5–7. https://api.oecdai.org/storage//policy-initiatives/Jul2025/fu_q68pcbgttddanwt.pdf.

El Peruano. 2025. "Decreto Supremo N 115-2025-PCM: Decreto Supremo que aprueba el Reglamento de la Ley N° 31814, Ley que promueve el uso de la inteligencia artificial en favor del desarrollo económico y social del país" [Supreme Decree No. 115-2025-PCM that approves the Regulation of Law No. 31814 to promote the development and use of artificial intelligence for the economic and social development of the country]. [In Spanish.] *Normas Legales* September 9: 4–13. https://busquedas.elperuano.pe/dispositivo/NL/2436426-1.

Enendu, Chiamaka. 2025. "Meta Threatens to Cut Off Facebook in Nigeria over Huge Fines: Report." *News* (blog), May 2. https://www.bbc.com/news/articles/ckgrwxp5r15o.

Epoch AI. 2026. "AI Models." Updated April 27, Epoch AI. https://epoch.ai/data/ai-models.

Fisher, Angelina, and Thomas Streinz. 2022. "Confronting Data Inequality." *Columbia Journal of Transnational Law* 60 (3): 829–956. https://www.jtl.columbia.edu/volume-60/confronting-data-inequality-xyrkf.

Fryc, Rafal. 2026. "Incentives or Obligations? The U.S. Regulatory Approach to Voluntary AI Governance Standards." *Future of Privacy Forum* (blog), updated March 25. https://fpf.org/blog/incentives-or-obligations-the-u-s-regulatory-approach-to-voluntary-ai-governance-standards/.

Galvagna, Christine. 2023. "Inclusive AI Governance: Civil Society Participation in Standards Development." Discussion Paper, The Future of Regulation Series,

Ada Lovelace Institute. https://www.adalovelaceinstitute.org/report/inclusive-ai-governance/.

Gebru, Timnit, Jamie Morgenstern, Briana Vecchione, et al. 2021. "Datasheets for Datasets." *arXiv:1803.09010v8 [cs.DB]*, December 1, Cornell University. https://doi.org/10.48550/ARXIV.1803.09010.

Gillespie, Nicole, Steven Lockey, Tabi Ward, Alexandria Macdade, and Gerard Hassed. 2025. *Trust, Attitudes and Use of Artificial Intelligence: A Global Study 2025*. University of Melbourne; KPMG International. https://assets.kpmg.com/content/dam/kpmgsites/xx/pdf/2025/05/trust-attitudes-and-use-of-ai-global-report.pdf.

Gordon-Tapiero, Aylet, Alexandra Wood, and Katrina Ligett. 2023. "The Case for Establishing a Collective Perspective to Address the Harms of Platform Personalization." *Vanderbilt Journal of Entertainment and Technology Law* 25 (4): 635–89. https://scholarship.law.vanderbilt.edu/jetlaw/vol25/iss4/1/.

Guio Español, Armando, and Pascal D. Koenig. 2025. "Regulatory Sandboxes for AI in the Majority World: A Learning-Centric Approach to Legal Adaptation." *Cambridge Forum on AI: Law and Governance* 1 (December): e42. https://doi.org/10.1017/cfl.2025.10015.

Habuka, Hiroki. 2025. "Japan's Agile AI Governance in Action: Fostering a Global Nexus Through Pluralistic Interoperability." Report, Center for Strategic and International Studies. https://www.csis.org/analysis/japans-agile-ai-governance-action-fostering-global-nexus-through-pluralistic.

Hennessy, Orla, Roxana Radu, and Nora von Ingersleben-Seip. 2026. "Who Leads AI Standardization? Geopolitics in a Fragmented Standards Landscape." RegulAite Working Paper 05/2026, University of Amsterdam. https://www.regulaite.eu/images/pdf/HennessyRaduvonIngerslebenSeip2026.pdf.

IEWG (International Enforcement Cooperation Working Group). 2021. "Report." Global Privacy Assembly, Secretariat, National Privacy Commission, the Philippines. https://globalprivacyassembly.com/wp-content/uploads/2021/10/1.3e-version-4.0-International-Enforcement-Cooperation-Working-Group-adopted.pdf.

ISO (International Organization for Standardization). 2025. "ISO Policy Brief: Harnessing International Standards for Responsible AI Development and Governance." ISO. https://www.iso.org/files/live/sites/isoorg/files/publications/en/PUB100498.pdf.

Jones, Emily. 2023. "Digital Disruption: Artificial Intelligence and International Trade Policy." *Oxford Review of Economic Policy* 39 (1): 70–84. https://doi.org/10.1093/oxrep/grac049.

Koros, Chebet, and Florence Ogonjo. 2025. "The Nwulite Obodo Open Data License: A New Licence for Sharing African Datasets." *Digital Rights* (blog), February 17. https://cipit.strathmore.edu/the-nwulite-obodo-open-data-license-a-new-licence-for-sharing-african-datasets/.

Lancieri, Filippo, Laura Edelson, and Stefan Bechtold. 2024. "AI Regulation: Competition, Arbitrage and Regulatory Capture." Center for Law and Economics Working Paper 11/2024, Swiss Federal Institute of Technology Zurich. https://doi.org/10.3929/ETHZ-B-000708626.

Laurer, Moritz, Andrea Renda, and Timothy Yeung. 2021. "Clarifying the Costs for the EU's AI Act." *AI, Digitalisation and Innovation* (blog), September 24. https://www.ceps.eu/clarifying-the-costs-for-the-eus-ai-act/.

Lee, Angie. 2024. "Māori Speech AI Model Helps Preserve and Promote New Zealand Indigenous Language." *NVIDIA* (blog), January 16. https://blogs.nvidia.com/blog/te-hiku-media-maori-speech-ai/.

Lee, Kwok Kin, Holly Krambeck, and Claudia Calderon. 2025. "2025 Highlights: Driving Data for Development." *Updates* (blog), December 15. https://datapartnership.org/updates/2025-highlights-driving-data-for-development/.

Leslie, David, Christopher Burr, Mhairi Aitken, Michael Katell, Morgan Briggs, and Cami Rincon. 2022. *Human Rights, Democracy, and the Rule of Law Assurance Framework for AI Systems: A Proposal*. Alan Turing Institute. https://doi.org/10.5281/ZENODO.5981676.

Livingstone, Grace. 2024. "Anger Mounts over Environmental Cost of Google Datacentre in Uruguay." *Global Development* (blog), August 1. https://www.theguardian.com/global-development/article/2024/aug/01/uruguay-anger-environmental-cost-google-datacentre-carbon-emissions-toxic-waste-water.

Lu, Sylvia. 2022. "Data Privacy, Human Rights, and Algorithmic Opacity." *California Law Review* 110 (6): 2087–147. https://doi.org/10.15779/Z38804XM07.

Mantelero, Alessandro, and Maria Samantha Esposito. 2021. "An Evidence-Based Methodology for Human Rights Impact Assessment (HRIA) in the Development of AI Data-Intensive Systems." *Computer Law and Security Review* 41 (July): 105561. https://doi.org/10.1016/j.clsr.2021.105561.

Marchant, Gary E., Braden R. Allenby, and Joseph R. Herkert, eds. 2011. *The Growing Gap Between Emerging Technologies and Legal-Ethical Oversight: The Pacing Problem*. International Library of Ethics, Law and Technology Series 7. Springer Nature. https://doi.org/10.1007/978-94-007-1356-7.

Morales, Humberto, Francisco García, Sean Muzquiz, Jose Manuel Marquez, Juan Carlos Torra, and Damián Gómez. 2024. "Amendment to the Federal Labor Law Related to Digital Platforms in Mexico." *Holland & Knight Alert* (blog), December 27. https://www.hklaw.com/en/insights/publications/2024/12/reforma-a-la-ley-federal-del-trabajo-en-materia-de-plataformas.

Mumbi, Lucy. 2026. "Activists Move to Court to Stop AI Rollout in Kenya over Rights Concerns." *Technology* (blog), February 5. https://eastleighvoice.co.ke/technology/287597/activists-move-to-court-to-stop-ai-rollout-in-kenya-over-rights-concerns.

Ng, Jeremy. 2025a. "Algorithmic Advertising as a Wicked Problem." *Georgetown Journal of International Law* 56 (3): 755–801. https://www.law.georgetown.edu/international-law-journal/in-print/volume-56/volume-56-number-3-spring-2025/algorithmic-advertising-as-a-wicked-problem/.

Ng, Jeremy. 2025b. "Multilateral Development Banks and the Legal Fabric of Global Data and AI Governance." In *Oxford Intersections: AI in Society*, edited by Philipp Hacker. Oxford University Press. https://doi.org/10.1093/9780198945215.003.0042.

OECD (Organisation for Economic Co-operation and Development). 2023. "Regulatory Sandboxes in Artificial Intelligence." OECD Digital Economy Paper 356, OECD. https://doi.org/10.1787/8f80a0e6-en.

Okorie, Chijioke I., and Melissa Omino. 2025. "Addressing Inequitable Openness in Licences for Sharing African Data and Datasets Through the Nwulite Obodo Open Data Licence." *Law, Technology and Humans* 7 (3): 94–106. https://lthj.qut.edu.au/article/view/4001.

OMB (Office of Management and Budget). 2025. "Accelerating Federal Use of AI Through Innovation, Governance, and Public Trust." Memorandum M-25-21, OMB, Executive Office of the President. https://www.whitehouse.gov/wp-content/uploads/2025/02/M-25-21-Accelerating-Federal-Use-of-AI-through-Innovation-Governance-and-Public-Trust.pdf.

Oxford Institute of Technology and Justice. 2026. "Colombia." March, Blavatnik School of Government, University of Oxford. https://www.techandjustice.bsg.ox.ac.uk/research/colombia.

Paulger, Dominic. 2025. "Understanding Japan's AI Promotion Act: An 'Innovation-First' Blueprint for AI Regulation." *Future of Privacy Forum* (blog), July 5. https://fpf.org/blog/understanding-japans-ai-promotion-act-an-innovation-first-blueprint-for-ai-regulation/.

Radu, Roxana. 2026. "The Global Landscape of National AI Strategies." Background paper prepared for *World Development Report 2026: The Promise of Artificial Intelligence*, World Bank. https://www.worldbank.org/en/publication/wdr2026/brief/world-development-report-2026-background-papers.

Randolph, Christabel. 2025. "United States, California AI Policy: A Review of the 2025 Legislative Outcomes." *Journal of AI Law and Regulation* 2 (4): 417–22. https://doi.org/10.21552/aire/2025/4/16.

Rich, Motoko, Elisabetta Povoledo, and Elizabeth Dias. 2026. "Pope Leo Warns of Risks From A.I. in 42,300-Word Encyclical." *Europe* (blog), May 25. https://www.nytimes.com/2026/05/25/world/europe/pope-leo-encyclical.html.

Roberts, Huw, Emmie Hine, Mariarosaria Taddeo, and Luciano Floridi. 2024. "Global AI Governance: Barriers and Pathways Forward." *International Affairs* 100 (3): 1275–86. https://doi.org/10.1093/ia/iiae073.

Rotenberg, Marc. 2025. "The California Effect: AI Redux." *Journal of AI Law and Regulation* 2 (4): 360–63. https://doi.org/10.21552/aire/2025/4/7.

Ruohonen, Jukka, and Sini Mickelsson. 2023. "Reflections on the Data Governance Act." *Digital Society* 2 (March): 10. https://doi.org/10.1007/s44206-023-00041-7.

Sabel, Charles F., and Jonathan Zeitlin. 2008. "Learning from Difference: The New Architecture of Experimentalist Governance in the EU." *European Law Journal* 14 (3): 271–327. https://doi.org/10.1111/j.1468-0386.2008.00415.x.

Schipper, Tetiana. 2025. "Exploited Intelligence: AI, Cybercrime, and the Global South's Digital Struggle." *Journal of World Affairs* 2 (1): 50–71. https://doi.org/10.1177/29769442251405945.

Schüür, Friederike, Michael Birtwistle, Octavia Field Reid, Lara Groves, and Cam Rincon. 2026. "The UN Global Dialogue on AI Governance: The Case for a Global AI Governance Floor." *Ada Lovelace Institute Blog*, May 7. https://www.adalovelaceinstitute.org/blog/the-case-for-a-global-ai-governance-floor/.

Siegmann, Charlotte, and Markus Anderljung. 2022. "The Brussels Effect and Artificial Intelligence: How EU Regulation Will Impact the Global AI Market." *arXiv:2208.12645v1 [cs.CY]*, August 23, Cornell University. https://doi.org/10.48550/ARXIV.2208.12645.

Smuha, Nathalie A., and Karen Yeung. 2025. "The European Union's AI Act: Beyond Motherhood and Apple Pie?" In *The Cambridge Handbook of the Law, Ethics and Policy of Artificial Intelligence*, edited by Nathalie A. Smuha. Cambridge Law Handbooks Series. Cambridge University Press. https://www.cambridge.org/core/books/cambridge-handbook-of-the-law-ethics-and-policy-of-artificial-intelligence/european-unions-ai-act/D41DE1DB8D6A8C7319DB82598410F5DA.

Solow-Niederman, Alicia. 2023. "Can AI Standards Have Politics?" *UCLA Law Review Discourse* 71: 2–17. https://scholarship.law.gwu.edu/cgi/viewcontent.cgi?article=3006&context=faculty_publications.

Texas Legislature Online. 2025. "Texas Responsible Artificial Intelligence Governance Act." Enrolled June 22, Texas Legislative Council, Austin. https://capitol.texas.gov/BillLookup/Text.aspx?LegSess=89R&Bill=HB149.

Tironi, Martin, and Camila Albornoz. 2025. "Divergent Futures in a Damaged Territory: The Rise of Data Centers and Water Conflicts in Santiago de Chile." *Journal of Urban Technology* 32 (4): 51–68. https://www.tandfonline.com/doi/full/10.1080/10630732.2025.2546784#d1e221.

Tomei, Philip Moreira, Rupal Jain, and Matija Franklin. 2025. "AI Governance Through Markets." *arXiv:2501.17755v2 [econ.GN]*, March 5, Cornell University. https://doi.org/10.48550/arXiv.2501.17755.

Trajano, Karryl Kim Sagun. 2026. "What the Grok Bans in Southeast Asia Tell Us About AI Governance." *The Interpreter* (blog), January 19. https://www.lowyinstitute.org/the-interpreter/what-grok-bans-southeast-asia-tell-us-about-ai-governance.

Tsebee, Dorcas, and Ridwan Oloyede. 2024. "DPAs and AI Regulation in Africa." *News* (blog), November 6. https://iapp.org/news/a/dpas-and-ai-regulation-in-africa.

United Nations. 2026. "Preliminary Report of the Independent International Scientific Panel on AI: Evidence-Based Assessment of Opportunities, Risks and Impacts of Artificial Intelligence." Independent International Scientific Panel on Artificial Intelligence, United Nations. https://www.un.org/independent-international-scientific-panel-ai/sites/default/files/2026-07/en_Preliminary%20Report_.pdf.

United Nations High-Level Advisory Body on Artificial Intelligence. 2024. *Governing AI for Humanity: Final Report*. United Nations. https://www.un.org/sites

/un2.un.org/files/governing_ai_for_humanity_final_report_en.pdf.
Veale, Michael, Kira Matus, and Robert Gorwa. 2023. "AI and Global Governance: Modalities, Rationales, Tensions." *Annual Review of Law and Social Science* 19 (October): 255–75. https://doi.org/10.1146/annurev-lawsocsci-020223-040749.
Verhulst, Stefaan G., Adam Zable, Andrew Zahuranec, and Peter Addo. 2025. "Reimagining Data Governance for AI: Operationalizing a Social License for Data Reuse." Technical Report 78, Agence française de développement. https://www.afd.fr/sites/default/files/2025-05-01-53-37/RT_78_VA_BAT.pdf.
Viljoen, Salomé. 2021. "A Relational Theory of Data Governance." *Yale Law Journal* 131 (November): 573–654. https://www.yalelawjournal.org/feature/a-relational-theory-of-data-governance.
White & Case. 2025. "AI Watch: Global Regulatory Tracker, China." *Insight* (blog), September 22. https://www.whitecase.com/insight-our-thinking/ai-watch-global-regulatory-tracker-china.
World Bank. 2021. *World Development Report 2021: Data for Better Lives*. World Bank. https://doi.org/10.1596/978-1-4648-1600-0.
World Bank. 2024. *Global Trends in AI Governance: Evolving Country Approaches*. World Bank. https://doi.org/10.1596/42500.
World Bank. 2025a. "Digital Trade Regulatory Readiness (DTRR) Database." *Data: Interactive* (blog), September 10. https://www.worldbank.org/en/data/interactive/2025/09/10/digital-trade-regulatory-readiness-dtrr-database.
World Bank. 2025b. "Global Regulations, Institutional Development, and Market Authorities Perspective Toolkit (GRIDMAP): Data Markets Module." July, World Bank, Washington, DC. https://documents1.worldbank.org/curated/en/099082225093534862/pdf/P179766-0d673a3c-c406-4e92-9fb4-16f8a771eb87.pdf.
World Bank. 2025c. *World Development Report 2025: Standards for Development*. World Bank. https://doi.org/10.1596/978-1-4648-2275-9.

7 Spotlight 7

Overcoming Government Fragmentation in AI Policy

Bureaucratic fragmentation is the central obstacle to effective government policy regarding artificial intelligence (AI). AI confronts governments with a problem their organizational structures were not built to solve. As a general-purpose technology, AI cuts across nearly every domain of public administration, from health and finance to education, justice, and infrastructure, whereas public institutions are organized vertically around sectors, with their own mandates, budgets, and data systems. Weak interagency coordination has already been a barrier to earlier waves of public sector digital transformation in developing countries.[1] But AI raises the stakes. Unlike more sector-specific technologies that can be managed within a single institution, AI depends on shared inputs and generates effects that routinely cross institutional boundaries, creating pressure on governments already facing overlapping mandates, siloed systems, and weak incentives for collaboration.[2] These are not simply areas in which better coordination would produce marginal gains; they represent foundational conditions for governments to enable, use, and govern AI safely and effectively.

The consequences of fragmentation play out across each of government's three roles in the AI agenda. As *users* of AI, government agencies are prevented from pooling the data, infrastructure, and expertise needed to deploy systems effectively and at scale. As *enablers* of AI across the broader economy, these agencies must contend with weakened policy coherence, which limits the public investment needed to support innovation and sends mixed signals to firms and investors. As *regulators* of AI, agencies confront dangerous blind spots: Because AI systems routinely cut across sectors, institutions, and jurisdictions, siloed oversight can fail to detect risks that are systemic and scale rapidly and whose effects are sometimes difficult to reverse when the risks materialize.

At its root, fragmentation reflects the political economy of bureaucracy itself: overlapping mandates that no one has the authority to rationalize, turf protection by agencies guarding budgets and data, and weak incentives for officials to invest in collaboration when the benefits will accrue elsewhere.[3] Getting the organizational structure right is therefore not an administrative detail, but a central challenge for effective AI policy making. Without a strong framework for institutional coordination, agencies may work at cross-purposes, undermining the government's national vision for AI—repeating mistakes from previous waves of technological change in the public sector.[4] Yet the experience of the last decade suggests the challenge this represents can be met.

Policy makers can address the central challenge of fragmentation through a federated approach to institutional coordination

Evidence from earlier waves of government digital transformation suggests that the key to addressing such political economy constraints is a *federated approach* to institutional coordination. Such an approach combines two layers:

- A *horizontal coordination* layer that extends *across* government functions. This layer ensures that a cohesive vision for AI is being implemented across the entire government, preventing individual agencies from working at cross-purposes.
- A *vertical implementation* layer that sits with the line ministries, departments, and agencies responsible for AI deployment and policy within their domains, ensuring they remain engaged through their custodianship, but under the common standards, shared infrastructure, and strategic direction set by the horizontal coordination layer.

Table S7.1 summarizes, and figure S7.1 illustrates, this approach for each of government's roles as user, enabler, and regulator of AI.

Table S7.1 Implementing a two-layered federated approach to AI policy coordination

HORIZONTAL COORDINATION LAYER			
Module	**Description**	**Advantages**	**Challenges**
Center-of-government module	Coordination anchored in the prime minister's or president's office, a cabinet secretariat, or an equivalent central authority.	• Political authority to resolve disputes across ministries. • Strong signaling of priorities. • All three government roles simultaneously embraced.	• Heavy reliance on political attention, which can fluctuate. • Limited technical capacity at the center without dedicated staffing. • Risk of bottlenecks if too many decisions escalate upward.
Lead-agency module	A designated ministry or statutory body (often a digital or information and communication technology authority) given a crosscutting mandate to coordinate AI policy across government.	• Technical depth combined with a coordinating role. • Institutional continuity beyond political cycles. • Clear external point of contact for firms, citizens, and international partners.	• Often informal and contested authority over peer ministries. • Risk of being seen as encroaching on sectoral mandates. • Requirement for strong convening skills, not just technical expertise.

(Table continues next page)

Table S7.1 Implementing a two-layered federated approach to AI policy coordination *(continued)*

Module	Description	Advantages	Challenges
HORIZONTAL COORDINATION LAYER			
Interministerial council or committee module	A standing body that brings together ministers or senior officials from relevant ministries to align ministries on AI strategy, standards, and investments.	• Sectoral autonomy preserved and alignment enabled. • Low institutional cost. • Flexible and adaptable as the AI agenda evolves.	• Potential for slow decision-making based on consensus. • Lack of implementation capacity. • Effectiveness heavily dependent on political backing and quality of the council or committee's secretariat.
VERTICAL IMPLEMENTATION LAYER			
Extension module	Absorption of AI mandate into an existing institution (for example, a sectoral regulator takes on oversight of AI within its domain or a ministry adds AI responsibilities to an existing digital unit).	• Retention of existing domain expertise and institutional relationships. • Pragmatic and resource efficient; cost of new institutions avoided. • Faster to scale up than a new body.	• Risk of overstretching teams with existing workloads and limited capacity. • Potential lack of AI-specific technical expertise, even when domain expertise is strong. • Crosscutting AI issues potentially outside of mandate.
Specialization module	Establishment of a new dedicated institution to address functions specific to AI (for example, an AI safety institute, a standards body, or a central AI office).	• Seriousness of commitment. • Concentrated hubs of technical expertise. • Useful for functions that require dedicated capacity and independence (AI safety testing, standards setting, assurance infrastructure).	• High cost to establish and sustain. • Risk of "AI-washing" without adequate resources: institutions set up to "do AI" without creating meaningful change in practice. • Potential for mandate overlap with existing ministries, departments, and agencies if boundaries are not carefully drawn.

Source: WDR 2026 team, based on World Bank 2018, 2021, 2022.
Note: AI = artificial intelligence.

Figure S7.1 Applying a federated framework across government's three roles in the AI agenda

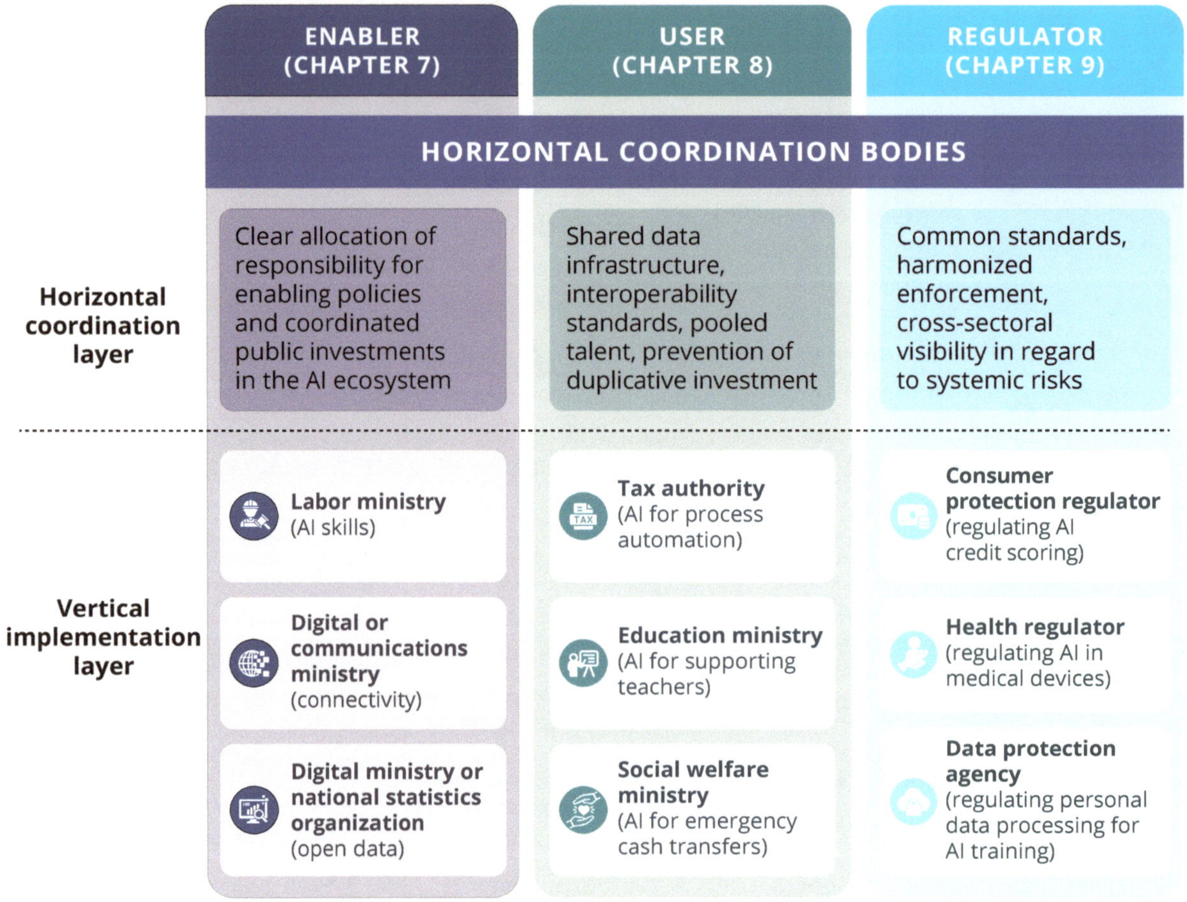

Source: WDR 2026 team.

Note: Bodies in the horizontal coordination layer include a center-of-government anchor, a lead agency, and an interministerial council. AI = artificial intelligence.

These modules are designed to be complementary rather than exclusive. As the case studies that follow show, countries can mix and match different modules in both the horizontal coordination and vertical implementation layers to solve local problems.

Countries' use of the specialization module largely tracks with income level. High-income countries are much more likely to have a dedicated AI agency than are low-income countries, just 9 percent of which have a specialized agency for AI (refer to figure S7.2).

Figure S7.2 Higher-income countries are more likely to have a dedicated AI agency

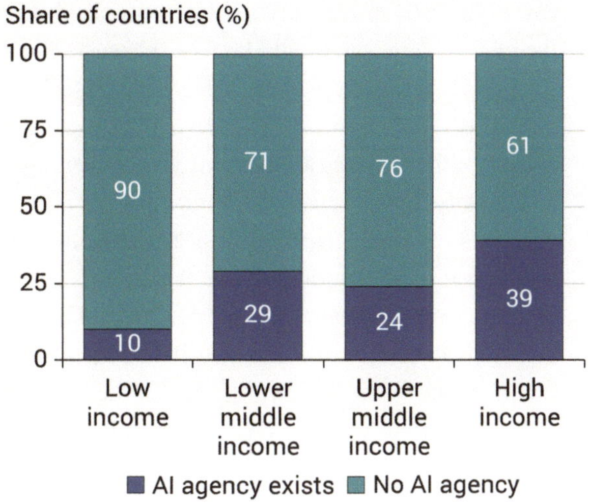

Source: WDR 2026 team.

Note: The figure shows the share of countries by income group that have a dedicated AI agency. The sample includes 20 low-income countries, 38 lower-middle-income countries, 49 upper-middle-income countries, and 69 high-income countries. AI = artificial intelligence.

Governments across very different contexts have adopted a federated framework and adapted it to suit their needs

What varies across countries that have implemented a federated framework for AI governance is not whether the framework's two layers are needed, but how they are built, in what sequence, and with what mix of modules.

Singapore: A mature model with fully operational horizontal coordination and vertical implementation layers

Singapore illustrates what a mature federated model looks like when both layers in the model are fully established and implemented. In Singapore's framework, policy strategy, operational rulemaking, technical assurance, research, and regional convening are allocated to specialized institutions cooperating under a common national direction: the National AI Strategy 2.0 and its guiding philosophy of "AI for the public good." The horizontal coordination layer is anchored in the Ministry of Digital Development and Information, which sets the country's overall strategy for digital development, public sector digitalization, and AI policy. The Infocomm Media Development Authority (IMDA), a statutory board within the ministry, is the lead operational agency for AI governance. Together these institutions provide strategic direction and common standards.

In the vertical implementation layer, Singapore employs both the extension and specialization modules of the framework. It does not have a single horizontal AI regulator. Instead, it uses the extension module to ensure that sectoral and domain regulators such as the Monetary Authority of Singapore, Competition and Consumer Commission of Singapore, and Personal Data Protection Commission Singapore apply responsible AI principles in the context of their existing mandates across financial regulation, competition, and data protection, respectively. Singapore has instituted two bodies specifically for the specialization module. The country's AI Verify Foundation, a public-private consortium, stewards the infrastructure underpinning Singapore's open-source testing. Seven premier members (Aicadium, Google, IBM, IMDA, Microsoft, Red Hat, and Salesforce) set the consortium's strategic direction, and a wider community of more than 220 members contributes to its codebase, benchmarks, and best practices. The Singapore AI Safety Institute, hosted by the Digital Trust Centre at Nanyang Technological University, operates in partnership with IMDA: IMDA handles baseline policy and international engagement, and the center drives technical work on testing and evaluation methodologies, safe model design, content assurance, and research relating to governance.

Arab Republic of Egypt: Creating a new horizontal coordination layer to coordinate existing players in vertical implementation

The Arab Republic of Egypt faced a different challenge: deliberately designing a horizontal coordination layer for its framework when none previously existed. In 2019, Egypt established its National Council for Artificial Intelligence as the country's supreme strategic body for AI policy, chaired by the Minister of Communications and Information Technology and bringing together relevant ministries, departments, and agencies alongside academic and industry experts. The council was approved by the Cabinet of Egypt and given a mandate to set central strategy and regulatory direction, combining center-of-government authority with a standing interministerial structure. Its executive arm, the Egyptian Center for Responsible AI, develops policies and standards and provides technical advice and capacity-building activities to line ministries.[5]

In the vertical implementation layer of its federated framework, Egypt relies predominantly on the extension module. Digital regulators, notably the country's National Telecom Regulatory Authority and its Personal Data Protection Center, apply their domain expertise to AI-specific tasks, including auditing systems for compliance with core principles of data protection such as data minimization (limiting the collection and processing of personal data to what is strictly necessary for a defined purpose) and purpose limitation (requiring that personal data be processed only for specific, explicit, and legitimate purposes). The choice of an extension module over a specialization module reflects a pragmatic stance in regard to capacity. Egypt is iteratively building AI competencies into institutions that are themselves still maturing: The Personal Data Protection Center became operational only in late 2025. The case of Egypt is instructive because it shows how the framework's horizontal coordination layer can be constructed quickly through political authority, whereas the vertical implementation layer can develop at a slower pace alongside institutional capacity building.

Bangladesh: Building AI on a backbone of digital-services delivery

Bangladesh illustrates a different starting point: one at which a substantial backbone for delivering digital services was built well before the country's AI policy agenda emerged and in which AI coordination is now being layered onto that existing infrastructure. The horizontal coordination layer of the country's AI policy framework is still under construction: The country's Information and Communication Technology (ICT) Division, under the Ministry of Posts, Telecommunications and Information Technology, is expected to lead policy, and the National AI Policy 2026–2030 (currently in draft during the writing of this Report) designates the National Data Governance Authority as the central coordinating and regulatory body for AI across government. The draft also creates an Independent Oversight Committee, an AI Project Implementation Cell inside the ICT Division, and an AI Innovation Fund, and it states that AI development for public service delivery shall be centrally coordinated by the ICT Division, with line ministries using shared platforms. None of this is yet operational. In practice, horizontal coordination defaults to the ICT Division supported by Aspire to Innovate (a2i), a whole-of-government digital innovation program hosted by the ICT Division that is in mid-transition from a donor-supported project into a statutory agency, has driven more than a decade of digitalization of the country's public services.[6]

In the framework's vertical implementation layer, existing line ministries in agriculture, health, and citizen services are deploying AI: an extension module by default rather than by deliberate design. The case of Bangladesh suggests that in lower-income settings, digital public infrastructure built before AI entered the policy conversation can become the foundation on which a federated AI architecture can later be constructed and that sequencing choices made in earlier waves of digital transformation shape what is possible later.

Conclusion

The AI policy coordination framework discussed in this spotlight shows how a federated approach to institutions solves key coordination challenges faced by policy makers. The framework's horizontal coordination layer handles fragmentation issues by ensuring a "whole-of-government" direction, whereas its vertical implementation layer addresses incentives by giving ministries, departments, and agencies a stake in the process of AI policy making and sufficient autonomy to carry out related responsibilities, but within a coordinated structure.

In all cases, the *functions* of these two layers are more important than the *form* they take.[7] The country case studies in this spotlight show that a range of institutions—from high-level cross-agency councils, to specialized responsible AI institutions, to existing ministries for information, communication, and technology—can be fit for their specific purposes, depending on local contexts, mandates, and capacity.

Notes

1. World Bank (2021, 2022).
2. Andrews et al. (2017); World Bank (2018).
3. De la Cruz et al. (2025); World Bank (2018).
4. World Bank (2018).
5. ECRAI (2026).
6. Refer to https://aipolicy.gov.bd/.
7. World Bank (2017, 2018).

References

Andrews, Matt J., Lant H. Pritchett, and Michael Woolcock. 2017. *Building State Capability: Evidence, Analysis, Action*. Oxford University Press. https://academic.oup.com/book/26994.

De la Cruz, Marco, Evrim Tan, Paula Muñoz, and Carlos Casas. 2025. "Unlocking the Value of Data Governance in Developing Countries: A Framework for Public Administration." *Electronic Journal of Information Systems in Developing Countries* 91 (6): e70043. https://doi.org/10.1002/isd2.70043.

ECRAI (Egyptian Center for Responsible AI). 2026. "Guide to Egypt's National AI Governance Framework." Document EG-NCAI-GOV-FW-2026-02, ECRAI, National Council for Artificial Intelligence, Quantum Computing, and Emerging Technologies. https://ai.gov.eg/SynchedFiles/ar/Resources/Guide%20to%20Egypt%E2%80%99s%20National%20AI%20Governance%20Framework.pdf.

World Bank. 2017. *World Development Report 2017: Governance and the Law*. World Bank. https://www.worldbank.org/en/publication/wdr2017.

World Bank. 2018. *Improving Public Sector Performance: Through Innovation and Inter-Agency Coordination*. Global Report: Public Sector Performance. Global Knowledge and Research Hub, World Bank. https://openknowledge.worldbank.org/server/api/core/bitstreams/aea43954-078e-5aa5-a712-94b1fc7a178a/content.

World Bank. 2021. *World Development Report 2021: Data for Better Lives*. World Bank. https://www.worldbank.org/en/publication/wdr2021.

World Bank. 2022. *Tech Savvy: Advancing GovTech Reforms in Public Administration*. Governance: Equitable Growth, Finance, and Institutions Insight Series. World Bank. https://documents.worldbank.org/en/publication/documents-reports/documentdetail/099400004112257749.

www.ingramcontent.com/pod-product-compliance
Lightning Source LLC
LaVergne TN
LVHW070624061126
851857LV00002B/10